Financial Transformations Beyond the COVID-19 Health Crisis

Transformations in Banking, Finance and Regulation

Print ISSN: 2752-5821
Online ISSN: 2752-583X

Series Editors: Sabri Boubaker
(*EM Normandie Business School, France & Swansea University, UK*)
Duc Khuong Nguyen
(*IPAG Business School, France*)

Presently, the banking and finance sectors evolve within a globalized and highly uncertain environment. Each business and financial decision requires careful consideration of country-specific and international factors due to high levels of shock transmission and volatility spillovers. Furthermore, it would be remiss to omit the COVID-19 health crisis, which caused harmful effects to all areas of the real economy and made profound changes in the way our firms, economies, and markets used to function.

Many other already well-known aspects, including the repercussions of quantitative easing policies, disruptive technologies in finance (e.g., FinTech, Big Data, Data Analytics, Artificial Intelligence, and Blockchains), as well as innovative financing instruments for startups (e.g., ICOs and crowdfunding) are currently revolutionizing banking and finance and posing numerous challenges to regulatory bodies and policymakers. Climate change emergencies also put pressure on governments and firms worldwide to improve policy on governance, corporate social responsibility, and sustainability practices.

This book series "Transformations in Banking, Finance, and Regulation" attempts to address these issues by focusing on transformative perspectives in banking and finance. Accordingly, it provides evidence-based guidance, recommendations, and pathways to assist businesses and policy decision-makers through an interdisciplinary and in-depth understanding of ongoing changes in the behavior of economic agents.

Published

Vol. 2 *Institutional Change and China Capitalism: Frontier of Cliometrics and its Application to China*
edited by Antoine Le Riche, Antoine Parent and Lei Zhang

Vol. 1 *Financial Transformations Beyond the COVID-19 Health Crisis*
edited by Sabri Boubaker and Duc Khuong Nguyen

Transformations in Banking, Finance and Regulation
Volume 1

Financial Transformations Beyond the COVID-19 Health Crisis

Editors

Sabri Boubaker
EM Normandie Business School, France &
Swansea University, UK

Duc Khuong Nguyen
IPAG Business School, France

World Scientific

NEW JERSEY • LONDON • SINGAPORE • BEIJING • SHANGHAI • HONG KONG • TAIPEI • CHENNAI • TOKYO

Published by

World Scientific Publishing Europe Ltd.
57 Shelton Street, Covent Garden, London WC2H 9HE
Head office: 5 Toh Tuck Link, Singapore 596224
USA office: 27 Warren Street, Suite 401-402, Hackensack, NJ 07601

Library of Congress Cataloging-in-Publication Data
Names: Boubaker, Sabri, editor. | Nguyen, Duc Khuong, 1978– editor.
Title: Financial transformations beyond the Covid-19 health crisis / editors,
Sabri Boubaker, EM Normandie Business School, France & Swansea University, UK,
Duc Khuong Nguyen, IPAG Business School, France.
Description: Hackensack, NJ : World Scientific, 2022. | Series: Transformations in banking, finance and regulation, 2752-5821 ; Volume 1
Identifiers: LCCN 2021026280 (print) | LCCN 2021026281 (ebook) |
ISBN 9781800610774 (hardcover) | ISBN 9781800610781 (ebook) |
ISBN 9781800610798 (ebook other)
Subjects: LCSH: Finance--Social aspects. | COVID-19 (Disease)--Social aspects. |
COVID-19 (Disease)--Economic aspects.
Classification: LCC HG101 .F57 2022 (print) | LCC HG101 (ebook) | DDC 332.02--dc23
LC record available at https://lccn.loc.gov/2021026280
LC ebook record available at https://lccn.loc.gov/2021026281

British Library Cataloguing-in-Publication Data
A catalogue record for this book is available from the British Library.

For any available supplementary material, please visit
https://www.worldscientific.com/worldscibooks/10.1142/Q0318#t=suppl

Desk Editors: Jayanthi Muthuswamy/Michael Beale/Shi Ying Koe

Typeset by Stallion Press
Email: enquiries@stallionpress.com

https://doi.org/10.1142/9781800610781_fmatter

Preface

The ongoing global health pandemic, driven by the SARS-CoV-2 infection (COVID-19), forced unusual measures such as social distancing and strict lockdowns in many countries. It has changed the world, brought about an unprecedented crisis, and shook up all finance and real economy sectors. It caused changes in many of our certainties and practices, including the foundations of the market-led version of capitalism and existing social models by bringing back social and health considerations at the forefront of firms' considerations, investors' strategies, and governments' agendas.

Health uncertainties and their increasing consequences for human life and activities have also required stronger and faster actions to shape the pathways toward sustainability. This health crisis seems to be the visible part of the iceberg since many other similar diseases can evolve in the future from epidemic to pandemic in a globalized world, as stated by the Global Preparedness Monitoring Board in its 2019 "A World at Risk" based on the WHO's survey and tracking data of 1,483 epidemic events in 172 countries during 2011–2018.[1]

When the WHO officially declared the novel coronavirus outbreak a pandemic on 11 March 2020, economic agents faced severe fear and anxiety about losing social interactions and psychological distress. They particularly anticipated a deep recession and a looming economic crisis, despite efforts and actions by governments around

[1]https://www.gpmb.org/annual-reports/annual-report-2019.

the world to increase liquidity and to provide significant rescue packages. In response to the possibly enormous economic consequences of the pandemic, international financial markets have witnessed a sharp stock market plunge during March 2020. They first corrected, then crashed, and after that remained highly volatile. The implied volatility index (VIX) rose more than 4.5 times from 18 February 2020 (14.83) to 16 March 2020 (82.69). Large panic selling triggered market-wide circuit-breakers four times in March 2020 to prevent US market crashes. This mechanism has been triggered only once before in 1997. Uncertainty is extreme, and the situation is fast evolving with no clear idea of the duration and depth of the economic slowdown, making it difficult for governments and policymakers to adopt appropriate fiscal and monetary policy responses.

Over the last two years, scholars have extensively researched the roots of the coronavirus, its transmission mechanisms, vaccines, and the economic and financial effects of the pandemic. It appears that combating COVID-19 leads to a global increase in anxiety, uncertainty, and depression as it has a multidimensional impact on society and economy, and new variants arise when the vaccination rate is unequal around the world, and vaccination hesitancy lowers the race to immunity (Callaway, 2021). Recent studies have attempted to quantify the COVID-19 effects on, among others, the most important economic issues such as financial markets behavior (Akhtaruzzaman *et al.*, 2021a,b,c; Rouatbi *et al.*, 2021; Aslam *et al.*, 2020), startups (Hoang *et al.*, 2021), corporate resilience (Beninger and Francis, 2021; Ding *et al.*, 2021), innovation (Markovic *et al.*, 2021; Zimmerling and Chen, 2021), and financial fragility (Clark *et al.*, 2021). However, more than ever before, further research is needed as many questions remain unanswered about how this pandemic situation impacts financial markets and their transformations. Moreover, historical episodes do not provide us with many lessons to better assess the economic and financial consequences of this unusual crisis.

This handbook is an effort to bring together an overview of the changes and insights about the transformations of the financial sector amid the COVID-19 pandemic. It specifically aims at providing readers, including investors, fund managers, corporate leaders, and policymakers, with new results, recent findings, and future perspectives related to the impact of COVID-19 on financial markets, firm behaviors, governance mechanisms, financing policies, and investment strategies. In terms of contributions, the handbook covers conceptual and empirical, and policy-driven chapters, using quantitative and qualitative methods alike, to achieve a broad picture of what happened and what is expected in the coming years.

The handbook is a collection of 27 chapters that fall into five parts. **Part I** includes *five* chapters and focuses on the macroeconomic effects of the pandemic. It covers topics such as government responses to health and socio-economic consequences (Linh Tu Ho and Christopher Gan), the public debt legacy under the pandemic effect (Anthony J. Makin), financial system stability and inequality (John L. Haracz), the interactions between international integration and real economy during the COVID-19 crisis (İlkay Şendeniz-Yüncü), and the economic recession risk (Alfredo Martín-Oliver and Florina Silaghi). **Part II** comprises *six* chapters and closely examines stock market behavior during the pandemic. It discusses extreme movements (Veni Arakelian), stock and CDS market reactions to COVID-19 (Moritz Johannes Herber and Matthias Scherf), intraday volatility responses (Jiayang Nie, Xiao Qiao, and Sibo Yan), foreign trading and market volatility (Zeynep Kantur and Gülserim Özcan), stock market comovements (Abdelkader Derbali, Mohamed Bechir Chenguel, Lamia Jamel, Meriem Jouirou, and Fathi Jouini), and short-term effects on Chinese stock markets (Huy Pham, Vikash Ramiah, Nisreen Moosa, Giancarlo Giudici, and Vijay Pereira). **Part III** features *five* chapters investigating the effects of the pandemic on financial institutions, money, and instruments, i.e., pandemic-driven insurance instruments (Marco Rossi), peer-to-peer lending markets (Asror Nigmonov and Hussein Daradkeh), equity crowdfunding (Francesca Battaglia, Francesco Busato, and Maria Manganiello), oil-gold relationships (Saroja Selvanathan and Eliyathamby A. Selvanathan), and Euro resilience (Stelios Markoulis and Neophytos Vasiliou). **Part IV** also includes *five* chapters and dedicates attention to the COVID-19 implications for corporate governance and finance, i.e., ESG compliance and firm performance (Jędrzej Białkowski and Anna Sławik), firm liquidity (Valdone Darškuviene, Bernadeta Goštautaite, Egidijus Kundelis, Dalius Misiūnas, and Siuzana Ščerbina-Dalibagienė), corporate board responses (Grazia Dicuonzo and Francesca Donofrio), firm-level return (Nidhi Kaicker, Radhika Aggarwal, and Raghav Gaiha), and business group affiliation (Shreya Biswas and Nivedita Sinha). **Part V** covers the *six* remaining chapters dealing with current and future transformations of the financial sector, i.e., EU banking system transformation (Magdalena Grothe and Antonio Sánchez Serrano), banking digitalization and sustainability (Frederic de Mariz), digital and disruptive transformations of firms (Wissem Ajili-Ben Youssef and Yves Rakotondratsimba), digital transformation and customer behavior (Jasmine T. Ha, Jason Q. Nguyen, and Quan V. Le), derivatives securities in emerging markets (Mazin A. M. Al Janabi), and changes in financial services and fund investing (Qiyu Wang).

We believe that this collection of high-quality chapters is a timely contribution to understanding the pandemic effects and brings valuable information for economic and financial actors to make informed decisions. We would like to take this occasion to thank all the contributors for their intellectual and thoughtful ideas. Our thanks also go to Dr. Natalie K. Watson (*Acquisitions Editor, World Scientific Publishing Europe*) and Jayanthi M (*Book Editor, Academic Consulting and Editorial Services, World Scientific Group*) for their helpful assistance during the preparations of this handbook.

References

Akhtaruzzaman, M., Boubaker, S. and Sensoy, A. (2021a). Financial contagion during COVID–19 crisis. *Finance Research Letters*, **38**, 101604.

Akhtaruzzaman, M., Boubaker, S., Chiah, M. and Zhong, A. (2021b). COVID–19 and oil price risk exposure. *Finance research letters*, **42**, 101882.

Akhtaruzzaman, M., Boubaker, S., Lucey, B.M. and Sensoy, A. (2021c). Is gold a hedge or a safe-haven asset in the COVID–19 crisis?. *Economic Modelling*, **102**, 105588.

Aslam, F., Aziz, S., Nguyen, D.K., Mughal, K.S. and Khan, M. (2020). On the efficiency of foreign exchange markets in times of the COVID-19 pandemic. *Technological Forecasting and Social Change*, **161**, 120261.

Beninger, S. and Francis, J.N. (2021). Resources for Business Resilience in a Covid-19 World: A Community-Centric Approach. *Business Horizons*.

Callaway, E. (2021). Beyond Omicron: what's next for COVID's viral evolution. *Nature*, **600**(7888), 204–207.

Clark, R.L., Lusardi, A. and Mitchell, O.S. (2021, May). Financial fragility during the COVID-19 pandemic. In *AEA Papers and Proceedings* (Vol. 111, pp. 292–296).

Ding, W., Levine, R., Lin, C. and Xie, W. (2021). Corporate immunity to the COVID-19 pandemic. *Journal of Financial Economics*, **141**(2), 802–830.

Hoang, H.V., Nguyen, C. and Nguyen, D.K. (2022). Corporate immunity, national culture and stock returns: Startups amid the COVID-19 pandemic. *International Review of Financial Analysis*, **79**, 101975.

Markovic, S., Koporcic, N., Arslanagic-Kalajdzic, M., Kadic-Maglajlic, S., Bagherzadeh, M. and Islam, N. (2021). Business-to-business open innovation: COVID-19 lessons for small and medium-sized enterprises from emerging markets. *Technological Forecasting and Social Change*, **170**, 120883.

Rouatbi, W., Demir, E., Kizys, R. and Zaremba, A. (2021). Immunizing markets against the pandemic: COVID-19 vaccinations and stock volatility around the world. *International Review of Financial Analysis*, **77**, 101819.

Zimmerling, A. and Chen, X. (2021). Innovation and possible long-term impact driven by COVID-19: Manufacturing, personal protective equipment and digital technologies. *Technology in Society*, **65**, 101541.

https://doi.org/10.1142/9781800610781_fmatter

About the Editors

Sabri Boubaker is Professor of Finance at EM Normandie Business School (France) and the School of Management of Swansea University (UK). He holds a Ph.D. in Finance from University of Paris Est (2006) and an H.D.R. degree (Habilitation for Supervising Doctoral Research) in 2010 from the same university. He has recently published many academic papers in international refereed journals, including *Journal of Corporate Finance, Journal of Banking and Finance, Journal of International Money and Finance, Financial Management, Journal of Business Ethics, Journal of Economics and Dynamics and Control, International Review of Financial Analysis, European Financial Management Journal, Review of Quantitative Accounting and Finance*, and *Journal of International Financial Markets, Institutions and Money.* Professor Boubaker has also edited many books on corporate finance and financial markets and serves on editorial boards of several peer-reviewed finance journals. He is the co-founder (with Duc Khuong Nguyen) of the Paris Financial Management Conference and Vietnam Symposium in Banking and Finance (VSBF).

Duc Khuong Nguyen is Professor of Finance and Deputy Dean for Research at IPAG Business School (France). He holds a Ph.D. in Finance from the University of Grenoble Alpes (France) and an H.D.R. (Habilitation for Supervising Scientific Research) in Management Science from University of Cergy-Pontoise (France), and completed an executive education program in "Leadership in Development" at Harvard Kennedy School (USA). He is also a Visiting Professor at International School, Vietnam National University (Hanoi, Vietnam). His research works focusing on asset pricing, emerging market finance, energy finance, and risk management have been published in *European Journal of Operational Research*, *Journal of Economic Dynamics and Control*, *Journal of Banking and Finance*, *Journal of International Money and Finance*, and *Macroeconomic Dynamics*, among others. Professor Nguyen has edited many books on corporate finance and financial markets issues and serves as subject and associate editors of several finance journals. He is the co-founder (with Sabri Boubaker) of the Paris Financial Management Conference and Vietnam Symposium in Banking and Finance (VSBF).

https://doi.org/10.1142/9781800610781_fmatter

About the Contributors

Radhika Aggarwal is a doctoral student of Management at the Faculty of Management Studies, University of Delhi, India. She holds a Bachelor's degree in Commerce from Hindu College, University of Delhi, and a Masters in Business Administration with a specialization in Finance from Ambedkar University Delhi, India. Her research interests include financial economics, international business, and public policy. She also assisted in the International Fund for Agricultural Development's Asia Pacific region in their research related to time-series analysis of food commodity prices in several states in India. Radhika teaches at Ambedkar University, Delhi, and has also previously worked in the University's planning division during an institutional review process.

Wissem Ajili-Ben Youssef is an Assistant Professor in Economics and International Finance at the ESLSCA — Paris Business School (France). Wissem Ajili's main research interests include the political economy of sovereign debt and international crisis management, economic and institutional approaches for public debt management, sovereign debt default, sovereign debt auditing, public debt viability, and the new approaches for sovereign debt management. She is also interested in risk management, emerging risks (cyber risk and climatic risk), derivatives (insurance-linked securities), digital disruptions in finance (FinTech, blockchain, cryptocurrencies), and Islamic finance. Wissem is a member of the Scientific Board of the *Journal of Entrepreneurship Education*. Dr. Ajili had presented her research findings in many international conferences such as the American Economic Association's Annual Meeting and the Canadian Economics Association's Annual Meeting.

Mazin A. M. Al Janabi is a Full Research-Professor of Finance & Banking and Financial Engineering, who recently retired from EGADE Business School, Tecnologico de Monterrey, Mexico. Before joining EGADE Business School, Professor Al Janabi worked for many years as a Full Research-Professor of Finance & Banking and Financial Engineering at UAE University (UAEU) in Abu Dhabi, UAE, and at Al Akhawayn University in Ifrane (AUI), Morocco, among other academic institutions. He holds a Ph.D. degree in Nuclear Engineering from the University of London, UK, and has more than 30 years of real-world experience in science & technology think tanks, engineering enterprises, financial markets, and academic institutions in many different roles. He has worked for top international financial groups (e.g. ING-Barings and BBVA) where he has held several senior management positions, such as Director of Global Market Risk Management, Head of Trading Risk Management, and Head of Derivative Products. Prof. Al Janabi has a strong interest in research and development within emerging economies and has several publications in international refereed journals, books, and chapters in books. Furthermore, his research and development in quantitative finance have been formally classified in the academic literatures as the "Al Janabi Model" for Liquidity Risk Management (Liquidity Adjusted Value-at-Risk, LVaR Model). Prof. Al Janabi has published in top-tier journals such as the following: *European Journal of Operational Research, Journal of Forecasting, International Review of Financial Analysis, Physica A: Statistical Mechanics and Its Applications, European Actuarial Journal, Annals of Operations Research, Applied Economics, Economic Modelling, Review of Financial Economics, Journal of Asset Management, Service Industries Journal, Journal of Modelling in Management, Studies in Economics and Finance, Emerging Markets Finance and Trade, Journal of Risk Finance, Journal of Banking Regulation*, and *Annals of Nuclear Energy*.

Veni Arakelian is an academic expert in Macrofinance and Financial Econometrics. She studied mathematics at the University of Athens, and holds a Ph.D. in Econometrics from Athens University of

Economics and Business, Greece. She has more than 15 years of experience in research, teaching, and working for the banking sector. She is also the author and co-author of several publications in leading scientific journals in finance, statistics, and econometrics. As a partner of two projects on FinTech, she delivers training on the developments to market regulators and authorities, bankers and companies. Her research interests are systemic risk, macroeconomic uncertainty, and the implications of both asset pricing and portfolio allocation. Veni currently works as a Senior Economist at the Division of Economic Research & Investment Strategy of Piraeus Bank. She is also an industry associate at UCL Center for Blockchain Technologies.

Francesca Battaglia is Associate Professor of Banking and Finance at the Department of Management Studies and Quantitative Methods, University of Naples, Parthenope, Italy, where she teaches "Risk Management in Banking" and "Financial Markets and Institutions." She received her Ph.D. in Banking and Finance from the University of Rome Tor Vergata. She serves as a member of the teaching board of the Doctorate "Governance, Management and Economics." Her research interests focus on risk management, securitization, corporate governance, systemic risk of financial intermediaries, and crowdfunding. She has published several papers in a number of peer-reviewed international journals in finance and economics. In 2015 she was awarded the Outstanding Teaching Award 2015 at the University of Naples Parthenope.

Jędrzej Białkowski (FRM, PRM) is a Professor at the University of Canterbury, New Zealand. Dr. Jędrzej Białkowski is engaged in research projects with well-established academic institutions in Australia (University of Melbourne), Germany (University of Münster), Poland (Jagiellonian University), and the US (University of Texas at Austin). His international cooperation resulted in 30 publications in peer-reviewed journals. He has published in top-ranked journals such as *Journal of Financial Economics*, *Journal of Banking and Finance*, *Journal of Derivatives*, and *Journal of Futures Markets*. Jędrzej has also had his work accepted by the top finance conferences: American Finance Association (AFA) and European Finance Association (EFA). His papers are frequently cited in top finance journals. Two of his papers in the area of Investments were awarded with the Best Paper Award in Investments Category by

Institute of Finance Professionals New Zealand (INFINZ). In 2019, he won a prestigious award — BLR Cup for Best Overall Paper — at the 2019 New Zealand Finance Colloquium. He serves as associate editor of the *Bulletin of Economic Research* journal.

Shreya Biswas is an Assistant Professor at the Department of Economics & Finance at the Birla Institute of Technology & Science, Pilani, Hyderabad Campus, India. She obtained her Ph.D. from Indira Gandhi Institute of Development Research, India. Her research interests include corporate governance issues and topics in household finance in India. She has published papers in international journals on the importance of board's social capital and board diversity for non-financial firms and banks in India. She has presented papers at several national and international conferences. Her research involves understanding the investment mistakes made by households and determinants of household portfolio in India along with what interventions can rectify such common investment mistakes. She has obtained research grants to analyze the socio-economic determinants of household portfolio in the Indian context and role of female directors on corporate boards.

Francesco Busato is Full Professor of Economics at the University of Naples "Parthenope," Italy; received his B.A. from University of Rome La Sapienza (summa cum laude), M.A. from Bocconi University and Ph.D. in Economics from Columbia University, United States. He served as Assistant Professor at University of Aaarhus Denmark, University of Rome III, as Associate Professor and next Full Professor at University of Naples Parthenope. He is the Head of Ph.D. Program of Economics, Statistics and Sustainability. Professor Busato teaches classes in topics such as finance, economics, and bachelor, master and Ph.D. level. He has published several papers in a number of peer-reviewed international journals in finance, economics (dynamic models) and sustainability.

Mohamed Bechir Chenguel is Assistant Professor in Finance at the Higher Institute of Informatics and Management of Kairouan, Kairouan University, Kairouan, Tunisia. His research interests include risk management, banking and market microstructure and Islamic finance. He has published articles, among others, in *International Journal of the Economics of Business, International Journal of Financial Engineering, International Journal of Decision Sciences,*

Risk and Management, International Journal of Research in Applied Sciences, and *International Journal of Business and Management Science.*

Hussein Daradkeh is a Ph.D. candidate at the University of Southern Queensland in Springfield, Australia. His research areas include corporate governance, corporate disclosure, and financial technology. Hussein holds an M.Sc. in Finance from the George Washington University in Washington D.C., USA, and an MBA specialized in International Finance from Virginia International University in Virginia, USA. He also holds a B.Sc. in Finance and Banking from Yarmouk University in Irbid, Jordan.

Valdonė Darškuvienė is Full Professor at ISM University of Management and Economics (Lithuania). Her research interests focus on corporate finance, corporate governance, and corporate social responsibility. She has served as Vice-President for Research at ISM (2015–2019) and Chair at the Department of Economics in 2016–2017. Previously she has held various positions and was awarded the title of Full Professor at Vytautas Magnus University (Lithuania). She is active in international research initiatives and networks. In 2014–2017 she served as expert at EC Horizon-2020 MSCA Advisory Group, which provides advice to the Commission regarding the Marie Skłodowska-Curie actions on skills, training and career development, as well as expert at EC Horizon-2020 Gender Advisory Group, which promotes implementation of gender dimension in research and innovation content as a cross-cutting issue in Horizon 2020 work programme. She is a member of scientific committee on public enterprises at CIRIEC (France) and expert at the Research Council of Lithuania.

Frederic de Mariz, Ph.D., is Executive Director at UBS and Lecturer at Columbia University and Sciences Po. His areas of expertise include the banking segment, FinTech, impact investing, and ESG. At UBS, he heads the Financial Institutions, FinTech, and ESG groups for Latin America. Frederic has 20 years of experience in investment banking, having worked in London, New York, Mexico City, and São Paulo. Prior experience includes positions at JP Morgan and Goldman Sachs. His team was consistently ranked among the top three in independent industry surveys, including #1 in Impact Investing by *Euromoney* (2017). At Columbia University

|SIPA, he teaches a class on innovative finance and impact investing. Frederic graduated from Columbia University |SIPA (MIA, 2005), La Sorbonne (MA in History, 2003), Sciences Po., Paris, (MPA, 2004), ESSEC, Paris (MBA, 2004). He completed his Ph.D. in Finance at University of São Paulo (FEA-USP, 2017) with a thesis on payments and financial inclusion. He has co-authored two books on sustainable finance and published numerous academic articles. He is a member of the Brazilian Banking Association (Febraban) and was an advisor to several microfinance institutions in Brazil.

Abdelkader Derbali is an Assistant Professor in Finance at Higher Institute of Informatics and Management of Kairouan, Kairouan University, Kairouan, Tunisia and at the Department of Administrative and Financial Sciences and Techniques, Community College, Taibah University, Saudi Arabia. His research interests include risk management, systemic risk, international finance, banking and market microstructure and Islamic finance. He has published articles, among others, in *Research in International Business and Management, Cogent Business & Management, Cogent Economic & Finance, Journal of Chinese Governance, The Chinese Economy, Finance Research Letters, International Journal of Financial Engineering, China Economic Journal, Pacific Accounting Review, Journal of Economics, Finance and Administrative Science, Human Systems Management, Journal of the Knowledge Economy, International Journal of Decision Sciences, Risk and Management, Journal of Asset Management, International Journal of Productivity and Quality Management, International Journal Of Management And Enterprise Development, Journal of Energy Markets*, and *International Journal of Trade and Global Markets.*

Grazia Dicuonzo is Associate Professor of Business Administration at the University of Bari Aldo Moro, Italy, where she teaches financial accounting, financial statement analysis and IAS/IFRS. She has a Ph.D. in Business Administration and she is eligible to Full Professor of Business Administration with (Italian) National Scientific Qualification. She is a member of the editorial board of the *International Journal of Digital Culture and Electronic Tourism* and *Management Control.*" She is also a MC Substitute of the Cost Project "Fintech and Artificial Intelligence in Finance." Her research interests are in the areas of smart technologies, risk disclosure, integrated reporting and non-financial information, and financial accounting. She is ad hoc reviewer for *Management Decision, Corporate Social Responsibility & Environmental Management, Business Strategy and the Environment, International Journal of Environmental Research and Public Health,* and *Technology Analysis & Strategic Management.*

Francesca Donofrio is a Ph.D. student in Business Administration at the University of Bari Aldo Moro, Italy. She has a degree in Economics and Finance and a Master's degree in Global Marketing Communication & Made in Italy. Her research interests are in the areas of corporate governance, corporate social responsibility, integrated reporting and non-financial information, smart technologies and artificial intelligence. She is an ad hoc reviewer for *Corporate Governance* published by Emerald.

Raghav Gaiha is (former) Professor of Public Policy, Faculty of Management Studies, University of Delhi, India. He has been Visiting Fellow/Scholar at Harvard, MIT, Stanford, Penn and University of Cambridge. He is currently (Hon.) Professorial Research Fellow, Global Development Institute, University of Manchester, UK and Research Affiliate, Population Studies, Centre, University of Pennsylvania, USA. He served as a Visiting Professor of Economics, University of Rome, Tor Vergata. He has undertaken consulting assignments with the World Bank, WIDER, Asian Development Bank, Food and Agricultural Organisation of the United Nations (FAO). IFAD is International Fund for Agricultural Development. He has published papers in *Journal of Development Economics, Economic Development and Cultural Change, Cambridge Journal of Economics*, and *World Development.* His research interests include inequality, poverty, nutrition, and aging.

Christopher Gan is the Professor in Accounting and Finance in the Faculty of Agribusiness and Commerce, Lincoln University, New Zealand. He is recognized internationally for research leadership in banking, microfinance, stock markets, and Asian financial economics. His approach is quantitative in nature with an applied focus. He aims to expand existing knowledge and develop recommendations for relevant agencies, government, and businesses. He actively collaborates with academics from other universities (particularly from Asia) and inspires the next young generation of scholars through postgraduate supervision. He has an extensive publication record (with numerous of his students as co-authors) in well-ranked peer reviewed journals and is regularly cited by other researchers. In 2017, he founded and presently leads the Lincoln University's Yunus Social Business Centre. The objectives of the Yunus Social Business Centre are to build awareness of social business, undertake training and education, provide mentoring, and support research on social business. It is the first Yunus Social Business Centre in New Zealand.

Giancarlo Giudici is Full Professor of corporate finance at Politecnico di Milano, Italy. He belongs to the faculty of MIP Graduate School of Business where he teaches finance. He wrote several publications on domestic and international journals on the topics of entrepreneurship, corporate financing, listings and IPOs, venture capital, and crowdfunding. He is the director of the Italian Observatories on Minibond and Crowdinvesting at Politecnico di Milano, School of Management. He led several projects financed by public and private entities on the topics of competitiveness and firm financing. He is adjunct professor at the Ton Duc Thang University in Ho Chi Minh City (Vietnam).

Bernadeta Goštautaitė is a Professor at the ISM University of Management and Economics in Vilnius. She earned a Master's degree from the University of Mannheim (Germany) and a Ph.D. from the ISM University of Management and Economics. Her research investigates how individuals adapt to diverse work-related changes, including individual changes, workplace transformations, and societal-level turbulences. She received Research Excellence Ph.D. Scholarship from the Research Council of Lithuania in 2013, Young Scholar Award from the Lithuanian Academy of Science (2017), Early Career Visiting Award provided from the Future of Work Institute (2020) at Curtin University (Australia), and Scholar of the Year Award from ISM University of Management and Economics (2015 and 2019). Professor Goštautaitė has almost 10 years of experience in human resources management and consulting.

Magdalena Grothe is Lead Economist at the European Central Bank. She is involved in the assessment of global financial stability issues and developments in global financial markets. In her previous roles, Magdalena worked on financial market modelling and the assessment of euro area inflation expectations within the European Central Bank, as well as on the assessment of risks to EU financial stability within the European Systemic Risk Board. Magdalena has published several articles in academic journals and contributed to many ECB and ESRB reports.

Jasmine T. Ha is an Assistant Professor at the Department of Sociology, Western University, London, ON, Canada and Regional Affiliate at the Center for Studies of Demography and Ecology, University of Washington, Seattle, USA. She received Doctorate training in Sociology and Demography at the University of Minnesota. Her research focuses on the integration of multi-dimensional social, economic, demographic, and spatial data to understand how people make climate adaptation decisions. Her research has been published in high-impact peered-review journals, including *Climatic Change, European Journal of Population*, and *Population, Space, and Place.*

John L. Haracz, B.A. (San Francisco State University), M.D. (Medical College of Wisconsin), Ph.D. (UCLA), M.P.H. (UC Berkeley). is a Visiting Scientist at Indiana University since 2013. He was Assistant Professor at California State University, East Bay; Research Analyst at the San Mateo County Health Department; Research Associate at the Medical College of Wisconsin, Indiana University, Albert Einstein College of Medicine, and the University of Miami School of Medicine. He had Visiting Scholar positions at UC Berkeley in the Goldman School of Public Policy, School of Public Health, and Department of Psychology. His work was presented at the Society for Neuroeconomics, Society for Neuroscience, Society of Biological Psychiatry, American Psychiatric Association, American Association for the Advancement of Science, Psychonomic Society, Chapman University Economic Science Institute, Claremont Graduate University Department of Economic Sciences, UC Berkeley Social Science Matrix, and Stanford Complexity Group. He received a National Research Service Award fellowship from the National Institutes of Health and a UC Berkeley University Fellowship. His research interests include the neuroeconomics of asset-price bubbles, niche construction as a basis for inequality, causes of excessive asset trading, and market design interventions for negative feedback with reflexive information.

Moritz Johannes Herber is currently pursuing an M.Sc. in Economics and Business Administration at Copenhagen Business School,

Denmark. He holds a B.Sc, in Business Administration from the University of Trier, Germany, which included a one-year exchange at BI Norwegian Business School, Norway.

Linh Tu Ho is a Lecturer in Investment Management in the Faculty of Agribusiness and Commerce, Lincoln University, New Zealand. She has about 10 years of teaching in international education institutions such as Canterbury College and Lincoln University in New Zealand, and Hue University in Vietnam. She has taught courses on investment economics, investment management, financial fundamentals, and management. She holds a Ph.D. in Economics from Lincoln University, New Zealand, and a Master's Degree in Enterprise Management from Huazhong University of Science and Technology, China. She published her work on topics such as initial public offerings and foreign direct investment. Her research interests include pandemic uncertainty, investment, stock performance, and government responses to rebuild the economies post pandemics. She presented at several leading conferences, including the Accounting and Finance Association of Australia and New Zealand Conference (AFAANZ), International Congress on Modelling and Simulation (MODSIM) in Australia, and New Zealand Association of Economists Annual Conference (NZAE).

Lamia Jamel is an Assistant Professor in Economic Sciences at the Department of Finance and Economics, College of Business Administration, Taibah University, Saudi Arabia. Her research interests include economic growth, financial development, financial economics, and pollution. She has published articles, among others, in *Cogent Economic & Finance, Journal of Investment Compliance, Corporate Law & Governance Review, Journal of Economics, Finance and Administrative Science, Journal of the Knowledge Economy, International Journal of Productivity and Quality Management, International Journal of Management and Enterprise Development*, and *Virtual Economics.*

Fathi Jouini is an Assistant Professor in Finance at the Faculty of Economic Sciences and Management of Sousse, Sousse University, Sousse, Tunisia. His research interests include financial markets, corporate governance, banking and market microstructure and Islamic finance. He has published articles, among others, in *International Journal of Critical Accounting, The Chinese Economy, EuroMed*

Journal of Management, International Journal of Governance and Financial Intermediation, International Journal of Management and Enterprise Development, Journal of Asset Management, International Journal of Innovation and Applied Studies, European Journal of Economics, Finance and Administrative Sciences, and *International Journal of Economics and Financial Issues.*

Meriem Jouirou is an Assistant Professor in Finance at the Higher Institute of Informatics and Management of Kairouan, Kairouan University, Kairouan, Tunisia. Her research interests include banking and market microstructure and Islamic finance. She has published articles, among others, in *International Journal of the Economics of Business, International Journal of Financial Engineering*, and *International Journal of Business and Management Science.*

Nidhi Kaicker is an Assistant Professor at the School of Business, Public Policy and Social Entrepreneurship, Ambedkar University Delhi, India. She holds a Master's Degree in Business Administration and a Ph.D. degree in Management. Her research interests include managerial economics, agricultural value chains, financial markets, and strategic management. She has published in several international peer-reviewed journals in these areas.

Zeynep Kantur earned her Ph.D. in Economics at Bilkent University. Currently she is an Assistant Professor of Economics at Başkent University and a Researcher at the Sustainable Economics and Finance Association (SEFIA). She was a visiting Ph.D. student at the Center for Research in International Economics (CREI), Spain in 2014. Her research interests include macroeconomics and monetary theory and has published articles on these topics in scientific journals.

Egidijus Kundelis is a doctorate student at ISM University of Management and Economics (Lithuania). His research interests focus on taxation, tax avoidance, and corporate finance. Egidijus has been a tax advisor for 19 years in PwC. He has vast experience in tax due diligence, international tax structuring, and corporate taxation projects for both Lithuanian-based and foreign multinational companies. He has advised a number of inbound investments to Lithuania as well as assisted Lithuanian investors in expanding their activities abroad. Egidijus holds an executive MBA from the Baltic Management Institute (Vytautas Magnus University, with HEC Paris, CBS, Copenhagen, NHH, Bergen, LSM, Louvain) and is a fellow member of ACCA (Association of Chartered Certified Accountants).

Quan V. Le is the Vice President of Academic Affairs and Professor of Economics at the University of Management and Technology (UMT) in Ho Chi Minh City, and Non-Resident Senior Research Fellow at the Institute for Circular Economy Development at Vietnam National University — Ho Chi Minh City. Prior to joining UMT, he was Eva Albers Professor of Economics and Director of the International Business Program at Seattle University. He also held administrative positions at several universities in Vietnam in recent years. He teaches primarily in the areas of international economics, macroeconomics, and economic development. His research is in the areas of entrepreneurship, governance, public health, and sustainability. His work has appeared in *International Review of Financial Analysis*, *Journal of International Money and Finance*, *International Journal of Entrepreneurship Behavior & Research*, and *Public Health*.

Anthony J. Makin is Professor of Economics at Griffith University and has previously taught at the University of Queensland and the National University of Singapore. He has served as an International Consultant Economist with the IMF Institute for Capacity Building, as Director of the Griffith APEC Study Centre and as an economist in the Australian federal departments of Finance, Foreign Affairs and Trade and Treasury. He is a member of the National Economic Panel of the Economic Society of Australia and the author of *International Money and Finance* (2016), Routledge, *Global Finance and the Macroeconomy* (2000), Macmillan, *Global Imbalances, Exchange Rates and Stabilization Policy* (2009), Springer, and *The Limits of Fiscal Policy* (2018), Springer as well as many articles in journals including *Journal of International Money and Finance, Economic Modelling, International Review of Economics and Finance, Empirical Economics, Economic Analysis and Policy, Economic Record, Applied Economics, The World Economy, Review of Development Economics, Business Economics, China and World Economy, Singapore Economic Review*, and *Journal of Asian Economics*.

Maria Manganiello received her B.Sc. in Business Economics and M.Sc. in Economic and Financial Sciences from the University of Naples Parthenope cum laude. She was awarded at the Chamber of Deputies in Rome as a young merit graduate for the attainment of the first-level degree, by obtaining a Master's degree in Global Marketing Communication & Made in Italy at the Italy–USA Foundation, in collaboration with the Ministry of Education, University and Research. She also completed the "Advanced Risk and Portfolio Management Marathon," a Master's-level program at the University of Rome, Tor Vergata. She is currently a third-year Ph.D. student in the International Program on Economics, Statistics, and Sustainability at the Department of Economic and Legal Studies of the University of Naples, Parthenope. Her professional interests include financial economics, quantitative risk management, FinTech, quantitative portfolio management, financial management, corporate finance, systemic risk, and real estate.

Stelios Markoulis is an Associate Professor of Finance at the Cyprus International Institute of Management, a member of the visiting faculty at the University of Cyprus and an Honorary Visiting Research Fellow at the Business School of City University, London. He has taught extensively and carried out research in the area of finance, where his current research interests focus on bank distress, bank regulation, and the effect of external shocks on the stock market and the foreign exchange market. Stelios also has an experience of 17 years in the banking industry, and in particular in the area of investment banking, where he worked as part of, or managed teams, that were in charge of transactions such as stocks and bonds, private and public offerings, mergers and acquisitions, company valuations and restructurings, among others.

Alfredo Martín-Oliver has been Associate Professor at the Business Department, Universitat de les Illes Balears (UIB) since 2011. He worked as a senior economist at the Bank of Spain from 2003–2010, and is currently on leave. Alfredo holds a Ph.D. in Economics and Management of Organizations from the University of Zaragoza (2010) and a Master's in Finance at CEMFI (2003). He has a teaching experience in graduate and postgraduate courses at UIB, Universitat Autònoma de Barcelona (UAB), and CUNEF. His research topics include banking, financial crisis and corporate finance, with publications in high-ranked journals of economics and finance. His work has been presented in national and international conferences.

He is the Principal Researcher of projects financed by public and private entities; his research has been awarded with grants from different public and private institutions. He has supervised a Ph.D. thesis at the Doctorate of Economics and Management Organization (UIB-UAB-UPNA) and has participated in several Working Groups at the European Central Bank.

Dalius Misiūnas is President and Senior Lecturer at ISM University of Management and Economics (Lithuania). His research interests focus on leadership, corporate governance, mergers and acquisitions, business development, project management, strategy, and planning. Hū was one of the authors of a study "Designing business insolvency model and its application for assessing implications of COVID-19 in Lithuania." He holds a Ph.D. in Industrial Automation from Lund University (2005, Sweden). Currently, he is teaching leadership in EMBA and Bachelor studies, leading ISM students CEO's club, representing ISM at The Lithuanian University Rectors' Conference, and is a member of the Advisory Council for Prime Minister on Economic Proposals for recovery and resilience plan. Dr. Misiūnas has also been involved in educational activities as a member of the Council of Higher Education of Lithuania, Chairman of the Council of KTU, and member of the Board of ISM. Previously he also has been CEO, board member, and participated in the raising capital in global financial markets.

Nisreen Moosa is a health economist, holding a Ph.D. from the University of South Australia. She also holds a Bachelor of Science degree from the University of Melbourne, a Bachelor of Health Science (RMIT), a Master of Clinical Chiropractic (RMIT) and a Graduate Certificate in Finance (RMIT). She had previously worked as a chiropractor before she embarked on a change of career in economics and finance. She has published papers in finance and health/environmental economics. She has also co-authored a book entitled *Eliminating the IMF: An Analysis of the Debate to Keep, Reform or Abolish the Fund*, in which she analyzed the effect of IMF operations on healthcare expenditure.

Jason Q. Nguyen is an Assistant Professor of Operations Management at the Ivey Business School, Western University, London, ON, Canada and Non-Resident Senior Research Fellow at the Institute for Circular Economy Development at Vietnam National University

– Ho Chi Minh City. He received his Ph.D. in Business Administration, specializing in Supply Chain and Operation Management at the Carlson School of Management, University of Minnesota, Twin Cities, USA. He uses his expertise in game theory, optimization, behavioral experiments, econometrics, and big data analytics to rigorously analyze how existing environmental regulations, policies and incentive mechanisms influence businesses' operational decisions, as well as other stakeholders' behaviors and perceptions. His work has been published in top-tiered peer-reviewed journals, including Management Science (Financial Times' 50), Manufacturing and Services Operations Management (Financial Times' 50), Service Science and Environmental and Resource Economics.

Jiayang Nie is an undergraduate student at University of California, Berkeley. Graduating with B.A. in Statistics in 2021, he will continue to pursue his academic interest in cross-disciplinary study of mathematics, statistics, and finance in a Master's program in Statistics or Financial Engineering. His research interests include intraday stock market momentum and estimating equity volatility models.

Asror Nigmonov obtained a Ph.D. in Economics from the University of Southern Queensland (Australia). He also holds an M.Sc. in Economics (University of Southern Denmark) and a B.Sc. (Honours) in Economics (University of Westminster). Asror Nigmonov's research focuses on FinTech lending practices and performance evaluation of financial institutions. His Ph.D. research is on "Evaluating Performance of Peer-to-peer (P2P) Lending Platforms." Prior to his Ph.D., Asror worked for MIFX Asset Management (Welltrado), which provides investment tools for managing and tracking investments in P2P loans.

Gülserim Özcan is an Assistant Professor of Economics at Atılım University, Turkey. She received a Ph.D. in Economics and M.A. in Economics from Bilkent University, and a B.Sc. in Economics from Middle East Technical University. During her Ph.D. studies, she worked as a Visiting Fellow at DIW (German Institute for Economic Research), Berlin in Germany in 2014. Between 2017 and 2018, she was a Postdoctoral Research Fellow at the Department of Economics at Bilkent University, and she served as an Economics Consultant at Republic of Turkey Ministry of Finance. As a consultant, she was responsible for monitoring technical assessments of economic developments and developing models for forecasting macroeconomics variables of the Turkish economy. She published in the areas of macroeconomics, monetary economics, and applied time series analysis.

Vijay Pereira (Ph.D., UK) is Full Professor of International and Strategic Human Capital Management in the People and Organizations Department at NEOMA Business School, France. He is also an adjunct Full Professor at the University of South Pacific (USP) Fiji. Professor Pereira is the Associate Editor (Strategic Management and Organization Behavior) for the *Journal of Business Research* and the Global Real Impact Editor for the *Journal of Knowledge Management*. Professor Pereira has unique experience in industry, consulting, and academia. He has a track record of attracting funding and has published widely, in over 150 outlets, including in leading international journals such as the *HRM US, Academy of Management Perspectives, Academy of Management Discoveries, Journal of Business Ethics, Journal of World Business, British Journal of Management, International Journal of HRM, Journal of Business Research, International Journal of Research in Marketing, Business History, International Marketing Review, Journal of International Management, International Business Review, Applied Psychology: An International Review* and *International Journal of Production Research*, among others. Professor Pereira has guest edited close to 20 special issues in top-tier journals and has published 12 books. He is currently on the editorial and advisory board for the journals *Production and Operations Management* (Listed in *Financial Times*), *Journal of Management Studies, International Journal of HRM, Asia Pacific Journal of Management, Asian Business & Management Journal*, and *South Asian History and Culture*. Professor Pereira is the elected Vice President of the Academy of International Business (Middle East and North Africa) and the Secretary of the Indian Academy of Management (an affiliate of the Academy of Management, US).

Huy Pham is a Lecturer in Finance at RMIT University in Vietnam and a regular member of American Finance Association. He obtained his Ph.D. from University of South Australia and worked at various universities in Australia and Vietnam prior to joining RMIT University. His research interests are in the fields of FinTech, cryptocurrencies, environmental finance, asset pricing, and empirical finance.

He has published his work in a wide range of academic journals, including *Accounting and Finance, Economic Modelling* and *Applied Economics* among many others. Huy has served as a referee for several journals including *Transportation Research Part E: Logistics and Transportation Review*, and *Economic Modelling*, among several others. He is often approached for expert comments on financial and economic issues from various local and international premium news outlets such as *Tech in Asia*, *Nikkei Asian Review*, and *Vietnam Investment Review*.

Xiao Qiao is an Assistant Professor at the School of Data Science at the City University of Hong Kong and a member of the Hong Kong Institute for Data Science. He is on the editorial board of the *Journal of Portfolio Management* and his research has been featured by *Forbes* and *Institutional Investor*. Prior to CityU, Xiao worked in the investment management industry, where he participated in the creation of two award-winning ETFs. He was a co-founder at Paraconic Technologies, an associate director at SummerHaven Investment Management, and a quantitative researcher at Hull Investments. Xiao received a B.S. in Economics from the Wharton School and a B.S. in Engineering from the School of Engineering and Applied Sciences at the University of Pennsylvania. He received a Ph.D. in Finance from the University of Chicago, where he was Nobel laureate Eugene Fama's teaching assistant.

Yves Rakotondratsimba is an Assistant Professor of Quantitative Finance at ECE Paris-Engineering School, INSEEC U, France. At present, Yves is working on predictive analyses, scenario generations, valuation, and hedging of financial derivatives. He is also developing solutions for the education under the combined effect of digital transformation, environmental transitions, and rise of DeepTech. Yves has published at least 70 academic publications, 38 of which are in mathematics. He has participated in at least 40 international finance conferences.

Vikash Ramiah is an Associate Professor in Finance at University of Wollongong in Dubai. Vikash has been teaching economics and finance courses at the University of South Australia, Royal Melbourne Institute of Technology, University of Melbourne, La Trobe University, and Australian Catholic University since 1999. He has published in reputable academic journals and supervises numerous

Ph.D. students. His industry experience involves ANZ investment banking, the Australian Stock Exchange, Finance and Treasury Association of Australia, Glomacs, and the Australian Centre for Financial Studies. Other services to the community includes being a research fellow for Institute of Global Business and Society, Cologne University of Applied Sciences, and Tianjin Academy of Environmental Science. He has established his leadership both domestically and internationally as he is appointed as a Professorial Research Associate at Victoria University, Adjunct Professor at Ton Duc Thang University, Adjunct Associate Professor at UniSA, and Professor at Global Humanistic University. He specializes in Applied Finance and his research areas are financial markets, behavioral finance, and environmental/sustainable finance.

Marco Rossi is the Founder of The Global Pandemic Shield Project, which he launched in response to the COVID-19 pandemic to provide tailored financial protection to businesses in the event of disease outbreaks. Previously, he worked for over 20 years at the IMF, covering design and implementation of sustainable economic policy strategies in a wide range of countries, reforms of the global financial system, analysis and assessment of economic and financial, local, regional, and global conditions and trends, and research. Prior to joining the IMF, he worked at the Bank of England, advising on topics relevant to the Bank's operations in the run-up to the European Monetary Union. He is the author of *Payment Systems in the Financial Markets* (McMillan Press 1998, https://link.springer.com/book/10.1007/978-1-349-26374-5). He has contributed to edited books by leading scientific publishers and has published in peer-review professional journals. He received his Ph.D. in Quantitative Economics jointly from the London School of Economics and the Catholic University of Louvain.

Antonio Sánchez Serrano is Principal Economist at the European Systemic Risk Board (since 2015), where he has worked intensively on financial stability and systemic risk analysis, with particular attention to the EU banking system. He has also been the Secretary of the Advisory Scientific Committee of the European Systemic Risk Board since August 2017. He has more than fifteen years of working experience gained at Banco de España and the European Central

Bank. Antonio has published several articles in academic journals and contributed to many ECB and ESRB reports.

Siuzana Ščerbina-Dalibagienė heads the division of Audit, Property Valuation and Insolvency Policy in the Ministry of Finance of the Republic of Lithuania and has extensive experience in drafting legislation in the fields of insolvency, restructuring and corporate law. She is one of the main drafters of the Law of Insolvency of Legal Entities (entered into force 2020). She is also responsible for the implementation of corporate insolvency reform in Lithuania and the establishment of an early warning system for business in financial difficulties. At the European Union level, she participates in European Council working parties and expert groups. She obtained her Ph.D. in Finance and also holds background in law. Her main research interests are insolvency, restructuring, corporate governance, and corporate law.

Matthias Scherf is a Research Fellow and Ph.D. student of Finance and Banking at the University of Trier, Germany. He holds a Master's degree in Business Administration, from the University of Trier, where he specialized in Accounting, Taxation, and Finance. His research interest includes behavioral finance, financial markets, and financial decision-making. Additionally, he teaches behavioral finance and information and decision theory at the same university.

Eliyathamby A. Selvanathan is a Professor in Econometrics in the Economics and Business Statistics Discipline at Griffith University. He publishes theoretical and applied work in consumer demand, index numbers, tourism economics, and energy economics. His publications have appeared in high-ranking journals such as *Review of Economic Studies, Economics Letters, Journal of Economics and Business Statistics, Review of Economics and Statistics, Journal of Econometrics, Energy Economics, Transportation Research, Marketing Science, Tourism Analysis, Tourism Economics, Applied Economics, Empirical Economics*, and *Economic Record*. He has published well over 100 journal articles and book chapters and 8 research monographs. He is a co-author of the best-selling Australasian statistics textbook *Business Statistics* (Selvanathan, E. Antony, Saroja Selvanathan, and Gerald Keller; Cengage AU, 2016). He has received several teaching awards for his undergraduate and postgraduate teaching as well as for Ph.D. supervision.

Saroja Selvanathan is a Professor of Econometrics in the Economics and Business Statistics Discipline at Griffith University. Her research interests include time series analysis, econometric modeling, and consumer demand. She has published well over 75 journal articles and 5 research monographs in the broad area of applied econometrics. She is a co-author of the best-selling Australian business statistics textbook, *Business Statistics* (Selvanathan, E. Antony, Saroja Selvanathan, and Gerald Keller; Cengage AU, 2016). She has received several teaching awards for her contribution to Postgraduate Statistics and Research Design training, and more recently she was awarded the Griffith University Vice-Chancellor's Award for Excellence in Research in the category of Ph.D. supervision. She is also the co-editor-in-chief for the *Journal of the Asia Pacific Economy.*

İlkay Şendeniz-Yüncü is an Assistant Professor of Finance at Middle East Technical University, Turkey. She obtained her B.S. and M.S. degrees in Civil Engineering as well as an MBA from the same university. She received her Ph.D. in Finance from Bilkent University in 2007 and subsequently conducted postdoctoral research at the University of California, Berkeley, and Tilburg University. She previously held positions of Instructor at Bilkent University, Lecturer at Tilburg University, Assistant Professor of Finance at IÉSEG School of Management, and Assistant Professor of Finance at MEF University. Her research interests are banking, finance-growth relationships, and financial markets. She has published in the *Journal of Banking and Finance, Journal of Corporate Finance, Finance Research Letters, Applied Economics*, and *Emerging Markets Finance and Trade.*

Florina Silaghi is a Serra Húnter Fellow, Lecturer in Finance at the Autonomous University of Barcelona since 2015. She obtained a Ph.D. in Finance at University of Rennes 1 (2014), including a visiting period at Cass Business School London, and a Master's in Economics and Finance at CEMFI Madrid (2010). Her main research interest is corporate finance, with a particular focus on corporate debt renegotiation, trade credit, risk management, and crowdfunding. She has published her work in reputable international journals, including the *Journal of Corporate Finance, Journal of Banking and*

Finance, and the *European Journal of Operational Research*. She has been awarded the Juan de la Cierva Incorporation Grant.

Nivedita Sinha is an Assistant Professor at the Department of Economics & Finance at the Birla Institute of Technology & Science, Pilani, Hyderabad Campus, India. She obtained her Ph.D. in Finance & Control from the Indian Institute of Management, Bangalore, India. Nivedita's research focuses on corporate governance and, in particular, principal–principal agency conflicts in family business groups. She has received project funding from her institute to study minority shareholder's protection and its relationship with the business group ownership structure. She also has research interests in the area of entrepreneurial finance.

Anna Sławik is an Assistant Professor at the Faculty of Management and Social Communication of the Jagiellonian University in Cracow, Poland. Her research focuses on stakeholder management, corporate social responsibility (CSR), sustainable and responsible investing (SRI), management control, and corporate communication. Anna obtained a Ph.D. in Economics, degree with honors, from the Jagiellonian University, and her dissertation title was "Stakeholder identification in the management of industrial companies under contemporary crisis conditions." She also holds an M.A. in Management and Marketing, and a B.A. in Journalism and Social Communication. Anna is an author of over 10 academic papers, as well as the book *Lobbying in Corporate Strategies: Five Interesting Case Studies*. Krakow: Jagiellonian University Press, 2009. Her recent research project focuses on the development and testing of the Methodology of Identification of Strategic Stakeholders (MISS). She has been involved in regular research cooperation with the University of Canterbury, New Zealand.

Neophytos Vasiliou has an MBA and an M.Sc. in Environmental Conservation and Management (Energy and Pollution) from the Open University of Cyprus. He also holds a B.Eng. and an M.Sc. in Electrical Engineering from the Cyprus University of Technology. Neophytos is an active independent researcher, currently working on the effect of external shocks on markets.

Qiyu Wang obtained her Master's degree in Financial Mathematics from the University of Minnesota, Twin Cities, 2008 and a Ph.D.

degree in Applied Mathematics from The Hong Kong Polytechnic University, 2017. She had studied at the University of Chicago. Previous, the author had worked for Deloitte, Nielsen, and State Street from 2011–2014. Currently, she is a Lecturer at the Zhejiang University of Finance and Economics, Hangzhou, China.

Sibo Yan is a Quantitative Economist at Freddie Mac and research associate of UCLA. He holds a Ph.D. from UCLA in both Economics and Statistics. Sibo's research interests include financial econometrics, risk management, and machine learning, with applications to high-frequency financial data. His work has been published in IGI Global Academic Publications, *Journal of Portfolio Management*, *International Review of Finance*, and IEEE Big Data Conference. He has taught economics and finance in UCLA and Pepperdine University. He is a member and reviewer of the INFINITI Conference on International Finance, and IGI Global Academic Publications and a certified financial risk manager at the Global Association of Risk Professionals.

https://doi.org/10.1142/9781800610781_fmatter

Contents

PART I

COVID-19: Macroeconomic Effects

https://doi.org/10.1142/9781800610781_0001

Chapter 1

Health and Socio-economic Consequences of the COVID-19 Pandemic: Government Responses and Recovery

Linh Tu Ho[*,†,‡] **and Christopher Gan**[†,§]

[*]*Faculty of Economics and Development Studies*
University of Economics, Hue University, Vietnam

[†]*Department of Financial and Business Systems*
Lincoln University, Christchurch 7647, New Zealand

[‡]*htlinh@hce.edu.vn; Linh.Ho@lincoln.ac.nz*
[§]*christopher.gan@lincoln.ac.nz*

Abstract

This chapter explores government responses to rebuild their economies post COVID-19. First, the chapter briefly reviews the background of the virus outbreak and its consequences that led to unprecedented actions of governments. Second, the chapter analyses the government responses to the COVID-19 pandemic to overcome the health–social–economic crisis in 129 countries from Africa (27), America (23), Asia (27), Europe (48), and Oceania (4). Next, the time-dependent expectations in rebuilding the economies are discussed. The chapter concludes with takeaway messages to address an uncertain future.

1.1. Introduction

The COVID-19 pandemic started as a humanitarian crisis but snowballed into an economic and social crisis. As the deadly virus continues to spread globally, it is grinding life to a halt in cities around the world. The virus knows no geographical or political boundaries; political systems; or ethnic, class, and religious divides. It does not discriminate, and no country is spared. China was the first to resort to a massive lockdown on January 23, 2020 (Yuan *et al.*, 2020) followed by Italy, Spain, France, and New Zealand (Hale *et al.*, 2020). Massive lockdown is necessary to slow the rapid spread of the deadly disease and buy time for health authorities and hospitals to prepare for a surge in patients. However, massive lockdown and social distancing measures have also carried economic and social consequences. There is a large number of studies on the impacts of the COVID-19 pandemic on human health, economics, and financial markets. For example, Fernandes (2020), using data as of March 2020, shows the evidence of negative shock of the COVID-19 pandemic on the global financial markets and the severe economic impacts worldwide based on scenarios of 1.5-month, 3-month, and 4.5-month shutdowns. Brodeaur *et al.* (2020) review the literature on economic, financial, and socio-economic consequences of social distancing and lockdown measures as of May 2020. Tisdell (2020) provides important insights into social issues and political pressures due to the COVID-19 pandemic. The world is scrambling to prevent a global health–social–economic recession. It is an unprecedentedly difficult time for many people, causing worries about job security, food security, access to hospitals, and the lack of human social interaction. More importantly, economic recessions have proven to carry an impact on what are known to be the social determinants of health, exacerbating economic, social, and health inequalities across populations. Therefore, it is important to evaluate government responses to contain the widely spread virus, mitigate its consequences, and rebuild the economies post COVID-19.

The objective of this chapter is to investigate government responses to the COVID-19 pandemic with a focus on fiscal and monetary policies in five continents including Africa, America, Asia, Europe, and Oceania. We select our sampled countries based on two policy trackers: "Policy Responses to COVID-19" by the International Monetary Fund (IMF, 2020b) and "Country Policy Tracker" by the Organisation for Economic Co-operation and Development (OECD, 2020b). As of July 1, 2020, the two policy trackers documented government responses in 129 countries from Africa (27), America (23), Asia (27), Europe (48), and Oceania (4). To our best knowledge, this chapter is the first to investigate the fiscal and monetary responses to the COVID-19 pandemic using a large number of sampled countries from five continents. Massinga *et al.* (2020) studied containment measures in response to the COVID-19 pandemic in Africa. An and Tang (2020) compared COVID-19 responses of five countries in East Asia (Taiwan, Hong Kong, South Korea, Singapore, and Japan) in terms of leadership competence, institutional infrastructure, and cultural compatibility. Han *et al.* (2020) examined the government responses using containment measures of nine nations in the Asia-Pacific region and Europe (Hong Kong, Japan, New Zealand, Singapore, South Korea, Germany, Norway, Spain, and the UK). However, none of these studies investigated fiscal and monetary policies that governments have implemented to combat the COVID-19 pandemic.

The chapter compares the government responses to the COVID-19 pandemic based on the 129 sampled countries from five continents to provide important lessons learned to respond to the pandemic. First, we present the health, social, and economic consequences of COVID-19 that led to drastic government actions. Next, we discuss the government responses using fiscal and monetary policies to mitigate the toxic effects of the COVID-19 pandemic. This is followed by a discussion of the time-dependent expectations, including debt, recession, and growth during and post COVID-19 pandemic. Finally, this chapter suggests urgent actions that policymakers have to adopt in an uncertain future because of the new waves of the virus and how to accelerate global economic recovery.

The chapter identified several key findings. In terms of the health–social–economic consequences, we initially found that the COVID-19 outbreak spread globally, with the unequal distribution of confirmed cases and deaths among the five continents. Although the outbreak started in Asia, America had the highest number of confirmed cases and reported most deaths as of June 15, 2021. Second, using data of pre-lockdown and lockdown periods across the five continents, we found that announcing lockdown orders early is associated with the lower number of confirmed cases and the shorter lockdown period. Third, contact tracing using technology was widely implemented across the five continents, which raises data privacy problems and security challenges. Fourth, protecting health workers and mental health services received greater attention during the outbreak, and countries from Europe, America, and Oceania implemented more measures to protect the elderly than countries in Asia and Africa. Fifth, the chapter confirms the economic and financial recession in 2020 as a result of the health crisis based on the World Uncertainty Index WUI (2020) and the Global Economic Policy Uncertainty Index EPU (2020).

Regarding the government responses to the COVID-19 pandemic, there were differences in implementing fiscal policies (employment and social support, tax measures, and health packages) and monetary policies among the five continents. However, corporate income tax was the most common tax measure implemented across the five continents to improve business cash-flow. Less than 50% of the sampled countries applied health system measures in response to the COVID-19 pandemic. The most common monetary measures implemented in the five continents were liquidity support, monetary policy rate cut, loan restructuring, and suspension of loan requirements or repayments. Importantly, although COVID-19 immediate responses were applied across the five continents as of July 2020, there was a lack of longer-term recovery measures to support households, stop the job crisis, and prevent social consequences.

Rebuilding the global economy post COVID-19 depends on whether new waves of the pandemic will emerge. The economies can enter into debt and recession for a long time before recovery. Based on the discussion of the high levels of public debt, global recession, and high risk of the second wave of COVID-19 pandemic, we conclude that it will take more than five years to economically recover post COVID-19 if the new outbreak emerges in 2021. However, the second wave of the COVID-19 pandemic emerged earlier than expected. For example, from August to November 2020, fresh outbreaks were reported in many countries such as Canada, Malaysia, Myanmar, and European countries such as Belgium, France, Germany, Italy, and the United Kingdom (ECDC, 2020c).

The new waves of COVID-19 pandemic, high levels of public debt, and global recession require pressing governmental action to rebuild the economies post COVID-19. The recommendations are:

(i) develop epidemiological models to prevent future pandemics while reopening economies;
(ii) implement immediate fiscal measures to save lives and buffer businesses using tax measures during the COVID-19 pandemic;
(iii) boost the health–social–economic recovery using longer-term measures to support households, stop job crisis and prevent social consequences; and
(iv) issue COVID-19 bonds to finance public investments without increasing the risk of public debt.

The chapter is organized as follows. Section 1.2 reviews the background of the virus outbreak and its consequences. Section 1.3 investigates the government responses to the COVID-19 pandemic to overcome the health–social–economic crisis. Section 1.4 discusses time-dependent expectations with recommended actions in rebuilding the economies. Section 1.5 concludes the chapter with takeaway messages to address the uncertain future.

1.2. COVID-19 and Consequences

1.2.1. *Health consequences*

1.2.1.1. *From one to thousand cases*

COVID-19 has spread over the world unprecedentedly. In December 2019, the first cases of COVID-19 were reported in China. As of June 15, 2021, 176,953,132 confirmed cases and 3,825,401 deaths from coronavirus outbreak were reported in 220 countries around the globe (Worldometer, 2021). The virus was first called 2019-nCoV, referring to the novel or 2019 coronavirus by the World Health Organization (WHO). Later in the outbreak, the WHO gave it the official name as Corona Virus Disease 2019 or COVID-19 on February 11, 2020 (WHO, 2020d).

According to the ECDC (2020a), the lowest number of confirmed cases was reported in Oceania, while America had the highest number of confirmed cases, followed by Asia and Europe. Figure 1.1 shows

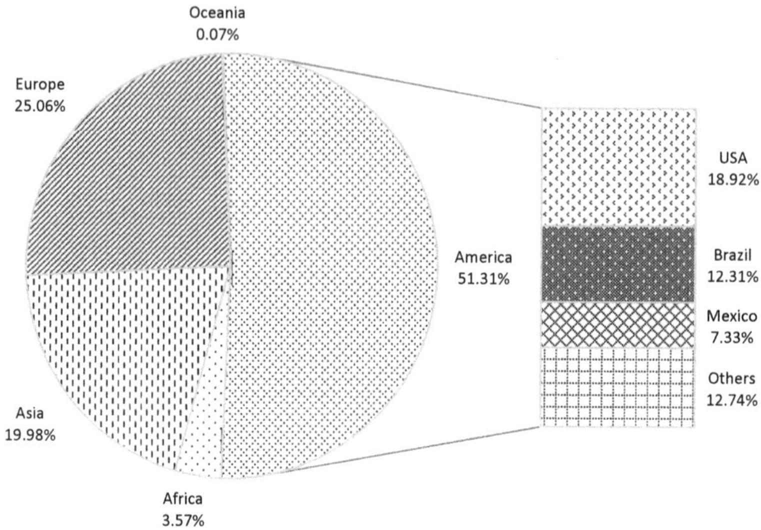

Figure 1.1. Distribution of COVID-19 deaths of the five continents.
Source: Authors' calculation as of November 20, 2020, based on data from Worldometer (2020b).

the number of COVID-19 deaths in the five continents. The two continents reporting the most deaths were America (51.31%) and Europe (25.06%) (see Figure 1.1). According to Worldometer (2021), as of June 15, 2021, the six countries experiencing the most deaths were the US (615,213), Brazil (488,228), India (377,061), Mexico (230,148), Peru (188,708), and the UK (127,907).

1.2.1.2. *Lockdown measures*

To reduce the rapid spread of the COVID-19 pandemic and eliminate the virus, governments applied containment measures including social distancing, lockdown, travel ban, school closure, cancellation of public events and places, and shutdown of most major economic activities. In terms of the lockdown measures, announcing lockdown policies that limit residents' movements and activities were not always prompt to contain the virus in some countries. The different periods from the first-case date to the lockdown start date (the pre-lockdown periods) and the lockdown periods are shown in Figures 1.2 and 1.3.

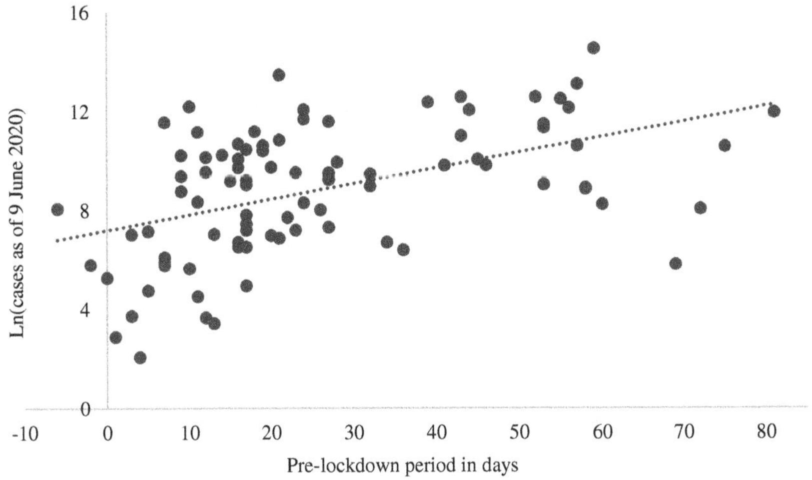

Figure 1.2. The relationship between pre-lockdown periods and the total confirmed COVID-19 cases of the five continents.

Note: The figure is for a sample of 88 countries including Africa (16), America (19), Asia (26), Europe (23), and Oceania (4). A negative value of the pre-lockdown period in days means a country went into lockdown before the first confirmed case was detected in the country.

Source: Authors' calculation as of June 9, 2020, based on data from ECDC (2020b), OECD (2020a), Hale *et al.* (2020), and Worldometer (2020a).

Figure 1.2 shows the total confirmed COVID-19 cases in natural logarithm as of June 9, 2020, and the pre-lockdown period using a sub-sample of 88 countries from Africa (16), America (19), Asia (26), Europe (23), and Oceania (4). Among the 88 countries, since the first-case date, 18 countries went straight into lockdown within the first 10 days of the outbreak, 38 countries went into lockdown between days 10 and 26, and more than 30 countries implemented the lockdown measure after day 26. The positive relationship between the total confirmed COVID-19 cases and the length of the pre-lockdown period is shown in Figure 1.2. This finding aligns with Yuan *et al.* (2020) estimation results of the effectiveness of early control measures (Wuhan's lockdown) in reducing infections in regions outside the outbreak (Wuhan) in China.

Figure 1.3 shows the averages of pre-lockdown and lockdown periods (in days) with standard deviations in the five continents. Based on data availability, Figure 1.3 consists of 76 sampled countries, with

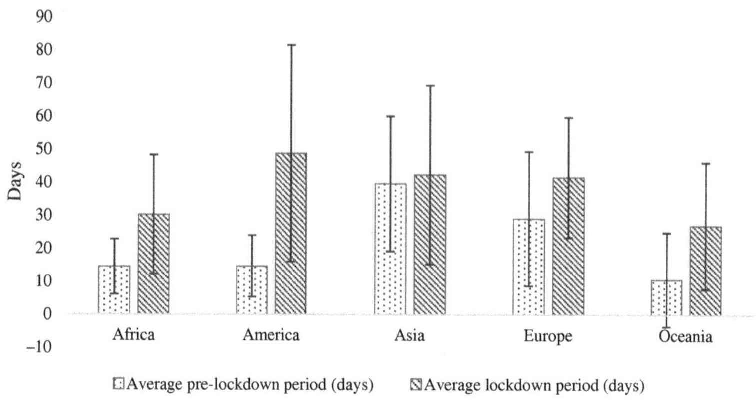

Figure 1.3. The average pre-lockdown and lockdown periods of the five continents.

Note: The figure is for a sample of 76 countries from Africa (15), America (15), Asia (22), Europe (21), and Oceania (3).

Source: Authors' calculation as of June 9, 2020, based on data from ECDC (2020b), OECD (2020a), Hale *et al.* (2020) and Worldometer (2020a).

15 in Africa, 15 in America, 22 in Asia, 21 in Europe, and 3 in Oceania. In general, Oceania outperformed America and Europe in eliminating the COVID-19 spread (see Figures 1.1 and 1.3). The countries in Oceania quickly went into lockdown on day 11 since the first reported case and remained lockdown for 27 days on average, whereas it took the countries in America 15 days to lockdown and 49 days to lift the lockdown on average (see Figure 1.3). These numbers in Europe are 30 days and 42 days, respectively (see Figure 1.3).

1.2.1.3. *Isolation, quarantine, and contact tracing*

Isolation, quarantine, and contact tracing are important containment measures to protect public health from disease outbreaks. Isolation and quarantine aim to separate a person from social activities during the incubation period of a virus (Moodley *et al.*, 2020). For COVID-19, most countries enforced all persons entering their borders to be mandatorily self-isolated or placed in a managed-isolation or quarantine facility from the date of entry for the incubation period of 14 days or up to 28 days (OECD, 2020b).

Contact tracing and testing contribute to the success of the containment measures (WHO, 2020b). Figure 1.4 describes measures of contact tracking, increasing healthcare supplies, and improving

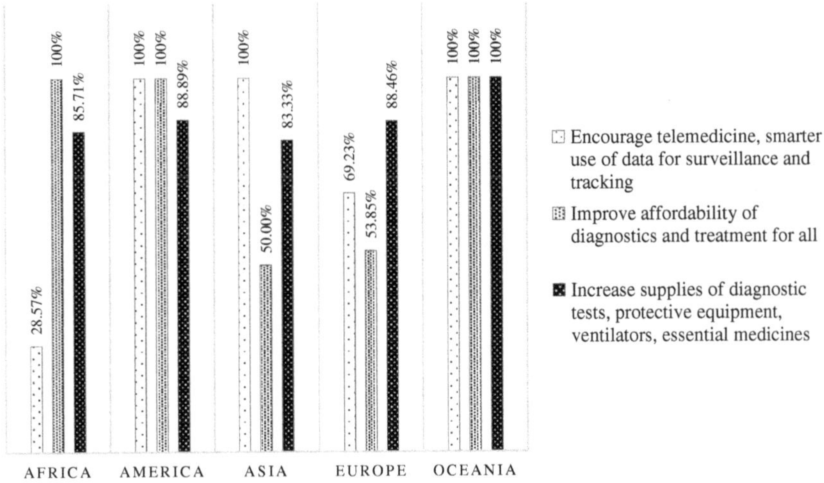

Figure 1.4. Contact tracing, healthcare supplies, and diagnostics and treatment of the five continents.

Note: The figure is for a sample of 50 countries from Africa (7), America (9), Asia (6), Europe (26), and Oceania (2).

Source: Authors' calculation as of June 24, 2020, based on the country policy tracker relating to health system response tracker by OECD (2020b) and the European Commission (EC)-OECD Science, Technology and Innovation Policy (STIP) Survey (Question 5) on responses to COVID-19 (EC/OECD, 2020).

diagnostic and treatment ability in 50 countries from Africa (7), America (9), Asia (6), Europe (26), and Oceania (2). Figure 1.4 shows 100% of countries in America, Asia, and Oceania applied technology for surveillance and tracking to combat the virus, whereas the rate is less than 30% in Africa and just above 69% in Europe. Overall, more than 80% of countries across the five continents increased medical supplies during the pandemic (see Figure 1.4). While all countries in Africa, America, and Oceania improved their capacities for diagnostics and treatment, Figure 1.4 reports about half of the countries in Asia and Europe increased their capacities.

1.2.2. *Social consequences*

1.2.2.1. *Working under pressure*

The containment measures of massive lockdown, isolation, and quarantine require workers and learners to change their normal way of working and learning to the digital modes. Digital work under lockdown brings opportunities for businesses and society to reduce vehicle emissions because of less travel and to work more flexibly (Richter, 2020). However, the closure of schools and non-essential businesses raised impending issues such as mental health, social connection, and finances (Pan, 2020). Although working from home ensures physical distance, digital work reduces workers' commitments in getting things done (Eckhardt, 2019), which can impact productivity and output. For some, going to work and meeting people would keep them sane. Richter (2020) finds that not only executives but also employees in Europe and New Zealand experienced stress because of working remotely with kids around, office-sharing with a partner, and lack of physical interactions. Besides, online meetings were stressful for many users because of unstable Internet connections and time-consuming nature of the sessions, which led to "Zoom fatigue" (Fosslien and West Duffy, 2020).

Online learning during the COVID-19 pandemic because of lockdown, isolation, and quarantine also creates pressure on learners. Students are not exempt from being affected by this deadly virus. Hyseni-Duraku and Hoxha (2020) find that students were under moderate levels of stress and mild psychological anxiety when studying online during lockdowns. Time management for many online assignments in limited space at home was reported as a key factor that caused students to be stressed and distracted during the lockdown (Hyseni-Duraku and Hoxha, 2020). Likewise, the working environment and technologies create more difficulties for users who do not normally work and study from home. Brewis (2020) finds that learning new ways of communication using different tools such as Zoom, Microsoft Teams, and Skype for various purposes during a short time created stress for workers and learners.

Data privacy and security are other technological issues that users are afraid of. Contact tracing using tracking applications and data-management tools helps countries combat the deadly COVID-19 spread. For example, some tracing applications include COVID-19 AO in Angola, GH COVID-19 Tracker App in Ghana, Alipay Health Code in China, TraceTogether in Singapore, COVIDSafe in Australia, NZ COVID Trace in New Zealand, CovidSafe in the US, COVID Shield in Canada, CoronApp in Colombia, Covi-ID in South Africa, NHS COVID-19 in the UK, and StopCovid in France. However, using applications to access individuals' location challenges application developers and authorities in terms of responsible data use. According to Zwitter and Gstrein (2020), while tracking-application users are concerned about their human rights and protection of their private information, there is a legal gap in data protection and privacy during this global health crisis.

1.2.2.2. *Social isolation and fear*

To contain the massive COVID-19 outbreak, implementing drastic measures such as lockdown, isolation, and quarantine can result in health-related issues such as mental health and domestic violence. According to Brooks *et al.* (2020), the side effects of quarantine on the psyche are anger, confusion, and post-traumatic stress. The health consequences due to isolation or quarantine can affect not only isolated people but also public health officials, politicians, and task-forces such as border controls, police, and military who support the healthcare system (Brooks *et al.*, 2020). People who are infected with the virus may also experience stress because of discriminatory feelings. Kassema (2020) finds that infected people experienced stress symptoms caused by quarantine, travel restrictions, discriminatory treatment, and fear of the virus spread.

Healthcare workers experienced mental symptoms during the COVID-19 pandemic. Cerami *et al.* (2020) find that Italian healthcare workers experienced distress and loneliness caused by COVID-19 pandemic. Cerami and co-authors emphasize the immediate need for healthcare policies and guidelines to manage the psychosocial distress crisis. Brewis (2020) finds the health and socio-economic impact on women working from home during lockdown because they had to meet job deadlines while spending more time with their partners and children. According to Brewis, female workers, especially women working in the healthcare sector, also experienced greater social and economic difficulties during the pandemic because they had to work under high pressure and stress in hospitals and take care of their homes after work.

The COVID-19 pandemic and its negative impact on parents affect children who play and study at home. While parents, especially mothers, faced work-from-home stress with financial problems, their parenting practices were more verbally and physically violent with their children at home (Lee and Ward, 2020). Staying at home and practicing physical distancing contributed to children's

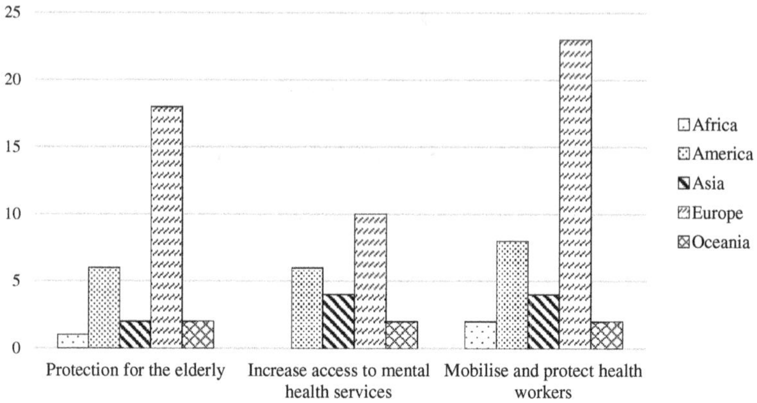

Figure 1.5. Mental health services and protection for the elderly and health workers of the five continents.

Note: The figure is for a sample of 50 countries from Africa (7), America (9), Asia (6), Europe (26), and Oceania (2).

Source: Authors' calculation as of June 24, 2020, based on data from OECD (2020b) and EC/OECD (2020).

emotional and behavioural changes (i.e. increased anxiousness and fear) (Hyseni-Duraku and Hoxha, 2020; Lee and Ward, 2020). WHO (2020a) reports an increase in at-home violence against children, partners, and the elderly. Therefore, with the guidance of WHO, countries responded to care for people who experience mental health symptoms and violence, including vulnerable people such as the elderly. Figure 1.5 shows the responses of 50 countries (by continent) which provide more access to mental health services and protect the elderly and health workers. In general, most countries paid more attention to protecting health workers and providing mental health services, while countries from Europe, America, and Oceania had more policies to protect the elderly than countries in Asia and Africa (see Figure 1.5).

1.2.3. *Economic consequences*

1.2.3.1. *Economic uncertainty*

The COVID-19 pandemic also caused economic uncertainty. The containment measures that limit all non-essential activities and mass gatherings worldwide to save people from the virus put the economies into a partly-frozen status. While some people can work and study remotely, organizations and companies producing goods and services need to suspend their operations. Therefore, gross domestic product (GDP) of most countries will go on a downfall spiral because of the restrictive containment measures (Kassema, 2020; OECD, 2020f; Pinshi, 2020). Closing businesses, especially in industries relating to retail sales, global travelling, and tourism, means unemployment and no income. Given the national shutdown of the economies, OECD (2020e) forecasts the impact of shutdowns on GDP in 2020 at about 25% for the US, France, Italy, and the UK, and around 30% for Spain and Germany.

The most severe economic recession is forecasted at the end of 2020. Figure 1.6 shows the economic outlook of selected countries (by continent) and the world. The outlook shows two scenarios of single-hit and double-hit (without and with the second wave of the virus spread, respectively). In terms of changes in the real GDP in

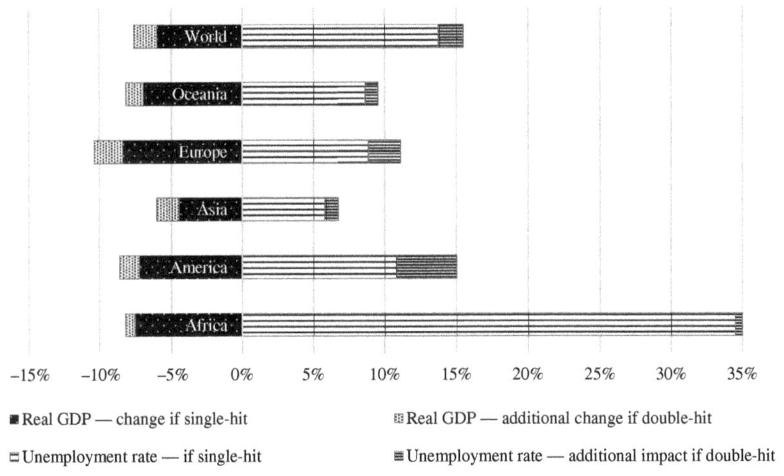

Figure 1.6. Estimated changes in real GDP and projected unemployment rate of the five continents.

Note: The figure is for a sample of 33 countries from Africa (1), America (4), Asia (3), Europe (23), and Oceania (2). The sample selection is based on the estimated data availability of real GDP change and the unemployment rate.

Source: Authors' calculation as of June 24, 2020, based on data from OECD (2020f,i,j).

2020 compared to 2019, Asia expects the least decrease, and Europe expects the hardest fall (see Figure 1.6). The unemployment rate in the fourth quarter of 2020 in America is projected to be higher than most of the other continents except for Africa. The forecast data of Africa is for only South Africa due to data unavailable in other African countries.

The COVID-19 pandemic also impacts global poverty by pushing millions of people into poverty. Mahler *et al.* (2020) forecasted 40–60 more million people in extreme poverty in their first estimation in April 2020, then updated the estimation two months later with two scenarios of baseline (single wave of COVID-19 pandemic) and downside (another wave of COVID-19 pandemic). It is estimated that 71 more million people are pushed into extreme poverty (at the international poverty line of US$1.90 per day) in the baseline scenario, and the figure jumps to 100 million people in the downside scenario (Mahler *et al.*, 2020). Sub-Saharan Africa and South Asia can be affected the hardest by the COVID-19 pandemic because the number of poor is expected to increase based on higher poverty lines of US$3.20 and US$5.50 per day (Mahler *et al.*, 2020).

1.2.3.2. *Financial volatility*

The financial crisis is projected to take place in 2020–2021 due to the economic uncertainty caused by the COVID-19 pandemic. A financial recession can result from increasing risk due to declines in stock prices, falls in currency values (Chowdhry and Goyal, 2000), strong volatilities, financial market dysfunction (Sukharev, 2020), and the uncertainty of the disease outbreaks (Pinshi, 2020). The WUI shows the different levels of uncertainty corresponding to different epidemics over time (see Figure 1.7). The WUI demonstrates the uncertainty level in 2020 is unprecedented and the worst over the last 50 years. The EPU shows the massive increases during the financial crises in 1998 and 2008 and the epidemics in 2002, 2012, and 2020 (see Figure 1.7).

The COVID-19 pandemic resulted in an enormous shock to the financial market. According to the Chicago Board Options Exchange (CBOE, 2020), the acceleration of the volatility index (VIX) associated with COVID-19 in 2020 (+207.65% on March 16,

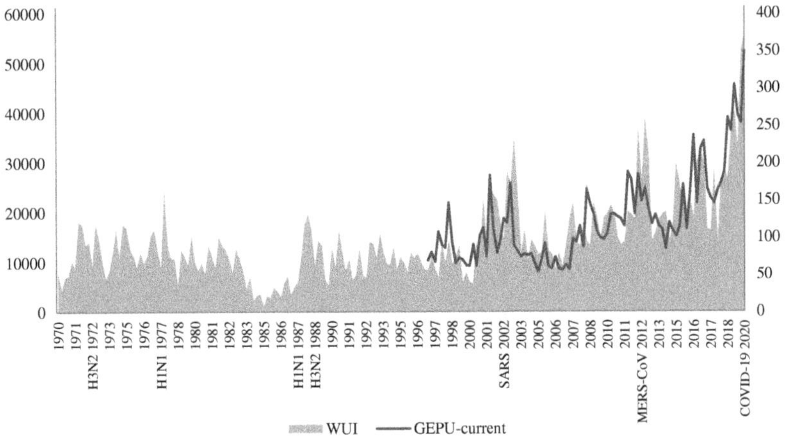

Figure 1.7. The World Uncertainty Index and Global Economic Policy Uncertainty Index.

Note: The outbreaks over time are based on Kilbourne (2006) and WHO (2020c).

Source: Authors' calculation as of June 30, 2020, based on data from WUI (2020) and EPU (2020).

2020) is steeper than the financial recession in 2008 (+200.63% on November 17, 2008). The S&P 500 index (SPX) also indicates the shrinking wave of the financial markets in March 2020 (CBOE, 2020) as a result of high volatility and economic uncertainty in 2020 (see Figure 1.7). As a result, the global economy faces the greatest recession triggered by the health crisis from COVID-19 pandemic (World Bank, 2020).

In conclusion, the COVID-19 pandemic led to massive containment measures that carry health, social, and economic consequences. To get through the health–social–economic crisis, governments' critical responses play important roles in fighting the deadly virus, protecting vulnerable people, securing jobs, and recovering the economies.

1.3. Government Responses to the COVID-19 Pandemic

Government responses to the COVID-19 pandemic are diversified and can be divided into four groups: fiscal policies, monetary policies, containment measures, and burden-sharing measures for private sectors. This section investigates the fiscal and monetary policies that help the economies get through the COVID-19 pandemic. The fiscal policies include employment and social support, tax measure, and health package. The monetary measures consist of mortgage extension, digital banking, and exchange rate management.

1.3.1. *Fiscal policies*

Fiscal policies are introduced to mitigate the economic impact of the COVID-19 pandemic. The policies include budgets to support businesses during the pandemic and restructuring budgets to minimize the effects of the health–social–economic crisis. The budgets include employment and social support, tax measures, and health packages. The fiscal measures play a vital role in supporting and rebuilding the economies during the health–social–economic crisis in 2020. Without the budgets, it would take governments years to restart their economies.

1.3.1.1. *Employment and social support*

The employment and social support policies are grouped into nine areas: wage or salary subsidy, social benefit, job protection, food program, one-off payment, essential-worker support, household payment, child-related support, and utility-bill support (OECD, 2020a). Table 1.1 summarizes the employment and social support policies of the five continents as of June 9, 2020. Overall, our sampled countries focused most on the social benefit policy, followed by the wage or salary subsidy. The food program and utility-bill support in Africa were more common than in other continents, whereas the child-related support was reported in many countries in Europe. The support for essential workers such as healthcare employees was the least common policy (only 11 of the 129 countries applied this policy) (see Table 1.1).

1.3.1.2. *Tax measure*

During the COVID-19 pandemic, the containment measures limited all non-essential businesses and activities, which seriously impacted individual and corporate incomes. Tax measures were implemented

Table 1.1. The number of countries with employment and social support policies across the five continents.

	Africa	**America**	**Asia**	**Europe**	**Oceania**	**Total**
Total number of countries	**27**	**23**	**27**	**48**	**4**	**129**
Wage or salary subsidy	4	9	7	29	2	51
Social benefit	11	10	10	31	2	64
Job protection	2	3	4	8	1	18
Food program	9	9	4	2	—	24
One-off payment	2	2	2	7	1	14
Essential-worker support	—	3	1	7	—	11
Household payment	4	8	4	4	—	20
Child-related support	2	2	3	13	1	21
Utility-bill support	8	6	3	4	1	22

Source: Authors' calculation as of June 9, 2020, based on the country policy tracker by OECD (2020a).

by most governments to respond to the COVID-19 pandemic. Among our 129 sampled countries, 114 countries implemented tax measures. The common types of tax measures are Corporate Income Tax (CIT), Value-Added Tax (VAT), Personal Income Tax (PIT), Social Security Contribution (SSC), and Property Tax. Table 1.2 summarizes how the tax policies by type were implemented to support the economies during the COVID-19 pandemic across the five continents as of June 9, 2020. The most common policies used were CIT and VAT in all continents, whereas SSC and property tax were the least common policies implemented (see Table 1.2 and Figure 1.8). Noticeably, among the 114 countries implementing tax measures, only one country, Spain, reformed all tax types as of June 9, 2020; 48 countries reformed both CIT and PIT; and 30 countries reformed CIT, PIT, and VAT (OECD, 2020a).

The tax measures were implemented for different purposes, such as the tax measure to enhance business cash-flow or household

Table 1.2. The number of countries with tax measures by types of taxes across the five continents.

	Africa	**America**	**Asia**	**Europe**	**Oceania**	**Total**
Total number of countries	**13**	**22**	**27**	**48**	**4**	**114**
CIT	8	15	17	31	4	75
VAT	4	15	14	31	1	65
PIT	5	12	12	30	1	60
SSC	4	5	7	23	2	41
Property tax	3	2	8	9	—	22

Note: According to OECD (2020a), Costa Rica (America) applied "income tax" that does not clarify whether it is PIT or CIT. Therefore, we assume that the income tax measure was for both PIT and CIT in Costa Rica.
Source: Authors' calculation as of June 9, 2020, based on the country policy tracker relating to tax policy and other measures by OECD (2020a).

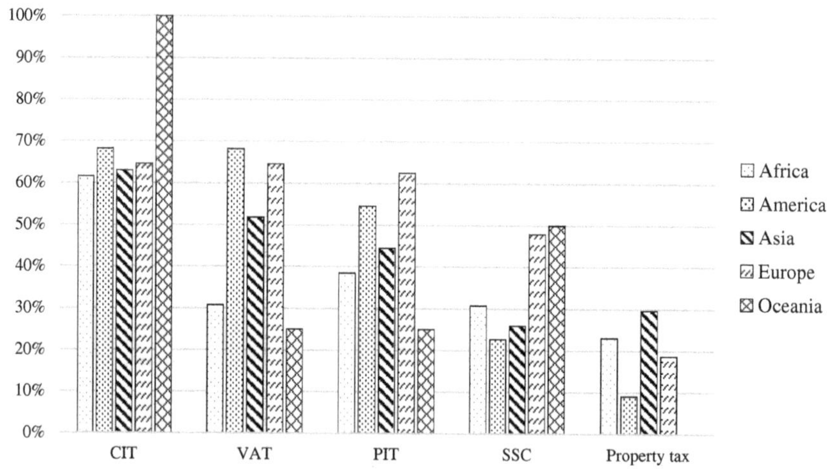

Figure 1.8. The percentage of countries with tax measures by type of taxes across the five continents.

Note: The figure is for a sample of 114 countries from Africa (13), America (22), Asia (27), Europe (48), and Oceania (4).

Source: Authors' calculation as of June 9, 2020, based on the country policy tracker relating to tax policy and other measures by OECD (2020a).

Table 1.3. The number of countries with tax measures by purpose across the five continents.

	Africa	America	Asia	Europe	Oceania	Total
Total number of countries	**13**	**22**	**27**	**48**	**4**	**114**
Measure to enhance business cash-flow	11	19	26	46	4	106
Measure to enhance household cash-flow	4	10	8	23	3	48
Tax policy - support consumption	3	4	7	9	—	23
Tax policy - support employment	1	5	4	16	2	28
Tax policy - support investment	3	2	5	2	3	15
Other tax policy measure	5	9	5	20	1	40

Source: Authors' calculation as of June 9, 2020, based on the country policy tracker relating to tax policy and other measures by OECD (2020a).

cash-flow, tax policy to support consumption, employment, or investment, and other tax policy measures. Table 1.3 shows the tax measures by purpose in the 114 countries. Most of the countries (106 of 114) focused on the measure to enhance business cash-flow (see Table 1.3 and Figure 1.9).

1.3.1.3. *Health package*

Governments spent their budgets on the health sector to respond to the COVID-19 pandemic. For example, the budgets include tax reductions for health sector workers in France; tax cuts for providers of health-related goods and services in Bosnia and Herzegovina and Brazil; encouragement in using non-cash payment method to prevent health risk in Denmark; policies to attract more healthcare

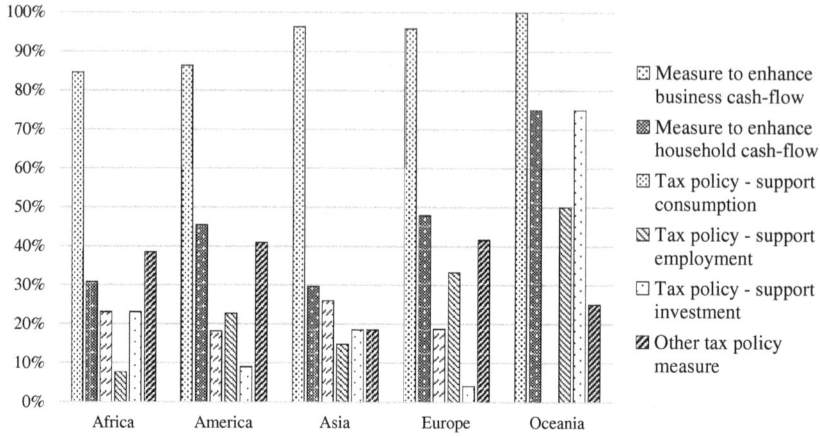

Figure 1.9. The percentage of countries with tax measures by purpose across the five continents.

Note: The figure is for a sample of 114 countries from Africa (13), America (22), Asia (27), Europe (48), and Oceania (4).

Source: Authors' calculation as of June 9, 2020, based on the country policy tracker relating to tax policy and other measures by OECD (2020a).

employees using benefit entitlements such as accommodation support in Colombia and the UK; free transport in Hungary and Turkey; or special allowance to frontline healthcare professionals in Japan (OECD, 2020a). However, among the 114 sampled countries, the OECD reported less than 50% of the countries that applied the measures to support the health sector (see Figure 1.10).

Table 1.4 lists the health system responses from the most to the least common across the five continents. The responses focus on supplies of diagnostic tests, protective equipment, ventilators, essential medicines; health worker protection; hospital beds and spaces; telemedicine, data surveillance and tracking; diagnostics and treatment; elderly protection; funding for the health system; vaccines and treatment; and mental health services.

1.3.2. *Monetary policies*

Governments implemented the expansionary monetary policy to support economic growth and maintain low unemployment rates during

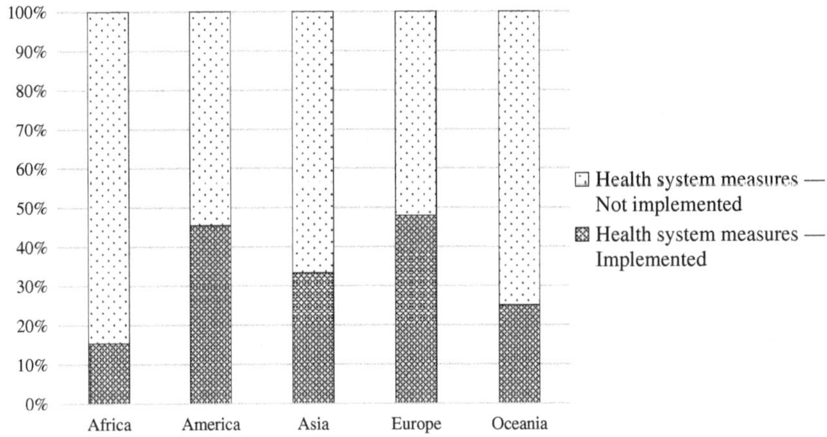

Figure 1.10. The percentage of countries with and without measures to support health sector across the five continents.

Note: The figure is for a sample of 114 countries from Africa (13), America (22), Asia (27), Europe (48), and Oceania (4).

Source: Authors' calculation as of June 9, 2020, based on the country policy tracker relating to tax policy and other measures by OECD (2020a).

the slowdown caused by the COVID-19 pandemic. To ease the liquidity stress and minimize an increase in the unemployment rate because of business closure, managing money supply and interest rates is crucial during this period. Central banks across countries worldwide cut monetary policy rates, bought back government bonds, and suspended bank dividends to increase the money supply. The policy also includes lowering the reserve requirements to allow banks to lend money at lower interest rates (loan encouraged) and encourage people to spend more instead of savings. Additionally, deferring loan repayments or suspending loan requirements was implemented to support businesses affected by the COVID-19 pandemic. Encouraging digital banking and managing exchange rates or balance of payments were also applied during the pandemic. Digital banking was encouraged or improved, such as waiving fees or increasing limits of online transactions.

Table 1.5 and Figure 1.11 show different monetary policies implemented by different continents in the first two quarters of 2020. Changes in monetary policies were recorded in 120 of 129 sampled

Table 1.4. The number of countries with health system responses across the five continents.

	Africa	America	Asia	Europe	Oceania	Total
Total number of countries	**7**	**9**	**6**	**26**	**2**	**50**
Supplies for testing, protection, treatment	6	8	5	23	2	44
Health worker protection	2	8	4	23	2	39
Hospital beds and spaces	5	9	4	18	2	38
Telemedicine, surveillance and tracking	2	9	6	18	2	37
Diagnostics and treatment	7	9	3	14	2	35
Protection for the elderly	1	6	2	18	2	29
Funding for the health system	7	4	2	11	2	26
Vaccines and treatment	1	4	5	12	1	23
Access to mental health services	0	6	4	10	2	22

Source: Authors' calculation as of June 24, 2020, based on data from OECD (2020b) and EC/OECD (2020).

countries with seven groups of measures (see Table 1.5). Figure 1.11 shows the most common monetary measures were liquidity support (more than 94% of 120 countries), monetary policy rate cut (85%), loan restructuring or encouraging the same (85%), and suspension of loan requirements or repayments (more than 73%). Among the five continents, the rate of implementing measures to encourage or improve digital banking is the highest in Africa (59.3%) (see Figure 1.11). Only a third of the countries in Europe implemented the exchange rate and balance of payment measures, which is the lowest compared to other continents (see Table 1.5 and Figure 1.11). In

Table 1.5. The number of countries with monetary policies by measure across the five continents.

	Africa	**America**	**Asia**	**Europe**	**Oceania**	**Total**
Total number of countries	**27**	**21**	**27**	**42**	**3**	**120**
Liquidity support	25	20	25	40	3	113
Monetary policy rate cut	25	13	24	37	3	102
Loan restructured or encouraged	19	19	23	38	3	102
Suspension of loan requirements or repayments	20	18	23	31	2	94
Exchange rate and balance of payments	10	13	16	14	3	56
Bank dividend suspended	2	2	6	26	2	38
Digital banking encouraged or improved	16	3	3	4	—	26

Source: Authors' calculation as of July 1, 2020, based on the policy tracker from IMF (2020b).

terms of suspending bank dividends, this measure was less common in Africa and America than in Asia, Europe, and Oceania.

1.4. Time-dependent Expectations

Recovering from the health–social–economic consequences worldwide takes time. Enterprises and organizations are hypothesized to resume their activities as soon as the containment measures such as border restrictions are lifted. However, this expectation is time-dependent. It is not because governments did not want to ease the containment measures, but the second wave of COVID-19 pandemic broke out in July 2020 in several countries such as Australia, Croatia, and Israel (Our World in Data OWID (2020). Melbourne in Australia went into a six-week lockdown from midnight on Wednesday July 8, 2020, for the second time to respond to the deadly wave of COVID-19 (Department of Health — Australian Government, 2020). The risk

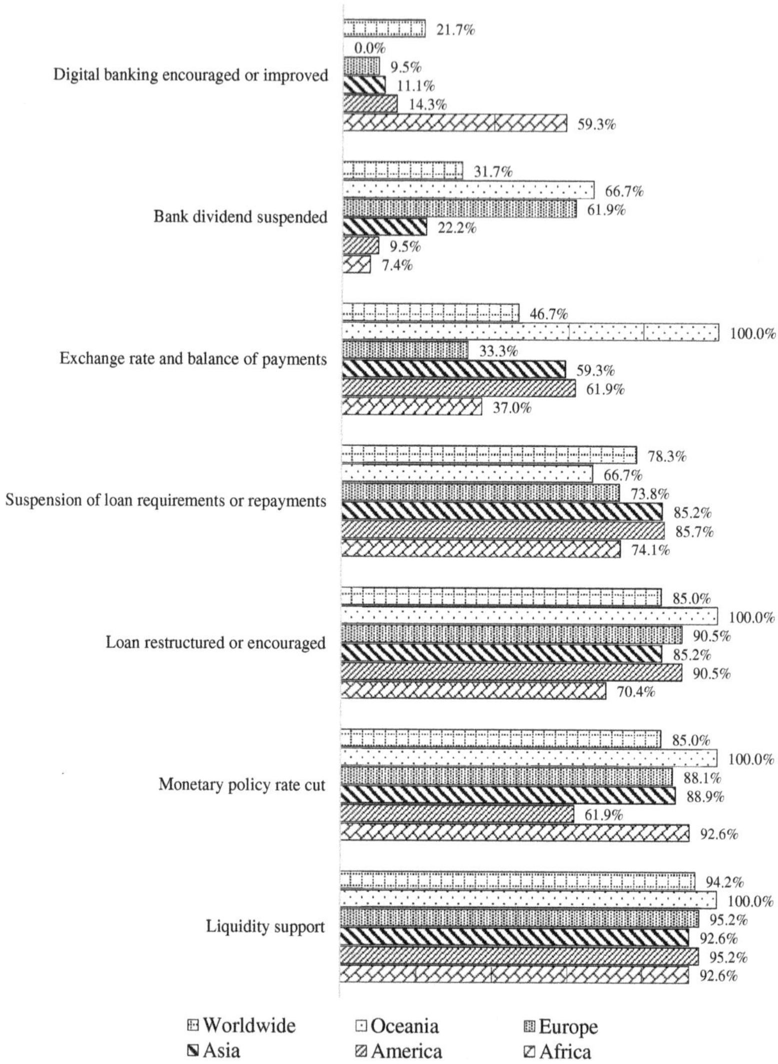

Figure 1.11. The percentage of countries with monetary policies by measure across the five continents.

Note: The figure is for a sample of 120 countries from Africa (27), America (21), Asia (27), Europe (42), and Oceania (3).

Source: Authors' calculation as of July 1, 2020, based on the policy tracker by IMF (2020b).

of containing the virus is growing every day. Although governments across continents continued to respond to the COVID-19 pandemic using fiscal and monetary policies, the economies can enter into debt and recession for a long time before recovery. The next sections discuss time-dependent expectations of debt, recession, and growth.

1.4.1. *Debt*

Fiscal and monetary measures were implemented to reduce the health–social–economic impact of COVID-19 pandemic but they have consequences. Public debt will be a challenge as a result of government financing during the pandemic. The IMF warned of public debt burden worldwide using forecast data of gross debt position in percent of GDP in 2020 and 2021 of 110 countries. Figure 1.12 shows that public debt will increase by 6.6% in Asia; 8.5% in America; and around 10% in Africa, Europe, and Oceania in 2020 compared to 2019. In 2021, public debt in Africa, Asia, and Oceania will continue to increase to the higher levels — especially, Oceania will experience the largest change (12.5%) compared to 2019 (see Figure 1.12).

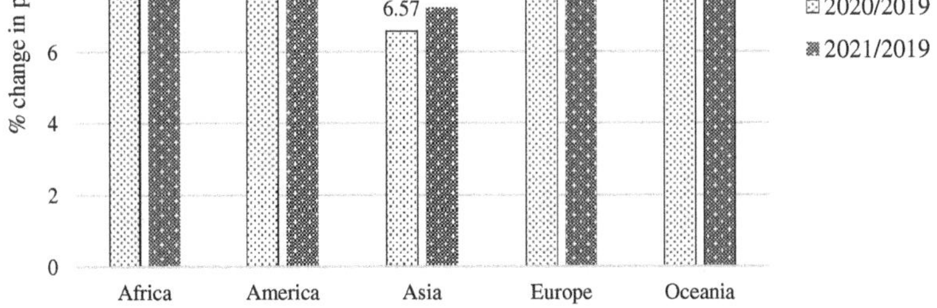

Figure 1.12. Forecast changes in public debt of the five continents.

Note: The figure is for a sample of 110 countries from Africa (28), America (14), Asia (32), Europe (33), and Oceania (3). The figure shows the estimated change in gross debt position or public debt (percent of GDP) across continents on average.

Source: Authors' calculation based on data from IMF (2020a).

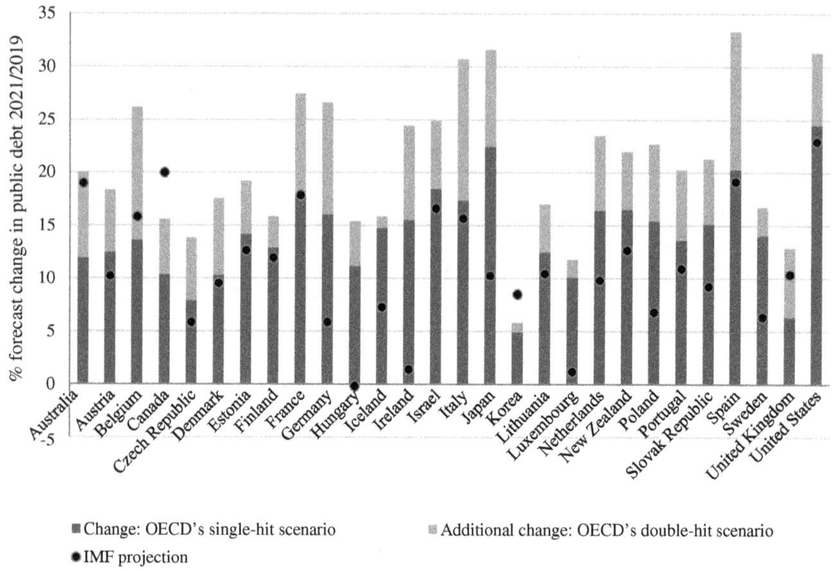

Figure 1.13. Public debt projections in selected countries 2019–2021.
Source: Authors' calculation based on data from OECD (2020c,d,f,g), and IMF (2020a).

Public debt projection by the OECD is less optimistic than that by the IMF (see Figure 1.13). OECD (2020f) projected that public debt of the US in 2021 compared to 2019 will increase 24.49% of GDP in the single-hit scenario or 31.32% of GDP in the double-hit scenario. Figure 1.13 shows that forecast changes in public debt in 2021 compared to 2019 will soar above a quarter of GDP in Belgium, France, Germany, Italy, Japan, Spain, and the US in the double-hit scenario. Forecast change in public debt of South Korea is expected the least (about 5%), whereas that of Canada, Czech Republic, Finland, Hungary, Sweden, and the UK are projected about 15% (see Figure 1.13). The high levels of debt will lead the global economy to an unusual crisis and an unpredictable recovery (IMF, 2020d).

1.4.2. *Recession*

The unusual crisis may lead the world economy to a recession before recovery. The recession consists of collapsed global economic activities and high unemployment rates. Containment measures such as border closures significantly impacted business activities. The airline is one of many industries hit hardest by the COVID-19 pandemic. To prevent infections, governments enacted international travel restrictions, which made the number of international flights drop dramatically. According to the International Civil Aviation Organization ICAO (2020a), compared to the same period in 2019, total global flights decreased by 45.57% in March 2020, and suddenly dropped 93% in April and May 2020 (see Figures 1.14 and 1.15). The sharp decline in the volume of flights significantly affected revenues of the airline industry worldwide. Figure 1.16 shows the total loss of the industry in the first five months in 2020 compared to 2019 by region based on data from ICAO (2020b).

Lifting border restrictions globally by the end of the year 2020 was expected. However, it is less likely possible until the COVID-19 vaccine is available. Despite a fear of the second wave of deadly COVID-19 pandemic, some countries have started to reopen their borders. According to World Nomads (2020), as of July 9, 2020, border restrictions were relaxed in 11 countries in Africa, 10 countries

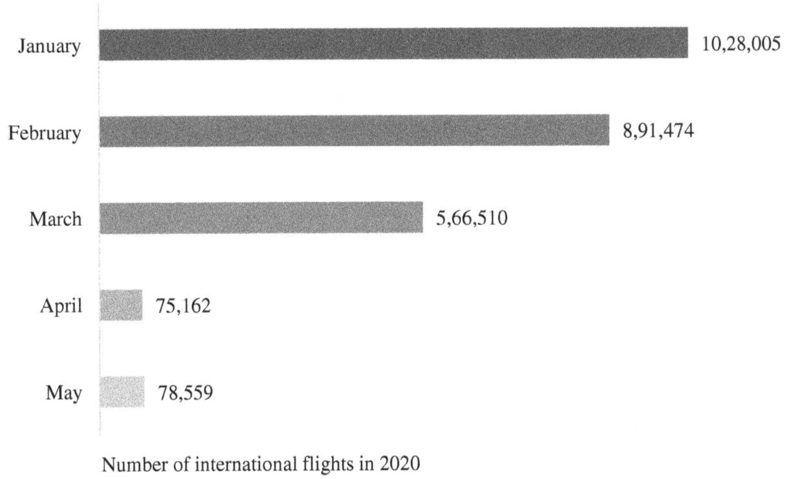

Figure 1.14. The number of international flights under border restrictions due to the COVID-19 pandemic.

Note: The figure shows the total number of international flights worldwide (excluding cargo) in the first five months in 2020.

Source: Authors' calculation based on data from ICAO (2020a).

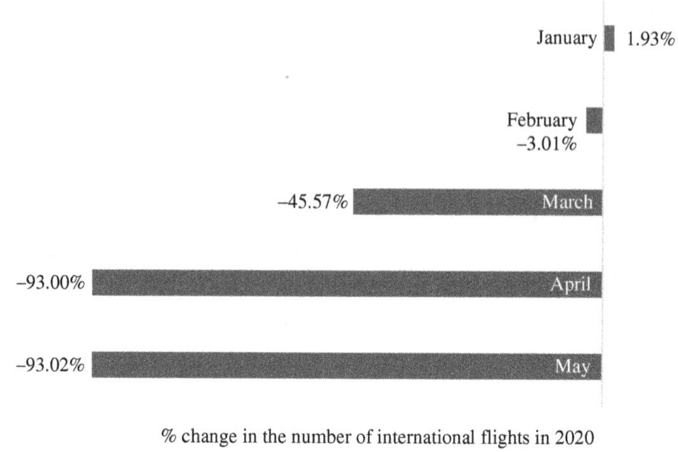

Figure 1.15. Changes in international flights under border restrictions due to the COVID-19 pandemic.

Note: The figure shows the % change in the total number of international flights worldwide (excluding cargo) in the first five months in 2020 compared to the same periods in 2019.

Source: Authors' calculation based on data from ICAO (2020a).

in South America, 11 countries in Asia, and 41 countries in Europe. Meanwhile, the second wave of COVID-19 pandemic prevents other countries from easing their border restrictions or forming "travel bubbles." Worldometer (2020a) recorded that the number of confirmed COVID-19 cases on July 9, 2020, increased in many countries such as the US (59,260 new cases as a daily record), Israel (1268 new cases), Ghana (641 new cases), Australia (173 new cases), and Croatia (91 new cases). If the second wave materializes, governments will further extend lockdown orders and border restrictions. As a result, reopening international routes to increase revenue is just a dream of the aviation industry. In April 2020, Airbus warned that it could take the airline industry five years to recover from the COVID-19 pandemic (*The Guardian*, 2020). However, the number of daily new cases worldwide continued to rise excessively in July 2020, and five years may not be enough for the recovery of this industry.

The collapse of the global economic activities due to the COVID-19 pandemic results in more unemployment and job losses, which turns the health pandemic into a job crisis worldwide. The World Travel and Tourism Council (2020) predicted that prolonged travel

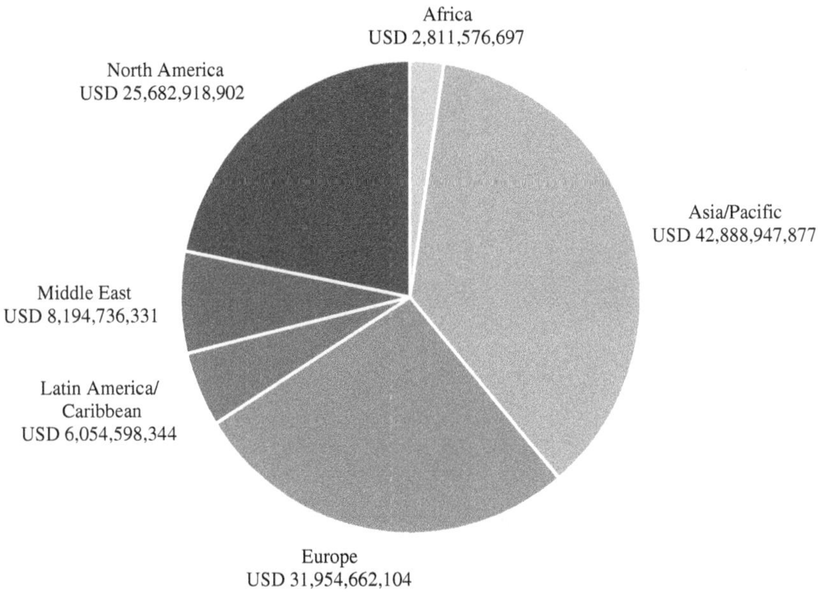

Figure 1.16. The total loss of revenue for air carriers by region due to the COVID-19 pandemic of the five continents.

Note: The figure shows the total loss of international and domestic air carriers in the first five months in 2020 compared to the same periods in 2019.

Source: Authors' calculation based on data from ICAO (2020b).

restrictions could put more than 197 million travel and tourism jobs at risk. To investigate the effect of the COVID-19 pandemic on the global employment market, we use data of unemployment rate from the IMF to calculate the change in the unemployment rate in 2009 compared to 2008, and in 2020 (projection) compared to 2019. Figures 1.17 to 1.21 show that the global employment market across the five continents will be very challenging in 2020. The COVID-19 pandemic impact on jobs is much greater than the global financial crisis in 2008, especially in the African countries of Mauritius and South Africa (see Figure 1.17); Israel and Kazakhstan in Asia (see Figure 1.18), Belize, the US, Nicaragua, Bolivia, and Honduras in America (see Figure 1.19); Fiji, New Zealand, and Australia in Oceania (see Figure 1.20); and Norway, Portugal, Poland, Romania, Czech Republic, Greece, Slovenia, Bulgaria, Croatia, the Netherlands, North Macedonia, Italy, Belarus, and Belgium in Europe (see Figure 1.21).

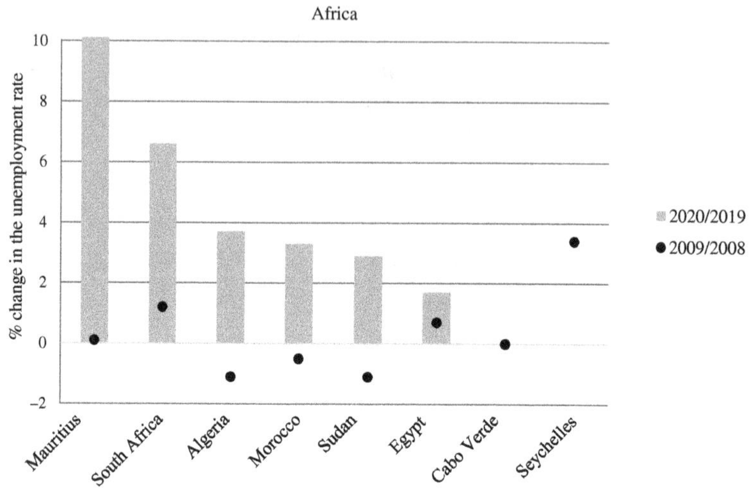

Figure 1.17. Changes in unemployment rate 2020/2019 compared to 2009/2008 in Africa.

Source: Authors' calculation based on data from IMF (2020c).

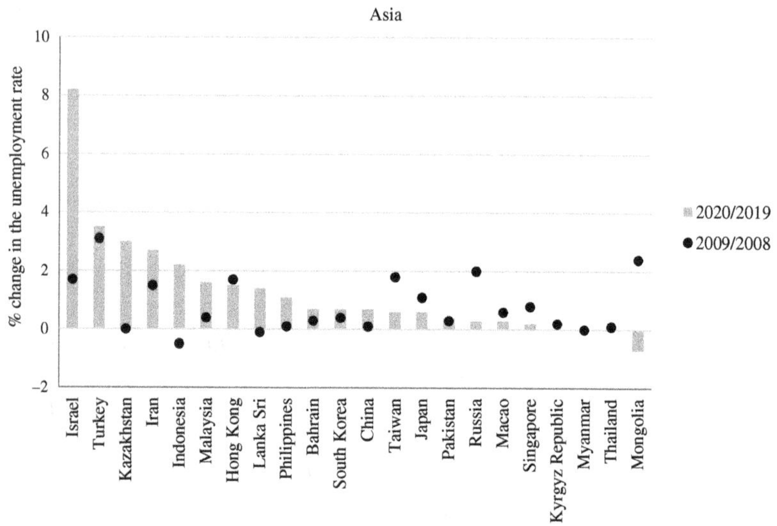

Figure 1.18. Changes in unemployment rate 2020/2019 compared to 2009/2008 in Asia.

Source: Authors' calculation based on data from IMF (2020c).

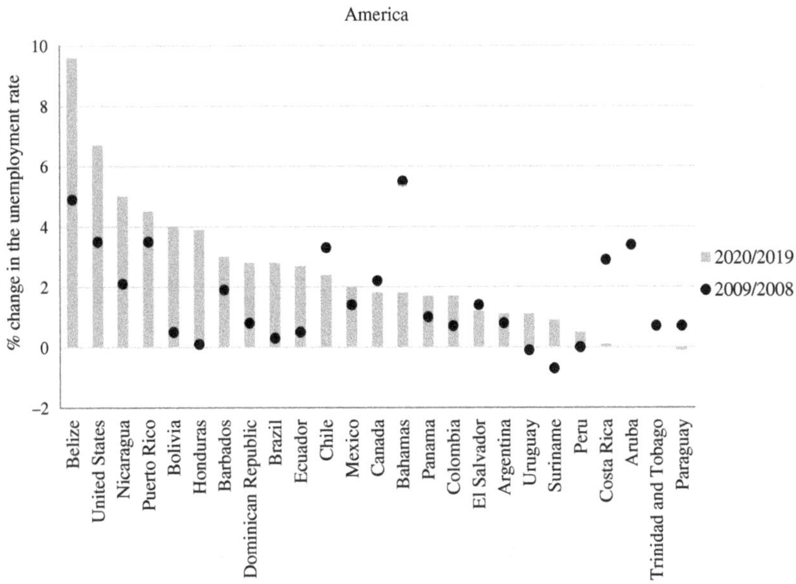

Figure 1.19. Changes in unemployment rate 2020/2019 compared to 2009/2008 in America.

Source: Authors' calculation based on data from IMF (2020c).

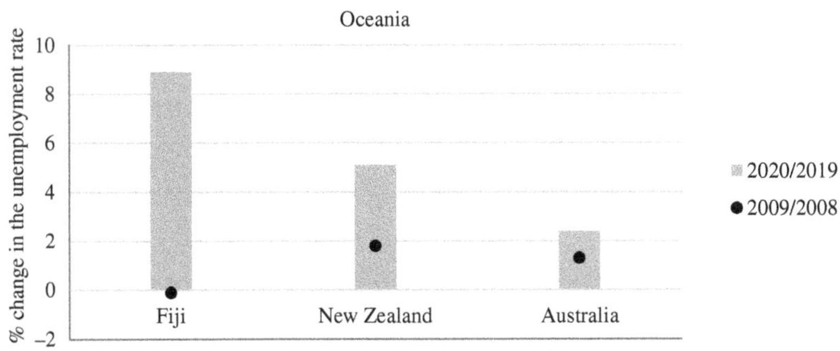

Figure 1.20. Changes in unemployment rate 2020/2019 compared to 2009/2008 in Oceania.

Source: Authors' calculation based on data from IMF (2020c).

1.4.3. *Growth*

The COVID-19 pandemic has led the global economy to a deep recession in all continents for the first time (see Figures 1.6 and 1.22).

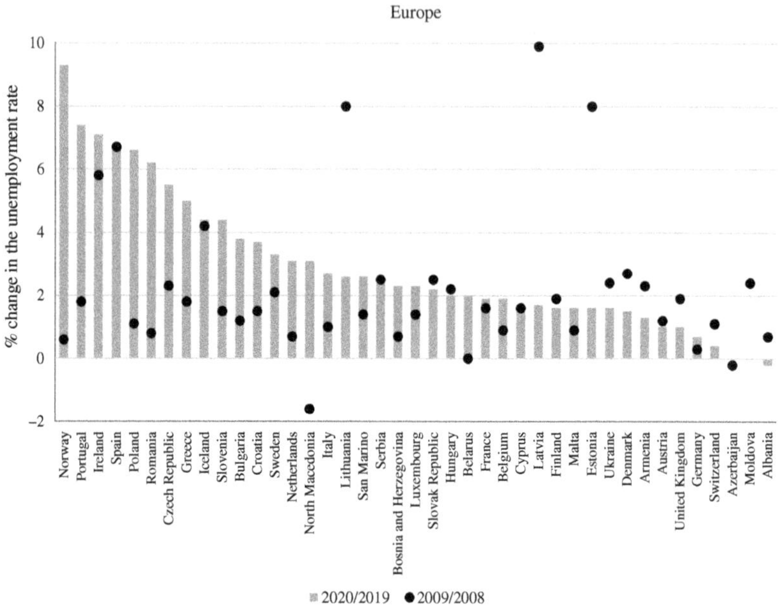

Figure 1.21. Changes in unemployment rate 2020/2019 compared to 2009/2008 in Europe.

Source: Authors' calculation based on data from IMF (2020c).

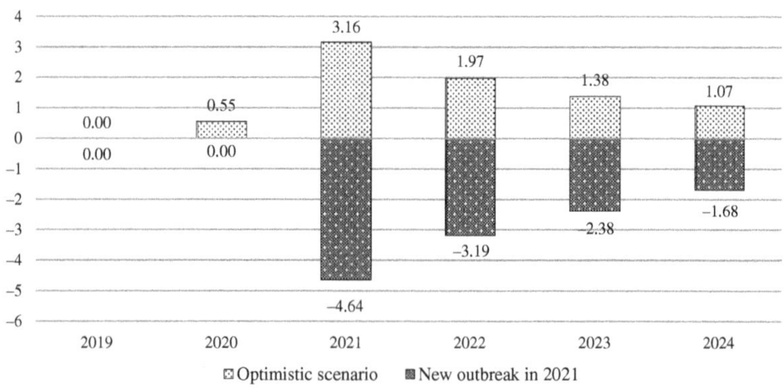

Figure 1.22. Uncertain recovery of the global economy.

Note: The figure shows the estimated change in world real GDP (%) compared to that in 2019 as a baseline. The optimistic scenario assumes a fast recovery beginning since the third quarter of 2020. The alternative scenario predicts an uncertain recovery because of a new outbreak in 2021.

Source: Authors' calculation based on data from IMF (2020d).

Global growth is estimated at –4.9% in 2020 by IMF (2020d), and at –6% in the single-hit scenario by OECD (2020e). In the optimistic scenario, global GDP is projected to return to the 2019 level in the fourth quarter of 2021 (IMF, 2020d; OECD, 2020e). However, the forecasts are highly uncertain because the impact of the second wave of COVID-19 pandemic is unpredictable. According to IMF (2020d), the recovery of the global economy depends on uncertain elements such as the prolonging of the pandemic and lockdown, job insecurity, social distancing, fear of business closures, global supply chain disruptions, and new workplace practices (work shift changes and workplace hygiene). In the alternative scenario of the new outbreak in 2021 by IMF (2020d), world real GDP is projected with a slow recovery until 2024 (see Figure 1.22). Therefore, the global economy may need at least five years to return to the 2019 level if another pandemic emerges in 2021.

Urgent actions are needed to support the recovery of the global economy. Reopening activities and borders while preventing a new wave of the virus plays a key role in the recovery. Countries should have an epidemiological model that can be implemented in different phases of a communicable disease. For example, OECD (2020h) developed a Strategic Public Health Planning framework for COVID-19 called the SPHeP-COVID model. The model is useful for policymakers to manage the pandemic using measures of public health interventions as early as possible to delay a massive lockdown and the health–social–economic consequences. Delaying or avoiding lockdowns while ensuring the healthcare systems' response to the COVID-19 pandemic is plausible so that business and social activities are not interrupted. Hence, economies will not be hit hard if another wave of the virus materializes. Building epidemiological models also help countries across continents be well prepared for a future pandemic caused by a new virus.

At the same time, governments have to manage the crisis efficiently and competently by implementing immediate and longer-term fiscal and monetary measures to support the health–social–economic recovery. In countries where the COVID-19 pandemic is still severe, immediate fiscal policies should focus on healthcare packages to save lives and relief on income tax to companies producing products related to life necessities and health protection. Monetary policies should continue to ease the liquidity stress and defer loan repayments for businesses. In countries where the pandemic is under control, fiscal policies should be reviewed to adapt to current situations and provide more support for households (IMF, 2020d) in the longer term. Measures to stop the job crisis and prevent a social crisis (OECD, 2020h) are needed. For example, the labour force may need to be retrained to return safely to workplaces or re-entering job markets, and mental health services are easily accessible and provided. In the long term, public investment in health care, infrastructure, and zero-emission systems should be considered as long as public debt can be mitigated. COVID-19 bonds, which are considered as Environmental, Social, and Governance (ESG) bonds, can be a solution to raise money without increasing public debt (Uzsoki, 2020). For example, a COVID-19 Response Sustainability Bond was issued on April 24, 2020, by Kookmin Bank in South Korea to support loans to small- and medium-sized enterprises affected by the pandemic (Hwang, 2020).

1.5. Conclusion

In conclusion, the COVID-19 pandemic has led to the health–social–economic crises. Among the government responses to COVID-19 pandemic, fiscal and monetary policies played key roles to help countries get through the COVID-19 pandemic and recover post COVID-19. However, the global economy has faced the greatest downfall and uncertain recovery. This chapter provides policy implications for governments to respond to COVID-19 pandemic and rebuild the economies. The new waves of COVID-19 pandemic, high levels of public debt, and health–social–economic recession require urgent actions from not only governments but also international organizations to accelerate the global economic recovery.

For each country, possible actions are:

- (i) develop epidemiological models to prevent future pandemics while reopening economies;
- (ii) implement immediate fiscal measures to save lives and buffer businesses using tax measures during the COVID-19 pandemic;
- (iii) support the health–social–economic recovery in the long term, such as measures to support households, stop job crisis, and prevent social consequences;

(iv) issue COVID-19 bonds to finance public investments without increasing the risk of public debt. In addition to these measures, it is the responsibility of citizens to self-quarantine and help the governments to tackle the economy recovery plans under the threat of the COVID-19 pandemic.

For international organizations, support for multidisciplinary coordination regionally and internationally is necessary to recover the global economy post COVID-19. For example, healthcare national programs in the US, such as the RECOVERY (CompREhensive Post-COVID CentER at Yale) program (Lutchmansingh *et al.*, 2020), should be extended geographically (to America and internationally) without being limited to one virus (COVID-19) as another pandemic may happen in the future. In the healthcare context, the roles of the WHO, ECDC, and UN are very important to develop the international capacity of pandemic preparedness and responses. In terms of trade and investment, countries in different regions should consider to strengthen their current trade agreements and develop new economic clusters for sustainable development. The world's largest free trade agreement, the Regional Comprehensive Economic Partnership (RCEP), was signed on November 15, 2020, by 15 Asia-Pacific countries (Association of Southeast Asian Nations [ASEAN], (2020)) as the first start for the international long-term economic recovery response to the pandemic. Therefore, the roles of economic, trade, and development organizations such as the WTO, Asia-Pacific Economic Cooperation (APEC), and OECD are vital to facilitate regional and global coordination to address social-economic recovery post COVID-19.

References

An, B.Y. and Tang, S.-Y. (2020). Lessons from COVID-19 responses in East Asia: Institutional infrastructure and enduring policy instruments. *The American Review of Public Administration*, **50**(6–7), 790–800. https://doi.org/10.1177/0275074020943707

Association of Southeast Asian Nations (2020). ASEAN hits historic milestone with signing of RCEP. Retrieved from https://asean.org/asean-hits-historic-milestone-signing-rcep/

Brewis, J. (2020). The health and socio-economic impact on menopausal women of working from home. *Case Reports in Women's Health*, **27**. https://doi.org/10.1016/j.crwh.2020.e00229

Brodeaur, A., Gray, D., Islam, A. and Bhuiyan, S. (2020). A Literature Review of the Economics of COVID-19. IZA Discussion Paper No. 13411. Available at SSRN: https://ssrn.com/abstract=3636640

Brooks, S.K., Webster, R.K., Smith, L.E., Woodland, L., Wessely, S., Greenberg, N. and Rubin, G.J. (2020). The psychological impact of quarantine and how to reduce it: Rapid review of the evidence. *The Lancet*, **395**, 912–920. https://doi.org/10.1016/S0140-6736(20)30460-8

Cerami, C., Santi, G.C., Galandra, C., Dodich, A., Cappa, S.F., Vecchi, T. and Crespi, C. (2020). COVID-19 outbreak in Italy: Are we ready for the psychosocial and economic crisis? Baseline findings from the longitudinal psycovid study. *Frontiers in Psychiatry,* **11**, 556. https://doi.org/10.3389/fpsyt.2020.00556

Chicago Board Options Exchange (2020). The Chicago Board Options Exchange VIX (CBOE Volatility Index) and the S&P 500 Index, January 2007-June 2020. Retrieved from the Chicago Board Options Exchange chart tool: http://www.cboe.com/delayedquote/advanced-charts

Chowdhry, B. and Goyal, A. (2000). Understanding the financial crisis in Asia. *Pacific-Basin Finance Journal,* **8**, 135–152. https://doi.org/10.1016/S0927-538X(00)00011-1

Department of Health — Australian Government (2020). COVID-19 in Victoria. Retrieved from https://www.health.gov.au/news/health-alerts/novel-coronavirus-2019-ncov-health-alert/coronavirus-covid-19-current-situation-and-case-numbers/covid-19-in-victoria (Accessed July 9, 2020).

Eckhardt, A., Endter, F., Giordano, A. and Somers, P. (2019). Three stages to a virtual workforce. *Management Information Systems Quarterly Executive,* **18**(1), 19–35. https://doi.org/10.17705/2msqe.00006

Economic Policy Uncertainty (2020). The Global Economic Policy Uncertainty (EPU) Index. Retrieved from: https://www.policyuncertainty.com/global_monthly.html

European Centre for Disease Prevention and Control (2020a). COVID-19 situation update worldwide, as of 23 July 2020. Retrieved from https://www.ecdc.europa.eu/en/geographical-distribution-2019-ncov-cases (Accessed July 24, 2020).

European Centre for Disease Prevention and Control (2020b). Download today's data on the geographic distribution of COVID-19 cases worldwide. Retrieved from https://www.ecdc.europa.eu/en/publications-data/download-todays-data-geographic-distribution-covid-19-cases-worldwide (Accessed June 9, 2020).

European Centre for Disease Prevention and Control (2020c). Download today's data on the geographic distribution of COVID-19 cases worldwide as of 16 November 2020. Retrieved from https://www.ecdc.europa.eu/en/publications-data/download-todays-data-geographic-distribution-covid-19-cases-worldwide (Accessed November 17, 2020).

European Commission/Organisation for Economic Co-operation and Development (2020). STIP compass: International database on Science, Technology and Innovation Policy (STIP), edition 6/24/2020. Retrieved from https://stiplab.github.io/Covid19/Q7.html (Accessed June 24, 2020).

Fernandes, N. (2020). Economic effects of coronavirus outbreak (COVID-19) on the world economy (November 5, 2020). IESE Business School Working Paper No. WP-1240-E. Retrieved from https://ssrn.com/abstract=3557504 or http://dx.doi.org/10.2139/ssrn.3557504

Fosslien, L. and West Duffy, M. (2020). How to combat Zoom fatigue. *Harvard Business Review*, April 29. Retrieved from https://hbr.org/2020/04/how-to-combat-zoom-fatigue

Han, E., Tan, M.J., Turk, E., Sridhar, D., Leung, G.M., Shibuya, K., ... Legido-Quigley, H. (2020). Lessons learnt from easing COVID-19 restrictions: An analysis of countries and regions in Asia Pacific and Europe. *Health Policy*, **396**(10261), 1525–1534. Retrieved from https://doi.org/10.1016/S0140-6736(20)32007-9

Hale, T., Angrist, N., Cameron-Blake, E., Hallas, L., Kira, B., Majumdar, S., Petherick, A., Phillips, T., Tatlow, H. and Webster, S. (2020). Oxford COVID-19 Government Response Tracker, Blavatnik School of Government. Retrieved from https://www.bsg.ox.ac.uk/research/research-projects/coronavirus-government-response-tracker#data (Accessed November 16, 2020).

Hwang, J. (2020). Kookmin Bank prints Korea's first Covid-19 bond. Retrieved from https://www.nasdaq.com/articles/kookmin-bank-prints-koreas-first-covid-19-bond-2020-04-24 (Accessed July 21, 2020).

Hyseni-Duraku, Z.H. and Hoxha, L. (2020). The impact of COVID-19 on higher education: A study of interaction among students' mental health, attitudes toward online learning, study skills, and changes in students' life. Retrieved from https://www.researchgate.net/publication/341599684_The_impact_of_COVID-19_on_higher_education_A_study_of_interaction_among_students'_mental_health_attitudes_toward_online_learning_study_skills_and_changes_in_students'_life

International Civil Aviation Organization (2020a). Flights among months including passenger — International, January-May 2019 vs 2020. Retrieved from https://data.icao.int/coVID-19/operational.htm (Accessed July 8, 2020).

International Civil Aviation Organization (2020b). Total loss of by region of air carrier registration – International & Domestic, Comparison January-May 2019 vs 2020. Retrieved from https://data.icao.int/co VID-19/economic.htm (Accessed July 8, 2020).

International Monetary Fund (2020a). Gross debt position, % of GDP (indicator). Retrieved from https://www.imf.org/external/datamapper/G_XWDG_G01_GDP_PT@FM/ADVEC/FM_EMG/FM_LIDC (Accessed July 8, 2020).

International Monetary Fund (2020b). Policy responses to COVID-19. Retrieved from https://www.imf.org/en/Topics/imf-and-covid19/Policy-Responses-to-COVID-19 (Accessed July 1, 2020).

International Monetary Fund (2020c). Unemployment rate, Percent (indicator). Retrieved from https://www.imf.org/external/datamapper/LUR@WEO/OEMDC/ADVEC/WEOWORLD/ALB/DZA/BIH/B GR (Accessed July 8, 2020).

International Monetary Fund (2020d). World Economic Outlook Update, June 2020. Retrieved from https://www.imf.org/en/Publications/WEO/Issues/2020/06/24/WEOUpdateJune2020 (Accessed July 8, 2020).

Kassema, J.J. (2020). COVID-19 outbreak: Is it a health crisis or economic crisis or both? Case of African counties. *Development Economic: Macroeconomic Issues in Development Economies eJournal*, **9**(51). https://doi.org/10.2139/ssrn.3559200

Kilbourne, E.D. (2006). Influenza pandemics of the 20th century. *Emerging Infectious Diseases*, **12**(1), 9–14. https://doi.org/10.3201/eid1201.05 1254

Lee, S.J. and Ward, K.P. (2020). Stress and parenting during the coronavirus pandemic (Research brief). Retrieved from https://www.par entingincontext.org/uploads/8/1/3/1/81318622/research_brief_stres s_and_parenting_during_the_coronavirus_pandemic_final.pdf

Lutchmansingh, D.D., Knauert, M.P., Antin-Ozerkis, D.E., Chupp, G., Cohn, L., Dela Cruz, C.S., …Possick, J.D. (2020). A clinic blueprint for post-COVID-19 RECOVERY: Learning from the past, looking to the future. *CHEST*. https://doi.org/10.1016/j.chest.2020. 10.067

Mahler, D.G., Lakner, C., Aguilar, R.A.C. and Wu, H. (2020). Updated estimates of the impact of COVID-19 on global poverty (Worldbank Blog). Retrieved from https://blogs.worldbank.org/opendata/updat ed-estimates-impact-covid-19-global-poverty

Massinga Loembé, M., Tshangela, A., Salyer, S.J., Varma, J.K., Ogwell Ouma, A.E. and Nkengasong, J.N. (2020). COVID-19 in Africa: The spread and response. *Nature Medicine*, **26**, 999–1003. https://doi.org/10.1038/s41591-020-0961-x

Moodley, K., Obasa, A. and London, L. (2020). Isolation and quarantine in South Africa during COVID-19: Draconian measures or proportional response? *South African Medical Journal*, **110**(6), 456–457. https://doi.org/10.7196/SAMJ.2020v110i6.14842

Organisation for Economic Co-operation and Development (2020a). Country policy tracker. Retrieved from https://www.oecd.org/coronavirus/country-policy-tracker/ (Accessed June 9, 2020).

Organisation for Economic Co-operation and Development (2020b). Country policy tracker. Retrieved from https://www.oecd.org/coronavirus/country-policy-tracker/ (Accessed June 24, 2020).

Organisation for Economic Co-operation and Development (2020c). Economic Outlook No 107 - June 2020 – Double-hit scenario. Retrieved from https://stats.oecd.org/viewhtml.aspx?datasetcode=EO107_INTERNET_2&lang=en

Organisation for Economic Co-operation and Development (2020d). Economic Outlook No 107 - June 2020 – Single-hit scenario. Retrieved from https://stats.oecd.org/viewhtml.aspx?datasetcode=EO107_INTERNET_1&lang=en

Organisation for Economic Co-operation and Development (2020e). *Evaluating the Initial Impact of COVID-19 Containment Measures on Economic Activity, OECD Policy Responses to Coronavirus (COVID-19)* (OECD Publishing, Paris). Retrieved from http://www.oecd.org/coronavirus/policy-responses/evaluating-the-initial-impact-of-covid-19-containment-measures-on-economic-activity-b1f6b68b/ (Accessed June 24, 2020).

Organisation for Economic Co-operation and Development (2020f). *OECD Economic Outlook, Volume 2020 Issue 1* (OECD Publishing, Paris). https://doi.org/10.1787/0d1d1e2e-en

Organisation for Economic Co-operation and Development (2020g). *OECD Economic Outlook: Statistics and Projections.* https://doi.org/10.1787/eo-data-en (Accessed July 8, 2020).

Organisation for Economic Co-operation and Development (2020h). *OECD Employment Outlook 2020: Worker Security and the COVID-19 Crisis.* Retrieved from https://www.oecd-ilibrary.org/sites/1686c758-en/1/3/1/index.html?itemId=/content/publication/1686c758-en&_csp_=fc80786ea6a3a7b4628d3f05b1e2e5d7&itemIGO=oecd&itemContentType=book (Accessed July 9, 2020).

Organisation for Economic Co-operation and Development (2020i). *Real GDP forecast* (indicator). https://doi.org/10.1787/b487f2cf-en (Accessed June 25, 2020).

Organisation for Economic Co-operation and Development (2020j). Unemployment rate forecast (indicator). https://doi.org/10.1787/1f84105b-en (Accessed June 25, 2020).

Our World in Data (2020). Daily new confirmed cases of COVID-19 per million people, in LOG as of 8 July 2020 [Graph]. Retrieved from https://ourworldindata.org/grapher/daily-new-confirmed-cases-of-covid-19-per-million-tests-per-case?country=AUS~HRV_GHA_ISR_NCL_PNG_USA

Pan, S.L., Cui, M. and Qian, J. (2020). Information resource orchestration during the COVID-19 pandemic: A study of community lockdowns in China. *International Journal of Information Management.* https://doi.org/10.1016/j.ijinfomgt.2020.102143

Pinshi, C.P. (2020). COVID-19 uncertainty and monetary policy. *Munich Personal RePEc Archive.* Retrieved from https://mpra.ub.uni-muenchen.de/100184/

Richter, A. (2020). Locked-down digital work. *International Journal of Information Management.* https://doi.org/10.1016/j.ijinfomgt.2020.102157

Sukharev, O.S. (2020). Economic crisis as a consequence COVID-19 virus attack: Risk and damage assessment. *Quantitative Finance and Economics*, **4**(2), 274–293. https://doi.org/10.3934/QFE.2020013

Tisdell, C.A. (2020). Economic, social and political issues raised by the COVID-19 pandemic, *Economic Analysis and Policy*, **68**, 17–28, ISSN 0313-5926. https://doi.org/10.1016/j.eap.2020.08.002

The Guardian (2020). Airlines may not recover from COVID-19 crisis for five years, says Airbus. Retrieved from https://www.theguardian.com/business/2020/apr/29/airlines-may-not-recover-from-covid-19-crisis-for-five-years-says-airbus (Accessed July 9, 2020).

Uzsoki, D. (2020). Financing COVID-19 stimulus: Will high levels of public debt come back to haunt us? Retrieved from https://www.iisd.org/blog/financing-covid-19-stimulus (Accessed July 21, 2020).

World Bank (2020). *Global Economic Prospects, June 2020* (World Bank, Washington, DC). https://doi.org/10.1596/978-1-4648-1553-9

World Health Organization (2020a). Addressing violence against children, women and older people during the COVID-19 pandemic: Key actions. Retrieved from https://www.who.int/publications/i/item/WHO-2019-nCoV-Violence_actions-2020.1 (Accessed June 24, 2020).

World Health Organization (2020b). Contact tracing in the context of COVID-19 (Interim Guidance). Retrieved from https://www.who.int/publications/i/item/contact-tracing-in-the-context-of-covid-19 (Accessed June 24, 2020).

World Health Organization (2020c). Disease outbreaks by year. Retrieved from https://www.who.int/csr/don/archive/year/en/ (Accessed June 30, 2020).

World Health Organization (2020d). Naming the coronavirus disease (COVID-19) and the virus that causes it. Retrieved from https://www.who.int/emergencies/diseases/novel-coronavirus-2019/technical-guidance/naming-the-coronavirus-disease-(covid-2019)-and-the-virus-that-causes-it (Accessed June 14, 2020).

World Nomads (2020). COVID-19 travel alert: Which countries have open borders? Retrieved from https://www.worldnomads.com/travel-safety/worldwide/worldwide-travel-alerts (Accessed July 9, 2020).

World Travel and Tourism Council (2020). More than 197m travel & tourism jobs will be lost due to prolonged travel restrictions, according to new research from WTTC. Retrieved from https://wttc.org/News-Article/More-than-197m-Travel-Tourism-jobs-will-be-lost-due-to-prolonged-travel-restrictions (Accessed July 9, 2020).

World Uncertainty Index (2020). World Uncertainty Index (WUI): Global. Retrieved from https://worlduncertaintyindex.com/

Worldometer (2020a). Reported cases and deaths by country, territory, or conveyance. Retrieved from https://www.worldometers.info/coronavirus/#countries (Accessed July 9, 2020).

Worldometer (2020b). Reported cases and deaths by country, territory, or conveyance. Retrieved from https://www.worldometers.info/coronavirus/#countries (Accessed November 20, 2020).

Worldometer (2021). Reported cases and deaths by country or territory. Retrieved from https://www.worldometers.info/coronavirus/#countries (Accessed June 15, 2021).

Yuan, Z., Xiao, Y., Dai, Z., Huang, J., Zhang, Z. and Chen, Y. (2020). Modelling the effects of Wuhan's lockdown during COVID-19, China. *Bulletin of the World Health Organization*, **98**(7), 484–494. https://doi.org/10.2471/blt.20.254045

Zwitter, A. and Gstrein, O.J. (2020). Big data, privacy and COVID-19 – learning from humanitarian expertise in data protection. *Journal of International Humanitarian Action*, **5**, 4. https://doi.org/10.1186/s41018-020-00072-6

https://doi.org/10.1142/9781800610781_0002

Chapter 2

The Pandemic's Pernicious Public Debt Legacy

Anthony J. Makin
Griffith Business School, Griffith University, Australia
t.makin@griffith.edu.au

Abstract
This chapter focuses on the rise in global public debt resulting from the fiscal responses of governments around the world to the COVID-19 crisis. After outlining key features of the global fiscal response, the chapter briefly evaluates their efficacy before assessing the resurgence of thinking that neglects the risk high public debt poses. It then proposes fiscal and other reform measures needed to address the public debt legacy, stressing the need to reduce government spending, and the size of government in advanced economies in particular, to ensure public debt sustainability and a revival of economic growth going forward.

2.1. Introduction

The COVID-19 health crisis caused havoc in financial markets and plagued economies worldwide, with the severity of the economic symptoms varying according to how quickly the virus spread and how strictly government lockdown restrictions were applied. From March 2020 it sparked global financial contagion with major stock market crashes in the US, Europe, and Asia, resulting in huge short-term losses for investors, unprecedented volatility, and risk levels.[1] Major central banks responded immediately, lowering official interest rates to, or near, zero to alleviate financial market uncertainty and minimize the negative impact on real economic activity.

Under these circumstances, governments also directly countered with expansive fiscal policies to mitigate the economic impact of the lockdowns on business and private sector employment. Despite these palliative macroeconomic measures, the IMF (2020a) estimated a 5% fall in world Gross Domestic Product (GDP) in 2020, higher for advanced economies, at around 8%, than for developing and emerging economies, at around 3%. Effective unemployment rates have exceeded 10% in many economies as a result.

The scale of the fiscal response of advanced economy governments to the COVID-19 crisis (hereafter "the CVC") to lockdowns has been gargantuan, with boosts to health expenditure, income transfers, and welfare payments, as well as wage subsidies to firms to stem a heft in short-term unemployment.[2] The IMF has estimated fiscal actions have run close to US$12 trillion or 12% of global GDP, with around half due to additional government spending or reduced revenue, and the other half due to liquidity support, government loans, guarantees, and capital injections by the public sector. The IMF has also advocated further temporary fiscal stimulus through increased public investment with an emphasis on inclusive and environmentally sustainable infrastructure projects.

While a fiscal response was obviously necessary to address the health imperative and stop the rise in unemployment levels, there needs to be greater recognition of the negative future consequences of the massive rise in public debt that has occurred, a topic hitherto largely neglected in the literature.

Many economic questions arise about the macroeconomic policy response to the CVC. Specifically, was the fiscal injection for the economic side effects of the lockdown an overdose? How serious will the associated hike in nations' public debt be, and what risks does

[1]For related discussion see Akhtaruzzaman *et al.* (2021), Caggiano *et al.* (2020), Zhang *et al.* (2020), and Sharif *et al.* (2020).

[2]The IMF details the policy responses of its member countries at https://www.imf.org/en/Topics/imf-and-covid19/Policy-Responses-to-COVID-19.

that pose? And what budgetary and structural reform policies are needed to address the deficits and public debt while assisting economic recovery?

This chapter aims to address these questions, focusing mainly on the fiscal elements of the CVC response and its economy-wide side effects. While literature on examining the impact of the CVC on financial markets and economies worldwide has grown, to date the fiscal side effects have been largely neglected. After outlining and quantifying key features of the fiscal response, the chapter briefly evaluating the budget response before considering the resurgence of crude Keynesianism and highlighting the risks of the public debt legacy. It then focuses on budget and other reform measures, stressing the need to reduce government spending and the size of government to ensure fiscal sustainability and stronger economic growth.

2.2. The Nature and Scale of the Fiscal Response

The IMF estimated a peak global fiscal deficit of around 14% of world GDP this year, a 10% rise from last year and almost three times the global deficit following the Global Financial Crisis (GFC).

2.2.1. *Key fiscal elements*

Elements of the fiscal support include:

- extra health spending;
- cash flow support and investment incentives for businesses;
- wage subsidies;
- payroll tax relief for businesses; and
- income support to households, including for childcare and via discounted utility bills.

The fiscal response to the CVC ensures that governments around the world will experience large budget deficits and escalating public debt for the foreseeable future (see Figure 2.1).

Pre-CVC gross public debt levels were already high worldwide. Public debt has since ballooned and, at over 100% of world GDP, now exceeds the immediate post World War II peak and is the highest ever recorded (IMF, 2020b) (see Figure 2.2).

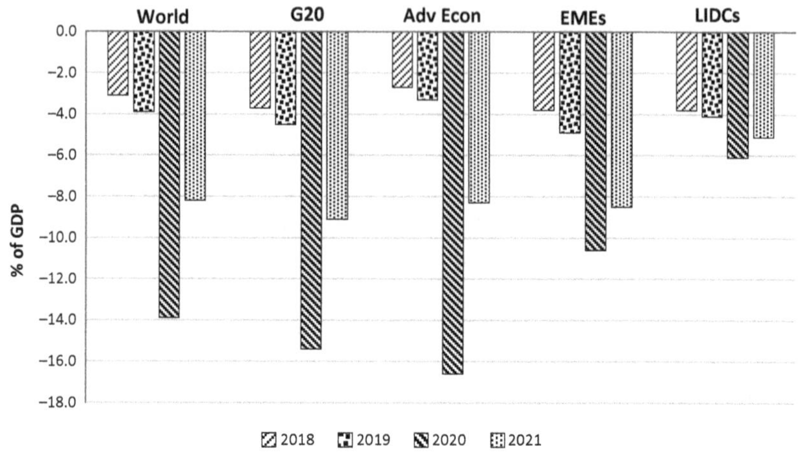

Figure 2.1. Overall fiscal balance, % Gross Domestic Product. LIDCs: Low income developing countries; EMEs: Emerging Market Economies; Adv Econ: Advanced Economies.

Source: IMF, World Economic Outlook (2020).

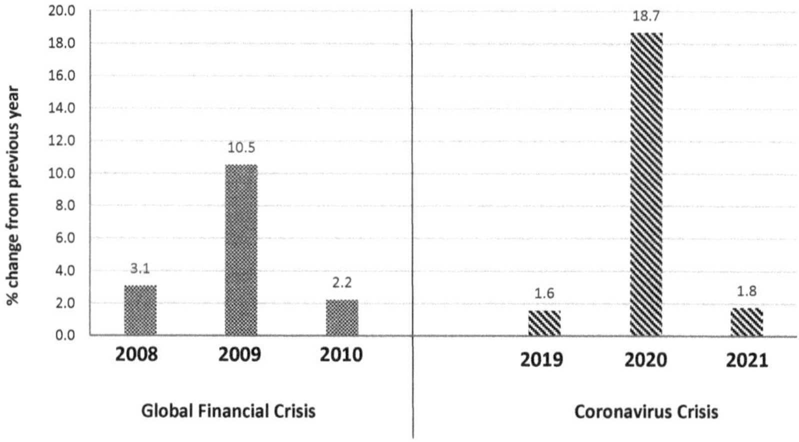

Figure 2.2. Change in government gross debt: GFC versus CVC.

Source: IMF, World Economic Outlook (2020).

Additionally, there is a range of "off-balance sheet" support measures, most notably official loans and government guarantees for bank loans. The IMF estimated total global government support amounted to around US$11 trillion, with around half of that in the form of

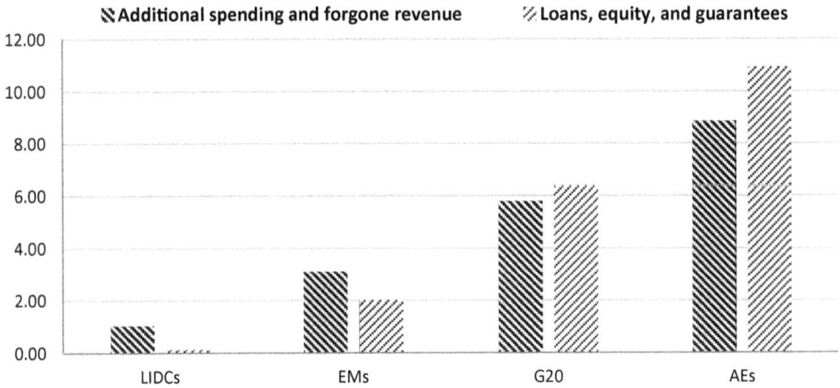

Figure 2.3. Fiscal measures in response to the CVC: Select country groups.
Source: IMF, World Economic Outlook (2020).

off-balance sheet assistance (see Figure 2.3). To the extent these off-balance sheet loans — as contingent liabilities of governments — are not repaid, they will add that much more to public debt.

2.3. Evaluating the Macroeconomic Policy Response

The IMF estimated total global government support amounted to around US$11 trillion, with around half of that in the form of off-balance sheet assistance. To the extent these off-balance sheet loans — as contingent liabilities of governments — are not repaid, they will exacerbate nations' fiscal imbalances. Government support provided in emerging and low-income developing countries was mostly direct fiscal support.

At the world level, the IMF estimated a peak global fiscal deficit of around 14% of world GDP in 2020, a 10% deficit rise on the previous year. This was some three times larger than the post-GFC deficit.

2.3.1. *Needed supply side support*

A macroeconomic policy response was necessary, and what transpired had elements directed at supporting the supply side of the economy and the demand side. The monetary policy response to ease liquidity and assist cash flow provided support for both aggregate supply and demand, as did new investment incentives for firms, and wage subsidy programs for firms that suffered a fall in revenue.

While there have been flaws in the operation of some economies' expensive wage subsidy programs, in principle these have been more justifiable than the other crude Keynesian elements of the fiscal response aimed at boosting aggregate demand. Indeed, more efficiently designed low-cost wage subsidy schemes that directly preserve employment on the aggregate supply side of economies provides a possible prototype for dealing with future "black swan" emergencies.

Providing ample liquidity through monetary measures involving the central bank and commercial banks is warranted in a crisis situation, as it can easily be withdrawn subsequently. On the other hand, the massive fiscal policy response to the CVC in many countries paralleled the macroeconomic response to the GFC. Although the causes of the two crises bear no similarity, in both instances large budget deficits caused public debt levels to escalate (see Figure 2.2).

2.3.2. *Ill-advised demand-side "stimulus"?*

However, other elements of the fiscal response aimed at the aggregate demand side were not only extravagant but also ill-advised, particularly those aimed at boosting household spending via increased bonus payments to pensioners and other welfare recipients. These replicated the cash transfer element of fiscal "stimulus" responses to the GFC.

Why governments, including Australia and the US, chose this fiscal option is puzzling for several reasons. First, it was at odds with government lockdown restrictions, including "stay at home" advice and limits on the provision of goods and services to essential services. Pensioners of all groups, for instance, were not supposed to be out spending.

Second, economic theory suggests that as these payments were one-off and hence temporary, they were more likely to be saved than spent, yet at significant cost to government saving. If they were spent, they also added to imports, detracting from GDP. Effectively a subsidy to retailers, such payments were an inefficient, duplicative, and ineffective means of preserving employment, especially since wage subsidies were devised for that explicit purpose.

Third, for some countries like Australia, the US, Canada, and New Zealand, larger budget deficits were funded by new government borrowing, much from abroad, worsening government balance sheets and causing further deterioration in the governments' negative net worth. To the extent they were directly or indirectly funded by central banks by buying government bonds (effectively "printing money"), this is likely to result in high inflation, as subsequently discussed further.

Key questions arise about and how best to address the macroeconomic side effects of the costly fiscal policy response. Before doing so, a digression on the fallacies of Keynesian thinking follows to provide necessary background for the remedial fiscal measures proposed subsequently.

2.4. Resurgent Crude Keynesianism

The CVC fiscal response cannot be understood with reference to textbook macroeconomic theory, but its consequences can, as can the implications of future fiscal policy options. Inevitably, interpretations of the macroeconomic role and efficacy of budgetary policy are coloured by views of how it is transmitted in the macroeconomy. At the risk of oversimplification, these perspectives, as well as those about the policy significance of public debt, can be categorised as either Keynesian or non-Keynesian.[3] Keynesianism, however, takes many forms.

2.4.1. *Keynesian schools of thought*

Since the Great Depression, a range of different schools of Keynesian thought have emerged, each variant purporting to convey what Keynes *really* meant. Doctrinal differences between these schools — for instance about the role of money, the significance of inflexible wages and prices, the rationality of financial markets, and the importance of capitalism itself — parallel differences between sects of the same religious faith.

[3]Some views were not necessarily held by John Maynard Keynes himself, who declared late in life that he was not a Keynesian. See Hutchison (1977).

The main Keynesian schools to emerge over the years have been the neo-Keynesian, the post-Keynesian, the new Keynesian, and Modern Monetary Theory (MMT), the crudest being the fundamentalist post-Keynesian and MMT perspectives. At the crudest level, Keynesianism is founded on the basic principles espoused in Keynes' *General Theory of Employment, Interest and Money.*

For fundamentalists, the message of this book is that economies are best managed by increasing government spending to reduce unemployment, drawing inspiration from the concluding chapter, where Keynes asserted — wrongly as it turned out — that in the post-Depression era "... somewhat comprehensive socialisation of investment will prove the only means of securing an approximation to full employment" (p. 378) and that "The central controls necessary to ensure full employment will, of course, involve a large extension of the traditional functions of government" (p. 379).

All these Keynesian schools, to varying degrees, have been at odds with the free market-oriented approaches of the monetarist, new classical, and Austrian schools that stemmed from classical economics originating in Adam Smith (1776) *The Wealth of Nations.* When Keynesian thinking previously dominated macro-policymaking in the 1970s, monetarist and new classical economists convincingly argued that inert fiscal policy was superior to fiscal activism. Milton Friedman (1962) has to this day been the most influential non-Keynesian thinker since the Depression, along with Friedrick Hayek (1995), a contemporary of Keynes.

In the Keynesian tradition, private consumption, investment, and government spending, as well as net exports in open economy extensions, determine aggregate demand, national income, and employment in the short run. Whereas in the classical and neoclassical tradition, national income is best explained as a supply-side phenomenon with reference to saving, capital accumulation, workforce expansion, and productivity.

2.4.2. *MMT*

Since the GFC, the so-called MMT, a deeply fundamentalist Keynesian approach, has surfaced as an alternative way of conducting macroeconomic policy. MMT's main point is that fiscal policy in the form of increased government spending should replace monetary policy as the macroeconomic instrument for steering the economy, and hence employment levels, via aggregate demand management. MMT assumes more government spending and higher public debt are inconsequential; and that if monetization of public debt is inflationary, government should just raise taxes to control it.

MMT has a bland, yet deceptive, name, for it is in essence a rebranding of discredited old closed- economy Keynesian ideas from the 1930s. In other words, it is old wine in a seemingly new bottle. Labelling this approach as something new is therefore misleading. So is referring to it as a monetary approach when it advocates fiscal policy (not monetary policy) as the key to macroeconomic management. As a theory, it is also at odds with reality, especially regarding the inflationary consequences of public debt monetization.

2.4.3. *Counter-arguments*

The main counter-theories to Keynesianism are:

(i) the loanable funds approach, which implies that extra government spending must be funded. It thereby either crowds out domestic private investment, increases foreign borrowing and the external debt, or leads to a combination of both;
(ii) the textbook open economy model[4] that proposes government spending puts upward pressure on interest rates which induces capital inflow from abroad. That in turn appreciates the currency and worsens international competitiveness, crowding out net exports. This assumes an unchanged monetary policy stance, but in the current context, to the extent central banks keep interest rates low through massive bond purchases, exchange rate appreciation will be dampened; and
(iii) Ricardian Equivalence, which implies crowding out of private consumption as households save to meet future tax obligations to repay public debt.[5]

Together, these approaches suggest that increased government spending, particularly public consumption, fails to stimulate national

[4]Known as the Mundell–Fleming model (Fleming, 1962; Mundell, 1963), this approach is expounded in all reputable intermediate-level university textbooks. See Mankiw (2020) for instance.

[5]Makin (2018) elaborates on these perspectives.

income and employment. In sum, these non-Keynesian perspectives, backed by a body of empirical evidence, tell us extra government spending aimed at bolstering aggregate demand side has offsetting effects elsewhere in the economy that negate its purpose. Lastly, there is the:

(iv) the intergenerational inequity argument that it is unfair for future generations to repay public debt incurred by the present generation.[6]

2.5. The Legacy of High Public Debt

It was once a tenet of Keynesian economics that public debt was not a problem because "we owed public debt to ourselves." This implied governments could run up public debt, without worrying unduly because its citizens and local financial institutions within the economy earned interest on it. This is false when governments borrow mainly from abroad to cover their budget deficits. This can worsen international competitiveness, further drain national income, lower economic growth, and risk high inflation. Moreover, the public debt is bequeathed to future generations to repay.

If public debt reflects funding of productive public investment in infrastructure and human capital, it can enhance economic growth. However, the global fiscal response to the CVC was overwhelmingly unproductive as it has not been matched by new assets on the government balance sheet. Moreover, there are reasons to doubt whether increased infrastructure spending would be an effective means of reducing CVC induced unemployment as discussed further later.

2.5.1. *Worsened competitiveness*

For small, open economies, government bonds issued to fund budget deficits can entice strong capital inflow from abroad. To the extent that strengthens the real exchange rate, it will worsen the economy's international competitiveness, thereby harming net exports by lifting imports and curbing exports. In this way the exchange rate could

[6]See Buchanan (1958).

mimic the behaviour of the Australian dollar in response to the Australian government's counterproductive fiscal response to the GFC.

The exchange rate subsequently began appreciating to historical highs (over AU$1.10 against the US$) in part due to belated spending "stimulus" that induced foreign capital inflow to buy Australian government debt. This severely worsened Australia's competitiveness and euthanised parts of the manufacturing sector.[7]

2.5.2. *The risk to credit ratings*

With budget deficits and public debt set to escalate, the creditworthiness of many nations will obviously be threatened. Creditworthiness downgrades would have the following economy-wide impact. First, interest rates on government bonds would rise instantly to reflect a higher risk premium, the rise depending on the bond market's reaction. If the central government credit rating is downgraded, the loss could automatically flow on to credit ratings for provincial governments.

Second, the downgrade would influence the entire interest rate spectrum, affecting mortgage and commercial loan rates. Third, it would dent household and business confidence, slowing consumption, construction, and business investment. Moreover, if world interest rates rise, this will further add to the public debt interest burden and enlarge the national income drain. Once lost, credit ratings can take years of fiscal repair to restore.

2.5.3. *Lower economic growth*

Uncertainty about how and when large fiscal deficits and high public debt levels will be addressed can weaken business confidence, which in turn implies lower private investment that translates to lower tax revenue than otherwise. As governments around the world continue to soak up funds to cover budget deficits and refinance maturing public debt previously incurred, the availability of funds for private investment also shrinks. This implies future global growth will be lower because economies' productive capital stocks will be lower.

---

[7]Makin and Pearce (2016) provides more detailed analysis.

Numerous empirical studies suggest a 10% increase of public debt is associated with a 0.2% decrease of economic growth.[8] While seemingly small on an annual basis, it means a significant national income loss over the longer term due to compounding. Moreover, these studies assume no widespread credit rating downgrades for borrower countries in the interim, or 1994-like bond market crisis that saw global interest rates spike around 2%.

2.5.4. *Higher inflation*

Lastly, history shows that there is a very big risk of higher inflation taking hold globally — perhaps with a lag of a few years — if central banks continue buying huge volumes of public debt, expanding domestic money supplies in the process. It has been known since Roman times that excessive money supply growth fuels inflation and can at worst lead to hyperinflation, as has been well documented in the voluminous academic literature.[9] High inflation in the 1970s prompted the original monetarist attack on Keynesianism, which could not explain it.

Inflation on a scale not experienced since then must rate as likely in light of the monetization of public debt that has already occurred, especially if there is a severing of international supply chains — including from China — that have kept production costs in advanced economies down. Low-cost production inputs, along with other cheap merchandise imports from China and other emerging economies, have contributed to low world inflation in recent decades. This low inflation has arguably been too low; so to the extent it rises initially may be welcome. However, preventing a rise in inflation above central bank target ranges could become a major future challenge for monetary policy.

When inflation is high, it tends to be more variable, which introduces additional uncertainty for business and complicates long-term planning decisions. These include the inconvenience and real cost to business of having to mark prices up very frequently (the so-called

[8]See for instance Afonso and Jalles (2013), Égert (2015), Gunarsa *et al.* (2019), Woo and Kumar (2015).

[9]Cagan (1956) is a classic empirical study of historical money-generated hyperinflations.

"menu cost" of inflation). If unanticipated, high inflation also causes arbitrary redistribution of wealth between borrowers and lenders in the economy. Hence in the 1970s, the saying that "inflation is theft" was popular as it conveyed the notion that inflation robbed those with accumulated savings.

There would also be extra inefficiencies because the price system would not clearly signal which relative prices are changing when all prices are rising. As a result, resources can be misallocated, reducing overall productivity and economic growth. This occurred around the world after the Keynesian fiscal excesses of the 1970s, resulting in prolonged stagflation — which in turn exacerbated unemployment.

2.6. Reducing Public Debt

Public debt will continue to grow in the coming years in the absence of substantial budget repair. Only via primary budget surpluses can public debt be paid down to prevent a vicious cycle of deficits and debt and preserve an economy's creditworthiness in the short term, and in the long term reduce the burden of public debt for future generations. The spending side of the budget is often ignored on the unproven Keynesian grounds that spending cuts reduce national income.

Yet from a macroeconomic perspective, fiscal repair generates additional national saving, improves credit availability, and puts downward pressure on the interest rates business face, as well as on the exchange rate which boosts international competitiveness.

2.6.1. *Public expenditure restraint*

Public finance theory tells us there are two basic rationales for public expenditure: (i) to correct for genuine market failure, which includes providing so-called "public goods," and (ii) to redistribute income. Comprehensive reviews of existing public spending programs of all levels of government could be instigated for public expenditure reform. These could assess whether existing programs meet at least the first of these principles. Addressing the second principle is most likely infeasible, given there will never be political consensus on what income and wealth distribution is fair.

Such a review would uncover a multiplicity of candidate items for expenditure reduction across all levels of government, including the duplication in health and education spending, industry assistance, public sector employee growth, and whether welfare payments could be more effectively means tested so the deserving poor benefit most.

2.6.2. *Is infrastructure spending any different?*

Infrastructure influences an economy's aggregate demand and supply sides by increasing demand through investment, while simultaneously adding to the capital stock. Crude Keynesian theory suggests that *any* form of government spending always boosts the economic activity, irrespective of its intrinsic economic worth, while any cut in government spending reduces it.

While deficit-financed spending on infrastructure can augment the economy's productive capacity if it passes rigorous cost-benefit tests, it can also slow national income if it manifests as debt-funded spending on public works; such as "roads and bridges to nowhere," as Japan's experience shows. Encouraging public–private partnerships is a way of minimising that risk.

However, there are good reasons to be skeptical about the macroeconomic benefits of ramping up government spending on infrastructure on this scale, especially if it has not been subjected to rigorous cost-benefit analysis on a project by project basis.

The key rationale for advocating more infrastructure spending is that it will create jobs and hence reduce the unacceptably high level of unemployment, an unquestionably worthy ideal. But economic recovery and reducing unemployment will depend on a revival of private sector activity, not government spending, because the private sector, especially the services industries, has overwhelmingly borne the brunt of the economic impact of the CVC.

Productive public infrastructure no doubt plays a pivotal role in the economy because it influences both aggregate demand and supply, increasing demand through investment, while adding to capacity via a larger capital stock. Yet increasing infrastructure spending without regard to its productivity is growth-limiting if it manifests as "roads and bridges to nowhere" that fail on cost-benefit grounds. Japan provides a case study on how over-reliance on infrastructure spending funded by world beating gross public debt around 250% of its GDP, rather than undertaking worthy fiscal consolidation, including tax reform, as well as domestic structural reform, retards economic growth.

Spending big on infrastructure to create employment is a straight replay of Keynes' 1930s advocacy of increased spending on "public works" during the Great Depression. But the industrial structure of advanced economies and their workforces have greatly changed since then. Today's labour force is more specialized than the workforce of the 1930s would have been. Back then, labour was more homogenous and hence more substitutable across industries. It would have been easier for displaced farm or factory workers, for instance, to be redeployed to other manual work on labour-intensive projects and there was greater incentive to do so as unemployment benefits where they existed were lower.

In contrast, advanced economies are now far more services-oriented and presently unemployed baristas or beauticians, for instance, are unlikely to be keen to switch to now more capital-intensive projects. Unproductive construction spending on projects in the non-tradable sector of the economy would also draw capital and labour away from tradable industries, worsening the economy's international competitiveness.

Moreover, infrastructure spending cannot be readily deployed, and inevitable lags occur, given delays in choosing the most viable projects, combining production inputs, and gaining the necessary planning approvals. Instead of focusing on government spending to boost aggregate demand, structural reform measures aimed at the supply side of the economy would be more effective in hastening economic recovery, most notably deregulation of business red and green tape, industrial relations reform, and lower company tax, or accelerated business investment allowances.

2.7. Conclusion

Unlike emergency monetary responses to increase liquidity and loosen credit availability, lavish government spending — particularly of the cash transfer and welfare support kind — cannot be readily withdrawn once announced and has lasting negative macroeconomic consequences.

Suddenly injecting government spending is not akin to injecting liquidity and bank credit via emergency monetary easing, because government spending has to be funded from elsewhere, in external borrower country cases, mostly from abroad. Walter Bagehot's (1873) classic dictum that central banks lend freely during crisis episodes still rings true for monetary policy.

But so does David Hume's (1777) even earlier dictum for fiscal policy. He said that because elected representatives make decisions to retain popular support and accordingly spend excessively under crisis conditions, "The practice of contracting debt will therefore almost infallibly be abused in every government."

High public debt harms business and household confidence to the extent it creates uncertainty about how the debt will be paid down via fiscal repair. This is inimical to private consumption and investment spending. As public debt limits expansion of the economy's capital stock, a key driver of economic growth, it means lower incomes for future generations. Relatedly, the intergenerational inequity argument suggests it is unfair for future generations to repay public debt incurred by the present generation.

Although world interest rates are presently very low, they must surely rise in coming years when public debt has to be refinanced, given the massive surge in public and private sector borrowing globally. Moreover, official interest rates will rise should inflationary pressures mount, as has historically been the case following large-scale public debt monetization by central banks.

To the extent that central banks continue to monetise public debt by buying government bonds (effectively "printing money"), the future could well be even worse, with slower economic growth, high unemployment, and high inflation. If economic history since Roman times is any guide, and there is no reason to doubt it, the money base expansion in advanced economies due to central bank monetization of public debt (either directly or indirectly via quantitative easing (QE)) will put upward pressure on the price level as economies recover, necessitating a rise in official interest rates. The lagged inflation response to money base growth has conventionally been assumed to be 18–24 months later. Under those conditions we would see history repeating the global "stagflation" of the 1970s.

A budget option for reducing the level of public debt is greater privatization of government assets, including sizeable real estate holdings. Though once-only sales proceeds could be used to pay down public debt, this option would not provide a lasting solution to the structural budget deficit problem.

The size of government in most advanced economies pre-CVC was already above its economic growth maximizing level.[10] Hence, government expenditure restraint should take precedence over raising taxes as the priority fiscal repair option for addressing the looming public debt problem. Reduced public spending — particularly on industry assistance and the overlap in spending at different levels of government in areas such as education and health — should therefore be central to the recovery program. This should be accompanied by tax reform as well as business deregulation and reforms to increase labour market flexibility to enhance productivity on economies' supply sides.

References

Afonso, A. and Jalles, J.T. (2013). Growth and productivity: The role of government debt. *International Review of Economics & Finance*, **25**, 384–407.

Akhtaruzzaman, M., Boubaker, S. and Sensoy, A. (2021). Financial contagion during COVID-19 crisis. *Finance Research Letters*, **38**, 101604.

Bagehot, W. (1873). *Lombard Street: A Description of the Money Market* (King, London; Reprinted Wiley, New York, 1999).

Buchanan, J. (1958). *Public Principles of Public Debt* (Liberty Fund, New York).

Cagan, P. (1956). The Monetary dynamics of hyperinflation. In *Studies in the Quantity Theory of Money*, Friedman, M. (ed.), (University of Chicago Press, Chicago), pp. 56–70.

Caggiano, G., Casteinuovo, E. and Kima, R. (2020). The global effects of COVID-19 uncertainty. *Economics Letters*, **194**, 1–5.

Égert, B. (2015). Public debt, economic growth and nonlinear effects: Myth or reality? *Journal of Macroeconomics*, **43**, 226–238.

[10]See Tanzi and Schuknecht (2000) and Makin and Pearce (2016).

Fleming, J. (1962). Domestic financial policies under fixed and under floating exchange rates. *IMF Staff Papers*, 12, 369–380.

Friedman, M. (1962). *Capitalism and Freedom* (University of Chicago Press, Chicago).

Gunarsa, S., Makin, A. and Rohde, N. (2020) Public debt in developing Asia: a help or hindrance to growth? *Applied Economics Letters, 2020*, **27**, 1400–1403.

Hayek, F. (1995). Contra Keynes and Cambridge. In *The Collected Works of F A Hayek*, Vol. 9, Caldwell, B. (ed.), (University of Chicago Press, Chicago), pp. 52–62.

Hume, D. (1777). *Essays, Moral, Political and Literary* (Liberty Fund, New York).

Hutchison, T. (1977). *Keynes versus the 'Keynesians'* (Institute of Public Affairs, London).

International Monetary Fund (2020a). *Fiscal Monitor* (International Monetary Fund, Washington, DC).

International Monetary Fund (2020b). *Australia, Article IV* (International Monetary Fund, Washington, DC).

Keynes, J.M. (1936). *The General Theory of Employment, Interest and Money* (Macmillan, London).

Makin, A. (2018). *The Limits of Fiscal Policy* (Palgrave Macmillan, UK).

Makin, A. and Pearce, J. (2016). Fiscal consolidation and Australia's public debt. *Australian Journal of Public Administration*, **75**(4), 424–440.

Mankiw, G. (2020). *Macroeconomics* (Worth, New York).

Mundell, R. (1963). Capital mobility and stabilization policy under fixed and flexible exchange rates. *Canadian Journal of Economics and Political Science*, **29**(4), 475–485.

Sharif, A., Aloui, C. and Yarovaya, L. (2020). COVID-19 pandemic, oil prices, stock market, geopolitical risk and policy uncertainty nexus in the US economy: Fresh evidence from the wavelet-based approach. *International Review of Financial Analysis*, **70**, 1–10.

Smith, A. (1776). *The Wealth of Nations* (Liberty Fund, New York).

Tanzi, V. and Schuknecht, L. (2000). *Public Spending in the 20th Century* (Cambridge University Press, Cambridge).

Woo, J. and Kumar, M. (2015). *Public Debt and Growth Economica*, **82**, 705–739.

Zhang, D., Hu, M. and Ji, Q. (2020). Financial markets under the global pandemic of COVID-19. *Finance Research Letters*, **36**, 1–6.

https://doi.org/10.1142/9781800610781_0003

Chapter 3

The Importance of Negative Feedback and Countervailing Measures for Financial System Stabilization and Constrained Inequality: A COVID-19–Induced Reminder

John L. Haracz

Department of Psychological and Brain Sciences
Indiana University
1101 E. 10th St., Bloomington, IN 47405, USA
jharacz@berkeley.edu

Abstract

Positive-feedback mechanisms destabilize asset markets and promote wealth or income inequality. The COVID-19 pandemic exposed mispricing in asset markets and triggered a price crash. The pandemic also exacerbated inequality. Runaway positive-feedback mechanisms can be counteracted by implementing negative-feedback loops for financial system stabilization. Asset markets are sorely lacking the types of negative-feedback loops that promote stability and equilibrium in biological or engineering systems. For introducing negative feedback into asset markets, investors could be fed back the prevalence of destabilizing investment strategies. A rise in this prevalence would warn investors to exit overheated asset markets, thereby cooling off these markets endogenously. Price bubbles in overheated markets represent a market-failure mode, in which prices fail to closely track asset fundamental value. To prevent this failure, a market design should feed back the prevalence of investors' destabilizing impulsive strategies, so traders could judge the degree of mispricing and voluntarily exit overheated markets. By exacerbating inequalities in income and health, the pandemic is also a reminder of the need for implementing countervailing measures to constrain inequality. These measures could include modest New-Deal–like programs that would be more readily implemented than the original New Deal in the US because existing government programs could be scaled up (e.g. housing vouchers for low-income renters, Medicaid, and the Earned Income Tax Credit). In summary, the widely recognized need for government spending in response to the pandemic should be seen as an opportunity to implement transformative measures aimed at stabilizing asset markets and constraining inequality.

3.1. Introduction

> *After all, there is an element in the readjustment of our financial system more important than currency, more important than gold, and that is the confidence of the people. Confidence and courage are the essentials of success in carrying out our plan. You people must have faith; you must not be stampeded by rumors or guesses. Let us unite in banishing fear. ... Together we cannot fail.*
>
> Franklin D. Roosevelt (2018 [1933], p. v)

> *God gave Noah the rainbow sign, No more water, the fire next time!*
>
> James Baldwin (1993 [1963], p. 106, italics in original)

3.1.1. *From fireside chats to the fire next time: COVID-19 exposes financial system and economic imbalances that promote social unrest*

The coronavirus disease 2019 (COVID-19) pandemic has illuminated global imbalances in financial systems and economies. These imbalances involve financial and economic structural issues that generate inequitable outcomes against the interests of many people. Financial system cycles and instability yield recessions with increased unemployment and financial insecurity that threaten to generate widespread social upheaval. The COVID-19 pandemic led to a stock market crash, an ongoing recession (at the time of writing), and increased income and health inequality. The pandemic's impact on employment levels and health has been particularly severe in socio-economically disadvantaged communities. High rates of COVID-19 morbidity and mortality afflicted Black and Latino populations as the Black Lives Matter movement gained momentum (Asante-Muhammad *et al.*, 2020; Chowkwanyun and Reed, Jr., 2020; Gross *et al.*, 2020; Mays and Newman, 2020; Mills and Battisto, 2020; Oppel, Jr. *et al.*, 2020; Overberg and Kamp, 2020). The disproportionate population-health impact of COVID-19 has followed longstanding patterns of inequality in health, income, and wealth among racial and ethnic groups (Chetty *et al.*, 2016; Diez Roux, 2020; Krieger, 2005; Laurencin and Walker, 2020; Maani and Galea, 2020).

3.1.2. *Proposed remedies for financial system and economic imbalances*

The present chapter, as a systematic literature review, proposes that governmental COVID-19 relief efforts should go beyond acute relief to address chronic financial system and economic structural issues that make disadvantaged populations bear the brunt of threats such as pandemics, recessions, earthquakes, and extreme weather events. Two specific classes of remedies are proposed, namely interventions that introduce negative-feedback loops into asset markets to promote financial system stability (see Section 3.2) and countervailing measures that constrain inequality (see Section 3.3).

Governmental and central bank responses to previous financial crises largely consisted of post-crisis rescue and recovery efforts, such as liquidity provisions for acute financial system stabilization supplemented with monetary and/or fiscal stimulus to alleviate economic contractions (Bernanke, 2012). On the other hand, the prevention of financial crises is relatively neglected by the literature (Roubini and Mihm, 2010). This deficit in the literature is addressed by the presently proposed market designs that feed back to investors the prevalence of destabilizing investment strategies. When this prevalence rises, investors may voluntarily reduce their exposure to excessively priced asset classes, thereby endogenously dampening price swings and forestalling major crashes.

A recurring theme among commentaries about the pandemic is that it presents a historic opportunity for policymakers to address financial and economic structural issues that perpetually generate inequitable outcomes, but are particularly adverse for disadvantaged populations during emergency conditions. For example, governments have been urged to develop pandemic recovery efforts that decrease poverty and inequality by addressing distributional issues head on (Desmond, 2020; Lin and Neely, 2020; Piketty, 2020; Pisani-Ferry, 2020; Santos and Alkire, 2020). Effectively tackling major structural issues would seem to require interventions that are sized to the task at hand, possibly approaching the scale of Great-Depression-era New Deal programs that alleviated poverty and inequality (Desmond, 2020). Unfortunately, current political leaders, at the time of this writing, largely lack the capacity for Roosevelt-like transformational leadership that offers steady reassurance in a fireside-chat setting (Roosevelt, 2018 [1933]). However, technological innovation (see Section 3.2) and election cycles in democracies around the world yield hope for the achievement of fundamental remedies, such as those presently proposed (see Sections 3.2 and 3.3).

While occasionally discussing other countries, this chapter focuses on the US due to its leadership tendencies in financial and economic trends. For example, international spillovers of income inequality (Kalliovirta and Malinen, 2020) and effects from expansionary (Bhattarai *et al.*, 2021) or tightened (Miranda-Agrippino and Rey, 2020) monetary policy have been found to originate in the US. These similarities in financial and economic trends across countries suggest that the potential effectiveness of the presently proposed policies may generalize internationally.

3.2. Negative Feedback for Financial System Stabilization

> *The most fundamental conviction of cybernetic theory is that it all comes down to messages (i.e., information) sent and responded to (i.e.,* feedback*). Faithful exchanges of information allow the machine, organism, or society to maintain a state of homeostasis. Information corrupted by various forms of noise leads to the opposite.*
>
> Doug Hill (2019 [1948], p. xi, emphasis added)

> *All purposeful behavior may be considered to require* negative feed-back.
>
> Arturo Rosenblueth, Norbert Wiener and Julian Bigelow (1943, p. 19, emphasis added)

> *Momentum, in my view, is the biggest embarrassment for efficient markets.*
>
> Eugene Fama (quoted by Amy Whyte [2016])

> *People are trading stocks with their cellphones on their living room couches with the television news blaring about the pandemic.*
>
> Robert J. Shiller (2020a)

3.2.1. *COVID-19 revealed that asset markets were overheated due to excessive positive feedback*

Negative-feedback loops keep well-controlled engineering systems operating smoothly and physiological metabolic pathways functioning within normal limits under conditions of homeostasis, which resembles the concept of equilibrium in economics. Unfortunately, asset markets are a very different matter due to inadequate negative feedback. In boom or bust scenarios, asset prices diverge greatly from what would be considered more reasonable asset values in stable market conditions that resemble the idealized equilibrium or market-clearing conditions of models for supply–demand interactions in economics or asset-pricing in finance. Asset mispricing may be driven partly by narratives about assets (e.g. "housing prices will keep rising" and "dot-com stocks are a great investment"). Narratives may drive asset-price bubbles by persuading investors to focus attention on supposedly positive aspects of assets (Shiller, 2019). Furthermore, narratives may elicit bubble-related herding (Baddeley, 2010; Stiglitz, 2011) by activating an evolutionary predisposition to group herding behavior seen also in non-human species (Haracz, 2013, 2021; Stépanoff, 2012). Consistent with an evolutionary predisposition to herding, animal survival is enhanced in groups, whereas experiments with human subjects found that subjective fear decreases as group size increases (Tedeschi *et al.*, 2020).

During an asset-price bubble, market participants engaged in herding (i.e. mimicking other participants' asset purchases) become willing to pay increasingly exorbitant prices for popular assets. This leads to a self-reinforcing acceleration of price increases. Far from being an efficient indicator of asset fundamental value, rising prices in this case generate positive feedback (Arthur, 2015; Barberis *et al.*, 2018; Battiston *et al.*, 2016; De Long *et al.*, 1990b; Hirshleifer, 2020; Leijonhufvud, 2014) by acting as heuristic signals for the elicitation of herding and further price rises. Prolonged price rises, as a major bubble builds over months or years, act as a signal that assets are gaining in popularity. Herding and heuristics will be discussed further in Section 3.2.2.

Among narratives that drove the fivefold increase in the S&P 500 index from March 9, 2009, (i.e. the nadir of the index during the Global Financial Crisis) to February 19, 2020 (i.e. the peak of the index before the COVID-19–induced price crash) were stories that proclaimed wonderful opportunities for the future growth of companies in the technology sector. Indeed, these narratives apparently survived the COVID-19 crash unscathed because five large tech companies have fueled the S&P 500's rise on the way to record levels since reaching a low on March 23, 2020 (DeCambre, 2020; O'Neill, 2020). This outperformance of the largest tech companies in the S&P 500 extends back to at least 2013 (Shefrin, 2019). Sell-side financial analysts showed evidence of an upward bias while formulating their target stock prices for these firms (i.e. a "growth opportunities bias" [Shefrin, 2019, p. 113]). As discussed in Section 3.2.2, the growth opportunities bias can be classified as a type of bubble bias because it may contribute to mechanisms involved in asset overpricing that drives bubble growth.

Against the backdrop of a high cyclically adjusted price earnings (CAPE) ratio for the US equity market (Shiller, 2020b), the COVID-19 pandemic triggered historically rapid asset devaluations (DeCambre, 2020). The pandemic-alleviating economic shutdown and social distancing were unavoidable (Atalan, 2020; López and Rodó, 2020), but introducing negative feedback into asset markets may dampen market swings and blunt the impact of recessions that follow market crashes. More generally, reducing the size of asset-price bubbles could decrease the economic impact of ensuing recessions.[1] Negative feedback may act as a nudge (Thaler and Sunstein, 2008) to reorient investors away from heuristics and biases that drive asset-price bubbles and crashes (Hawkins, 2011). These heuristics and biases are discussed in Section 3.2.2 before Section 3.2.3 describes specific forms of negative feedback for potential use as financial system stabilizers.

3.2.2. *Heuristics and biases involved in asset-price bubbles and crashes: The price heuristic and bubble or crash biases*

Numerous authors in the fields of economics, social psychology, evolutionary biology, psychiatry, sociology, and political science have described herding as behavioral conformity that tends to be more impulsive than deliberative (Morgan and Laland, 2012; Raafat *et al.*, 2009). The herding or conformity of decision-making is particularly prevalent in large groups of people who are confronted with uncertainty (Toyokawa *et al.*, 2019), so some degree of herding may be expected in markets with assets (e.g. stocks) that are not straightforward to valuate. Concerns about herding (i.e. decision-making that follows the decisions of others) have risen recently due to the potential of herding to destabilize financial markets and yield asset-price bubbles or crashes (Bursztyn *et al.*, 2014; Chang, 2014; Gärling *et al.*, 2009; Greenspan, 2013; Lux, 1995; Scharfstein and Stein, 1990). Therefore, signs of herding, in data yielded by digital technology (e.g. web analytics of impulsive investor interactions with online asset-trading platforms), may be candidate early-warning indicators for an emerging bubble. A high prevalence of these indicators among market participants could constitute information that is suitable for building a negative-feedback loop in asset markets. On a voluntary basis, these early-warning signals could be fed back to market participants for triggering self-regulatory actions. A high prevalence of herding among market participants could warn investors to exit potentially overheated asset markets, thereby cooling off these markets endogenously.

[1]Richard C. Koo, personal communication, March 30, 2020.

Besides web analytics of retail investors' impulsivity on asset-trading platforms, monitoring professional investors' investment strategies may also reveal signs of herding that are suitable for building negative-feedback loops in asset markets (see Section 3.2.3). These negative-feedback loops can prevent heuristics and biases that drive asset mispricing (Hawkins, 2011).

To clarify the role of cognitive distortions in asset-price bubbles and crashes, Haracz (2021) proposed the price heuristic hypothesis, which characterizes prices as heuristic signals that guide price heuristics or rules of thumb (i.e. prices can act as heuristic signals for eliciting price-based heuristics [Ceschi *et al.*, 2019; Gigerenzer and Gaissmaier, 2011; Hafenbradl *et al.*, 2016] or, in short, price heuristics). Price heuristics yield biased investment decisions involving bubble or crash biases that generate asset over- or under-valuations, respectively.

While evaluating the positive and negative aspects of potentially attractive assets, quantitatively minded investors deliberate about indicators of asset fundamental value (e.g. stock valuations are aided by applying discounted cash flow, residual income, or dividend discount models of valuation [Cassia and Vismara, 2009; Shefrin, 2019]). Deliberation may also involve assessing the degree to which an asset is over- or under-valued relative to fundamental value (Barberis *et al.*, 2018; Shefrin, 2019). Failing to engage in these types of deliberation could bias investors toward simply using asset-price changes as guides, or heuristics, to popular or unpopular assets, thereby letting investors fall under the spell of a bubble or crash bias, respectively. These biases promote trend-following investment strategies that may play a role in price bubbles and crashes.

During an asset-price bubble, market participants pay excessive prices for popular assets, thereby generating a self-reinforcing acceleration of price increases. Rather than efficiently indicating asset fundamental value, rising prices in this case generate positive feedback (Arthur, 2015; Barberis *et al.*, 2018; Battiston *et al.*, 2016; De Long *et al.*, 1990b; Hirshleifer, 2020; Leijonhufvud, 2014) by acting as heuristic signals (i.e. analogous to cues that become conditioned reinforcers during reinforcement learning) for the elicitation of herding and further price rises that can yield reinforcing realized gains. Asset prices that rise over months or years act as heuristic signals that assets are gaining in popularity.

In this view, prices guide decision-making by serving as signals for the use of simple price-based rules (i.e. price heuristics). Examples of prices acting as heuristic signals that elicit price heuristics include using prices for assessing the quality of products (Plassmann *et al.*, 2008; Shiv *et al.*, 2005), determining whether transaction terms are acceptable (Karmarkar *et al.*, 2015; Knutson *et al.*, 2007), gauging future prospects of inflation (de Haan and van den End, 2018), forecasting stock returns (Glaser *et al.*, 2019), applying technical analysis while making asset-trading decisions (Zhou, 2018), gaining information that other traders have about the fundamental values of assets (Bordalo *et al.*, 2021), developing price expectations based on the continuation of price trends (e.g. Schwaiger *et al.* [2020] found that financial professionals showed this trend-following use of prices), exploiting stock return momentum by adjusting portfolios to favor winners over losers (e.g. Stein [2009] and Asness *et al.* [2014] noted that institutional investors use this momentum investment strategy), guiding the design and implementation of algorithms for momentum trading (Ciliberti and Gualdi, 2020), assessing sentiment-related over- and under-valuation of assets (Shefrin, 2019; Zhou, 2018), allocating capital in a sometimes, but not always (Lim and Brooks, 2011), efficient manner, and detecting shifts in the balance between supply and demand (Arthur, 1994). In the supply–demand context, price functions as a heuristic signal between individual buyers and sellers who use heuristics based on price changes to detect shifts in the supply–demand balance. Particularly pertinent for the bubble bias is the use of past price paths by professional (Schwaiger *et al.*, 2020) and retail investors to predict future price trends. This positive-feedback dynamic may destabilize financial markets and decrease market efficiency.

The accuracy of asset valuation in financial models is limited because many variables in these models are related to the vagaries of human sentiment or emotion (Derman, 2011). The impact of sentiment on valuation, prices, and stock returns (Hill-Kleespie, 2019; Shefrin, 2019; Zhou, 2018) underscores the limited, heuristic nature of prices. This impact should motivate a departure from viewing prices as nearly infallible signals for the allocation of resources. It is not as if all pertinent information efficiently gets embedded into rapidly adjusting prices that accurately pinpoint the fundamental values of assets. More realistically, prices have rigidities that reflect limitations of individuals and firms. For example, as asset-related information becomes available, investors may respond by deploying inadequate attention (DellaVigna and Pollet, 2009; Hirshleifer *et al.*, 2011), whereas firms must choose how much information to acquire for setting prices (Stevens, 2020).

The price-heuristic hypothesis introduced above accommodates highly efficient markets as a special case, in which the price of an asset reflects all available information about the asset's fundamental value without sentiment-induced price distortions (Hill-Kleespie, 2019; Shefrin, 2019; Zhou, 2018). Besides sentiment, limited investor attention to publicly available information may also induce asset mispricing and restrict market efficiency (DellaVigna and Pollet, 2009; Hirshleifer *et al.*, 2011). News analytics used by trading algorithms enhance information incorporation into asset prices, but can include inaccurate analytics that produce short-term price distortions (von Beschwitz *et al.*, 2019). The limited, heuristic nature of prices may have been under-recognized due to the mystique of the efficient market hypothesis.

Prices can be used deliberatively, in the analysis of transaction terms relative to signs about the fundamental value of assets, or more impulsively, leading to biased judgments about the value and popularity of assets in boom or bust scenarios. Relative to optimal buy-and-hold investment strategies (Bogle, 2012), having a bubble (crash) bias makes investors herd on the basis of being suboptimally too optimistic (pessimistic) about potential stock returns. Similar to this proposed role for biases in investors' herding, Kienzler (2018) describes herding as a cognitive bias that influences the pricing practices of business managers. This herding may lead to mispricing getting baked into prices right from the start. These examples of mispricing arising from herding by investors or pricing managers support the presently proposed classification of prices as heuristic signals that give a partly informative idea about the value of assets and products rather than a precise reflection of market-wide information pertaining to fundamental value. The potential for herding-related mispricing in investment and product-pricing contexts raises the question of whether measurably rising levels of herding are associated with increases in mispricing. An affirmative answer is suggested by rising evidence of momentum-trading strategies by investment fund managers during the growing dot-com stock market bubble in the 1990s

(Barberis *et al.*, 2018; see Section 3.2.3). This evidence motivates a search for methodologies that could detect in real time a rising prevalence of herding among investors. In professional (Schwaiger *et al.*, 2020) and retail investors, the bubble bias associated with herding could generate a positive-feedback loop based on using past price increases to predict continuing upward trends. This potential for systemically destabilizing positive feedback (Arthur, 2015; Barberis *et al.*, 2018; Battiston *et al.*, 2016; De Long *et al.*, 1990b; Hirshleifer, 2020; Leijonhufvud, 2014) underscores the importance of introducing a stabilizing negative-feedback loop into financial systems (see Section 3.2.3).

Borrowing Charles Mackay's (2014 [1841]) terminology from his mid-19th-century, three-volume book, *Extraordinary Popular Delusions and the Madness of Crowds*, crowds can go mad in a variety of ways, so the bubble bias may be better understood as a collection of biases that potentially promote asset-price bubbles. For example, Section 3.2.1 described growth opportunities bias as a predisposition of sell-side financial analysts for assigning upwardly biased target stock prices to firms that are popular among buy-side institutional investors (Shefrin, 2019). Sell-side analysts' assessments of Tesla, Facebook, Alphabet, Amazon, and Netflix showed evidence of growth opportunities bias (Shefrin, 2019).

Another candidate bubble bias is extrapolation bias, also called "overextrapolation" or "extrapolative expectations" (Cassella and Gulen, 2018, p. 4346). Extrapolation bias is proposed to be associated with the representativeness heuristic (Gennaioli and Shleifer, 2018; Bordalo *et al.*, 2021). In this view, good news about a firm's earnings or other fundamental information encourages overestimated probabilities of future positive developments, such as the firm becoming the next Google. This overreaction to good news facilitates a bias toward extrapolating positive trends (e.g. increased stock returns) into the future. Extrapolation bias, particularly for positive trends, may have deep evolutionary roots. Like humans, monkeys prefer sequential rewards presented in a trend that is increasing in value, rather than decreasing, or flat (Blanchard *et al.*, 2014). This deeply ingrained trend bias for positive sequences could promote overextrapolation (Cassella and Gulen, 2018) and may be involved in the pervasive recurrence of asset-price bubbles over many centuries, in worldwide locations, and in a wide variety of asset classes (Reinhart and Rogoff, 2009). Extrapolation bias was examined in a study that used weekly survey data on expectations of stock returns (Cassella and Gulen, 2018). The results from retail and professional investors in the US is described in Section 3.2.3 because this study identified information that may be useful for building negative-feedback loops in asset markets.

Persuasion bias (DeMarzo *et al.*, 2003; Hirshleifer, 2020) and the related social transmission bias (Hirshleifer, 2020) are potential bubble biases that could facilitate the spread of narratives involved in driving asset-price bubbles (Shiller, 2019). Narratives about popular assets are likely to increase the probability that investors will remember these assets, so memory bias (Mechera-Ostrovsky and Gluth, 2018) may interact with the persuasion and social transmission biases in promoting bubbles. The memory bias arises when people favor remembered options over forgotten ones, even if a forgotten option is objectively optimal.

As a potential bubble bias, present bias (O'Donoghue and Rabin, 2015) may offer another plausible hypothetical mechanism for the generation of asset-price bubbles. Unlike patient investors with a buy-and-hold strategy, impatient stock "*renters*" (Bogle, 2012, p. 80, italics in original) with a present bias are more likely to "ride the bubble" (Barberis *et al.*, 2018, p. 221) while seeking to realize gains. This bubble riding could put upward pressure on stock prices as a bubble grows.

By promoting overconfidence, self-attribution bias (i.e. giving oneself undue credit [Daniel and Hirshleifer, 2015; Statman *et al.*, 2006]) is a candidate bubble bias. For example, noise traders (Campbell and Kyle, 1993; Chang, 2014; De Long *et al.*, 1990a; Lux and Marchesi, 1999; Shefrin and Statman, 1994) using relatively short-term investment strategies may misattribute positive returns in bull markets to their trading skills. Investor overconfidence may account for the finding that periods of high stock market returns are followed by increased trading volumes (Statman *et al.*, 2006). Rising stock prices could attract overconfident individual investors who trade excessively, but ultimately at a loss (Barber and Odean, 2000; Daniel and Hirshleifer, 2015; Grinblatt and Keloharju, 2009). Early evidence of excessive online trading by individual investors (Barber and Odean, 2002; Choi *et al.*, 2002; Glaser and Weber, 2007) is being corroborated by reports about trading on the Robinhood platform (see Section 3.2.3).

As the list of cognitive biases continues to grow (Ceschi *et al.*, 2019), further research may identify additional bubble biases among members of this list (e.g. optimism bias [Sharot, 2011]) or newly discovered biases. For promoting financial system stability, another potentially fruitful research direction is to determine whether bubble markers can be found among specific patterns of biased investor behaviors. As described in Section 3.2.3, these behavioral bubble markers may be useful for building negative-feedback loops to stabilize financial markets.

Financial markets are claimed to be suitable for the purpose of efficiently allocating capital (Fama, 1970, 1991). Negative feedback could facilitate this goal (see the above epigraph [Rosenblueth *et al.*, 1943]) by informing traders about an estimated prevalence of investors with impulsive, momentum, or trend-following trading strategies. When this prevalence rises, traders may stabilize overheated financial markets by exiting these markets, as outlined in Section 3.2.3.

3.2.3. *Cooling off overheated asset markets with real-time negative feedback*

Research is needed to determine how excessive positive feedback in asset markets might be counteracted by introducing negative-feedback loops into these markets, thereby promoting financial system stability and making markets more suitable for the purpose of efficiently allocating capital (Fama, 1991). This research should seek data that may yield behavioral bubble markers for self-regulatory negative feedback to dampen market swings. Candidate markers, to be discussed below, include data from professional investors showing rising prevalences of specific investing patterns during the growing dot-com bubble in the 1990s (Barberis *et al.*, 2018) and the rising stock market bubble before the crash in 2008–2009 (Gualdi *et al.*, 2016). The prevalence of momentum strategies (Barberis *et al.*, 2018) or portfolio overlap (Gualdi *et al.*, 2016) was found to increase gradually over years as these bubbles grew, so these prevalences may be useful for market-stabilizing negative feedback. These findings motivate the use of data analytics with machine learning to determine whether real-time data streams from professional or retail investors may yield potential behavioral bubble markers. The markers could be fed back to investors via financial news services or on online asset-trading platforms. By using the markers as early-warning signals for overheated markets, investors could exit these markets, thereby endogenously cooling off the markets.

The emotionality (Hill-Kleespie, 2019; Zhou, 2018), accessibility, and low cost (E*Trade, 2020; Knowledge@Wharton, 2018) of online trading may have played roles in recent massive stock market swings, including the dot-com bubble and crash, a doubling of the S&P 500 index before this index crashed in 2008–2009, a quintupling of the S&P 500 before the recent COVID-19–related crash, and a more than 50% rise in the S&P 500 that recouped the COVID-19–related losses (DeCambre, 2020). Large stock price increases that develop over years (e.g. the dot-com bubble as well as bubbles before and after the 2008–2009 crash) offer researchers opportunities for seeking bubble markers, which could clarify whether increased prices represent a bubble. For example, a price-bubble signal may be revealed at the behavioral level by analyzing investors' interactions with online trading platforms.

A behavioral price-bubble signal could be identified by designing and implementing a simplified asset-trading platform, scaled back from the likes of E*Trade's (2020) website with over 800 items on the site map. Simplification would ease the use of web analytic methods to monitor real-time prevalences of platform users showing impulsive trend-following behavior (i.e. herding [see Section 3.2.2]) or deliberative information-seeking behavior in association with asset trading. These prevalences could be offered as feedback on the platform and in financial market news services, so that a rising prevalence of impulsive agents (e.g. as in agent-based models discussed below) would warn investors to divest from assets with values that were inflated by purchases linked with trend-following behavior. For the goal of financial system stabilization, this feedback could serve as a self-regulatory mechanism based on the type of negative feedback that is found widely in engineering and biological systems (Rosenblueth *et al.*, 1943). The predictive accuracy of this negative feedback for identifying overheated markets could be assessed by applying predictive analytics with machine learning to investors' interactions with trading platforms.

Researchers at the Paul Woolley Centre for the Study of Capital Market Dysfunctionality note that "... investing boils down to a choice between two distinct strategies" (Ricardo Research, 2019, p. 4). These two broad strategies are modeled in extensive research with agent-based models of asset-price bubbles and/or asset prices, which include investor types that trade either deliberatively, based on information about the fundamental values of assets, or more impulsively while using trend-following, momentum, or chartist strategies (Alfi *et al.*, 2009; Barberis *et al.*, 2018; Campbell and Kyle, 1993; Chang, 2014; Chiarella and Di Guilmi, 2012; De Long *et al.*, 1990a; Grossman and Stiglitz, 1980; Hommes and in 't Veld, 2017; Hong and Stein, 1999; Lux and Marchesi, 1999; Shefrin and Statman, 1994; Zheng, 2020). This second "price-only investing" style was offered as a working definition of short-termism in asset management (Ricardo Research, 2019, p. 5). These models typically find that deliberative "fundamentalist" (Lux and Marchesi, 1999, p. 498; Alfi *et al.*, 2009, p. 387; Chiarella and Guilmi, 2012, p. 8; Hommes and in 't Veld, 2017, p. 105) agents stabilize asset markets, whereas the more impulsive agents, also called "noise traders" (Campbell and Kyle, 1993, p. 9; Chang, 2014, p. 91; De Long *et al.*, 1990a, p. 707; Lux and Marchesi, 1999, p. 498; Shefrin and Statman, 1994, p. 323), destabilize markets. Therefore, the method proposed above for providing negative feedback on trading platforms aims to detect in real time a rising prevalence of impulsive agents in order to give an early warning signal of overheating asset markets.

Besides the prevalence of impulsive trend-following traders using trading platforms, other data may serve as behavioral bubble markers for self-regulatory negative feedback to dampen market swings. Barberis *et al.* (2018) present a model of asset-price bubbles with extrapolative and fundamental traders. Extrapolative traders demand shares based on a growth signal derived from past price changes, but are disinclined to buy shares with a high value signal, which measures the difference between the price and a rational valuation of cash flow. Fundamental traders focus on rational valuations. The model yields bubbles that peak with a period of "wavering" (Barberis *et al.*, 2018, p. 204), when extrapolators are ambivalent about how to balance the conflicting growth and value signals. Consistent with the model, mutual and hedge funds showed evidence for wavering in their buying and selling of technology stocks near the dot-com bubble peak (Barberis *et al.*, 2018). Another finding is potentially suitable for identifying a bubble marker that could be used as negative feedback. During the growing dot-com bubble in the 1990s, mutual funds' trading of technology stocks showed a gradual increase in momentum-trading volume (Barberis *et al.*, 2018). Therefore, the volume of momentum trading by professional investors is a candidate bubble marker with potential usefulness for warning investors about an increased probability that stock prices will crash.

Gualdi *et al.* (2016) studied portfolio overlap (i.e. common holdings of securities across portfolios) shown in 13-F Securities and Exchange Commission filings by institutions (i.e. investment advisors, hedge funds, mutual funds, brokers, and private banking funds) during the period from 1999 to the end of 2013. During the years-long growth in stock prices before the Global Financial Crisis, institutional portfolio overlap gradually grew and peaked in 2007 just before the stock market crash. After reaching a low in 2009, portfolio overlap again grew to a level that exceeded the 2007 peak, leading the authors to conclude that these findings "... might question the stability of financial markets nowadays" (Gualdi *et al.*, 2016, p. 5). These results are consistent with Stein's (2009) proposal that institutional investors' crowded trades may push asset prices further away from what is justified by estimates of fundamental asset values. Gualdi *et al.* (2016) suggested that, in times of market euphoria, overlapping portfolios could help to generate self-reinforcing asset-price bubbles. Therefore, institutional portfolio overlap may join with professional investors' momentum-trading volume (Barberis *et al.*, 2018) as another candidate bubble marker with potential usefulness for negative feedback.

Cassella and Gulen (2018, p. 4384) noted that "... extrapolation is one of many known behavioral biases which may contribute to the rise and fall of fads," including market booms and busts. They studied the influence of extrapolation bias on stock returns expectations using data from the American Association of Individual Investors survey of retail investors and the Investor Intelligence Survey, which collects forecasts of stock market performance from US financial advisors' newsletters. Extrapolation bias, measured as the degree to which investors focused on recent returns while developing future returns expectations, was found to vary over time in association with major stock market swings. This measure rose gradually in the 1990s before falling after the dot-com bubble crashed. Extrapolation bias peaked again in 2007 just before the Global Financial Crisis.

Like portfolio overlap (Gualdi *et al.*, 2016), the bias then grew again through late 2013 to reach a level that exceeded the 2007 peak (Cassella and Gulen, 2018). Therefore, measures of portfolio overlap and extrapolation bias apparently may have been useful for detecting overvaluations in stock markets when market indices achieved record levels before the COVID-19–induced crash.

Cassella and Gulen (2018) also found that their measure of extrapolation bias moderated the capacity of price-scaled variables to predict stock returns. Low price-scaled variables (i.e. earnings-to-price, dividend-price, and book-to-market ratios) were followed by lower returns only when extrapolative bias was high. This finding suggests that an extrapolation-bias measure may facilitate the capacity of Viebig (2020) machine-learning methodology to predict stock returns on the basis of price-scaled variables. Using decades of MSCI data on worldwide equity markets up to 2016, support vector machines learned that the probability of abnormally low returns increases when markets trade at high valuation levels, as gauged by price-to-book ratios and dividend yields (Viebig, 2020). The machine-learning–based measure of probability for low future returns resembled measures of momentum trading volume (Barberis *et al.*, 2018), portfolio overlap (Gualdi *et al.*, 2016), and extrapolation bias (Cassella and Gulen, 2018) by showing a gradual increase as the dot-com bubble grew in the 1990s and as stock markets rose just before the Global Financial Crisis (Viebig, 2020). Like the portfolio overlap (Gualdi *et al.*, 2016) and extrapolation bias (Cassella and Gulen, 2018) measures, the machine learning gauge of overheated markets also peaked in 2007 just before the stock market crash associated with the Global Financial Crisis. The machine learning measure indicated that stock markets were overheated just before the COVID-19–related crash and in mid-August, 2020 — after markets recouped losses while reaching record levels (DeCambre and Wiltermuth, 2020; Shaban and Lynch, 2020).[2] The International Monetary Fund warned that the gap between rebounding asset prices and fundamentals was near historic highs (Lynch, 2020). Therefore, after three stock market crashes in this young century, markets already may be set up for a fourth.

[2]Jan Viebig, personal communication, August 14, 2020.

The machine learning measure is used for advising investor clients at Oddo BHF, a French-German financial services group.[3] Like the other reviewed measures (Barberis *et al.*, 2018; Cassella and Gulen, 2018; Gualdi *et al.*, 2016), the machine learning methodology potentially could be used for providing self-regulatory negative feedback that stabilizes markets.

Machine learning is becoming increasingly useful for analyzing large amounts of data while seeking early-warning indicators of financial crises. For example, Göbel and Araújo (2020) used machine learning to identify crisis-related macroeconomic indicators while searching for early-warning signals of banking and currency crises in 27 advanced or developing economies during the 1990s and just before the Global Financial Crisis. Machine learning could be useful for identifying specific combinations of presently reviewed measures (Barberis *et al.*, 2018; Cassella and Gulen, 2018; Gualdi *et al.*, 2016; Viebig, 2020) or other measures that may be used as market-stabilizing negative feedback.

Establishing a price-bubble signal for the above self-regulatory purpose may not require decades of research showing that a putative signal regularly precedes the peaks of major bubbles, which subsequently crash and result in prolonged recessions. The scale-free nature of relationships between changes in stock prices and transaction volumes suggest that the "larger abundance of data on smaller crises can provide quantifiable statistical laws for bubble formation and financial collapse on various scales" (Preis *et al.*, 2011, p. 7677). Therefore, candidate bubble markers could increasingly come into play during excessive price rises that yield either moderate market corrections or large crashes. A price-bubble signal (e.g. an increased prevalence of trend-following agents) could be useful for determining whether a stock price rise is excessive relative to fundamental parameters such as corporate earnings. Feeding back this price-bubble signal to stock trading platform and financial news service users could discourage herding and cool off overheated asset markets in a self-regulatory manner.

This feedback represents an introduction into asset markets of a potentially stabilizing negative-feedback loop, analogous to the many

[3]Jan Viebig, personal communication, August 14, 2020.

equilibrium-oriented, negative-feedback systems in physiology (Borgland and Dayas, 2019; Burdakov, 2019). The aim of implementing this feedback is to stabilize financial systems by inducing equilibria that are potentially as sustainable as the equilibria of physiology.

The COVID-19 pandemic has underscored the need for stabilizing asset markets with negative-feedback loops. While working from home, retail investors have been increasingly drawn to online trading platforms like Robinhood. Of the approximately six million online trading accounts opened in the first half of 2020, at least three million were with Robinhood (Salzman, 2020). Robinhood processed 4.5 million transactions per day in June 2020, more than any other broker and almost four times as many as rival E*Trade. Since retail investors played a significant role in driving the dot-com bubble (Griffin *et al.*, 2011), a sense of *déjà vu* might come from seeing Robinhood's platform design features that seem aimed to boost trading volume. With attractive features like confetti, users get nudged toward active stock trading rather than exchange-traded fund (ETF) purchases. This dynamic is consistent with a business model that results in most of Robinhood's revenue coming from payment for order flow. An addiction counselor who is a recovering drug addict warned that the experience of using Robinhood is not unlike the rush of other addictive behaviors (Salzman, 2020). Excessive enthusiasm for stock trading may also be generated by trading-oriented social media, such as Facebook groups and r/wallstreetbets, which is a Reddit subgroup. Posts on this Reddit forum encourage readers to bet on lottery-like speculative options (Buttonwood, 2020). These trader-oriented websites may promote the formation of social networks that support contagions of opinions about stocks (Jackson, 2019). Evidence of naïve trading patterns such as herding is found on Robintrack, a website that displays charts with superimposed timelines of changes in stock prices and the number of Robinhood users owning each stock (Schafer, 2019). Network effects may have led to 40,000 Robinhood accounts adding Tesla shares during a four-hour period when Tesla stock had an intraday rise of 16% before ending down by 3.1% (Ascarelli, 2020; Brush, 2020).

Network effects that promote destabilizing positive feedback can be counteracted by building negative-feedback loops into asset markets. This negative feedback could involve information about the degree that investors show evidence of momentum trading (Barberis *et al.*, 2018), portfolio overlap (Gualdi *et al.*, 2016), extrapolation bias (Cassella and Gulen, 2018), and impulsive interactions with trading platforms. Machine-learning–based estimates of market overheating may also be useful for negative feedback (Viebig, 2020). The negative feedback may serve as a controlling input that enables the nudging of financial system dynamics toward the desirable state of market stabilization (see Section 3.4).

3.3. Countervailing Measures for Constrained Inequality

> *The fire this time is burning for the same reasons it has so often in the past: that many African-Americans still live in places with the worst schools, the worst health care and the worst jobs; that the rules apply differently to black people; the fact, rammed home by Covid-19, that whenever America suffers misfortune, black America suffers most; a sense that the police are there to keep a lid on a city's poor, even as they protect wealthy suburbs. And, yes, the sheer intoxication that comes from belonging to a crowd that has suddenly found its voice, and which demands to be heard. . . . fear betrays Mr. Floyd's memory. The more America is united, the better it can strive to ensure that all its citizens are able to live by its founding ideals.*
>
> *The Economist* (2020, emphasis added)

> *The ongoing coronavirus pandemic has not only 'exposed the plight of the poor and the serious inequality that reigns in the world,' but even exacerbated them, Pope Francis said at the Wednesday [August 19, 2020] General Audience. . . . the Holy Father said our response to the pandemic must be twofold: 'finding a cure for this small but terrible virus,' but also curing 'a larger virus, that of social injustice, inequality of opportunity, marginalization, and lack of protection for the weakest.' . . . Pope Francis also warned against the 'scandal' of directing economic assistance during the pandemic primarily to 'industries that do not contribute to the inclusion of the excluded, the promotion of the least, the common good, or the care of creation' – which he proposed as four criteria for determining which industries should be helped. Looking ahead, Pope Francis said, 'if the virus were to intensify again in a world that is unjust to the poor and vulnerable, then we must change the world.'*
>
> Christopher Wells (2020)

> *When labor law enables working people to build organizations of* countervailing *power, the people can demand for themselves a more equitable nation. . . . For all workers to have the potential to build effective* countervailing *power, labor law must create pathways to collective power everywhere that corporate power impacts their lives: in the workplace and across industries, in the boardroom, and in our political system. . . . We know from history that when workers come together and collectively build organizations that are capable of* countervailing *the power of the wealthy and the power of corporations, the outcomes are profound.*
>
> Sharon I. Block and Benjamin I. Sachs (2020, emphasis added)

3.3.1. *COVID-19 exacerbated inequalities in wealth and health*

Despite US unemployment levels that exceeded those of the Great Recession (Kochhar, 2020; Rampell, 2020) and the potential for a "Greater Depression" (Levitz, 2020) or "pandemic depression" (Reinhart and Reinhart, 2020), the S&P 500 had, in April and May 2020, its best two-month performance since 2009 (Banerji and Chilkoti, 2020). In that year, US stocks similarly rebounded from the Global Financial Crisis relatively quickly, ahead of years-long high unemployment levels (DeSilver, 2014; Kochhar, 2020). Attesting to the breadth of the 2020 rebound, stocks, bonds, and commodities completed in July their strongest simultaneous four-month rise on record (Ramkumar, 2020) while the US unemployment rate remained elevated at 10.2% (US Bureau of Labor Statistics, 2020). The asset-owning investor class clearly enjoys a level of resiliency that eludes most wage earners in the US. This differential resiliency supports an observation made by Janet L. Yellen, former Chair of the Board of Governors of the US Federal Reserve System: "The stock market isn't the economy" (Long, 2020). Numerous commentators have made similar observations about the post-COVID-19 diverging prospects of stock markets and the real economy (Carlsson-Szlezak *et al.*, 2020; Long, 2020; Lynch, 2020; Rampell, 2020; Vigna, 2020).

The divergence between stocks and the real economy is associated with growing wealth and income inequality during recent decades (Kalliovirta and Malinen, 2020; Piketty *et al.*, 2018; Zucman, 2019).

Subjecting the long-run dynamics of inequality to an econometric analysis revealed that income inequality in the US is the driver of income inequality in other developed countries (Kalliovirta and Malinen, 2020). Stock ownership is increasingly concentrated among a small sliver of the US population perched atop the wealth distribution. Federal Reserve data indicate that the top 10% of Americans by wealth owned 87% of all stock outstanding in the first quarter of 2020. Over the past decade, that share has grown from 82.4% in 2009. Meanwhile, the percentage of Americans who own stock, either directly or via mutual or retirement funds, is dropping. It fell to 55%, according to an April 2020 Gallup poll, down from a high of 67% in 2002 (Vigna, 2020).

Inequality is shaped by political and economic institutions, which are themselves shaped by inequality in interactions that potentially involve positive feedback (Acemoglu and Robinson, 2015; Block and Sachs, 2020). If left unimpeded by countervailing forces (Galbraith, (1993 [1952]); Reich, 2020), this positive-feedback dynamic can gain momentum, as noted by Sharon I. Block and Benjamin I. Sachs (2020, p. 10), leaders of the Labor and Worklife Program at Harvard Law School, who claim that "... we face dual crises of inequality that reinforce and exacerbate each other in a vicious cycle: as economic wealth gets more and more concentrated, the wealthy build greater and greater political power that they, in turn, translate into favorable policies that lead to even more profound concentrations of wealth. And on and on." In short, "... those with great wealth use it to gain power and then utilize that power to accumulate more wealth ... " (Reich, 2020, p. 17).

This self-serving influence on institutions is a form of environmental engineering, or niche construction, that was conserved through much of evolution due to its effective fitness-enhancing capacity (Odling-Smee *et al.*, 2003). Niche construction is defined as the alteration of the environment by organisms, by which they "modify at least some of the natural selection pressures present in their own, and in each other's, local environments" (Odling-Smee *et al.*, 2003, p. 1). Although humans "are the ultimate niche constructors" (Odling-Smee *et al.*, 2003, p. 28), niche construction is found in many other species of animals, plants, and unicellular microorganisms. Among species, humans are uniquely effective at extracting benefits from manipulating the environment. Niche construction is described as one of the most important social processes that shaped the evolutionary history of humans (Fogarty *et al.*, 2012). Odling-Smee *et al.* (2003) concluded that the human niche construction capacity may have been amplified by modern technology.

Liberalization of financial system regulations has played a role in boosting income inequality to extreme levels not seen since the prelude to the 1929 stock market crash (Kalliovirta and Malinen, 2020; Manish and O'Reilly, 2019). Manipulative easing of the financial market regulatory environment is a prime example of how social niche construction can favor or disfavor high or low socio-economic status populations, respectively, with regard to fitness, wealth, and health. This manipulation is typically conducted in socially constructed networks of lobbyists and politicians (Johnson and Kwak, 2010; Solimine, 2020). In this example, social niche construction (Boehm and Flack, 2010; Odling-Smee, 2010) involves using money to favorably shape one's environment. Offshore tax havens, where wealthy individuals have stashed at least US$7.6 trillion (Zucman, 2015), are an attractive form of niche construction. In summary, an evolutionary perspective that takes into account niche construction (Laland and Brown, 2011; Odling-Smee, 2010) draws attention to the social construction of markets and could potentially explain how social niche construction may yield inequities in wealth and health.

The COVID-19 pandemic is boosting inequality to even more extreme levels. Pandemic-related job loss is concentrated among low-wage earners (Asante-Muhammad *et al.*, 2020; Bartik *et al.*, 2020; Cox, 2020; Mays and Newman, 2020; Mills and Battisto, 2020; Oppel, Jr. *et al.*, 2020; Overberg and Kamp, 2020; Reinhart and Reinhart, 2020). Formerly middle-class workers in the US and Europe are falling into poverty (Desmond, 2020; Stancati, 2020). The World Bank estimates that the pandemic will push 60 million people worldwide into extreme poverty (Reinhart and Reinhart, 2020). COVID-19 morbidity and mortality are highest among racial and ethnic minorities in the US. This racial and ethnic distribution of COVID-19 cases and fatalities follows the distribution of chronic disorders that are risk factors for COVID-19 (e.g. hypertension, diabetes, obesity, cardiovascular disease, and chronic obstructive pulmonary disease [Laurencin and Walker, 2020; Xie *et al.*, 2021]).

Coinciding with Black Lives Matter protests, awareness of the predilection for COVID-19 to affect disadvantaged populations has reached the highest levels of the US Federal Reserve System, at least in efforts at data interpretation, if not yet in the implementation of policy (Bostic, 2020; Powell, 2020; Siegel, 2020; Timiraos, 2020). Raphael W. Bostic, the President and CEO of the Federal Reserve Bank of Atlanta, is the first Black president to lead one of the Federal Reserve's regional banks. He indicated that the Federal Reserve's tools are blunt instruments that are not readily applied for specific goals, such as reducing racial inequities and bringing about a more inclusive economy (Siegel, 2020).

The Black Lives Matter protests intensified at the end of the summer of 2020, when an unarmed Black man was shot seven times in his back by a White police officer who was shooting from point-blank range in Kenosha, Wisconsin (*Associated Press*, 2020). In ensuing protests, fires were set in Kenosha, Madison, which is the capital of Wisconsin, Oakland, California, and Portland, Oregon (Ailworth and Wernau, 2020; Guarino *et al.*, 2020; KGO, ABC7 News, 2020; Maturen, 2020). Jacob Blake survived the shooting, but was hospitalized with paralysis below his waist. Two days after that shooting, a White supporter of the pro-police Back the Blue countermovement allegedly shot and killed two Black Lives Matter protesters in Kenosha (Craig, 2020). Kenosha is at the shore of Lake Michigan between Milwaukee, Wisconsin, and Chicago, Illinois, which are two cities that exemplify the racial disparities in the effects of COVID-19. Blacks make up 30% of the population in Chicago, but have over 50% of COVID-19 cases and more than 70% of deaths from the disease (Asante-Muhammad and Sim, 2020). In Milwaukee County, Blacks represent 25% of the population, but account for almost 75% of the deaths from COVID-19 (Asante-Muhammad *et al.*, 2020).

3.3.2. *Constraining inequality with countervailing measures*

Without constraints, runaway niche construction could yield record-setting inequality in uncharted territory beyond the gilded age. Given current levels of social unrest, increases in inequality seem risky. Regarding Black Lives Matter protests, Atlanta Federal Reserve President Bostic (2020) noted that "the economic inequality adds fuel to the underlying oppression that is now driving the protesters." Therefore, additional increases in inequality risk igniting further social upheaval. Inequality prevailing in the 1920s was attenuated by countervailing measures associated with New Deal programs (e.g. Social Security, unemployment insurance, bank deposit insurance, refinancing of home and farm mortgages, works programs like the Civilian Conservation Corps and Works Progress Administration, and Securities and Exchange Commission regulations (Asante-Muhammad *et al.*, 2020; Desmond, 2020; Schlesinger Jr., 1958). Compared to these and other New Deal programs that were started from scratch to span multiple sectors of the US economy, New-Deal–like programs today could be more readily implemented by being more modest in scope while expanding current government programs, such as housing vouchers for low-income renters, Medicaid, and the Earned Income Tax Credit (Desmond, 2020).

After the pandemic outbreak, British Prime Minister Boris Johnson announced emergency spending measures and said "This is the moment for a Rooseveltian approach to the UK" (Faulconbridge *et al.*, 2020). Ursula von der Leyen, President of the European Commission, is promoting a Green Deal for the European Union that requires actions across all economic sectors to achieve no net emissions of greenhouse gases by 2050 (European Commission, 2020).

Proposed programs for reducing inequality in the US include a universal basic income (UBI) (Asante-Muhammad *et al.*, 2020; AuYeung, 2020), wealth tax (Piketty, 2020), and job guarantees (Tcherneva, 2020). UBI programs are underway in Alaska, Stockton, California, and Jackson, Mississippi, and are planned for other cities across the US.

Some government spending programs could pay for themselves by yielding valuable benefits. For example, several early-childhood programs were found to boost the skills of disadvantaged children (Garcia *et al.*, 2020; Kirp, 2007). Garcia *et al.* (2020) studied two closely related early-childhood programs offering free childcare in North Carolina. Participants in the Carolina Abecedarian Project or the Carolina Approach to Responsive Education program were followed from 8 weeks of life through their mid-30s. The programs showed a 13.7% per annum tax-adjusted internal rate of return and a 7.3 tax-adjusted benefit/cost ratio. Rather than asking whether we can afford these programs, perhaps a better question is whether we can continue to afford going without an expansion of these programs.

Expanding early-childhood programs would address the acute need for childcare during recovery from the pandemic (Roecker and Vitali, 2020), the chronic disparities in access to quality early-childhood programs among racial and ethnic populations (Kirp, 2007; Williams and Lerner, 2019), and academic achievement gaps in these populations (Cohen *et al.*, 2006; Williams and Lerner, 2019). Compared to Whites, Black and Latino students show academic achievement gaps starting early in school (Cohen *et al.*, 2006; Williams and Lerner, 2019). Early education programs, such as Head Start and Early Head Start, should be expanded because they yield cost-effective improvements in the academic achievement, behavior, and cognitive skills of disadvantaged children (Heckman, 2007; Johnson *et al.*, 2019; Kirp, 2007; Lee, 2019). A nurse home visitation program also may be useful for this purpose because this program yielded long-term improvements in academic achievement and cognitive skills as well as reduced childhood mortality from preventable causes (Kitzman *et al.*, 2019). Knudsen *et al.* (2006, p. 10161) concluded that "the most cost-effective strategy for strengthening the future American workforce is to invest greater human and financial resources in the social and cognitive environments of children who are disadvantaged, beginning as early as possible. ... Stated simply, skills beget skills, success breeds success, and the provision of positive experiences early in life is considerably less expensive and more effective than the cost and effectiveness of corrective intervention at a later age."

Public policies that strengthen labor-market institutions also should be considered because strong unions have a constraining effect on income inequality (Block and Sachs, 2020; Jaumotte and Buitron, 2020; Reich, 2020; VanHeuvelen, 2020). COVID-19 may boost interest in building unions because non-unionized workers in the US have found the need to take actions, such as strikes, due to pandemic-related concerns about working conditions (Eidelson, 2020). US workers, particularly in the service sector, increasingly are realizing that weak labor protections make them more vulnerable to the coronavirus (Leibenluft, 2020).

3.4. Conclusion

> *A control process operates on the output of a system in such a way as to bring the system back to the desired behavior (set point), by means of* negative feedback.
>
> Bruce J. West (2006, p. 264, emphasis added)

> *Successful public health interventions reduce the cost, risk, and complexity of the needed economic policy response. However, where virus control is lacking, aggressive economic policy can offset shortcomings in health care policy. The U.S. is a case in point. Hopes that rich nations would easily control the virus were quickly dashed as it became clear that a specific mix of institutional capabilities – including health policy, government coordination, communication, and support in civil society – mattered more than economic heft.*
>
> Philipp Carlsson-Szlezak, Paul Swartz, and Martin Reeves (2020)

> *Though I may not be here with you, I urge you to answer the highest calling of your heart and stand up for what you truly believe. In my life I have done all I can to demonstrate that the way of peace, the way of love and nonviolence is the more excellent way. Now it is your turn to let freedom ring.*
>
> *When historians pick up their pens to write the story of the 21st century, let them say that it was your generation who laid down the heavy burdens of hate at last and that peace finally triumphed over violence, aggression and war. So I say to you, walk with the wind, brothers and sisters, and let the spirit of peace and the power of everlasting love be your guide.*
>
> John Lewis (2020)

3.4.1. *Financial systems, economies, and population health can be rebalanced*

This chapter has reviewed evidence of imbalances in financial systems and economies as the COVID-19 pandemic spread worldwide. The pandemic revealed asset mispricing as stock markets crashed. Longstanding inequalities in wealth and health were exacerbated by the pandemic. Fortunately, rebalancing mechanisms can be made available to prevent excessive asset mispricing and further growth of unequal outcomes in the wealth and health of populations (see Sections 3.4.2 and 3.4.3).

3.4.2. *Market designs for implementing negative feedback to stabilize asset markets*

Evidence for excessive positive feedback in stock markets (e.g. price-related herding among Robinhood users (Schafer, 2019; [see

Section 3.2.3]) motivates the implementation of negative feedback for market stabilization. Behavioral markers of asset-price bubbles could be fed back to investors via financial news services, online asset-trading platforms, or an online dashboard displaying early warning signals of financial system instability (Battiston *et al.*, 2016). By using the markers as warnings for overheated markets, investors could sell assets, thereby endogenously stabilizing the markets. As reviewed above (see Section 3.2.3) and summarized below, candidate behavioral bubble markers are emerging. If further research supports the reliability of these bubble markers, efficient methods could be made available for investors to monitor the markers (e.g. via news services, trading platforms, or an online dashboard [Battiston *et al.*, 2016]).

The presently proposed specific forms of this negative feedback (see Section 3.2.3) are initial steps toward design solutions in the application of market design to asset markets for enhancing stability. Among many applications to promote market stability and efficiency, market design was applied in developing the American medical residency matching program (Roth, 2008) and auctions for wireless spectrum (Milgrom and Segal, 2020) or chemical emission allowances (Porter *et al.*, 2009). In asset markets, design solutions have been implemented to counteract perceived adverse effects of high-frequency trading (Osipovich, 2019). However, market design is inadequately exploited for seeking preventive solutions to the devastating market failures of asset-price bubbles and crashes. By proposing that financial markets are inherently efficient, the longstanding, but increasingly questioned, efficient markets hypothesis (EMH) may have discouraged seeking market designs for mitigating bubbles and crashes. Proponents of the EMH have argued against the existence of asset-price bubbles (Fama, 2014). Counterarguments offer supportive evidence for bubbles (e.g. reports that upcoming negative asset returns are predictable based on changes in economic factors during steep asset-price rises [Greenwood *et al.*, 2019]).

In potential market-stabilizing design solutions, candidate markers for use as negative feedback include measures of momentum trading volume (Barberis *et al.*, 2018), portfolio overlap (Gualdi *et al.*, 2016), extrapolation bias (Cassella and Gulen, 2018), price-scaled variables Viebig (2020), and investors' interactions with trading platforms (see Section 3.2.3). Further research may identify additional candidate negative-feedback measures not directly associated with investor behavior. For example, analyses of large run-ups in securities prices of US and international industries revealed that price-crash probabilities, but not timing, could be predicted based on increases in stock return volatility, stock issuance, accelerated price changes, and altered price scaled variables (Greenwood *et al.*, 2019). Indices of investor sentiment have been developed as potential indicators of mispriced assets (Lehnert, 2020; Vidal-Tomas and Alfarano, 2020). Battiston *et al.* (2016) envisioned that early warning signals of financial system instability could be presented in almost real time on an online dashboard. Such signals could be made widely available for individuals to plan investment strategies (Haracz, 2021). Alternatively, the indicators could be dedicated for financial system monitoring by regulators, who would take countercyclical stabilizing actions (e.g. adjusting caps on loan-to-value ratios for mortgages and increasing capital requirements for banks [Bernanke, 2012; Bogle, 2012; Evans, 2011]).

Applying the above negative feedback to networks of asset traders could be guided by control theory of complex networks, which is derived from studies of social, biological, and physical networks (Egerstedt, 2011; Liu *et al.*, 2011; Solimine, 2020). Fortunately for the presently proposed application to traders, social networks were found to be particularly amenable to control by introducing a control input (Egerstedt, 2011; Liu *et al.*, 2011). Applying control theory to study the spread of opinions in a model of corrupted political networks, Solimine (2020) found that an input-induced opinion shift had spillovers into the opinions of other network members. Therefore, inputting negative feedback into trader networks could have spillover effects that would facilitate the spread of news about early evidence of an overheating market. In this way, trader networks that ordinarily may spread destabilizing herding-related opinions (Schafer, 2019) could absorb negative feedback that would encourage a switch to spreading market-stabilizing opinions about rising evidence for asset mispricing.

Asset prices convey sentiment-related information that elicits herding as well as information pertaining to asset fundamental value. Efficient markets are hypothesized to self-correct price distortions when astute investors trade with an eye on fundamental value-related information (i.e. “sophisticated traders may cause these ‘bubbles’ to burst before they have a chance to really get under way" [Fama, 1965, p. 38]). After three stock market crashes already in this young century, and a fourth that may be foretold by signs of market overheating during recovery from the COVID-19–induced crash (see Section 3.2.3), it is difficult to reconcile such jarring market downturns with the notion of an efficiently correcting market. Implementing negative feedback may dampen distortion-related price fluctuations by prompting investors to be more disciplined about taking into account asset fundamental values. This dampening could involve decreases in both the time and size scales of price swings. Stabilized stock markets with dampened price swings may attract more investment, so companies could gain funds for product innovation to fuel a sustainable boost of the economy.

3.4.3. *Countervailing and public health measures to constrain wealth and health inequality*

As the pandemic emerged, balancing public health and economic policy responses has become a challenge for many countries. The US mix of policy responses is being criticized for prioritizing attempts to promote economic recovery while inadequately focusing on public health (Sharfstein *et al.*, 2020). In this view, the "failed" (Sharfstein *et al.*, 2020; Sharfstein and Benjamin, 2020) US response to the pandemic is an almost predictable outcome of chronically insufficient funding for public health agencies, such as the Centers for Disease Control and Prevention (CDC) (Interlandi, 2020; Maani and Galea, 2020). In February, 2020, the CDC began distributing to states diagnostic test kits that were meant to detect severe acute respiratory syndrome coronavirus 2 (SARS-CoV-2), the novel coronavirus responsible for COVID-19. However, these tests failed to yield valid results due to contamination introduced during the CDC's development of the tests (Patel, 2020; Sharfstein *et al.*, 2020). This delay in developing tests was resolved when state laboratories developed diagnostic tests (Sharfstein *et al.*, 2020). Furthermore, the CDC was slow to launch a series of critical population studies for characterizing the basic epidemiologic features of COVID-19 (Diez Roux, 2020). Besides underfunding, the CDC also suffered from political interference: "Nearly from the start of the pandemic, the president has sidelined, muzzled and disempowered the [CDC], an agency with perhaps the highest concentration of infectious disease expertise in the world. ... injecting politics into medical science is dangerous and potentially fatal" (The Editorial Board, *The New York Times*, 2020).

To protect some of the public health workforce from underfunding and political interference (Maani and Galea, 2020), core public health data collection on the prevalence of diseases in specific populations could be taken over by central bank researchers in collaboration with public health experts. The Federal Reserve's mandate of maintaining labor market strength and price stability could encompass monitoring labor market quality by analyzing data on disease prevalence in racial and ethnic populations. This would enable initial steps toward the elusive goal of targeting Federal Reserve policies to specific populations (Bostic, 2020; Siegel, 2020; Timiraos, 2020). Securing this critical disease-prevalence data collection within the Federal Reserve would prevent lapses in obtaining important epidemiologic data (e.g. the above-noted delay in collecting pandemic-related data [Diez Roux, 2020] may have been prevented in this way).

Wealth and health inequalities across racial and ethnic populations could be mitigated by the coordinated actions of central banks and lawmakers who implement fiscal policy. For example, the Federal Reserve could use labor market quality data to recommend fiscal policies aimed at improving the health and financial status of specific populations. Mary Pittman, President and CEO of the Public Health Institute, noted that "... corporate leaders want and need resilient communities and a healthy workforce" (Benjamin and Komlos, 2020). These business interests would be supported by the Federal Reserve's monitoring of workforce quality. The private sector benefits from public health interventions aimed at health promotion and chronic disease prevention (McDaid *et al.*, 2015).

To monitor workforce quality, the Federal Reserve could maintain a data dashboard that includes population-specific measures, such as disease prevalence, life expectancy, income, wealth, education levels, and unemployment rates. The dashboard also could include other statistics on human capital and well-being, as recommended by the High-Level Group on the Measurement of Economic Performance and Social Progress (Stiglitz *et al.*, 2018). The disease prevalence data would facilitate monitoring of progress toward decreasing health inequities (e.g. mitigating the high rates of pre-existing diseases that are COVID-19 risk factors in minority groups [see Section 3.3.1]).

The dashboard also could include the prevalence of disorders found at high rates in White populations. For example, Whites showed a higher lifetime prevalence of mental disorders compared to Blacks, Latinos, and Asians (Alvarez *et al.*, 2019). Finally, to assess progress toward reducing inequality and achieving a more inclusive economy (Cohen, 2019), the dashboard could include the Gini coefficient as a measure of income or wealth inequality (Raffinetti *et al.*, 2015). The Gini coefficient can be modified to take into account experienced inequality (Bowles and Carlin, 2020).

Reviewed above are countervailing measures that have the potential of decreasing inequalities in income, wealth, and health (see Section 3.3.2). Parallel inequalities in household income and consumption-based carbon emissions (Chancel and Piketty, 2015; Kartha *et al.*, 2020) suggest that constraining income and wealth inequality could beneficially affect climate change by reducing the excessive carbon emissions of wealthy households. This potential mitigation of climate change adds to justifications and motivation for implementing proposed countervailing measures (see Section 3.3.2). Some of these measures approach the scale of New Deal programs that mitigated inequality in the Great Depression era and afterward. It remains to be seen whether present-day lawmakers are up to the task of designing and implementing countervailing measures at this scale. If not, then a future generation may have to encourage newly elected lawmakers to accomplish this task, as in the spirit of the epigraph from US Congressman John Lewis (2020), a civil rights leader who has the last word here: "Now it is your turn to let freedom ring."

References

Acemoglu, D. and Robinson, J.A. (2015). The rise and decline of general laws of capitalism. *Journal of Economic Perspectives*, **29**(1), 3–28.

Ailworth, E. and Wernau, J. (2020). Kenosha, Wis., protests over Jacob Blake police shooting turn violent. *Wall Street Journal*, August 24. Retrieved from https://www.wsj.com/articles/violence-flares-in-kenosha-wis-after-video-shows-police-shooting-black-man-11598278903 (Accessed September 10, 2020).

Alfi, V., Cristelli, M., Pietronero, L. and Zaccaria, A. (2009). Minimal agent based model for financial markets I. Origin and self-organization of stylized facts. *European Physical Journal B*, **67**, 385–397.

Alvarez, K., Fillbrunn, M., Green, J.G., Jackson, J.S., Kessler, R.C., McLaughlin, K.A., Sadikova, E., Sampson, N.A. and Alegría, M.

(2019). Race/ethnicity, nativity, and lifetime risk of mental disorders in US adults. *Social Psychiatry and Psychiatric Epidemioloy*, **54**, 553–565.

Arthur, W.B. (1994). *Increasing Returns and Path Dependence in the Economy* (University of Michigan Press, Ann Arbor).

Arthur, W.B. (2015). *Complexity and the Economy* (Oxford University Press, New York).

Asante-Muhammad, D., Collins, C. and Ocampo, O. (2020). White supremacy is the pre-existing condition: Eight solutions to ensure economic recovery reduces the racial wealth divide. Institute for Policy Studies. 19 June. Retrieved from https://ips-dc.org/white-supremacy-preexisting-condition-eight-solutions-economic-recovery-racial-wealth-divide (Accessed July 9, 2020).

Asante-Muhammad, D. and Sim, S. (2020). Racial health and economic disparities are two sides of the same coin. Institute for Policy Studies. 13 May. Retrieved from https://ips-dc.org/racial-health-and-economic-disparities-are-two-sides-of-the-same-coin (Accessed July 9, 2020).

Ascarelli, S. (2020). Tesla's earnings report is next moment of truth for bulls and bears. MarketWatch. 18 July. Retrieved from https://www.marketwatch.com/story/weekend-reads-teslas-earnings-report-is-next-moment-of-truth-for-bulls-and-bears-2020-07-17 (Accessed August 17, 2020).

Asness, C., Frazzini, A., Israel, R. and Moskowitz, T. (2014). Fact, fiction, and momentum investing. *Journal of Portfolio Management*, **40**(5), 75–92.

Associated Press (2020). Protests erupt after police shoot Black man in southeastern Wisconsin. *Wall Street Journal*. 24 August. Retrieved from https://www.wsj.com/articles/protests-erupt-after-police-shoot-black-man-in-southeastern-wisconsin-11598243826 (Accessed September 10, 2020).

Atalan, A. (2020). Is the lockdown important to prevent the COVID-19 pandemic? Effects on psychology, environment and economy-perspective. *Annals of Medicine and Surgery*, **56**, 38–42.

Au-Yeung, A. (2020). Jack Dorsey donates $3 million to U.S. mayors for universal basic income pilot programs in 15 cities. *Forbes*. 9 July. Retrieved from: https://www.forbes.com/sites/angelauyeung/2020/07/09/jack-dorsey-donates-3-million-to-us-mayors-for-universal-basic-income-pilot-programs-in-15-cities/ (Accessed August 17, 2020).

Baddeley, M. (2010). Herding, social influence and economic decision-making: socio-psychological and neuroscientific analyses. *Philosophical Transactions of the Royal Society B: Biological Sciences*, **365**(1538), 281–290.

Baldwin, J. (1993 [1963]). *The Fire Next Time* (Vintage International, New York).

Banerji, G. and Chilkoti, A. (2020). Stocks notch big monthly gains. *Wall Street Journal.* 29 May. Retrived from https://www.wsj.com/articles/global-stock-markets-dow-update-05-29-2020-11590727422 (Accessed May 31, 2020).

Barber, B.M. and Odean, T. (2000). Trading is hazardous to your wealth: The common stock investment performance of individual investors. *Journal of Finance*, **55**, 773–806.

Barber, B.M. and Odean, T. (2002). Online investors: Do the slow die first? *Review of Financial Studies*, **15**, 455–488.

Barberis, N., Greenwood, R., Jin, L. and Shleifer, A. (2018). Extrapolation and bubbles. *Journal of Financial Economics*, **129**(2), 203–227.

Bartik, A.W., Bertrand, M., Lin, F., Rothstein, J. and Unrath, M. (2020). Measuring the labor market since the onset of the COVID-19 crisis. Institute for Research on Labor and Employment. 4 August. Retrieved from https://irle.berkeley.edu/post-six-measuring-the-labor-market-since-the-onset-of-the-covid-19-crisis (Accessed August 17, 2020).

Battiston, S., Farmer, J.D., Flache, A., Garlaschelli, D., Haldane, A.G., Heesterbeek, H., Hommes, C., Jaeger, C., May, R. and Scheffer, M. (2016). Complexity theory and financial regulation: Economic policy needs interdisciplinary network analysis and behavioral modeling. *Science*, **351**, 818–819.

Benjamin, D. and Komlos, D. (2020). A public health expert says the pandemic is the tip of the iceberg when it comes to health, equity, and social justice. *Forbes.* 27 July. Retrieved from https://www.forbes.com/sites/benjaminkomlos/2020/07/27/a-public-health-expert-says-the-pandemic-is-the-tip-of-the-iceberg-when-it-comes-to-health-equity-and-social-justice/ (Accessed August 17, 2020).

Bernanke, B.S. (2012). The effects of the Great Recession on central bank doctrine and practice. *B.E. Journal of Macroeconomics*, **12**(3), Article 21.

Bhattarai, S., Chatterjee, A. and Park, W.Y. (2021). Effects of US quantitative easing on emerging market economies. *Journal of Economic Dynamics & Control*, **122**, 104031.

Blanchard, T.C., Wolfe, L.S., Vlaev, I., Winston, J.S. and Hayden, B.Y. (2014). Biases in preferences for sequences of outcomes in monkeys. *Cognition*, 130, 289–299.

Block, S.I. and Sachs, B.I. (2020). Clean slate for worker power: Building a just economy and democracy. Labor and Worklife Program, Harvard Law School. Retrieved from https://lwp.law.harvard.edu/clean-slate-project (Accessed July 5, 2020).

Boehm, C. and Flack, J.C. (2010). The emergence of simple and complex power structures through social niche construction. In Guinote, A. and Vescio, T.K. (eds.). *The Social Psychology of Power* (Guilford Press, New York), pp. 46–86.

Bogle, J.C. (2012). *The Clash of the Cultures: Investment vs. Speculation* (Wiley, Hoboken, NJ).

Bordalo, P., Gennaioli, N., Kwon, S.Y. and Shleifer, A. (2021). Diagnostic bubbles. *Journal of Financial Economics*, **141**, 1060–1077.

Borgland, S.L. and Dayas, C. (2019). Hypothalamic control of homeostasis. *Neuropharmacology*, **154**, 1–3.

Bostic, R. (2020). A moral and economic imperative to end racism. Federal Reserve Bank of Atlanta. 12 June. Retrieved from https://www.frbatlanta.org/about/feature/2020/06/12/bostic-a-moral-and-economic-imperative-to-end-racism (Accessed August 17, 2020).

Bowles, S. and Carlin, W. (2020). Inequality as experienced difference: a reformulation of the Gini coefficient. *Economics Letters*, **186**, 108789.

Brush, M. (2020). 7 risks for Tesla's stock that Robinhood traders would be wise to heed. *MarketWatch*. 15 July. Retrieved from https://www.marketwatch.com/story/robinhood-traders-would-be-wise-to-heed-these-seven-risks-for-teslas-stock-2020-07-15 (Accessed August 17, 2020).

Buttonwood. (2020). Bubble-hunting has become more art than science. *The Economist*, 19 August. Retrieved from https://www.economist.com/finance-and-economics/2020/08/19/bubble-hunting-has-become-more-art-than-science (Accessed September 10, 2020).

Burdakov, D. (2019). Reactive and predictive homeostasis: Roles of orexin/hypocretin neurons. *Neuropharmacology*, **154**, 61–67.

Bursztyn, L., Ederer, F., Ferman, B. and Yuchtman, N. (2014). Understanding mechanisms underlying peer effects: Evidence from a field experiment on financial decisions. *Econometrica*, **82**, 1273–1301.

Campbell, J.Y. and Kyle, A.S. (1993). Smart money, noise trading and stock price behavior. *Review of Economic Studies*, **60**, 1–34.

Carlsson-Szlezak, P., Swartz, P. and Reeves, M. (2020). Taking stock of the Covid-19 recession. *Harvard Business Review*, 14 August. Retrieved from https://hbr.org/2020/08/taking-stock-of-the-covid-19-recession (Accessed August 17, 2020).

Cassella, S. and Gulen, H. (2018). Extrapolation bias and the predictability of stock returns by price-scaled variables. *Review of Financial Studies*, **31**, 4345–4397.

Cassia, L. and Vismara, S. (2009). Valuation accuracy and infinity horizon forecast: Empirical evidence from Europe. *Journal of International Financial Management & Accounting*, **20**, 135–165.

Ceschi, A., Costantini, A., Sartori, R., Weller, J. and Di Fabio, A. (2019). Dimensions of decision-making: An evidence-based classification of heuristics and biases. *Personality and Individual Differences*, **146**, 188–200.

Chancel, L. and Piketty, T. (2015). Carbon and inequality: From Kyoto to Paris. Paris School of Economics. 3 November. Retrieved from http://piketty.pse.ens.fr/files/ChancelPiketty2015.pdf (Accessed December 15, 2020).

Chang, S.-K. (2014). Herd behavior, bubbles and social interactions in financial markets. *Studies in Nonlinear Dynamics and Econometrics*, **18**, 89–101.

Chetty, R., Stepner, M., Abraham, S., Lin, S., Scuderi, B., Turner, N., Bergeron, A. and Cutler, D. (2016). The association between income and life expectancy in the United States, 2001-2014. *JAMA*, **315**, 1750–1766.

Chiarella, C. and Di Guilmi, C. (2012). The fiscal cost of financial instability. *Studies in Nonlinear Dynamics & Econometrics*, **16**(4), 3.

Choi, J.J., Laibson, D. and Metrick, A. (2002). How does the Internet affect trading? Evidence from investor behavior in 401(k) plans. *Journal of Financial Economics*, **64**, 397–421.

Chowkwanyun, M. and Reed, Jr., A.L. (2020). Racial health disparities and COVID-19: caution and context. *New England Journal of Medicine*, 6 May. Retrieved from https://www.nejm.org/doi/full/10.1056/NEJMp2012910 (Accessed May 31, 2020).

Ciliberti, S. and Gualdi, S. (2020). Portfolio construction matters. *Journal of Portfolio Management*, **46**(7), 46–57.

Cohen, G.L., Garcia, J., Apfel, N. and Master, A. (2006). Reducing the racial achievement gap: A social-psychological intervention. *Science*, **313**, 1307–1310.

Cohen, J. (ed.) (2019). *Economics After Neoliberalism* (Boston Review, Cambridge, MA).

Cox, J. (2020). Worries grow over a K-shaped economic recovery that favors the wealthy. *CNBC*. 4 September. Retrieved from https://www.cnbc.com/2020/09/04/worries-grow-over-a-k-shaped-economic-recovery-that-favors-the-wealthy.html (Accessed September 10, 2020).

Craig, T. (2020). U.S. political divide becomes increasingly violent, rattling activists and police. *Washington Post*. 27 August. Retrieved from https://www.washingtonpost.com/national/protests-violence/2020/08/27/3f232e66-e578-11ea-970a-64c73a1c2392_story.html (Accessed September 10, 2020).

Daniel, K. and Hirshleifer, D. (2015). Overconfident investors, predictable returns, and excessive trading. *Journal of Economic Perspectives*, **29**(4), 61–88.

DeCambre, M. (2020). Why the S&P 500 is knocking on the door of its first record close in 6 months. *MarketWatch.* 11 August. Retrieved from https://www.marketwatch.com/amp/story/why-the-s-p-500-is-knocking-on-the-door-of-its-first-record-close-in-6-months-11597176257 (Accessed August 17, 2020).

DeCambre, M. and Wiltermuth, J. (2020). Nasdaq, S&P 500 close at record highs as big tech and working-from-home shares drive gains. *MarketWatch.* 1 September. Retrieved from https://www.marketwatch.com/story/dow-futures-see-subdued-action-but-tech-stocks-look-ready-to-extend-run-up-to-start-september-trade-2020-09-01 (Accessed September 10, 2020).

de Haan, L. and van den End, J.W. (2018). The signalling content of asset prices for inflation: Implications for quantitative easing. *Economic Systems*, **42**, 45–63.

DellaVigna, S. and Pollet, J.M. (2009). Investor inattention and Friday earnings announcements. *Journal of Finance*, **64**, 709–749.

De Long, J.B., Shleifer, A., Summers, L.H. and Waldmann, R.J. (1990a). Noise trader risk in financial markets. *Journal of Political Economy*, **98**, 703–738.

De Long, J.B., Shleifer, A., Summers, L.H. and Waldmann, R.J. (1990b). Positive feedback investment strategies and destabilizing rational speculation. *Journal of Finance*, **45**, 379–395.

DeMarzo, P.M., Vayanos, D. and Zwiebel, J. (2003). Persuasion bias, social influence, and unidimensional opinions. *Quarterly Journal of Economics*, **118**, 909–968.

Derman, E. (2011). *Models.Behaving.Badly. Why Confusing Illusion with Reality Can Lead to Disaster, on Wall Street and in Life* (Free Press, New York).

DeSilver, D. (2014). More and more Americans are outside the labor force entirely. Who are they? Pew Research Center. 14 November. Retrieved from https://www.pewresearch.org/fact-tank/2014/11/14/more-and-more-americans-are-outside-the-labor-force-entirely-who-are-they (Accessed August 23, 2020).

Desmond, M. (2020). Can America's middle class be saved from a New Depression? *New York Times Magazine.* 26 May. Retrieved from https://www.nytimes.com/interactive/2020/05/26/magazine/coronavirus-milwaukee-unemployment-jobs.html (Accessed May 31, 2020).

Diez Roux, A.V. (2020). Population health in the time of COVID-19: Confirmations and revelations. *Milbank Quarterly*, **98**, 629–640.

Eidelson, J. (2020). When working means deadly risk, backlash brews. *Bloomberg Businessweek*. 7 April. Retrieved from https://www.bloomberg.com/news/articles/2020-04-07/coronavirus-marks-the-best-and-worst-time-for-workers-to-strike (Accessed August 17, 2020).

Egerstedt, M. (2011). Degrees of control. *Nature*, **473**, 158–159.

E*Trade (2020). New to online investing. E*Trade Financial Corporation. Retrieved from https://us.etrade.com/planning (Accessed December 2, 2020).

European Commission (2020). A European Green Deal: Striving to be the first climate-neutral continent. Retrieved from https://ec.europa.eu/info/strategy/priorities-2019-2024/european-green-deal_en (Accessed September 9, 2020).

Evans, C.L. (2011). The international financial crisis: Asset price exuberance and macroprudential regulation. In Demirgüç-Kunt, A., Evanoff, D.D. and Kaufman, G.G. (eds.). *The International Financial Crisis: Have the Rules of Finance Changed?* (World Scientific, Singapore), pp. 3–71.

Fama, E.F. (1965). The behavior of stock-market prices. *Journal of Business*, **38**, 34–105.

Fama, E.F. (1970). Efficient capital markets: A review of theory and empirical work. *Journal of Finance*, **25**, 383–417.

Fama, E.F. (1991). Efficient capital markets: II. *Journal of Finance*, **46**, 1575–1617.

Fama, E.F. (2014). Two pillars of asset pricing. *American Economic Review*, **104**, 1467–1485.

Faulconbridge, G., Holton, K. and Schomberg, W. (2020). UK's Johnson pledges 'Rooseveltian' spending boost after COVID hit. *Reuters*, 29 June. Retrieved from https://www.reuters.com/article/us-health-coronavirus-britain-johnson/uks-johnson-pledges-rooseveltian-spending-boost-after-covid-hit-idUSKBN2400NN (Accessed August 17, 2020).

Fogarty, L., Rendell, L. and Laland, K.N. (2012). The importance of space in models of social learning, cultural evolution and niche construction. *Advances in Complex Systems*, **15** (01n02), 1150001.

Galbraith, J.K. (1993 [1952]). *American Capitalism: The Concept of Countervailing Power* (Routledge, New York).

García, J.L., Heckman, J.J., Leaf, D.E. and Prados, M.J. (2020). Quantifying the life-cycle benefits of an influential early childhood program. *Journal of Political Economy*, **128**, 2502–2541.

Gärling, T., Kirchler, E., Lewis, A. and van Raaij, F. (2009). Psychology, financial decision making, and financial crises. *Psychological Science in the Public Interest*, **10**, 1–47.

Gennaioli, N. and Shleifer, A. (2018). *A Crisis of Beliefs: Investor Psychology and Financial Fragility* (Princeton University Press, Princeton, NJ).

Gigerenzer, G. and Gaissmaier, W. (2011). Heuristic decision making. *Annual Review of Psychology*, **62**, 451–482.

Glaser, M., Iliewa, Z. and Weber, M. (2019). Thinking about prices versus thinking about returns in financial markets. *Journal of Finance*, **74**, 2997–3039.

Glaser, M. and Weber, M. (2007). Overconfidence and trading volume. *Geneva Risk and Insurance Review*, **32**, 1–36.

Göbel, M. and Araújo, T. (2020). Indicators of economic crises: A data-driven clustering approach. *Applied Network Science*, **5**, 44.

Greenspan, A. (2013). *The Map and the Territory: Risk, Human Nature, and the Future of Forecasting* (Penguin, New York).

Greenwood, R., Shleifer, A. and You, Y. (2019). Bubbles for Fama. *Journal of Financial Economics*, **131**, 20–43.

Griffin, J.M., Harris, J.H., Shu, T. and Topaloglu, S. (2011). Who drove and burst the tech bubble? *Journal of Finance*, **66**, 1251–1290.

Grinblatt, M. and Keloharju, M. (2009). Sensation seeking, overconfidence, and trading activity. *Journal of Finance*, **64**, 549–578.

Gross, C.P., Essien, U.R., Pasha, S., Gross, J.R., Wang, S.-Y. and Nunez-Smith, M. (2020). Racial and ethnic disparities in population-level Covid-19 mortality. *Journal of General Internal Medicine*, **35**, 3097–3099.

Grossman, S. and Stiglitz, J.E. (1980). On the impossibility of informationally efficient markets. *American Economic Review*, **70**(3), 393–408.

Gualdi, S., Cimini, G., Primicerio, K., Di Clemente, R. and Challet, D. (2016). Statistically validated network of portfolio overlaps and systemic risk. *Scientific Reports*, **6**, 39467.

Guarino, M., Berman, M., Peiser, J. and Witte, G. (2020). 17-year-old charged with homicide after shooting during Kenosha protests, authorities say. *Washington Post*. 26 August. Retrieved from https://www.washingtonpost.com/nation/2020/08/26/jacob-blake-kenosha-police-protests (Accessed September 10, 2020).

Hafenbradl, S., Waeger, D., Marewski, J.N. and Gigerenzer, G. (2016). Applied decision making with fast-and-frugal heuristics. *Journal of Applied Research in Memory and Cognition*, **5**, 215–231.

Haracz, J.L. (2013). Neuroeconomics of asset-price bubbles: A potential role for herding. Society for Neuroeconomics, 11th Annual Meeting, Lausanne, Switzerland.

Haracz, J.L. (2021). Neuroeconomics of asset-price bubbles: Neuroimaging, FinTech, and market design for the prediction and prevention of major bubbles. SSRN. 25 March. Retrieved from https://ssrn.com/abstract=3366527 (Accessed July 11, 2021).

Hawkins, R.J. (2011). Lending sociodynamics and economic instability. *Physica A*, **390**, 4355–4369.

Heckman, J.J. (2007). The economics, technology, and neuroscience of human capability formation. *Proceedings of the National Academy of Science USA*, **104**, 13250–13255.

Hill, D. (2019 [1948]). Foreword. In *Cybernetics, or Control and Communication in the Animal and the Machine*, Reissue of the 1961 2nd ed., Wiener, N. (ed.), (MIT Press, Cambridge, MA).

Hill-Kleespie, A. (2019). The good the bad and the trending: Microblogging sentiment and short term momentum. *9th Miami Behavioral Finance Conference 2018.* 6 June. Retrieved from https://ssrn.com/abstract=2906380 (Accessed August 17, 2020).

Hirshleifer, D. (2020). Presidential Address: Social transmission bias in economics and finance. *Journal of Finance*, **75**, 1778–1831.

Hirshleifer, D., Lim, S.S. and Teoh, S.H. (2011). Limited investor attention and stock market misreactions to accounting information. *Review of Asset Pricing Studies*, **1**, 35–73.

Hommes, C. and in 't Veld, D. (2017). Booms, busts and behavioural heterogeneity in stock prices. *Journal of Economic Dynamics and Control*, **80**, 101–124.

Hong, H. and Stein, J.C. (1999). A unified theory of underreaction, momentum trading, and overreaction in asset markets. *Journal of Finance*, **54**, 2143–2184.

Interlandi, J. (2020). Why we're losing the battle with Covid-19: The escalating crisis in Texas shows how the chronic underfunding of public health has put America on track for the worst coronavirus response in the developed world. *New York Times*, 14 July. Retrieved from https://www.nytimes.com/2020/07/14/magazine/covid-19-public-health-texas.html (Accessed August 17, 2020).

Jackson, M.O. (2019). *The Human Network: How Your Social Position Determines Your Power, Beliefs, and Behaviors* (Vintage Books, New York).

Jaumotte, F. and Buitron, C.O. (2020). Inequality: Traditional drivers and the role of union power. *Oxford Economic Papers*, **72**, 25–58.

Johnson, A.D., Finch, J.E. and Phillips, D.A. (2019). Associations between publicly funded preschool and low-income children's kindergarten readiness: The moderating role of child temperament. *Developmental Psychology*, **55**, 623–636.

Johnson, S. and Kwak, J. (2010). *13 Bankers: The Wall Street Takeover and the Next Financial Meltdown* (Vintage Books, New York).

Kalliovirta, L. and Malinen, T. (2020). Non-linearity and cross-country dependence of income inequality. *Review of Income and Wealth*, **66**, 227–249.

Karmarkar, U.R., Shiv, B. and Knutson, B. (2015). Cost conscious? The neural and behavioral impact of price primacy on decision making. *Journal of Marketing Research*, **52**, 467–481.

Kartha, S., Kemp-Benedict, E., Ghosh, E., Nazareth, A. and Gore, T. (2020). The Carbon Inequality Era: An assessment of the global distribution of consumption emissions among individuals from 1990 to 2015 and beyond. Joint Research Report. Stockholm Environment Institute and Oxfam International. 21 September. Retrieved from https://www.sei.org/publications/the-carbon-inequality-era (Accessed December 15, 2020).

KGO, ABC7 News (2020). Jacob Blake protest: Crowds yell 'burn it down' while lighting fires, breaking windows in Oakland, police say. 27 August. Retrieved from https://www.msn.com/en-us/news/crime/jacob-blake-protest-crowds-yell-burn-it-down-while-lighting-fires-breaking-windows-in-oakland-police-say/ar-BB18pGyH (Accessed September 10, 2020).

Kienzler, M. (2018). Value-based pricing and cognitive biases: An overview for business markets. *Industrial Marketing Management*, **68**, 86–94.

Kirp, D.L. (2007). *The Sandbox Investment: The Preschool Movement and Kids-First Politics* (Harvard University Press, Cambridge, MA).

Kitzman, H., Olds, D.L., Knudtson, M.D., Cole, R., Anson, E., Smith, J.A., Fishbein, D., DiClemente, R., Wingood, G., Caliendo, A.M., Hopfer, C., Miller, T. and Conti, G. (2019). Prenatal and infancy nurse home visiting and 18-year outcomes of a randomized trial. *Pediatrics*, **144**(6), e20183876.

Knowledge@Wharton (2018). Siegel vs. Shiller: Is the stock market overvalued? 18 September. Retrieved from http://knowledge.wharton.upenn.edu/article/siegel-shiller-stock-market (Accessed August 17, 2020).

Knudsen, E.I., Heckman, J.J., Cameron, J.L. and Shonkoff, J.P. (2006). Economic, neurobiological, and behavioral perspectives on building America's future workforce. *Proceedings of the National Academy of Science USA*, **103**, 10155–10162.

Knutson, B., Rick, S., Wimmer, G.E., Prelec, D. and Loewenstein, G. (2007). Neural predictors of purchases. *Neuron*, **53**, 147–156.

Kochhar, R. (2020). Unemployment rose higher in three months of COVID-19 than it did in two years of the Great Recession. Pew Research Center. 11 June. Retrieved from https://www.pewresearch.org/fact-tank/

2020/06/11/unemployment-rose-higher-in-three-months-of-covid-19-than-it-did-in-two-years-of-the-great-recession (Accessed August 23, 2020).

Krieger, N. (ed.) (2005). *Embodying Inequality: Epidemiologic Perspectives* (Baywood, Amityville, NY).

Laland, K. and Brown, G. (2011). Niche construction and human behavioral ecology: Tools for understanding work. In Levin, R., Laughlin, S., De La Rocha, C. and Blackwell, A. (eds.). *Work Meets Life: Exploring the Integrative Study of Work in Living Systems* (MIT Press, Cambridge, MA), pp. 113–131.

Laurencin, C.T. and Walker, J.M. (2020). A pandemic on a pandemic: Racism and COVID-19 in Blacks. *Cell Systems*, **11**, 9–10.

Lee, K. (2019). Impact of Head Start quality on children's developmental outcomes. *Social Work in Public Health*, **34**, 239–250.

Lehnert, T. (2020). Fear and stock price bubbles. *PLoS ONE*, **15**(5), e0233024.

Leibenluft, J. (2020). The pandemic hurts countries that don't value workers. *Foreign Affairs*, 19 August. Retrieved from https://www.foreignaffairs.com/articles/united-states/2020-08-19/pandemic-hurts-countries-dont-value-workers (Accessed September 10, 2020).

Leijonhufvud, A. (2014). Economics of the crisis and the crisis of economics. *European Journal of the History of Economic Thought*, **21**, 760–774.

Levitz, E. (2020). Why our economy may be headed for a decade of depression. *New York Magazine*, 22 May. Retrieved from https://nymag.com/intelligencer/2020/05/why-the-economy-is-headed-for-a-post-coronavirus-depression-nouriel-roubini.html (Accessed August 17, 2020).

Lewis, J. (2020). Together, you can redeem the soul of our nation. *New York Times*, 30 July. Retrieved from https://www.nytimes.com/2020/07/30/opinion/john-lewis-civil-rights-america.html (Accessed September 9, 2020).

Lim, K.-P. and R. Brooks. (2011). The evolution of stock market efficiency over time: A survey of the empirical literature. *Journal of Economic Surveys*, **25**, 69–108.

Lin, K.-H. and Neely, M.T. (2020). *Divested: Inequality in the Age of Finance* (Oxford University Press, New York).

Liu, Y.-Y., Slotine, J.-J. and Barabási, A.-L. (2011). Controllability of complex networks. *Nature*, **473**, 167–173.

Long, H. (2020). The recession is over for the rich, but the working class is far from recovered. *Washington Post*, 13 August. Retrieved from https://www.washingtonpost.com/business/2020/08/13/recession-is-over-rich-working-class-is-far-recovered (Accessed August 17, 2020).

López, L. and Rodó, X. (2020). The end of social confinement and COVID-19 re-emergence risk. *Nature Human Behaviour*, **4**, 746–755.

Lux, T. (1995). Herd behaviour, bubbles and crashes. *The Economic Journal*, **105**, 881–896.

Lux, T. and Marchesi, M. (1999). Scaling and criticality in a stochastic multi-agent model of a financial market. *Nature*, **397**, 498–500.

Lynch, D.J. (2020). As stock prices hit record high, economy trails behind. *Washington Post*, 18 August. Retrieved from https://www.washingtonpost.com/business/2020/08/18/stocks-economy-coronavirus (Accessed September 10, 2020).

Maani, N. and Galea, S. (2020). COVID-19 and underinvestment in the public health infrastructure of the United States. *Milbank Quarterly*, **98**, 250–259.

Mackay, C. (2014 [1841]). *Extraordinary Popular Delusions and the Madness of Crowds* (CreateSpace, Middletown, DL).

Manish, G.P. and O'Reilly, C. (2019). Banking regulation, regulatory capture and inequality. *Public Choice*, **180**, 145–164.

Maturen, S. (2020). Wisconsin calls out National Guard after unrest over police shooting of Black man. *Reuters*. 24 August. Retrieved from https://www.msn.com/en-us/news/crime/black-man-shot-injured-by-police-in-wisconsin-city-curfew-imposed/ar-BB18ikbe (Accessed September 10, 2020).

Mays, J.C. and Newman, A. (2020). Virus is twice as deadly for Black and Latino people than whites in N.Y.C. *New York Times*, 8 April. Retrieved from https://www.nytimes.com/2020/04/08/nyregion/coronavirus-race-deaths.html (Accessed May 31, 2020).

McDaid, D., Sassi, F. and Merkur, S. (eds.) (2015). *Promoting Health, Preventing Disease: The Economic Case* (Open University Press, Maidenhead, Berkshire, UK).

Mechera-Ostrovsky, T. and Gluth, S. (2018). Memory beliefs drive the memory bias on value-based decisions. *Scientific Reports*, **8**, 10592.

Milgrom, P. and Segal, I. (2020). Clock auctions and radio spectrum reallocation. *Journal of Political Economy*, **128**, 1–31.

Mills, C.K. and Battisto, J. (2020). Double jeopardy: COVID-19's concentrated health and wealth effects in Black communities. Federal Reserve Bank of New York, August. Retrieved from https://www.newyorkfed.org/search?text=double+jeopardy&application=ny_pub&sources=ny_pub (Accessed August 5, 2020).

Miranda-Agrippino, S. and Rey, H. (2020). U.S. monetary policy and the global financial cycle. *Review of Economic Studies*, **87**, 2754–2776.

Morgan, T.J.H. and Laland, K.N. (2012). The biological bases of conformity. *Frontiers in Neuroscience*, **6**, 87.

Odling-Smee, J. (2010). Niche inheritance. In Pigliucci, M. and Muller, G.B. (eds.). *Evolution: The Extended Synthesis* (MIT Press, Cambridge, MA), pp. 175–207.

Odling-Smee, F.J., Laland, K.N. and Feldman, M.W. (2003). *Niche Construction: The Neglected Process in Evolution* (Princeton University Press, Princeton, NJ).

O'Donoghue, T. and Rabin, M. (2015). Present bias: Lessons learned and to be learned. *American Economic Review*, **105**(5), 273–279.

O'Neill, J. (2020). Are financial markets none the wiser? Project Syndicate, 6 August. Retrieved from https://www.project-syndicate.org/commentary/financial-market-outlook-august-2020-by-jim-o-neill-2020-08 (Accessed August 17, 2020).

Oppel, Jr., R.A., Gebeloff, R., Lai, K.K.R., Wright, W. and Smith, M. (2020). The fullest look yet at the racial inequity of coronavirus. *New York Times*, 5 July. Retrieved from https://www.nytimes.com/interactive/2020/07/05/us/coronavirus-latinos-african-americans-cdc-data.html (Accessed August 17, 2020).

Osipovich, A. (2019). More exchanges add 'speed bumps,' defying high-frequency traders. *Wall Street Journal*, 29 July. Retrieved from https://www.wsj.com/articles/more-exchanges-add-speed-bumps-defying-high-frequency-traders-11564401611 (Accessed November 29, 2020).

Overberg, P. and Kamp, J. (2020). Covid-19 deaths strike early for many minorities. *Wall Street Journal*, 16 August. Retrieved from https://www.msn.com/en-us/news/us/covid-19-deaths-strike-early-for-many-minorities/ar-BB181rxv (Accessed August 17, 2020).

Patel, N.V. (2020). Why the CDC botched its coronavirus testing. *MIT Technology Review*, 5 March. Retrieved from https://www.technologyreview.com/2020/03/05/905484/why-the-cdc-botched-its-coronavirus-testing (Accessed August 17, 2020).

Piketty, T. (2020). Economist Thomas Piketty: Coronavirus pandemic has exposed the "violence of social inequality." *Democracy Now*, 30 April. Retrieved from https://www.democracynow.org/2020/4/30/thomas_piketty (Accessed August 5, 2020).

Piketty, T., Saez, E. and Zucman, G. (2018). Distributional national accounts: Methods and estimates for the United States. *Quarterly Journal of Economics*, **133**, 553–609.

Pisani-Ferry, J. (2020). The challenges of the post-pandemic agenda. Project Syndicate, 27 July. Retrieved from https://www.project-syndicate.org/commentary/harsh-uncertain-economic-transition-after-covid19-by-jean-pisani-ferry-2020-07 (Accessed August 17, 2020).

Plassmann, H., O'Doherty, J., Shiv, B. and Rangel, A. (2008). Marketing actions can modulate neural representations of experienced pleasantness. *Proceedings of the National Academy of Sciences USA*, **105**, 1050–1054.

Porter, D., Rassenti, S., Shobe, W., Smith, V. and Winn, A. (2009). The design, testing and implementation of Virginia's NOx allowance auction. *Journal of Economic Behavior & Organization*, **69**, 190–200.

Powell, J.H. (2020). Introductory comments. Board of Governors of the Federal Reserve System. 19 June. Retrieved from https://www.federalreserve.gov/newsevents/speech/powell20200619a.htm (Accessed August 17, 2020).

Preis, T., Schneider, J.J. and Stanley, H.E. (2011). Switching processes in financial markets. *Proceedings of the National Academy of Sciences USA*, **108**, 7674–7678.

Raafat, R.M., Chater, N. and Frith, C. (2009). Herding in humans. *Trends in Cognitive Sciences*, **13**, 420–428.

Raffinetti, E., Siletti, E. and Vernizzi, A. (2015). On the Gini coefficient normalization when attributes with negative values are considered. *Statistical Methods & Applications*, **24**, 507–521.

Ramkumar, A. (2020). Investors set aside coronavirus worries, driving a 'melt-up' in markets. *Wall Street Journal*, 26 July. Retrieved from https://www.wsj.com/articles/investor-anxiety-turns-to-greed-driving-risky-market-melt-up-11595755801 (Accessed September 3, 2020).

Rampell, C. (2020). The U.S. has two economies: How much longer will the losing side stand for that? *Washington Post*, 20 August. Retrieved from https://www.washingtonpost.com/opinions/2020/08/20/us-has-two-economies-how-much-longer-will-losing-side-stand-that (Accessed September 10, 2020).

Reich, R.B. (2020). *The System: Who Rigged It, How We Fix It* (Alfred A. Knopf, New York).

Reinhart, C. and Reinhart, V. (2020). The pandemic depression: The global economy will never be the same.*Foreign Affairs*, September/October. Retrieved from https://www.foreignaffairs.com/articles/united-states/2020-08-06/coronavirus-depression-global-economy (Accessed August 27, 2020).

Reinhart, C.M. and Rogoff, K.S. (2009). *This Time Is Different: Eight Centuries of Financial Folly* (Princeton University Press, Princeton, NJ).

Ricardo Research, (2019). A model of imperfection. Ricardo Research Limited, February. Retrieved from https://ricardoresearch.com/idea/a-model-of-imperfection (Accessed May 1, 2020).

Roecker, M. and Vitali, A. (2020). Child care providers struggle as need for services remain for many. *NBC News*, 31 August. Retrieved from https://www.msn.com/en-us/news/us/child-care-providers-struggle-as-need-for-services-remain-for-many/ar-BB18xSOK (Accessed September 10, 2020).

Roosevelt, F.D. (2018 [1933]). *The Fireside Chats of Franklin Delano Roosevelt: Radio Addresses to the American People Broadcast Between 1933 and 1944* (CreateSpace, Scotts Valley, CA).

Rosenblueth, A., Wiener, N. and Bigelow, J. (1943). Behavior, purpose and teleology. *Philosophy of Science*, **10**, 18–24.

Roth, A.E. (2008). What have we learned from market design? *The Economic Journal*, **118**, 285–310.

Roubini, N. and Mihm, S. (2010). *Crisis Economics: A Crash Course in the Future of Finance* (Penguin, New York).

Salzman, A. (2020). Robinhood turned millions of people stuck at home into investors: What's next for the app? Barron's. 14 August. Retrieved from https://www.marketwatch.com/articles/what-is-robinhood-apps-next-act-its-already-mastered-the-stock-market-game-51597451777 (Accessed August 17, 2020).

Santos, J.M. and Alkire, S. (2020). Keeping poverty reduction front and center. Project Syndicate. 29 July. Retrieved from https://www.project-syndicate.org/commentary/multidimensional-poverty-measures-in-pandemic-response-by-juan-manuel-santos-and-sabina-alkire-2020-07 (Accessed August 17, 2020).

Schafer, B. (2019). Robintrack: The coolest investing site you've never heard of. Market Brothers Media, 18 May. Retrieved from https://medium.com/swlh/robintrack-the-coolest-investing-site-youve-never-heard-of-838f9445c9fc (Accessed July 14, 2020).

Scharfstein, D.S. and Stein, J.C. (1990). Herd behavior and investment. *American Economic Review*, **80**, 465–479.

Schlesinger, Jr., A.M. (1958). *The Coming of the New Deal: 1933-1935* (HoughtonMifflin, New York).

Schwaiger, R., Kirchler, M., Lindner, F. and Weitzel, U. (2020). Determinants of investor expectations and satisfaction: A study with financial professionals. *Journal of Economic Dynamics & Control*, **110**, 103675.

Shaban, H. and Lynch, D.J. (2020). U.S. stocks hit record high, ending shortest bear market in history. *Washington Post*, 18 August. Retrieved from https://www.washingtonpost.com/business/2020/08/18/stocks-record-high-sp-500 (Accessed September 10, 2020).

Sharfstein, J.M. and Benjamin, G.C. (2020). The exceptional American relationship to public health: Why the United States has failed so spectacularly to control COVID-19. *Foreign Affairs*, 26 August.

Retrieved from https://www.foreignaffairs.com/articles/united-states/2020-08-26/exceptional-american-relationship-public-health (Accessed September 10, 2020).

Sharfstein, J.M., Becker, S.J. and Mello, M.M. (2020). Diagnostic testing for the novel coronavirus. *JAMA*, **323**, 1437–1438.

Sharot, T. (2011). The optimism bias. *Current Biology*, **21**, R941–R945.

Shefrin, H. (2019). Valuation bias and limits to nudges. *Journal of Portfolio Management*, **45**(5), 112–124.

Shefrin, H. and Statman, M. (1994). Behavioral capital asset pricing theory. *Journal of Financial and Quantitative Analysis*, **29**, 323–349.

Shiller, R.J., (2019). *Narrative Economics: How Stories Go Viral & Drive Major Economic Events* (Princeton University Press, Princeton, NJ).

Shiller, R.J. (2020a). Predictions for the coronavirus stock market. *New York Times*, 2 April. Retrieved from https://www.nytimes.com/2020/04/02/business/stock-market-predictions-coronavirus-shiller.html (Accessed August 17, 2020).

Shiller, R.J. (2020b). Online data Robert Shiller. Retrieved from http://www.econ.yale.edu/~shiller/data.htm (Accessed August 17, 2020).

Shiv, B., Carmon, Z. and Ariely, D. (2005). Placebo effects of marketing actions: Consumers may get what they pay for. *Journal of Marketing Research*, **42**, 383–393.

Siegel, R. (2020). To narrow racial and economic disparities, Atlanta Fed chief Raphael Bostic is rethinking what the Fed's mandate means. *Washington Post*, 21 August. Retrieved from https://www.washingtonpost.com/business/2020/08/21/bostic-fed-race-economy (Accessed September 10, 2020).

Solimine, P.C. (2020). Political corruption and the congestion of controllability in social networks. *Applied Network Science*, **5**, 23.

Stancati, M. (2020). As the coronavirus lockdown eases, Italy confronts an epidemic of poverty. *Wall Street Journal*, 21 May. Retrieved from https://www.wsj.com/articles/as-the-coronavirus-lockdown-eases-italy-confronts-an-epidemic-of-poverty-11590058801 (Accessed May 31, 2020).

Statman, M., Thorley, S. and Vorkink, K. (2006). Investor overconfidence and trading volume. *Review of Financial Studies*, **19**, 1531–1565.

Stein, J.C. (2009). Presidential Address: Sophisticated investors and market efficiency. *Journal of Finance*, **64**, 1516–1548.

Stépanoff, C. (2012). Human-animal 'joint commitment' in a reindeer herding system. *HAU: Journal of Ethnographic Theory*, **2**(2), 287–312.

Stevens, L. (2020). Coarse pricing policies. *Review of Economic Studies*, **87**, 420–453.

Stiglitz, J.E. (2011). Rethinking macroeconomics. What failed, and how to repair it. *Journal of the European Economic Association*, **9**, 591–645.

Stiglitz, J.E., Fitoussi, J.-P. and Durand, M. (2018). *Beyond GDP: Measuring What Counts for Economic and Social Performance* (OECD, Paris).

Tedeschi, E., Armand, S., Buyalskaya, A., Silston, B. and Mobbs, D. (2020). Subjective fear dilutes as group size increases. *PsyArXiv*, 19 June. Retrieved from https://psyarxiv.com/r2yhn (Accessed July 11, 2021).

Tcherneva, P.R. (2020). *The Case for a Job Guarantee* (Polity, Cambridge, UK).

Thaler, R. and Sunstein, C. (2008). *Nudge: Improving Decisions About Health, Wealth, and Happiness* (Yale University Press, New Haven, CT).

The Economist (2020). Police violence, race and protest in America. 4 June. Retrieved from https://www.economist.com/leaders/2020/06/04/police-violence-race-and-protest-in-america (Accessed August 17, 2020).

The Editorial Board (2020). Politicizing medical science will cost American lives. *The New York Times.* 24 August. Retrieved from https://www.nytimes.com/2020/08/24/opinion/trump-fda-coronavirus.html (Accessed September 10, 2020).

Timiraos, N. (2020). WSJ in conversation with Atlanta Fed President Raphael Bostic. *Wall Street Journal*, 3 September. Retrieved from https://www.wsj.com/articles/transcript-wsj-in-conversation-with-atlanta-fed-president-raphael-bostic-11599175116 (Accessed September 10, 2020).

Toyokawa, W., Whalen, A. and Laland, K.N. (2019). Social learning strategies regulate the wisdom and madness of interactive crowds. *Nature Human Behaviour*, **3**, 183–193.

US Bureau of Labor Statistics. (2020). *Economic News Release: Employment Situation Summary.* 7 August. Retrived from https://www.bls.gov/news.release/metro.nr0.htm (Accessed August 26, 2020).

VanHeuvelen, T. (2020). The right to work, power resources, and economic inequality. *American Journal of Sociology*, **125**, 1255–1302.

Vidal-Tomás, D. and Alfarano, S. (2020). An agent-based early warning indicator for financial market instability. *Journal of Economic Interaction and Coordination*, **15**, 49–87.

Viebig, J. (2020). Exuberance in financial markets: Evidence from machine learning algorithms. *Journal of Behavioral Finance*, **21**, 128–135.

Vigna, P. (2020). When the stock market and economy seem disconnected. *Wall Street Journal*, 21 August. Retrieved from https://www.wsj.

com/articles/when-the-stock-market-and-economy-seem-disconnected-11598002220 (Accessed September 10, 2020).

von Beschwitz, B., Keim, D.B. and Massa, M. (2019). First to 'read' the news: News analytics and algorithmic trading. *Review of Asset Pricing Studies*, **10**, 122–178.

Wells, C. (2020). Pope at Audience: Healing the world is an opportunity to build something better. *Vatican News*, 19 August. Retrieved from https://www.vaticannews.va/en/pope/news/2020-08/healing-the-world-an-opportunity-to-build-something-different.html (Accessed September 10, 2020).

West, B.J. (2006). *Where Medicine Went Wrong: Rediscovering the Path to Complexity* (World Scientific, Singapore).

Whyte, A. (2016). Asness debunks Fama's views on momentum: The debate over whether investors can capture returns from momentum strategies 'should be put to bed,' according to the founder of AQR. Chief Investment Officer. 7 February. Retrieved from https://www.ai-cio.com/news/asness-debunks-famas-views-on-momentum (Accessed August 17, 2020).

Williams, P.G., Lerner, M.A., AAP Council on Early Childhood, and the AAP Council on School Health (2019). School readiness. *Pediatrics*, **144**(2), e20191766.

Xie, J., Zu, Y., Alkhatib, A., Pham, T.T., Gill, F., Jang, A., Radosta, S., Chaaya, G., Myers, L., Zifodya, J.S., Bojanowski, C.M., Marrouche, N.F., Mauvais-Jarvis, F. and Denson, J.L. (2021). Metabolic syndrome and COVID-19 mortality among adult Black patients in New Orleans. *Diabetes Care*, **44**, 188–193.

Zheng, H. (2020). Coordinated bubbles and crashes. *Journal of Economic Dynamics & Control*, **120**, 103974.

Zhou, G. (2018). Measuring investor sentiment. *Annual Review of Financial Economics*, **10**, 239–259.

Zucman, G. (2015). *The Hidden Wealth of Nations: The Scourge of Tax Havens* (University of Chicago Press, Chicago).

Zucman, G. (2019). Global wealth inequality. *Annual Review of Economics*, **11**, 109–138.

https://doi.org/10.1142/9781800610781_0004

Chapter 4

New Evidence on the Interactions Between International Integration and Real Economy During the COVID-19 Crisis

İlkay Şendeniz-Yüncü

Department of Business Administration
Middle East Technical University
Üniversiteler Mah Dumlupınar
Blv No: 1 06800 Çankaya Ankara, Turkey

sendeniz@metu.edu.tr

Abstract

This study investigates the relationships between economic and financial integration and the real economy before and during the COVID-19 pandemic in G7 countries. In our global and integrated world, the economic effects of the COVID-19 pandemic are inevitable. Trade restrictions have led to the slowdown of economic and financial activities, decreased the level of international integration, and decelerated the economic growth of countries. The results of this chapter document a positive and significant effect of trade measures and foreign direct investment (FDI) inflows on gross domestic product (GDP) per capita. The close connection between international integration and the real economy implies that the downward movement of integration due to the pandemic has an adverse impact on economic growth. International cooperation should be improved in order to develop effective policy measures on international trade and investment flows to countries to maintain economic recovery following the COVID-19 pandemic.

4.1. Introduction

The globalization process has attracted much attention in finance and economics literature. While some argue that globalization is beneficial, providing new investment and financing opportunities, others claim that globalization can lead to overborrowing, higher vulnerabilities, exposure to volatile international markets, and eventually crises. International integration provides access to an international pool of resources that may affect domestic investment and growth.

International economic integration is a major factor influencing globalization. Export and import volumes and trade openness, i.e. the total value of exports and imports volumes as a share of gross domestic product (GDP), are good measures of economic integration. Literature provides support for a relationship between openness to the global capital market and economic growth (Bekaert *et al.*, 2001; Edwards, 2001; Quinn, 1997; Schularick and Steger, 2006). Hummels *et al.* (2001) and Yi (2003) examine the relationship between trade growth and the world economy and suggest that increasing the share of trade in an economy would have major effects on economic growth. Lee *et al.* (2017) document trade openness as one of the crucial stimuli to economic growth, through knowledge transfer, capitalization of comparative advantage, and access to direct investment.

International financial integration is another major factor influencing economic growth in a global world, which also needs to be considered for the existence of strong economic integration. Edison *et al.* (2002) define international financial integration as the degree to which an economy does not restrict cross-border transactions. Giannetti *et al.* (2002) state that close trade partners may also be more closely integrated financially, suggesting a close relationship between economic integration and financial integration. Lane and Milesi-Ferretti (2003) investigate the connection of trade in goods and services with trade in assets and mention the contribution of trade openness to increased international financial integration. Lane and Milesi-Ferretti (2003) state that goods trade may matter for several reasons. First, trade in goods directly entails corresponding financial transactions, such as trade credit, transportation costs, and export insurance. Second, as in the theoretical model of Obstfeld and Rogoff (2000), financial asset trade is the mirror image of goods trade.

In their model, there is a close connection between the gains from international financial diversification and the extent of goods trade: trade costs create an international wedge between marginal rates of substitution and hence limit the gains to asset trade. Third, goods trade and financial positions are jointly determined in some situations, as is often the case with foreign direct investment (FDI), given the importance of intra-firm intermediate trade. Finally, openness in goods markets may increase the willingness to conduct cross-border financial transactions, reducing financial home bias (a "familiarity" effect). Following the above literature, Vo and Daly (2007) investigate the relationship between trade in goods and services and trade in assets. They find increased openness in international trade is associated with increased international financial integration and conclude that trade openness, domestic credit, and economic growth are quite successful candidates to act as drivers of international financial integration. Chambet and Gibson (2008) show a significantly positive relationship between the level of financial integration and the import or export concentration, and discuss the links connecting international trade to financial markets. A large part of the goods trade directly entails corresponding financial transactions, such as trade credit or export insurance, as well as hedging transactions.

In addition to the relationship between economic and financial integration, there is a debate on the relationship between financial integration and economic growth in literature. Edison *et al.* (2002) discuss the conflicting predictions about the growth effects of international financial integration. On the one hand, there are some theories suggesting that financial integration facilitates risk-sharing and thereby enhances production specialization, capital allocation, and economic growth (Acemoglu and Zilibotti, 1997; Obstfeld, 1994). Baele *et al.* (2004) state that financial integration and development of financial markets are likely to contribute to economic growth by removing frictions and barriers to exchange and by allocating capital more efficiently. In the standard neoclassical growth model, financial integration eases the flow of capital to capital-scarce countries, with positive output effects. Financial integration may enhance the functioning of domestic financial systems through the intensification of competition and the importation of financial services, with positive growth effects (Klein and Olivei, 2000; Levine, 2001). Lee *et al.* (2017) define financial integration as high capital mobility as well as the removal of barriers with regard to international investment, such as transaction costs, information costs, and cultural bias, which enhances international risk-sharing through a diminution in consumption volatility and raises financial stability, thus leading to higher economic growth. They also document that financial integration, which can be achieved by liberalizing controls on international trade, augments domestic investment. On the other hand, according to some other theories, financial integration in the presence of pre-existing distortions can actually inhibit growth. Boyd and Smith (1992) show that financial integration in countries with weak institutions and policies — e.g. weak financial and legal systems — may actually induce a capital outflow from capital-scarce countries to capital-abundant countries with better institutions, and predict that financial integration will promote growth only in countries with sound institutions and good policies (also see Henry, 2000). Schmukler and Vesperoni (2001) argue that if there exists any negative effect of financial liberalization, countries with more developed domestic markets should be less concerned about opening up their financial systems.

In the existence of the above discussions on the close relationship between international integration and the real economy, we faced the COVID-19 pandemic. On March 11, 2020, the World Health Organization (WHO) declared that COVID-19 was a pandemic. Immediately after the declaration, governments adopted a range of restrictions in order to prevent the spread of the virus. Governments implemented precautions such as lockdowns and prevented public gatherings, banned travel, and closed schools. However, contractions in production, transport and trade restrictions, and limits on FDI caused disruption and slowdown of economic and financial activities. In a global world, the effects of the COVID-19 pandemic on economic and financial integration are inevitable. Restrictions decreased the level of international integration, which also decelerated the economic growth of countries. McKibbin and Fernando (2020) state that companies across the world, dependent upon inputs from China, have started experiencing contractions in production. The United Nations Conference on Trade and Development (UNCTAD) presented the joint report of the Committee for the Coordination of Statistical Activities (CCSA) and 36 international organizations and documented a cut in global trade values by 3% in the first quarter of 2020, with global trade projection of a quarter-on-quarter decline of 27% (UNCTAD, 2020a). Vidyaa and Prabheeshb (2020) measure the trade interconnectedness among the 15 leading trading economies before and after the COVID-19 outbreak. Using Trade Network Analysis and Artificial Neural Networks, they show a reduction in trade interconnectedness, connectivity, and density among countries due to the pandemic, and forecast a significant decline for the rest of 2020. They also argue that while there is a visible change in the structure of the trade network, China's central position in the network is not affected by the pandemic. Agarwal and Mulenga (2020) discuss market failures in most countries around the world and a decline in global economic growth prospects due to the pandemic. They add that the pandemic poses a threat to international trade and is likely to erode the gains made toward trade liberalization over the past few decades. Its adverse effects on trade are projected to be more severe than those of the 2008–2009 Global Financial Crisis because it has impacted both aggregate demand and supply, leading to disruption in global value chains, especially in the trade of essential goods and services. In their study, Agarwal and Mulenga (2020) investigate the adverse effects of COVID-19 in least-developed countries in Africa, due to their high dependence on trade and low levels of diversification, and list a series of policy recommendations for those countries to motive for development of a post-pandemic recovery plan.

This chapter investigates the relationships of economic integration as well as financial integration with the real economy before and during COVID-19 pandemic for G7 countries. Findings of this study show that trade measures and FDI inflows have significant positive effects on GDP per capita, implying a strong relationship between international integration and economic growth. Beginning with the COVID-19 pandemic, a sharp decrease in the volumes of exports and imports as well as economic activity is observed. FDI flows were already struggling before the COVID-19 pandemic, and there has been a sharp decrease in 2020. The uncertainty due to the COVID-19 pandemic has not ended, and the impact of the pandemic on international trade, FDI flows, economic activity, and thus economic growth of countries will depend on the success of both public health and economic policy responses. Countries need to improve international cooperation and develop recovery policies to support international trade and investment flows for the post–COVID-19 world.

The rest of the chapter proceeds as follows: Section 4.2 introduces data and summary statistics; Section 4.3 presents international trade as a measure of economic integration; Section 4.4 presents FDI as a measure of financial integration; Section 4.5 discusses economic integration, financial integration, and real economy relationships; and Section 4.6 concludes the chapter.

4.2. Data and Summary Statistics

In this study, analyses are conducted for the G7 countries, which are among the ones that are mostly affected from COVID-19 pandemic, considering their high number of confirmed cases per population. UNCTAD (2020b) reports that the Americas account for 50% of all confirmed cases in the world and 53% of all recorded deaths attributable to COVID-19. Europe is the second largest contributor overall, accounting for 20% of cases and 24% of deaths. Besides, G7 countries account for 45.17% of global GDP as of 2019, according to the World Bank.[1] According to UNCTAD (2020b), due to the pandemic, the US is expected to experience negative output growth in 2020 at −5.4%, and European countries are also expected to suffer significant negative growth in 2020, with France at −8.1%, Germany at −4.9%, Italy at −8.6%, and the UK at −9.9%. It is also pointed out that in the first half of the year, global FDI flows were down 49% compared to 2019, and developed economies experienced the biggest fall, a decline of 75%, while FDI flows to developing economies decreased by only 16%.[2] All those statistics are reasons to select G7 countries as the sample in this chapter. Recent research investigating the economic and financial effects of the COVID-19 pandemic also show interest in G7 countries due to similar reasons.[3]

The total confirmed cases per population of the sample countries for the first 11 months of 2020 are shown in Figure 4.1. Data source

[1]https://data.worldbank.org/indicator/NY.GDP.MKTP.CD.

[2]See UNCTAD (2020b).

[3]Among others, see Akhtaruzzaman *et al.* (2021) that examine how financial contagion occurs through financial and non-financial firms between China and G7 countries during the COVID-19 period.

for the confirmed cases is WHO.[4] As shown in Figure 4.1, the number of confirmed cases increased drastically in the sample countries, especially in March and April 2020, being the first outbreak, and in October and November 2020, being the second outbreak.

As an indicator of real economy, real GDP per capita is used in the analyses. Exports value (goods), imports value (goods), and trade openness are the measures of international trade, which represents the economic integration. FDI inflows and outflows are selected as indicators for financial integration. Economic activity is represented by production of total industry (index).[5] Sample period is selected to be 2013Q1–2020Q2, not to overlap with the Global Financial Crisis (2007–2009) and European sovereign debt crisis (2010–2012), as mentioned in

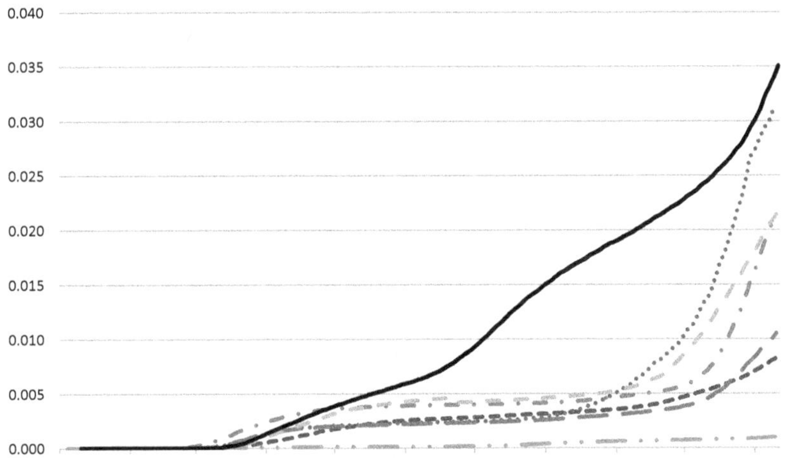

Figure 4.1. COVID-19 confirmed cases per population for G7 countries, period: January 2020–November 2020.

Note: This figure presents the number of total confirmed cases per population for G7 countries to be provide more information about the effects of COVID-19 for different countries with different ranges of population, between January 2020–November 2020.

[4]https://covid19.who.int/table.

[5]Data source for the variables is OECD.stat, https://stats.oecd.org/.

Table 4.1. Names, abbreviations, and descriptions of the variables and data sources used in the empirical analyses.

Variable name	Abbreviation	Description	Data source
Real GDP per capita	RGDPC	Real GDP per capita, log, US Dollars, s.a.	OECD.stat
Economic activity	ACT	Production of total industry, index, 2015 = 100, s.a.	OECD.stat
Exports value (goods)	EXP	Exports in goods, log, US Dollars, billions, s.a.	OECD.stat
Imports value (goods)	IMP	Imports in goods, log, US Dollars, billions, s.a.	OECD.stat
Trade openness	OPE	Total value of exports and imports volumes, share of GDP	Calculated
FDI inflows	FDI_in	Foreign direct investment, financial inflows, US Dollars, millions	OECD.stat
FDI outflows	FDI_out	Foreign direct investment, financial outflows, US Dollars, millions	OECD.stat

Table 4.2. Descriptive statistics for the variables.

	Real GDP per capita	Activity	Exports	Imports	Trade openness	FDI inflows	FDI outflows
Mean	46421.48	100.93	199.61	226.85	0.10	18835.93	20592.22
Median	44883.50	100.75	141.27	162.58	0.10	7783.50	14311
Maximum	66009	111.10	423.09	644.33	0.18	240161	122413
Minimum	35880	78.33	76.74	80.08	0.04	−72473	−131118
Std. Dev.	6995.74	4.57	113.70	157.87	0.04	35243.14	32826.98
Observations	210	210	210	210	210	206	206

Akhtaruzzaman *et al.* (2021). Monthly data is also available for the economic activity, export and import values for the period 2013M1–2020M9.

Table 4.1 presents names, abbreviations, descriptions, and data sources for the variables. Descriptive statistics are presented in Table 4.2.

4.3. International Trade as a Measure of Economic Integration

International trade, a major indicator of economic integration, has an effect on the growth of economies in today's integrated world, as discussed in the literature. Export and import volumes of countries show the level of trade openness and economic integration of those countries. The World Trade Organization WTO (2020) reports that although international trade has not faced problems with respect to healthcare products as a result of a pandemic before, there are lessons that may be learned from the previous introductions of export prohibitions and restrictions in the context of food shortages. According to the report, between 2007 and 2012, the world experienced a tightening of the food market and increased price volatility, which could be used as a reference point to understand the impact of export prohibitions and restrictions in a time of crisis. For the period 2007–2012, 251 export-restrictive measures were introduced, only 88 of which remained in place after 2012, when the world food market was no longer facing a critical shortage situation. No new notifications were made after the crisis.

Similarly, immediately after the spread of the COVID-19 pandemic, sharp decreases were observed in international trade levels in many countries, including G7 economies. Growth in trade in goods and services declined in the first quarter of 2020, and experienced a much more dramatic decline in the second quarter. Figure 4.2 presents the production of industry index, as an indicator of economic activity, as well as exports and import volumes for G7 countries between 2013M1–2020M6. A downward movement is observed in all series due to the COVID-19 pandemic.

4.4. FDI as a Measure of Financial Integration

Financial integration (as proxied by the size of FDI flows) and its effects on the host economy have been investigated in the literature,

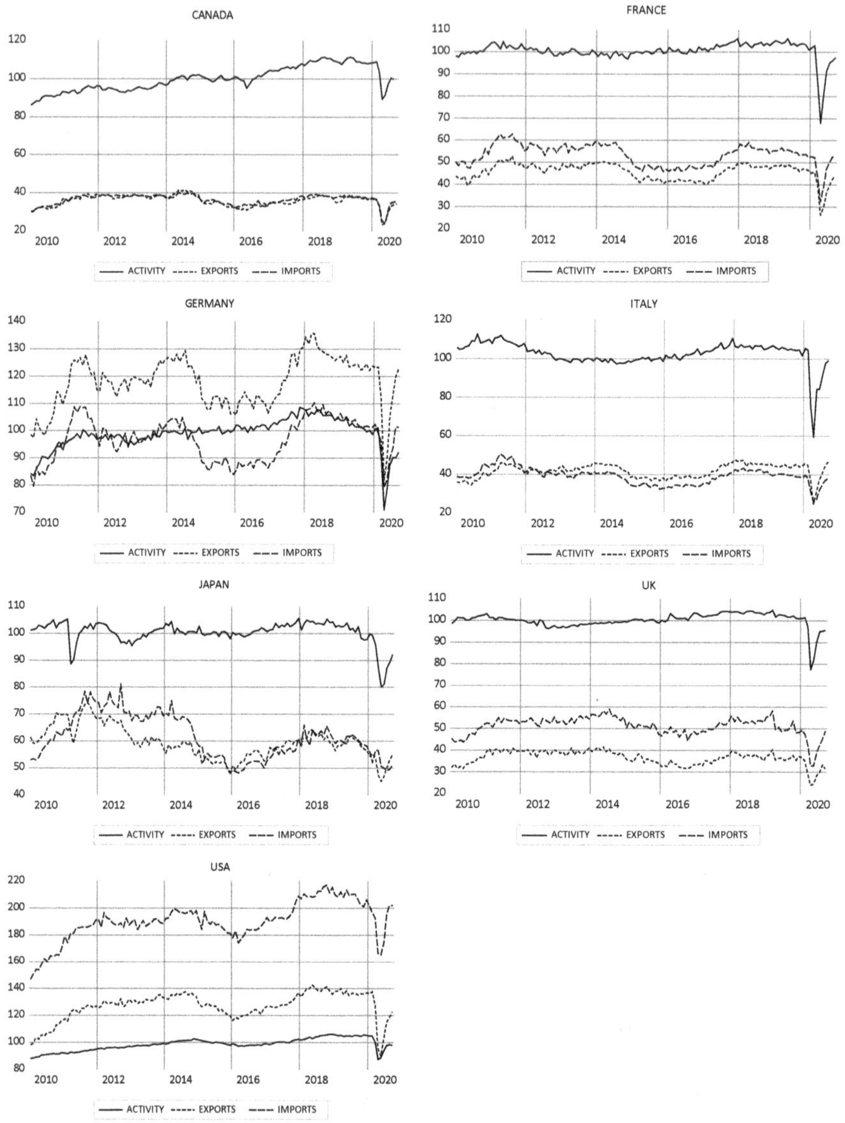

Figure 4.2. Economic activity (index), export value and import value, (USD billions), period: 2013M1–2020M9.

Note: This figure presents the sharp decrease in the economic activity, exports and imports volumes due to the COVID-19 pandemic (in US$ billions).

suggesting the positive effects of FDI on economic growth. Agénor (2003) defines the rate of real output growth and the degree of trade openness as the two most statistically significant determinants of FDI. The size of capital flows, particularly in the form of FDI, can be seen as an adequate proxy for the degree of financial openness. Agénor (2003) describes the relationship between financial integration and growth to be bidirectional, i.e. capital inflows may have a positive effect on growth, but growth in turn tends to stimulate the inflow of FDI. Iamsiraroj (2016) describes trade openness, economic freedom, and an investment-friendly climate among key determinants of FDI. Due to the dynamic relationships between FDI and economic growth, these elements influence FDI into the country and potentially stimulate economic growth through FDI inflows. International transfers are significant features of the global economy, and FDI is one of the most important components of such transfers. Most countries target to attract FDI into their economies as they expect long-term economic growth from additional stable resources in host countries. While most studies examine the impact of FDI on developing economies,[6] Lucas (1990), Gourinchas and Jeanne (2013), and Carbonell and Werner (2018) argue that FDI is mainly received by developed countries. According to the review of empirical literature by Carbonell and Werner (2018), it seems that any positive effect of FDI on growth is largest among developed countries, since they have the absorptive capacity to benefit from the foreign investment.

Immediately after our world faced the COVID-19 pandemic, governments implemented various policies in order to decrease the spread and effects of the pandemic. Along with the policies to limit the spread of the pandemic, FDI flows also decreased sharply with strategic firm decisions and economic disruptions. According to the COVID-19 reports of the Organisation for Economic Co-operation and Development (OECD), the eventual impact on FDI flows will depend on the success of both public health and economic policy

[6]See Pehlivan and Kirkpatrick (1992), Denizer (2000), Prasad *et al.* (2005), Giannetti and Ongena (2012), Şendeniz-Yüncü (2021), and Selvarajan and Ab-Rahim (2020), among others.

responses. OECD (2020) documents that FDI flows were already struggling before the COVID-19 pandemic and are expected to fall by more than 30% in 2020 even under the most optimistic scenario for the success of the public health and economic support policy measures taken by governments to address the COVID-19 pandemic and the resulting recession. UNCTAD (2020b) also predicts that global FDI flows will decrease by up to 40% in 2020, projected to decrease further in 2021 and only begin to recover in 2022 at the earliest. During and after the COVID-19 crisis, FDI may be used to support economies by means of financial support to their affiliates, assisting governments in addressing the pandemic, and through linkages with local firms.[7]

4.5. Economic Integration, Financial Integration, and Real Economy Relationships

The Panel Least Squares (LS) regression model below (Eq. 4.1) investigates the economic integration, financial integration and the real economy relationships for G7 countries for the period of 2013Q1–2020Q2.

$$\begin{aligned} RGDPC_{i,t} &= \alpha + \beta_1 ACT_{i,t} + \beta_2 EXP_{i,t} + \beta_3 IMP_{i,t} \\ &\quad + \beta_4 OPE_{i,t} + \beta_5 FDI\_in_{i,t} + \beta_6 FDI\_out_{i,t} + \varepsilon_{i,t}. \end{aligned} \quad (4.1)$$

In the model, the dependent variable is the real GDP per capita (RGDPC), as an indicator of the real economy. Explanatory variables are the economic activity (ACT), exports (EXP), imports (IMP), trade openness (OPE), FDI inflow (FDI_in), and FDI outflow (FDI_out). ε is the error term, and i and t represent the country and time, respectively. Panel LS regression results are presented in Table 4.3.

The models in Table 4.3 present positive significant effects of exports, imports, and trade openness on the real GDP per capita, providing evidence of the strong relationship between economic integration and the real economy. FDI inflows, an indicator of financial integration, also has a significant positive effect on the real GDP per capita. The close connection between the variables implies that

[7]See OECD (2020) for a detailed discussion.

Table 4.3. Effect of international integration on the real economy.

Dependent variable: RGDPC			
Models	(1)	(2)	(3)
ACT	0.012***	0.011***	0.011***
	(0.003)	(0.009)	(0.003)
EXP		0.121***	
		(0.033)	
IMP	0.126***		0.143***
	(0.032)		(0.028)
OPE			0.073*
			(0.038)
FDI_in	0.040***	0.048***	0.039***
	(0.010)	(0.008)	(0.008)
FDI_out	0.009	0.014	0.015
	(0.012)	(0.012)	(0.010)
Constant	7.507***	7.530***	7.507***
	(0.430)	(0.436)	(0.436)
Number of observations	154	154	154
R-squared	0.751	0.742	0.779
Adjusted R-squared	0.745	0.735	0.772

Note: This table presents the relationships between economic and financial integration and the real economy, derived using the panel LS method. The dependent variable is RGDPC. Logarithmic values are used for the variables. The estimated coefficient is given on the first line for each item, with the standard error reported in parentheses on the second line; the corresponding significance level appears on the first line adjacent to the estimated coefficient. ***Significant at 1%; *significant at 10%.

the downward movement of economic integration as well as financial integration due to the COVID-19 pandemic has an adverse impact on the real economy. This finding is in line with the existing literature, which predicts an adverse effect of trade restrictions and FDI limits on economic growth.

Agarwal and Mulenga (2020) investigate the adverse effects of COVID-19 on international trade in least-developed countries in Africa, and argue that the external restrictive policy shocks threaten to expose the continent to severe health and economic risks. Therefore they suggest countries to exercise a degree of caution while implementing restrictive policies during the ongoing crisis to ensure a continuous and unhindered supply of medical goods and basic foodstuffs to least-developed countries.

WTO (2020) reports that, due to the pandemic, governments placed export restrictions to ensure sufficient domestic supply of key products and to keep the domestic prices lower than world prices. However, if the country is a large exporter of a good on which the export prohibition or restriction is enacted, the negative effects of export restrictions can be substantial. The decrease in the supply of a good in the world would cause an increase in the world price of that good, which may later reduce the incentive of producers to manufacture the goods domestically. Besides, such restrictions can also push other exporters to introduce similar restrictions to keep domestic prices low. In a global crisis, as in the case of COVID-19 pandemic, this situation may become a major issue. At the end, we may come up with a disturbed global value chain and inefficiencies in production processes. Lamy and Pedrosa (2020) argue that while 60 governments had placed some form of export curb on medical supplies as of March 27, 2020, export restrictions are questionable. Mentioning the agreement of G20 trade ministers that the emergency measures designed to tackle COVID-19 must not create unnecessary barriers to trade or disruption to global supply chains, Lamy and Pedrosa (2020) discuss the government crisis-response policies that need to be separated into those taken to stem the spread of the virus and those taken to bridge the gap between supply and demand of key products to fight the disease.

UNCTAD (2020b) reminds that, for all forms of cross-border investments, projections for 2020 and beyond seem to be uncertain. In terms of FDI flows, with a second wave of the pandemic undermining efforts toward a general economic recovery, the decline of the first half of 2020 could persist longer, making the forecast additional decline of 2021 sharper. The outlook for investment flows will depend on the duration of the health crisis and the effectiveness of policy interventions to mitigate the economic effects of the pandemic.

4.6. Conclusion

In a globalized and strongly connected world, the economic effects of the COVID-19 pandemic on international integration is inevitable. Contractions in production and transport, trade restrictions and limits on FDI caused disruption and slowdown of economic and financial activities and decreased the level of international integration, which also retarded the economic growth of countries.

This study analyses the relationships of economic and financial integration with the real economy before and during COVID-19 pandemic for G7 countries. The results of the study provide evidence of positive significant effects of exports, imports, and trade openness on the real GDP per capita, implying a strong relationship between economic integration and the real economy. FDI inflows, an indicator of financial integration, also has a significant positive effect on real GDP per capita, which provides evidence of a strong link between financial integration and the real economy.

Beginning with the COVID-19 pandemic, a sharp decrease in the volumes of exports and imports as well as economic activity is observed. FDI flows are also decreasing drastically due to the pandemic. The close connection between trade variables, FDI, and the real economy implies that the downward movement of economic integration as well as financial integration due to the COVID-19 pandemic has an adverse impact on the real economy. All shortcomings and negative results of export restrictions and limits on FDI are expected to lead the world to improve international cooperation and develop recovery policies on trade and financial integration. During and after the COVID-19 crisis, policies to improve FDI processes by means of assisting governments and the local firms may help the growth of economies. With the help of effective policy moves on international trade and investment flows to mostly affected countries, it may be possible to support economies during the recovery period following the pandemic.

References

Acemoglu, D. and Zilibotti, F. (1997). Was Prometheus unbound by chance? Risk diversification, and growth. *Journal of Political Economy*, **105**, 709–751.

Agarwal, P. and Mulenga, M.C. (2020). Impact of COVID-19 on international trade: Lessons for African LDCs. *Working paper*. Center for Economic Studies and Planning, Jawaharlal Nehru University and Mulungushi University.

Agénor, R. (2003). Benefits and costs of international financial integration: Theory and facts. *The World Economy*, **26**(8), 1089–1118.

Akhtaruzzaman, Md, Boubaker, S. and Sensoy, A. (2021). Financial contagion during COVID–19 crisis. *Finance Research Letters*, Vol. 38, 101604.

Baele, L., Ferrando, A., Hördahl, P., Krylova, E. and Monnet, C. (2004). Measuring financial integration in the Euro area. ECB Occasional Paper No. 14.

Bekaert, G., Harvey, R. and Lundblad, C. (2001). Does financial liberalization spur growth? NBER Working Paper No. 8245.

Boyd, J.H. and Smith, B.D. (1992). Intermediation and the equilibrium allocation of investment capital: Implications for economic development. *Journal of Monetary Economics*, **30**, 409–432.

Carbonell, J.B. and Werner, R.A. (2018). Does foreign direct investment generate economic growth? A new empirical approach applied to Spain, *Economic Geography*, **94**(4), 425–456.

Chambet, A. and Gibson, R. (2008). Financial integration, economic instability and trade structure in emerging markets. *Journal of International Money and Finance*, **27**(4), 654–675.

Denizer, C. (2000). Foreign entry in Turkey's banking sector, 1980–97. Policy Research Working Paper, 2462.

Edison, H., Levine, R., Ricci, L. and Sløk, T. (2002). International financial integration and economic growth. *Journal of International Money and Finance*, **21**, 749–776.

Edwards, S. (2001). Capital mobility and economic performance: Are emerging economies different? NBER Working Paper No. 8076 (January).

Giannetti, M., Guiso, L., Jappelli, T., Padula, M. and Pagano, M. (2002). Financial market integration. Corporate Financing and Economic Growth Final Report.

Giannetti, M. and Ongena, S. (2012). Lending by example: Direct and indirect effects of foreign bank presence in emerging markets. *Journal of International Economics*, **86**(1), 167–180.

Gourinchas, P.O. and Jeanne, O. (2013). Capital flows to developing countries: The allocation puzzle. *Review of Economic Studies*, **80**(4), 1484–1515.

Henry, P.B. (2000). Do stock market liberalizations cause investment booms? *Journal of Financial Economics*, **58**, 301–334.

Hummels, D. Ishii, J. and Yi, K. (2001). The nature and growth of vertical specialization in world trade. *Journal of International Economics*, **54**(1), 75–96.

Iamsiraroj, S. (2016). The foreign direct investment–economic growth nexus. *International Review of Economics & Finance*, **42**, 116–133.

Klein, M. and Olivei, G. (2000). Capital account liberalization, financial depth, and economic growth. Unpublished, Tufts University, Somerville, MA, USA.

Lamy, P. and Pedrosa, E. (2020). Economics: Trade and connectivity in the Post-COVID-19 world, Chapter 6. In Challenges and Opportunities in the Post-COVID-19 World. World Economic Forum, Insight Report, Switzerland. May, 28–31.

Lane, P.R. and Milesi-Ferretti, G.M. (2003). International financial integration. Institute for International Integration Studies Discussion Paper.

Lee, P.L., Chin, L., Law, S.H. and Azman-Saini, W.N.W. (2017). Do integrated economies grow faster? Evidence from domestic equity holdings. *Economics Bulletin*, **37**(4), 2905–2916.

Levine, R. (2001). International financial liberalization and economic growth. *Review of International Economics*, **9**, 688–702.

Lucas, R.E. Jr. (1990). Why doesn't capital flow from rich to poor countries? *American Economic Review*, **80**(2), 92–96.

McKibbin, W. and Fernando, R. (2020). The global macroeconomic impacts of COVID-19: Seven scenarios. CAMA Working Paper 19/2020.

Obstfeld, M. (1994). Risk-taking, global diversification, and growth. *American Economic Review*, **84**, 1310–1329.

Obstfeld, M. and Rogoff, K. (2000). The six major puzzles in international macroeconomics: Is there a common cause? NBER Working Paper Series, Vol. 7777.

OECD (2020). Investment policy responses to COVID-19, Foreign direct investment flows in the time of COVID-19. Retrieved from www.oecd.org/coronavirus.

Pehlivan, H. and Kirkpatrick, C. (1992). The impact of transnational banks on developing countries' banking sector: An analysis of the Turkish experience, 1980-89. *British Journal of Middle Eastern Studies*, **19**(2), 186–201.

Prasad, E., Rogoff, K., Wei, S.J. and Kose, M.A. (2005). Effects of financial globalization on developing countries: Some empirical evidence, In: Tseng, W., Cowen, D. (eds). *India's and China's Recent Experience with Reform and Growth. Procyclicality of Financial Systems in Asia.* Palgrave Macmillan, London, 201–228.

Quinn, D. (1997). The correlates of change in international financial regulation. *American Political Science Review*, **91**(3), 531–551.

Schmukler, S.L. and Vesperoni, E. (2001). Globalization and firms' financing choices: Evidence from emerging economies. IMF Working Paper No.01/95.

Schularick, M. and Steger, T.M. (2006). Does financial integration spur economic growth? New evidence from the first era of financial globalization. CESIFO Working Paper No. 1691.

Selvarajan, S.K. and Ab-Rahim, R. (2020). Financial integration and economic growth: Should Asia emulate Europe? *Journal of Economic Integration*, **35**(1), 191–213.

Şendeniz-Yüncü, İ. (2021). Relationship between foreign direct investment as a measure of financial integration and economic growth in emerging markets. Working Paper. Middle East Technical University.

UNCTAD (2020a). How Covid-19 is changing the world: A statistical perspective, 2020. Committee for the Coördination of Statistical Activities (CCSA). Retrieved from www.unctad.org.

UNCTAD (2020b). Impact of the COVID-19 pandemic on trade and development: Transitioning to a new normal, UNCTAD/OSG/2020/1 - 19 Nov 2020. Retrieved from www.unctad.org.

Vidyaa, C.T. and Prabheeshb, K.P. (2020). Implications of COVID-19 pandemic on the global trade networks. *Emerging Markets Finance and Trade*, **56**(10), 2408–2421

Vo, X.V. and Daly, K.J. (2007). The determinants of international financial integration. *Global Finance Journal*, **18**(2), 228–250.

WTO (2020). Information note: Export prohibitions and restrictions, 23 April 2020, p. 8. Retrieved from https://www.wto.org/english/tratop_e/covid19_e/export_prohibitions_report_e.pdf, (Accessed December 01, 2020).

Yi, K.M. (2003). Can vertical specialization explain the growth of world trade? *Journal of Political Economy*, **111**(1), 52–102.

https://doi.org/10.1142/9781800610781_0005

Chapter 5

Great Recession: Mere Dry Run for COVID-19?

Alfredo Martín-Oliver[*,‡] **and Florina Silaghi**[†,§]

[*]*Universitat des Illes Balears*
Ctra. Valldemossa km 7.5
07122 Palma de Mallorca, Islas Baleares, Spain

[†]*Universitat Autònoma de Barcelona*
Campus de Bellaterra, 08193 Barcelona, Spain

[‡]*alfredo.martin@uib.es*
[§]*florina.silaghi@uab.cat*

Abstract

The immediate real effects of the COVID-19 crisis are far more dramatic than those of the Great Recession of 2008. Moreover, the initial stock market plunge to the World Health Organization's announcement on March 11, 2020, declaring COVID-19 a pandemic reached levels unseen since 1997. This has led commentators to qualify the Great Recession as a mere dry run for COVID-19. This chapter compares the reaction of the stock and credit default swap market to Lehman bankruptcy filing announcement with their reaction to the COVID-19 announcements. Cumulative returns and spread changes over a period of 30 calendar days following the event are also analyzed. Moreover, we investigate the effects of both adverse shocks and stimulus announcements by industry. We find that the credit default swap (CDS) market reaction is not statistically different in the two outbreaks, implying a similar increase in perceived credit risk. For the stock market, however, although the initial response

[§]Corresponding author.

to COVID-19 is significantly larger, the post-shock effects over 30 calendar days were significantly larger for the Lehman announcement.

5.1. Introduction

The ongoing COVID-19 pandemic has disrupted personal lives across the world, with half of the world's population affected by a lockdown. Besides the tragic health impact, this crisis will have important economic consequences (Barro *et al.*, 2020). The collapse in global output and the potential unemployment and firm bankruptcies that it might cause have led commentators to label this crisis as the worse economic downturn since the Great Depression, far worse than the Great Recession of 2008.[1] In fact, some claim that the latter was a "mere dry run for today's economic catastrophe" (Rogoff, 2020).

Although it is still too early to quantify the economic impact of COVID-19, financial markets have already responded with dramatic movements and global financial market risk has increased (Zhang, 2020). The financial markets' reaction to the COVID-19 pandemic captures investors' expectations regarding its potential economic consequences. The goal of the present study is to empirically analyze whether COVID-19 actually had a far stronger immediate impact on financial markets than the Great Recession using a sample of credit default swap (CDS) trading US firms. While both events caused strong reactions of financial markets and unprecedented interventions by the Federal Reserve (FED), they are of different nature and their effects are not alike. The fundamental difference between the two crises is that while the Great Recession originated in the financial sector with the Lehman Brothers' collapse, COVID-19 is a health crisis that started outside the financial sector. By its nature, COVID-19 implied a disruption in economic activities due to broken supply chains, lockdowns, and mobility restrictions. This in turn caused a cash flow shortfall of uncertain duration for corporations. Moreover, while the Great Recession initially started as a financial crisis which disrupted the supply of credit, and whose effects on the real economy were experienced later on, the real effects of

[1]https://blogs.imf.org/2020/04/14/the-great-lockdown-worst-economic-downturn-since-the-great-depression/.

the COVID-19 were immediate and much more severe. COVID-19 pushed most economies into unprecedented contractions, with the US Gross Domestic Product (GDP) plunging 31.4% in the second quarter of 2020. This difference is also reflected in overall market sentiment. During the Great Recession, news sentiment showed a V-shaped pattern, although the stock market exhibited a U-shaped pattern. In contrast, during COVID-19, despite a V-shaped stock market pattern, news sentiment follows a U-pattern. Therefore, the stock market optimism is not translating into more positive economic news (Buckman *et al.*, 2020).

The two crises also triggered different policy responses from the Federal Reserve and the US government. For the Great Recession, the Troubled Asset Relief Program (TARP, consisting of US$700 billion) was announced on September 19, 2008, and September 22, 2008. For COVID-19, the Federal Reserve stated on March 23, 2020, that it would buy Treasuries "in the amounts needed to support smooth market functioning and effective transmission of monetary policy to broader financial conditions and the economy." It also announced two facilities to support credit to large corporations. Moreover, a US$2 trillion stimulus deal to offset the economic damage of coronavirus was announced on March 25, 2020. The policy measures taken during COVID-19 thus went beyond those during the Great Recession.

To analyze whether the COVID-19 actually had a far stronger immediate impact on financial markets than the Great Recession, we will investigate the stock and CDS markets' reactions to announcements such as the WHO's announcement on March 11, 2020, declaring COVID-19 a pandemic, and the one of Lehman Brother bankruptcy filing on September 15, 2008. Looking beyond the stock market reaction to the CDS market reaction is important since CDS contracts are supposed to reflect credit risk, and previous evidence shows distinct reactions of the two markets to diverse corporate announcements (Jorion, 2007; Norden, 2004).[2] Besides analyzing

[2]The analysis could also be done for the bond market. However, previous literature has shown that CDS spreads reflect changes in credit risk more accurately and quickly than corporate bond yield spreads (Blanco *et al.*, 2005), therefore CDS spreads are used as a preferred market benchmark for credit risk (Blanco *et al.*, 2005; Longstaff *et al.*, 2005).

the immediate reaction of the general market, we also examine post-shock effects over 30 calendar days to be able to capture the impact of policy measures, and the potential mitigating effect that they can have on the initial reaction to the negative shocks. Moreover, we look at the heterogeneous effect of these two crises on investment-grade and speculative-rated firms and across different industries. Indeed, given the distinct nature of the crises, the impact across sectors will be different, with some industries facing more hardships than others.

Our chapter is related to the quickly emerging literature on the effect of the COVID-19 crisis on financial markets. Ramelli and Wagner (2020) provide a first analysis of cross-sectional stock price responses of US firms to COVID-19 with a focus on international exposure. In international samples, Ru *et al.* (2020) show that the stock market reaction is faster and stronger in countries that suffered from the 2003 SARS outbreak, while Gerding *et al.* (2020) find that stock prices reacted more strongly in countries with higher debt-to-GDP ratio. However, most of the studies focus on the stock market reaction. A notable exception is the study by Fahlenbrach *et al.* (2020), who analyze both stock and CDS markets' reaction to news about the COVID-19 crisis, as we do. Nevertheless, they focus on how the reaction differs across firms with different financial flexibility (leverage, cash holdings). In contrast, we compare the stock and CDS market reaction during COVID-19 to that during the Great Recession. A related study by Schiereck *et al.* (2016) compares bank share prices and CDS spreads' reactions to the Brexit announcement with the reactions to the Lehman Brothers' bankruptcy filing. They find that Brexit was not another Lehman moment for banks.

Our results for the event days show that the drop in stock prices and the increase in CDS spreads are of a similar magnitude for both crises. We conclude that, at least on the short-term and with the COVID-19 health crisis ongoing, the financial market reaction does not support the common perception that the COVID-19 is far worse than the Great Recession. Despite a larger initial stock market plunge during COVID-19, the stock market seems to have partially recovered since then. This can be explained by the lack of investment opportunities in a context characterized by low (even negative) returns on bonds, which pushes investors to invest in the stock market, thus opening a gap between the stock market and the real economy. Regarding the heterogeneous effects by industry, while the financial industry suffered the most during the Great Recession, the most affected industry that we identify in the current crisis is the energy sector, while sectors such as communications and technology are among the least affected. Our industry-level stock market results for COVID-19 are consistent with contemporaneous evidence by Ramelli and Wagner (2020). Our work complements their results by analyzing the CDS market reaction as well.

The rest of this chapter is organized as follows. Section 5.2 offers a full description of our data set and the methodology used in this study. Section 5.3 provides our empirical results. Finally, Section 5.4 concludes.

5.2. Database and Empirical Strategy

5.2.1. *Database*

We use daily information of CDS spreads and equity prices from January 1, 2008, to April 8, 2020, of public US firms obtained from Datastream. The firms in our sample belong either to the Credit Default Swap Index (CDX) investment-grade or CDX high-yield indices, which include the most liquid CDS-trading US firms. Our sample includes 156 US firms with 5-year CDS (the most liquid and most popularly traded CDS contracts) for senior unsecured debt with a no restructuring clause, and a total of 511,497 (502,888) daily observations of equity returns (CDS spreads). We focus on the US for a couple of reasons. First, while both crises are global, they have had a major impact in the US: the Lehman Brothers' bankruptcy is the biggest bankruptcy in the history of the US, whereas the US has the highest number of COVID-19 cases in the world at the time of writing. Second, focusing on the US also allows us to analyze the impact of the aggressive policy measures taken by the US Federal Reserve.

5.2.2. *Empirical strategy*

We posit different analyses to study the impact of negative shocks and policy measures on CDS and stock prices during the COVID crisis. In each analysis, we compare the effects in the COVID crisis with those in the Lehman crisis. We also compare their different impacts depending on whether the firm is listed in the high-yield or investment-grade CDX indexes. We expect that reactions in the stock prices will have the opposite sign than in CDS, since negative (positive) shocks are expected to decrease (increase) future cash flows and, thus, increase (decrease) credit risk.

First of all, notice that our setup is not the typical event study in which only a sub-sample of firms is affected by a shock (i.e. announcement of earnings, M&A). Instead, all the firms in the market are affected by the shock, though possibly with different intensities. Moreover, while in the typical event study the event day is different for each firm, in our case all firms are affected at the same time.

Our first analysis consists of studying the average immediate impact on CDS and equity markets during the days of the negative shock, and the average effect on the markets during a 30-calendar-day window after the outbreak of each crisis. This will allow us to assess the strength of the initial negative shock and whether it has been mitigated or accentuated during the following days. To estimate the immediate effects, we estimate an OLS regression using the equity returns and CDS changes in the window [−1,1] as dependent variable, explained with dummies that identify the relevant days. The coefficients of the dummies will inform of the average stock return and the average CDS change in the days included in the window. We use all the daily observations between January 1, 2008, until April 8, 2020, during a complete economic cycle (from crisis to crisis).[3] To analyze the effect during the 30-day window, we estimate an OLS regression using daily equity returns and CDS changes as dependent variable, explained with a dummy that identifies the 30 calendar days after the COVID-19 (Lehman) crisis outbreak, which we set in March 11, 2020 (September 15, 2008). The purpose is to learn whether the immediate effects have been mitigated or accentuated during the days after the event date.

Our second analysis complements the previous one, assessing the market reaction to the announcement of policy measures.

[3]We also estimate our models for two separate estimation windows of 120 days corresponding to the events of the two crises, as standard in the event study literature (Doidge and Dyck, 2015; Schiereck *et al.*, 2016). Our results are robust to these specifications.

The purpose is to study whether policy stimulus are effective tools to mitigate the negative shocks observed in the markets at the outburst of each crisis, and whether they can be considered the determinants of a (at least partial) recovery of stock prices and CDS spreads during the days after the initial negative shock.

The third analysis compares the different effects studied above, by industry. Here, we estimate two empirical models, one for CDS spreads and another for stock returns. The models include a dummy variable that identifies the industry of the corresponding firm. In the CDS spread (stock return) model, we include the median CDS change[4] across firms (the return of the S&P 500 index) during the corresponding day, to account for the market evolution, and we allow for a different coefficient by industry. Finally, the models include dummy variables that identify the relevant dates, and whose coefficients will inform of the average impact on CDS spreads (equity returns) during that day. Notice that we allow for different α and β for each industry,[5] in order to estimate the different abnormal reaction at industry level for each event day, after taking into account the expected average value resulting from the CAPM coefficients α and β.

Regarding the event dates, for adverse shocks regarding the Great Recession we take September 15 and 16, 2008, corresponding to the Lehman bankruptcy. For COVID-19 we analyze four different event days:

(i) January 30, 2020, when the WHO declared COVID-19 a public health emergency of international concern and when the US reported its first confirmed case of person-to-person transmission of the virus;
(ii) February 28, 2020, when the WHO raised the global risk of spread of COVID-19 from "high" to "very high;"
(iii) March 9, 2020, when Italy declared lockdown;

[4]Similarly, Batta *et al.* (2016) and Du (2017) use the cross-sectional mean across all CDS on the same day as the benchmark for CDS spreads to compute abnormal spreads.

[5]The advantage of a joint estimation is that it takes into account the correlations across industries, resulting in higher efficiency of the estimation; and that it allows for tests of coefficients across industries.

(iv) March 11, 2020, when the WHO declared the global COVID-19 outbreak a pandemic.

For policy measures announcements for the Great Recession, two announcements referring to TARP (consisting of 700 billion US dollars) were made on September 19, 2008, and September 22, 2008. Finally, for COVID-19 we consider two dates:

(i) March 23, 2020, when the FED announced an unlimited Quantitative Easing (QE) policy;
(ii) March 25, 2020, when a US$2 trillion stimulus deal to offset the economic damage of coronavirus was announced.

5.3. Main Results

5.3.1. *Aggregate reaction to negative shocks: Stock market vs CDS*

Table 5.1 presents the general reaction of both stock and CDS markets to the adverse shocks corresponding to the Lehman bankruptcy and the COVID-19 crisis. First of all, as expected, there exists a negative reaction on both markets for both crises, with a drop in stock prices and an increase in CDS spreads. For the COVID-19 crisis, we observe a significant negative reaction on the dates of the initial announcements of January 30, 2020 and February 28, 2020. Nevertheless, these reactions are of a small magnitude. On the contrary, on March 9 and 11, 2020, with the lockdown of Italy and the declaration of COVID-19 a pandemic, both markets' reactions are of a very large magnitude, similar to, and even larger than those during the Great Recession.[6] For the stock market, the sum of the returns for the days March 9 and 11, 2020 in the window [−1,1] is −19.86%, statistically larger (in absolute values, p-value < 0.000) than the sum of stock returns for the days September 15 and 16, 2008, which amounted to −13.29%. For the CDS market, spread changes (CS) amount to

[6]Contemporaneous evidence from Fahlenbrach *et al.* (2020) shows that firms with less financial flexibility experience worse stock returns and larger increases in CDS spreads. At the same time, they benefit more from policy measures.

Table 5.1. General stock and CDS market reaction to adverse shocks.

	Adverse shocks							
	Great recession			**COVID-19**				
	Lehman bankruptcy (9/15/08)	**Lehman bankruptcy (9/16/08)**	**30 days post-shock**	**WHO: interna-tional concern (1/30/20)**	**WHO: very high risk (02/28/20)**	**Italy Lockdown (03/09/20)**	**WHO: COVID as pandemic (3/11/20)**	**30 days post-shock**
Equity	-0.038^{***}	-0.095^{***}	-0.012^{***}	-0.026^{***}	-0.014^{***}	-0.076^{***}	-0.122^{***}	-0.002^{**}
	(−7.028)	(−17.778)	(−16.714)	(−4.800)	(−2.793)	(−14.760)	(−23.744)	(−2.552)
CDS	109.691^{**}	57.027^{***}	8.684^{***}	3.385	21.150^{***}	117.057^{***}	124.817^{***}	9.683^{***}
	(19.785)	(10.286)	(−12.305)	(0.627)	(3.917)	(21.677)	(23.114)	(−14.086)

Note: t-ratios in parentheses. ***, ** = statistical significance at 1% and 5%, respectively. This table shows the average equity returns and CDS changes during the days of adverse shocks for the Lehman crisis (Columns 2–3) and the COVID-19 crisis (Columns 5–8). The coefficients of each row belong to the same OLS regression, that relates the dependent variable (CDS changes or equity returns) with the dummy variables that identify the event days. Columns 4 and 9 show the average equity returns and CDS changes during the 30-calendar-day window after the shock of the Lehman crisis (September 15, 2008) and the COVID-19 crisis (March 9, 2020) respectively. The coefficients are obtained from the same OLS regression, that relates the equity returns/CDS changes with dummy variables that identify the 30-day window after the outbreak of each crisis.

241.84 and 166.72 basis points for the days March 9 and 11, 2020, and September 15 and 16, 2008, respectively, and they are not statistically different in the two crises. This implies that the increase in the overall perceived firms' credit risk is similar in the two outbreaks. The first takeaway is thus that the CDS market's reaction to the declaration of COVID-19 a pandemic is of the same order of magnitude as in the Great Recession, while the immediate stock market's reaction is larger for COVID-19.

In Columns 4 and 9 of Table 5.1, we report the cumulative returns and spreads, respectively, over the window (0, 30) calendar days after September 15, 2008, and March 9, 2020, respectively. In the case of Lehman, we find negative and significant post-shock effects for both the equity and the CDS markets. Nevertheless, in the case of COVID-19, although we find a negative and significant reaction in the CDS market, for the stock market, the effect is relatively small and significant only at 5%, suggesting that the stock market has partially recovered.

These results are further confirmed in Figure 5.1, which plots the equity and CDS market reactions to both crises for the 30 calendar days post-event. Although the stock market exhibits a much larger initial plunge in early March 2020 compared to the one of September 2008, it has since partially recovered, opening a gap between the stock market and the real economy. This can be explained by the current context of lack of alternative investment opportunities, with bond markets offering negative returns. On the contrary, the CDS market exhibits an increasing trend for both outbreaks reflecting a similar rise in credit risk. Moreover, both the immediate and post-shock reactions of the CDS market are of a similar magnitude comparing the two crises.

In Table 5.2, we split the sample into investment-grade firms (panel A) and speculative-rated firms (panel B). We can observe that speculative-rated firms show more negative stock returns and higher increases in CDS spreads. This is particularly the case during the COVID-19 crisis, when the CDS market reaction is much larger for speculative-rated firms, reflecting a large increase in credit risk for financially distressed firms given the potential liquidity and solvency problems caused by the pandemic. In figures, the change spread on March 9 and 11, 2020, was of around 33 and 46 basis points for investment-grade firms, respectively, while for

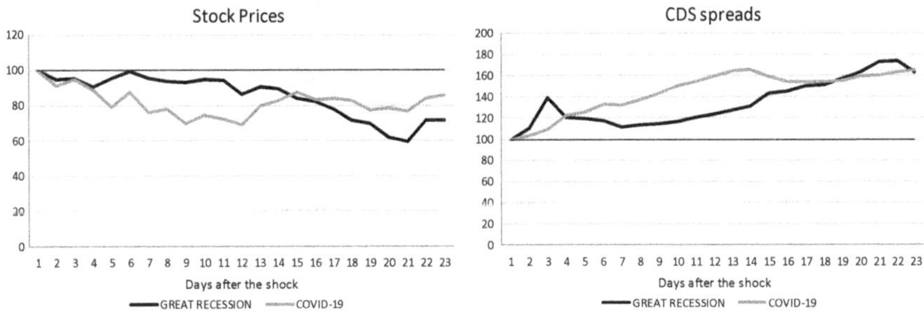

Figure 5.1. Stock and CDS market reaction to Lehman and COVID-19.

Note: This figure shows stock prices and CDS spreads for the two crises (black line: Great Recession; gray line COVID-19). Day 0 is September 12, 2008, for the Great Recession and March 6, 2020, for COVID-19. Stock prices and CDS spreads are normalized to 100 on day 0.

speculative-rated firms it was of around 227 and 229 basis points, respectively.

5.3.2. *Aggregate reaction to stimulus announcements: Stock market vs CDS*

As we have seen from the post-shock effects in Table 5.1, the initial negative reactions were attenuated 30 calendar days after the adverse shocks. This section analyses whether this mitigation was (at least partly) due to timely policy measures announcements. Table 5.3 presents the stock and CDS market reaction to stimulus announcements for both crises. For the Great Recession, two announcements referring to the TARP were made on September 19, 2008, and September 22, 2008. We note a positive reaction on both markets on these dates, although the positive effect only partially offset the negative shock of the previous days in both markets.

For COVID-19, similarly, a US$2 trillion stimulus deal to offset the economic damage of the coronavirus was announced on March 25, 2020, triggering a positive reaction on both markets. Nevertheless, on March 23, 2020, when the FED announced an unlimited QE policy, the reactions differed. While the stock market reacts positively, there is a negative and significant reaction for CDS spreads with an increase in spreads. However, we verify that the CS for the window [0,1] is not significant. Since the CDS market is dominated

Table 5.2. Stock and CDS market reaction to adverse shocks: Investment-grade versus speculative.

Panel A. Investment-grade firms

	Adverse shocks for investment-grade firms							
	Great recession			**COVID-19**				
	Lehman bankruptcy (9/15/08)	**Lehman bankruptcy (9/16/08)**	**30 days post-shock**	**WHO: international concern (1/30/20)**	**WHO: very high risk (02/28/20)**	**Italy lockdown (03/09/20)**	**WHO: COVID as pandemic (3/11/20)**	**30 days post-shock**
Equity	-0.034^{***}	-0.086^{***}	-0.010^{***}	-0.025^{***}	-0.014^{***}	-0.071^{***}	-0.116^{***}	-0.001
	(-8.558)	(-21.462)	(-19.003)	(-6.184)	(-3.496)	(-17.790)	(-29.161)	(-1.387)
CDS	107.064^{***}	36.472^{***}	3.987^{***}	2.231	10.001^{***}	33.398^{***}	46.030^{***}	2.084^{***}
	(-32.991)	(-11.239)	(-8.676)	(-0.708)	(-3.174)	(-10.601)	(-14.61)	(-4.672)

Table 5.2. (*Continued*)

Panel B. Speculative-rated firms

	Adverse Shocks for Speculative-rated Firms							
	Great recession			COVID-19				
	Lehman bankruptcy (9/15/08)	Lehman bankruptcy (9/16/08)	30 days post-shock	WHO: interna-tional concern (1/30/20)	WHO: very high risk (02/28/20)	Italy lockdown (03/09/20)	WHO: COVID as pandemic (3/11/20)	30 days post-shock
Equity	−0.042***	−0.107***	−0.014***	−0.025**	−0.015	−0.082***	−0.130***	−0.003**
	(−3.801)	(−9.704)	(−9.562)	(−2.430)	(−1.460)	(−8.025)	(−12.666)	(−2.2)
CDS	115.147***	84.045***	14.892***	4.882	35.876***	227.687***	229.752***	19.728***
	(−9.575)	(−6.989)	(−9.862)	(−0.415)	(−3.052)	(−19.373)	(−19.548)	(−13.368)

Note: t-ratios in parentheses. ***, ** = statistical significance at 1% and 5%, respectively. This table shows the average equity returns and CDS changes during the days of adverse shocks for the Lehman crisis and the COVID crisis for the subsamples of investment-grade firms (Panel A) and speculative-rated firms (Panel B). The coefficients of each row belong to the same OLS regression, that relates the dependent variable (CDS changes or equity returns) with the dummy variables that identify the event days.

Table 5.3. Stock and CDS market reaction to stimulus announcements.

	Stimulus announcements			
	TARP program (9/19/2008)	**TARP program (9/22/2008)**	**Unlimited QE (3/23/2020)**	**\$2tn stimulus program (3/25/2020)**
Equity	0.048***	−0.017***	0.054***	0.183***
	(8.997)	(−3.217)	(10.374)	(35.513)
CDS	−25.014***	−16.693***	60.811**	−49.375**
	(−4.512)	(−3.011)	(11.261)	(−9.143)

Note: t-ratios in parentheses. ***, ** = statistical significance at 1% and 5%, respectively. This table shows the average equity returns and CDS changes during the days of stimulus announcements for the Lehman crisis and the COVID-19 crisis. The coefficients of each row belong to the same OLS regression, that relates the dependent variable (CDS changes or equity returns) with the dummy variables that identify the event days.

by sophisticated investors unlike the equity market, these findings might suggest that given that the FED had recurred to QE in the Great Recession, the unlimited QE policy announced by the FED did not come as a surprise to these investors. An alternative explanation is that these sophisticated investors have an information advantage, the CDS market being a preferred venue for informed trading (Batta *et al.*, 2016). Although the stimulus deal agreed by the White House and the Senate was likely expected as well, its unprecedented size was probably unexpected and positively received by the CDS market. Comparing policy measures effects in the two crises, while they appear to have a large impact in the case of Lehman, the positive reaction to policy measures announcements in the case of COVID-19 is smaller (see Figure 5.1).

5.3.3. *Stock and CDS market reactions by industry*

We now analyze the differences in the market reactions to the two crises across industries. We first verify in unreported results that all industries have a negative reaction (significant for almost all industries) in both markets (equity and CDS) for both Lehman and

COVID-19.[7] Table 5.4 reports the CAR and CAS over the window [−1,1] in a model including the market return. Therefore, the reactions of each industry need to be interpreted relative to the overall (negative) market reaction.

We observe that in the case of Lehman, the most affected sector is by far the financial sector since this was a financial crisis caused by the subprime mortgages. On the contrary, for COVID-19, a pandemic that led to lockdowns across the world, it is the energy sector that has the most negative reaction, given the power demand reduction as the economy slowed down. Nevertheless, there are two sectors, communications and technology, which appear to be the least affected in the COVID crisis. Indeed, the lockdown led to many companies embracing work-from-home and schools and university across the world switched to virtual teaching, making massive use of online communication and increasing demand for video-conferencing technology. This has benefited companies in these sectors such as Zoom, which saw its share price soar from below US$70 in January 2020 to US$150 by the end of March 2020 (Neate, 2020). Moreover, the utilities sector shows a stronger negative stock price reaction compared to the market, and this holds in both crises. Interestingly, one of the least affected sectors in the Lehman crisis, consumer cyclical, is among the most affected sectors in the case of COVID-19. Indeed, during the COVID-19 crisis, this sector, including retail stores, restaurants, auto and auto-part manufacturers, was severely affected by the lockdown, as it not considered as essential business and work-from-home was not an option.

Table 5.4 also presents the average abnormal returns during the days of announcements of policy measures to fight the consequences of the crisis, by industry. We focus on the sectors that are more severely affected by the negative shocks, i.e. financial for Lehman and energy for COVID-19, to analyze whether the policy measures (at least partially) offset the severity of the negative shocks suffered during the outbreak of each crisis. For the Lehman crisis, we observe that the stock prices of financial companies reacted positively to the TARP announcement. Nevertheless, the CDS market does not seem

[7]Given the results of the initial analysis, we now focus on the two most important dates for COVID-19: March 9 and 11, 2020.

Table 5.4. Stock and CDS market reaction to adverse shocks and stimulus announcements by industry.

Adverse shocks

		Basic materials	Commun-ications	Consumer cyclical	Consumer non-cyclical	Energy	Finan-cial	Indus-try	Tech-nology	Utili-ties
15–16 Sep-08	Equity	−0.003	−0.024**	0.019**	0.000	0.008	−0.080***	0.008	0.003	−0.059***
		(−0.265)	(−2.166)	(2.534)	(0.026)	(0.776)	(−6.136)	(0.769)	(0.222)	(−3.813)
	CDS	−27.539**	−21.793*	−48.901***	−12.923	−30.512**	419.169***	−11.012	−9.036	14.462
		(−2.014)	(−1.782)	(−5.839)	(−1.443)	(−2.493)	(33.109)	(−0.900)	(−0.572)	(0.863)
9–11 Mar-20	Equity	−0.000	0.009	−0.017**	−0.008	−0.086***	−0.014	−0.004	−0.011	−0.028**
		(−0.026)	(0.778)	(−2.319)	(−1.014)	(−8.585)	(−1.174)	(−0.397)	(−0.767)	(−2.024)
	CDS	18.615	−28.360**	36.752***	3.896	630.564***	−24.011**	4.353	−30.387*	9.819
		(1.422)	(−2.476)	(4.540)	(0.445)	(53.416)	(−1.970)	(0.345)	(−1.931)	(0.624)

Table 5.4. (*Continued*)

Stimulus announcements

		Basic materials	Commun-ications	Consumer cyclical	Consumer non-cyclical	Energy	Finan-cial	Indus-try	Tech-nology	Utili-ties
19-22 Sep-08	Equity	0.007	0.010	−0.049***	−0.022***	0.062***	0.070***	−0.023**	−0.021	0.032**
		(0.544)	(0.905)	(−6.369)	(−2.798)	(5.946)	(5.362)	(−2.125)	(−1.454)	(2.109)
	CDS	8.928	7.693	−5.189	3.742	6.924	−19.817	4.081	19.561	−0.911
		(0.659)	(0.635)	(−0.626)	(0.422)	(0.572)	(−1.580)	(0.337)	(1.251)	(−0.055)
23-25 Mar-20	Equity	−0.030**	−0.048***	0.054***	−0.009	−0.016*	0.035***	0.023**	0.003	0.017
		(−2.409)	(−4.304)	(7.492)	(−1.226)	(−1.694)	(2.897)	(2.084)	(0.216)	(1.211)
	CDS	17.311	44.300***	187.140***	2.850	−11.413	41.728***	−2.205	57.832***	6.739
		(1.323)	(3.871)	(23.134)	(0.325)	(−0.968)	(3.426)	(−0.175)	(3.679)	(0.428)

Note: t-ratios in parentheses. ***, **, * = statistical significance at 1%, 5%, and 10%, respectively. This table shows the average abnormal CDS changes and average abnormal equity returns by industry. All the coefficients presented in the row Equity come from the same OLS regression that relates the average equity returns with the interaction of dummy variables that identify the event day and dummy variables that identify the type of industry. The estimation includes industry fixed effects and a beta-specific coefficient of the S&P 500 returns, R_{Mt}, for each industry. The coefficients presented in the row CDS come from the same OLS regression that relates the average CDS changes with the interaction of dummy variables that identify the event day and dummy variables that identify the type of industry. The estimation includes industry fixed effects and a beta-specific coefficient for each industry of the variable average abnormal CDS changes across industries, $\overline{CS}_{Mt}$.

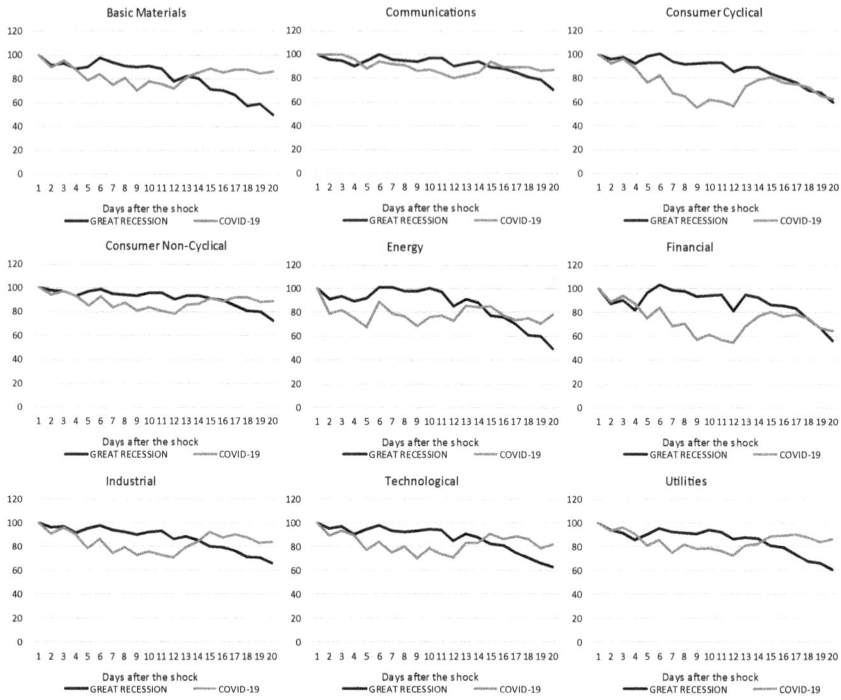

Figure 5.2. Stock market reaction by industry.

Note: This figure shows the stock market reaction by industry for the two crises (black line: Great Recession; gray line: COVID-19). Day 0 is September 12, 2008, for the Great Recession and March 6, 2020, for COVID-19. Stock prices are normalized to 100 on day 0.

to show a negative abnormal decrease in credit risk for those firms. As for the COVID-19 crisis, we observe that the announcement of policy measures had no impact on the on the perceived credit risk of firms in the energy sector most affected by the initial shock.

Finally, Figures 5.2 and 5.3 present the equity and CDS market reactions, respectively, to both crises for the 30 calendar days post-event by industry. We observe a larger initial stock market plunge for COVID-19 compared to the Great Recession across all sectors. However, the recovery over the 30 calendar days post-event is also larger for almost all sectors during the COVID-19 than during the Great Recession. The technological sector more than fully recovered the initial loss suffered during COVID-19, in line with the findings

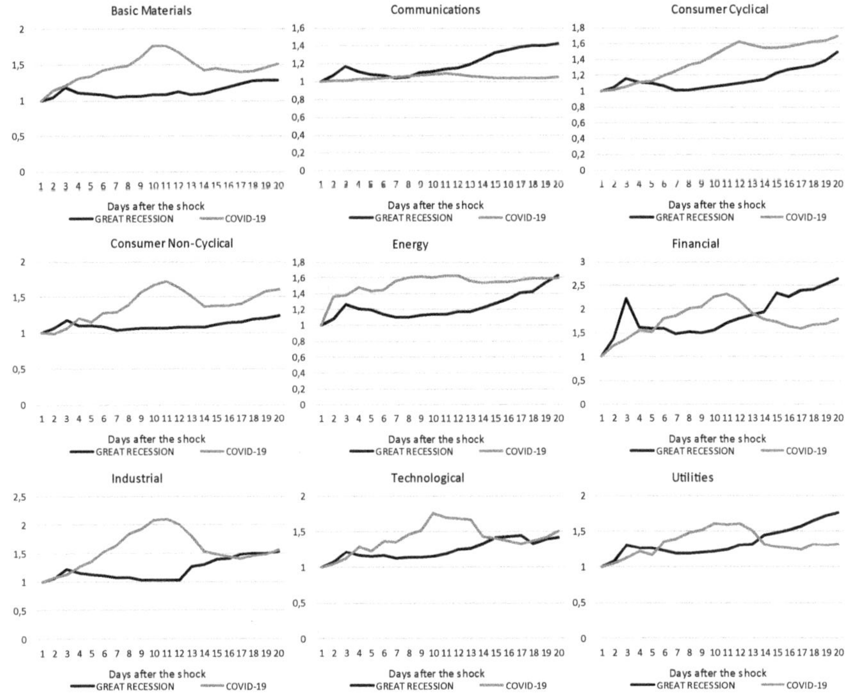

Figure 5.3. CDS market reaction by industry.

Note: This figure shows the CDS market reaction by industry for the two crises (black line: Great Recession; gray line: COVID-19). Day 0 is September 12, 2008, for the Great Recession and March 6, 2020, for COVID-19. Stock prices are normalized to 100 on day 0.

from Table 5.4. The negative reaction in the CDS market (increase in CDS spreads) appears to be larger for COVID-19 since policymakers took a longer time to announce stimulus packages. Nevertheless, the decrease in CDS spreads following stimulus announcements is evident across almost all sectors, particularly for COVID-19.

5.4. Conclusions

Our analyses of the stock and CDS market reactions to the Lehman bankruptcy announcement and the declaration of COVID-19 a pandemic suggest that, at least from the current perspective of investors, the Great Recession of 2008 was not a mere dry run for COVID-19.

Although the initial stock market reaction to COVID-19 was significantly larger than the one to Lehman's bankruptcy, the stock market has since partially recovered. Moreover, the CDS market reaction to COVID-19 is of a similar magnitude to the one during the Great Recession. In fact, our analysis of post-shock effects shows a significantly larger decrease in stock returns for the Great Recession over the 30 calendar days following the adverse shocks, not for COVID-19. Furthermore, the CDS market results are again not significantly different in both crises implying a similar increase in perceived firms' credit risk.

Finally, we can draw some policy implications from our analysis of policy responses. In case of similar shocks in the future, in order to stabilize financial markets, a prompt and ambitious policy response is needed to be able to restore the trust of the investors and the normal functioning of the markets. The response has to include not only monetary policy, i.e. central banks providing liquidity provisions, but also, and more importantly, fiscal policy to provide support to corporations through measures such as loan schemes with government guarantees, direct grants, or deferred tax payments.

Acknowledgments

Florina Silaghi, Serra Húnter Fellow, and Alfredo Martín-Oliver gratefully acknowledge financial support from the Ramón Areces Foundation. Florina Silaghi also thanks the support of the Spanish Ministry of Economics and Competitiveness (Project ECO2017-86054-C3-1-R).

References

Barro, R.J., Ursua, J.F. and Weng, J. (2020). The coronavirus and the great influenza pandemic: Lessons from the "Spanish Flu" for the coronavirus's potential effects on mortality and economic activity. NBER Working Papers No. w26866.

Batta, G.E., Qiu, J. and Yu, F. (2016). Credit derivatives and analyst behavior. *The Accounting Review*, **91**, 1315–1343.

Blanco, F., Brennan, S. and Marsh, I. (2005). An empirical analysis of the dynamic relationship between investment grade bonds and credit default swaps. *Journal of Finance*, **60**, 2255–2281.

Buckman, S.R., Shapiro, A.H. and Wilson, D.J. (2020). Comparing news sentiment in the time of COVID-19 to the 2008 financial crisis. *San Francisco FED Blog*, May 27.

Doidge, C., Dyck, A., 2015. Taxes and corporate policies: Evidence from a quasi natural experiment. *Journal of Finance*, **70**(1), 45–89.

Du, L. (2017). The CDS market reaction to restatement announcements. *Journal of Business Finance & Accounting*, **44**, 1015–1035.

Fahlenbrach, R., Rageth, K. and Stulz, R. (2020). How valuable is financial flexibility when revenue stops? Evidence from the COVID-19 crisis. *Review of Financial Studies* (forthcoming).

Gerding, F., Thorsten M. and Nagler, F. (2020). Sovereign debt and equity returns in the face of disaster. Working Paper.

Jorion, P. (2007). Good and bad credit contagion: Evidence from credit default swaps. *Journal of Financial Economics*, **84**, 860–883.

Krugman, P. (2020). Crashing Economy, Rising Stocks: What's going on? *The New York Times*, May 6.

Longstaff, F.A., Mithal, S. and Neis, E. (2005). Corporate yield spreads: Default risk or liquidity? New evidence from the credit default swap market. *Journal of Finance*, **60**, 2213–2253.

Neate, R. (2020). Zoom booms as demand for video-conferencing tech grows. *The Guardian*, March 31.

Norden, L.(2004). Informational efficiency of credit default swap and stock markets: The impact of credit rating announcements. *Journal of Banking & Finance*, **28**, 2813–2843.

Ramelli, S. and Wagner, A.F. (2020). Feverish stock price reactions to COVID-19. *The Review of Corporate Finance Studies*, **9**(3), 622–655.

Rogoff, K. (2020). The 2008 financial crisis will be seen as a dry run for COVID-19 cataclysm. *The Guardian*, April 8.

Ru, H., Yang, E. and Zou, K. (2020). Combating the COVID-19 pandemic: The role of the SARS imprint. *Management Science* (forthcoming).

Schiereck, D., Kiesel, F. and Kolaric, S. (2016). Brexit: (Not) another Lehman moment for banks? *Finance Research Letters*, **19**, 291–297.

The Economist (2020). A dangerous gap: The market vs the real economy. May 7.

Zhang, D., Hu, M. and Ji, Q. (2020). Financial markets under the global pandemic of COVID-19. *Finance Research Letters*, **36**, 101528.

PART II
COVID-19: Stock Market Behavior

https://doi.org/10.1142/9781800610781_0006

Chapter 6

Extreme Events: What Are US Stock Market Sectors Afraid of More?

Veni Arakelian

Economic Analysis and Investment Strategy, Piraeus Bank
Vasilissis Sofia 94 & Kerasountos 1, Athens, Greece

arakelianv@piraeusbank.gr

Abstract

We examine the reaction of US stock market sectors to a stock market bubble, a terrorist attack, two pandemics, a financial crisis, an industrial disaster, and an unexpected positive event. Although the indices belong to the same local market and are expected to show uniform responses to shocks, the degree of stock market reactions differs significantly. Especially, with regard to the COVID-19 outbreak, there is clear evidence that the US stock market sector indices positively over-reacted to this unanticipated event. An explanation is the effect of the unconventional measures adopted immediately to combat the crisis.

6.1. Introduction

Every time an extreme event occurs, the weakness not only of the financial markets but also of the societies themselves in predicting and dealing with it is revealed. Economists are frequently asked to measure the effects of an economic event on the value of firms. The event studies are both vast and have a long history, dating back to 1933 when Dolley (1933) examined the effects of stock splits on stock prices. His study considered 95 splits from 1921 to 1931, and concluded that the price increased in 57 of the cases, while it declined in only 26 instances. The next 30 years resulted in an upgrade to the level of sophistication of event studies (see, e.g. Baker (1956), Baker (1957), and Ashley (1962)), including the removal of the general stock market price movements and the dissociation of confounding events. In the late 1960s, Ball and Brown (1968) considered the information content of earnings, and Fama *et al.* (1969) introduced the methodology to study how a firm-specific event[1] or market-wide information, such as the trade deficit, the change in market regulations, or central bank quantitative easing programs, affects the performance indicators of the firm. Other fields where the event study is used are the law and economics, to measure for example the impact of a change in the regulatory environment on the value of a firm (e.g. Schwert (1981), or, in legal liability cases, to assess damages (e.g. Mitchell and Netter (1994)).

The study of extreme events seems to be a difficult problem, but the construction of a measure that will reflect the reaction to the event is not particularly difficult, while the value of such information is great as it will provide the impact of a particular event on the value of a business. This measure can be constructed based on security prices observed over a relatively short period, which incorporates the rationale that all the information is captured by the security prices. On the contrary, direct productivity-related measures may require many months or even years of observation.

The extreme events do not always originate endogenously but also arise from external factors, such as terrorist attacks, environmental disasters, and pandemics. In all cases, the common feature is the rarity of the event. For example, it will not be an exaggeration to say that COVID-19 took the markets by surprise and that the stock markets showed a laggard reaction. For example, the major global stock market index, the S&P 500 index, soared to its peak in February 2020, and then reached its trough on March 9, 2020, falling by 7% in 4 minutes and triggering a circuit breaker for the

[1]Some other examples of firm-specific events are mergers and acquisitions, earnings announcements, bonus dividend distribution, bonus share, new debt, or equity issuance.

first time since the financial crisis of 2007–2008 and halting trading for 15 minutes. The volatility levels were similar to those seen during the financial crisis of 2007. The comparison of this pandemic crisis with the previous crisis was inevitable and was accompanied by media speculation about the onset of another Great Depression. The unanticipated event of the COVID-19 pandemic resulted in one of the biggest price shocks the energy market experienced since the first oil shock of 1973. Brent crude prices dipped below US$20 a barrel, losing nearly 70% in value, with storage capacity approaching its limits.

Several authors have studied the effects of COVID-19, either in terms of performance or of volatility in a variety of asset classes and countries, adopting different methodological approaches. Ciner (2020) studied the predictive ability of a relatively large number of variables from currency, bond, and commodity markets of US stock returns during the COVID-19 crisis. Le *et al.* (2020) compared a wide range of assets, such as exchange rates, commodities, equity indices, US Treasury bonds, and Bitcoin, and showed that there exists an asymmetric response in the tail dependencies to the COVID-19 crisis for various asset classes, where the effect in the left tail is stronger and more prevalent than that in the right tail. Sherif (2020) studied the UK Dow Jones Islamic stock market index, and the findings suggest a strong and statistically significant relationship between the COVID-19 pandemic and the performance of the conventional stock market index. Mirza *et al.* (2020) evaluated the impact of COVID-19 on different types of actively managed funds in Europe to conclude that social entrepreneurship funds outperformed their counterparts during the outbreak. The results remained robust for volatility timing with evidence of this phenomenon for social funds. The Treasury funds were positive during the first stage but as the epidemic escalated, the cumulative abnormal returns became negative. On the other hand, Pástor and Vorsatz (2020) analyzed the performance and the flows of US actively managed equity mutual funds in the US during the COVID-19, concluding that most active funds underperform passive benchmarks during the crisis, contradicting a popular hypothesis. Heyden and Heyden (2020), adopting an event study approach, examined the short-term market reactions of US and European stocks after the announcement of the first death due to COVID-19 in a given country and found that stocks reacted in a significantly negative manner. The authors also report that the stock returns are negatively affected by the announcements of country-specific fiscal policies, whereas the monetary policy measures have the potential to calm markets, which both are either intensified or lessened by firm-specific characteristics such as tangible assets, liquidity, and institutional holdings. Salisu and Vob (2020) studied the effect on the stock markets using news related to COVID-19 and found that health-related news have a negative and statistically significant effect on stock returns, indicating that returns decline as more information is sought on health issues since the pandemic outbreak. Similarly, Albulescu (2020) investigated the effect of the official announcements of the new cases of COVID-19 infection and fatality ratio to conclude that the S&P 500 realized volatility is enhanced. Additionally, the implications in volatility of major stock markets like that of the US, Germany, and Italy during COVID-19 are as high as that of the financial crisis of 2007, contrary to that of China and Japan (see Ali *et al.* (2020)). Lyócsa *et al.* (2020) highlighted the predictive ability of Google searches about COVID-19 on stock market price variations.

In this study, we compare the reaction of 38 US sector stock indices facing extreme events that originated from different sources. Schnusenberg and Madura (2014) and this study differ from the majority of the event study papers, as they both focus on stock indices rather than on individual stocks. As the authors mention, in using stock indices, the potential bias due to firm size and the bid–ask spread is avoided. Additionally, such research is valuable to investors as for most of the indices a variety of Exchange Traded Funds (ETFs) are available, allowing investors to invest in stock market indices. Therefore the existence of abnormal returns in response to newly arriving information is relevant from an investment perspective, revealing the possible arbitrage opportunities. Moreover, in this way, the stock market inefficiencies are highlighted. Therefore, we examine the reaction under a stock market bubble (dot-com bubble, March 31, 2000), a terrorist attack (September 11, 2001), pandemics (SARS outbreak, July 5, 2003; coronavirus disease 2019, hereafter COVID-19, outbreak, March 11, 2020), a financial crisis (Lehman Brothers Collapse, September 15, 2008), and an industrial disaster (Gulf of Mexico oil spill, September 8, 2010). On the contrary, we evaluate the reaction when an unexpected positive event happened, and we choose that to be the

President of ECB, Mario Draghi's; "Whatever it takes" statement (July 26, 2012), which marked the turnaround of the euro crisis. The absence of a quantitative definition of an extreme event drives a re-evaluation of their consequences, and the market participants seek new ways to protect their investments, adding new features of diversification.

The chapter is organized as follows: Section 6.2 reviews the event study methodology; Section 6.3 describes the data used; in Section 6.4, we discuss the results; and in Section 6.5, we conclude.

6.2. Event Study Design

The literature studying the econometrics of the event studies is vast (see e.g. MacKinlay, 1997, Campbell *et al.* (1997), Binder (1998), Kothari and Warner (2007), Brooks (2019)). The stages of an event study are rather commonly known and have only little differences depending on the exact method of implementation. Campbell *et al.* (1997) summarized them into the following steps:

(1) Event definition,
(2) Selection criteria,
(3) Normal and abnormal return measurement,
(4) Estimation procedure,
(5) Testing procedure,
(6) Empirical results,
(7) Interpretation of results and conclusions.

6.2.1. *Event definition*

As a start, the *event date*, i.e. the date on which the market receives the unanticipated information for the first time, must be specified. This is not always straightforward, either due to the reporting delays among the news providers or the need to be first identified by an organization. For example, in the case of COVID-19, the official date of the event is March 11, 2020, when the World Health Organization determined that i.e. COVID-19 is a pandemic. Next, an event window must be defined, how many trading days before and after the event will be included. For example, for an earnings announcement event study with daily data, a one-day event window is usually assumed

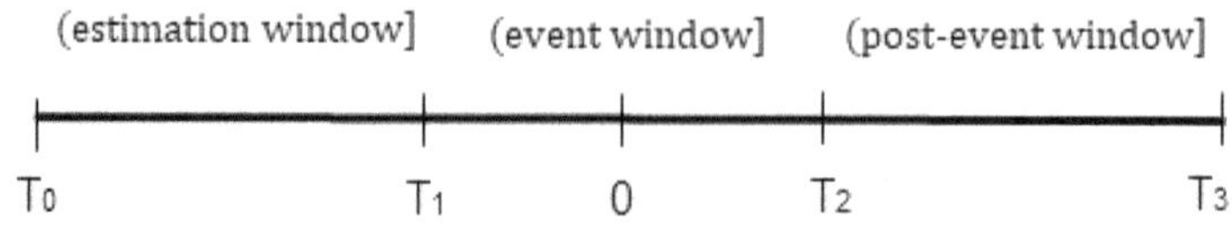

Figure 6.1. Event study time span.

to capture the price effects of the announcement after the closing of the stock market on the announcement day. In this study, we follow this assumption as well. Finally, an estimation period is defined to examine how the stock returns should have behaved in the absence of the event. In this study, the estimation period is 120 days (a quarter) and, the same is assumed for the post-event window. Figure 6.1 shows the period of the event study.

6.2.2. *Selection criteria*

At this point, the *selection criteria* for the inclusion of a firm are determined. Some features might be market capitalization, industry representation, or data availability.

6.2.3. *Normal and abnormal returns*

A very important step is the calculation of the *abnormal returns*. To define what an abnormal return is, it is first required to define what a *normal return* is. Then the abnormal returns are defined as the disturbance term of the model estimated, which is calculated on an out-of-sample basis. Statistical and economic methods are two categories of the approaches used, which are mainly based on whether the behavior of asset returns follow some statistical assumptions or some economic arguments concerning investor behavior. For the $i = 1, 2, \ldots, J$ assets, the distributional assumption that the asset i returns are jointly a random sample from a normal distribution is sufficient for the *constant mean return model*:

$$\begin{aligned} R_{i,t} &= \mu_i + \epsilon_{i,t} \\ E(\epsilon_{i,t}) &= 0 \\ Var(\epsilon_t) &= \sigma_i^2, \end{aligned} \tag{6.1}$$

and although it is a strong assumption, inferences using the normal return models tend to be robust to deviations from this (MacKinlay, 1997). Additionally, the assumption can be easily modified to accommodate autocorrelation and heteroskedasticity of the returns. The model in although very simple bids more sophisticated models yielding similar results (Brown and Warner, 1980, Brown and Warner, 1985). The second statistical model we examine is the *market model*

$$\begin{aligned} R_{i,t} &= \alpha_i + \beta_i R_{m,t} + \epsilon_{i,t} \\ E(\epsilon_{i,t}) &= 0 \\ Var(\epsilon_{i,t}) &= \sigma_i^2, \end{aligned} \tag{6.2}$$

whose potential improvement over the constant mean return model is the reduction of the variance of the abnormal returns by removing the return related to the variation in the market return, R_m.

The constant mean model assumes that the expected return is equal to a constant, which can differ across the indices, and abnormal return is equal to the difference between the observed return, R_i, and the predicted return. The model is consistent with the Capital Asset Pricing Model (CAPM) (Litner, 1965; Sharpe, 1964). Under the assumption that security has constant systematic risk and that the efficient frontier is stationary, the Arbitrage Pricing Model (APT) (Ross, 1976) also predicts that a security's expected return is constant. The market model is consistent with the APT if all securities have a systematic risk of unity. Additionally, the CAPM and the APT can be used to obtain more constrained normal returns models than those of the statistical models. The null hypothesis of the over-reaction is equivalent to investigate if the residual portfolio returns measured relative to the single-period CAPM, equals zero. First, De Bondt and Thaler (1985) provide evidence of over-reaction after large price changes, hypothesizing that extreme movements in stock prices are followed by movements in the opposite direction to correct the initial observation, which is not consistent with the efficient market hypothesis. Later, Brown *et al.* (1988) develop and test the uncertain information hypothesis as a means of explaining the response of rational, risk-averse investors to the arrival of unanticipated information. Of course, cases cannot be excluded where the over-reaction is due to misspecification errors attributed to a single beta CAPM model.

6.2.3.1. *Estimation of abnormal returns*

As is already mentioned, the abnormal returns are calculated as the out-of-sample residual of the expected model assumed. On top of the decision of which model is the right one, we have to choose how to cumulate the abnormal returns. There are two methods: the cumulative abnormal returns and the buy-and-hold abnormal returns. The difference between them is that of arithmetic versus geometric sums. In this study, we use the cumulative abnormal returns (hereafter CAR), given by the following equation:

$$AR_{i,t} = R_{i,t} - E(R_{i,t})$$

$$CAR_{i,t} = \sum_{t=T_1}^{T_2} AR_{i,t}. \tag{6.3}$$

6.2.4. *Testing*

The goal is to find whether the event had impact or no impact on the returns. The null hypothesis is assumed as no abnormal returns, no unusual return volatility, etc. Under the null of no abnormal performance, the test statistics based on the standardized abnormal performance will be asymptotically normal distributed (as the estimation window increases)

$$AR_{i,t} \sim N(0, \sigma^2(AR_{i,t})), \tag{6.4}$$

where the variance of the abnormal returns $\sigma^2(AR_{it})$ is estimated in various ways. For the constant mean or the market model, the estimated variance is given by

$$\hat{\sigma}^2(AR_{i,t}) = \frac{1}{T-k} \sum_{t=T_0}^{T_1} \hat{u}_{i,t}^2, \tag{6.5}$$

where k is the number of the independent variables and $T = T_1 - T_0$ is the estimation window. In certain case, the variance is adjusted to reflect the errors from the estimation of the coefficients (for details, see Brooks (2019)).

To test the hypothesis that the cumulative abnormal returns or the buy-and-hold abnormal returns exist, either parametric or non-parametric tests are used. The traditional t-statistics used to identify the abnormal returns over an event window from T_1 to T_2 is:

$$t_{CAR_i} = \frac{\sum_{t=T_1}^{T_2} \widehat{AR}_{i,t}}{\sigma(CAR_i(T_1, T_2))} \tag{6.6}$$

or

$$t_{CAR_i} = \frac{\sum_{t=T_1}^{T_2} \widehat{AR}_{i,t}}{\sqrt{T_2 - T_1 + 1}\hat{\sigma}(AR_{i,t})} \sim N(0, 1). \tag{6.7}$$

On the other hand, popular non-parametric tests free of distributional assumptions on returns are the Sign Test, which assumes symmetry in returns, and the Rank Test, which allows for non-symmetry in returns (see Corrado (1989)).

6.2.5. *Empirical results*

The presentation of the empirical results and the diagnostics can be fruitful. For example, there are cases where only a few firms heavily influence the empirical results, a fact that it is important for gauging the importance of the results.

6.2.6. *Interpretation and conclusions*

Ideally, the empirical results will lead to insights about the mechanisms by which the event affects security prices. Additional analysis may be included to distinguish between competing explanations.

6.3. Data

We apply the proposed methodologies to the daily data of 38 US sector stock indices, including the S&P 500 index, which serves as the benchmark. We choose from:

- *FTSE Russell Group* 8 indices:
  - The *Russell 1000 Total Return Index* consists of the largest 1,000 companies in the Russell 3000 Index, representing the universe of large capitalization stocks from which most active managers typically select. The *Russell 2000 Total Return Index*

brings vivid detail to the investable small cap market measuring the performance of those Russell 3000 companies with lower price-to-book ratios and lower forecasted growth values. Academic and practitioner research confirms that large-cap stocks behave differently than small-cap stocks and that performance is variable. There are sub-periods during which the Russell 1000 outperforms the Russell 2000 and vice versa.

— The *Russell 1000 Value Index* measures the performance of those Russell 1000 companies with lower price-to-book ratios and lower forecasted growth values, whereas the *Russell 2000 Value Index* measures that of Russell 2000 companies. *The Russell 2000 Dividend Growth Index* is designed to represent the performance of companies of *Russell 2000 Index* that have successfully increased their dividend payments over a period of 10 years. Companies are screened for liquidity and dividend status and then selected and equal-weighted, subject to a maximum sector weight of 30%.

— The *Russell 1000 Growth/Value Index* measures the relative performance of a combination of their component indices, the *Russell 1000 Growth Index* and the *Russell 1000 Value Index*, and a cash component. It represents a positive weighting on the *Russell 1000 Growth Index* and a negative weighting on the *Russell 1000 Value Index*. The weight for both component indices will be reset to (+/-)100% on a daily basis with no cost of borrowing or margin requirement and no interest on cash. It is designed to provide a benchmark for market participants looking to measure the relative performance of a growth compared with value investment theme.

- *S&P Global Group* 28 indices:

— The *S&P US 600 Small Cap Index* and the *S&P 500 Mid Cap Index* are taken as representatives of the size investing from the S&P Global Group. We also include 10 sectoral indices, which are composed of those companies included in the S&P 500 that are classified as members of the GICS of the specified sector, namely *S&P 500 Cons. Discret./ Commun. Services/ Cons. Staples/ Energy/ Financials/ Health Care/ Industrials/ Inform. Tech/ Materials/ Utilities Index.*

— *S&P 500 Dividend Aristocrats Index* measures the performance of S&P 500 companies that have increased dividends every year for the last 25 consecutive years, treating each constituent as a distinct investment opportunity without regard to its size by equally weighting each company. *The S&P 500 Buyback Index* is designed to measure the performance of the top 100 stocks with the highest buyback ratios in the S&P 500. *The S&P 500 High Beta Index* measures the performance of 100 constituents in the S&P 500 that are most sensitive to changes in market returns, designed for investors initiating a bullish strategy or making a directional bet on current markets. The *S&P 500 Pure Value (Growth) Index* is a style-concentrated index designed to track the performance of stocks that exhibit the strongest value (growth) characteristics by using a style-attractiveness-weighting scheme. The *S&P 500 High Dividend Index* serves as a benchmark for income-seeking equity investors, measuring the performance of 80 high-yield companies within the S&P 500 and is equally weighted to best represent the performance of this group, regardless of constituent size. The *S&P 500 Quality Index* is designed to track high-quality stocks in the S&P 500 by quality score, which is calculated based on return on equity, accruals ratio, and financial leverage ratio. The *S&P 500 Momentum Index* is designed to measure the performance of securities in the S&P 500 universe that exhibit persistence in their relative performance. The *S&P 500 Quality — Lowest Quintile Index* is designed to measure the performance of the 100 lowest-ranked stocks in the S&P 500 based on quality score. Quality scores are calculated based on return on equity, accruals ratio, and financial leverage ratio.

- *MSCI Group* 2 indices:

— The *MSCI World High Dividend Yield Index* is based on the *MSCI World Index* and includes large- and mid-cap stocks across 23 Developed Markets (DM) countries. The index is designed to reflect the performance of equities in the parent index (excluding REITs) with higher dividend income and quality characteristics than average dividend yields that are both sustainable and persistent. The index also applies quality screens and reviews 12-month past performance to omit stocks with potentially deteriorating fundamentals that could force them to cut or reduce dividends.

— The *MSCI USA Quality Index*, which is based on the MSCI USA Index, its parent index, includes large- and mid-cap stocks in the US equity market. The index aims to capture the performance of quality growth stocks by identifying stocks with high-quality scores based on three main fundamental variables: high return on equity (ROE), stable year-over-year earnings growth, and low financial leverage. The MSCI Quality Indices complement the existing MSCI Factor Indices and can provide an effective diversification role in a portfolio of factor strategies.

Daily data are frequent enough to isolate the event from the prior- and post-event period. Tables 6.1–6.7 show the descriptive statistics of the daily returns for 120 days before the event. To save space, we present only the top and bottom 10 performing indices.

6.4. Application and Discussion of the Results

We apply the event study methodology described and choose to discuss the results for a post-event window of 120 days. Most of the studies focus on short-term dynamics, on the 1-day CAR or 60-days CAR (e.g. Brown *et al.* (1988)). We extend the window to avoid the effect of the large fluctuations of the stock indices and to capture the impact of any reforms or financial aid adopted to cope with the unexpected event. Additionally, many investors choose short investment period that.

Tables 6.8 and 6.9 show the statistically significant post-event cumulative abnormal returns. Our results have two important implications. First, although the indices belong to the same local market and are expected to show uniform responses to shocks, the degree of stock market reactions differs significantly. Consequently, investors could benefit from portfolio diversification. Furthermore, since all the events examined are unanticipated, the magnitude of abnormal performance reflects the impact of that type of event on the indices' valuation. Second, the non-zero abnormal

Table 6.1. The table contains the descriptive statistics of the daily returns for the period $t = -120, -119, \ldots, t = 1$.

Top 10	Mean	Median	Max	Min	Std. dev.	Skewness	Kurtosis
S&P US 600 SC Index	1.457	0.815	17.945	−3.561	2.890	1.715	10.430
Russell 2000 Growth Index	0.383	0.666	4.296	−6.054	1.978	−0.724	3.402
S&P 500 INFO TECH Index	0.340	0.74	4.14	−5.52	2.156	−0.487	2.488
S&P 500 Pure Growth Index	0.328	0.34	5.37	−5.77	2.065	−0.168	3.143
S&P 500 Momentum Index	0.275	0.438	3.709	−5.042	1.858	−0.563	2.750
Russell 2000 Index	0.265	0.45	3.608	−4.444	1.549	−0.541	3.150
S&P 500 High Beta Index	0.251	0.4	6.17	−5.46	2.013	−0.365	3.309
Russell 1000 Growth Index	0.204	0.349	4.675	−4.6613	1.759	−0.021	3.350
S&P Mid Cap Index	0.165	0.28	6.15	−3.56	1.539	0.249	4.108
MSCI USA Cyclical Sectors Index	0.153	0.145	4.73	−4.52	1.608	−0.264	3.444

(*Continued*)

Table 6.1. (*Continued*)

Bottom 10	Mean	Median	Max	Min	Std. dev.	Skewness	Kurtosis
S&P 500 Div Aristocrat Index	−0.133	−0.155	6.698	−4.156	1.530	1.147	7.091
Russell 1000 Dividend Growth Index	−0.142	−0.287	6.759	−2.913	1.358	1.559	9.085
Russell 2000 Dividend Growth Index	−0.148	−0.126	4.349	−2.287	0.868	1.079	8.006
S&P 500 High Dividend Index	−0.157	−0.1825	6.061	−2.806	1.321	1.226	7.560
S&P 500 Low Volatility Index	−0.159	−0.18	5.92	−3.04	1.296	1.105	7.106
MSCI USA Defense Sectors Index	−0.190	−0.26	4.77	−2.86	1.458	0.945	4.619
Russell 1000 Value/Growth Index	−0.213	0.01	3.92	−3	1.196	−0.001	3.446
S&P 500 Energy Index	−0.252	−0.645	8.27	−4.02	2.131	0.820	4.018
S&P 500 Consumer Staples Index	−0.320	−0.52	7.88	−8.88	1.955	0.387	7.775
MSCI World High Dividend Yield Index	−1.920	−1.555	2.79	−7.55	4.039	−0.205	1.478

Note: The $t = 0$ is assumed to be the date associated to the dot-com bubble, March 31, 2000.

Table 6.2. The table contains the descriptive statistics of the daily returns for the period $t = -120, -119, \ldots, t = 1$.

Top 10	Mean	Median	Max	Min	Std. dev.	Skewness	Kurtosis
Russell 1000 Value/Growth Index	0.138	0.1	2.29	−2.77	0.851	−0.474	3.766
S&P 500 Energy Index	0.027	0	3.86	−2.88	1.097	0.054	3.704
Russell 2000 Dividend Growth	−0.021	0	1.539	−1.659	0.762	−0.061	2.235
S&P 500 High Dividend Index	−0.033	0.075	2.237	−2.122	0.736	−0.222	3.333
S&P 500 Low Volatility Index	−0.042	−0.04	2.01	−1.64	0.596	0.199	4.208
S&P 500 Pure Value Index	−0.044	0.085	2.06	−2.4	0.871	−0.594	3.296
Russell 1000 Dividend Growth Index	−0.051	0	2.269	−1.821	0.638	−0.163	4.470
S&P US 600 Index	−0.058	−0.069	2.733	−2.201	1.079	0.233	2.948
Russell 2000 Value Index	−0.064	0.044	1.959	−1.996	0.865	−0.183	2.424
S&P 500 Div Aristocrat Index	−0.066	−0.031	2.74503	−1.874	0.723	0.110	4.501

(Continued)

Table 6.2. (*Continued*)

Bottom 10	Mean	Median	Max	Min	Std. dev.	Skewness	Kurtosis
S&P 500 Financials Index	−0.208	−0.22	3.28	−2.19	0.964	0.345	3.984
MSCI USA Quality USD Index	−0.209	−0.165	2.82	−2.7	1.145	0.198	2.871
S&P 500 Quality — Lowest Quintile Index	−0.232	−0.18	3	−2.44	1.214	0.230	2.596
S&P 500 Growth Index	−0.236	−0.16	3.4	−2.72	1.243	0.278	2.809
MSCI USA Cyclical Sectors Index	−0.266	−0.115	4.16	−3.18	1.359	0.218	3.390
Russell 1000 Growth Index	−0.277	−0.176	3.777	−2.997	1.432	0.299	2.955
S&P 500 Cons Discret Index	−0.295	−0.195	3.263	−4.137	1.385	−0.221	3.615
S&P 500 Pure Growth Index	−0.300	−0.31	5.07	−3.98	1.847	0.277	3.148
S&P 500 INFO TECH Index	−0.387	−0.14	7.32	−5.81	2.500	0.265	3.513
S&P 500 High Beta Index	−0.405	−0.59	6.74	−6.3	2.704	0.295	3.073

Note: The $t = 0$ is assumed to be the date associated to the September 11, 2001 terrorist attack.

Table 6.3. The tables contain the descriptive statistics of the daily returns for the period $t = -120, -119, \ldots, t = 1$.

Top 10	**Mean**	**Median**	**Max**	**Min**	**Std. dev.**	**Skewness**	**Kurtosis**
S&P 500 High Beta Index	0.471	0.35	6.79	−5.36	2.130	0.116	3.199
S&P 500 Utilities Index	0.362	0.27	3.88	−2.21	1.158	0.642	4.116
S&P 500 Commun Services Index	0.360	0.395	8.36	−4.57	1.770	0.592	5.656
S&P 500 Pure Value Index	0.353	0.285	3.31	−3.28	1.210	−0.154	2.886
S&P 500 High Dividend Index	0.335	0.2145	2.889	−3.317	1.135	−0.127	3.082
S&P 500 Financials Index	0.333	0.24	4.3	−3.7	1.333	−0.116	3.695
S&P 500 Quality-Lowest Quintile Index	0.324	0.305	3.4	−3.42	1.213	−0.209	3.324
S&P 500 Value Index	0.308	0.366	3.475	−3.534	1.214	−0.176	3.448
S&P 500 Cons Discret Index	0.308	0.14285	4.8366	−4.7201	1.445	0.205	4.246
S&P Mid Cap Index	0.296	0.14	3.16	−3.13	1.102	0.067	3.140

Bottom 10	**Mean**	**Median**	**Max**	**Min**	**Std. dev.**	**Skewness**	**Kurtosis**
S&P 500 Quality Index	0.224	0.044	3.518	−3.493	1.170	0.128	3.436
S&P 500 Health Care Index	0.200	0.34	3.14	−3.48	1.217	−0.219	3.195
S&P 500 Growth Index	0.200	0.015	3.64	−3.51	1.196	0.219	3.437
MSCI USA Defense Sectors Index	0.185	0.05	2.69	−2.74	0.964	−0.243	3.123
MSCI USA Quality Index	0.175	0	3.55	−3.37	1.115	0.161	3.705
Russell 2000 Dividend Growth Index	0.173	0	2.408	−1.851	0.876	0.262	2.760
S&P 500 INFO TECH Index	0.158	−0.035	5.4	−4.21	1.687	0.397	3.466
S&P 500 Consumer Staples Index	0.141	0.175	2.65	−2.78	0.974	0.006	3.208
S&P 500 Energy Index	0.135	0.09	2.4	−2	0.931	0.145	2.750
Russell 1000 Value/ Growth Index	0.060	0.03	0.94	−0.85	0.393	0.144	2.812

Note: The $t = 0$ is assumed to be the date associated to the SARS outbreak, July 5, 2003.

Table 6.4. The tables contain the descriptive statistics of the daily returns for the period $t = -120, -119, \ldots, t = 1$.

Top 10	Mean	Median	Max	Min	Std. dev.	Skewness	Kurtosis
Russell 2000 Dividend Growth	0.067	0	5.652	−4.065	1.856	0.390	3.464
Russell 1000 Value/ Growth Index	0.014	−0.095	1.88	−1.34	0.660	0.451	2.848
Russell 2000 Value Index	0.002	0.133	4.604	−3.286	1.680	0.370	3.065
S&P 500 Consumer Staples Index	−0.010	−0.04	2.33	−2.5	1.015	0.055	3.075
S&P US 600 Index	−0.017	0.146	3.486	−3.146	1.445	0.122	2.881
Russell 1000 Dividend Growth Index	−0.018	−0.0195	4.744	−3.469	1.636	0.340	3.254
S&P 500 Div Aristocrat Index	−0.024	−0.064975	3.7693	−3.18001	1.483	0.241	3.028
Russell 2000 Index	−0.032	0.0015	3.72	−3.488	1.519	0.113	2.811
S&P 500 Health Care Index	−0.044	0.055	2.94	−2.59	1.084	0.067	3.243
S&P 500 Low Volatility	−0.051	0.07	2.67	−2.63	1.024	0.113	3.599

Table 6.4. (*Continued*)

Bottom 10	Mean	Median	Max	Min	Std. dev.	Skewness	Kurtosis
S&P 500 Pure Value Index	−0.184	−0.295	6.01	−5.18	2.112	0.268	3.165
S&P 500 Momentum Index	−0.194	−0.14	3.168	−4.174	1.243	−0.137	3.144
S&P 500 Quality — Lowest Quintile Index	−0.202	−0.235	5.72	−5.17	1.859	0.152	3.424
S&P 500 Financials Index	−0.208	−0.6	12.3	−6.74	3.009	0.684	4.781
S&P 500 INFO TECH Index	−0.214	−0.16	2.78	−3.55	1.419	−0.208	2.470
S&P 500 Commun Services Index	−0.235	−0.565	3.35	−3.36	1.520	0.415	2.828
MSCI World High Dividend Yield Index	−0.244	−0.35	3.65	−2.88	1.174	0.680	3.594
S&P 500 High Beta Index	−0.247	−0.17	9.01	−7.8	2.711	0.088	3.864
S&P 500 Energy Index	−0.249	−0.49	5.59	−6.41	1.952	0.130	3.646
S&P 500 Utilities Index	−0.295	−0.105	2.42	−3.32	1.305	−0.351	2.389

Note: The $t = 0$ is assumed to be the date associated to the Lehman Brothers collapse, September 15, 2008.

Table 6.5. The tables contain the descriptive statistics of the daily returns for the period $t = -120, -119, \ldots, t = 1$.

Top 10	**Mean**	**Median**	**Max**	**Min**	**Std. dev.**	**Skewness**	**Kurtosis**
S&P 500 Materials Index	0.038	−0.03	3.91	−4.41	1.858	−0.135	2.561
S&P 500 Utilities Index	0.027	0.1	3.12	−3.21	1.143	−0.350	3.945
Russell 1000 Value/ Growth Index	−0.003	−0.07	0.92	−0.97	0.355	0.613	3.977
S&P 500 High Dividend Index	−0.020	−0.066	3.045	−3.524	1.274	−0.336	3.764
S&P 500 Commun Services Index	−0.023	0.005	2.42	−2.7	0.984	−0.046	3.149
S&P 500 Pure Growth Index	−0.036	−0.01	4.34	−4.27	1.788	−0.148	3.083
S&P 500 Low Volatility Index	−0.043	0.03	2.33	−3.03	1.001	−0.448	4.119
Russell 2000 Growth Index	−0.060	−0.171	4.005	−4.66	1.995	−0.214	2.739
S&P 500 Quality -Lowest Quintile Index	−0.063	−0.17	4.24	−4.41	1.739	−0.165	3.071
MSCI World High Dividend Yield Index	−0.067	0.08	2.75	−2.91	1.171	−0.513	3.548

Table 6.5. (*Continued*)

Bottom 10	Mean	Median	Max	Min	Std. dev.	Skewness	Kurtosis
S&P 500 Value Index	−0.117	−0.136	3.357	−4.036	1.460	−0.223	3.332
S&P 500 Financials Index	−0.120	−0.175	4.45	−4.72	2.037	−0.016	2.755
Russell 2000 Value Index	−0.122	−0.073	4.678	−5.503	2.110	−0.271	2.960
S&P 500 Pure Value	−0.124	−0.11	4.21	−4.84	1.792	−0.305	3.263
S&P 500 Quality Index	−0.130	−0.102	2.954	−3.695	1.264	−0.309	3.747
S&P 500 Industrials Index	−0.135	−0.165	3.86	−4.58	1.758	−0.335	3.362
S&P 500 INFO TECH Index	−0.139	−0.23	3.66	−3.84	1.442	−0.054	3.345
S&P 500 Cons Discret Index	−0.144	−0.0991	3.5226	−3.8083	1.639	−0.193	2.858
S&P 500 High Beta Index	−0.147	−0.305	5.4	−5.54	2.428	−0.111	2.837
S&P 500 Energy Index	−0.163	−0.2	4.91	−4.43	1.720	0.305	3.636

Note: The $t = 0$ is assumed to be the date associated to the Gulf of Mexico oil spill, September 8, 2010.

Table 6.6. The tables contain the descriptive statistics of the daily returns for the period $t = -120, -119, \ldots, t = 1$.

Top 10	Mean	Median	Max	Min	Std. dev.	Skewness	Kurtosis
S&P 500 Commun Services	0.103	0.1	2.79	−1.83	0.897	−0.060	2.819
S&P 500 Utilities Index	0.090	0.175	1.23	−1.33	0.533	−0.169	2.608
S&P 500 Low Volatility Index	0.064	0.08	1.57	−1.4	0.621	−0.020	3.121
S&P 500 Consumer Staples Index	0.047	−0.05	1.85	−1.66	0.671	0.122	3.656
S&P 500 High Dividend Index	0.030	−0.018	1.678	−1.769	0.730	−0.076	2.965
Russell 1000 Value/Growth Index	0.012	0.085	0.8	−1.13	0.360	−0.477	3.329
S&P 500 Div Aristocrat Index	0.010	−0.02036	2.25155	−2.10359	0.880	0.058	3.240
MSCI USA Defensive Sectors Index	0.009	0	2.05	−2	0.812	0.088	3.072
S&P 500 Health Care Index	−0.001	0.04	1.85	−1.77	0.825	−0.063	2.524
S&P500 Momentum Index	−0.003	0.0405	2.051	−2.504	0.905	−0.344	3.504

Table 6.6. *(Continued)*

Bottom 10	Mean	Median	Max	Min	Std. dev.	Skewness	Kurtosis
Russell 2000 Growth Index	−0.080	−0.104	3.101	−3.479	1.397	−0.071	2.819
S&P Mid Cap Index	−0.100	−0.04	2.83	−3.17	1.223	−0.142	3.184
MSCI USA Cyclical Sectors Index	−0.112	−0.155	2.84	−3.04	1.196	0.115	3.231
S&P 500 Quality -Lowest Quintile Index	−0.130	−0.27	2.86	−3.18	1.253	−0.018	2.849
S&P 500 INFO TECH Index	−0.133	−0.235	3.3	−2.73	1.309	0.451	3.241
S&P 500 Financials Index	−0.150	−0.27	2.97	−3.71	1.406	−0.045	2.936
S&P 500 Pure Value Index	−0.199	−0.31	3.08	−3.3	1.343	0.026	2.679
S&P 500 High Beta Index	−0.223	−0.4	3.86	−4.06	1.726	0.157	2.857

Note: The $t = 0$ is assumed to be the date associated to the "Whatever it takes," statement by the president of ECB on July 26, 2012.

Table 6.7. The tables contain the descriptive statistics of the daily returns for the period $t = -120, -119, \ldots, t = 1$.

Top 10	**Mean**	**Median**	**Max**	**Min**	**Std. dev.**	**Skewness**	**Kurtosis**
S&P 500 Utilities Index	0.038	0.235	5.86	−5.64	1.291	−0.137	12.678
S&P500 Momentum Index	−0.016	0.1075	5.343	−6.036	1.282	−0.246	11.309
S&P 500 Consumer Staples Index	−0.029	0.095	5.48	−4.41	1.114	0.666	12.976
S&P 500 Low Volatility Index	−0.031	0.095	5.06	−6.22	1.237	−0.636	12.675
S&P 500 Health Care Index	−0.033	0.05	5.81	−5.19	1.325	0.386	8.631
S&P 500 INFO TECH Index	−0.039	0.245	6.6	−7.56	1.711	−0.450	8.385
Russell 1000 Growth Index	−0.048	0.1107	5.3061	−6.8963	1.418	−0.623	10.074
S&P 500 Growth Index	−0.060	0.125	5.44	−7.23	1.432	−0.717	10.781
MSCI USA Quality Index	−0.064	0.11	5.26	−6.55	1.394	−0.488	9.732
S&P 500 Commun Services	−0.078	0.1	4.53	−6.21	1.273	−0.925	9.541

Table 6.7. (*Continued*)

Bottom 10	Mean	Median	Max	Min	Std. dev.	Skewness	Kurtosis
S&P 500 Buyback	−0.283	−0.15	5.06	−9.17	1.547	−1.423	12.442
Russell 2000 Index	−0.284	−0.246	3.041	−9.36	1.393	−2.372	17.188
S&P500 High Dividend Index	−0.288	−0.117	4.015	−10.966	1.564	−2.708	20.659
S&P 500 Materials Index	−0.291	−0.135	4.15	−9.26	1.537	−1.591	12.947
S&P 500 Financials Index	−0.320	−0.11	6.04	−10.91	1.769	−1.624	14.344
S&P US 600 Index	−0.326	−0.121	3.142	−9.643	1.445	−2.266	16.490
S&P 500 High Beta Index	−0.341	0.01	6.49	−12.8	2.009	−1.987	14.989
Russell 2000 Value Index	−0.353	−0.248	3.014	−10.25	1.448	−2.720	20.180
S&P 500 Pure Value Index	−0.436	−0.135	5.66	−11.92	1.813	−2.163	16.415
S&P 500 Energy Index	−0.602	−0.405	5	−20.08	2.486	−4.183	33.075

Note: The $t = 0$ is assumed to be the date associated to the COVID-19 outbreak, March 11, 2020.

Table 6.8. Cumulative abnormal returns calculated using the constant mean model as the normal return.

Event day 120	Dot-com bubble	September 11 terrorist attack	SARS outbreak	Lehman Brothers collapse	Gulf of Mexico oil spill	"Whatever it takes"	COVID-19 outbreak
	31/03/00	11/09/01	06/07/03	15/09/08	08/09/10	26/07/12	11/03/20
Russell 2000 Index	−34.169**	37.805	−27.668**	10.598*	51.263**	23.493*	74.683
Russell 2000 Value Index	−0.226*	27.758	−28.647	11.737*	50.470**	24.850*	74.425
Russell 2000 Growth Index	−58.827	48.093	−26.643**	9.832*	51.680	22.088*	74.975
Russell 2000 Dividend Growth Index	15.102*	15.007*	−17.282*	−2.628*	33.708*	13.430*	29.367**
Russell 1000 Index	−21.680*	35.493	−22.612*	−20.631*	38.793	21.560*	46.660
Russell 1000 Growth Index	−27.425*	48.202	−19.627*	16.125*	41.553	22.046*	43.733
Russell 1000 Value Index	−15.790*	24.254	−25.752	25.644	35.970*	21.083	49.554
Russell 1000 Value/Growth Index	11.653*	−23.918	−6.040*	9.496*	−5.617*	−0.851*	1.287*
Russell 1000 Dividend Growth Index	6.628*	13.927**	−21.835*	3.102*	31.101**	13.830*	35.766
MSCI USA Cyclical Sectors Index	−32.153*	52.666	−13.947*	15.437*	41.636	29.132**	50.864
MSCI USA Defensive Sectors Index	10.540*	11.474*	−22.825**	8.479*	30.038	6.962*	32.728
MSCI World High Dividend Yield Index	339.290	8.496*	−21.935**	−1.706*	17.317*	19.505*	28.552
MSCI USA Quality Index	−11.087*	40.059	−15.345*	8.991*	36.135	20.465*	37.034
S&P 500 Energy Index	16.712*	15.493*	−9.075*	35.009*	57.123	24.222*	109.572

S&P 500 Financials Index	−14.640*	28.028	−32.523**	47.808*	34.280*	36.870	76.000
S&P 500 Health Care Index	21.288*	29.235**	−32.740	3.904*	26.595**	11.571*	28.683*
S&P 500 Info Tech Index	−42.540*	87.997	13.92*	22.984*	47.629	26.743*	46.398
S&P 500 Cons Discret Index	−25.034*	64.150	−23.765*	6.867*	48.406	25.473**	45.741
S&P 500 Utilities Index	1.393*	1.852*	−39.442	40.416	0.873*	−19.160	−3.138*
S&P 500 Cons Staples Index	39.030*	4.809*	−14.591*	−6.400*	23.158**	−10.17*	18.579*
S&P 500 Industrials Index	−13.556*	41.765	−22.983*	15.322*	44.475	26.258**	42.523
S&P 500 Materials Index	−25.409*	25.569*	−14.692*	−0.258*	32.662*	22.666*	84.621
S&P 500 Communic Services	−31.720*	17.696*	−47.710	37.224**	16.753*	−14.743*	30.078**
S&P Mid Cap Index	−15.365*	26.552	−21.226*	19.950*	41.093*	28.730*	67.253
S&P US 600 SC Index	−226.594	21.361*	−28.043**	5.648*	50.414	20.027*	73.690
S&P 500 Value Index	−15.084*	31.366	−26.331**	24.248*	36.653**	23.196*	44.854
S&P 500 Growth Index	−17.383*	40.676	−18.080*	14.497*	39.478	17.324*	43.380
S&P 500 Div Aristocrat Index	1.523*	14.676*	−26.034**	11.973*	25.524*	13.808*	43.351
S&P 500 Buyback Index	−14.214*	23.771	−20.607*	18.566*	34.839	23.372**	58.613
S&P 500 High Beta Index	−32.891*	88.815	−38.401*	56.757*	56.227**	54.543	81.072
S&P 500 Low Volatility Index	15.309*	11.472*	−18.903**	4.921*	19.323*	−4.024*	20.051*
S&P 500 Pure Value Index	2.595*	15.094*	−27.223**	23.523*	42.714**	50.909	89.285
S&P 500 Pure Growth Index	−36.918*	61.390	−25.720*	16.690*	42.556**	25.071*	53.108
S&P500 High Dividend Index	16.869*	6.766*	−28.763	8.191*	18.499*	2.617*	59.199
S&P 500 Quality Index	−5.675*	31.209	−21.009*	16.606*	40.261	21.840*	39.984
S&P500 Momentum Index	−31.544*	29.951	−23.773	20.772*	41.769	9.831*	37.582
S&P 500 Quality-Lowest Quintile Index	−26.461*	42.962*	−30.904	18.722*	34.543*	35.270	47.213
S&P 500 Index	−16.106*	36.318	−22.163*	20.323*	38.108	20.002*	44.607

Note: Statistical significant cumulative abnormal returns at 1% (5%) level are denoted with "**" ("*").

Table 6.9. Cumulative abnormal returns calculated using the market model as the normal return.

Event day 120	Dot-com bubble	September 11th terrorist attack	SARS outbreak	Lehman Brothers collapse	Gulf of Mexico oil spill	"Whatever it takes"	COVID-19 outbreak
	31/03/00	11/09/01	05/07/03	15/09/08	08/09/10	26/07/12	11/03/20
Russell 2000 Index	−22.988*	7.695*	−8.855*	−10.662*	51.263	−1.483*	32.787
Russell 2000 Value Index	8.160*	4.657*	−10.791*	−11.526*	50.470	1.248*	31.509
Russell 2000 Growth Index	−45.834	9.954	−6.846*	−9.435*	51.680	−4.266*	34.017
Russell 2000 Dividend Growth Index	21.013	−4.538*	−3.770*	−26.996	33.708	−3.658*	−4.766*
Russell 1000 Index	−5.599	−0.704*	−0.862*	0.724*	38.793	1.270	2.229
Russell 1000 Growth Index	−9.216*	0.023*	3.092*	−17.36*	41.553	1.093*	−1.149*
Russell 1000 Value Index	−2.798*	−1.622*	−5.031**	3.549	35.970	1.470*	5.598*
Russell 1000 Value/Growth Index	6.430*	−1.601*	−8.035*	5.255*	−5.617*	0.481*	2.143
Russell 1000 Dividend Growth Index	18.111*	−4.536*	−4.218*	−20.332	31.101	−3.606*	−4.738
MSCI USA Cyclical Sectors Index	−15.731	6.840**	10.067	−10.040**	41.636	5.852	3.994
MSCI USA Defensive Sectors Index	22.786**	−7.946*	−6.206*	−3.671*	30.038	−8.453	−6.022*
MSCI World High Dividend Yield Index	344.867	−7.388*	−7.682*	−12.454*	17.317	4.468*	−1.255
MSCI USA Quality Index	4.616*	2.053*	4.815*	−7.414**	36.135	0.072*	−7.137

S&P 500 Energy Index	25.628*	0.101*	1.903*	24.447*	57.123	0.826*	43.465
S&P 500 Financials Index	3.818*	0.296*	−8.795*	8.329*	34.280	11.039**	21.798
S&P 500 Health Care Index	38.576	5.858*	−13.016*	−10.113	26.595	−3.393*	−9.952*
S&P 500 info Tech Index	−24.376*	12.212*	29.254	3.719*	47.629	2.856*	−6.137*
S&P 500 Cons Discret Index	−9.545	21.169	2.013*	−20.031**	48.406	5.412*	75.47*
S&P 500 Utilities Index	9.642*	−7.909*	−27.101	28.252	0.873	−25.618	−33.770
S&P 500 Cons Staples Index	52.208	−7.335*	1.350*	−19.096	23.158	−12.474	−12.390**
S&P 500 Industrials Index	2.980*	3.559*	0.083*	−7.699*	44.475	3.705*	−2.907
S&P 500 Materials Index	−12.153*	−4.864*	8.696*	−18.272*	32.662	−0.390*	38.739
S&P 500 Communic Services	−16.616*	14.004*	−22.125*	19.230*	16.753	−25.725	−8.678**
S&P Mid Cap Index	−1.076*	−3.905*	−2.113*	1.389*	41.093	5.521*	23.791
S&P US 600 SC Index	−212.323	−6.032*	−9.794*	−14.854	50.414	−4.120*	31.024
S&P 500 Value Index	−0.886*	0.573*	−3.999*	0.567*	36.653	2.457*	1.255
S&P 500 Growth Index	0.410*	−1.280*	3.923*	−25.92*	39.478	−2.079*	−2.054
S&P 500 Div Aristocrat Index	14.716	−6.650*	−5.808**	−9.376	25.524	−3.086*	4.300
S&P 500 Buyback Index	1.169*	−3.064	0.587*	−3.923	34.839	2.768*	10.351
S&P 500 High Beta Index	−12.156*	8.326*	−2.529*	19.379*	56.227	21.740	21.236
S&P 500 Low Volatility Index	25.245	−4.278*	−3.437	−9.781**	19.323	−15.335	−14.993
S&P 500 Pure Value Index	12.774*	−10.190*	−6.980*	−5.847*	42.714	25.588	34.209

(Continued)

Table 6.9. (*Continued*)

Event day 120	Dot-com bubble	September 11th terrorist attack	SARS outbreak	Lehman Brothers collapse	Gulf of Mexico oil spill	"Whatever it takes"	COVID-19 outbreak
S&P 500 Pure Growth Index	−17.578*	3.176*	1.447*	−1.963*	42.556	2.995*	6.026
S&P500 High Dividend Index	27.161	−13.375	−9.879*	−19.692**	18.499	−10.880	11.788**
S&P 500 Quality Index	11.470*	1.063*	0.472*	−1.548*	40.261	1.097*	−3.484*
S&P500 Momentum Index	−13.617	10.558	−7.819	6.444*	41.769	−6.858**	−2.010*
S&P 500 Quality -Lowest Quintile Index	−10.151*	3.323*	−8.755	−8.445*	34.543	11.341	2.361*

Note: Statistical significant cumulative abnormal returns at 1% (5%) level are denoted with "**" ("*").

returns found are inconsistent with the hypothesis that security prices adjust quickly to reflect new information fully. The intuition behind the differences in the results of the constant mean model and market model is that the former focuses on the returns to each index around its event. We test whether or not the cumulative abnormal returns on the sample indices are statistically significantly different from zero. The latter takes into account market-wide movements that occurred at the same time that the indices experienced events. Additionally, a notable remark is that the statistically significant post-event cumulative abnormal returns tend to be mostly positive, except in the SARS outbreak and the Lehman Brothers collapse. An environmental disaster like the one caused by the Gulf of Mexico oil spill did not yield any CAR except in two indices.

Table 6.10 shows the average daily CAR implied by the two models considering only the statistically significant CAR. The reactions to the September 11 terrorist attack are less severe than those thought initially. However, the economy in the US in the months before the terrorist attack showed signs of weakness, raising fears that the event would push both the economy and stock market into a steep decline. The constant model implies an average daily CAR of 25% and the market model, −0.2%. A notable result is also obtained comparing the SARS and the COVID-19 outbreaks. Regarding the sign of the average CAR, only in the SARS outbreak event, both are negative, contrary to the COVID-19 pandemic, in which both are positive. An explanation is that the policies adopted to combat these two crises were different. The Federal Reserve Bank (FED) has maintained negative or rock-bottom interest rates and aggressively expanded quantitative easing program, reactivating the Term Asset-Backed Securities Loan Facility — first established in late 2008 — and also established the Paycheck Protection Program Liquidity Facility to provide liquidity against payroll loans guaranteed by the Treasury. Before the financial crisis of 2007, in no other cases, the market experienced such low interest rates. Similarly, after the COVID-19 outbreak emerged, the FED's quick response indicates lesson. Bhar and Malliaris (2020), making a preliminary comparison between the financial crisis of 2007 and COVID-19, mention that the FED's balance sheet increased from about US$1 trillion in late 2008

Table 6.10. Daily average cumulative abnormal return based on 120-days window.

Model	Dot-com bubble	September 11 terrorist attack	SARS outbreak	Lehman brothers collapse
Constant mean model	−6.5%	25%	−19%	13.6%
Market model	4.9%	−0.2%	−2.9%	−3.5%
Model	**Lehman Mexico oil spill**	**Gulf of it takes**	**Whatever COVID-19 outbreak**	
Constant mean model	29.6%	15.8%	40.8%	
Market model	−1.97%	−0.4%	5.6%	

Note: Only statistical significant cumulative abnormal returns are considered to the calculations.

to US$4.5 trillion in late 2014 and remained at that level during 2015–2017, whereas its balance sheet expanded to US$7 trillion in late May 2020 in brief period of US two months. Nevertheless, considerations are expressed about these intensive policy measures to save the troubled financial markets (see, e.g. Zhang *et al.* (2020)). The measures have to mitigate the effects of the widespread infection of the population, the millions of deaths, the lockdown of cities, and many other health measures, leading to economic depressions around the world (Barro *et al.*, 2020). Furthermore, these policies may have positive implications in the short run. Still, they may create inconsistencies between investors' short-term and long-term expectations (Gormsen and Koijen, 2020) or increase the systemic risk significantly at the time (see Yang and Zhou, 2017).

6.5. Conclusions

This chapter analyses the impact of various unanticipated events on the returns of US stock market sector indices. Although the indices belong to the same local market and are expected to show uniform responses to shocks, the degree of stock market reactions differs significantly. Especially, with regard to the COVID-19 outbreak, there is clear evidence that the US stock market sector indices positively over-reacted to this unanticipated event. An explanation is the policies adopted to combat the crisis. Policy reactions to contain the virus are necessary; however, the continuous non-conventional policy interventions may cause long-term problems. Nevertheless, the short-term response of the US sector stock indices in response to the event and the measures adopted are vital for policymakers, investors, academicians, portfolio managers, and researchers.

Disclaimer

This study should not be reported as representing the views of the Piraeus Bank. The views expressed are those of the author and do not necessarily reflect those of the Piraeus Bank.

Appendix

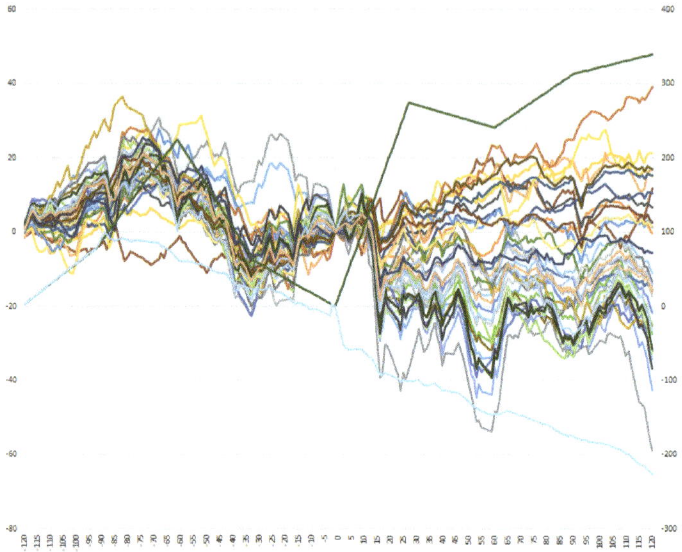

(a)

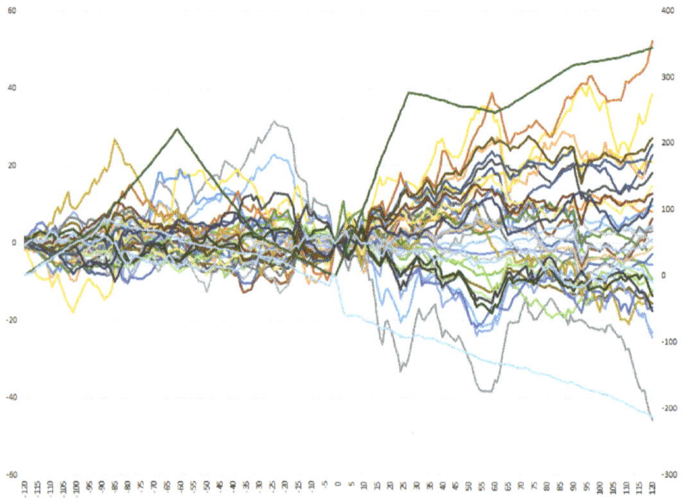

(b)

Figure 6A.1. Dot-com bubble. (a) Plot of cumulative abnormal returns calculated using the constant mean model as the normal return. (b) Plot of cumulative abnormal returns calculated using the market model as the normal return.

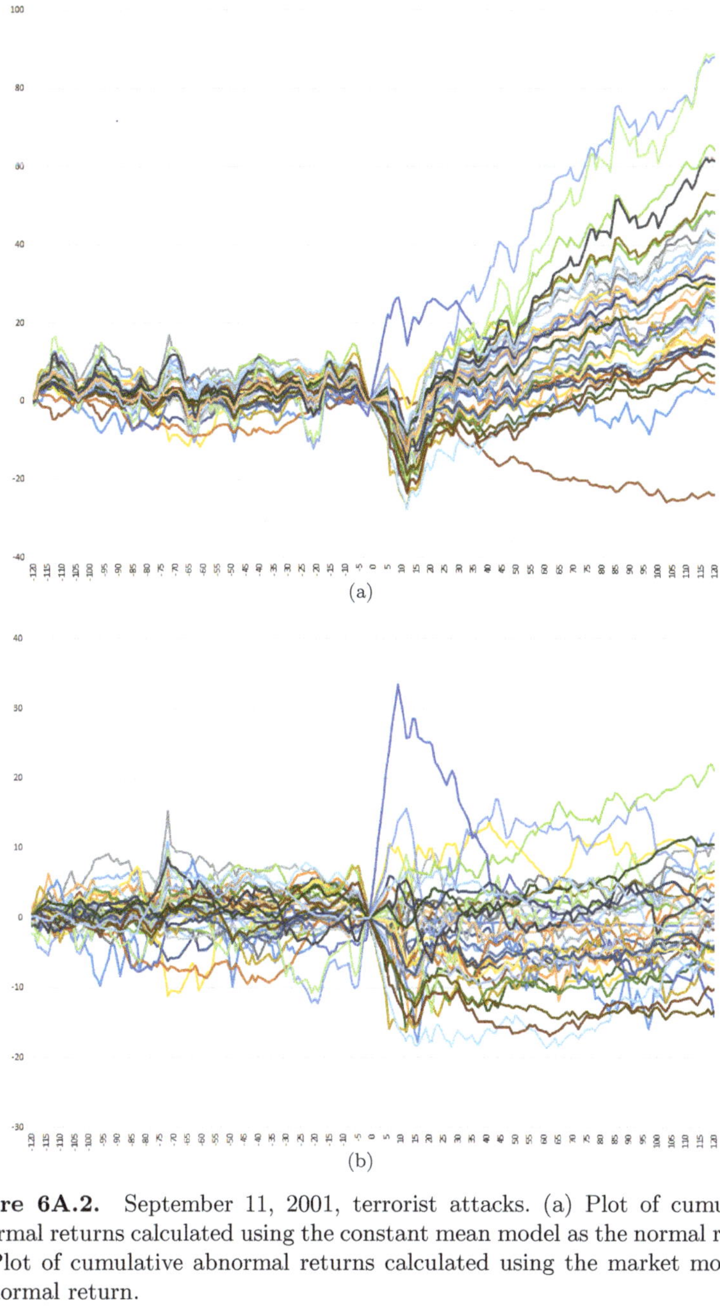

Figure 6A.2. September 11, 2001, terrorist attacks. (a) Plot of cumulative abnormal returns calculated using the constant mean model as the normal return. (b) Plot of cumulative abnormal returns calculated using the market model as the normal return.

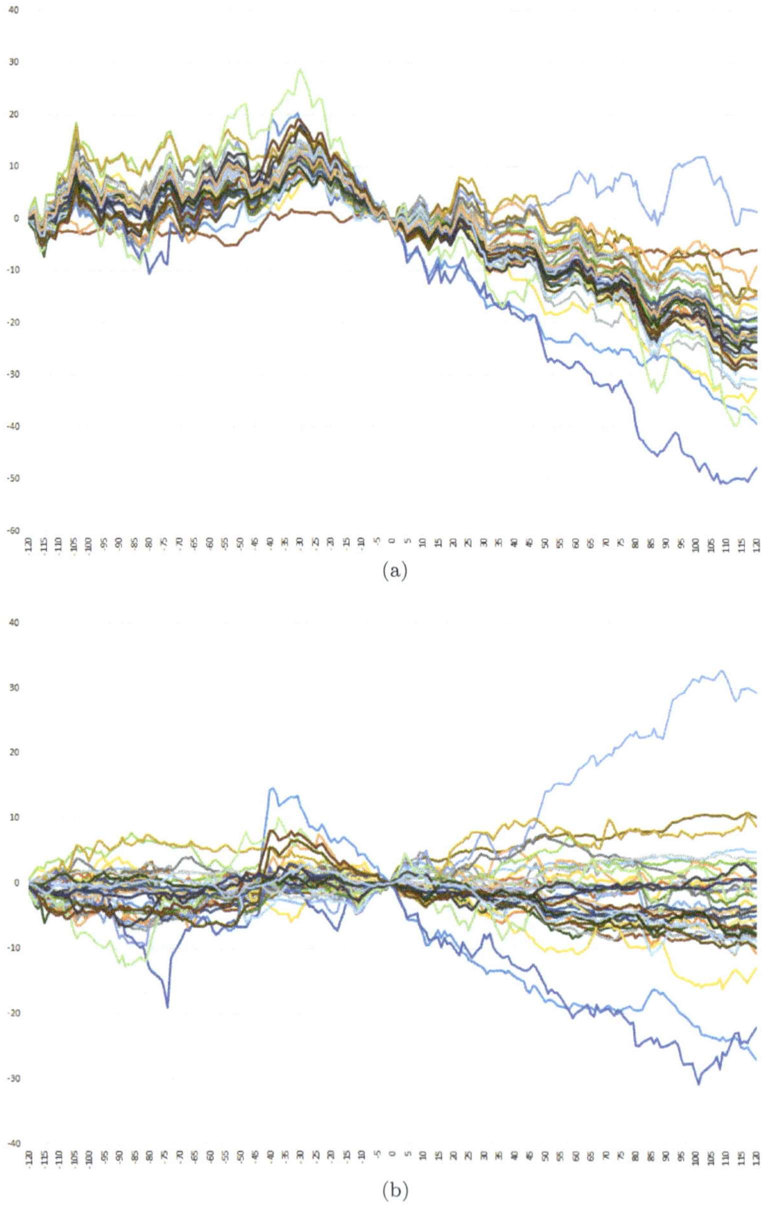

Figure 6A.3. SARS. (a) Plot of cumulative abnormal returns calculated using the constant mean model as the normal return. (b) Plot of cumulative abnormal returns calculated using the market model as the normal return.

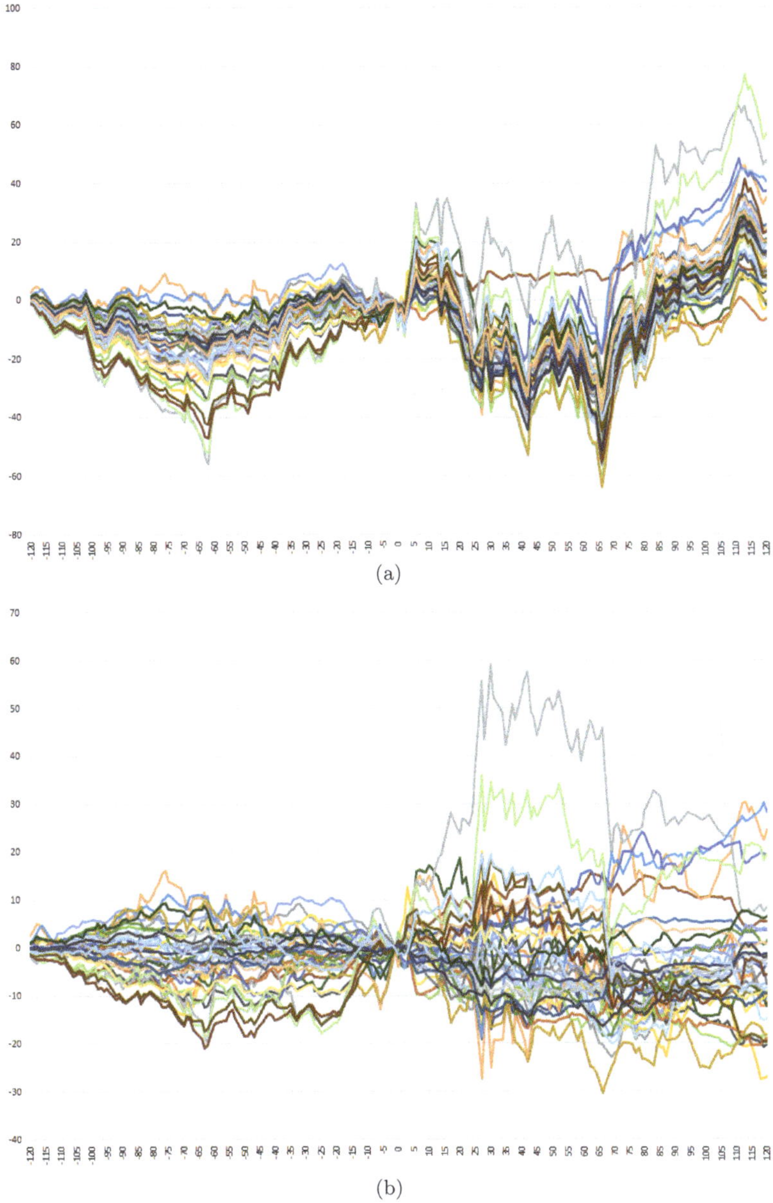

Figure 6A.4. Lehman Brothers collapse. (a) Plot of cumulative abnormal returns calculated using the constant mean model as the normal return. (b) Plot of cumulative abnormal returns calculated using the market model as the normal return.

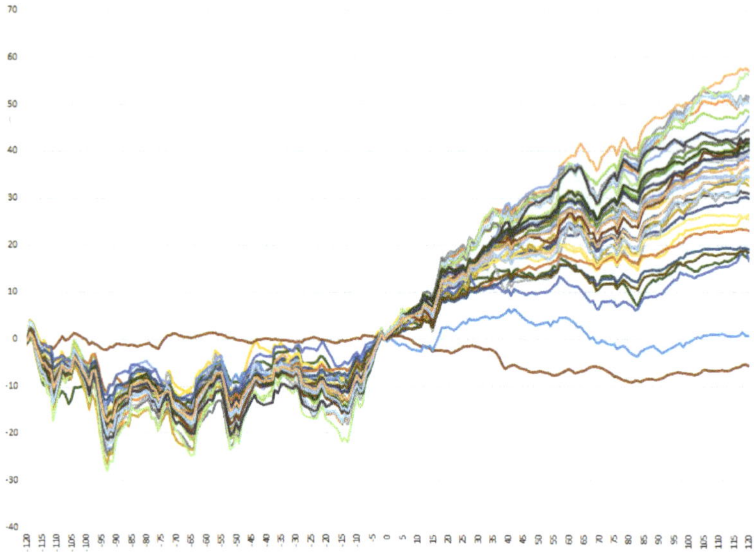

(a)

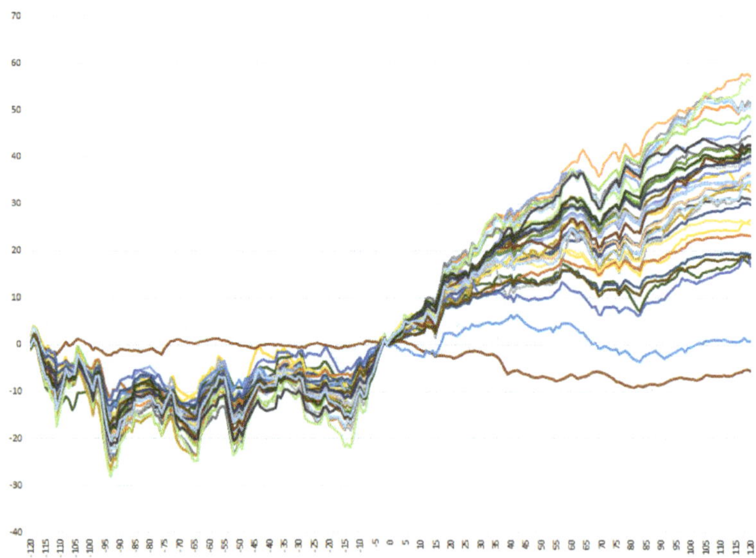

(b)

Figure 6A.5. BP oil spill in gulf of Mexico, 2010. (a) Plot of cumulative abnormal returns calculated using the constant mean model as the normal return. (b) Plot of cumulative abnormal returns calculated using the market model as the normal return.

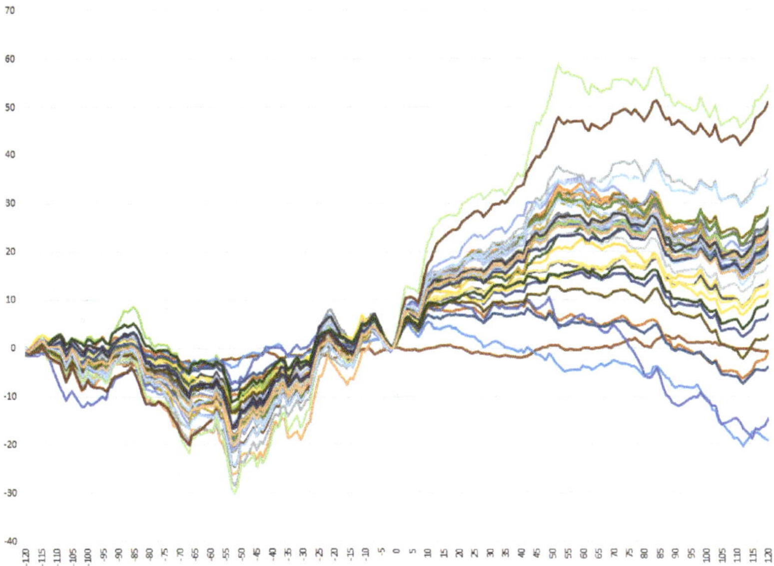

(a)

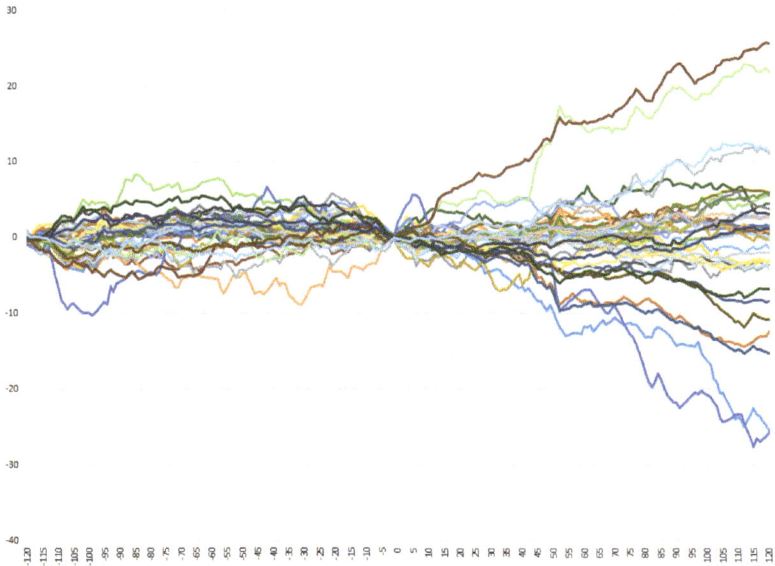

(b)

Figure 6A.6. "Whatever it takes" statement by the president of ECB. (a) Plot of cumulative abnormal returns calculated using the constant mean model as the normal return. (b) Plot of cumulative abnormal returns calculated using the market model as the normal return.

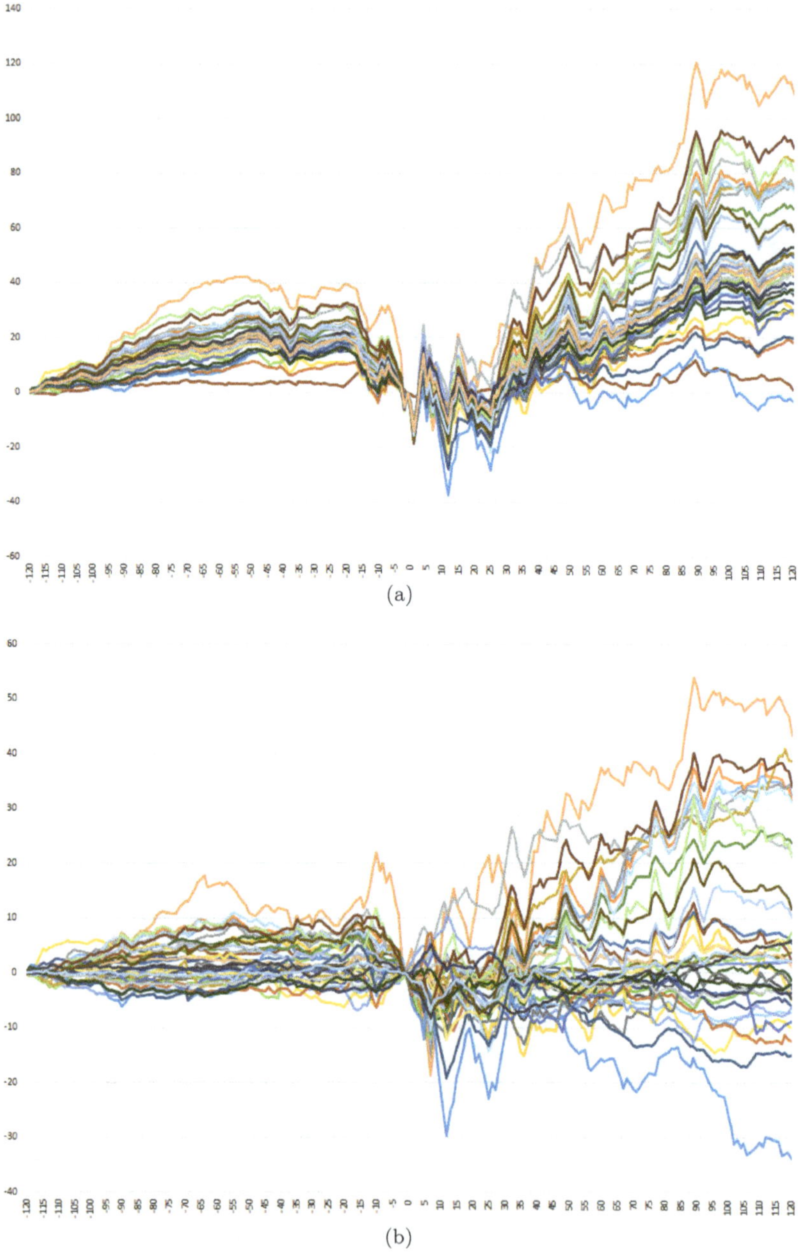

(a)

(b)

Figure 6A.7. COVID-19. (a) Plot of cumulative abnormal returns calculated using the constant mean model as the normal return. (b) Plot of cumulative abnormal returns calculated using the market model as the normal return.

Acknowledgement

This paper has received funding from the European Union's Horizon 2020 research and innovation program "FIN-TECH: A Financial supervision and Technology compliance training programme" under the grant agreement No 825215 (Topic: ICT-35-2018, Type of action: CSA). Also, it is based upon work from COST Action 19130, supported by COST (European Cooperation in Science and Technology).

References

Albulescu, C. (2020). COVID-19 and the united states financial markets' volatility. *Finance Research Letters*, **38**, 101699.

Ali, M., Alam, N. and Rizvi, S.A.R. (2020). Coronavirus (COVID-19) — an epidemic or pandemic for financial markets. *Journal of Behavioral and Experimental Finance*, **27**, 100341.

Ashley, J.W. (1962). Stock prices and changes in earnings and dividends. *Journal of Political Economy*, **70**(1), 82–85.

Baker, C. (1956). Effective stock splits. *Harvard Business Review*, **34**(1), 101–106.

Baker, C. (1957). Stock splits in a bull market. *Harvard Business Review*, **35**(3), 72–79.

Ball, R. and Brown, P. (1968). An empirical analysis of accounting income numbers. *Journal of Accounting Research*, **6**(2), 159–178.

Barro, R., Ursúa, J. and Weng, J. (2020). The coronavirus and the great influenza pandemic: Lessons from the "spanish flu" for the coronavirus's potential effects on mortality and economic activity. NBER Working Papers 26866, National Bureau of Economic Research, Inc.

Bhar, R. and Malliaris, A. (2020). Modeling U.S. monetary policy during the global financial crisis and lessons for COVID-19. *Journal of Policy Modeling*, **43**(1), 15–33.

Binder, J. (1998). The event study methodology since 1969. *Review of Quantitative Finance and Accounting*, **11**, 111–137.

Brooks, C. (2019). *Introductory Econometrics for Finance*, 4th edn, (Cambridge University Press).

Brown, K.C., Harlow, W. and Tinic, S.M. (1988). Risk aversion, uncertain information, and market efficiency. *Journal of Financial Economics*, **22**(2), 355–385.

Brown, S.J. and Warner, J.B. (1980). Measuring security price performance. *Journal of Financial Economics*, **8**(3), 205–58.

Brown, S.J. and Warner, J.B. (1985). Using daily stock returns: The case of event studies. *Journal of Financial Economics*, **14**(1), 3–31.

Campbell, J.Y., Lo, A.W. and MacKinlay, A.G. (1997). *The Econometrics of Financial Markets*, Princeton University Press.

Ciner, C. (2020). Stock return predictability in the time of COVID-19, *Finance Research Letters*, **38**, 101705.

Corrado, C.J. (1989). A nonparametric test for abnormal security price performance in event studies. *Journal of Financial Economics*, **23**, 385–395.

De Bondt, W.F.M. and Thaler, R. (1985). Does the stock market overreact? *The Journal of Finance*, **40**(3), 793–805.

Dolley, J. (1933). Characteristics and procedure of common stock split-ups. *Harvard Business Review*, **11**, 316–326.

Fama, E.F., Fisher, L., Jensen, M.C. and Roll, R. (1969). The adjustment of stock prices to new information. *International Economic Review*, **10**(1), 1–21.

Gormsen, N. and Koijen, R. (2020). Coronavirus: Impact on stock prices and growth expectations. *The Review of Asset Pricing Studies*, **10**(4), 574–597.

Heyden, K. and Heyden, T. (2020). Market reactions to the arrival and containment of COVID-19: An event study. *Finance Research Letters*, **38**, 101745.

Kothari, S. and Warner, J.B. (2007). Econometrics of event studies. In *Handbook of Empirical Corporate Finance, Handbooks in Finance*, Eckbo, B.E. (ed.), (Elsevier, San Diego), pp. 3–36.

Le, T.H., Do, H.X., Nguyen, D.K. and Sensoy, A. (2020). Covid-19 pandemic and tail-dependency networks of financial assets. *Finance Research Letters*, **38**, 101800.

Litner, J. (1965). The valuation of risky assets and the selection of risky investments in stock portfolios and capital budgets. *Review of Economics and Statistics*, **47**(1), 13–37.

Lyócsa, S., Baumöhl, E., Výrost, T. and Molnár, P. (2020). Fear of the coronavirus and the stock markets. *Finance Research Letters*, **36**, 101735.

MacKinlay, A.C. (1997). Event studies in economics and finance. *Journal of Economic Literature*, **35**(1), 13–39.

Mirza, N., Naqvi, B., Rahata, B. and Rizvic, S.K.A. (2020). Price reaction, volatility timing and funds' performance during COVID-19. *Finance Research Letters*, (36), 101657.

Mitchell, M.L. and Netter, J.M. (1994). The role of financial economics in securities fraud cases: Applications at the securities and exchange commission. *The Business Lawyer*, **49**(2), 545–590.

Pástor, L. and Vorsatz, M.B. (2020). Mutual Fund Performance and Flows during the COVID-19 Crisis. *The Review of Asset Pricing Studies*, **10**(4), 791–833.

Ross, S.A. (1976). The arbitrage theory of capital asset pricing. *Journal of Economic Theory*, **13**(3), 341–360.

Salisu, A.A. and Vob, X.V. (2020). Predicting stock returns in the presence of COVID-19 pandemic: The role of health news. *International Review of Financial Analysis*, **71**, 101546.

Schnusenberg, O. and Madura, J. (2014). Do U.S. stock market indexes over - or underreact?. *The Journal of Financial Research*, **24**(2), 179–204.

Schwert, G. (1981). Using financial data to measure the effect of regulation. *Journal of Law and Economics*, **24**, 121–157.

Sharpe, W.F. (1964). Capital asset prices: A theory of market equilibrium under conditions of risk. *Journal of Finance*, **19**(3), 425–442.

Sherif, M. (2020). The impact of coronavirus (COVID-19) outbreak on faith-based investments: An original analysis. *Journal of Behavioral and Experimental Finance*, **28**, 100403.

Yang, Z. and Zhou, Y. (2017). Quantitative easing and volatility spillovers across countries and asset classes. *Management Science*, **63**(2), 333–354.

Zhang, D., Hu, M. and Ji, Q. (2020). Financial markets under the global pandemic of COVID-19. *Finance Research Letters*, **36**, 101528.

https://doi.org/10.1142/9781800610781_0007

Chapter 7

Rational Behavior or Mere Panic? The Effects of the COVID-19 Pandemic on the Stock Markets

Moritz Johannes Herber[*,‡] **and Matthias Scherf**[†,§]

[*]*Copenhagen Business School, Copenhagen, Denmark*

[†]*University of Trier, Trier, Germany*

[‡]*moritz-herber@gmx.de*

[§]*scherfm@uni-trier.de*

Abstract

The negative effect of market sentiment on asset prices is well known in behavioral finance. In this study, we examine the effect of panic over the COVID-19 pandemic on the stock market. We find a significant negative effect of the panic caused by the pandemic on country indices of India, Italy, Germany, and the US, while for China and South Korea, we find no effect. To measure panic, we used data on COVID-19–related search results from Google, Naver, and Baidu. Controlling for cases and recoveries from COVID-19 showed that the panic over the pandemic had a greater impact on individual country indices than the pandemic itself.

7.1. Introduction

COVID-19 is keeping the world in suspense at the time of writing. Due to its rapid spread and sometimes poor preparation, hospitals

[§]Corresponding author.

and medical staff in many countries have been completely overburdened (Reuters, 2020a). In addition to the news about the medical care situation and the public discussion about the new virus, misleading rumors and conspiracy theories were circulating around the world shortly after the outbreak. Therefore, driven by social media, not only did the virus spread rapidly but so did the panic in society (Depoux *et al.*, 2020).

The novel SARS-CoV-2 virus, which is also simply known as the coronavirus, originated in Wuhan, China, and has spread to more than 213 countries and territories at the time of writing this chapter. More than 58 million cases and over 1 million deaths have been reported at the beginning of November 2020 according to the John Hopkins University (JHU). While the virus originated in China, the US, India, and the EU became hotspots of the pandemic and contributed to spreading the virus around the world (BBC, 2020a), with more than 33 million cases in the US, 29 million cases in India and 32 million cases in the EU by June 2021, according to JHU (OCHA, 2020). To avoid confusion, this chapter will focus on the disease caused by the novel coronavirus and use the term COVID-19, following the name of the WHO (World Health Organization and others, 2020a).

Furthermore, COVID-19 has had a big impact on the economy. The worldwide projected GDP growth rate is estimated to be −3,5% (International Monetary Fund (IMF) 2021). Some countries have been hit harder than others. While China has a positive projected GDP growth rate (1.8%), most other countries will have a negative growth rate according to the Organisation for Economic Co-operation and Development (OECD). The respective numbers for the US, India, Germany, and Italy are −3.8%, −10.2%, −5.4%, and −10.5% (OECD, 2020).

The influence of the virus can also be observed in the financial markets. On March 9, 2020, major stock indices lost about 10% of their value. This marks the highest daily loss since the attacks of September 11, 2001. Losses were even greater than those during the Global Financial Crisis of 2008. (Daube, 2020). Additionally, the financial Volatility Index (VIX), which is known to measure the "fear" circulating in financial markets, was recorded to be higher in March 2020 than it was during the Global Financial Crisis of 2008 (Leduc *et al.*, 2020). The COVID-19 pandemic has also affected oil prices (Sharif *et al.*, 2020), with oil being used as a commodity for

Figure 7.1. MSCI World Index price chart.
Source: Own representation based on data from investing.com (2020).

hedging in some mutual funds. Thus, altogether COVID-19 brings great uncertainty to the economy worldwide.

By contrast, Figure 7.1 shows that the MSCI World Index fully recovered by the beginning of September 2020, while the COVID-19 pandemic is still ongoing at the time of writing. This leaves the question of whether the sharp drops in the country's indices in March are a result of new information absorbed by rational investors or a result of panic about the uncertainty that arises from the social and economic impact of the virus?

Negative moods, such as panic, can lead to investors becoming more risk averse. They can be more pessimistic about future returns than the facts would suggest. Kaplanski and Levy (2010) note that stock market drops that are driven by fear tend to recover quickly. Because the recovery is relatively short compared to the still ongoing pandemic, we assume the following: "Investors did not act rationally during the COVID-19 pandemic. Panic had a greater impact on share prices than the actual facts."

This chapter studies the development of selected stock indices in China, Germany, India, Italy, South Korea, and the US in relation to the thesis of this work. China is studied as the first human cases of COVID-19 have been reported in Wuhan, China. In order to get a better picture of the Asian region, India and South Korea are also included. South Korea was one of the first countries affected while the pandemic reached India with a considerable delay. To take

European stock markets into account, Germany and Italy are examined. Germany is characterized by a low number of deaths per million inhabitants, while in Italy more than 24,000 had already died of COVID-19 on April 20, 2020. (OCHA, 2020) This chapter also looks at the US, which is the country with the most cases at the time of writing. As of June 2021 over 33 million cases have been confirmed in the US alone (World Health Organization and others, 2020b).

The results of this study show that panic has indeed a bigger impact on the stock market than the actual facts for India, Italy, Germany, and the US, while this cannot be confirmed for China and South Korea. We found that for India, Italy, Germany, and the US, a 1% increase in panic results in an average loss of 3–4% on the respective stock markets. Panic is measured by the search volume of keywords related to the novel coronavirus in the search engines Google, Naver, and Baidu. The key facts regarding the virus, such as the number of COVID-19 cases, do not show a significant effect or, contrary to expectations, show a weak positive effect on the respective country stock index.

Thus, this work contributes to the efforts aimed to identify key drivers behind the strong price drops in March 2020. Moreover, the chapter provides further evidence that investor sentiment plays an important role in describing returns and challenges the efficient market hypothesis (EMH). This is in line with Baker *et al.* (2012), who find that investor sentiment plays an important role in the prediction of market returns and that sentiment is "contagious" across markets.

The chapter is structured as follows. After providing the theoretical background of this work in Section 7.2, which includes a brief overview of the COVID-19 pandemic, the data, methodology as well as the hypothesis will be presented in ensuing sections. The last section contains concluding remarks about the study.

7.2. Theoretical Background

People show different levels of risk-taking attitudes depending on their mood. According to Yuen and Lee (2003), people with depressed moods have a lower willingness to take risks. Further studies support this relation. Lerner *et al.* (2004) found that emotions, such as fear and anger, have a dramatic impact on economic transactions.

These results can also be applied to investors trading on stock markets. According to Sperling *et al.* (2008), emotional components (such as panic in the population) play an important role in the pricing of a commodity and consequently in the price correction of shares traded on stock exchanges. Furthermore, international stock exchanges and financial centers are particularly sensitive to such affective disorders. (Sperling *et al.*, 2008). Bash and Alsaifi (2019) found a strong negative impact of fear, arising from uncertainty about Jamal Khashoggi's disappearance, on stock returns in Saudi Arabia. Kaplanski and Levy (2010) further show that negative sentiment of investors following aviation disasters results on average in a bigger price decline than the direct economic loss would warrant. The authors argue that if a stock market crash occurred due to an actual economic loss rather than the mood of the investors, there would not be any reversal effect. The existence of price reversals, therefore, suggests irrational behavior by market participants (Kaplanski and Levy, 2010). This reversal could also be seen after the initial sharp decline in international stock indices at the beginning of the COVID-19 pandemic. Figure 7.1 shows a clear price reversal of the MSCI World Index after its sharp decline in March 2020.

If people are affectively involved, as in the COVID-19 pandemic, this has an impact on their risk tolerance. Negative moods such as panic can make people more pessimistic, which in turn can reduce their willingness to take risks (Yuen and Lee, 2003). As a possible consequence, investors turn away from the stock market. Looking at the current media coverage of the COVID-19 pandemic, it can be assumed that it causes emotions such as fear and panic. This chapter deliberately refrains from analyzing the media coverage; instead, the influence of panic on the share price development will be measured directly.

A closer look at the stock market development reveals that the German and American indices show a very similar development. The DAX reached its trough on March 18, 2020 (8,442 points), while the DJIA hit rock bottom on March 23, 2020 (18,592 points). In addition, the SSE Composite Index reached its minimum on March 23, 2020 (5,320 points). However, the Chinese benchmark index already recorded significant price drops of more than 7% daily at the beginning of February 2020. This is probably due to the fact that COVID-19 affected China much earlier than most other countries.

While the number of cases in China flatlined at a level of around 80,000 at the beginning of March, COVID-19 did not spread noticeably in Germany and the US until mid-March. The pandemic reached Italy somewhat earlier than Germany, but the development in the number of infected persons showed a similar pattern. In the period considered in this chapter, India recorded only a few confirmed cases of COVID-19 (OCHA, 2020). Nevertheless, the stock market in India also plummeted significantly. All these events bear evidence to the irrational behavior of the market participants, at least in part.

On the other hand, we have the assumption of efficient markets, in which rational market participants trade securities and any potential mispricing is corrected immediately. Goldberg and von Nitzsch (2004) further state the following conditions for rationality: Market participants need unbiased information on which they base their decisions and they must not be misled by emotions such as panic. If one follows the efficient market hypothesis (EMH), no significant delay should be assumed. According to the thesis, the financial market reflects at any time all available information (Fama, 1970). Because key data about the spread of the novel coronavirus (e.g. COVID-19 cases) is reported daily, this means that according to the EMH, asset prices should reflect that information.

The price of a share depends on the expectations of the market participants regarding the future development of a variety of factors. These factors may include expected future corporate profits, the overall economic situation, or expected changes in interest rates. It should be noted that it is impossible to identify all factors and therefore only parts of the variance of share prices can be explained by publicly available information (Cutler *et al.*, 1988).

If the number of COVID-19 cases is high, negative economic consequences are likely. Döhrn (2020) distinguishes between direct and indirect effects of the virus. An obvious direct effect is that people infected with the virus cannot perform their jobs. Döhrn (2020) also argues that the labor supply may even be impaired in the long term if there are many deaths due to COVID-19. Indirect effects describe the consequences of measures to contain the virus, such as the shutdown of stores and production facilities. International trade in goods is also being restricted and entire industries are collapsing, such as the tourism industry (Döhrn, 2020).

7.2.1. *The COVID-19 pandemic*

The novel coronavirus originated in the Chinese city of Wuhan in December 2019 and has since been spreading around the world. Figure 7.2 displays the exponential spread of COVID-19 between January 22, 2020, and April 20, 2020. As of June 15, 2021 JHU counted 176,274,200 COVID-19 cases worldwide.

On March 11, 2020, the WHO declared the COVID-19 outbreak a pandemic. The countries were called upon to react quickly and decisively. In response to the global spread of COVID-19, governments took drastic measures. As early as January 23, 2020, the Chinese central government imposed a lockdown in Wuhan with the aim to contain the spread of the virus. Far-reaching measures were also taken in Beijing, such as the cancellation of all Chinese New Year celebrations (BBC, 2020b). Other countries followed with similar measures, including Italy, which imposed a strict curfew (BBC, 2020c). On March 14, 2020, US President Trump imposed a travel ban to the US for travellers from 26 European countries (BBC, 2020d).

7.3. Data, Methodology, and Hypothesis

This section presents the relevant data and explains the methodology of the analysis. This is followed by a presentation of the exact hypotheses.

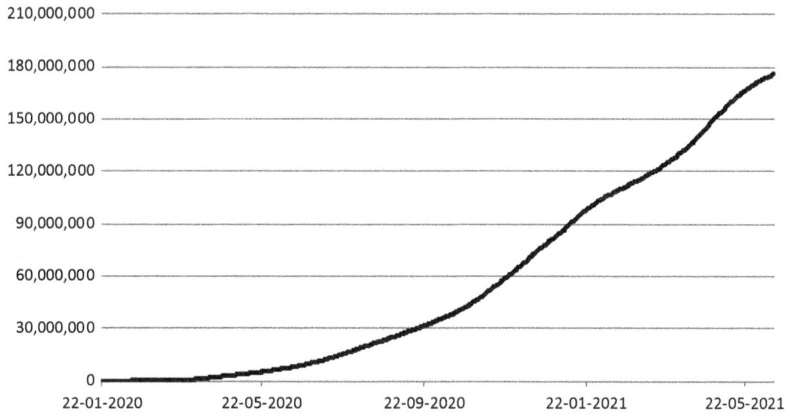

Figure 7.2. Number of COVID-19 cases worldwide.
Source: Own representation based on data from OCHA — HDX, 2020.

7.3.1. *Sample data*

To track the stock market development, a representative benchmark index is used to examine each country (see Table 7.1). For the endogenous variable Return t, daily data is available, except for the weekends when stock exchanges are closed. Other exceptions include country-specific stock exchange holidays. To calculate the corresponding returns, the selected benchmark index of each country under study is used. The data is collected from the investing.com website (investing.com, 2020).

China is included in the analysis as it is the country of origin of COVID-19 (Ayittey *et al.*, 2020).To get an overview of the Asian region, South Korea and India are also included in the analysis. South Korea was already severely affected by COVID-19 in February 2020 (OCHA, 2020). Despite a still relatively low number of COVID-19 cases, India imposed a curfew in the entire country in March 2020 (Gettleman and Schultz, 2020).

To get an idea of the situation in Europe, Germany and Italy are also included in the analysis. Compared to the rest of Europe, the COVID-19 situation in Germany is characterized by a low number of deaths (4,862 deaths, as of April 20, 2020), while in Italy more than 24,000 people died of COVID-19 in the same time period (OCHA, 2020). At times, the healthcare system in northern Italy was so overburdened that patients could no longer be treated, and doctors had to triage the patients (Horowitz, 2020). This study also looks at the US. As of April 20, 2020, there were over 780,000 confirmed COVID-19 cases in the US alone. Due to time constraints, only these countries are analyzed in this study.

Table 7.1. Benchmark indices of the countries studied.

Country	Indices
China	SSE Composite Index (Shanghai Stock Exchange Composite Index)
Germany	DAX (Deutscher Aktienindex)
India	BSE Sensex (Bombay Stock Exchange Sensitivity Index)
Italy	FTSE MIB (Financial Times Stock Exchange Milano Italia Borsa)
South Korea	KOSPI (Korea Composite Stock Price Index)
US	DJIA (Dow Jones Industrial Average)

For exogenous variables, key facts and variables measuring panic are used. The variables that measure the facts in the COVID-19 pandemic are hereinafter referred to as "fact variables." These display the daily changes in worldwide and country-specific confirmed cases and recoveries from COVID-19. The underlying data is obtained from the Humanitarian Data Exchange, which is compiled by JHU in collaboration with a variety of partners (OCHA, 2020). The datasets are updated daily, are accessible to everyone free of charge, and contain data starting from January 22, 2020.

The counterpart to the fact variables are the "panic variables." For this purpose, variables that represent the panic in the population are identified. The data for the panic variables is obtained from the databases of three different search engines. The collected data contains information about the number of search queries for selected terms. The identified panic variables are then combined into a "Panic Index" (see Section 7.3.2.1). Google Trends was used for Germany, India, Italy, and the US. Google Trends is a service which enables the analysis of search terms. In addition to direct comparisons of different search terms, the data can also be filtered by region. The results are normalized to a relative scale from 0 to 100 (depending on time and location) and do not allow any conclusions to be drawn about absolute numbers. Even with the same search interest in different regions, the total volume of searches can differ. As of November 2019, Google's market share of all search queries in these four countries was over 80%; in India, for example, it was 96.63% (StatCounter, 2019). For this reason, only Google Trends data is considered for these four countries. Looking at South Korea, it was noted that South Koreans have increasingly used the national search engine for search queries related to COVID-19. The data for South Korea is therefore obtained from the Naver database. Here too, search queries are recorded as relative frequencies on a scale from 0 to 100. Unfortunately, the Naver Data Lab cannot filter by region. However, since Naver is used almost exclusively in South Korea, this inaccuracy is accepted to be able to continue the analysis.

In China, the most widely used search engine is Baidu, with a market share of 68.66% as of March 2020 (StatCounter, 2020). This study, therefore, uses the trend function of Baidu as the source for the panic variables for China. Unlike Naver and Google, Baidu provides information on the absolute number of search queries. In addition to the number of search queries in the search engine itself, Baidu also provides another data set, which will be named "information index." The information index shows the daily number of news, shares, likes, comments, and redirects for the searched term. The panic variables from the information index are marked with an (info).

The analysis is limited to the period from January 22, 2020 to April 20, 2020. Although COVID-19, as the name suggests, emerged already in December 2019, the data from JHU (fact variables) is only available as of January 22, 2020.

7.3.2. *The model*

The analysis of this chapter is intended to provide clarity about the extent to which the price drops in the context of the COVID-19 pandemic can be explained rationally (or by facts) or can be attributed to irrational behavior. In simple terms, the goal is to find out whether facts or panic had greater influence on the share price development.

To test our hypothesis, we run the following regression:

$$R_t = \beta_0 + \sum_{1=1}^{2} \beta_{1i} F_{it} + \beta_2 FW_t + \beta_3 P_t + \sum_{j=1}^{4} \beta_{4i} R_{t-j} + \beta_5 D_t + \varepsilon_t, \quad (7.1)$$

R_t is the daily rate of return of the individual country index, β_0 is the regression intercept, F_{it} are the variables that represent the current state of the corona pandemic, this includes the country's number of daily new cases and recoveries. In addition to the fact variables of the countries studied, the global fact variables are also considered. FW_t is the variable representing the total daily new cases globally. This should give information about the extent to which national returns can be explained by the worldwide spread of COVID-19, e.g. the situation in other countries. P_t is an index variable that is calculated from different individual variables that measure the panic surrounding the corona pandemic. To control for serial correlation, we include the jth previous day's rate of return, denoted by R_{t-i}, and to control for the "Monday effect," we include a dummy variable D_{it} for Monday; this approach is similar to Kaplanski and Levy (2010). This is done to control for non-random movements in the regression (Cross, 1973). The Monday effect describes below-average returns on Mondays as compared to the other days of the week (Cho *et al.*, 2007).

The estimation method used in the empirical analysis is the Generalized Least Squares (GLS) estimation. The GLS regression allows for efficient estimations in the presence of error terms u_t whose variance is not constant (heteroscedasticity), as well as correlating error term u_t, or in other words trends in the data (autocorrelation).

7.3.2.1. *Fact variables and panic variables*

First, the selection of the fact variables is justified. The number of COVID-19 cases and the number of recoveries from COVID-19 are considered as fact variables. The two figures provide a good overview of the actual development (factual situation) of the COVID-19 pandemic in individual countries. The collection of data, e.g. different test methods used or number of tests performed, will not be discussed further; for more information see Worldometer.info (2020). For the analysis, the cumulative case numbers are converted into daily changes. If expectations change, the security prices also adjust. Based on these considerations, it is therefore assumed that the higher the number of cases (bad news), the more pessimistic the economic expectations. In the case of convalescents, the opposite effect is expected (good news).

To measure panic, selected search queries from Google, Naver, and Baidu are used as described. Studies found correlations between the transaction volume of the companies represented in the S&P 500 and the search volume of the corresponding company names (Preis *et al.*, 2010). The problem with this approach is that it cannot be deduced from the search queries whether the terms were searched for due to panic or other motives. For later interpretation, however, it is of great importance that the search terms used are closely related to the market panic prevailing in society. While the search for "social distancing" suggests the goal of rational self-information, an increased search for "COVID-19 symptoms" suggests the presence of fear and panic in the population, according to Springer *et al.* (2020). Other studies found a correlation between the spread rate of COVID-19 and the search term "washing hands," but not between the spread rate of COVID-19 and the search term "mouth-nose protection." Lin *et al.* (2020) believe that the search term "washing hands" partly reflects an increased awareness of the danger of COVID-19 (also fear and panic) but may also indicate proactive action by people. This proactive action subsequently led to a decreasing rate of spread. In contrast, the increased search for "mouth and nose protection" probably reflects the panic and fear of the population over COVID-19, as argued by Lin *et al.* (2020). The authors also justify this with possible fear of a lack of mouth and nose protection equipment (Lin *et al.*, 2020).

The panic variable "mouth-nose protection" is therefore included in the Panic Index. Furthermore, "hand sanitizer" is used as a panic variable for the Panic Index. The use of this variable can be justified in the same way as the use of the search term "mouth-and-nose protection." While the use of "hand sanitizer" was increasingly recommended, the availability was limited. This may have led to the fear of not being able to find the product. As a result, people increasingly searched online (BBC, 2020e). Toilet paper is the third "panic product" and, thus, a panic variable. Again, availability was temporarily limited, and the demand was high (Scottie, 2020). If one follows the previous logic, it also makes sense to use the search term "corona symptoms" as a panic variable (Springer *et al.*, 2020). The high degree of uncertainty about the course of COVID-19 in each individual case generates fear. Another factor possibly contributing to the uncertainty is the similarity of the symptoms of influenza and COVID-19 (CDC, 2020). In addition, the search terms "coronavirus" and "COVID-19" are also included as panic variables. It is assumed that an increased search for these terms also reflects panic in society.

For the US analysis, the search term "weapon store" is additionally used as a panic variable. American citizens increasingly stocked up on weapons and ammunition out of fear and panic. Background checks on firearms in the period from February 21, 2020, to March 1, 2020, reached the third highest level since 1998 (Taskinsoy, 2020). Such an increase cannot be explained by rational arguments.

In the analysis of India, the search term "Hinduism" is included as a panic variable. This is justified by the fact that people increasingly turn to faith in times of crisis (Chapman, 1994). Moreover, in India, the fear of COVID-19 is causing tensions between different religious groups (Gettleman *et al.*, 2020). It is, therefore, assumed that an increased search for "Hinduism" can be related to uncertainty and panic.

In order to accurately measure the panic and to analyze its influence on the stock markets, the identified panic variables are combined into the Panic Index. This is necessary as it might be the case that the search data for "face mask" is significantly influenced by a political decision. To take this into account, an index is formed that gives less weight to the individual panic variables. This makes it easier to interpret the results of the analysis later. To build the index score from the panic variables, first the z-scores of the panic variables i (search terms) are calculated at each time t. The z-scores are calculated as follows:

$$z_{it} = \frac{(x_{it} - \mu_i)}{\sigma_i}, \tag{7.2}$$

where

z_{it} = z-score of the search term i at time t;
x_{it} = search volume of the search term i at the time t;
μ_i = average value of the search volume for search term i;
σ_i = standard deviation of the search volume for search term i.

By forming the z-scores, the variables are standardized. After standardization, the mean value of each measurement series is 0 and the standard deviation is 1.

To form the index, the average of all panic variables (search terms) i (1, 2, 3, ..., n) at time t is calculated:

$$Index\_Score_t = \frac{1}{n} \sum_{i=1^n} z_{it}. \tag{7.3}$$

The same methodology is used to create the Panic Index (info) with the panic variables (info) for the models of China.

In addition to the selection of relevant facts and panic variables, the following must be taken into account: the timing of the effect of the exogenous variables on stock prices depends on the one hand on the speed with which the information reaches investors and on the other hand on how quickly they react to the new information. As real-time data is available, a no-time-delayed impact on stock prices is possible. Investors have access to the latest information and can adjust their trading in the financial markets accordingly. Again, if one follows the EMH, no significant impact delay can be assumed; in other words the financial market reflects all available information at all times (Fama, 1970). However, trading hours on stock exchanges are limited. Information that reaches investors after the stock exchange closes can, at the earliest, influence the return of the next day. In practice, investors may not use real-time data to inform themselves on the latest developments of COVID-19 but check for updates once a day. The same applies for the panic variables. To take this problem into account, the fact variables as well as the Panic Index of a specific day are "lagged" by one and two days. The models are denoted as: Without Lag, Lag1, and Lag2. This means that in the model with Lag2, the daily return of February 21 is to be explained by the values of the fact variables and the Panic Index of February 19 (a delay of two days). The control variables that measure the global facts are also delayed accordingly. Thus, three regressions are performed for each country.

7.3.3. *Hypothesis*

This section summarizes the assumptions made in the previous section and the factors identified as relevant. For this purpose, hypotheses are derived which will be tested statistically in the empirical analysis that follows. The hypotheses concerning the fact variables are as follows:

Hypothesis 1: "The higher the number of COVID-19 cases, the lower the return on the stock market."
Hypothesis 2: "The higher the number of people recovered from COVID-19, the higher the return on the stock market."
As explained in Section 7.2.2, an increased search volume for the panic variables is likely to indicate panic in the society. As a possible consequence, investors turn away from the stock markets. This leads to the following assumption.
Hypothesis 3: "The higher the Panic Index, the lower the return on the stock market."

7.4. Results

In this section, the results of the analysis are presented, and the hypotheses are examined using empirical models. The results of the analysis can be found in the appendix (Tables 7.A.1–7.A.6). First, the hypotheses of the fact variables are tested (Hypotheses 1 and 2):

7.4.1. *Regarding Hypothesis 1*

First, we look at the fact variable Cases. In the regressions for China, South Korea, India, the US, and Germany, no significant influence of the variable on the return could be proven. A similar result can be observed for Italy. Although the number of COVID-19 cases may have an influence on the FTSE MIB, the direction of the effect is unclear. For example, the corresponding coefficient in the Italian model (Without Lag) is positive (0.0000203) and in the model Lag1 negative (−0.0000192). Additionally, the numbers are so small that they only make a difference of about −0.2 (0.2) basis points.

Based on the analyses, Hypothesis 1 cannot be confirmed. Therefore, based on the preliminary considerations in Section 7.2.2, the positive influence of the variable Cases (country), as observed in the data for Italy cannot be explained.

In addition to the country-specific cases, the effect of the cases worldwide has been considered. The control variable Cases Worldwide has no significant impact on the Chinese, South Korean, US, and German benchmark indices. For India and Italy, a direct effect (Without Lag) can be observed, which is positive for India and negative for Italy. But the effect for both is even smaller than the country level effect at 0.01 and −0.01 basis points. Therefore, the hypothesis of the impact of the global cases can only be confirmed for Italy.

7.4.2. *Regarding Hypothesis 2*

In the regressions for China, South Korea, India, Germany, and the US, no significant influence of the variable Recoveries (country) on the return could be observed. The situation is different in the Italian model (Without Lag). Here, the number of COVID-19 recoveries has a statistically significant impact on the returns (0.0000256).

The direction of the effect is also consistent with Hypothesis 2: an increasing number of recoveries in Italy appears to have a positive effect on the FTSE MIB.

Based on the analyses carried out in this study, Hypothesis 2 can hence be accepted only for the data for Italy. But then again, the impact is very small at about 0.3 basis points. The data from other examined countries does not provide any evidence that would suggest a correlation between the number of recoveries and the share price.

7.4.3. *Regarding Hypothesis 3*

The regressions for India, Italy, the US, and Germany confirm that panic has a negative and greater impact on stock market returns compared to fact variables of the coronavirus. Yet, this thesis could not be confirmed for China and South Korea.

For India, Italy and the US, Hypothesis 3 is supported by the results of the analysis. The model for India — Without Lag (Lag 1) — shows a significant negative (negative) correlation between the Panic Index and the return. The results for Italy and the US show an immediate effect on the respective country index as opposed to India where it stretches over two days. This is shown by the significant Panic Index in the models Italy (US) — Without Lag — as well as in the model India – Without Lag (Lag1). If the Panic Index rises by 1%, the individual country index falls 4.5% (Italy), 4.6% (US) and 3.5% (India). To evaluate the thesis of this study for Italy, the model Without Lag will be considered. It should be noted here that the significant influence of the fact variable Recovered (Italy) and the Panic Index are simultaneous. If we now compare the coefficients of the two variables, we find that the influence of the Panic Index is stronger. While an increase in the number of convalescents by 1% is estimated to increase returns by 0.00203% on average, a decrease in the Panic Index by 1% increases returns by 4.5% on average.

On that basis, the thesis for Italy can be accepted. Panic had a stronger influence than the relevant facts. Thus, investors did not act rationally.

A possible explanation for the strong influence of panic on stock prices could be the so-called "herd instinct." Herd instinct is the simultaneous action of individuals or companies. In this context, the behavior of market participants can lead to uncertainty in the financial markets and result in rapid price declines. A trigger for the herd instinct in financial markets can be irrational panic, as it was the case during the COVID-19 pandemic (Ionescu, 2012). Studies show a correlation between herd instinct and panic in stock markets. For example, herd instincts in the British stock market were demonstrated during the 2007 financial crisis (Economou *et al.*, 2018).

The Panic Index also has a significant influence on the return for the German models. The model Germany — Lag1 — shows the expected effect. If the Panic Index increases, the DAX is expected to fall by an average of approximately 2%. Model Germany – Lag2 also shows a significant influence of the Panic Index, but the coefficients are positive (contradiction to Hypothesis 3). Studies find such "reversals" of returns especially after sharp price drops (Cox and Peterson, 1994). The initial price decline can be interpreted as an "overreaction" of the market (Atkins and Dyl, 1990). According to deBondt and Thaler (1985), a possible explanation for this is the irrational behavior of the investors who are strongly influenced by current, unexpected, and dramatic events. This overreaction can then be followed by a price reversal. Such a reversal is also more likely if the price change cannot be explained by "fundamentals," e.g. company announcements (Da *et al.*, 2014). Thus, the thesis of this chapter can be agreed for Germany. As described, a possible reversal effect can be attributed to the irrational behavior of the investors.

The estimation for the model of China only shows a significant impact for the model Lag 2. Here, the Panic Index (info) has a significant effect. However, the coefficients are positive and, therefore, opposite of what was expected. Therefore, Hypothesis 3 cannot be confirmed for China.

For South Korea, the Panic Index does not have a significant effect on the share price.

Even if panic in these countries had no direct influence on the collapse of national stock markets, the price trend could have been driven by herd effects across markets. Panic may therefore have had an indirect impact on the Chinese and South Korean stock markets. An indication of such a cross-market herd effect is the performance of the Chinese leading index SSE Composite in the period from January 22, 2020, to April 20, 2020. While the index had already fallen by more than 7% at the beginning of January but then recovered, the index fell again significantly in March, despite stable infection figures in China. Studies show that, for example, a crisis on the American stock exchange can have a domino effect on the financial markets of other countries, regardless of their economic policy situation. Such an irrational mechanism based on collective panic was already observed during the SARS pandemic in 2003, according to Sperling *et al.* (2008). Collective panic describes an affectively irrational reaction that cannot be logically understood. (Sperling *et al.*, 2008) Another explanation for interdependencies between financial centers is the increasingly networked global economy. Information that is relevant for one market is usually just as relevant for other markets. Study results suggest that markets react very quickly to information that is reflected in the prices of another market (Černy and Koblas, 2005).

7.5. Concluding Remarks

The aim of this work was to investigate the influence of COVID-19 on stock markets. More precisely, the goal was to analyze to what extent the price developments could be explained by rational behavior or by panic. The hypothesis was put forward that investors did not act rationally during the COVID-19 pandemic and that the price falls could be better explained by the panic than by the facts. Using GLS regression, China, South Korea, India, Italy, Germany, and the US were examined for this purpose.

The results of the analysis support the thesis for the stock markets in India, Italy, Germany, and the US. Based on the respective data, the models of these countries show that panic had a greater influence on the stock price development than the facts. When panic increased among the population, the returns of the national leading indices fell significantly. With reference to the statements of Goldberg and von Nitzsch (2004), it can be concluded from the results of the analysis that investors did not behave rationally during the COVID-19 pandemic, as emotions played a central role. This has important implications for equity investors, especially if we compare the time the S&P 500 took to recover during the COVID-19 pandemic and after the Global Financial Crisis. While the S&P 500 took 1,107 days to recover after 2008 (Reuters, 2020b), the index recovered three times faster in the COVID-19 pandemic. Important implications for investors are that they should be aware of the role emotions play in markets during a downturn. Therefore, investors should look closely at the impact such crises have on their investments and should not get caught up in the emotions of the market. For contrarian investors, such crises might yield good investment opportunities.

Based on the data from China and South Korea, however, the hypothesis cannot be accepted. Nevertheless, even for these countries, due to the interdependence of the financial market, at least an indirect effect of the panic on the national stock markets is quite conceivable. This makes it more difficult for investors to benefit from international diversification, exposing them to higher risk.

The methodological and theoretical limitations of this work are as follows. It is assumed that if the chosen fact variables have a stronger influence than the panic variables, it can be concluded that investors act rationally. Goldberg and von Nitzsch (2004) assumed for rational acting that investors are fully equipped with undistorted information and do not let themselves be influenced by emotions in their decisions. However, it can be questioned as to what extent rationality can be inferred from the influence of the fact variables used. Although the fact variables represent undistorted information, they are not sufficient to fully inform investors about the COVID-19 pandemic. In order to make valid statements about the rationality of the market participants, a variety of other factors, such as political decisions, should be taken into account (Maqbool *et al.*, 2018). For example, the ban on entry into the US announced by the US President Donald Trump on March 12, 2020, had a strong impact on the financial markets (Rodrigo, 2020). As a result of such a far-reaching decision with consequences for companies and entire industries e.g. tourism industry, share price changes due to changed expectations can be rational, even if they cannot be explained by the case numbers (fact variables).

Not only the fact variables provide only limited information on the rationality of investors, but also the use of panic variables or the Panic Index has its limits in mapping panic and its influence on stock markets. In this study, only a relatively small number of panic variables were used for the Panic Index. To improve the significance of the results of the analysis, a larger number of variables should be identified and used in future work.

Another factor not considered by either the factual variables or the Panic Index is the influence of institutions, e.g. central banks, on stock markets. Among other things, the market expects security and predictability from central banks. If this confidence is violated, an "overreaction," i.e. an excessive reaction of the market, can occur. While the statement "whatever it takes" (July 26, 2012) by the then President of the European Central Bank (ECB) Draghi had a calming or positive effect on the markets, the statement by ECB President Lagarde on March 12, 2020, "[...] it is not the task of a central bank to lower the yield premiums of individual countries," is likely to have had the opposite effect, according to Daube (2020). In order to better understand the drivers of the sharp falls in share prices, future analyses should also look more closely at the economic situation before the pandemic. Daube (2020) suggests that the markets were already "vulnerable" in the beginning of 2020. Such a state of affairs may possibly exacerbate the effects of the panic on the stock markets.

In conclusion, despite the methodological limitations of the models, this work demonstrates the impact of panic over COVID-19 on stock markets.

Appendix

Table 7.A.1. Empirical results for China.

	Without Lag	**Lag1**	**Lag2**
Intercept	0.006	0.005	−0.025
	(0.707)	(0.711)	(0.094)
R_{t-x}	−0.783	−0.645	−0.695
	(0.000)	(0.000)	(0.000)
R-t2	−0.457	−0.384	−0.389
	(0.008)	(0.032)	(0.015)
R-t3	−0.198	−0.075	0.010
	(0.234)	(0.650)	(0.952)
R-t4	0.167	−0.062	−0.024
	(0.252)	(0.679)	(0.869)
Cases (global)	0.000	−0.000	0.000
	(0.739)	(0.466)	(0.113)
Mon	−0.010	0.011	−0.008
	(0.057)	(0.435)	(0.152)
Cases (country)	0.000	−0.000	0.000
	(0.439)	(0.680)	(0.322)
Recovered (country)	0.000	−0.000	0.000
	(0.511)	(0.557)	(0.176)
Panic Index	0.003	−0.014	−0.009
	(0.771)	(0.148)	(0.076)
Panic Index (info)	−0.011	−0.010	0.016
	(0.075)	(0.192)	(0.010)
AIC	−161.646	−156.374	−161.525

Note: Regression results for the following regression: $R_t = \beta_0 + \sum_{1=1}^{2} \beta_{1i} F_{it} + \beta_2 FW_t + \beta_3 P_t + \sum_{j=1}^{4} \beta_{4i} R_{t-j} + \beta_5 D_t + \varepsilon_t$, where R_t is the daily return of the individual country indices, Fit are the country-specific fact variables, i.e. COVID-19 cases and recoveries; FW_t are the global confirmed COVID-19 cases; P_t is the Panic Index; R_{t-j} are the returns of the jth previous days; and D_t is a dummy variable for Monday (Mon). The variables Cases (country/global) Recovered (country), and the Panic Index are lagged one and two days for the Model Lag1 and Lag2. The analyzed period is January 22, 2020 to April 20, 2020. The regression coefficients are presented in the first line and the corresponding p-values in brackets. AIC is the Akaike-Information-Criterion.

Table 7.A.2. Empirical results for South Korea.

	Without Lag	**Lag1**	**Lag2**
Intercept	−0.005	−0.011	−0.018
	(0.746)	(0.415)	(0.226)
R-t1	−0.707	−0.647	−0.711
	(0.000)	(0.000)	(0.000)
R-t2	−0.265	−0.266	−0.221
	(0.119)	(0.130)	(0.238)
R-t3	0.009	0.026	0.025
	(0.956)	(0.875)	(0.890)
R-t4	−0.006	−0.017	0.005
	(0.968)	(0.907)	(0.973)
Cases (global)	0.000	0.000	0.000
	(0.932)	(0.246)	(0.113)
Mon	−0.013	−0.007	−0.015
	(0.079)	(0.478)	(0.055)
Cases (country)	0.000	0.000	0.000
	(0.893)	(0.787)	(0.607)
Recovered (country)	0.000	0.000	0.000
	(0.261)	(0.255)	(0.848)
Panic Index	−0.018	−0.010	0.001
	(0.070)	(0.266)	(0.937)
AIC	−154.212	−146.643	−140.240

Note: Regression results for the following regression: $R_t = \beta_0 + \sum_{1=1}^{2} \beta_{1i} F_{it} + \beta_2 FW_t + \beta_3 P_t + \sum_{j=1}^{4} \beta_{4i} R_{t-j} + \beta_5 D_t + \varepsilon_t$, where R_t is the daily return of the individual country indices, Fit are the country-specific fact variables, i.e. COVID-19 cases and recoveries; FW_t are the global confirmed COVID-19 cases; P_t is the Panic Index; R_{t-j} are the returns of the jth previous days; and D_t is a dummy variable for Monday (Mon). The variables Cases (country/global) Recovered (country), and the Panic Index are lagged one and two days for the Model Lag1 and Lag2. The analyzed period is January 22, 2020 to April 20, 2020. The regression coefficients are presented in the first line and the corresponding p-values in brackets. AIC is the Akaike-Information-Criterion.

Table 7.A.3. Empirical results for India.

	Without Lag	Lag1	Lag2
Intercept	−0.029	−0.025	−0.009
	(0.021)	(0.015)	(0.371)
R-t1	−0.591	−0.412	−0.406
	(0.000)	(0.002)	(0.018)
R-t2	−0.333	−0.270	−0.081
	(0.048)	(0.066)	(0.595)
R-t3	−0.229	−0.104	0.029
	(0.211)	(0.468)	(0.854)
R-t4	−0.264	−0.180	−0.028
	(0.090)	(0.155)	(0.844)
Cases (global)	0.000	0.000	0.000
	(0.035)	(0.089)	(0.174)
Mon	−0.022	0.004	−0.034
	(0.039)	(0.779)	(0.005)
Cases (country)	0.000	0.000	0.000
	(0.702)	(0.543)	(0.412)
Recovered (country)	0.000	0.000	0.000
	(0.723)	(0.914)	(0.413)
Panic Index	−0.040	−0.035	−0.007
	(0.016)	(0.002)	(0.502)
AIC	−129.608	−130.248	−113.148

Note: Regression results for the following regression: $R_t = \beta_0 + \sum_{1=1}^{2} \beta_{1i} F_{it} + \beta_2 FW_t + \beta_3 P_t + \sum_{j=1}^{4} \beta_{4i} R_{t-j} + \beta_5 D_t + \varepsilon_t$, where R_t is the daily return of the individual country indices, Fit are the country-specific fact variables, i.e. COVID-19 cases and recoveries; FW_t are the global confirmed COVID-19 cases; P_t is the Panic Index; R_{t-j} are the returns of the jth previous days; and D_t is a dummy variable for Monday (Mon). The variables Cases (country/global) Recovered (country), and the Panic Index are lagged one and two days for the Model Lag1 and Lag2. The analyzed period is January 22, 2020 to April 20, 2020. The regression coefficients are presented in the first line and the corresponding p-values in brackets. AIC is the Akaike-Information-Criterion.

Table 7.A.4. Empirical results for Italy.

	Without Lag	**Lag1**	**Lag2**
Intercept	−0.037	0.009	−0.037
	(0.010)	(0.813)	(0.239)
R-t1	−0.686	−0.803	0.981
	(0.000)	(0.000)	(0.000)
R-t2	−0.370	−0.506	−0.549
	(0.011)	(0.008)	(0.006)
R-t3	−0.210	−0.121	−0.264
	(0.148)	(0.518)	(0.187)
R-t4	−0.022	0.041	−0.148
	(0.850)	(0.776)	(0.329)
Cases (global)	0.000	0.000	0.000
	(0.050)	(0.334)	(0.740)
Mon	−0.009	−0.004	−0.021
	(0.195)	(0.737)	(0.032)
Cases (country)	0.000	0.000	0.000
	(0.000)	(0.030)	(0.114)
Recovered (country)	0.000	0.000	0.000
	(0.030)	(0.669)	(0.382)
Panic Index	−0.045	−0.011	−0.010
	(0.000)	(0.240)	(0.264)
AIC	−150.8658	−140.240	−125.766

Note: Regression results for the following regression: $R_t = \beta_0 + \sum_{1=1}^{2} \beta_{1i} F_{it} + \beta_2 FW_t + \beta_3 P_t + \sum_{j=1}^{4} \beta_{4i} R_{t-j} + \beta_5 D_t + \varepsilon_t$, where R_t is the daily return of the individual country indices, Fit are the country-specific fact variables, i.e. COVID-19 cases and recoveries; FW_t are the global confirmed COVID-19 cases; P_t is the Panic Index; R_{t-j} are the returns of the jth previous days; and D_t is a dummy variable for Monday (Mon). The variables Cases (country/global), Recovered (country), and the Panic Index are lagged one and two days for the Model Lag1 and Lag2. The analyzed period is January 22, 2020 to April 20, 2020. The regression coefficients are presented in the first line and the corresponding p-values in brackets. AIC is the Akaike-Information-Criterion.

Table 7.A.5. Empirical results for Germany.

	Without Lag	**Lag1**	**Lag2**
Intercept	−0.016	−0.018	−0.014
	(0.602)	(0.433)	(0.548)
R-t1	−0.862	−0.819	−0.669
	(0.000)	(0.000)	(0.000)
R-t2	−0.602	−0.530	−0.323
	(0.002)	(0.003)	(0.065)
R-t3	−0.360	−0.225	−0.115
	(0.058)	(0.229)	(0.530)
R-t4	−0.168	0.008	−0.026
	(0.242)	(0.953)	(0.868)
Cases (global)	0.000	0.000	0.000
	(0.318)	(0.186)	(0.715)
Mon	−0.016	−0.003	−0.010
	(0.034)	(0.751)	(0.185)
Cases (country)	0.000	0.000	0.000
	(0.305)	(0.455)	(0.413)
Recovered (country)	0.000	0.000	0.000
	(0.376)	(0.693)	(0.807)
Panic Index	−0.041	−0.021	0.022
	(0.066)	(0.042)	(0.011)
AIC	−140.217	−132.929	−131.635

Note: Regression results for the following regression: $R_t = \beta_0 + \sum_{1=1}^{2} \beta_{1i} F_{it} + \beta_2 FW_t + \beta_3 P_t + \sum_{j=1}^{4} \beta_{4i} R_{t-j} + \beta_5 D_t + \varepsilon_t$, where R_t is the daily return of the individual country indices; Fit are the country-specific fact variables, i.e. COVID-19 cases and recoveries; FW_t are the global confirmed COVID-19 cases; P_t is the Panic Index; R_{t-j} are the returns of the jth previous days; and D_t is a dummy variable for Monday (Mon). The variables Cases (country/global), Recovered (country), and the Panic Index are lagged one and two days for the Model Lag1 and Lag2. The analyzed period is January 22, 2020 to April 20, 2020. The regression coefficients are presented in the first line and the corresponding p-values in brackets. AIC is the Akaike-Information-Criterion.

Table 7.A.6. Empirical results for the US.

	Without Lag	**Lag1**	**Lag2**
Intercept	−0.042	−0.016	−0.011
	(0.017)	(0.292)	(0.490)
R-t1	−1.025	−0.867	−0.894
	(0.000)	(0.000)	(0.000)
R-t2	−0.454	−0.213	−0.255
	(0.014)	(0.270)	(0.180)
R-t3	−0.285	−0.044	−0.020
	(0.129)	(0.822)	(0.918)
R-t4	−0.305	−0.141	−0.122
	(0.034)	(0.334)	(0.420)
Cases (global)	0.000	0.000	0.000
	(0.100)	(0.982)	(0.423)
Mon	−0.010	−0.004	−0.013
	(0.298)	(0.794)	(0.209)
Cases (country)	0.000	0.000	0.000
	(0.474)	(0.701)	(0.210)
Recovered (country)	0.000	0.000	0.000
	(0.669)	(0.834)	(0.681)
Panic Index	−0.046	−0.008	0.005
	(0.006)	(0.536)	(0.600)
AIC	−121.270	−106.984	−104.435

Note: Regression results for the following regression: $R_t = \beta_0 + \sum_{1=1}^{2} \beta_{1i} F_{it} + \beta_2 FW_t + \beta_3 P_t + \sum_{j=1}^{4} \beta_{4i} R_{t-j} + \beta_5 D_t + \varepsilon_t$, where R_t is the daily return of the individual country indices; Fit are the country-specific fact variables, i.e. COVID-19 cases and recoveries; FW_t are the global confirmed COVID-19 cases; P_t is the Panic Index; R_{t-j} are the returns of the jth previous days; and D_t is a dummy variable for Monday (Mon). The variables Cases (country/global), Recovered (country), and the Panic Index are lagged one and two days for the Model Lag1 and Lag2. The analyzed period is January 22, 2020 to April 20, 2020. The regression coefficients are presented in the first line and the corresponding *p*-values in brackets. AIC is the Akaike-Information-Criterion.

References

Atkins, A.B. and Dyl, E.A. (1990). Price reversals, bid-ask spreads, and market efficiency. *Journal of Financial and Quantitative Analysis*, **25**(4), 535–547.

Ayittey, F.K., Dzuvor, C., Ayittey, M.K., Chiwero, N.B. and Habib, A. (2020). Updates on Wuhan 2019 novel coronavirus epidemic. *Journal of Medical Virology*, **92**(4), 403.

Baker, M., Wurgler, J. and Yuan, Y. (2012). Global, local, and contagious investor sentiment. *Journal of Financial Economics*, **104**(2), 272–287.

Bash, A. and Alsaifi, K. (2019). Fear from uncertainty: An event study of Khashoggi and stock market returns. *Journal of Behavioral and Experimental Finance*, **23**, 54–58.

BBC (2020a). Covid-19 pandemic: Tracking the global coronavirus outbreak, November 23. Retrieved from https://www.bbc.com/news/world-51235105. Accessed 23.11.2020.

BBC (2020b). China coronavirus: Lockdown measures rise across Hubei province, May 18. https://www.bbc.com/news/world-asia-china-51217455. Accessed 18.05.2020 Publication: 23.01.2020

BBC (2020c). Coronavirus: Italy extends emergency measures nationwide. Retrieved from https://www.bbc.com/news/world-europe-51810673. Accessed 18.05.2020 Publication: 10.03.2020.

BBC (2020d). Coronavirus: US travel ban on 26 European countries comes into force, June 7. Retrieved from:https://www.bbc.com/news/world-us-canada-51883728. Accessed: 18.05.2020 Publication date: 14.03.2020.

BBC (2020e). Coronavirus: Where has all the hand sanitiser gone? June 7. Retrieved from: https://www.bbc.com/news/stories-52126847. Accessed: 07.06.2020 Publication: 02.04.2020.

CDC (2020). Symptoms of Coronavirus. Centres for Disease control and Prevention, May 13. Retrieved from: https://www.cdc.gov/coronavirus/2019-ncov/symptoms-testing/symptoms.html. Accessed: 18.05.2020 Publication date: 13.05.2020.

Černy, A. and Koblas, M. (2005). Stock market integration and the speed of information transmission: The role of data frequency in cointegration and Granger causality tests. *Journal of International Business and Economics*, **1**(1), 110–120.

Chapman, G.C. (1994). What God can help? Trinity and pop religions of crisis. *CrossCurrents*, **44**(3), 316–331.

Cho, Y.-H., Linton, O. and Whang, Y.-J. (2007). Are there Monday effects in stock returns: A stochastic dominance approach. *Journal of Empirical Finance*, **14**(5), 736–755.

Cox, D.R. and Peterson, D.R. (1994). Stock returns following large one-day declines: Evidence on short-term reversals and longer-term performance. *The Journal of Finance*, **49**(1), 255–267.

Cross, F. (1973). The behavior of stock prices on Fridays and Mondays. *Financial Analysts Journal*, **29**(6), 67–69.

Cutler, D.M., Poterba, J.M. and Summers, L.H. (1988). What moves stock prices? National Bureau of Economic Research.

Da, Z., Liu, Q. and Schaumburg, E. (2014). A closer look at the short-term return reversal. *Management Science*, **60**(3), 658–674.

Daube, C.H. (2020). The Corona Virus Stock Exchange Crash. Working Paper. ECONSTOR. Retrieved from https://www.econstor.eu/handle/10419/214881. Accessed 15.06.2021.

de Bondt W.F.M. and Thaler, R. (1985). Does the stock market overreact? *The Journal of Finance*, **40**(3), 793–805.

Depoux, A., Martin, S., Karafillakis, E., Preet, R., Wilder-Smith, A. and Larson, H. (2020). The pandemic of social media panic travels faster than the COVID-19 outbreak. *Journal of Travel Medicine*, March 3 [online].

Döhrn, R. (2020). *Auswirkungen der COVID-19 Epidemie auf die chinesische Wirtschaft-eine erste Abschätzung*. RWI Materialien.

Economou, F., Hassapis, C. and Philippas, N. (2018). Investors' fear and herding in the stock market. *Applied Economics*, **50**(34–35), 3654–3663.

Fama, E.F. (1970). Efficient capital markets: A review of theory and empirical work. *The Journal of Finance*, **25**(2), 383–417.

Gettleman, J. and Schultz, K. (2020). Modi orders 3-week total lockdown for all 1.3 billion Indians. *The New York Times*. Retrieved from https://www.Nytimes.Com/2020/03/24/world/asia/india-Coronavirus-Lockdown.Html.

Gettleman, J., Schultz, K. and Raj, S. (2020). In India, coronavirus fans religious hatred. *The New York Times*, April 12. Retrieved from https://www.nytimes.com/2020/04/12/world/asia/india-coronavirus-muslims-bigotry.html. Accessed: 22.04.2020 Publication date: 12.04.2020.

Goldberg, J. and Nitzsch, R. von. (2004). *Behavioral finance: gewinnen mit Kompetenz;[verbessern Sie die Trefferquote Ihrer Anlageentscheidungen deutlich!]*. FinanzBuch Verlag.

Horowitz, J. (2020). Italy's health care system groans under coronavirus—a warning to the world. *The New York Times*. https://www.nytimes.com/2020/03/12/world/europe/12italy-coronavirus-health-care.html. Accessed: 12.04.2020 Publication date: 12.03.2020.

Investing.com (2020). Indices. Retrieved from https://www.investing.com/indices/. Accessed: 05.05.2020 Publication date.

Ionescu, C. (2012). The herd behavior and the financial instability. *Annals of the University of Petroşani. Economics*, **12**, 129–140.

Kaplanski, G. and Levy, H. (2010). Sentiment and stock prices: The case of aviation disasters. *Journal of Financial Economics*, **95**(2), 174–201.

Leduc, S. and Liu, Z., *et al.* (2020). The uncertainty channel of the coronavirus. *Economic Letters*.

Lerner, J.S., Small, D.A. and Loewenstein, G. (2004). Heart strings and purse strings: Carryover effects of emotions on economic decisions. *Psychological Science*, **15**(5), 337–341.

Lin, Y.-H., Liu, C.-H. and Chiu, Y.-C. (2020). Google searches for the keywords of "wash hands" predict the speed of national spread of COVID-19 outbreak among 21 countries. *Brain, Behavior, and Immunity*.

Maqbool, N., Hameed, W. and Habib, M. (2018). Impact of political influences on stock returns. *International Journal of Multidisciplinary Scientific Publication (IJMSP)*, **1**(1), 1–6.

OCHA (2020). Novel Coronavirus (COVID-19) Cases Data. Retrieved from https://data.humdata.org/dataset/novel-coronavirus-2019-ncov-cases. Accessed: 13.05.2020 Publication date = Accessed date.

OECD (2020). Global outlook less pessimistic, but risks and uncertainty remain high. Retrived from https://www.oecd.org/economic-outlook/. Accessed: 03.09.2020 Publication date.

Preis, T., Reith, D. and Stanley, H.E. (2010). Complex dynamics of our economic life on different scales: Insights from search engine query data. *Philosophical Transactions of the Royal Society A: Mathematical, Physical and Engineering Sciences*, **368**(1933), 5707–5719.

Reuters (2020a). Germany treats first Italians as coronavirus care crosses borders. https://www.reuters.com/article/us-health-coronavirus-germany-italy-idUSKBN21B2GL. Accessed: 20.06.2020 Publication date: 24.03.2020.

Reuters (2020b). S&P recovery will be far faster than 2008: Citigroup. Retrieved from https://www.reuters.com/article/us-usa-stocks-citigroup-idUSKBN22V15W. Accessed: 20.06.2020 Publication date: 19.05.2020.

Rodrigo, C. (2020). Panic grips financial markets after U.S. travel curbs, ECB move. *Reuters*. https://www.reuters.com/article/us-global-markets-idUSKBN20Z00B. Accessed: 14.07.2020 Publication date: 12.03.2020.

Scottie, A. (2020). The psychology behind why toilet paper, of all things, is the latest coronavirus panic buy. *CNN*, June 7. Retrieved from https://edition.cnn.com/2020/03/09/health/toilet-paper-shortages-novel-coronavirus-trnd/index.html. Accessed: 07.06.2020 Publication date: 09.03.2020

Sharif, A., Aloui, C. and Yarovaya, L. (2020). COVID-19 pandemic, oil prices, stock market, geopolitical risk and policy uncertainty nexus in the US economy: Fresh evidence from the wavelet-based approach. *International Review of Financial Analysis*, 101496.

Sperling, W., Bleich, S. and Reulbach, U. (2008). Black Monday on stock markets throughout the world-A new phenomenon of collective panic disorder? A psychiatric approach. *Medical Hypotheses*, **71**(6), 972–974.

Springer, S., Menzel, L. and Zieger, M. (2020). Google Trends provides a tool to monitor population concerns and information needs during COVID-19 pandemic. *Brain, Behavior, and Immunity.*

StatCounter (2019). Share of desktop search traffic originating from Google in selected countries as of November 2019 [Graph]. Retrieved from https://www.statista.com/statistics/220534/goo41gles-share-of-search-market-in-selected-countries/. Accessed: 13.05.2020 Publication date = Accessed date.

StatCounter (2020). Market share of search engines in China as of March 2020, based on pageview. Retrieved from https://www.statista.com/statistics/253340/market-share-of-search-engines-in-china-pageviews/. Accessed: 13.05.2020 Publication date = Access date.

Taskinsoy, J. (2020). Coronavirus pandemic: The US induced great panic of the 21st century. Available at SSRN 3610749.

World Health Organization and others (2020a). WHO Director-General's remarks at the media briefing on 2019-nCoV on 11 February 2020.

World Health Organization and others (2020b). Coronavirus disease 2019 (COVID-19): Situation report, 82.

Worldometer.info (2020). Covid-19 corona virus pandemic, June 5. Retrieved from https://www.worldometers.info/coronavirus/. Accessed: 05.06.2020.

Yuen, K.S.L. and Lee, T.M.C. (2003). Could mood state affect risk-taking decisions? *Journal of Affective Disorders*, **75**(1), 11–18.

https://doi.org/10.1142/9781800610781_0008

Chapter 8

COVID-19 Effects on Intraday Stock Market Behavior

Jiayang Nie[*,§], Xiao Qiao[†,¶], and Sibo Yan[‡,]**

[*]*University of California, Berkeley, California*

[†]*City University of Hong Kong, Hong Kong*

[‡]*University of California, Los Angeles, California*

[§]*jnie@berkeley.edu*

[¶]*xiaoqiao@cityu.edu.hk*

[**]*kavanster@g.ucla.edu*

Abstract

This chapter investigates the stock market implications of COVID-19 using high-frequency data. Our analysis covers three aspects. First, we compare intraday volatility patterns of the S&P 500 during COVID-19 with those before COVID-19. Second, we document changes to intraday return predictability of the S&P 500 before and during COVID-19. Third, we examine the Heston (1993) stochastic volatility model during COVID-19 and compare to previous market events. Our empirical findings suggest that, during COVID-19, there is more disagreement among market participants in processing new information, and market makers are more concerned about inventory risk.

8.1. Introduction

The COVID-19 pandemic has massively transformed our lives. Over 100 countries have implemented some form of lockdown in response to the pandemic, restricting the movement of a significant fraction of the world's population, which has greatly strained the global economy.

The rapid spread of COVID-19 also has had a major impact on financial markets, creating historically high levels of uncertainty.

Researchers have responded quickly to the onset of the COVID-19 pandemic. Novel literature centered around the financial market impact of COVID-19 has developed in a relatively short time frame. For example, Seven and Yilmaz (2020) examine the significant losses of equity markets worldwide in the first quarter of 2020 and find that fiscal support is positively associated with the subsequent recovery. Shehzad *et al.* (2020) apply the asymmetric power GARCH model to global equity markets and find that in some markets, COVID-19 resulted in higher volatility than the Global Financial Crisis (GFC), but in other markets, the GFC was associated with higher levels of volatility. These papers, and many others, have expanded our understanding of the financial market implications of COVID-19 in a timely manner, serving the important purpose of keeping policymakers and investors informed.

While the literature around COVID-19 effects on financial markets has developed quickly, there has been limited insight into the intraday behavior of the stock market. We do not have a good grasp on the interaction among market participants throughout the trading day, or the resulting implications for market efficiency and risk management. We fill this gap by investigating the US stock market behavior before and during COVID-19 using high-frequency data, which allow us to compute more accurate volatility measures and provide a more granular view of stock market behavior.

Our investigation follows three dimensions: the diurnal pattern of realized volatility, intraday return predictability, and the Heston (1993) model fit to intraday data. First, we construct realized volatility of the S&P 500, and we compare the intraday volatility pattern for trading days before and during COVID-19. Existing literature has document that intraday volatility tends to follow a "U" or a reverse "J" shape, with higher values near the open and the close (Andersen and Bollerslev, 1997; Harris, 1986). This observation can be attributed to clustered information incorporation into market prices at the open and market makers' inventory concerns at the market close. Consistent with the literature, we find that 30-minute realized volatilities follow a reverse "J" shape — highest at the open, lowest in the middle of the day, and high again in the final 30 minutes — for our full sample from 1998 to 2020. We divide the full sample into the COVID-19 period and the non-COVID period, and we find that intraday volatility is higher in every 30-minute interval during COVID-19 than the non-COVID sample: the percentage differences of 30-minute volatilities range between 68% and 149%. The annualized value of 30-minute volatilities averages 26% during COVID-19 versus 14% in the non-COVID sample. We also compare the intraday volatility pattern during COVID-19 to those in the 2001 recession and the Great Recession (2008). Volatilities during COVID-19 are 22–104% higher than the values in the 2001 recession, but do not appear to be significantly higher than those in the Great Recession.

The shape of diurnal volatility sheds light on potential changes in the behavior of market participants in different market events. We observe a "U" shape in the Great Recession and a reverse "J" shape during the 2001 recession. In contrast, there is a "J" shape during COVID-19: volatility is high at the open, low throughout the day, and highest in the final 30 minutes of trading. Furthermore, the opening and closing half-hours during COVID-19 have higher volatilities than the same half-hour periods in both the Great Recession and the 2001 recession. News about COVID-19 is often released in the evening after market close. Given our fear and lack of understanding of this novel disease, market participants can have a wide range of different interpretations of new information, which can contribute to elevated volatility at the market open. Concerns about uncertainty and market instability may motivate market makers to carry reduced overnight inventory during COVID-19 than usual, which may lead to higher volatility toward the end of the trading day as market makers trade more aggressively to reduce their inventory.

The second dimension we examine is intraday return predictability of the S&P 500 returns. We expand the analysis in Gao *et al.* (2018) to use non-overlapping, 30-minute returns to predict the returns in the final 30 minutes of the trading day. Using a different sample than Gao *et al.* (2018), we confirm there is strong predictive power for the final half-hour returns using the 1st and 12th half-hours. A 1% increase in the 1st and 12th half-hours is associated with a six- and ten-basis-point increase in the final half-hour, which is economically large considering that expected returns for the full trading day is about four basis points. Differing from Gao *et al.* (2018), we also uncover predictability for other half-hour periods, which can carry positive or negative coefficients depending on the time of day.

During COVID-19, the returns in the first half-hour continue to have strong positive predictive power for the returns in the final half-hour, but the general pattern for intraday predictability is different from the patterns for the full sample, the 2001 recession, or the Great Recession. In the COVID-19 sample, the most predictive periods for the final half-hour returns can be found in the middle of the trading day, rather than at the beginning or at the end. Furthermore, the economic magnitude of the predictive coefficients in the COVID-19 sample is several times larger compared to other samples.

Intraday return predictability is consistent with investors splitting up their orders into multiple trading sessions (Bogousslavsky, 2016), but this channel does not explain why the predictive coefficients are much larger during COVID-19. We conjecture that elevated inventory risk for market makers may be associated with the unique intraday return predictability pattern during COVID-19. Market makers who provide liquidity must trade in the same direction to unload their inventory. For example, if there is selling pressure during the trading day and market makers buy to meet this demand, they must sell before the market close to offset their long positions — downward price pressure during the trading day would lead to downward price pressure in the closing hours. If market makers are especially sensitive about inventory risk during COVID-19, the direction of order flow during the trading day may become more prominently related to the direction of flow in the closing hours. To the extent price pressure is reflected in returns, we would also observe stronger return predictability.

To complement our reduced-form analysis of volatility and predictability, we also take a structural approach to understand the behavior of volatility during COVID-19. We estimate the stochastic volatility model of Heston (1993) using intraday realized volatilities. The stochastic volatility process in the Heston (1993) model succinctly summarize the behavior of volatility using three parameters: speed of mean-reversion, long-run volatility, and volatility of volatility. We follow Ellickson *et al.* (2018) to estimate these parameters using the generalized method of moments (GMM; Hansen, 1982).

During COVID-19, mean-reversion of the volatility process was found to be lower compared to the recent past, indicating that volatility is behaving in less predictable ways and can deviate from its long-run average value for extended periods. The long-run volatility parameter in the Heston (1993) model is higher during COVID-19 than the preceding years, but not as high as the estimates during the Great Recession. Similarly, the volatility of volatility parameter is also high during COVID-19, but not as high as the values during the Great Recession. From the perspective of the Heston (1993) model, while COVID-19 is associated with increased volatility and the uncertainty around volatility, these increases are not unprecedented. The values are comparable to the period in 2008 around the Great Recession.

This chapter fits into the burgeoning literature on the COVID-19 implications for financial markets. Albulescu (2020) uses robust least squares to show increases in volatility associated with COVID-19. Zhang *et al.* (2020) demonstrate that global equity market volatilities and correlations have increased substantially in response to the pandemic. Just and Echaust (2020) use a Markov switching model to illustrate how the relationship between the S&P 500 returns and implied volatility changed during COVID-19. Compared to these papers, our focus on intraday returns and volatility patterns provides a new perspective and expands our understanding of the financial effects of COVID-19.

This chapter is also related to three additional strands of literature, tied together through the lens of COVID-19. The literature on intraday volatility patterns at least goes back to Wood *et al.* (1985) and Harris (1986). More recently, Andersen and Bollerslev (1997) illustrate how to incorporate seasonality into GARCH-family models for a better statistical fit of intraday volatility. The primary source we refer to for the intraday return predictability literature is Gao *et al.* (2018), who document significant predictive power in the 1st and 12th half-hours of the trading day for the final half-hour returns on the S&P 500. There is a great amount of literature available on modeling and estimating stochastic volatility models. Ellickson *et al.* (2018) demonstrate that fitting Heston (1993) models to high-frequency data can capture the empirical behavior of intraday realized volatility. Compared to these papers, our contribution is to connect these seemingly disparate literatures through the lens of COVID-19. Through three complementary exercises studying intraday volatility and returns, we gain a better understanding of how COVID-19 has impacted the US stock market on an intraday level.

The chapter is organized as follows. Section 8.2 studies the diurnal volatility patterns in COVID-19. Section 8.3 compares intraday return predictability before and during COVID-19. Section 8.4 explores the Heston (1993) model. Section 8.5 concludes.

8.2. Diurnal Volatility Pattern during COVID-19

8.2.1. *Data*

Intraday market data come from the New York Stock Exchange (NYSE) Euronext Trades and Quotes (TAQ) database. We obtain one-minute level data aggregated from the trade component of TAQ for the SPDR S&P 500 ETF, SPY. Data fields include the timestamp, open, high, low, close in each minute during NYSE trading hours. We use the closing price to calculate return bars, which are then used to compute volatility and longer-horizon return series. Our sample is from January 1998 to June 2020.

8.2.2. *Intraday volatility*

There is a well-documented diurnal pattern in volatility — squared price changes during the course of a trading day tend to form a "U" or a reverse "J" shape with larger fluctuations near the open and the close (Andersen and Bollerslev, 1997; Harris, 1986). This pattern can be attributed to clustered information dissemination at the market open and inventory concerns at the market close. We compare the pattern in intraday volatility before and during COVID-19 to assess whether information dissemination or inventory considerations are different between COVID and non-COVID periods.

We take the COVID-19 sample to be from February 1, 2020, to the end of our data set on June 8, 2020. The pandemic certainly did not end on June 8, and many countries continue to struggle with COVID-19 past this date. However, to facilitate research progress we had to fix our sample.

For each trading day, we construct realized volatilities in the following way. We compute one-minute log returns r_t of the S&P 500, and we define the cumulative sum of squared returns S_t as follows:

$$S_t = \sum_{t_i<t} r_{t_i}^2, \tag{8.1}$$

where r_{t_i} is the return from t_{i-1} to t_i. Realized variance is calculated in the same way as Corradi and Distaso (2006):

$$RV_{t,t+j} = S_{t+j} - S_t. \tag{8.2}$$

We compute realized variances for each half-hour of the trading day. The realized half-hour variances are annualized through multiplying by 13×252, then we take the square root for annualized volatility figures.

The 13 half-hour volatilities have similar time series variation and are highly correlated with one another. Figure 8.1 plots the time series of realized volatilities from the 1st half-hour, from 9:30 am to 10 am Eastern Time, and the 13th (final) half-hour, from 3:30 pm to 4 pm Eastern Time. The two times series track each other closely; they have a correlation of 0.8. For the ease of exposition, other half-hour volatilities are not shown on the figure, but they are also highly correlated with the 1st and 13th half-hours. The half-hour volatilities

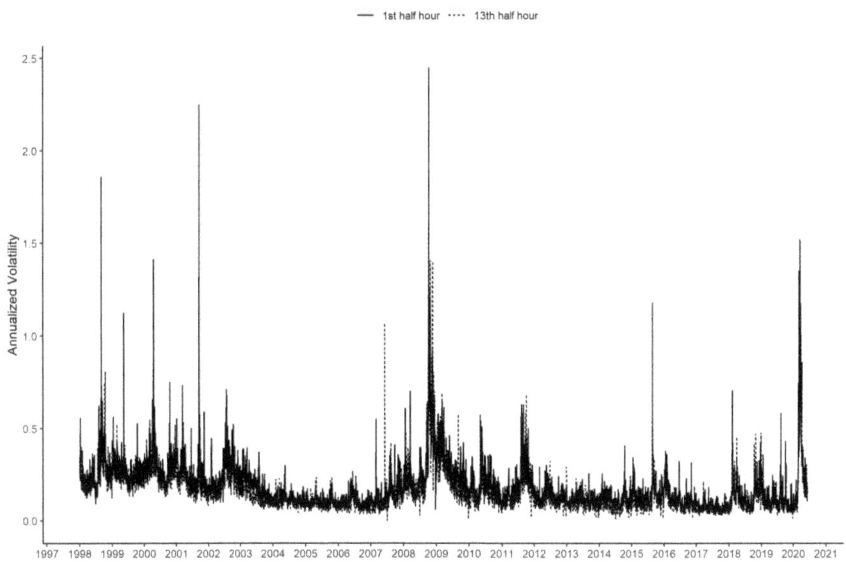

Figure 8.1. Time series variation of 1st and 13th half-hour volatilities.

Note: This figure plots the time series of realized volatilities from the 1st half-hour (9:30–10:00 am Eastern Time) and the 13th half-hour (3:30–4:00 pm Eastern time). Realized volatilities are annualized through multiplying by $\sqrt{13 \times 252}$.

also move together closely with the daily realized volatility as well as the VIX index.

Although the 1st and 13th half-hour volatilities tend to co-move, they do not always behave in the same way. During 2001 and 2008, when macroeconomic conditions were poor, the 1st half-hour volatility was much higher than the 13th half-hour: in late 2001, the annualized volatility of the 1st half-hour jumped to over 200%, whereas the 13th half-hour volatility did not exceed 50%. In 2008, both volatilities rose sharply, with the 1st half-hour reaching almost 250% and the 13th half-hour passing 200%. There were also episodes, such as in 2007 and 2020, when the 13th half-hour volatility exceeded the 1st half-hour volatility. These differences illustrate that the diurnal pattern in volatility is time varying. Depending on the environment, we could see a "U," "J," or a reverse "J."

We calculate the time series averages of half-hour realized volatilities for the full sample, from January 1998 to June 2020. Figure 8.2 plots these intraday volatilities. The average volatility of the first

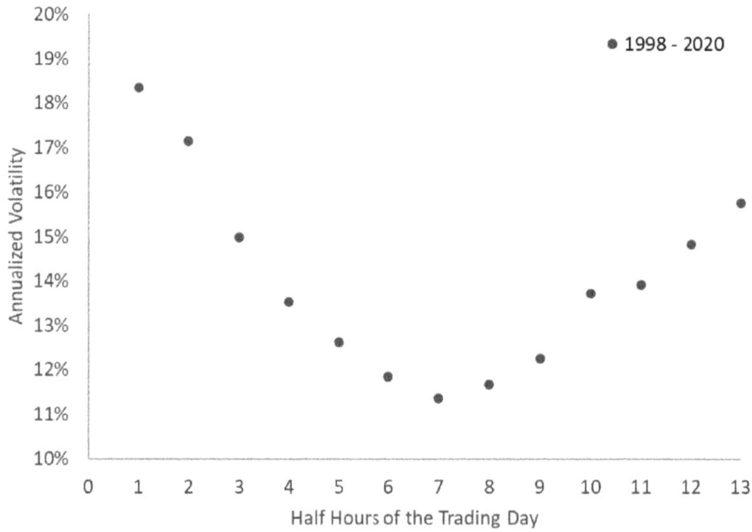

Figure 8.2. Unconditional diurnal volatility pattern.

Note: This figure plots the time series averages of realized volatilities by 30-minute intervals through the trading day. Half-hour volatilities are annualized through multiplying by $\sqrt{13 \times 252}$. The sample is from January 1998 to June 2020.

half-hour is the highest, the second half-hour is the second highest, and the final half-hour is the third highest. Trading hours in the middle of the day have markedly lower average volatilities than the values at market open or market close. This reverse "J" shape is consistent with the literature on intraday volatility, at least going back to Wood *et al.* (1985) and Harris (1986).

We turn our attention to comparing COVID-19 and non-COVID periods. Our COVID-19 sample starts on February 1, 2020. The first case of COVID-19 in the US was identified on January 20 (Holshue *et al.*, 2020). On January 30, the World Health Organization (WHO) declared a global health emergency, drawing the world's attention to the severity of COVID-19. January 31 marked the first major policy response to COVID-19: The Trump Administration restricted travel from China, further raising public awareness of the pandemic.

Our COVID-19 sample ends on June 8, 2020. The COVID-19 pandemic continues past this date, but we feel it is important to study existing data in a timely manner rather than to wait, much as the medical field has done. Insights from the medical research community have greatly improved our understanding of COVID-19 and influenced public policy responses, even though many results are based on limited data. Our understanding of COVID-19 will continue to evolve as additional data become available.

Figure 8.3 compares the diurnal volatility pattern during COVID-19 with the pattern in the non-COVID period. The non-COVID period includes all trading days prior to February 1, 2020. Volatility is significantly elevated during the COVID-19 sample than the non-COVID sample — each half-hour volatility is higher in the COVID-19 sample than the non-COVID sample, and the average of all 13 half-hour volatilities is 26% during COVID-19 versus 14% outside of COVID-19. The lowest half-hour volatility during COVID-19, which occurs in the sixth half-hour between 12 pm and 12:30 pm Eastern Time, is 21.5% — higher than the highest half-hour volatility in the non-COVID sample.

Volatility differences between the COVID and non-COVID periods are economically significant. During COVID-19, percentage differences in volatility to non-COVID days range from 68% (10th half-hour) to 149% (13th half-hour). COVID-19 presented the real economy with substantial challenges, which translated to higher uncertainty for investors in financial markets.

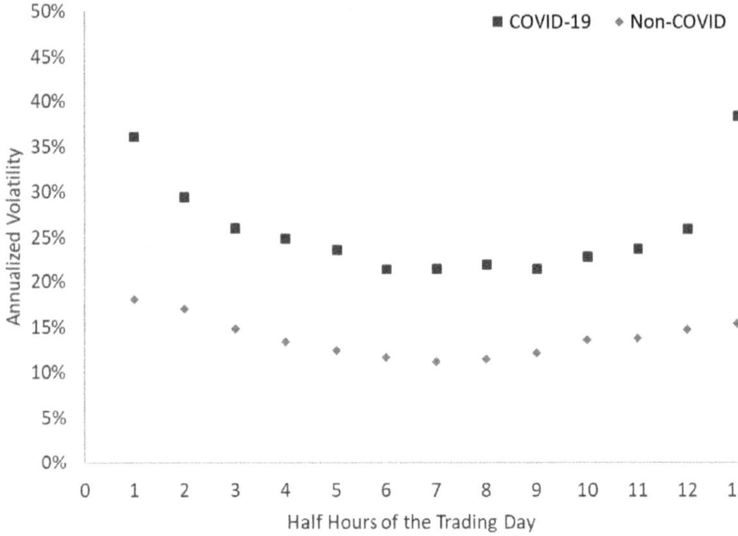

Figure 8.3. Diurnal volatility pattern in COVID-19.

Note: This figure plots the time series averages of realized volatilities by 30-minute intervals through the trading day. The COVID-19 period goes from February 1, 2020, to June 8, 2020 (the end of our sample), and the non-COVID period covers the remaining trading days from January 1998 to January 2020. Half-hour volatilities are annualized through multiplying by $\sqrt{13 \times 252}$.

The intraday volatility shape is also somewhat different between the COVID-19 and non-COVID periods. During COVID-19, we observe a "J" shape: at the beginning of the trading day, volatility is 36%, which gradually decreases throughout the trading day until around lunchtime (12 pm to 2 pm) before rising back up to end the trading day at 38%, slightly higher than the first half-hour. In the non-COVID sample, intraday volatility appears more like a reverse "J" shape. Volatility starts the day at 18% in the first half hour, which gradually decreases toward the middle of the day before rising back to 15% in the last half-hour.

The boom and bust of the technology sector in the late 1990s led to an economic recession in 2001, and the 2008 GFC was associated with the Great Recession. In these recessions, concerns about the real economy, rather than a pandemic, drove changes to the stock market. We compare the diurnal volatility pattern during COVID-19 to the recessions of 2001 and 2008. We refer to the National Bureau of

Economic Research (NBER) dating of US Business Cycle Expansions and Contractions for the recession dates. According to the NBER, the 2001 recession began in April 2001 and ended in November 2001. The Great Recession began in January 2008 and ended in June 2009.

Figure 8.4 compares the intraday volatility pattern during COVID-19 with those from the 2001 and 2008 recessions. Compared to the 2001 recession, intraday volatilities during COVID-19 are higher in every half-hour interval. The average across 13 half-hours for the 2001 recession is 18.5%, which is 40% lower than the 26% average during COVID-19. Looking at each half-hour separately, percentage differences in volatility are 22% (2nd half-hour) to 104% (13th half-hour) between COVID-19 and the 2001 recession.

Volatility levels during the Great Recession are clearly higher than those during the 2001 recession. Compared to volatilities in

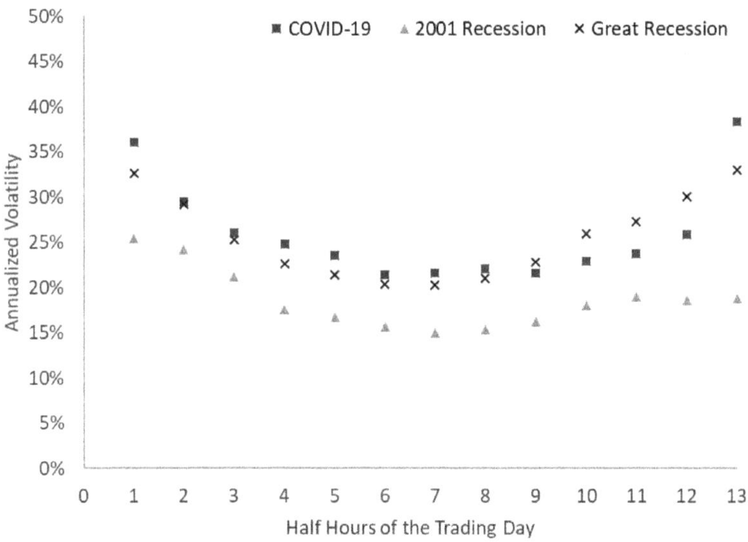

Figure 8.4. A comparison of diurnal volatility in COVID-19 and recessions.

Note: This figure plots the time series averages of realized volatilities by 30-minute intervals through the trading day. The COVID-19 period goes from February 1, 2020, to June 8, 2020 (the end of our sample). We use the NBER recession dates: the 2001 recession began on April 1, 2001, and ended November 30, 2001. The Great Recession began on January 1, 2008, and ended June 30, 2009. Half-hour volatilities are annualized through multiplying by $\sqrt{13 \times 252}$.

the Great Recession, COVID-19 volatility levels are not significantly higher. The 13 half-hour volatilities average to 25.5% during the Great Recession, almost as high as during COVID-19 (26%). COVID-19 volatilities tend to be higher in the first half of the trading day, but the volatilities during the Great Recession are higher in the afternoon from 1:30 pm to 3 pm Eastern time.

The shape of intraday volatility also differs across the stress events. Intraday volatility during COVID-19 makes a "J" shape — the final half-hour volatility is higher than the first half-hour, and the middle half-hours are the lowest. In comparison, the 2001 recession shows a reverse "J" shape, with the first half-hour volatility exceeding the final half-hour. Volatilities in the Great Recession show a symmetrical "U" shape: average volatility is 32.6% in the first half-hour, almost identical to 33% in the final half-hour.

What do the different intraday volatility patterns mean? Almost all earnings and major economic news are released before the market opens, so the market typically opens at such a level that reflects the new information (Gao *et al.*, 2018). Elevated volatility at the beginning of trading day reflects information processing by the market participants; disagreement among market participants leads to fluctuations in prices. Institutional investors tend to place strong emphasis on the closing stock prices (Cushing and Madhavan, 2000; Foucault *et al.*, 2005)). Market makers are also concerned with the closing minutes of the trading day, seeking to unload inventory to avoid overnight risk exposure. Volatility near the end of a trading day reflects inventory concerns as well as institutional investor's concerns about market stability.

During COVID-19, volatilities are higher than other samples for the opening and closing half-hours. News about COVID-19 is often released in the evening, after the end of the trading day. Given our limited understanding of COVID-19, investors may have drastically different assessments of new information, which can contribute to disagreement about new price levels, leading to elevated volatility at the beginning of the trading day. The same concern about uncertainty and market instability could lead to high volatility toward the end of the trading day. Market makers are especially motivated to not take on overnight risk during COVID-19, since inventory risk is magnified as the overall volatility in financial markets is substantially higher.

8.3. Intraday Return Predictability

Gao *et al.* (2018) document that the S&P 500 returns in the 1st and 12th half-hour of the trading day have significant predictive power for the returns in the final half-hour. Their findings are consistent with investors splitting up their order into multiple trading sessions (Bogousslavsky, 2016), or informed trading in the last half-hour in the same direction as the first half-hour. We expand this analysis to document the predictive power of each half-hour, thereby constructing an intraday pattern of the predictive coefficients for the S&P 500. We compare the predictability pattern before and during COVID-19 to see whether the pandemic has caused any changes to this intraday market dynamic.

We follow Gao *et al.* (2018) to divide the trading day into 13 half-hour intervals. We run predictive regressions forecasting the final half-hour of S&P 500 returns:

$$r_{t,13} = \alpha + \beta r_{t,j} + \epsilon_t, \tag{8.3}$$

where $r_{t,13}$ is the return on the S&P 500 index in the 13th half-hour on day t; $r_{t,j}$ is the return in the jth half-hour; and β is the predictive coefficient. We are interested in the sign and magnitude of β.

Table 8.1 presents the predictive regression results. Consistent with the findings in Gao *et al.* (2018), our full-sample results from 1998 to 2020 shows strong predictive power for the 1st and 12th half-hours.[1] A 1% increase in the returns in the first 30 minutes of the trading day is associated with a six-basis-point increase in the final half-hour, and a 1% increase in the 12th half-hour returns is associated with a ten-basis-point increase in the final half-hour. Considering that the expected returns for the S&P 500 is about three or four basis points for the entire day, these predictive coefficients are economically large. Both coefficients are statistically significant at the 1% level, consistent with the statistical significance shown in Gao *et al.* (2018).

Aside from the 1st and 12th half-hours, Gao *et al.* (2018) do not emphasize the forecasting power of other periods. We find that the 2nd, 4th, 5th, and 11th half-hours all exhibit some predictability for

[1]The sample in Gao *et al.* (2018) is from 1993 to 2013.

Table 8.1. Intraday return predictability of half-hour returns.

Half-Hour	**1**	**2**	**3**	**4**	**5**	**6**
Time (Eastern US)	**9:30 am–10 am**	**10 am–10:30 am**	**10:30 am–11 am**	**11 am–11:30 am**	**11:30 am–12 pm**	**12 pm–12:30 pm**
1998–2020	0.06***	0.06***	0.03	0.03*	0.11***	0.00
	(9.1)	(4.0)	(1.6)	(1.7)	(5.2)	(0.1)
COVID-19	0.08*	0.25	−0.67***	−0.10	0.61**	−0.11
	(1.8)	(1.4)	(−3.7)	(−0.7)	(2.3)	(−0.4)
Great Recession	0.17***	0.02	0.03	−0.03	−0.50***	0.12
	(3.9)	(0.2)	(0.2)	(−0.3)	(−3.6)	(0.9)
2001 recession	0.01	−0.03	−0.01	−0.12	−0.04	−0.13
	(0.4)	(−0.5)	(−0.1)	(−1.3)	(−0.4)	(−1.2)
Half-Hour	**7**	**8**	**9**	**10**	**11**	**12**
Time (Eastern US)	**12:30 pm–1 pm**	**1 pm–1:30 pm**	**1:30 pm–2 pm**	**2 pm–2:30 pm**	**2:30 pm–3 pm**	**3 pm–3:30 pm**
1998–2020	−0.05**	−0.01	−0.07***	0.03	0.05***	0.10***
	(−2.1)	(−0.4)	(−3.1)	(1.6)	(2.7)	(6.5)
COVID-19	−0.07	−0.16	−0.19	0.03	0.40**	−0.03
	(−0.4)	(−0.7)	(−0.8)	(0.1)	(2.2)	(−0.1)
Great Recession	0.04	0.03	0.16	−0.18*	0.00	0.14
	(0.3)	(0.2)	(1.1)	(−1.7)	(0.0)	(1.4)
2001 recession	0.06	−0.07	−0.23**	0.02	−0.20**	0.21***
	(0.6)	(−0.6)	(−2.3)	(0.3)	(−2.3)	(2.5)

Note: This table presents the forecasting coefficients in the following predictive regressions:

$$r_{t,13} = \alpha + \beta r_{t,j} + \epsilon_t,$$

where $r_{t,13}$ is the return of the S&P 500 index in the 13th half-hour of the trading day (3:30 pm to 4 pm Eastern Time) on day t, and $r_{t,j}$ is the return in the jth half-hour. T-statistics are shown in parentheses. Statistical significance at the 10%, 5%, and 1% levels are shown with *, **, ***, respectively.

the 13th half-hour with positive coefficients of varying magnitudes, whereas the 7th and 9th half-hours have significantly negative coefficients. In particular, the 2nd, 5th, and 11th half-hours have positive coefficients that are significant at the 1% level. These predictive coefficients are on the same magnitude as those for the 1st and 12th half hours. The 4th half-hour shows a smaller coefficient of 0.03, significant at the 10% level. The 7th and 9th half-hours show predictive coefficients of –0.05 and –0.07, significant at the 5% and 1% levels, which are about the same size as the 1st half-hour but with the opposite sign. Predictability for the final half-hour of S&P 500 returns does not appear to be limited to the 1st and 12th half-hours; other half-hour intervals also exhibit significant predictability.

Intraday return predictability during COVID-19 shows a different pattern compared to the full sample. Since our COVID-19 sample only spans four months, we must be aware of sampling variation when interpreting the results. In a small sample, the point estimates are consistent, but the sizable standard errors make statistical inference more difficult. With this caveat in mind, let us compare the predictive coefficients during COVID-19 with those from the full sample.

In the COVID-19 sample, we continue to observe significant predictability in the 1st half-hour, and the predictive coefficient of 0.08 is close to the full-sample estimate of 0.06. Given the much shorter sample of COVID-19 compared to the full sample, the statistical significance on this coefficient is lower — it is significant at the 10% level, rather than the 1% level for the full sample. We also find significant predictive power for the 5th and 11th half-hours, consistent with the full-sample results. However, we no longer observe predictability for the 12th half-hour. In fact, its predictive coefficient during COVID-19 has a negative point estimate of –0.03, which stands in contrast to the full-sample estimate of 0.10. The 3rd half-hour, which does not predict the final half-hour in the full sample, shows a negative and large coefficient during COVID-19. Evidently, serial correlation of intraday returns shows substantial differences during COVID-19 compared to the full sample.

The economic magnitude of return predictability during COVID-19 also appears to be different compared to the full sample. The size of predictive coefficients is up to six times larger compared to the coefficients in the full sample. Even time periods that do not show statistically significant predictability may contain economically large coefficients, such as 0.25 for the 2nd half-hour, which is two to four times larger compared to the full sample predictive coefficients.

The Great Recession and the 2001 recession are associated with substantial negative shocks to the financial markets, although for different reasons than the COVID-19 pandemic. During the Great Recession, the first half-hour is the only period that contains a significant and positive predictive coefficient for the final half-hour of S&P 500 returns. The 5th and 10th half-hours have economically large negative coefficients: a 1% increase in the S&P 500 returns between 11:30 am and 12 pm is associated with a 50-basis point decrease of the S&P 500 returns between 3:30 pm and 4 pm, and a 1% increase in returns between 2 pm and 2:30 pm is associated with an 18-basis-point decrease. While the predictive coefficients are economically large for the 6th and 12th half-hours, they are not statistically significant at conventional levels.

In the 2001 recession, the morning trading hours do not exhibit predictive power for the final 30 minutes of S&P 500 returns. The 9th and 11th half-hours have rather large negative coefficients, –0.23 and –0.20. These values imply that a 1% increase in the 9th or 11th half-hour returns is associated with a 23- or 20-basis-point decline in the final half-hour of the S&P 500. The 12th half-hour has an economically and statistically large positive predictive coefficient for the 13th half-hour.

The Great Recession and the 2001 recession exhibit different patterns for intraday return predictability. For the Great Recession, the morning trading hours have stronger predictability, whereas the afternoon hours have stronger predictability during the 2001 recession. Return predictability during COVID-19 also appears to follow a distinct pattern, not resembling either recession. The most predictive periods are during the middle of the trading day, rather than at the beginning or toward the end, and the economic magnitude of return predictability is greater than any other period. Indeed, COVID-19 appears to have disrupted the normal stock market dynamics over the course of the trading day. While the channel proposed by Bogousslavsky (2016) still may be consistent with return predictability in the COVID-19 sample, predictive coefficients much larger than other samples suggest there may be additional drivers.

The diurnal volatility pattern during COVID-19 suggests more trading toward the end of the day, perhaps due to market makers concerned about increased inventory risk during a highly uncertain period. To the extent intraday returns reflect the demand of market participants, market makers who take the offsetting side of these transactions must trade in the same direction to unload their inventory. For example, if there is selling pressure during the trading day and market makers buy to meet this demand, they must sell before the market closes to offset their long positions. Selling pressure during the trading day translates to selling pressure of market makers at the end of the trading day, and any downward price pressure in these time periods would lead to a positive relationship between the returns. If market makers are especially sensitive about inventory risk during COVID-19, the direction of order flow during the trading day may become more prominently related to the direction of order flow in the closing hours. To the extent returns reflect demand, we would observe stronger return predictability.

8.4. Intraday Stochastic Volatility

Ellickson *et al.* (2018) show that the instantaneous volatility process can be described by the Heston (1993) model of stochastic volatility. We estimate Heston models using intraday data before and during COVID-19 to compare model parameters such as the volatility of volatility and the mean-reversion speed of the stochastic volatility component. This structural approach complements our reduced-form volatility analysis to uncover differences in volatility dynamics before and during COVID-19.

The stochastic volatility model of Heston (1993) assumes that price $X(t)$ follows a stochastic differential equation:

$$dX_t = \mu X_t dt + \sqrt{V}_t dW_t, \tag{8.4}$$

where W_t is a Brownian motion, μ is the instantaneous mean, and $\sqrt{V}_t$ is the conditional volatility. The variance process V_t follows its own stochastic process:

$$dV_t = \kappa(\underline{c} - V_t)dt + \gamma\sqrt{V}_t dB_t, \tag{8.5}$$

where B_t is a second Brownian motion, possibly correlated with W_t; $\underline{c}$ is the asymptotic mean of the variance process, also known as the long-term equilibrium level of variance since V_t mean-reverts towards $\underline{c}$; and κ is the rate of mean-reversion for the variance process V_t. A larger κ means faster reversion to the long-run variance level $\underline{c}$, whereas a smaller value for κ indicates slower mean-reversion. γ is the "volatility of volatility" that determines the variance of V_t.

A typical calibration of the Heston (1993) model uses Equations (8.4) and (8.5) to calculate parameter values from prices and returns. Ellickson *et al.* (2018) advocate estimating Equation (8.5) using intraday realized volatility, because realized volatility can provide a more precise measurement of the latent volatility process (Andersen and Bollerslev, 1997). We follow the estimation strategy laid out in Ellickson *et al.* (2018), which uses the generalized method of moments (Hansen, 1982) to estimate the model parameters. Because we do not use Equation (8.4) in our estimation strategy, the drift parameter μ and the correlation between the two Brownian motions are not parameters of interest. We focus on the three parameters in Equation (8.5): mean-reversion speed κ, the long-run variance $\underline{c}$, and the volatility of volatility γ.

We estimate the Heston (1993) model using 30-minute realized volatilities. At the end of each month, we use the preceding two months (44 trading days, $13 \times 44 = 572$ observations) to estimate the Heston model. We obtain three series that allow us to investigate the time variation in the stochastic volatility process.

Figure 8.5 plots the mean-reversion parameter over time. For the ease of exposition, we present the three-month moving average. A larger value indicates a stronger tendency to revert to the long-run average volatility level, whereas a smaller value indicates weaker mean-reversion and a greater likelihood that the volatility deviates from the long-run average for an extended period.

From 1998 to 2020, the average mean-reversion parameter value is 0.28. There is substantial variation around this average value, especially before 2005. During times of economic stress, such as the recession in 2001 and the Great Recession of 2008, the mean-reversion parameter tends to decrease to around 0.1. In the COVID-19 sample, we observe a similar decrease in this mean-reversion parameter to a level below the unconditional average. It appears the uncertainty created by COVID-19 is associated with volatility behaving in less predictable ways, deviating from its average value for longer periods.

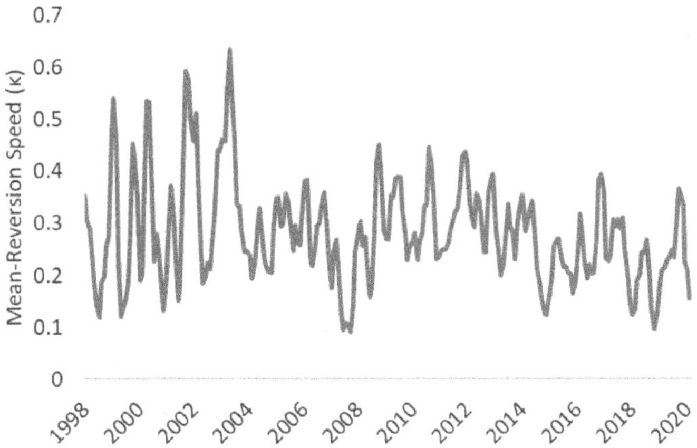

Figure 8.5. Mean-reversion speed of stochastic volatility in the Heston (1993) model.

Note: This figure shows the mean-reversion parameter in the Heston (1993) model, as a three-month moving average. Each month, the Heston (1993) model is estimated using two months (44 trading days) of 30-minute realized volatilities. The sample is from January 1998 to May 2020.

Figure 8.6 presents the long-run volatility in the Heston model from 1998 to 2020. This parameter was subdued in the mid-2000s and in the 2010s, consistent with the low VIX index during those periods. We observe a large positive move during the Great Recession and a similar sharp rise during COVID-19. However, the level of long-run volatility during the Great Recession is higher than the level during COVID-19. While the long-run volatility during COVID-19 appears quite high locally, especially compared to the single-digit VIX environment just prior to the pandemic, the long-run volatility parameter during the Great Recession is twice as high as the value during COVID-19. This finding is consistent with Figure 8.1, which shows that intraday realized volatility during COVID-19 is high relative to recent years, but not as high as the most volatile months during the Great Recession.

Figure 8.7 presents the volatility of volatility parameter in the Heston (1993) model. The prominent peak of the volatility of volatility parameter during the Great Recession resembles the long-run volatility pattern in Figure 8.6. During crisis periods, not only is market volatility higher than usual but also it is more difficult to precisely measure volatility. The volatility of volatility parameter dropped to

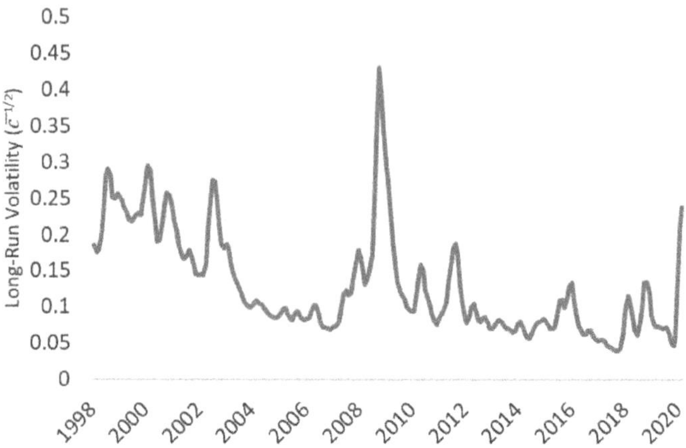

Figure 8.6. Long-run volatility in the Heston (1993) model.

Note: This figure shows the long-run volatility parameter in the Heston (1993) model, as a three-month moving average. We take the square root of the long-run variance, $\underline{c}$ to be the long-run volatility. Each month, the Heston (1993) model is estimated using two months (44 trading days) of 30-minute realized volatilities. The sample is from January 1998 to May 2020.

Figure 8.7. Volatility of volatility in the Heston (1993) model.

Note: This figure shows the volatility of volatility parameter in the Heston (1993) model, as a three-month moving average. Each month, the Heston (1993) model is estimated using two months (44 trading days) of 30-minute realized volatilities. The sample is from January 1998 to May 2020.

very low values in the decade following the Great Recession, and only rose again in the COVID-19 sample. Although the volatility of volatility parameter during COVID-19 appears large compared to the preceding years, it is not as high as during the Great Recession. Indeed, there were numerous disruptions to the financial sector as well as the real economy during the Great Recession.

Prior to 2005, intraday trading was not as developed as the succeeding years. During this period, trading volumes were relatively low, as there were often large time gaps between valid trades. As such, intraday data prior to 2005 reflect poorer data quality in a less mature and less liquid market. In the preceding figures, the apparent noise in the Heston (1993) model parameters prior to 2005 is reflective of this underlying shift in market maturity and microstructure.

The Heston (1993) model gives us a structural way of looking at the behavior of volatility during COVID-19. The three parameters governing the stochastic volatility process shed light on the behavior of intraday volatility. First, the mean-reversion parameter is lower during COVID-19 than earlier years, because volatility behaves in less predictable ways during COVID-19 and can deviate from its long-term average for extended periods. This behavior is similar to that observed in the Great Recession, and the mean-reversion parameter estimate during COVID-19 resembles the value in the Great Recession.

Second, the long-run volatility parameter in the Heston (1993) model is higher during COVID-19 than recent years prior to COVID, but not as high as the long-run volatility estimate in the Great Recession. COVID-19 certainly marks significant disruptions and uncertainty in the financial markets, but apparently to a lesser extent than the most volatile times during the Great Recession. Third, volatility of volatility tells us about the uncertainty around volatility and how precisely we can estimate it. The uncertainty associated with COVID-19 has translated into higher volatility of volatility compared to recent years, but not as high as the values during the Great Recession.

8.5. Conclusion

In this chapter, we provide a unique perspective of the financial market implications of COVID-19 using intraday data. Consistent with existing studies, we find higher intraday volatility during COVID-19 compared to non-COVID periods. Volatilities in COVID-19 are also higher than those in the 2001 recession, but not significantly higher than the volatilities in the Great Recession. In fact, the most volatile months during the Great Recession are more volatile than the COVID-19 sample.

Stock return predictability during COVID-19 shows strong predictive power for the trading hours in the middle of the day, rather than at the beginning or at the end as Gao *et al.* (2018) documented. Our intraday volatility and return predictability results suggest that during COVID-19, there is more investor disagreement about new information and market makers are more concerned about inventory risk. GMM estimation of the Heston (1993) stochastic volatility model reveals that while COVID-19 is associated with increased volatility and uncertainty, this uncertainty is comparable to the Great Recession.

While the stock market has become more volatile as a response to COVID-19, some market participants may be well-positioned to benefit from such volatility. The economically large intraday return predictability is not only important in characterizing the behavior of stock market returns but also economically significant for investors who have the resources to implement trading strategies that capture this empirical observation. In a similar vein, with higher inventory risk, market makers who are able to appropriately manage their inventory risk during COVID-19 may be rewarded with a stronger competitive position. With fewer market makers willing to take inventory risk, the economic profit of market-making activities also likely goes up. On the flip side, investors who are not positioned to benefit from the elevated volatility levels would be better served by taking a long-term view rather than focus on the elevated day-to-day stock market fluctuations.

The far-reaching effects of COVID-19 will take time to be fully understood. In order to formulate appropriate policy responses as well as prepare for the next pandemic, we need to better understand not only the medical and social effects surrounding COVID-19 but also its implications for financial markets. While we take a step toward improving our understanding of the financial market impact of COVID-19, much more remains to be done. It would be interesting to study market reactions to particular events, such as the first confirmed infection in the US or the unscheduled Federal Open Market

Committee meetings of the Federal Reserve. Establishing a connection between intraday volatility patterns and investor behavior could be another fruitful direction.

Acknowledgments

We thank the editors Sabri Boubaker and Duc Nguyen. We also thank Carrie Wang for helpful discussions. All errors are our own.

References

Albulescu, C.T. (2020). COVID-19 and the United States financial markets' volatility. *Finance Research Letters*, 101699.

Andersen, T.G. and Bollerslev, T. (1997). Intraday periodicity and volatility persistence in financial markets. *Journal of Empirical Finance*, **4**, 115–158.

Andersen, T.G., Bollerslev, T., Diebold, F.X. and Labys, P. (2003). Modeling and forecasting realized volatility. *Econometrica*, **71**, 579–625.

Bogousslavsky, V. (2016). Infrequent rebalancing, return autocorrelation, and seasonality. *Journal of Finance*, **71**, 2967–3006.

Corradi, V. and Distaso, W. (2006). Semi-parametric comparison of stochastic volatility models using realized measures. *Review of Economic Studies*, **73**, 635–667.

Cushing, D. and Madhavan, A. (2000). Stock returns and trading at the close. *Journal of Financial Markets*, **3**, 45-67.

Ellickson, B., Sun, M., Whang, D. and Yan, S. (2018). Estimation a local Heston model. SSRN 3108822.

Foucault, T., Kadan, O. and Kandel, E. (2005). Limit order book as a market for liquidity. *Review of Financial Studies*, **18**, 1171–1217.

Gao, L., Han, Y., Li, S. and Zhou, G. (2018). Market intraday momentum. *Journal of Financial Economics*, **2**, 394–414.

Hansen, L.P. (1982). Large sample properties of generalized method of moments estimators. *Econometrica*, **50**(4), 1029–1054.

Harris, L. (1986). A transaction data study of weekly and intraday patterns in stock prices. *Journal of Financial Economics*, **16**, 99–117.

Heston, S.L. (1993). A closed-form solution for options with stochastic volatility with applications to bond and currency options. *Review of Financial Studies*, **6**, 327–343.

Holshue, M. L., DeBolt, C., Lindquist, S., Lofy, K.H., Wiesman, J., Bruce, H., Spitters, C., Ericson, K., Wilkerson, S., Tural, A. and Diaz, G.

(2020). First case of 2019 novel coronavirus in the United States. *New England Journal of Medicine*, **382**, 929–936.

Just, M. and Echaust, K. (2020). Stock market returns, volatility, correlation and liquidity during the COVID-19 crisis: Evidence from the Markov switching approach. *Finance Research Letters*, **37**(C), 101775.

Seven, U. and Yilmaz, F. (2020). World equity markets and COVID-19: Immediate response and recovery prospects. *Research in International Business and Finance*, **56**, 101349.

Shehzad, K., Liu, X. and Kazouz, H. (2020). COVID-19's disasters are perilous than Global Financial Crisis: A rumor or fact? *Finance Research Letters*, **36**, 101669.

Wood, R.A., McInish, T.H. and Ord, J.K. (1985). An investigation of transaction data for NYSE stocks. *Journal of Finance*, **25**, 723–739.

Zhang D., Hu, M. and Ji, Q. (2020). Financial markets under the global pandemic of COVID-19. *Financial Research Letters*, **36**, 101528.

https://doi.org/10.1142/9781800610781_0009

Chapter 9

The Short-Term Effects of COVID-19 on China's Stock Market

Huy Pham[*,], Vikash Ramiah[†,††], Nisreen Moosa[‡,‡‡], Giancarlo Giudici[§,§§], and Vijay Pereira[¶,¶¶]**

[*]*School of Business and Management, RMIT University, Vietnam*

[†]*Faculty of Business, University of Wollongong, Dubai, United Arab Emirates*

[‡]*School of Commerce, University of South Australia, Adelaide, Australia*

[§]*Politecnico di Milano, Milan, Italy*

[¶]*Humanities and Social Sciences Faculty, Khalifa University, Abu Dhabi, United Arab Emirates*

[**]*huy.phamnguyenanh@rmit.edu.vn*
[††]*VikashRamiah@uowdubai.ac.ae*
[‡‡]*nisreen.moosa@mymail.unisa.edu.au*
[§§]*giancarlo.giudici@polimi.it*
[¶¶]*vijay.pereira@port.ac.uk*

Abstract

We investigate the impact of COVID-19 on 36 sectors of China's stock market as classified by Thomson Reuters Eikon. By applying the event study methodology, we examine short-term changes of up to 10 days in stock prices and returns following events pertaining to COVID-19 for the period between December 31, 2019, and March 10, 2020. The evidence captures the gloomy effect of the virus on the Chinese market. We find statistically significant negative abnormal returns following many events across sectors, whereby the most significant effect is widely observed on February 4, 2020. The results are supported by various robustness tests including those of Corrado (1989) and Chesney *et al.* (2011), as well as allowing for market integration. In addition, we document changes in systematic risk by using various ARCH models such as GARCH (1,1), TARCH, PARCH, and EGARCH. We find several spikes — instant changes in systematic risk — in the travel and leisure sector while pharmaceuticals and biotechnology and healthcare equipment and services sectors seem to benefit from the pandemic.

9.1. Introduction

COVID-19, which is a new (or novel) strain of coronavirus, originated in Wuhan, China, in late December 2019. This virus is extremely contagious — by June 2021, it had infected approximately one eighty two million people worldwide. The mortality rate of COVID-19 (around 2%) is, however, much lower than that of SARS (around 10%). At the time of writing, the virus is still spreading rapidly and the death toll is mounting.

COVID-19 has already caused a profound impact on the global economy. The airline sector, for instance, as been one of the worst hit as airlines are grounding their fleets. The pandemic is hurting the tourism and hospitality sector as many countries have entered into lockdown and banned outbound and inbound travel. Another sector that is likely to take a significant hit is the automobile industry, whereby the interruption of production in China has disturbed the supply chain. While the economic cost of COVID-19 is unclear, it is beyond doubt going to be massive. Early indicators of the economic consequences of the outbreak appear in the stock market, which motivates us to investigate how this public health crisis is affecting return and risk in the stock market. Several studies have examined the effects of the impact of COVID-19 on China's stock market. Huo and Qiu (2020) find China's stock market overreacted during the pandemic lockdown and that overreactions are stronger for stocks with lower institutional ownership. In addition, Al-Awadhi *et al.* (2020) show that the Chinese stocks reacted negatively to both the daily growth in total confirmed cases and the daily growth in total cases of death caused by COVID-19. Other studies such as those by Zhang *et al.* (2020) and Ashraf (2020) examine how COVID-19 affects risk and return in various markets. They find that stock markets exhibit a quick response to COVID-19 pandemic and substantial increases in volatility are found in global markets. However, these studies have three significant shortcomings: (i) ignorance of the stock market reaction before the lockdown, (ii) lack of robustness tests, and (iii) failure to show how COVID-19 affects both risk and return of every sector in China. Since the Chinese government has implemented strict regulations on social and economic activities, such as lockdown and regional traffic and travel restrictions (Wang *et al.*, 2020), it is important to assess how China's stock market reacts to each stage of COVID-19. Therefore, our study attempts to examine how COVID-19 affects the risk and return of China's stock market since the first confirmed case of COVID-19 in China.

We apply the event-study methodology of Brown and Warner (1983), and follow the procedure suggested by (Pham *et al.*, 2019), to examine the effects of COVID-19 on the Chinese stock market. The event-study methodology is considered the most suitable for this purpose since there are daily updates on events pertaining to the spread of the virus. Several robustness tests are employed to verify the results, including the Corrado (1989) non-parametric ranking test, the Chesney *et al.* (2012) parametric conditional distribution approach, and the market integration approach. Furthermore, we use various ARCH-type models (such as GARCH (1,1), TARCH, PARCH, and EGARCH) to determine how the sectoral systematic risks changed following the outbreak. In general, we find that COVID-19 negatively impacts the Chinese stock market in the sense that negative reactions outnumber and outweigh the positive ones. The outbreak also has a widespread effect on the market as our results indicate that 35 out of 36 Chinese sectors were affected by the COVID-19 events. Moreover, we find several spikes — instant changes in systematic risk — in the travel and leisure sector, which is one of the most affected sectors, whereas healthcare-related sectors seem to benefit from this pandemic as they experience declining systematic risk.

The remainder of the chapter is structured as follow. In Section 9.2, the relevant literature is reviewed. In Section 9.3, the data and methodology used in the study are presented. The empirical findings are discussed in Section 9.4. Section 9.5 is reserved for concluding remarks.

9.2. Literature Review

Several studies have examined the impact of health crises on the economy. Brainerd and Siegler (2003), for instance, examine the connection between the influenza epidemic and US economic growth over the period 1918–1930. By controlling for numerous factors (including initial income, density, urbanization, human capital, climate, the sectoral composition of output, geography, and the legacy of slavery) the results indicate a large and robust positive effect of the influenza epidemic on per capita income growth across states during the 1920s. This seems to be a reflection of recovery from the pandemic.

Lee and McKibbin (2003) use a G-cubed model to determine that epidemics, such as SARS, cause a reduction in consumer demand, particularly for travel and retail services. This phenomenon is not only observed in the affected countries but also in other countries due to psychological shock. Siu and Wong (2020) examine the effect of SARS in Hong Kong and find that several industries, such as consumer goods and services where human contact is inevitable, are hit the hardest. Au *et al.* (2005) also assess the effects of SARS on Hong Kong and find that the tourism industry was heavily affected, with a higher magnitude than the September 11 terrorist attack. Another study by Overby *et al.* (2004) shows that retail, travel, and tourism industries were seriously affected due to the SARS outbreak since China and Hong Kong were the epicenters of SARS.

From the behavioral finance perspective, a change in social mood may have an adverse effect on stock market performance. Prechter (1979; 1999) and Prechter and Parker (2007) suggest that social mood can be reflected in stock market indices as investors tend to react in the aftermath of an event. Saunders (1993), Nofsinger and Kim (2003), Hirshleifer and Shumway (2003), and Prechter *et al.* (2012) find a positive correlation between social mood and stock prices, whereby a negative social mood can lead to a substantial decline in stock prices. This proposition is supported by Bollen *et al.* (2011) and Gilbert and Karahalios (2010), whose results indicate responsiveness of financial markets to changes in social sentiment.

Furthermore, the fears of infectious diseases may also cause a stir in social sentiment that subsequently affects stock market performance. For example, Donadelli *et al.* (2017) investigate the effect of disease-related news (including SARS, H1N1, and Ebola) on investor mood and pharmaceutical companies' stock prices in the US from 2003 to 2014, and find that the news has "a positive and significant effect on pharmaceutical firms' stock returns" and that the effects last longer than one day. However, they also find that the fear caused by disease-related news has a negative impact on investor sentiment and subsequently leads to a negative effect on stock prices. Ichev and Marinč (2018) find that the Ebola outbreak hurt financial markets such that the effects are stronger on those companies that have exposure to the US and West African countries.

This study focuses on the unprecedented COVID-19 outbreak, which was considered a public health emergency of international concern by WHO on January 30, 2020, and was declared as a pandemic on March 11, 2020. We examine the effect of the outbreak on Chinese stock returns. This study contributes to the literature by determining how investors in various sectors behave during these extraordinary circumstances and how investor behavior is reflected in stock prices. Since we cannot assume that all sectors will be affected in a similar manner, it is important to find out how each sector is affected by the outbreak. We hypothesize that equity holders respond negatively when a perceived riskier environment is expected to have an adverse effect on returns.

Furthermore, Ichev and Marinč (2018) examine how the implied volatility of the US stock market, as reflected through VIX and VXO, changed following the Ebola outbreak and find that the outbreak affected the extent of perceived risk. Their results show a significant surge of VIX and VXO on the day of the event and that the magnitude of the effect is more adverse for highly volatile stocks. These findings imply that a negative investor mood can affect the stock market adversely. We expect that sectors requiring more human interaction or bringing more transmission risk (such as travel and leisure and industrial transportation) will be highly volatile as a result of COVID-19. Accordingly, we hypothesize that these sectors are negatively affected by the outbreak and that they experience an increase in systematic risk. On the other hand, sectors that are vital for the fight against the virus, such as pharmaceuticals and biotechnology, will benefit from the outbreak. Hence we anticipate that these sectors experience a decline in systematic risk.

9.3. Methodology

The daily stock return of a company c in a sector s is calculated as the first log difference (or the log ratio) of stock prices. Hence

$$R_{cst} = \ln\left(\frac{P_{cst}}{P_{cst-1}}\right), \tag{9.1}$$

where P_{cst} is the stock price index (adjusted for dividends, etc) for company c in sector s at time t. Following Brown and Warner (1985) and Ramiah *et al.* (2016), the *ex-post* abnormal returns (AR_{cst}) for each listed company is calculated as the difference between the observed return of company c in sector s on event day t, and the expected return of that company on the same day, $E(R_{cst})$. This gives:

$$AR_{cst} = R_{cst} - E(R_{cst}). \tag{9.2}$$

The expected daily return, $E(R_{cst})$, is estimated using the Capital Asset Pricing Model (CAPM) over the previous 260 observed daily returns. Hence,

$$E(R_{cst}) = \beta^0_{cst} + \beta^1_{cst}(r_{mkt} - r_{ft}) + \varepsilon_{cst}, \tag{9.3}$$

where r_{mkt} is the return on the market index and r_{ft} is the risk-free rate. β^0_{cst} and β^1_{cst} are, respectively, the intercept and the slope of the CAPM and ε_{cst} is the error term.

The daily abnormal return for a sector, AR_{st}, is obtained by averaging the abnormal returns of each company within the sector, which gives

$$AR_{st} = \frac{1}{N}\sum\nolimits_{c=1}^{N} AR_{cst}. \tag{9.4}$$

The standard t-statistic, which is used to find out if the abnormal return is statistically significant, is calculated as

$$t_{AR_{st}} = \frac{AR_{st}}{SD(AR_{st})}, \tag{9.5}$$

where $SD(AR_{st})$ is the standard deviation of abnormal return over the previous 260 days.

According to the efficient market hypothesis (EMH), the market reacts instantly to any available information. In the absence of market efficiency, market participants may over- or under-react to an event or announcement. To investigate this possibility, the cumulative abnormal return (CAR) is estimated over n trading days by using the equation

$$CAR_{stn} = \sum\nolimits_{t=1}^{n} AR_{stn}. \tag{9.6}$$

The t-statistic of estimated CAR is calculated as

$$t_{CAR_{stn}} = \frac{CAR_{stn}}{SD(CAR_{stn})}. \tag{9.7}$$

By examining the significance of CARs, we find out whether or not the market exhibits mean reversion.

Following Pham *et al.* (2019), several robustness checks will be used to validate the results generated from the event study. A criticism of the parametric t-test is that daily abnormal returns are not necessarily normally distributed. In particular, the distribution might exhibit fat tails and positive skewness, leading to positive or negative bias. Hence, when the assumption of normality of abnormal returns is violated, the parametric t-test may not be appropriate and a non-parametric test will be more powerful in detecting a false null hypothesis of zero abnormal returns. Accordingly, we use (as robustness tests) the non-parametric ranking test developed by Corrado (1989) and the Chesney *et al.* (2011) non-parametric conditional distribution approach. To apply the Corrado (1989) ranking test, abnormal returns are transformed into ranks from 1 to 260 over the combined period of 260 days (the estimation period and event window). We then compare the ranks with the expected average rank under the null hypothesis of no abnormal returns. This test, however, only provides the direction but not the magnitude of change. From a statistical point of view, the results of the non-parametric ranking test are valid since it deals with non-normality, particularly when the distribution is skewed and/or leptokurtic (Ataullah *et al.*, 2011).

The Chesney *et al.* (2011) non-parametric conditional distribution approach is used to reveal the outliers that are generally located in the tails of a particular distribution. For this purpose, the kernel regression technique is used, as it does not assume any underlying distribution in the estimation process. The event has an extreme effect on the market only when the conditional cumulative probability of the return on the general index (which is less than or equal to what is observed on the event date) is less than 0.05.

Since the Chinese market is integrated with Asian, European, and the US markets, these markets are likely to exert some influence on observed abnormal returns (ARs). Following Chesney *et al.* (2011) and Graham and Ramiah (2012), three market risk premia are added to the CAPM to control for spillover effects: (i) a market premium for Asia $\tilde{r}_{mkt}^{Asia} - \tilde{r}_{ft}^{Asia}$, (ii) another for Europe $\tilde{r}_{mkt}^{Europe} - \tilde{r}_{ft}^{Europe}$, and (iii) one for the US $\tilde{r}_{mkt}^{US} - \tilde{r}_{ft}^{US}$. Accordingly, the model appears as follows:

$$\begin{aligned} AR_{st}^{int} = \frac{1}{N}\sum_{c=1}^{N}\Bigg[\ln\left(\frac{P_{cst}}{P_{cst-1}}\right) - [\beta_{cst}^{0} + \beta_{cst}^{1}(r_{mkt} - r_{ft})] \\ + \beta_{cst}^{2}(\tilde{r}_{mkt}^{Asia} - \tilde{r}_{ft}^{Asia}) + \beta_{cst}^{3}(\tilde{r}_{mkt}^{Europe} - \tilde{r}_{ft}^{Europe}) \\ + \beta_{cst}^{4}(\tilde{r}_{mkt}^{US} - \tilde{r}_{ft}^{US}) + \varepsilon_{cst}\Bigg], \end{aligned} \tag{9.8}$$

where β_{cst}^{2}, β_{cst}^{3} and β_{cst}^{4} are the coefficients on the market risk premia for Asia, Europe, and the US, respectively, and ε_{cst} is the error term. The standard t-statistic is used to determine if the re-estimated abnormal returns are statistically significant.

Following Ramiah *et al.* (2016) and Pham *et al.* (2018), various risk models are used to capture the changes in sectoral systematic risk produced by COVID-19. The GARCH model of Bollerslev (1986) is specified as:

$$\begin{aligned} \tilde{r}_{st} - \tilde{r}_{ft} = \beta_{s}^{0} + \beta_{s}^{1}\left[\tilde{r}_{mt} - \tilde{r}_{ft}\right] + \beta_{s}^{2}\left[\tilde{r}_{mt} - \tilde{r}_{ft}\right] * AD_{t} \\ + \sum_{j=1}^{p}\alpha_{j}(\tilde{r}_{s} - \tilde{r}_{f})_{t-j} + \sum_{j=1}^{q}\emptyset_{j}\varepsilon_{t-j}. \end{aligned} \tag{9.9}$$

Equation (9.9) is used to test for the aggregate change in systematic risk by adjusting the CAPM in such a way as to incorporate interaction variables and control for autocorrelation. $\tilde{r}_{st}$, $\tilde{r}_{ft}$, and $\tilde{r}_{mt}$ are sectoral return, return on the risk-free asset, and market return, respectively. An aggregate dummy variable (AD) is incorporated, taking the value of one on the announcement date(s) and zero otherwise. β_s^0 is the intercept of the regression equation, β_s^1 is the systematic risk of the sector, and β_s^2 captures the aggregate change in the sectoral risk following the announcements. p and q represent significant lags in the autocorrelation function since we include appropriate AR and MA terms. The GARCH (1,1) model is used to capture volatility clustering that occurs within the daily time series, whereby relatively higher volatility occurs on Mondays and Fridays than the rest of the week. As a robustness check, we also use TARCH, EGARCH, and PARCH models.

Equation (9.9) does not capture the individual effect of each COVID-19–related announcement on each sector. Therefore, we create an individual instant dummy (*IID*) variable for each announcement (or event) to capture instant changes in systematic risk. The *IID* has a value of one on the announcement date and zero otherwise. Each *IID* is multiplied by the market risk premium to obtain 36 interaction variables whose coefficients represent the instant change in systematic risk caused by each event. The model is then written as follows:

$$\tilde{r}_{st} - \tilde{r}_{ft} = \beta_s^0 + \beta_s^1[\tilde{r}_{mt} - \tilde{r}_{ft}] + \sum\nolimits_{g=1}^{36} \beta_{s,g}^2[\tilde{r}_{mt} - \tilde{r}_{ft}] * IID_g + \sum_{j=1}^{p} \alpha_j \left(\tilde{r}_s - \tilde{r}_f\right)_{t-j} + \sum_{j=1}^{q} \emptyset_j \varepsilon_{t-j}. \tag{9.10}$$

The number of *IIDs* in Equation (9.10) may cause multicollinearity, which can be dealt with by creating continuous short-term dummy (*CD*) variables that take the value of one for a longer period (more than one day) after the event. Equation (9.11) is then rewritten as follow:

$$\tilde{r}_{st} - \tilde{r}_{ft} = \beta_s^0 + \beta_s^1[\tilde{r}_{mt} - \tilde{r}_{ft}] + \sum\nolimits_{g=1}^{36} \beta_{s,g}^2[\tilde{r}_{mt} - \tilde{r}_{ft}] * CD_g + \sum_{j=1}^{p} \alpha_j \left(\tilde{r}_s - \tilde{r}_f\right)_{t-j} + \sum_{j=1}^{q} \emptyset_j \varepsilon_{t-j}. \tag{9.11}$$

For instance, the *CD* for event 1 takes the value of zero prior to December 31, 2019, and one thereafter. Likewise, the *CD* for event 2 takes the value of zero prior to January 5, 2020, and one until the last day of the sample. The *CD*s for other events are constructed in a similar manner.

9.4. Data and Empirical Results

Table 9.1 presents a brief summary of the events surrounding the development of COVID-19. The early cases of COVID-19 were reported by China to WHO on December 31, 2019, which in turn declared the virus as a global emergency on January 30, 2020.[1] We use daily stock prices, market indices, and the risk-free rate for the period between January 1, 2015, to March 10, 2020, obtained from Thomson Reuters Eikon.[2] As we observed the impact of COVID-19 at a sectoral level, several sectoral portfolios were constructed, based on the classification used by Thomson Reuters Eikon. In addition, we collect data on Asia, the US, and Europe from Thomson Reuters Eikon for our robustness tests.

Table 9.2 reports overall market reactions of China, Asia, the US, and Europe following each COVID-19 event. In general, the Chinese stock market was hit much earlier compared to other stock markets since the virus originated in China. The highest negative reaction was observed on Monday, February 3, 2020, when there was an exponential rise in confirmed cases and deaths in the country. In addition, we observe that 35 out of 36 Chinese sectors reacted to COVID-19, with 30 of them experiencing mixed reactions. The results show the dominance of negative reactions. In addition, we detect a structural break on February 4, 2020, for several sectors, including travel and leisure, beverages, construction and materials, electricity, general retailers, industrial transportation, oil producers, personal goods, and real estate investment and services.[3]

Table 9.3 reports statistically significant positive and negative abnormal returns (and their t-statistics) arising in response to the COVID-19 events. The corresponding results of the robustness tests are reported in Table 9.4. Two sectors were affected positively — banks and fixed-line telecommunication — and three sectors were affected negatively — beverages, leisure goods, and life insurance. The effects of COVID-19 on the banks and fixed-line

[1]The events are collected from https://www.aljazeera.com/news/2020/01/timeline-china-coronavirus-spread-200126061554884.html as of March 10, 2020.

[2]For estimation purpose, we must collect our data for a longer period compared to the timeline of our events.

[3]The results are not reported for brevity purpose.

Table 9.1. COVID-19 events.

Event date	Event number	Description
31/12/2019	1	China alerted WHO to several cases of pneumonia in Wuhan.
7/01/2020	2	The officials announced they had identified a new virus, according to the WHO.
11/01/2020	3	China announced its first death.
13/01/2020		WHO reported a case in Thailand.
16/01/2020	4	Japan's health ministry reported a confirmed case.
17/01/2020	5	A second death was reported in Wuhan.
20/01/2020	6	China reported a third death and more than 200 infections. Asian countries ramped up measures to block the spread of the virus.
22/01/2020	7	The death toll in China jumped to 17 with more than 550 infections. European airports stepped up checks on flights from Wuhan.
23/01/2020	8	Wuhan, Xiantao, and Chibi were placed under effective quarantine on January 23 as air and rail departures were suspended.
24/01/2020	9	The death toll in China is 26 with more than 830 infections.
		The number of cities under lockdown in Hubei rose to 13.
27/01/2020	10	Travel restrictions were imposed on a further five cities in Hubei province. Hong Kong declared a virus emergency.
		The death toll rose to 56, with almost 2,000 cases confirmed as travel restrictions were increased in Hong Kong.
		New cases were confirmed in the US, Taiwan, Thailand, Japan, and South Korea.
		The death toll in China rose to 106, with 100 in Hubei province.
30/01/2020	11	The WHO declared coronavirus a global emergency as the death toll in China jumped to 170, with 7,711 cases reported. India and the Philippines confirmed their first cases.
31/01/2020	12	The number of confirmed cases in China jumped to 9,809. Russia, Spain, Sweden, and the UK confirmed their first cases of the virus.

(*Continued*)

Table 9.1. (*Continued*)

Event date	Event number	Description
3/02/2020	13	China reported 57 new fatalities, bringing its death toll to at least 361. New cases were confirmed in Australia, Canada, Germany, Japan, Singapore, the US, the United Arab Emirates (UAE), and Vietnam. The first death outside of China was reported in the Philippines.
4/02/2020	14	China states the death toll rose to 425 people. Hong Kong also reported one death, bringing the global fatalities to 427. The first case was confirmed in Belgium.
5/02/2020	15	More flights evacuating US citizens returned from Wuhan and the WHO reaffirmed there was "no known effective treatment" for the coronavirus.
6/02/2020	16	The death toll in mainland China rose to 563. First known human-to-human transmission in Malaysia and the number of people infected in Europe reached 30.
7/02/2020	17	Mainland China confirmed the death toll had reached at least 636.
10/02/2020	18	A US citizen died in Wuhan in what appears to be the first confirmed foreign death. A Japanese man in his 60s with a suspected coronavirus infection also died in hospital in Wuhan. China had 908 confirmed deaths and a total of 40,171 infections
11/02/2020	19	The WHO announced that the new coronavirus would be called "COVID-19." Meanwhile, deaths in China reached 1,016, with 42,638 infections recorded.
12/02/2020	20	The death toll in mainland China hit 1,113, with 44,653 infections recorded.
13/02/2020	21	The death toll in mainland China hit 1,300. Japan confirmed its first death from the virus.
14/02/2020	22	China reported 121 more deaths, bringing to the total number across the mainland to nearly 1,400.
17/02/2020	23	1,770 deaths reported in mainland China and 70,548 cases. Japan confirmed 99 new cases of the virus onboard the quarantined Diamond Princess cruise ship.

Table 9.1. (*Continued*)

Event date	Event number	Description
18/02/2020	24	China's daily infection figures drop below 2,000 for the first time since January, with 1,868 deaths. Russia bans entry to Chinese citizens from February 20.
19/02/2020	25	Iran reported two deaths from the coronavirus. China's daily infection figures drop below 2,000 for the second straight day, with 2,004 deaths.
20/02/2020	26	South Korea reported its first death from the coronavirus. China reported the death toll had risen to 2,118.
21/02/2020	27	South Korea reported its second death and 100 new confirmed cases. In mainland China, the death toll reached 2,236 as the confirmed cases of the infection rose above 75,400. Israel reported its first confirmed case of the coronavirus. In Italy, the region of Lombardy reported the first local transmission of the virus with three new cases.
24/02/2020	28	Iran confirmed the sixth death. A seventh death was reported in northern Italy. Kuwait, Bahrain, Iraq, Afghanistan, and Oman all reported their first cases of the virus. The number of cases in South Korea ballooned to 833, with 7 deaths. The death toll in China rose to 2,595 among 77,262 confirmed cases.
25/02/2020	29	Iran reached 95 cases with 15 deaths. China's reported cases continued to plateau, with 518 new infections and 71 new deaths. South Korea's confirmed cases rose to 977 while Italy's reached 229.
26/02/2020	30	The global death toll neared 2,800 with a total of about 80,000 confirmed infections. Norway, Romania, Greece, Georgia, Pakistan, North Macedonia, and Brazil all detected their first cases of the coronavirus.
27/02/2020	31	Estonia, Denmark, Northern Ireland, and the Netherlands reported their first coronavirus cases. 82,000 infections worldwide with more than 2,800 deaths. Italy's infections jumped to 650 with 17 deaths.

(*Continued*)

Table 9.1. (*Continued*)

Event date	Event number	Description
28/02/2020	32	Lithuania and Wales reported their first coronavirus cases, with Netherlands and Georgia reporting their second.
2/03/2020	33	South Korea's total infections of 3,150 with 17 deaths. Iran also reported 593 confirmed cases with 43 deaths. First coronavirus case in Qatar, Saudi Arabia, Tunisia, and Jordan.
3/03/2020	34	Italy and Iran announced the death toll in the country reached 77.
9/03/2020	35	Nearly 3,500 deaths and infected another 102,000 people across more than 90 countries. China reported 99 new cases. China's exports plunging 17.2% in the first two months of the year. Iran has 4,747 reported cases and 124 deaths.
		Saudi authorities locked down the eastern Qatif region in a bid to contain the fast-spreading virus. In Italy, the government imposed a strict quarantine in the state of Lombardy and 14 other areas in the north.
		Germany reported its first two deaths, with at least 1,100 confirmed cases in the country.
10/03/2020	36	A total of 54 people died in Iran, while in Italy, 168 new fatalities were recorded. Lebanon and Morocco reported their first deaths from the virus, while Democratic Republic of the Congo, Panama, and Mongolia confirmed their first cases of infection.

telecommunication sectors were negligible since these reactions took place past the peak of the outbreak in China. Since the services of banks and telecommunication companies are required even during a pandemic, it is not difficult to explain why these two sectors are the least affected by the virus. The findings are consistent with those of Huo and Qiu (2020) in the short-term effect context.

On the other hand, we observe that beverages, leisure goods, and life insurance sectors were negatively affected by the outbreak and that most of these reactions appeared during the peak period. The beverages sector, for instance, experienced a negative abnormal return of –3.87% (with a t-statistic of –5.11) on February 4, 2020,

Table 9.2. Stock market reactions to COVID-19 events (%) in different regions.

Event date	Event number	China	US	Asia	Europe
31/12/2019	1	0.44	0.29	−0.43	0.06
7/01/2020	2	1.00	−0.28	0.63	−0.21
13/01/2020	3	1.05	0.70	1.26	−0.01
16/01/2020	4	−0.33	0.83	0.45	−0.02
17/01/2020	5	−0.12	0.39	0.43	0.56
20/01/2020	6	0.98	0.00	−0.13	−0.24
22/01/2020	7	0.50	0.03	1.22	−0.21
23/01/2020	8	−3.15	0.11	−1.40	−1.06
24/01/2020	9	0.00	−0.91	0.13	0.74
27/01/2020	10	0.00	−1.59	0.00	−2.36
30/01/2020	11	0.00	0.31	−3.39	−0.75
31/01/2020	12	0.00	−1.79	−0.47	−0.65
3/02/2020	13	−8.41	0.72	−0.02	−0.05
4/02/2020	14	1.56	1.49	2.10	1.46
5/02/2020	15	1.85	1.12	0.40	0.91
6/02/2020	16	2.28	0.33	2.52	0.18
7/02/2020	17	0.42	−0.54	−0.81	−0.55
10/02/2020	18	0.86	0.73	−0.87	−0.22
11/02/2020	19	0.21	0.17	1.30	0.89
12/02/2020	20	1.20	0.64	1.09	0.41
13/02/2020	21	−0.74	−0.16	−0.11	−0.55
14/02/2020	22	0.41	0.18	0.32	−0.19
17/02/2020	23	2.69	0.00	0.16	0.23
18/02/2020	24	0.58	−0.29	−1.92	−0.60
19/02/2020	25	−0.44	0.47	0.52	0.59
20/02/2020	26	1.98	−0.38	−0.43	−0.77
21/02/2020	27	0.72	−1.06	−1.42	0.01
24/02/2020	28	0.54	−3.41	−2.75	−3.85
25/02/2020	29	−0.05	−3.07	1.08	−1.69
26/02/2020	30	−1.79	−0.38	−1.06	0.16
27/02/2020	31	0.18	−4.52	−0.19	−2.91
28/02/2020	32	−4.42	−0.83	−2.26	−3.43
2/03/2020	33	3.40	4.50	0.97	1.66
3/03/2020	34	0.88	−2.85	0.69	1.33
9/03/2020	35	−3.46	−7.90	−4.61	−6.50
10/03/2020	36	2.10	4.82	1.52	−2.40
	MAX	3.40	4.82	2.52	1.66
	MIN	−8.41	−7.90	−4.61	−6.50

Table 9.3. Positive and negative sectoral reactions following COVID-19 events (%).

Sector	Event date	AR	t-stat	CAR2	t-stat	CAR5	t-stat	CAR10	t-stat
Positive reaction									
Banks	26/02/2020	2.08	2.62	0.87	0.79	−0.12	−0.07	0.20	0.09
Fixed-line telecommunications	21/02/2020	3.13	2.19	4.80	2.34	1.05	0.34	−2.75	−0.67
Negative reaction									
Beverages	4/02/2020	−3.87	−5.11	−1.66	−1.48	0.07	0.04	−2.80	−1.03
Leisure goods	17/01/2020	−1.52	−2.07	−0.31	−0.29	−1.03	−0.55	−1.20	−0.47
	4/02/2020	−1.79	−2.42	0.93	0.90	1.79	1.01	0.60	0.26
Life insurance	5/02/2020	−2.59	−2.18	−2.74	−1.74	−4.21	−1.79	−5.88	−1.81
	24/02/2020	−2.50	−2.13	0.30	0.19	−0.67	−0.29	−2.42	−0.77

Note: The table shows the statistically significant positive and negative reactions with their respective t-statistic of up to 10 days following COVID-19 events.

Table 9.4. Mixed sectoral reactions following COVID-19 events (%).

Sector	Event date	AR	t-stat	CAR2	t-stat	CAR5	t-stat	CAR10	t-stat
Aerospace & defense	4/02/2020	−3.36	−2.63	0.36	0.21	0.34	0.12	6.24	1.64
	17/02/2020	3.90	3.01	2.66	1.48	1.87	0.68	−1.33	−0.35
	28/02/2020	−2.91	−2.22	1.81	1.00	3.09	1.12	2.18	0.58
Alternative energy	4/02/2020	−3.92	−4.85	−0.67	−0.60	0.06	0.03	3.18	1.35
	12/02/2020	2.48	3.08	−1.08	−0.96	0.80	0.45	−0.88	−0.38
	18/02/2020	1.87	2.31	0.10	0.09	−2.36	−1.32	−3.53	−1.52
Automobiles & parts	6/01/2020	1.34	2.02	2.47	2.61	1.19	0.77	0.36	0.17
	4/02/2020	−2.96	−4.27	0.11	0.11	1.67	1.12	2.71	1.38
	10/02/2020	2.11	3.07	−0.66	−0.68	−1.15	−0.77	1.09	0.55
	28/02/2020	−1.89	−2.72	0.27	0.28	0.60	0.40	0.22	0.11
Chemicals	4/02/2020	−2.24	−3.91	1.09	1.47	1.20	1.03	2.78	1.79
	11/02/2020	−1.19	−2.11	0.16	0.22	1.58	1.34	1.48	0.95
	18/02/2020	1.45	2.50	−0.18	−0.24	−0.10	−0.09	−0.29	−0.19
	10/03/2020	−1.19	−2.08	0.00	0.00	0.00	0.00	0.00	0.00
Construction & materials	4/02/2020	−3.85	−7.30	−1.04	−1.31	0.53	0.40	0.42	0.21
	10/02/2020	1.60	2.74	−0.31	−0.37	−0.82	−0.57	−0.78	−0.37
	26/02/2020	3.80	6.32	1.01	1.18	5.90	4.08	5.83	2.71
	2/03/2020	2.30	3.84	2.59	3.06	2.62	1.80	2.52	1.17
Electricity	3/02/2020	−1.77	−3.05	−2.71	−3.08	−2.90	−2.12	−3.51	−1.88
	4/02/2020	−2.52	−4.30	−1.12	−1.25	−0.24	−0.17	−0.58	−0.30
	25/02/2020	−1.56	−2.58	2.56	2.83	2.68	1.88	5.33	2.76
	26/02/2020	2.26	3.72	0.95	1.05	1.48	1.04	3.07	1.59

(Continued)

Table 9.4. (*Continued*)

Sector	Event Date	AR	*t*-stat	CAR2	*t*-stat	CAR5	*t*-stat	CAR10	*t*-stat
Electronic equipment & services	4/02/2020	−2.73	−3.42	−0.82	−0.72	0.62	0.32	4.56	1.79
	18/02/2020	2.15	2.68	0.09	0.08	3.39	1.77	−1.26	−0.51
	24/02/2020	2.47	3.08	−1.35	−1.19	−3.61	−1.88	−5.29	−2.15
	26/02/2020	−1.93	−2.40	−2.37	−2.08	−3.56	−1.86	−2.78	−1.13
Financial services	4/02/2020	−3.88	−3.19	−2.03	−1.18	−2.69	−1.04	−2.87	−0.81
	20/02/2020	3.49	2.82	−1.98	−1.14	−0.84	−0.32	1.07	0.34
Food & drug retailers	3/02/2020	2.01	2.81	−1.51	−1.53	0.32	0.21	−3.71	−1.63
	4/02/2020	−1.62	−2.26	1.86	1.96	1.34	0.88	−1.66	−0.74
	6/02/2020	1.76	2.56	0.08	0.09	−2.56	−1.72	−5.24	−2.33
Food producers	4/02/2020	−2.48	−2.87	2.34	1.93	3.53	1.89	4.62	1.91
	10/02/2020	3.49	4.03	−2.01	−1.66	−1.39	−0.73	−0.96	−0.40
	11/02/2020	−2.22	−2.57	0.39	0.32	1.09	0.57	0.54	0.23
Forestry & paper	4/02/2020	−3.66	−5.17	−0.60	−0.58	1.74	1.08	0.91	0.39
	10/02/2020	1.83	2.54	−0.56	−0.53	−1.78	−1.06	−1.32	−0.56
	26/02/2020	2.33	3.17	0.97	0.90	2.98	1.78	5.50	2.33
Gas, water & multiutilities	3/02/2020	−2.59	−3.47	−2.04	−2.03	0.69	0.48	−2.42	−1.27
	4/02/2020	−1.89	−2.52	0.40	0.40	1.19	0.82	−0.06	−0.03
	7/02/2020	1.74	2.35	−0.95	−0.95	−2.52	−1.71	−2.61	−1.34
General industrials	4/02/2020	−2.47	−3.70	0.61	0.64	0.92	0.56	0.13	0.05
	26/02/2020	1.92	2.91	−1.09	−1.15	0.02	0.01	0.57	0.25
General retailers	22/01/2020	−1.27	−2.31	−0.87	−1.12	−0.79	−0.65	−5.34	−3.11
	3/02/2020	−1.53	−2.79	−3.05	−3.97	−1.70	−1.49	−3.62	−2.24
	4/02/2020	−3.21	−5.87	−0.11	−0.15	0.65	0.58	0.29	0.18

	10/02/2020	1.59	3.02	−1.38	−1.90	−1.91	−1.67	−1.97	−1.18
	26/02/2020	1.73	3.22	0.34	0.45	1.00	0.85	3.12	1.87
Healthcare equipment & services	23/01/2020	3.19	3.16	−0.40	−0.25	−0.88	−0.32	15.96	4.34
	3/02/2020	8.95	8.53	6.62	4.07	3.55	1.31	−0.28	−0.08
	4/02/2020	3.46	3.28	4.57	2.79	−2.47	−0.91	−3.42	−0.93
	5/02/2020	3.16	2.95	0.08	0.05	−5.43	−2.01	−9.10	−2.48
	10/02/2020	−3.14	−2.92	−2.37	−1.44	−3.83	−1.41	−3.88	−1.06
	11/02/2020	−2.56	−2.38	−1.33	−0.80	−0.95	−0.35	0.88	0.24
	19/02/2020	−2.53	−2.22	−1.19	−0.69	1.34	0.49	2.35	0.65
	24/02/2020	3.34	2.93	−0.81	−0.47	0.73	0.27	6.14	1.69
	26/02/2020	−3.01	−2.64	1.50	0.87	1.01	0.37	3.37	0.93
Household goods & Home construction	22/01/2020	−1.16	−2.48	−0.82	−1.24	−0.68	−0.62	−3.99	−2.44
	4/02/2020	−2.74	−5.75	−0.60	−0.90	0.13	0.12	0.44	0.27
	18/02/2020	1.08	2.21	−0.18	−0.26	−2.02	−1.81	0.61	0.36
	26/02/2020	1.70	3.46	0.59	0.85	2.37	2.15	3.08	1.84
Industrial engineering	4/02/2020	−3.15	−5.26	−0.01	−0.02	1.73	1.30	3.43	1.84
	7/02/2020	1.37	2.33	0.37	0.45	−0.06	−0.04	2.36	1.26
	10/02/2020	1.26	2.14	−0.66	−0.80	−0.83	−0.61	1.77	0.94
	18/02/2020	1.64	2.73	0.16	0.19	0.98	0.73	3.03	1.63
	26/02/2020	1.27	2.12	−0.05	−0.06	1.44	1.07	2.56	1.37
Industrial metals & mining	4/02/2020	−3.16	−4.62	−1.14	−1.21	1.62	1.12	2.43	1.22
	6/02/2020	−1.56	−2.27	2.10	2.24	2.89	1.99	2.72	1.37
	10/02/2020	1.98	2.88	0.89	0.95	0.95	0.65	0.43	0.21
	26/02/2020	2.22	3.22	−0.77	−0.82	0.46	0.32	0.69	0.35

(Continued)

Table 9.4. (*Continued*)

Sector	Event date	AR	*t*-stat	CAR2	*t*-stat	CAR5	*t*-stat	CAR10	*t*-stat
Industrial transportation	3/02/2020	−1.48	−2.65	−3.99	−5.11	−3.77	−3.10	−5.02	−2.74
	4/02/2020	−4.16	−7.47	−0.08	−0.10	0.12	0.10	−0.73	−0.39
	24/02/2020	−1.37	−2.31	1.33	1.60	1.77	1.34	5.95	2.98
	26/02/2020	2.25	3.81	0.19	0.23	1.95	1.46	4.61	2.30
	9/03/2020	2.38	4.01	−0.01	−0.01	−0.01	−0.01	−0.01	0.00
Media	6/01/2020	1.96	2.43	0.29	0.24	−1.20	−0.64	−2.83	−1.07
	7/01/2020	1.89	2.35	−2.28	−1.92	−2.53	−1.34	−5.00	−1.88
	20/01/2020	−2.51	−3.02	−1.46	−1.19	−1.62	−0.83	−1.17	−0.44
	4/02/2020	−2.21	−2.63	3.12	2.57	3.04	1.63	2.57	1.00
	11/02/2020	−1.81	−2.17	−1.58	−1.29	−0.48	−0.25	−4.79	−1.86
	13/02/2020	−1.73	−2.06	−0.83	−0.68	−1.47	−0.79	−2.46	−0.96
	18/02/2020	1.93	2.29	−2.57	−2.10	−4.31	−2.31	−5.15	−2.01
	19/02/2020	−1.85	−2.19	−1.13	−0.93	−1.65	−0.88	−2.32	−0.90
Mining	6/01/2020	1.84	2.55	0.77	0.79	−2.56	−1.71	−4.23	−1.95
	3/02/2020	−1.56	−2.13	−2.00	−1.98	−1.46	−0.93	−0.94	−0.43
	4/02/2020	−2.57	−3.49	0.07	0.07	1.32	0.85	2.62	1.21
Oil equipment	6/01/2020	3.28	3.06	−0.75	−0.49	−5.26	−2.42	−4.90	−1.74
	7/01/2020	−2.46	−2.29	−0.26	−0.17	−1.93	−0.88	−1.29	−0.46
	4/02/2020	−4.69	−4.21	−1.21	−0.76	0.56	0.25	0.19	0.07
	25/02/2020	−2.52	−2.25	0.84	0.52	0.75	0.33	0.19	0.07
Oil producers	6/01/2020	4.50	4.43	0.52	0.37	−5.93	−2.84	−7.18	−2.67
	7/01/2020	−2.91	−2.86	−1.00	−0.72	−2.78	−1.32	−4.28	−1.58

	3/02/2020	−2.35	−2.25	−4.18	−2.83	−4.38	−1.98	−5.00	−1.78
	4/02/2020	−4.26	−4.05	−0.25	−0.17	−0.13	−0.06	−0.56	−0.20
	24/02/2020	−2.33	−2.15	0.66	0.44	1.27	0.56	4.85	1.69
	26/02/2020	2.62	2.41	0.99	0.66	0.65	0.29	2.79	0.97
Personal goods	22/01/2020	−1.23	−2.39	−0.03	−0.04	0.19	0.16	−0.43	−0.27
	4/02/2020	−1.70	−3.28	2.24	3.12	1.91	1.71	1.41	0.85
	5/02/2020	1.26	2.43	2.40	3.33	0.92	0.81	−0.05	−0.03
	7/02/2020	1.41	2.73	−1.75	−2.41	−3.03	−2.59	−3.06	−1.79
	11/02/2020	−1.92	−3.70	−0.31	−0.43	−0.51	−0.41	−0.19	−0.11
	28/02/2020	1.38	2.37	0.21	0.26	4.24	3.37	3.32	1.91
	9/03/2020	1.70	2.93	−2.62	−3.20	−2.62	−2.09	−2.62	−1.52
	10/03/2020	−2.62	−4.51	0.00	0.00	0.00	0.00	0.00	0.00
Pharmaceutical & biotechnology	31/12/2019	1.85	2.73	−0.88	−0.93	−1.00	−0.65	0.22	0.10
	20/01/2020	1.67	1.98	1.31	1.04	2.94	1.40	7.89	2.83
	22/01/2020	−3.10	−3.65	1.66	1.31	1.58	0.75	12.14	4.37
	23/01/2020	1.68	1.98	−0.05	−0.04	−0.13	−0.06	11.46	4.14
	3/02/2020	5.06	5.89	5.57	4.37	0.58	0.28	−3.14	−1.16
	4/02/2020	2.05	2.38	4.52	3.54	−2.85	−1.37	−5.04	−1.87
	5/02/2020	3.52	4.07	−1.80	−1.41	−7.04	−3.40	−10.20	−3.79
	7/02/2020	−2.79	−3.24	−4.57	−3.58	−6.72	−3.24	−9.59	−3.56
	10/02/2020	−3.19	−3.70	−2.05	−1.61	−3.72	−1.79	−5.68	−2.11
	9/03/2020	1.92	2.19	−2.18	−1.67	−2.18	−1.04	−2.18	−0.81
	10/03/2020	−2.18	−2.49	0.00	0.00	0.00	0.00	0.00	0.00

(Continued)

Table 9.4. (*Continued*)

Sector	Event date	AR	*t*-stat	CAR2	*t*-stat	CAR5	*t*-stat	CAR10	*t*-stat
Real estate investment & services	3/02/2020	−1.20	−1.98	−4.00	−4.69	−3.61	−2.63	−2.38	−1.13
	4/02/2020	−3.77	−6.27	−0.92	−1.07	0.30	0.22	1.36	0.64
	26/02/2020	2.96	4.54	−0.10	−0.11	3.54	2.44	2.85	1.34
Software	7/02/2020	3.79	3.61	−3.35	−2.26	−2.49	−1.10	−2.21	−0.79
	26/02/2020	−2.27	−2.11	−0.02	−0.01	−0.59	−0.25	−3.49	−1.23
Support services	17/01/2020	−1.24	−2.12	−0.93	−1.14	−1.89	−1.49	−2.21	−1.28
	4/02/2020	−3.27	−5.58	0.83	1.04	1.45	1.20	2.91	1.75
	7/02/2020	1.59	2.75	−0.97	−1.22	−0.78	−0.64	0.25	0.15
	11/02/2020	−1.61	−2.78	0.28	0.35	1.46	1.18	0.25	0.15
	25/02/2020	−1.36	−2.30	2.04	2.50	2.28	1.83	4.36	2.56
Technology hardware & equipment	4/02/2020	−2.68	−2.73	−0.16	−0.12	1.27	0.61	6.73	2.44
	7/02/2020	2.47	2.47	−1.04	−0.75	1.33	0.63	4.39	1.59
	18/02/2020	2.21	2.18	−1.24	−0.88	4.10	1.92	−1.70	−0.62
	24/02/2020	3.32	3.26	−1.78	−1.25	−4.84	−2.25	−6.78	−2.46
	26/02/2020	−2.59	−2.53	−3.04	−2.14	−4.24	−1.97	−2.41	−0.87
	10/03/2020	2.59	2.58	0.00	0.00	0.00	0.00	0.00	0.00
Travel & leisure	20/01/2020	−1.95	−3.20	−2.03	−2.28	−3.04	−2.04	−4.38	−1.94
	3/02/2020	−1.38	−2.15	−4.93	−5.11	−3.65	−2.44	−4.12	−1.85
	4/02/2020	−5.27	−8.19	−0.28	−0.28	1.95	1.29	2.32	1.03
	7/02/2020	1.30	1.98	0.93	0.95	0.29	0.19	3.29	1.45
	19/02/2020	2.04	3.09	−0.06	−0.06	−1.26	−0.82	−0.11	−0.05
	24/02/2020	−2.27	−3.44	1.07	1.09	1.94	1.27	3.87	1.69
	26/02/2020	2.24	3.37	0.87	0.87	1.15	0.75	2.77	1.21

Note: The table shows the statistically significant mixed reactions with their respective *t*-statistic of up to 10 days following COVID-19 events.

when the death toll rose to 425 people and the number of infections stood at 20,438 people. On the same day, the leisure goods sector recorded a negative abnormal return of –1.79% (with a t-statistic of –2.42). These findings are supported by at least one of the robustness tests. An epidemic can cause a major disruption of consumption (Jung *et al.*, 2016), hence there is less demand for beverage products or leisure goods that would subsequently have an adverse effect on the revenues of these two sectors. These findings are consistent with those of Siu and Wong (2020), Overby *et al.* (2004) and Au *et al.* (2005). Moreover, we find that the life insurance sector exhibited a negative abnormal return of –2.59% (with a t-statistic of –2.18) and –2.50% (with a t-statistic of -2.13) on February 5, 2020 (when China reported 490 deaths and 24,324 cases of infections) and on February 24, 2020 (when the death toll rose to 2,595 among 77,262 confirmed cases). These negative reactions can be attributed to the losses incurred by life insurance firms, as a result of paying out life insurance policies, and to investor expectations that the outbreak would become so severe that it would eventually lead to a surge in the death toll. One interesting observation is that the effects of these events did not last long. The results show that most cumulative abnormal returns for 2, 5, and 10 days after the event are not statistically significant, with the exception of CAR2 of the fixed-line telecommunication sector. The findings of negative reactions to an increase in reported deaths and confirmed cases are in line with those of Al-Awadhi *et al.* (2020).

The results show that 30 out of 35 sectors exhibit mixed reactions, including general retailers, healthcare equipment and services, household goods and home construction, industrial transportation, pharmaceutical and biotechnology, and travel and leisure (Tables 9.5 and 9.6). It is worthwhile to focus on the reaction of healthcare equipment and services and pharmaceutical and biotechnology sectors, since their activities are highly relevant to the outbreak. These two sectors recorded most cases where positive reactions outweigh negative reactions. The reactions could be attributed to the highly contagious nature of the coronavirus, leading to a surge in the demand for healthcare equipment and medicine.

On the other hand, sectors such as industrial transportation and travel and leisure tend to suffer, as the results show that negative reactions overshadow positive reactions in these sectors. As a

Table 9.5. Robustness tests for positive and negative sectoral reactions following COVID-19 events.

Sector	Event date	Corrado	Chesney		Market integration	
			CP	*t*-stat	AR (%)	t-stat
Positive reaction						
Banks	26/02/2020	2.20	0.47	0.07	1.98	2.65
Fixed-line telecommunications	21/02/2020	2.06	0.47	0.08	3.39	2.37
Negative reaction						
Beverages	4/02/2020	−2.60	0.50	0.00	−3.84	−5.04
Leisure goods	17/01/2020	−1.72	0.07	1.73	−1.24	−1.74
	4/02/2020	−1.53	0.09	1.57	−1.22	−1.72
Life insurance	5/02/2020	−1.94	0.10	1.46	−2.60	−2.26
	24/02/2020	−2.02	0.40	0.26	−1.11	−0.97

result of the COVID-19 outbreak, most transportation means have been suspended, both locally and internationally. The 14-day quarantine rules applied in most countries have led to a massive reduction in transportation and travel demand, exerting substantial negative effects on the underlying sectors. The negative effects on the two sectors seem to be long-lasting as we find that the reactions continue in a downward direction for up to 10 days after some event dates, including February 3, 2020 (when China reported 57 new fatalities, bringing the death toll to at least 361 and the number of cases to 17,205 people across the country) and February 4 (when the death toll rose to 425 people and the number of infected people stood at 20,438).

Another issue that requires an investigation is the effects of the COVID-19 outbreak on risk. To address this issue, we study the effects of the virus on the systematic risk of 36 sectors. Equation (9.9) is used to capture the aggregate change in systematic risk, whereas Equations (9.10) and (9.11) are used to capture instant and short-term changes in systematic risk following the underlying events.

Table 9.7 presents the aggregate change in systematic risk following events. The results show that 12 out of 36 sectors experienced an aggregate decrease in systematic risk. Based on the GARCH (1,1)

Table 9.6. Robustness tests for mixed sectoral reactions following COVID-19 events.

Sector	Event date	Corrado	Chesney		Market integration	
			CP	t-stat	AR (%)	t-stat
Aerospace & defense	4/02/2020	−1.62	0.49	0.01517	−2.64	−2.28
	17/02/2020	2.14	0.24	0.75365	3.62	3.04
	28/02/2020	−0.15	0.03	2.34395	−2.82	−2.33
Alternative energy	4/02/2020	−3.40	0.05	2.08008	−3.76	−4.81
	12/02/2020	2.21	0.25	0.72785	2.83	3.61
	18/02/2020	2.47	0.36	0.38852	1.31	1.65
Automobiles & parts	6/01/2020	1.71	0.36	0.37484	1.25	1.99
	4/02/2020	−2.27	0.24	0.76339	−2.70	−4.11
	10/02/2020	2.98	0.02	2.7154	1.94	2.98
	28/02/2020	−2.61	0.02	2.78904	−1.91	−2.88
Chemicals	4/02/2020	−2.42	0.05	1.95626	−1.86	−3.33
	11/02/2020	−1.68	0.48	0.05422	−1.10	−2.00
	18/02/2020	2.03	0.35	0.3969	0.66	1.17
	10/03/2020	−2.02	0.03	2.37284	−1.35	−2.41
Construction & materials	4/02/2020	−3.30	0.02	2.83769	−3.60	−7.07
	10/02/2020	2.67	0.09	1.54976	1.47	2.59
	26/02/2020	3.58	0.50	0.00031	3.61	6.19
	2/03/2020	2.71	0.40	0.27055	2.57	4.42
Electricity	3/02/2020	−2.10	0.25	0.73484	−1.44	−2.50
	4/02/2020	−1.91	0.50	0.00208	−2.33	−4.01
	25/02/2020	−3.19	0.05	1.9849	−1.53	−2.54
	26/02/2020	3.37	0.50	0.0128	2.19	3.63
Electronic equipment & services	4/02/2020	−1.32	0.19	0.96169	−2.86	−3.93
	18/02/2020	−1.06	0.39	0.29743	1.58	2.10
	24/02/2020	0.67	0.49	0.03558	1.33	1.76
	26/02/2020	−0.78	0.37	0.33918	−2.01	−2.65
Financial services	4/02/2020	−0.54	0.49	0.03717	−3.60	−3.06
	20/02/2020	−0.36	0.49	0.02398	3.36	2.80
Food & drug retailers	3/02/2020	−1.68	0.50	0.00	2.39	3.30
	4/02/2020	−3.43	0.02	2.74	−1.46	−2.01
	6/02/2020	−3.04	0.20	0.92	1.86	2.65
Food producers	4/02/2020	−2.70	0.50	0.01	−1.96	−2.32
	10/02/2020	−2.59	0.03	2.45	3.40	4.02
	11/02/2020	−3.64	0.25	0.73	−1.96	−2.32
Forestry & paper	4/02/2020	−2.54	0.39	0.30	−3.21	−4.68
	10/02/2020	−3.50	0.46	0.12	1.75	2.50
	26/02/2020	−3.50	0.49	0.02	2.21	3.12

(*Continued*)

Table 9.6. (*Continued*)

Sector	Event date	Corrado	Chesney		Market integration	
			CP	t-stat	AR (%)	t-stat
Gas, water & multiutilities	3/02/2020	−2.50	0.19	0.98	−1.68	−2.29
	4/02/2020	−2.64	0.20	0.91	−1.53	−2.07
	7/02/2020	0.60	0.05	2.00	1.59	2.18
General industrials	4/02/2020	−2.40	0.05	2.03	−2.04	−3.18
	26/02/2020	−0.35	0.17	1.06	1.70	2.70
General retailers	22/01/2020	−2.79	0.06	1.83	−1.07	−2.02
	3/02/2020	−1.80	0.14	1.22	−0.94	−1.77
	4/02/2020	−2.74	0.03	2.46	−2.97	−5.60
	10/02/2020	−4.34	0.43	0.18	1.51	2.95
	26/02/2020	0.16	0.48	0.06	1.77	3.38
Healthcare equipment & Services	23/01/2020	−0.14	0.41	0.25	3.28	3.37
	3/02/2020	−1.98	0.04	2.10	8.67	8.57
	4/02/2020	−1.84	0.20	0.93	3.12	3.08
	5/02/2020	0.49	0.16	1.10	2.14	2.08
	10/02/2020	−1.27	0.49	0.03	−2.70	−2.62
	11/02/2020	0.54	0.44	0.15	−1.99	−1.92
	19/02/2020	−2.01	0.04	2.29	−2.23	−2.03
	24/02/2020	−1.41	0.44	0.15	3.45	3.14
	26/02/2020	−0.52	0.02	2.84	−2.37	−2.15
Household equipment	22/01/2020	−3.89	0.02	2.76	−1.08	−2.40
	4/02/2020	−2.63	0.50	0.00	−2.46	−5.31
	18/02/2020	−1.20	0.20	0.94	0.77	1.62
	26/02/2020	−0.18	0.49	0.03	1.62	3.40
Industrial engineering	4/02/2020	−2.63	0.50	0.00	−2.82	−5.11
	7/02/2020	−0.06	0.09	1.53	1.03	1.89
	10/02/2020	−3.58	0.02	2.93	1.08	1.98
	18/02/2020	−0.26	0.35	0.41	1.15	2.06
	26/02/2020	0.10	0.05	1.99	1.40	2.52
Industrial metals & mining	4/02/2020	−1.27	0.50	0.01	−2.94	−4.37
	6/02/2020	−2.94	0.42	0.20	−1.22	−1.81
	10/02/2020	−3.69	0.02	2.68	1.79	2.66
	26/02/2020	−0.87	0.49	0.02	2.02	2.99

Table 9.6. (*Continued*)

Sector	Event date	Corrado	Chesney CP	Chesney t-stat	Market integration AR (%)	Market integration t-stat
Industrial transportation	3/02/2020	−2.92	0.02	2.76	−1.15	−2.11
	4/02/2020	−2.53	0.50	0.00	−4.11	7.48
	24/02/2020	−1.48	0.05	1.99	−1.77	−3.01
	26/02/2020	1.32	0.49	0.03	2.26	3.85
	9/03/2020	−0.40	0.50	0.00	2.04	3.47
Media	6/01/2020	1.92	0.45	0.14	1.94	2.45
	7/01/2020	−2.42	0.41	0.25	2.00	2.52
	20/01/2020	−3.96	0.49	0.02	−2.67	−3.26
	4/02/2020	−1.61	0.50	0.01	−1.79	−2.16
	11/02/2020	−0.91	0.48	0.04	−1.58	−1.90
	13/02/2020	1.25	0.46	0.10	−2.02	−2.42
	18/02/2020	−0.66	0.01	3.57	1.73	2.07
	19/02/2020	−2.53	0.47	0.08	−1.54	−1.84
Mining	6/01/2020	−1.91	0.06	1.92	1.74	2.44
	3/02/2020	−2.66	0.04	2.17	−0.91	−1.27
	4/02/2020	1.46	0.24	0.78	−2.23	−3.10
Oil equipment	6/01/2020	−3.05	0.03	2.50	3.29	3.07
	7/01/2020	−3.96	0.46	0.10	−2.36	−2.21
	4/02/2020	−0.51	0.50	0.00	−4.55	−4.08
	25/02/2020	−3.16	0.05	2.00	−2.45	−2.19
Oil producers	6/01/2020	−2.60	0.19	0.95	4.57	4.48
	7/01/2020	−2.90	0.45	0.14	−2.87	−2.82
	3/02/2020	−1.23	0.11	1.42	−2.30	−2.20
	4/02/2020	−2.04	0.50	0.00	−4.25	−4.04
	24/02/2020	−0.31	0.40	0.26	−2.32	−2.14
	26/02/2020	−0.84	0.46	0.11	2.46	2.26
Personal goods	22/01/2020	−1.89	0.04	2.16	−1.07	−2.12
	4/02/2020	−2.13	0.02	2.57	−1.42	−2.84
	5/02/2020	−0.25	0.26	0.69	1.30	2.59
	7/02/2020	−1.57	0.13	1.27	1.25	2.48
	11/02/2020	−1.65	0.44	0.16	−1.79	−3.55
	28/02/2020	−2.59	0.49	0.02	1.31	2.36
	9/03/2020	−1.98	0.30	0.57	0.65	1.18
	10/03/2020	−2.04	0.08	1.69	−2.51	−4.58

(*Continued*)

Table 9.6. (*Continued*)

Sector	Event date	Corrado	Chesney CP	Chesney t-stat	Market integration AR (%)	Market integration t-stat
Pharmaceutical & biotechnology	31/12/2019	0.20	0.06	1.85	1.84	2.78
	20/01/2020	−1.23	0.08	1.69	1.48	1.72
	22/01/2020	−3.24	0.48	0.04	−2.70	−3.11
	23/01/2020	0.54	0.17	1.07	1.91	2.19
	3/02/2020	−1.79	0.03	2.35	5.90	6.72
	4/02/2020	−0.82	0.32	0.51	2.19	2.49
	5/02/2020	0.63	0.49	0.03	3.78	4.27
	7/02/2020	−3.36	0.43	0.19	−2.88	−3.27
	10/02/2020	−3.81	0.49	0.03	−3.47	−3.93
	9/03/2020	−0.54	0.48	0.05	1.57	1.77
	10/03/2020	−3.18	0.38	0.33	−1.63	−1.83
Real estate investment & services	3/02/2020	−3.51	0.01	3.12	−0.90	−1.49
	4/02/2020	−2.37	0.50	0.00	−3.67	−6.09
	26/02/2020	−0.24	0.50	0.00	2.94	4.47
Software	7/02/2020	0.16	0.50	0.01	3.38	3.31
	26/02/2020	−1.52	0.01	3.04	−2.00	−1.90
Support services	17/01/2020	−0.42	0.48	0.06	−0.39	−0.68
	4/02/2020	−2.71	0.50	0.00	−3.18	−5.55
	7/02/2020	−1.22	0.49	0.03	1.44	2.55
	11/02/2020	−0.39	0.41	0.24	−1.12	−1.98
	25/02/2020	−3.73	0.09	1.53	−1.40	−2.41
Technology hardware & equipment	4/02/2020	−2.31	0.09	1.58	−2.81	−3.02
	7/02/2020	0.92	0.14	1.19	1.95	2.02
	18/02/2020	−0.02	0.03	2.42	1.61	1.64
	24/02/2020	1.67	0.49	0.02	1.94	1.97
	26/02/2020	−2.33	0.31	0.54	−2.46	−2.49
	10/03/2020	−3.18	0.50	0.00	2.50	2.58
Travel & leisure	20/01/2020	−1.43	0.05	2.02	−2.04	−3.32
	3/02/2020	−2.76	0.06	1.91	−1.22	−1.89
	4/02/2020	−1.82	0.50	0.00	−5.66	−8.74
	7/02/2020	−2.30	0.28	0.63	1.17	1.77
	19/02/2020	−3.51	0.49	0.03	1.93	2.87
	24/02/2020	0.78	0.50	0.01	−2.54	−3.78
	26/02/2020	0.21	0.49	0.03	2.18	3.23

Table 9.7. Aggregate changes in systematic risk following all COVD-19 events.

			Aggregate change in systematic risk									
Sector	Beta	*t*-stat	OLS	*t*-stat	GARCH (1,1)	*z*-stat	TARCH	*z*-stat	EGARCH	*z*-stat	PARCH	*z*-stat
Decrease in Systematic Risk												
Beverages	1.04	80.92	−0.12	−3.05	−0.13	−5.59	−0.12	−5.75	−0.12	−5.98	−0.11	−5.37
Construction & materials	1.16	145.65	−0.07	−3.11	−0.16	−4.36	−0.13	−10.84	−0.13	−10.10	−0.13	−10.70
Electricity	1.09	115.80	−0.17	−6.20	−0.11	−2.23	−0.04	−2.83	−0.03	−2.08	−0.05	−3.40
Food & drug retailers	1.09	105.16	−0.35	−3.08	−0.35	−2.60	−0.35	−6.89	−0.33	−7.82	−0.33	−7.57
Gas, water & multiutilities	1.11	104.00	−0.11	−2.55	−0.08	−1.12	−0.06	−2.41	−0.06	−2.03	−0.06	−2.43
General retailers	1.11	134.99	−0.09	−3.46	−0.10	−2.48	−0.09	−5.66	−0.09	−6.04	−0.09	−5.74
Healthcare equipment & services	1.24	87.37	−0.86	−23.90	−0.98	−33.93	−0.93	−26.48	−0.93	−28.36	−0.93	−26.44
Industrial transportation	1.1	133.97	−0.12	−5.67	−0.13	−3.58	−0.09	−7.05	−0.07	−5.60	−0.09	−7.18
Personal goods	1.07	131.55	−0.17	−5.50	−0.12	−6.75	−0.15	−7.36	−0.15	−8.49	−0.15	−8.08
Pharmaceuticals & biotechnology	1.09	109.16	−0.47	−16.20	−0.49	−18.49	−0.48	−7.79	−0.50	−12.22	−0.49	−8.26
Real estate investment & Services	1.09	112.98	−0.10	−3.56	−0.09	−6.48	−0.08	−6.41	−0.08	−6.33	−0.08	−6.48
Travel & leisure	1.06	134.47	−0.12	−5.69	−0.18	−5.04	−0.19	−10.18	−0.18	−9.51	−0.18	−9.49
Increase in Systematic Risk												
Electronic equipment & services	1.19	118.87	0.18	3.21	0.19	1.98	0.21	11.00	0.15	5.17	0.20	10.04

Note: We only report statistically significant results for brevity purpose. The results of other sectors are available upon request.

model, the sector of healthcare equipment and services, and that of pharmaceuticals and biotechnology recorded the biggest decline of –0.98 (with a z-statistic of –33.93) and –0.49 (with a z-statistic of –18.49) respectively. The main reason for these declines is that these two sectors benefit from the outbreak due to the increase in demand for ventilators and medicines required for COVID-19 treatment. These results are fully supported by other models, including TARCH, EGARCH and PARCH.

One interesting observation is that most sectors did not exhibit an aggregate change in systematic risk since the outcome of these events may offset each other. The results based on Equation (9.10), which is used to capture instant changes in systematic risk following each event, show the travel and leisure sector became much riskier during the outbreak. The highest instant increase in systematic risk materialized on January 24, 2020 (event 9) when the death toll was 26, with more than 830 infections, while the number of cities under lockdown in Hubei rose to 13, affecting 41 million people. Figure 9.1 shows beta for each sector over the 36 events. On the contrary, the pharmaceuticals and biotechnology sector seems to benefit from the outbreak, as it became less risky, with the highest instant decline in

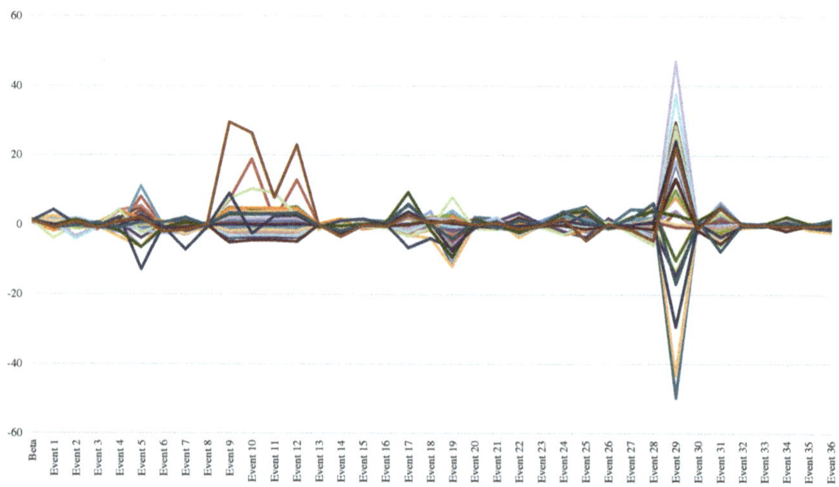

Figure 9.1. Instant changes in systematic risk of all sectors in China following COVID-19 events.

Note: Data of this figure is available upon request.

systematic risk materializing on January 17, 2020 (event 5) when a second death was reported in Wuhan (Figure 9.1). In addition, we observe a diamond risk structure on February 25, 2020 (event 29), but we cannot confirm if this structure was caused by the outbreak, since it had gone past its peak by that time. This phenomenon appears to be largely driven by the events outside China that led to declining oil prices amid fears of the virus spreading to more countries.

Furthermore, when Equation (9.11) is used to examine the short-term changes in systematic risk, we observe a wave-like movement. The travel and leisure sector, for instance, might have experienced an increase in systematic risk following event 5, when a second death was reported in Wuhan, but the surge is offset by a decline on the following day (event 10) when the death toll rose to 106 with 4,515 infected people (Figure 9.2). However, the magnitude of the decline is smaller than that of the increase, which is why the sector ends up being riskier from the investors' perspective. The results show that most sectors behave in a similar manner (Figure 9.2).

9.5. Conclusion

COVID-19 is one of the worst pandemics in human history as it ravages countries worldwide. In this study, we examine the effects of the

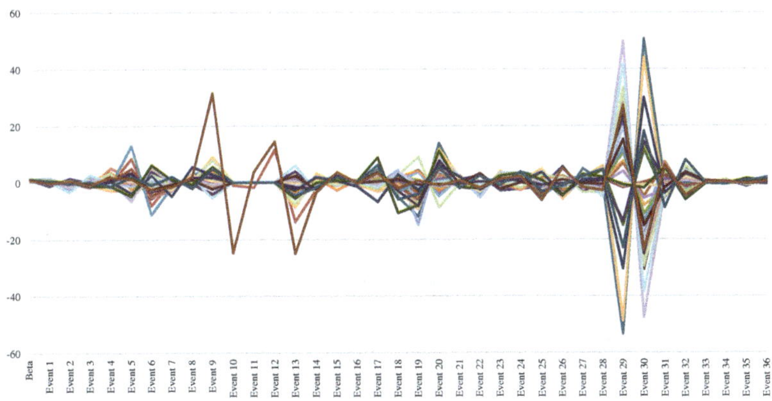

Figure 9.2. Short-term changes in systematic risk of all sectors following COVID-19 events.

Note: Data of this figure is available upon request.

outbreak on China where the virus originated. Our results show that most sectors are affected by the virus and that the effects are most conspicuous during the peak of the outbreak. In addition, we find a dominant number of negative reactions in the sectors that are badly hit by the virus and these effects tend to be short term. Our results show that beverages, leisure goods, and life insurance sectors were negatively affected by COVID-19, especially during the peak period. During the outbreak, the healthcare system and medical products are the most important for the country, hence the healthcare equipment and services and pharmaceuticals and biotechnology sectors tend to exhibit a better performance as shown by positive abnormal returns and decreases in systematic risk. These results provide a significant implication for the governments around the world whereby they should focus on supporting those sectors that were or anticipate to be hit the hardest during the outbreak such as beverages, leisure goods, or transportation by providing appropriate support packages to ensure a swift economic recovery after the outbreak.

One drawback of this study is that we cannot draw a general conclusion for the global economy as to how the outbreak affects each sector in every country. Therefore, a wide avenue of research involves an investigation of the effects of COVID-19 at sectoral levels in more countries. Research endeavors in this area will provide a more general picture of the widespread impact of this pandemic.

References

Al-Awadhi, A., Alsaifi, K., Al-Awadhi, A. and Alhammadi, A. (2020). Death and contagious infectious diseases: Impact of the COVID-19 virus on stock market returns. *Journal of Behavioral and Experimental Finance*, **27**, 100326.

Ashraf, B.N. (2020). Stock markets' reaction to COVID-19: Cases or fatalities?. *Research in International Business and Finance*, **54**, 101249.

Ataullah, A., Song, X. and Tippett, M. (2011). A modified Corrado test for assessing abnormal security returns. *The European Journal of Finance*, **17**(7), 589–601.

Au, A.K.M., Ramasamy, B. and Yeung, M.C.H. (2005). The effect of SARS on the Hong Kong tourism industry: An empirical evaluation. *Asia Pacific Journal of Tourism Research*, **10**(1), 85–95.

Bollen, J., Mao, H. and Zeng, X. (2011). Twitter mood predicts the stock market. *Journal of Computational Science*, **2**(1), 1–8.

Bollerslev, T. (1986). Generalized autoregressive conditional heteroskedasticity. *Journal of Econometrics*, **31**(3), 307–327.

Brainerd, E. and Siegler, M.V. (2003). The economic effects of the 1918 influenza epidemic. CEPR Discussion Papers No 3791.

Brown, S. J. and Warner, J.B. (1985). Using daily stock returns: The case of event studies. *Journal of Financial Economics*, **14**(1), 3–31.

Chesney, M., Reshetar, G. and Karaman, M. (2011). The impact of terrorism on financial markets: an empirical study. *Journal of Banking and Finance*, **35**, 253–267.

Corrado, C.J. (1989). A non-parametric test for abnormal security price performance in event studies. *Journal of Financial Economics*, **23**, 385–395.

Donadelli, M., Kizys, R. and Riedel, M. (2016). Globally dangerous diseases: Bad news for main street, good news for Wall Street? *Journal of Financial Markets*, **35**, 84–103.

Gilbert, E. and Karahalios, K. (2010). Widespread worry and the stock market. In *The Proceedings of the Fourth International AAAI Conference on Weblogs and Social Media, Washington*, Association for the Advancement of Artificial Intelligence (ed.), (AAAI Press, California), pp. 58–65.

Graham, M.A. and Ramiah, V. (2012). Global terrorism and adaptive expectations in financial markets: evidence from Japanese equity market. *Research in International Business and Finance*, **26**, 97–119.

Hirshleifer, D. and Shumway, T. (2003). Good day sunshine: Stock returns and the weather. *Journal of Finance*, **58**(3), 1009–1032.

Huo, X. and Qiu, Z. (2020). How does China's stock market react to the announcement of the COVID-19 pandemic lockdown? *Economic and Political Studies*. DOI:10.1080/20954816.2020.1780695.

Ichev, R. and Marinč, M. (2018). Stock prices and geographic proximity of information: Evidence from the Ebola outbreak. *International Review of Financial Analysis*, **56**, 153–166.

Jung, H., Park, M., Hong, K. and Hyun, E. (2016). The impact of an epidemic outbreak on consumer expenditures: An empirical assessment for MERS Korea. *Sustainability*, **8**(5), 454.

Lee, J. and McKibbin, W.J. (2004). Globalisation and disease: The case of SARS. *Asian Economic Papers*, **3**(1), 113–131.

Nofsinger, J. and Kim, K. (2003). Regaining investor confidence, Chapter 14. In *Infectious Greed: Restoring Confidence in America's Companies* (Pearson, London), 274–264.

Overby, J., Rayburn, M., Hammond, K. and Wyld, D.C. (2004). The China syndrome: The impact of the SARS epidemic in Southeast Asia. *Asia Pacific Journal of Marketing and Logistics*, **16**(1), 69–94.

Pham, H.N.A., Ramiah, V. and Moosa, I. (2019). The effects of environmental regulation on the stock market: The French experience. *Accounting and Finance*, **60**(4), 3279–3304.

Pham, H.N.A., Ramiah, V., Moosa N., Huynh, T. and Pham, N. (2018). The financial effects of Trumpism. *Economic Modelling*, **74**, 264–274.

Prechter, R.R. Jr. (1979). What's going on? In *The Elliot Wave Theorist* (New Classics Library, Georgia, USA).

Prechter, R.R.Jr. (1999). *The Wave Principle of Human Social Behavior and the New Science of Socionomics* (New Classics Library, Georgia).

Prechter, R.R. Jr. and Parker, W.D. (2007). The financial/economic dichotomy in social behavioral dynamics: The socionomic perspective. *Journal of Behavioral Finance*, **8**(2), 84–110.

Prechter, R.R., Goel, D., Parker, W.D. and Lampert, M. (2012). Social mood, stock market performance, and U.S. presidential elections. *SAGE Open*, **2**(4), 215824401245919.

Ramiah, V., Pham, H.N.A. and Moosa, I. (2016). The sectoral effects of Brexit on the British economy: Early evidence from the reaction of the stock market. *Applied Economics*, **49**(26), 2508–2514.

Saunders, E.M.J. (1993). Stock prices and Wall Street weather. *American Economic Review*, **83**(5), 1337–1345.

Siu, A. and Wong, Y.C.R. (2004). Economic impact of SARS: The case of Hong Kong. *Asian Economic Papers*, **3**(1), 62–83.

Wang, Y., Wang. J. and Wang, X. (2020). COVID-19, supply chain disruption and China's hog market: A dynamic analysis. *China Agricultural Economic Review*, **12**(3), 427–443.

Zhang, D., Hu, M. and Ji, Q. (2020). Financial markets under the global pandemic of COVID-19. *Finance Research Letters*, **36**, 101528.

https://doi.org/10.1142/9781800610781_0010

Chapter 10

Impact of the Severity of the COVID-19 Pandemic on the Interaction Between Foreign Trading and Stock Market Volatility

Zeynep Kantur[*,‡] **and Gülserim Özcan**[†,§]

[*]*Department of Economics Başkent University, Ankara 06790, Turkey*

[†]*Department of Economics Atılım University, Ankara 06830, Turkey*

[‡]*zeynepkantur@baskent.edu.tr*
[§]*gulserim.ozcan@atilim.edu.tr*

Abstract

This chapter investigates the impact of the severity of the COVID-19 pandemic on stock markets by focusing on the relationship between foreign trading and stock market volatility. We use a panel data set of a selection of countries from February 3, 2020, to April 30, 2020. We first document that foreign trading is positively related to the stock market volatility. Next, we show that, as the severity of the pandemics increases, the link between foreign trading and stock market volatility weakens. Moreover, we find that increased health- and economics-related safety measures strengthen the relation between foreign trading and stock market volatility. We believe that the results of the analysis are crucial for policymakers to maintain financial stability during uncertain times.

10.1. Introduction

The liberalization of the financial markets increased the accessibility of foreign investors to the stock markets. The significance of the role of international investors is more imperative in some countries. Huang and Yang (2000) showed the impact of financial liberalization on stock market volatility is equivocal. In South Korea, Mexico, and Turkey, the presence of foreign trading leads to higher volatility. On the other hand, in Argentina, Chile, Malaysia, and the Philippines, foreign trading has a stabilizing effect.

Under uncertain times and events, the behavior of foreign investors is erratic, which has an impact on the relationship between stock market volatility and foreign trading. Caporale *et al.* (2020) explored international investors' trading activity during both the Asian and Global Financial Crises. The stock market volatility was lower during the Asian Financial Crisis compared to Global Financial Crisis due to the different attitudes of the investors. The most significant "black swan event" that the world has ever experienced after the liberalization of the financial system is the COVID-19 pandemic. Hence, the impact of the pandemic should also be explored by revisiting the relation between stock market volatility and foreign trading behavior. We focus on international investor sentiment because the information asymmetries between domestic and foreign traders soar during abnormal times. Herding and erratic behavior of the foreign traders during obscure events leads to significant fluctuations in the stock market.

The COVID-19 pandemic and the ensuing health-related policy interventions have induced negative changes in investors' sentiment and complicated worldwide economic and financial prospects. Especially for countries prone to frequent foreign investment outflows and inflows, fluctuations in stock markets are more severe during unfamiliar times. The pandemic's future effects are still highly uncertain; thus, it would be interesting to investigate the incorporation of the information on COVID-19 into the relationship between foreign trading and the performance of stock market indices as measured by volatility.

To explore the impact of the severity of COVID-19 on the relationship between foreign trading and stock market performance, we use panel fixed effects regression on a sample of developed and emerging countries over the course of the pandemic during its early stages. Our country list covers Indonesia, the Philippines, South Africa, South Korea, Turkey, Taiwan, Thailand, and the United Arab Emirates (UAE). We focus on the early impact of the pandemic; hence our sample covers February 3, 2020 to April 30, 2020. Our results indicate that as the severity of the disease increases, the relationship between stock market volatility and foreign trading weakens.

After the Global Financial Crisis, financial stability has become an imperative policy concern for policymakers. Therefore, some safety measures have been taken by the governments and central banks in order to minimize the impact of COVID-19 on the financial markets. In this chapter, we also study the influence of policy interventions on the examined relation during this period. Following the related literature, we use stringency, containment, and government response indices provided by Hale *et al.* (2020) to represent the safety measures taken by countries. According to our findings, safety measures counteract the impact of the pandemics on the link between stock market volatility and foreign trading.

This chapter proceeds as follows. Section 10.2 summarizes the related literature. Section 10.3 introduces the data and Section 10.4 describes the empirical methodology. Section 10.5 analyses the link between foreign trading and stock market volatility during the COVID-19 pandemic and explores the impact of safety measures during this period on the relation. Section 10.6 concludes.

10.2. Related Literature

The relationship between foreign trading and stock market volatility is studied extensively for normal and abnormal times and emerging and developed countries. The findings of the pre-pandemic are decidedly mixed for both groups; some studies found evidence supporting the hypothesis that foreign trading has a stabilizing effect on the volatility of the stock market. Wang (2007) documents a strong contemporaneous relationship between foreign equity trading and market volatility in Indonesia and Thailand. Similarly, Chiang and Chan (2017) finds that foreign ownership lowers stock market volatility in Taiwan due to the improvements in disclosure and operations. As discussed by Vo (2015), international investors have access to better quality information and efficiently control their transaction costs.

On the contrary, some studies show international trading leads to an increase in stock market volatility. Jeon and Moffett (2010) study the herding behavior of international investors in Korea and find evidence of a significant impact of foreign trading on stock returns. Chen *et al.* (2013) discuss that higher foreign trading in China leads to higher stock return volatility due to the strengthening impact of liquidity. Umutlu and Shackleton (2015) examine the daily equity trading by different investor groups in the Korean Stock Exchange. According to the findings, foreign trading has an increasing impact on stock market volatility. Using Norwegian stock market data, Che (2018) also shows a positive correlation between foreign trading and stock market volatility. Umutlu *et al.* (2013) explore a similar relationship by employing foreign equity purchases and sales data in Turkey. The findings suggest that the net foreign equity flow is positively related to average stock return volatility even after controlling for market return, liquidity, market development, and volatility persistency effects.

Hence, there is still no consensus over the impact of foreign trading, and the link should be re-examined for the COVID-19 pandemic. Some stock markets experienced the worst sell-offs on fears that the COVID-19 pandemic will cause a recession, and some stock markets experienced limited impact. Therefore, in this chapter, we seek to contribute to this discussion and aim at answering the following question: How does the interaction between foreign ownership and stock market volatility respond to the severity of the COVID-19 pandemic?

10.3. Data

In this chapter, we investigate the financial markets' reaction to the COVID-19 pandemic by considering three variable categories (i) financial data, (ii) severity of the COVID-19 pandemic, and (iii) government interventions and policies, including containment policies, interventions in the healthcare sector, and economic stimulus packages.

10.3.1. *Financial data*

We analyze the relationship between stock price volatility and foreign trading. The sample period is February 3, 2020, to April 30, 2020, and the data frequency is daily for a five-day week (Monday to Friday). We use a sample of emerging and advanced countries, i.e. Indonesia, the Philippines, South Africa, South Korea, Taiwan, Thailand, Turkey, and the UAE.[1] Considering different country groups, we aim to document whether the impact of COVID-19 on the stock market volatility exhibits heterogeneity across developed and emerging economies. The financial data are obtained from Thomson Reuters Datastream.

We use the leading national stock price indices of the countries that are listed above. For Indonesia, we employ the IDX Composite Index, for the Philippines the PSEI Index, for South Africa FTSE/JSE Africa All Share Index, for South Korea KOSPI Index, for Turkey BIST National 100 Index, for Taiwan TAIEX Index, for Thailand the Bangkok SET Index, and for the UAE ADX General Index.

Figure 10.1 illustrates the normalized stock prices indices. We observe the sharp decline starts at the beginning of March for all countries in our sample.

We use daily purchase and sale values in local currencies of foreign investors. As a measure of foreign trading, we employ buy-sell imbalance. The nature of our data allows us to examine the relationship between stock prices and trading on a daily basis. The selection of countries was, in part, determined due to the availability of foreign trading data in daily frequency. For the reference interest rate, we collect overnight interbank rates for the Philippines, South Africa, South Korea, Taiwan, Thailand, and Turkey, and the weekly interbank rates for Indonesia and the UAE. Finally, as for the exchange rate, we use Indonesian Rupiah to United States (US) Dollar, Philippine Peso to US Dollar, South Africa Rand to US Dollar, South Korean Won to US Dollar, Thai Baht to US Dollar, Taiwan New Dollar to US Dollar to US Dollar, Turkish Lira to US Dollar, and UAE Dirham to

[1]The set of countries included in our analysis was, in part, determined due to the availability of data.

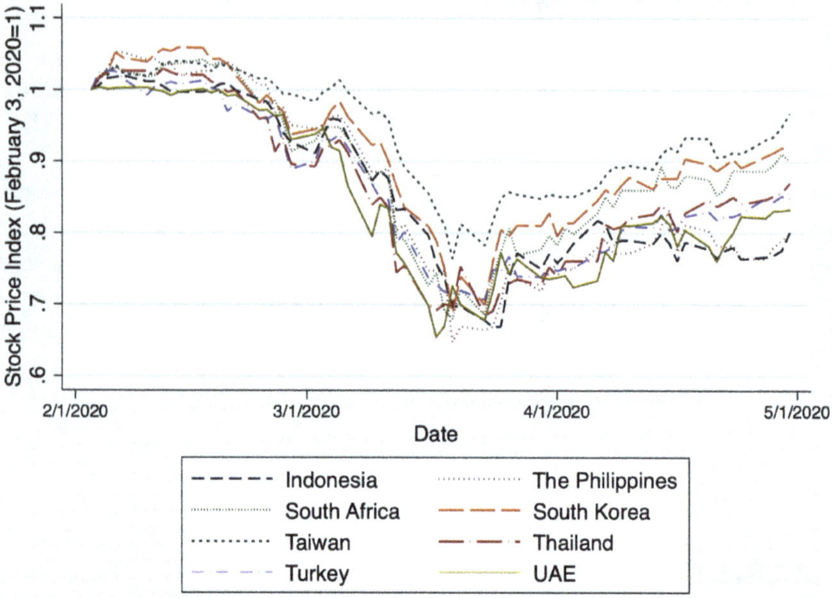

Figure 10.1. Stock price indices.

Note: The figure shows the normalized stock prices indices.

US Dollar. Table 10.1 summarizes the primary variables, data transformations, and their sources.

10.3.2. *Construction of pandemic severity indices*

We gather data of coronavirus cases for each country from the Oxford COVID-19 Government Response Tracker. We measure the growth rate of confirmed cases in each country and the world in the spirit of Alfaro *et al.* (2020) by taking the log-differences of the confirmed COVID-19 cases between dates $t-1$ and $t-2$.

$$Case_t = \ln(1 + C_{t-1}) - \ln(1 + C_{t-2}). \tag{10.1}$$

$$World\ Case_t = \ln(1 + W_{t-1}) - \ln(1 + W_{t-2}). \tag{10.2}$$

Table 10.1. Data description.

Variable	Definition	Data source
Financial variables		
Stock price index	Daily growth in the stock price index (%)	Thomson Reuters database
Foreign	Daily change in the foreign ownership market value (Foreign Purchases – Foreign Sales)	
Interest rate	Daily change in the benchmark interbank rate	
Dollar rate	Daily growth in national currency per Dollar (%)	
Country dummy	Emerging Country Indicator [Country Dummy = 1, if EM, Country Dummy = 0, otherwise]	Author's calculations
Policy-related variables		
Stringency	COVID-19 Government Response Stringency Index. It aggregates nine response indicators including school closures, workplace closures, and travel bans. It is rescaled to create a score between 0 and 100 (100 = strictest)	Hale *et al.* (2020)
Containment	COVID-19 Containment and Health Index. It aggregates 11 policy response indicators including school closures, workplace closures, travel bans, testing policy and contact tracing, rescaled to a value from 0 to 100 (100 = strictest)	
Gov response	COVID-19 Overall Government Response Index. It aggregates all indicators including containment and closure, health system, and economic stimulus measures, rescaled to a value from 0 to 100 (100 = strictest)	

(*Continued*)

Table 10.1. (*Continued*)

Variable	Definition	Data source
Pandemic-related variables		
Case	Growth in confirmed cases in each country	The Oxford COVID-19 Government Response Tracker and Author's Calculations
World case	Growth in confirmed global cases	
Death	Growth in confirmed number of deaths in each country	

Note: This table describes the variables used in the empirical analysis, describes how the variable is computed/measured, and acknowledges the source of information.

Here, the basis for predicted cumulative cases for day t is information on day $t-1$ since the number of infections on day $t-1$ is observed after the market closes on that day but before the market opens on the next day. This prediction can be compared to the forecast made with day $t-2$ information.

We also take the log-differences of the confirmed deaths in each country as follows:

$$Death_t = \ln(1 + D_{t-1}) - \ln(1 + D_{t-2}). \tag{10.3}$$

To further investigate the effect of the pandemic, we develop four pandemic severity indices.

$$Severity\text{-}I_{i,t} = Case_{i,t}/WorldCase_t. \tag{10.4}$$

$$Severity\text{-}II_{i,t} = \ln(C_{i,t-1}/W_{t-1})/\ln(C_{i,t-2}/W_{t-2}). \tag{10.5}$$

$$Severity\text{-}III_{i,t} = Death_{i,t}/Case_{i,t}. \tag{10.6}$$

$$Severity\text{-}IV_{i,t} = Case_{i,t}. \tag{10.7}$$

Severity-I and Severity-II indices are designed to provide information about the severity of the pandemic relative to the rest of the world. On the other hand, Severity-III and Severity-IV provide information about the countries' exposure to the pandemic. Severity-III could be interpreted as the treatment quality in hospitals and the hospital capacity in countries.

10.3.3. *Government policies*

We utilize data on government responses to the pandemic collected by Hale *et al.* (2020). The dataset classifies government intervention data into three sub-categories: (i) containment and closure, (ii) health system, and (ii) economic stimulus. All the indicators are available on a daily basis and are computed on an ordinal scale. In terms of the containment and closure, school closing, workplace closing, cancellation of public events, restrictions on gatherings size, public transport closure, stay-at-home requirements, restrictions on internal movement, and international travel restrictions are represented. Health system interventions include public information campaigns, testing policies, and contact tracing. Economic stimulus summarizes information on income support and debt/contract relief for households. We use aggregated indices from these individual measures provided by Hale *et al.* (2020). The Containment Index represents the first sub-category; the overall Stringency Index represents a measure of the intensity of non-medical government interventions during the pandemic, including containment measures and public information campaigns; and the overall Government Response Index aggregates all sub-categories. Aggregate indices are rescaled to create scores 0 to 100.

10.3.4. *Descriptive statistics*

Table 10.2 reports summary statistics of the main variables. The mean value of the stock market price is −0.2, which shows that, on average, sample countries experienced approximately 0% loss in stock markets. Minimum and maximum values are −13.34 and +10.19, respectively, which show that stock indexes swung between negative 13% and positive 10%. The mean value of foreign trading is −0.08 (in billion national currencies) with a standard deviation of 0.26. The mean interest rate is −0.02 basis points with a standard deviation of 0.12 basis points, implying that the reference rate is not moving much in our sample period. The mean exchange rate is 0.10 basis points. The minimum and maximum values are −3.05 and +4.57, respectively.

The indices for government safety measures, i.e. stringency, containment, and government response, have means lying between 45 and 50, with standard deviations in the range of 28–31, showing

Table 10.2. Summary statistics.

Variable	Obs	Mean	SD	Min	Max
Stock price index	520	−0.20	2.82	−13.34	10.19
Foreign	520	−0.08	0.26	−1.75	0.66
Interest rate	520	−0.02	0.12	−1.54	0.49
Dollar rate	520	0.10	0.77	−3.05	4.57
Stringency	520	46.57	30.87	0.00	100.00
Containment	520	49.35	28.41	0.00	96.97
Gov response	520	44.44	26.56	0.00	91.67
Case	520	0.08	0.14	0.00	1.19
World case	520	0.06	0.05	0.01	0.29
Deaths	520	0.05	0.12	0.00	1.39

Note: This table reports the summary statistics of main variables over the period from February 3, 2020, to April 30, 2020, for eight countries: number of observations (Obs), mean (Mean), standard deviation (SD), minimum (Min), maximum (Max).

that policymakers of the countries in our sample have taken considerable action to compensate for COVID-19.

The average daily growth in COVID-19 confirmed cases is 8%, with a wide standard deviation of 14%. Following a similar trend, the average daily change in deaths is 5%, with a standard deviation of 12%. The average daily growth in worldwide confirmed cases is 5%, with a lower standard deviation of 5%.

10.4. Methodology

We use panel fixed effects regression on a sample of developed and emerging countries over the pandemic period. Panel data analysis is preferred over the event-study methodology because the spread of disease is not one point of time event but evolves over time. Furthermore, this method has the advantage of allowing to control for unobserved heterogeneity among countries, and minimizes issues such as multicollinearity and heteroscedasticity by using both time-series and cross-sectional variation in the data. Our baseline empirical model establishes that stock market volatility depends on foreign trading and country-specific variables, as shown in

Equation (10.8).

$$\Delta Stock\,Price_{i,t} = \mu_i + \beta_0 Foreign_{i,t} + \beta_1 \Delta Interest\,Rate_{i,t} + \beta_2 \Delta Dollar\,Rate_{i,t} + \beta_3 Policy_{i,t} + \varepsilon_{i,t}, \tag{10.8}$$

where μ_i denotes the country-fixed effects. As the dependent variable, $\Delta Stock\,Price_{i,t}$, we use the daily percentage change in the leading national stock price index of country i at time t. The main explanatory variable, $Foreign_{i,t}$ is purchase–sale imbalance by foreign investors. As a measure for the short rate, we employ daily change in the reference interest rate, $\Delta Interest\,Rate_{i,t}$. $\Delta Dollar\,Rate_{i,t}$ is the daily percentage change in local currency per dollar. Finally, $Policy_{i,t}$ denotes the government response to the pandemic discussed in the previous section.

Next, we include interacting terms in order to account for the heterogeneity across the sample countries. We let foreign trading interact with the indices for the severity of the pandemic in Equation (10.9). This allows us to show that countries heavily affected by the pandemic respond differently from countries with moderate severity.

$$\begin{aligned}\Delta Stock\,Price_{i,t} = {} & \mu_i + \beta_0 Foreign_{i,t} + \beta_1 \Delta Interest\,Rate_{i,t} \\ & + \beta_2 \Delta Dollar\,Rate_{i,t} + \beta_3 Policy_{i,t} \\ & + \beta_4 Severity_{i,t} + \beta_5 Severity_{i,t} * Foreign_{i,t} \\ & + \varepsilon_{i,t}.\end{aligned} \tag{10.9}$$

Finally, to further investigate the effect of the government safety measures on the stock price–foreign trading relationship, we include interaction terms with government intervention indices as follows:

$$\begin{aligned}\Delta Stock\,Price_{i,t} = {} & \mu_i + \beta_0 Foreign_{i,t} + \beta_1 \Delta Interest\,Rate_{i,t} \\ & + \beta_2 \Delta Dollar\,Rate_{i,t} + \beta_3 Policy_{i,t} \\ & + \beta_4 Severity_{i,t} + \beta_5 Severity_{i,t} * Foreign_{i,t} \\ & + \beta_6 Policy_{i,t} * Foreign_{i,t} + \varepsilon_{i,t}.\end{aligned} \tag{10.10}$$

10.5. Results

In this section, we present the results of our empirical analysis in a way that allows us to compare emerging countries with the whole sample.

10.5.1. *Main regression results*

Table 10.3 reports the estimated coefficients for the panel model on the stock market. First, we find a positive and significant correlation between foreign trading and stock market volatility, suggesting that the stock market responds positively to the net foreign trading. Furthermore, the stock market volatility responds negatively to the appreciation of local currency against the US Dollar, consistent with theoretical predictions. Exchange rate movements affect the values of a firm's outstanding payables and receivables denominated in foreign currencies. Hence, stock price indices decline as the local currency depreciates. On average, 1% appreciation of Dollar against local currency reduces the stock price index by 1.5%. Although central banks lowered their interest rates in response to the pandemic, we found no significant monetary policy response during the analyzed period.

We also examine the impacts of safety measures taken by the policymakers to reduce the unfavorable effects of the pandemic on the economy. The effects of stringency, containment, and government response indices are similar both qualitatively and quantitatively, implying conduct of these policies elevate the stock market prices and counteract the impact of the pandemic.

10.5.2. *The impact of severity of the pandemic*

We also allow for the interaction terms between four different severity indices and foreign trading. Hence, we are interested in whether the impact of foreign trading is affected by COVID-19. The inclusion of interaction terms enables us to understand how our analysis is influenced by the severity of the pandemic. As discussed above, we use different severity indices that take a snapshot of each country's COVID-19 case and death status relative to the world. For all of the indices, the estimated coefficients of the interaction terms are negative and highly significant in emerging economies. For the whole

Table 10.3. Impact of foreign trading on stock price volatility and severity of pandemic.

	All countries					Emerging economies				
Panel A	**(I)**	**(II)**	**(III)**	**(IV)**	**(V)**	**(I)**	**(II)**	**(III)**	**(IV)**	**(V)**
Foreign	1.726**	1.753**	1.804**	1.781**	1.740**	1.022***	1.301***	1.292***	1.082***	1.184***
	(0.631)	(0.623)	(0.516)	(0.631)	(0.526)	(0.048)	(0.072)	(0.053)	(0.044)	(0.056)
Stringency	0.016***	0.016***	0.016***	0.015***	0.016***	0.015***	0.015***	0.016***	0.014***	0.016***
	(0.002)	(0.002)	(0.002)	(0.002)	(0.002)	(0.002)	(0.002)	(0.002)	(0.002)	(0.002)
Interest rate	−0.019	−0.098	−0.286	−0.001	−0.157	−0.026	−0.213	−0.314	−0.037	−0.183
	(0.966)	(0.954)	(0.899)	(0.977)	(0.923)	(1.021)	(0.965)	(0.936)	(1.024)	(0.968)
Dollar rate	−1.505***	−1.491***	−1.474***	−1.492***	−1.486***	−1.470***	−1.452***	−1.454***	−1.452***	−1.457***
	(0.122)	(0.123)	(0.116)	(0.125)	(0.118)	(0.132)	(0.134)	(0.124)	(0.133)	(0.128)
Severity-I		−0.036***					−0.068			
		(0.010)					(0.036)			
Severity-I × Foreign		**−0.009**					**−0.154*****			
		(0.005)					**(0.014)**			
Severity-II			−1.511**					−1.503*		
			(0.570)					(0.619)		
Severity-II × Foreign			**−1.788**					**−5.554*****		
			(2.206)					**(0.504)**		
Severity-III				1.578					1.841	
				(1.135)					(1.274)	
Severity-III × Foreign				**−2.227*****					**−1.747*****	
				(0.626)					**(0.198)**	

(Continued)

Table 10.3. *(Continued)*

	All countries					Emerging economies				
Panel A	**(I)**	**(II)**	**(III)**	**(IV)**	**(V)**	**(I)**	**(II)**	**(III)**	**(IV)**	**(V)**
Severity-IV					−0.747					−0.772
					(0.418)					(0.407)
Severity-IV × Foreign					**0.068**					**−1.916*****
					(1.350)					**(0.469)**
Constant	−0.638***	−0.574***	−0.618***	−0.603***	−0.594***	−0.745***	−0.649***	−0.709***	−0.701***	−0.696***
	(0.077)	(0.075)	(0.080)	(0.075)	(0.083)	(0.094)	(0.093)	(0.095)	(0.088)	(0.096)
Observations	520	520	520	520	520	390	390	390	390	390
Panel B										
Foreign	1.737**	1.766**	1.817***	1.791**	1.752**	1.031***	1.319***	1.305***	1.090***	1.194***
	(0.633)	(0.625)	(0.517)	(0.633)	(0.527)	(0.048)	(0.073)	(0.053)	(0.044)	(0.055)
Containment	0.017***	0.017***	0.017***	0.016***	0.017***	0.016***	0.016***	0.017***	0.015***	0.016***
	(0.002)	(0.002)	(0.002)	(0.002)	(0.002)	(0.002)	(0.002)	(0.002)	(0.002)	(0.002)
Interest rate	−0.034	−0.114	−0.305	−0.017	−0.171	−0.040	−0.232	−0.330	−0.053	−0.196
	(0.962)	(0.950)	(0.897)	(0.973)	(0.924)	(1.017)	(0.963)	(0.934)	(1.021)	(0.969)

Table 10.3 (*Continued*)

	All countries					Emerging economies				
Panel B	**(I)**	**(II)**	**(III)**	**(IV)**	**(V)**	**(I)**	**(II)**	**(III)**	**(IV)**	**(V)**
Dollar rate	−1.510***	−1.496***	−1.479***	−1.497***	−1.491***	−1.475***	−1.456***	−1.459***	−1.457***	−1.462***
	(0.121)	(0.123)	(0.116)	(0.125)	(0.118)	(0.131)	(0.134)	(0.123)	(0.132)	(0.128)
Severity-I		−0.037***					−0.070			
		(0.010)					(0.035)			
Severity-I × Foreign		**−0.010***					**−0.158*****			
		(0.005)					**(0.014)**			
Severity-II			−1.537**					−1.512*		
			(0.558)					(0.598)		
Severity-II × Foreign			**−1.839**					**−5.647*****		
			(2.223)					**(0.499)**		
Severity-III				1.609					1.873	
				(1.143)					(1.282)	
Severity-III × Foreign				**−2.205****					**−1.720*****	
				(0.633)					**(0.199)**	
Severity-IV					−0.746					−0.767*
					(0.397)					(0.377)
Severity-IV × Foreign					**0.062**					**−1.937*****
					(1.360)					**(0.448)**
Constant	−0.726***	−0.664***	−0.712***	−0.686***	−0.684***	−0.802***	−0.708***	−0.771***	−0.755***	−0.757***
	(0.070)	(0.070)	(0.078)	(0.072)	(0.076)	(0.084)	(0.087)	(0.089)	(0.082)	(0.087)
Observations	520	520	520	520	520	390	390	390	390	390

(*Continued*)

Table 10.3. *(Continued)*

	All countries					Emerging economies				
Panel C	**(I)**	**(II)**	**(III)**	**(IV)**	**(V)**	**(I)**	**(II)**	**(III)**	**(IV)**	**(V)**
Foreign	1.719**	1.751**	1.799***	1.774**	1.730**	1.033***	1.319***	1.302***	1.092***	1.188***
	(0.613)	(0.607)	(0.499)	(0.614)	(0.510)	(0.048)	(0.071)	(0.049)	(0.044)	(0.050)
Gov response	0.018***	0.018***	0.018***	0.017***	0.018***	0.017***	0.017***	0.018***	0.016***	0.018***
	(0.002)	(0.002)	(0.002)	(0.002)	(0.002)	(0.002)	(0.002)	(0.002)	(0.002)	(0.002)
Interest rate	−0.037	−0.116	−0.299	−0.020	−0.156	−0.046	−0.232	−0.325	−0.057	−0.183
	(0.970)	(0.959)	(0.907)	(0.982)	(0.936)	(1.024)	(0.973)	(0.946)	(1.030)	(0.982)
Dollar rate	−1.507***	−1.494***	−1.478***	−1.495***	−1.491***	−1.470***	−1.453***	−1.456***	−1.453***	−1.460***
	(0.122)	(0.123)	(0.116)	(0.125)	(0.119)	(0.131)	(0.134)	(0.123)	(0.132)	(0.128)
Severity-I		−0.035***					−0.068			
		(0.010)					(0.035)			
Severity-I × Foreign		**−0.011***					**−0.158*****			
		(0.005)					**(0.013)**			
Severity-II			−1.459**					−1.438*		
			(0.533)					(0.569)		
Severity-II × Foreign			**−1.888**					**−5.594*****		
			(2.172)					**(0.458)**		
Severity-III				1.581					1.841	
				(1.142)					(1.283)	
Severity-III × Foreign				**−2.209*****					**−1.736*****	
				(0.617)					**(0.200)**	

Table 10.3. *(Continued)*

	All countries					Emerging economies				
Panel C	**(I)**	**(II)**	**(III)**	**(IV)**	**(V)**	**(I)**	**(II)**	**(III)**	**(IV)**	**(V)**
Severity-IV					−0.630					−0.659
					(0.365)					(0.339)
Severity-IV × Foreign					**0.055**					**−1.875*****
					(1.322)					**(0.430)**
Constant	−0.705***	−0.639***	−0.683***	−0.665***	−0.663***	−0.775***	−0.680***	−0.738***	−0.728***	−0.730***
	(0.058)	(0.060)	(0.064)	(0.067)	(0.071)	(0.075)	(0.084)	(0.078)	(0.078)	(0.083)
Observations	520	520	520	520	520	390	390	390	390	390

Note: Fixed-effects estimation controls for country-fixed effects. The dependent variable is the daily percentage change in the leading stock market index. Robust standard errors clustered by country are in parentheses. $^{***}p < 0.01$, $^{**}p < 0.05$, $^{*}p < 0.1$.

Table 10.4. Impact of safety measures on the relationship between stock market volatility and foreign trading.

	All countries				Emerging economies			
Panel A	**(I)**	**(II)**	**(III)**	**(IV)**	**(I)**	**(II)**	**(III)**	**(IV)**
Stringency × Foreign	**0.025***** **(0.004)**	**0.026***** **(0.006)**	**0.023***** **(0.004)**	**0.025***** **(0.004)**	**0.022***** **(0.002)**	**0.020***** **(0.002)**	**0.019***** **(0.002)**	**0.021***** **(0.002)**
Severity-I × Foreign	−0.011* (0.006)				−0.171*** (0.016)			
Severity-II × Foreign		−1.480 (2.147)				−5.170*** (0.486)		
Severity-III × Foreign			−2.153** (0.656)				−1.664*** (0.196)	
Severity-IV × Foreign				0.107 (1.508)				−2.048*** (0.478)
Panel B								
Containment × Foreign	**0.037***** **(0.005)**	**0.037***** **(0.006)**	**0.035***** **(0.004)**	**0.036***** **(0.004)**	**0.027***** **(0.002)**	**0.025***** **(0.003)**	**0.025***** **(0.002)**	**0.027***** **(0.002)**

Table 10.4. *(Continued)*

	All countries				Emerging economies			
Panel B	**(I)**	**(II)**	**(III)**	**(IV)**	**(I)**	**(II)**	**(III)**	**(IV)**
Severity-I × Foreign	−0.018* (0.008)				−0.178*** (0.015)			
Severity-II × Foreign		−1.432 (2.103)				−5.211*** (0.478)		
Severity-III × Foreign			−2.114** (0.657)				−1.644*** (0.197)	
Severity-IV × Foreign				−0.047 (1.583)				−2.198*** (0.465)
Panel C								
Gov response × Foreign	**0.036*** (0.003)**	**0.035*** (0.004)**	**0.033*** (0.002)**	**0.035*** (0.003)**	**0.028*** (0.002)**	**0.025*** (0.003)**	**0.025*** (0.002)**	**0.027*** (0.002)**
Severity-I × Foreign	−0.016* (0.008)				−0.173*** (0.014)			
Severity-II × Foreign		−1.340 (2.116)				−5.125*** (0.441)		

(Continued)

Table 10.4 (*Continued*)

	All countries				Emerging economies			
Panel C	**(I)**	**(II)**	**(III)**	**(IV)**	**(I)**	**(II)**	**(III)**	**(IV)**
Severity-III × Foreign			-2.125^{**}				-1.650^{***}	
			(0.663)				(0.200)	
Severity-IV × Foreign				0.153				-2.039^{***}
				(1.589)				(0.439)
Observations	520	520	520	520	390	390	390	390

Notes: Fixed effects estimation controls for country fixed effects. The dependent variable is the daily percentage change in the leading stock market index. Robust standard errors clustered by country are in parentheses. $^{***}p < 0.01$, $^{**}p < 0.05$, $^{*}p < 0.1$.

sample, the significance is achieved only for Severity-III index, which is related to the quality of treatment in countries. A more considerable increase in the COVID-19 cases weakens the impact of foreign trading on the stock price volatility. All other coefficients broadly unchanged when the interaction effects are included in the regression.

10.5.3. *Impact of safety measures*

Table 10.4 summarizes the impact of safety measures taken by the policymakers on the relationship between foreign trading and stock price growth. All safety measures related interaction terms enter significantly with a positive sign. The questioned relationship becomes stronger as the precautions are being taken by the policymakers.

10.6. Conclusion

The effect of foreign trading on the stock market development is an enigma during normal and abnormal times. The bulk of literature attempts to answer this Delphic relation by focusing on particular events such as the Asian Financial Crisis, Global Financial Crisis, etc. In this chapter, we contribute to the related literature by answering the following question: How does the interaction between foreign trading and stock market volatility respond to the severity of the COVID-19? In order to answer this question, we use a panel data set of a selection of emerging and advanced countries from February 3, 2020, to April 30, 2020. We also focus on the effectiveness of safety measures taken during the sample period. Our findings can be summarized as follows: first, the stock market is sensitive to the severity of the pandemic. As the severity of COVID-19 increases, the impact of foreign trading on the volatility of the stock market is mitigated. Next, after controlling for the lockdown measures, the link between stock prices and foreign trading falls with the severity of the pandemic.

References

Alfaro, L., Chari, A., Greenland, A.N. and Schott, P.K. (2020). Aggregate and firm-level stock returns during pandemics, in real time. NBER Working Paper No:w26950.

Caporale, G.M., Karanasos, M., Yfanti, S. and Kartsaklas, A. (2020). Investors' trading behaviour and stock market volatility during crisis periods: A dual long-memory model for the Korean Stock Exchange. *International Journal of Finance & Economics*, 1–21.

Che, L. (2018). Investor types and stock return volatility. *Journal of Empirical Finance*, **47**, 139–161.

Chen, Z., Du, J., Li, D. and Ouyang, R. (2013). Does foreign institutional ownership increase return volatility? Evidence from China. *Journal of Banking & Finance*, **37**(2), 660–669.

Chiang, Y.-C. and Chan, M.-H. (2017). Foreign ownership and firm-level stock return volatility in Taiwan. *Investment Management and Financial Innovations*, **14**(3), 261–269.

Hale, T. *et al.* (2020). Oxford COVID-19 Government Response Tracker. Blavatnik School of Government Working Paper, 31.

Huang, B.-N. and Yang, C.-W. (2000). The impact of financial liberalization on stock price volatility in emerging markets. *Journal of Comparative Economics*, **28**(2), 321–339.

Jeon, Q.J. and Moffett, M.C. (2010). Herding by foreign investors and emerging market equity returns: Evidence from Korea. *International Review of Economics and Finance*, **19**, 698–710.

Umutlu, M., Akdeniz, L. and Altay, A. (2013). Foreign equity trading and average stock-return volatility. *The World Economy*, **36**(9), 1209–1228.

Umutlu, M. and Shackleton, M.B. (2015). Stock-return volatility and daily equity trading by investor groups in Korea. *Pacific-Basin Finance Journal*, **34**, 43–70.

Vo, X.V. (2015). Foreign ownership and stock return volatility — Evidence from Vietnam. *Journal of Multinational Financial Management*, **30**, 101–109.

Wang, J. (2007). Foreign equity trading and emerging market volatility: Evidence from Indonesia and Thailand. *Journal of Development Economics*, **84**(2), 798–811.

https://doi.org/10.1142/9781800610781_0011

Chapter 11

COVID-19 Pandemic and Co-movement Dynamics Among American and European Stock Markets

Abdelkader Derbali[*,§], **Mohamed Bechir Chenguel**[*,¶], **Lamia Jamel**[†,**], **Meriem Jouirou**[*,††], **and Fathi Jouini**[‡,‡‡]

[*]*Department of Finance and Accounting, Higher Institute of Informatics and Management of Kairouan, Kairouan University, Tunisia*

[†]*Department of Finance and Economics, College of Business Administration, Taibah University, Saudi Arabia*

[‡]*Department of Finance and Accounting, Faculty of Economic Sciences and Management of Sousse, Sousse University, Tunisia*

[§]*derbaliabdelkader@outlook.fr*
[¶]*bechir.chenguel@gmail.com*
[**]*lajamel@yahoo.fr*
[††]*jouirou.meriem@gmail.com*
[‡‡]*fathi_75@hotmail.fr*

Abstract

This chapter presents a crucial perspective to the predictive capacity of confirmed cases and deaths from COVID-19 surprises in the US and

[§]Corresponding author.

publication announcements for the correlation between financial stock market indices during the period from August 1, 2019 to August 31, 2020 using the DCC-GARCH(1,1) specifications. We use a sample composed of two major financial stock market indices in the US (S&P500 and Dow Jones) and 10 European stock market indices. To capture the unexpected factor of the COVID-19 surprises in the US, we use the Kuttner's (2001) methodology. From our empirical results, we present a considerable DCC between financial stock market indices in the US and Europe, especially in the epidemic of COVID-19. We confirm that the estimated DCC begins to react considerably more in the case of COVID-19 pandemic surprises than the period without the COVID-19 pandemic spread. Then, we prove that the COVID-19 pandemic has a short-term effect on the financial stock market indices of the selected countries. Additionally, we find that the influence of the COVID-19 pandemic on international financial stock markets has a bidirectional spillover effect between the US and chosen European countries. Finally, we confirm the financialization of European financial stock market indices.

11.1. Introduction

As the COVID-19 pandemic continues to spread around the world and countries are faced with the reality of trying to contain the virus and protect their populations, it is not surprising that it is also having a direct impact on the global foreign exchange market. To examine the current effects of the coronavirus on the foreign exchange market, it is important to review the timeline. Since the first case in Wuhan, China, in December 2019, the virus has spread at an alarming rate throughout China in January and February, with the number of deaths exceeding that of the 2002–2003 SARS epidemic on February 9, 2020. During this period, cases began to appear in other Asian countries, including Taiwan, Japan, and South Korea, and spread to the Middle East, Europe, Australia, and North America. On March 12, the World Health Organization (WHO) declared the new coronavirus outbreak a pandemic, with confirmed cases and deaths continuing to rise. At the end of March, China and other Asian countries were slowly recovering from the pandemic, with fewer cases being reported each day, while Europe became the new epicenter of the virus, with numbers steadily increasing across the continent. In particular, Italy, which has the highest number of deaths to date, is still struggling to control the pandemic despite the extreme preventive measures now in place, meaning that the long-term effects of COVID-19 are still unclear but could be devastating for all of Europe. On the other side of the Atlantic, the number of cases in the US continues to increase and, as they are reportedly slow to implement effective containment measures, the WHO predicts that the US will become the new epicenter in the coming weeks.

The number of deaths in Italy now exceeds that of China, and other major countries such as Spain, Germany and France are also experiencing increased pressure on health services and financial reserves in the fight against COVID-19, which explains the downward trend in the EUR/USD since the beginning of the year is 2020. Although the European Central Bank (ECB) announced on March 12, 2020 that it would inject €750 billion into the economy to help manage the financial fallout from the coronavirus, this has done little to boost the confidence of investors who prefer the US dollar as a more stable currency. In the UK, the introduction of security measures against the virus was slow, which had an impact on confidence in the pound sterling. With the Bank of England further reducing base interest rates to 0.1%, the current account deficit, and the continued uncertainties due to Brexit, investors are selling the pound sterling, which is lowering its value. However, the good news is that other EU countries are learning from the mistakes made by the countries most affected by the coronavirus in the early stages of the pandemic by introducing stricter coping strategies immediately rather than waiting. It is believed that this proactive approach could contribute to recovery in the long term, putting them in a better position to accelerate economic recovery.

The COVID-19 pandemic is found by numerous investigations to be extremely transmittable, which describes why it has rapidly propagated throughout human-to-human spread to various worldwide nations and states (Ahmad *et al.*, 2020; Arshad *et al.*, 2020; Harapan *et al.*, 2020). With the aim of tackling the COVID-19 pandemic, numerous nations across the world have implemented several radical procedures such as enforcing social separation, preventing excessive travel, and prohibiting parishioners. By the end of March 2020, more than 100 nations worldwide had enforced numerous lockdown constraints, considerably and negatively affecting their social, financial, cultural, and economic movements and events (Nicola *et al.*, 2020). Dutta *et al.* (2020) examine the time-varying correlations among gold and oil markets to investigate whether gold is a reliable haven portfolio asset for the international crude oil market during the COVID-19 pandemic period. The findings of the time-varying correlations achieved across the DCC-GARCH model show that gold is a secure haven portfolio asset for the global crude oil market. Also, Bitcoin reacts only as a diversifier for crude oil. Then, the findings further indicate that the portfolio risk is diminished when investors incorporate oil and gold in their portfolio instead of buying assets in oil and Bitcoin markets.

Mensi *et al.* (2020) investigate the effects of COVID-19 pandemic on the multifractality of gold and oil prices founded on higher and down movements. They use the Asymmetric Multifractal Detrended Fluctuation Analysis (A-MF-DFA) methodology on a 15-min interval intra-day dataset. Their empirical findings reveal robust proof of asymmetric multifractality that rises as the fractality scale rises. Furthermore, they demonstrate that multifractality is particularly great in the weakness (benefit) movement for Brent oil (gold), and this surplus asymmetry has been highlighted through the COVID-19 outbreak. Gharib *et al.* (2020) investigate the causal nexus among crude oil and gold spot prices to evaluate how the COVID-19 pandemic has influenced them. They examine West Texas Light crude oil (WTI) and gold prices during the period of study from January 4, 2010, to May 4, 2020. They remark frequent periods of moderate explosivity in WTI and gold markets. Additionally, they demonstrate a bilateral contagion impact of bubbles in oil and gold markets through the current coronavirus pandemic.

He *et al.* (2020) examine the direct effects and transmission of COVID-19 on international financial stock markets such as in China, Italy, South Korea, France, Spain, Germany, Japan, and the US. They utilize standard *t*-tests and non-parametric Mann–Whitney tests as an appropriate econometric methodology. Also, they analyze a daily return dataset relative to the used international financial stock markets in China, Italy, South Korea, France, Spain, Germany, Japan, and the US. They conclude that the coronavirus has a negative and crucial but short-term influence on the employed financial stock markets of affected countries. Additionally, they find that the impact of the coronavirus on the studied international financial stock markets has bidirectional transmission influences between

Asian financial stock markets and European and American financial stock markets.

Additionally, Sansa (2020) examines the influence of COVID-19 on the international financial stock markets throughout the period of study from March 1, 2020 to March 25, 2020 in China and the US. Then, he validates that there is a positive and significant nexus between the COVID-19 confirmed cases and the international financial stock markets used in his study (i.e. Shanghai Stock Exchange and New York Dow Jones) during the period from March 1, 2020 to March 25, 2020 in China and in the US. Also, this empirical result concludes that COVID-19 had a significant influence on the international financial stock markets during the period from March 1, 2020 to March 25, 2020 in China and the US.

COVID-19 has significantly influenced international financial markets worldwide. It generated an extraordinary degree of risk, affecting shareholders to tolerate considerable deficits a minimum number of day in the week. In March 2020, the stock market in the US reached the an important pics in the volatilities of the US stock market four times in ten days. The most important stock markets registered in the US, such as the Dow Jones Industrial Average (DJIA) and Standard & Poor's 500 Index (S&P500), declined considerably (Wagner, 2020). Numerous international equity markets across the world suffered their quickest index decline in history. Stock markets in Europe, Africa, and Asia also tumbled (Ashraf, 2020; Zhang *et al.*, 2020). Assuming the dramatic arrangements detected lately in numerous international financial markets worldwide, various current researchers have utilized numerous experimental methods to examine the ultimate impacts of COVID-19 on international stock market returns and level of risks in various influenced nations and states such as China, US, Japan, Korea, Singapore, Germany, Italy, and UK (Ali *et al.*, 2020; Liu *et al.*, 2020; Sharif *et al.*, 2020; Zhang *et al.*, 2020).

This chapter delivers an essential perspective on the predictive capacity of confirmed cases and deaths due to COVID-19 in the US and their production and publication of news for the relationship between financial stock market indices in US and in Europe during the period of study from August 1, 2019 to August 31, 2020. Then, we utilize a daily dataset for the two major stock market indices in the US (S&P500 and Dow Jones) and ten European stock market indices (RTS from

Russia, FTSE100 from UK, DAX from Germany, IBEX35 from Spain, CAC40 from France, AEX from Netherlands, SMI from Suisse, PSI from Portugal, ASE from Greece, and FTSE from Italia). To empirically examine the unanticipated component of the confirmed cases and deaths due to COVID-19 in the US, we use the Kuttner (2001) methodology and utilize the number of confirmed cases and deaths due to COVID-19 in the US to capture the surprise factor. Also, we employ the methodology of DCC-GARCH (1,1) (Generalized Autoregressive Conditional Heteroskedasticity-Dynamic Conditional Correlation) as founded by Engle (2002) to assess the nexus among the financial stock market in the US and Europe. From the empirical results, we find an important DCC between the American financial stock market indices and selected European financial stock market indices, especially during COVID-19. We prove that the DCC among American financial stock market indices and selected European financial stock market indices begin to react significantly and considerably more during COVID-19 compared to the period without COVID-19. Our empirical investigations imply that the COVID-19 pandemic has a short-term impact on the stock market indices of the selected countries. Additionally, we find that the effect of the COVID-19 pandemic on international stock markets has bidirectional spillover influence in the US and select European countries. Also, we prove the financialization of the European stock market indices. Finally, we assume that the COVID-19 pandemic explains the spillover effects of the American stock market index on select European countries by using DCC-GARCH specifications.

The rest of this chapter is organized as follow: Section 11.2 clearly describes the econometric methodology used in this chapter. Section 11.3 presents the data employed in this research. Section 11.4 focuses on the empirical results of the effect of confirmed cases and deaths due to COVID-19 in the US and its connection among American and European financial stock markets indices. Section 11.5 provides the conclusion. Finally, Section 11.6 presents policy implications of our chapter.

11.2. Econometric Methodology

In this research, the econometric method utilized to assess the relationship between American and European financial stock markets returns and volatilities in response to COVID-19 pandemic shocks in the US is founded on the DCC multivariate technique, as recommended by Engle (2002). To accomplish the reaction of European financial stock markets returns correlated with American financial stock markets returns to the surprise component, we operate the Generalized Autoregressive Conditional Heteroskedasticity technique. Therefore, the Generalized Autoregressive Conditional Heteroskedasticity (1,1) model is applied through the following equation:

$$h_t = \omega + \alpha\varepsilon_{t-1}^2 + \beta h_{t-1}, \tag{11.1}$$

where ω, α, and β represent the parameters that need to be measured. The estimate dynamic conditional correlation (DCC) matrix R_t of the standardized disturbances ε_t can be given by the following matrix:

$$R_t = \begin{bmatrix} 1 & q_{12t} \\ q_{21t} & 1 \end{bmatrix}, \tag{11.2}$$

where $\varepsilon_t = D_t^{-1} r_t$. The return matrix R_t is determined through the following equation:

$$R_t = Q_t^{*-1} Q_t Q_t^{*-1}, \tag{11.3}$$

where Q_t indicates the time varying covariance matrix of ε_t and Q_t^{*-1} presents the reversed diagonal matrix along among the square root of the diagonal components of Q_t. Q_t^{*-1} can be corresponding to the following matrix:

$$Q_t^{*-1} = \begin{bmatrix} 1/\sqrt{q_{11t}} & 0 \\ 0 & 1/\sqrt{q_{22t}} \end{bmatrix}. \tag{11.4}$$

The Generalized Autoregressive Conditional Heteroskedasticity — DCC (1,1) is suggested by the following equation:

$$Q_t = \omega + \alpha\varepsilon_{t-1}\varepsilon_{t-1}' + \beta Q_{t-1}, \tag{11.5}$$

with $\omega = (1 - \alpha - \beta)\overline{Q}$, where, $\overline{Q}$ is the unconditional covariance of the standardized disturbances ε_t. ω, α, and β indicate the parameters that need to be estimated. In this chapter, we add to the existing financial and economic literature by incorporating an exogenous indicator in the DCC-GARCH (1,1) model, which assesses the

COVID-19 shock in the US. Thus, the estimated equation is presented as follows:

$$Q_t = \omega + \alpha \varepsilon_{t-1} \varepsilon'_{t-1} + \beta Q_{t-1} + \gamma S_t, \qquad (11.6)$$

where S_t implies the unanticipated COVID-19 shock announcements at the period t. The surprise indicate the informations about the COVID-19 shock in the US. The surprise is measured by the COVID-19 confirmed and death cases in the US.

Using the Kuttner (2001) methodology, we compute the surprise factor as the scaled version of change in the one-day COVID-19 confirmed and death cases at an occurrence date (d identified as a pronouncement of COVID-19 confirmed and death cases in the US). The use of Kuttner (2001) measures in this chapter is justified by the importance of assessing the surprises component issued by the COVID-19 outbreak. Obviously, the shock factor for each COVID-19 confirmed and death case change in the US is offered by the following formula:

$$S = \frac{D}{D-d}(f_d - f_{d-1}), \qquad (11.7)$$

where f_d implies the number of COVID-19 confirmed/death cases at the end of the statement day d in the US, f_{d-1} indicates the number of COVID-19 confirmed/death cases at the end of the publication day $(d-1)$ in the US, and D represents the number of days in the month. The nomination of all variables are presented in Table 11.1.

11.3. Data

In this section, we expand upon the data employed in our chapter, which comprise a daily time series of returns and volatilities of two major stock market indices in the US (S&P500 and Dow Jones) and ten European stock market indices (RTS from Russia, FTSE100 from UK, DAX from Germany, IBEX35 from Spain, CAC40 from France, AEX from Netherlands, SMI from Switzerland, PSI from Portugal, ASE from Greece, and FTSE from Italy). Thus, in the framework to examine the impact of the announcements of confirmed and death cases due to COVID-19 in the US, we focus on the anticipated and

Table 11.1. Variable codification.

No.	Region	Stock market index code	Country
1	USA	DJ	USA
2		S&P500	USA
3	Europe	AEX	Netherlands
4		ASE	Greece
5		CAC40	France
6		DAX	Germany
7		FTSE	Italia
8		FTSE100	United Kingdom
9		IBEX35	Spain
10		PSI	Portugal
11		RTS	Russia
12		SMI	Suisse

surprise factors in the COVID-19 confirmed cases and deaths variation in the US. The data sample used here incorporates the period of study from August 1, 2019 to August 31, 2020. Also, the data utilized in this chapter is acquired from three data resources.[1] The selection of COVID-19 confirmed cases and death cases variation in the US is supported by two factors: (1) it presents the highest number of COVID-19 confirmed cases (nine million confirmed cases) and (2) it presents the highest number of death due to the COVID-19 pandemic (May 2, 2020 death cases). The selected stock market indices are justified by two reasons: (1) we choose S&P500 and Dow Jones because they are the major and important stock market indices in the US and (2) we use the ten European stock market indices based on their important capitalizations and because their countries are the most influenced by the COVID-19 pandemic.

Furthermore, we declare that all stock market price indices of the two major stock market indices in the US and the ten European stock market indices are transformed into logarithmic forms. Subsequently, we utilize the logarithmic of return, such as $r_t = \ln(p_t/p_{t-1})$, where

[1]The three data sources are https://markets.businessinsider.com/currencies, https://fr.investing.com/ and https://data.europa.eu/euodp/en/home.

p_t indicates the stock market price index at the moment t and p_{t-1} indicates the stock market price index at the moment $t-1$.

11.3.1. *American and European stock market indices*

In Table 11.2, we recap the descriptive statistics relative to the daily returns of two major stock market indices in the US, i.e. S&P500 and Dow Jones. Based the findings presented in Table 11.2, we observe that the smallest mean of return is equal to 4.06E-05 for Dow Jones but the highest mean is equal to 0.000465 for S&P500. For the expected volatility of the daily estimated return of S&P500 and Dow Jones, which is determined by the standard deviation statistic, we find that Dow Jones exhibits daily volatility of 0.010095 versus S&P500 with a volatility of 0.009027.

The estimated statistics of skewness show a negative sign for the two employed stock market indices (S&P500 and Dow Jones). The negative sign associated with the skewness statistic recommends that the estimated distribution of S&P500 and Dow Jones is asymmetrical to the left. Additionally, the estimated statistics of kurtosis are outstanding to the unity (1). Furthermore, the value of the Jarque–Bera, skewness, and kurtosis statistics reveals the rejection of the null hypothesis comparative to the normal dispersion of S&P500 and Dow Jones.

Table 11.3 summarizes the statistical characteristics for the conditional volatility of the employed American stock market indices.

Table 11.2. Descriptive analysis for the daily returns of American stock market indices.

	DJ	**S&P500**
Mean	0.0004	0.0004
Std. Dev.	0.0100	0.0090
Skewness	−1.3975	−0.9215
Kurtosis	13.512	13.089
Jarque–Bera	1365.6	1214.0
Observations	277	277

Note: This table present a summary of descriptive statistics of daily returns for American stock market indices. The study period is from August 1, 2019 until August 31, 2020.

Table 11.3. Descriptive analysis for the daily conditional volatilities of American stock market indices.

	DJ	**S&P500**
Mean	0.0009	0.0008
Std. Dev.	0.0002	0.0001
Skewness	3.3995	3.4759
Kurtosis	14.378	14.487
Jarque–Bera	2027.7	2080.7
Observations	277	277

Note: This table summarizes a summary of descriptive statistics of daily conditional volatilities for American stock market indices. The study period is from August 1, 2019 until August 31, 2020.

Table 11.4. Unit root test.

Method	**Statistic**	**Prob.***	**Cross-sections**	**Obs.**
Null: Unit root (assumes common unit root process)				
Levin, Lin & Chu	−75.199	0.0000	2	538
Null: Unit root (assumes individual unit root process)				
Im, Pesaran–Shin W-stat	−5.4423	0.0000	2	538
ADF–Fisher Chi-square	40.506	0.0000	2	538
PP–Fisher Chi-square	256.27	0.0000	2	552

Note: This table summarizes unit root test of daily returns of the employed American stock market indices. The study period is from August 1, 2019 to August 31, 2020. *Probabilities for Fisher tests are computed using an asymptotic Chi-square distribution. All other tests assume asymptotic normality.

We demonstrate that in mean the higher conditional volatility is for Dow Jones (9.92E-05) followed by S&P500 (8.03E-05).

Then, the Levin–Lin–Chu test, Im–Pesaran–Shin test, Augmented Dickey–Fuller test, and Phillips–Perron test applied to the two major stock market indices in the US are presented in Table 11.4. In our chapter and from Table 11.4, we conclude that all employed American stock market indices are stationary in level, with regard to the Lin–Chu test, Im–Pesaran–Shin test, Augmented Dickey–Fuller test, and Phillips–Perron test.

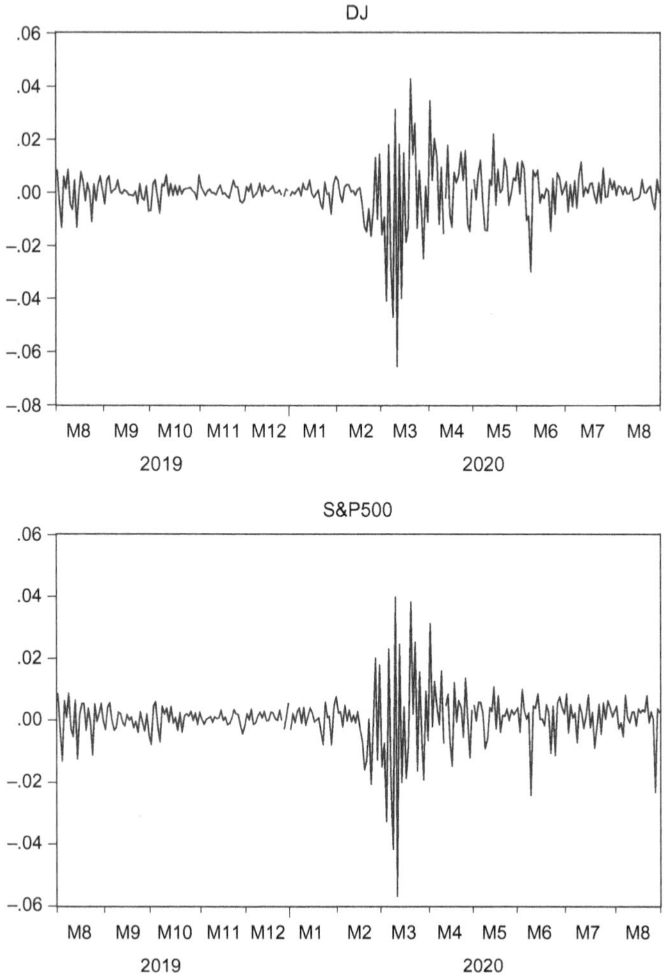

Figure 11.1. The evolution of the daily returns of the American stock market indices during the period of study from August 1, 2019 to August 31, 2020.

Figure 11.1 presents the evolution of the daily returns of American stock market indices. It can be seen that the studied American stock market indices have some peaks in their return evolutions. The breaks are exhibited especially in March and April 2020 during the COVID-19 pandemic. These months are marked by the high level of COVID-19 confirmed cases and deaths in all countries worldwide, especially in the US. Figure 11.2 presents the progression of the

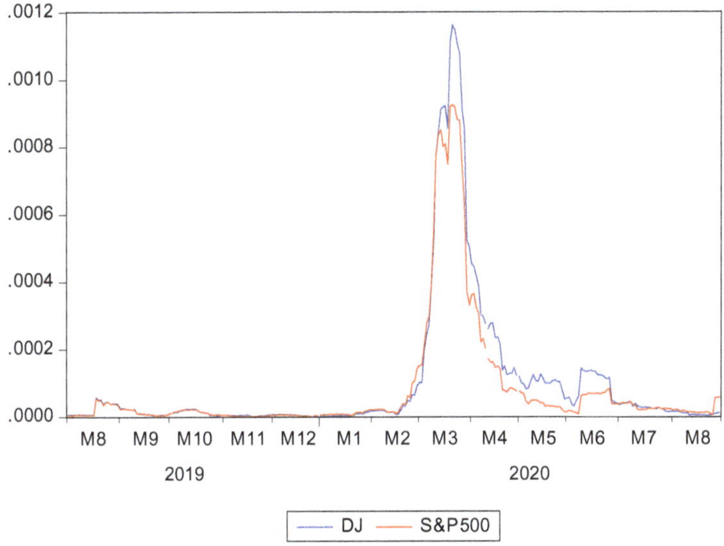

Figure 11.2. The evolution of the daily conditional volatilities of the American stock market indices through the period of study from August 1, 2019 to August 31, 2020.

conditional volatilities of the American stock market indices. It can be seen that the conditional volatilities of American stock market indices achieve their maximum in March and April 2020.

In Table 11.5, we summarize the descriptive statistics relative to the daily returns of European stock market indices, such as RTS from Russia, FTSE100 from UK, DAX from Germany, IBEX35 from Spain, CAC40 from France, AEX from Netherlands, SMI from Switzerland, PSI from Portugal, ASE from Greece, and FTSE from Italy. From the results presented in this table, we find that the lowest mean of return is equal to −0.000451 for ASE but the highest mean is equal to 0.000967 for CAC40. For the anticipated volatility of the daily return, which is determined by the standard deviation statistic, we find that the highest value is equal to 0.025976 for the DAX index and the lowest value is for SMI (0.006676).

The estimated statistics of skewness show a negative sign for seven European stock market indices, i.e. SMI, PSI, IBEX35, FTSE, DAX, ASE, and AEX. However, we find a negative sign for three European stock market indices, i.e. RTS, FTSE100, and CAC40. The negative sign associated with the skewness statistic recommends that the

Table 11.5. Descriptive analysis for the daily returns of European stock market indices.

	SMI	**RTS**	**PSI**	**IBEX35**	**FTSE100**	**FTSE**	**DAX**	**CAC40**	**ASE**	**AEX**
Mean	0.0001	0.0001	0.0001	−0.0004	0.0003	−0.0002	−0.0007	0.0009	−0.0004	0.0001
Std. Dev.	0.0066	0.0102	0.0086	0.0084	0.0073	0.0190	0.0259	0.0258	0.0121	0.0074
Skewness	−0.7282	1.5321	−1.0422	−1.9220	1.2856	−3.6513	−1.8219	2.1671	−1.2789	−1.1908
Kurtosis	15.578	12.170	14.080	17.617	13.348	34.414	17.983	17.659	12.446	13.435
Jarque–Bera	1850.6	1079.1	1467.1	2636.5	1312.2	12005	2744.3	2697.2	1105.5	1322.2
Observations	277	277	277	277	277	277	277	277	277	277

Note: This table presents a summary of descriptive statistics of daily returns for European stock market indices. The study period is from August 1, 2019 until August 31, 2020.

estimated distribution of SMI, PSI, IBEX35, FTSE, DAX, ASE, and AEX is asymmetrical to the left. However, the positive sign associated with the skewness statistic recommends that the estimated distribution of RTS, FTSE100, and CAC40. Furthermore, the estimated statistics of kurtosis are superior to the unity (1). Additionally, the estimated values of Jarque–Bera, skewness, and kurtosis statistics confirm the refusal of the null assumption relative to the normal dispersion of used European stock market indices.

Table 11.6 summarizes the descriptive statistical features for the conditional volatility of the used European stock market indices. Then, we find that in mean the greater conditional volatility of is for CAC40 (0.000665), however, the lowest conditional volatility is for (8.03E-05).

Subsequently, the Levin–Lin–Chu test, Im–Pesaran–Shin test, Augmented Dickey–Fuller test, and Phillips–Perron test are applied to the two major stock market indices in the US, as summarized in Table 11.7. In our chapter and from Table 11.7, we demonstrate that all employed European stock market indices are stationary in level based on the Lin–Chu test, Im–Pesaran–Shin test, Augmented Dickey–Fuller test, and Phillips–Perron test.

Figure 11.3 shows the progress of the daily returns of European stock market indices. It can be seen that the utilized European stock market indices have important breaks in their return progressions. These breaks are exhibited especially in March and April 2020 during the COVID-19 pandemic. These months are evidenced by the elevated intensity of COVID-19 confirmed cases and deaths in all countries in the world, especially in the European countries such as France, Spain, Italy, Russia, UK, Germany, Netherlands, and Switzerland. In addition, Figure 11.4 shows the evolution of the conditional volatilities of the European stock market indices. It can be seen that the conditional volatilities of European stock market indices achieve their maximum in March and April 2020. This period is evidenced by the elevated intensity of COVID-19 confirmed cases and deaths in most European countries.

11.3.2. *The unconditional correlation matrix*

Table 11.8 summarizes the most important statistical characteristics for the unconditional correlation matrix among Dow Jones and

Table 11.6. Descriptive analysis for the daily conditional volatilities of European stock market indices.

	ASE	**AEX**	**CAC40**	**DAX**	**FTSE**	**FTSE100**	**IBEX35**	**PSI**	**SMI**	**RTS**
Mean	0.0001	0.0005	0.0006	0.0006	0.0003	0.0005	0.0006	0.0007	0.0004	0.0001
Std. Dev.	0.0002	0.0008	0.0012	0.0011	0.0007	0.0008	0.0001	0.0001	0.0007	0.0001
Skewness	3.2481	3.3852	3.4897	3.4433	4.0248	3.1351	3.7557	3.7259	3.3576	3.0348
Kurtosis	13.343	15.218	15.622	15.619	18.369	13.312	17.140	16.761	15.141	12.461
Jarque–Bera	1721.9	2252.0	2401.2	2385.5	3474.2	1681.1	2958.9	2826.6	2221.8	1458.4
Observations	277	277	277	277	277	277	277	277	277	277

Note: This table summarizes a summary of descriptive statistics of daily returns for European stock market indices. The study period is from August 1, 2019 until August 31, 2020.

Table 11.7. Unit root test.

Method	Statistic	Prob.*	Cross-sections	Obs.
Null: Unit root (assumes common unit root process)				
Levin, Lin & Chu	−45.6057	0.0000	10	2752
Null: Unit root (assumes individual unit root process)				
Im–Pesaran–Shin W-stat	−46.3552	0.0000	10	2752
ADF–Fisher Chi-square	1071.29	0.0000	10	2752
PP–Fisher Chi-square	1327.59	0.0000	10	2760

Note: This table summarizes unit root test of daily returns of the employed European stock market indices. The used period is from August 1, 2019 to August 31, 2020. *Probabilities for Fisher tests are computed using an asymptotic Chi-square distribution. All other tests assume asymptotic normality.

European stock market indices. From the unconditional correlation showed in this table, we prove that Dow Jones has a positive correlation with European stock market indices (especially ASE, FTSE, DAX, and PSI). This result proves that COVID-19 shocks justify the spillover impacts of Dow Jones in European stock market indices. Furthermore, Table 11.8 summarizes the most crucial statistical attributes for the unconditional correlation matrix between S&P500 and selected European stock market indices. From this table, we find S&P500 have a positive connection with selected European stock market indices (especially ASE, FTSE, DAX, and PSI) during the period of study.

Table 11.9 recapitulates the generally essential statistical attributes for the unconditional correlation matrix between S&P500 and European stock market indices. Using the unconditional correlation presented in this table, we provide evidence that S&P500 present a positive and important correlation with European stock market indices (especially ASE, FTSE, DAX, and PSI). This finding demonstrates that COVID-19 shockwaves can substantiate the spillover influences of S&P500 in selected European stock market indices.

Additionally, Tables 11.8 and 11.9 show important and positive unconditional correlation between some European stock market indices such as, between "AEX" and "ASE and IBEX35," between

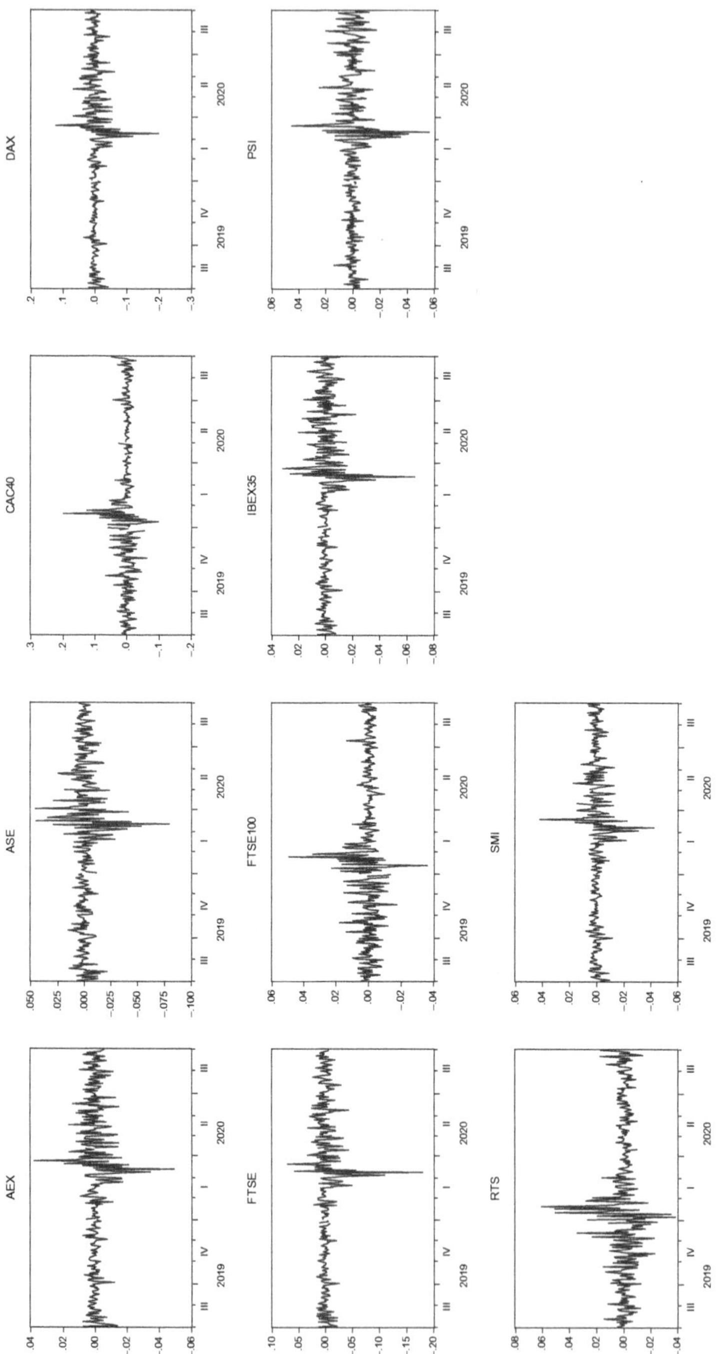

Figure 11.3. The evolution of the daily returns of the European stock market indices during the period of study from August 1, 2019 to August 31, 2020.

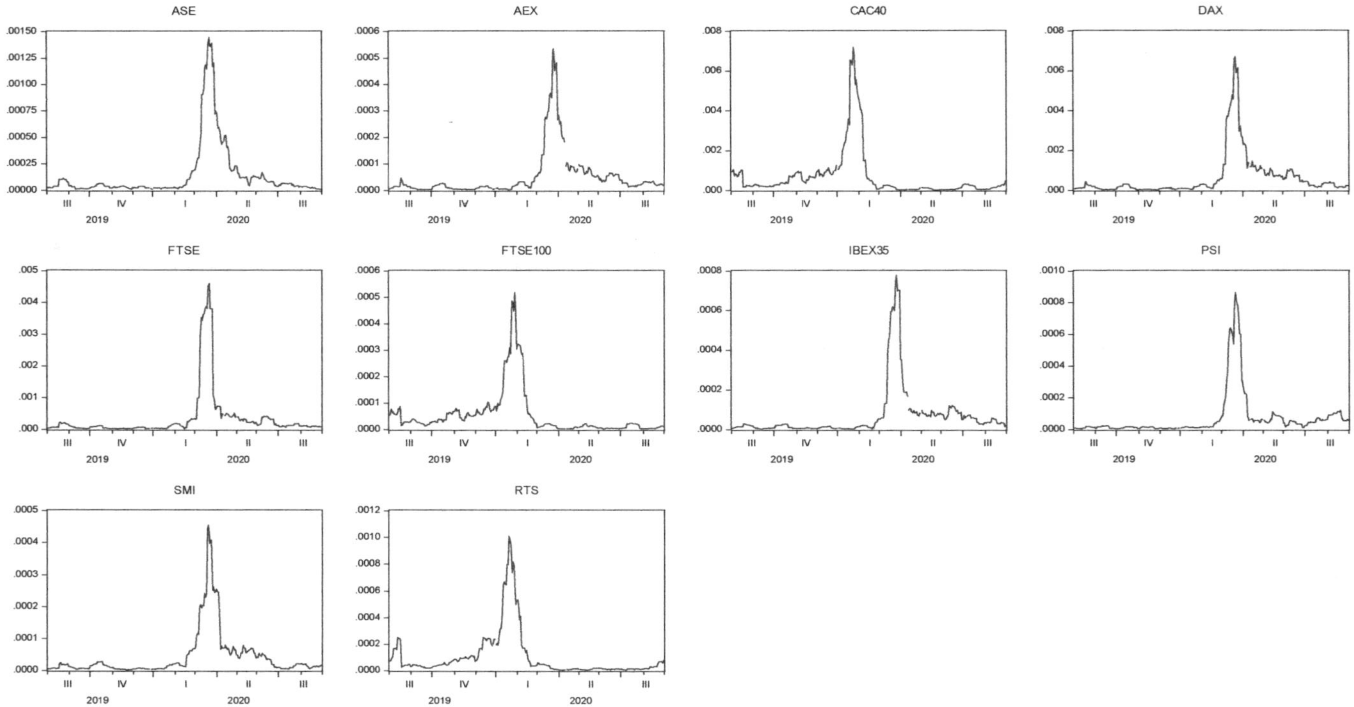

Figure 11.4. The evolution of the daily conditional volatilities of the European stock market indices through the period of study from August 1, 2019 to August 31, 2020.

Table 11.8. Unconditional correlation between Dow Jones and European stock market indices.

	DJ	AEX	ASE	CAC40	DAX	FTSE	FTSE100	IBEX35	PSI	RTS	SMI
DJ	1,000	0,057	**0,787**	0,021	**0,586**	**0,574**	−0,043	−0,079	**0,683**	−0,033	0,004
AEX	0,057	1,000	0,089	−0,011	0,185	0,182	0,003	**0,874**	0,158	0,021	0,047
ASE	**0,787**	**0,089**	1,000	−0,008	**0,520**	**0,516**	−0,049	−0,025	**0,557**	−0,041	−0,004
CAC40	0,021	−0,011	−0,008	1,000	0,028	0,057	0,295	0,009	−0,027	0,260	−0,131
DAX	**0,586**	0,185	**0,520**	0,028	1,000	**0,802**	0,013	0,115	**0,524**	0,005	0,057
FTSE	**0,574**	0,182	**0,516**	0,057	**0,802**	1,000	0,021	0,112	**0,511**	0,027	0,043
FTSE100	−0,043	0,003	−0,049	0,295	0,013	0,021	1,000	0,012	−0,015	0,001	0,014
IBEX35	−0,079	**0,874**	−0,025	0,009	0,115	0,112	0,012	1,000	0,060	0,030	0,081
PSI	**0,683**	0,158	**0,557**	−0,027	**0,524**	**0,511**	−0,015	0,060	1,000	−0,047	0,054
RTS	−0,033	0,021	−0,041	0,260	0,005	0,027	0,001	0,030	−0,047	1,000	−0,011
SMI	0,004	0,047	−0,004	−0,131	0,057	0,043	0,014	0,081	0,054	−0,011	1,000

Note: This table shows the unconditional correlation matrix between daily returns of Dow Jones and European stock market indices. The data period is from August 1, 2019 to August 31, 2020.

Table 11.9. Unconditional correlation between S&P500 and European stock market indices.

	S&P500	**AEX**	**ASE**	**CAC40**	**DAX**	**FTSE**	**FTSE100**	**IBEX35**	**PSI**	**RTS**	**SMI**
S&P500	1,000	0,046	**0,714**	0,033	**0,509**	**0,527**	−0,035	−0,072	**0,656**	−0,036	0,031
AEX	0,046	1,000	0,089	−0,011	0,185	0,182	0,003	**0,874**	0,158	0,021	0,047
ASE	**0,714**	**0,089**	1,000	−0,008	**0,520**	**0,516**	−0,049	−0,025	**0,557**	−0,041	−0,004
CAC40	0,033	−0,011	−0,008	1,000	0,028	0,057	0,295	0,009	−0,027	0,260	−0,131
DAX	**0,509**	0,185	**0,520**	0,028	1,000	**0,802**	0,013	0,115	**0,524**	0,005	0,057
FTSE	**0,527**	0,182	**0,516**	0,057	**0,802**	1,000	0,021	0,112	**0,511**	0,027	0,043
FTSE100	−0,035	0,003	−0,049	0,295	0,013	0,021	1,000	0,012	−0,015	0,001	0,014
IBEX35	−0,072	**0,874**	−0,025	0,009	0,115	0,112	0,012	1,000	0,060	0,030	0,081
PSI	**0,656**	0,158	**0,557**	−0,027	**0,524**	**0,511**	−0,015	0,060	1,000	−0,047	0,054
RTS	−0,036	0,021	−0,041	0,260	0,005	0,027	0,001	0,030	−0,047	1,000	−0,011
SMI	0,031	0,047	−0,004	−0,131	0,057	0,043	0,014	0,081	0,054	−0,011	1,000

Note: This table shows the unconditional correlation matrix between daily returns of S&P500 and European stock market indices. The bolded numbers indicate the correlations which are superior than 0.5. The data period is from August 1, 2019 to August 31, 2020.

"ASE" and "DAX, FTSE, and PSI," between "DAX" and "FTSE and PSI," and between "FTSE" and "PSI." So, we confirm the dynamic dependence among European financial stock markets, especially in Germany, Spain, Greece, Italy, and Portugal.

11.3.3. *COVID-19 surprises*

Table 11.10 summarizes the descriptive statistics founded on a sample of COVID-19 confirmed cases and deaths from August 1, 2019 through August 31, 2020. The period under consideration covers a total of 139 COVID-19 confirmed case surprises (SCC) and 130 COVID-19 death case surprises in the US (SDC). The mean values of the variations of the COVID-19 SCC and SDC in the US are, respectively, 0.000678 and 0.000678. In addition, it is crucial to reveal that the standard deviation (which measures the risk) of the COVID-19 SDC (1.042793) is superior to those of COVID-19 SCC (0.637709). This result recommends that the COVID-19 SDC is more important and significant compared to the COVID-19 SCC in the US.

Table 11.10. Descriptive statistics for the surprises components in the US.

	SCC	SDC
Mean	0.0006	0.0570
Std. Dev.	0.6377	1.0427
Skewness	−5.1757	1.1522
Kurtosis	89.461	28.018
Jarque–Bera	87518	7285.3
Observations	277	277

Note: This table summarizes the descriptive statistics for COVID-19 confirmed cases and death cases declaration surprises in the US. The period of study is from August 1, 2019 until August 31, 2020. The COVID-19 confirmed cases and death cases declarations shocks are collected from the https://data.europa.eu/euodp/en/home. The sample period includes 139 confirmed cases announcements and 130 death cases declarations in the US. Then, we follow the Kuttner (2001) approach and specify the discovered surprises by utilizing the one-day change in COVID-19 confirmed cases and death cases for each day.

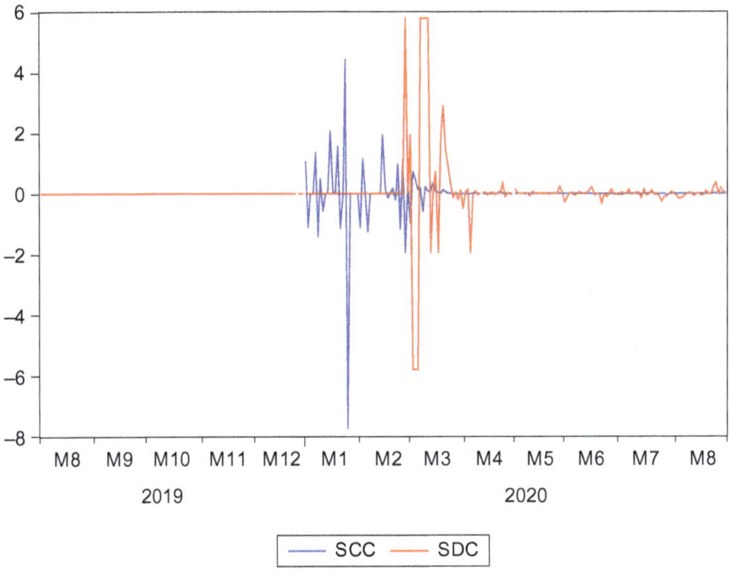

Figure 11.5. The evolution of the COVID-19 confirmed case (SCC) and death case (SDC) surprises in the US during the period August 1, 2019 to August 31, 2020.

Figure 11.5 shows the daily evolution of the COVID-19 confirmed case and death case surprises in the US during the period of study from August 1, 2019 to August 31, 2020. Based on this figure, we remark that the COVID-19 confirmed case surprises is more volatile than the COVID-19 death case surprises in the US. The greatest volatility of COVID-19 confirmed case surprises is observed during the period from January to March 2020. However, the highest level of the volatility of COVID-19 death case shocks is observed during the period from March to April 2020.

11.4. Empirical Results

In the investigational assessment of this chapter, we explore the effect of the COVID-19 news in the US on the dynamic conditional correlation among two major US stock market indices (S&P500 and Dow Jones) and ten European stock market indices (RTS from

Russia, FTSE100 from UK, DAX from Germany, IBEX35 from Spain, CAC40 from France, AEX from the Netherlands, SMI from Switzerland, PSI from Portugal, ASE from Greece, and FTSE from Italy). The econometric approach used in this chapter is based on the DCC-GARCH (1.1) specification introduced by Engle (2002). Also, the data sample runs across the period of study from August 1, 2019 to August 31, 2020. Then, we employ the approach founded by Kuttner (2001), which has established predominant in the scholarly literature in finance and economics. Particularly, we utilize the changes in the COVID-19 confirmed cases and death cases shocks in the US.

Table 11.11 summarizes the descriptive statistics for the estimated dynamic conditional correlation among Dow Jones and the selected European stock market indices. From this table, we determine that the bigger dynamic conditional correlation is among Dow Jones and PSI (0.984853) followed by ASE (0.949767), FTSE (0.931574), and DAX (0.928463). This result suggests the importance of the dependence between financial stock markets in the US and Europe mainly during the COVID-19 pandemic.

Table 11.12 summarizes the descriptive statistics for the estimated dynamic conditional correlation among S&P500 and the selected European stock market indices. From the results of this table, we show that the greater dynamic conditional correlation is between S&P500 and PSI (0.974821) followed by ASE (0.957519), IBEX35 (0.942573), and AEX (0.935087). This finding recommends the importance of the dynamic dependence between the US financial stock market and the European financial stock markets mainly during the COVID-19 pandemic.

From Figures 11.6 and 11.7, which present the evolution of DCC between the American stock market indices and the selected European stock market indices during the period August 1, 2019 to August 31, 2020, we find that highest peaks of their correlations are observed in the period from February to March 2020. This period coincides with the higher propagation of COVID-19, especially in Europe and the US.

Tables 11.13 and 11.14 recap the empirical results of the estimation of the DCC-GARCH (1,1) between the two major stock market indices in the US (S&P500 and Dow Jones) and ten European stock market indices (RTS from Russia, FTSE100 from UK,

Table 11.11. Descriptive statistics for DCC between Dow Jones and the selected European stock market indices.

	AEX	ASE	CAC40	DAX	FTSE	FTSE100	IBEX35	PSI	RTS	SMI
Mean	−0.0276	0.412	0.0914	0.2400	0.2217	0.0282	−0.0628	0.4019	−0.0262	0.0585
Std. Dev.	0.3579	0.3084	0.2069	0.3798	0.3861	0.3101	0.3344	0.3183	0.3390	0.3671
Skewness	0.4786	−0.3369	−0.3273	−0.0993	−0.4404	−0.6743	0.6078	−0.4794	0.0624	0.2157
Kurtosis	2.7173	2.1714	3.0616	2.2638	2.5977	3.0896	3.4922	2.6824	2.0363	2.1281
Jarque–Bera	11.497	13.166	49.919	56.710	10.822	21.087	19.854	11.776	10.897	10.920
Observations	277	277	277	277	277	277	277	277	277	277

Note: This table gives brief statistics of DCC among Dow Jones and the selected European stock market indices. The data period is from August 1, 2019 until August 31, 2020.

Table 11.12. Descriptive statistics for DCC between S&P500 and the selected European stock market indices.

	AEX	ASE	CAC40	DAX	FTSE	FTSE100	IBEX35	PSI	RTS	SMI
Mean	−0.0723	0.4332	0.0956	0.2894	0.2952	0.0188	−0.0667	0.3325	−0.0269	0.0612
Std. Dev.	0.3657	0.3477	0.2361	0.3834	0.3509	0.2991	0.3605	0.3660	0.3409	0.4154
Skewness	0.5229	−0.5124	−0.0300	−0.4958	−0.5596	−0.3983	0.6979	−0.3204	0.3052	0.0252
Kurtosis	2.9642	2.4721	2.3283	2.7647	2.7934	3.1071	3.0104	2.2584	2.7129	2.0118
Jarque–Bera	12.641	15.338	52.489	11.988	14.951	74.592	22.489	11.087	52.528	11.298
Observations	277	277	277	277	277	277	277	277	277	277

Note: This table gives brief statistics of DCC among S&P500 and the selected European stock market indices. The data period is from August 1, 2019 until August 31, 2020.

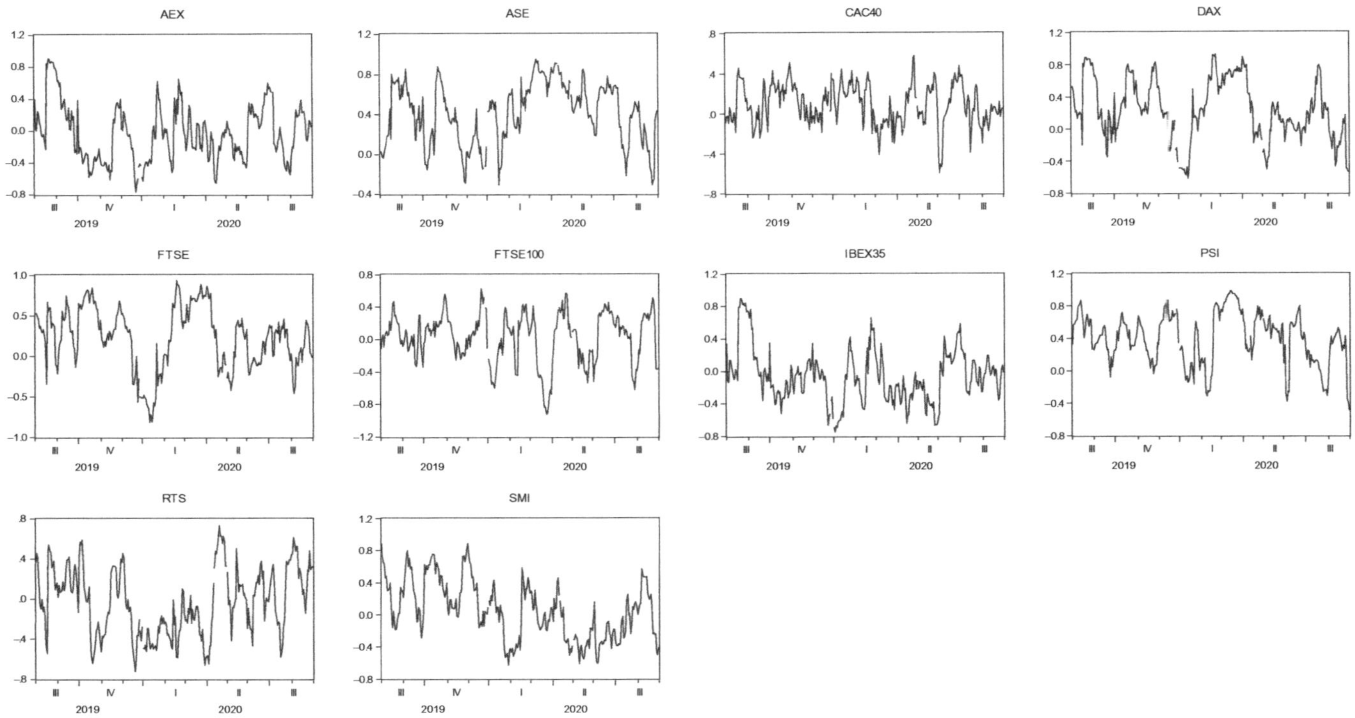

Figure 11.6. The evolution of the DCC between Dow Jones and the selected European stock market indices during the period August 1, 2019 to August 31, 2020.

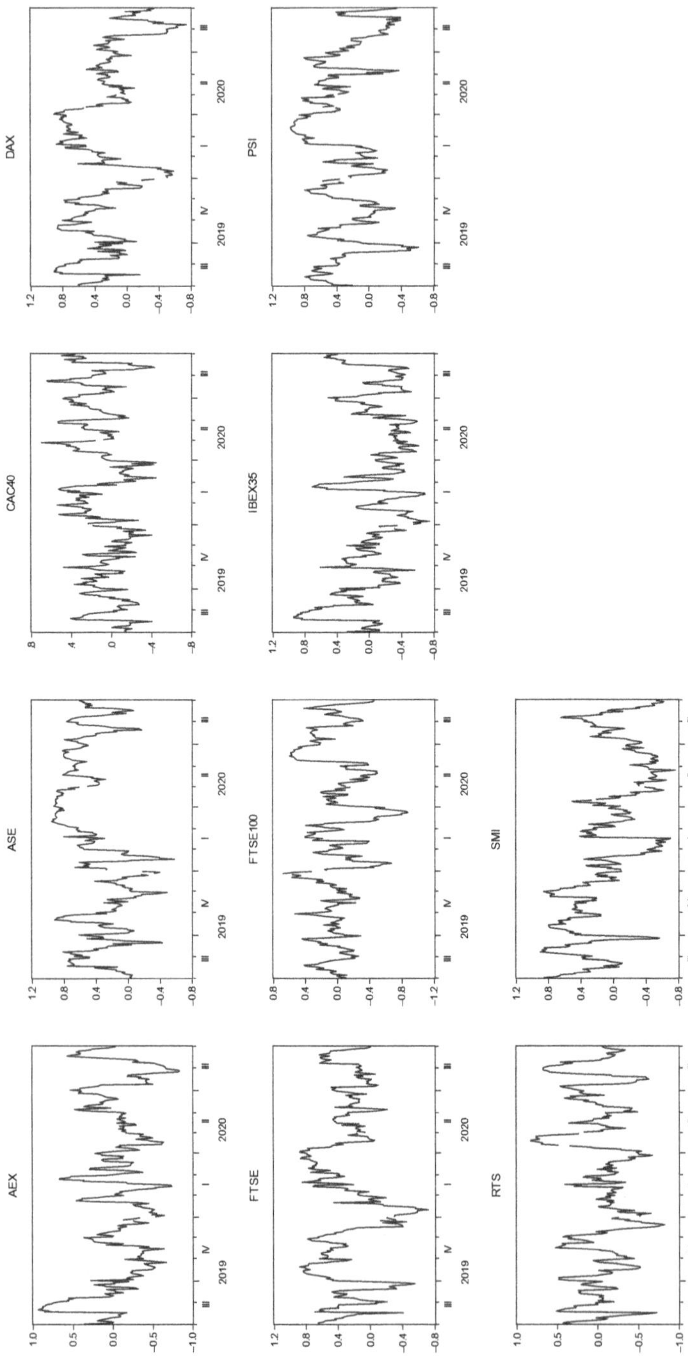

Figure 11.7. The evolution of the DCC between S&P500 and the selected European stock market indices during the period August 1, 2019 to August 31, 2020.

Table 11.13. The estimation results of DCC-GARCH (1,1) between Dow Jones and the selected European stock market indices.

Parameters	ω_i	α_i	β_i	COVID-19 SCC	COVID-19 SDC
DCC between	0.0566	0.0122	0.9607	−0.1728	
DJ and AEX	(4.61)**	(15.00)*	(42.18)*	(−21.75)*	
	0.0955	0.0115	0.9722		−0.0819
	(4.49)**	(14.11)*	(61.83)*		(−13.21)*
DCC between	0.0756	0.0824	0.9105	−0.1500	
DJ and ASE	(4.73)**	(16.21)*	(38.71)*	(−23.92)*	
	0.0438	0.1275	0.8699		−0.0955
	(3.65)**	(14.31)*	(41.29)*		(−13.08)*
DCC between	0.0735	0.0796	0.9165	−0.1480	
DJ and	(4.84)**	(12.43)*	(38.34)*	(−20.87)*	
CAC40	0.0538	0.0658	0.9212		−0.0801
	(4.10)**	(11.48)*	(42.81)*		(−12.19)*
DCC between	0.0256	0.0100	0.9607	−0.1072	
DJ and DAX	(4.13)**	(14.57)*	(33.97)*	(−19.38)*	
	0.0546	0.0918	0.8807		−0.0673
	(4.72)**	(14.93)*	(31.90)*		(−10.38)*
DCC between	0.0544	0.1052	0.8819	−0.1175	
DJ and FTSE	(4.85)**	(11.43)*	(37.88)*	(−21.46)*	
	0.0700	0.1073	0.8737		−0.0735
	(4.60)**	(11.56)*	(36.91)*		(−13.92)*
DCC between	0.0438	0.1032	0.8816	−0.1491	
DJ and	(4.86)**	(11.79)*	(40.83)*	(−20.82)*	
FTSE100	0.0724	0.1125	0.8634		−0.0795
	(4.49)**	(13.32)*	(41.11)*		(−14.00)*
DCC between	0.0028	0.1425	0.8493	−0.1376	
DJ and	(4.87)**	(12.49)*	(51.03)*	(−20.81)*	
IBEX35	0.0619	0.1182	0.8622		−0.0819
	(4.93)**	(11.83)*	(53.22)*		(−15.72)*
DCC between	0.0720	0.0827	0.8931	−0.1272	
DJ and PSI	(4.81)**	(9.47)*	(48.29)*	(−22.96)*	
	0.0466	0.0971	0.8827		−0.0827
	(4.52)**	(11.33)*	(46.67)*		(−12.58)*

(*Continued*)

Table 11.13. (*Continued*)

Parameters	ω_i	α_i	β_i	COVID-19 SCC	COVID-19 SDC
DCC between	0.0751	0.1008	0.8719	−0.1085	
DJ and RTS	(4.01)**	(14.00)*	(41.01)*	(−23.11)*	
	0.0708	0.1184	0.8670		−0.0958
	(4.00)**	(13.33)*	(38.00)*		(−12.11)*
DCC between	0.0385	0.0734	0.9173	−0.1527	
DJ and SMI	(4.77)**	(11.09)*	(33.40)*	(−25.01)*	
	0.0852	0.0894	0.8839		−0.0855
	(4.78)**	(10.08)*	(30.51)*		(−10.70)*

Note: This table summarizes the estimated coefficients from DCC-GARCH (1.1) model. Then, to empirically evaluate this specification, we utilize daily volatility timeseries of returns of two major stock market indices in the US (S&P500 and Dow Jones) and ten European Stock market indices (RTS from Russia, FTSE100 from UK, DAX from Germany, IBEX35 from Spain, CAC40 from France, AEX from Netherlands, SMI from Switzerland, PSI from Portugal, ASE from Greece, and FTSE from Italy) through the period of study from August 1, 2019 to August 31, 2020. Statistical significance at the 1% and 5% level is designated by * and **, respectively.

DAX from Germany, IBEX35 from Spain, CAC40 from France, AEX from Netherlands, SMI from Switzerland, PSI from Portugal, ASE from Greece, and FTSE from Italy) in the presence of COVID-19 confirmed case and death cases surprises in the US. Various notable ends emerge from this empirical investigation. First, we demonstrate that COVID-19 confirmed cases surprises and COVID-19 death cases surprises in the US affect the dynamic conditional correlation between the two major stock market indices in the US and ten European stock market indices. The negative sign of the coefficients of the COVID-19 confirmed cases and death case surprises suggests that the variations in the confirmed and death cases of COVID-19 in the US decrease the mean concentration of volatility of the American and European financial stock markets. Given the impact of COVID-19 confirmed and death case surprises in the US on the dynamic conditional correlation among the two major stock market indices in US and ten European stock market indices in this chapter, the empirical findings presented in Tables 11.12 and 11.13 show that the

Table 11.14. The estimation results of DCC-GARCH (1,1) between S&P500 and the selected European stock market indices.

Parameters	ωi	α_i	β_i	COVID-19 SCC	COVID-19 SDC
DCC between	0.0766	0.0899	0.9073	−0.0046	
S&P500 and	(5.31)**	(13.92)*	(36.01)*	(−10.11)*	
AEX	0.0673	0.1176	0.8645		−0.0673
	(5.22)**	(14.08)*	(38.91)*		(−12.11)*
DCC between	0.0837	0.1059	0.8732	−0.1005	
S&P500 and	(5.46)**	(14.59)*	(56.91)*	(−19.01)*	
ASE	0.0735	0.0622	0.9173		−0.5326
	(5.37)**	(13.60)*	(48.32)*		(−15.76)*
DCC between	0.0571	0.0825	0.8955	−0.0973	
S&P500 and	(5.08)**	(14.44)*	(41.01)*	(−17.17)*	
CAC40	0.0648	0.1173	0.8655		−0.8519
	(5.45)**	(15.10)*	(45.00)*		(−14.13)*
DCC between	0.0700	0.1089	0.8719	−0.0829	
S&P500 and	(5.29)**	(14.67)*	(43.10)*	(−18.00)*	
DAX	0.0978	0.0956	0.9000		−0.0693
	(5.25)**	(14.08)*	(53.78)*		(−13.97)*
DCC between	0.0843	0.1020	0.8716	−0.1127	
S&P500 and	(5.04)**	(13.91)*	(50.98)*	(−19.01)*	
FTSE	0.0944	0.0953	0.8750		−0.0988
	(5.79)**	(13.61)*	(48.75)*		(−12.52)*
DCC between	0.0610	0.1152	0.8746	−0.1278	
S&P500 and	(4.21)**	(14.57)*	(45.35)*	(−17.63)*	
	0.0751	0.0988	0.9011		−0.1785
FTSE100	(4.08)**	(14.76)*	(46.57)*		(−12.58)*
DCC between	0.0722	0.0672	0.9273	−0.1146	
S&P500 and	(4.77)**	(15.09)*	(45.51)*	(−17.62)*	
IBEX35	0.0852	0.0769	0.9017		−0.1302
	(5.42)**	(13.48)*	(50.59)*		(−13.46)*
DCC between	0.0917	0.0865	0.0942	−0.1045	
S&P500 and	(4.80)**	(14.95)*	(48.82)	(−16.84)*	
PSI	0.0831	0.1095	0.8737		−0.1385
	(5.73)**	(13.45)*	(47.64)*		(−13.28)*

(Continued)

Table 11.14. (*Continued*)

Parameters	ωi	α_i	β_i	COVID-19 SCC	COVID-19 SDC
DCC between S&P500 and RTS	0.0845	0.0731	0.9016	−0.9299	
	(5.38)**	(14.16)*	(44.37)*	(−19.91)*	
	0.0591	0.0665	0.9205		−0.1407
	(5.94)**	(15.76)*	(50.49)*		(−12.19)*
DCC between S&P500 and SMI	0.0837	0.0855	0.8955	−0.0945	
	(5.37)**	(16.12)*	(51.13)*	(−17.13)*	
	0.0944	0.0855	0.9007		−0.1755
	(4.01)**	(14.25)*	(52.11)*		(−15.73)*

Note: This table summarizes the estimated coefficients from DCC-GARCH (1.1) model. Then, to empirically evaluate this specification, we utilize daily volatility timeseries of returns of two major stock market indices in the US (S&P500 and Dow Jones) and ten European Stock market indices (RTS from Russia, FTSE100 from UK, DAX from Germany, IBEX35 from Spain, CAC40 from France, AEX from Netherlands, SMI from Switzerland, PSI from Portugal, ASE from Greece, and FTSE from Italy) through the period of study from August 1, 2019 to August 31, 2020. Statistical significance at the 1% level is designated by *. Values ** in parentheses show the t-Student.

COVID-19 SDC in the US is more important than the COVID-19 SCC.

In this context, we assume that the significant difference between COVID-19 SCC and COVID-19 SDC in the US and their influence on the DCC among the two major stock market indices in the US and ten European stock market indices. The empirical findings of our chapter demonstrate that the recent COVID-19 pandemic present a significative and negative but short-term effect on international financial stock markets indices and that the influence of the COVID-19 pandemic on financial stock market indices has bidirectional spillover impacts amongst American and European financial stock markets. Our results are similar to those found in various recent investigations such as Dutta *et al.* (2020), Mensi *et al.* (2020), He *et al.* (2020), Sansa (2020), Ashraf (2020), and Zhang *et al.* (2020).

Furthermore, we demonstrate a clarification which proves that the summation of the estimated volatility coefficients ($\alpha+\beta$) is very adjacent to the unity (1), in the estimations of all DCC among the two major stock market indices in the US and ten European stock market indices observed, demonstrating the higher persistence of estimated volatility between American and European financial stock markets in the presence of the COVID-19 SCC and the COVID-19 SDC in the US. Then, we validate an imperative potential explanation, which demonstrates that such persistence gets along with the phenomena of financialization of international financial stock market indices and the recent health crisis, such as the two major stock market indices in the US and ten European stock market indices and COVID-19 (Chebbi and Derbali, 2015; Chebbi and Derbali, 2016a,b; Creti *et al.*, 2013; Derbali and Jouini, 2019; Derbali and Bouzgarrou, 2020; Derbali *et al.*, 2020a,b). Finally, our empirical findings in this chapter underline the importance of utilizing the method of DCC-GARCH (1,1) in justifying the time-varying dynamic relationship between American and European financial stock markets in the health crisis of 2020.

Furthermore, and in observing the daily time series, we validate that the changes in the estimated shock components in COVID-19 SCC and SDC in the US have accomplished an indispensable situation in the enhancements of volatility of most significant investment portfolio such as financial stock market indices. This result is not surprising. One explanation is that considering the significant and important impact of the American economy on the world economy, the announcement linked to the changes in COVID-19 confirmed and death case shocks in the US may significantly and pointedly influence foreign economic fundamentals and consequently the estimated volatility of American and European financial stock markets. In addition, the significant effect of the COVID-19 confirmed and death case shocks in the US on the European financial stock markets can be corroborated by the propagation of the COVID-19 pandemic in the US, which is the most affected country worldwide at the time of writing.

11.5. Conclusion

The nexus amongst American and European financial stock markets have generated significant literature through the preceding two decades. Moreover, several significant developments have been provided in application to increase the estimated findings. Amongst these improvements, we observe the presence of the monetary policy surprises in the estimated volatility paradigms, political insecurities surprises, and health crisis surprises (especially after the COVID-19 pandemic). These classes of surprises in volatility representations strength are affected by country-specific political, economic, and financial measures and local and international political, economic, and financial effects (e.g. the financial and economic crisis of 2007, European sovereign-debt crisis of 2010, Arab Spring in 2011, Federal Open Market Committee monetary policy, European Central Bank monetary policy, and COVID-19 pandemic).

In this chapter, we examine the time-varying links between the two major stock market indices in the US (S&P500 and Dow Jones) and ten European stock market indices (RTS from Russia, FTSE100 from UK, DAX from Germany, IBEX35 from Spain, CAC40 from France, AEX from Netherlands, SMI from Switzerland, PSI from Portugal, ASE from Greece, and FTSE from Italy) over the period of study from August 1, 2019 until August 31, 2020. To do so, we utilize the DCC-GARCH (1.1) approach with integrating of COVID-19 confirmed and death case surprises in the US. The empirical findings of our chapter indicate a considerable dynamic conditional correlation between American and European financial stock markets if COVID-19 confirmed and death case surprises are incorporated in variance specifications.

Therefore, these conclusions confirm the financialization phenomena of American and European financial stock markets. Additionally, our results linked to the intensity of the tenacity of volatility specifications are sensitive to the presence of COVID-19 confirmed and death case shocks into the DCC-GARCH (1,1) estimations. Furthermore, the estimated dynamic conditional correlations between American and European financial stock markets commence to respond considerably further in the case of COVID-19 confirmed cases announcements than the COVID-19 death cases news in the US. Additionally, we prove that the performance of every international financial stock market containing selected indices suggests that European financial stock market indices cannot be judged as a homogeneous and a standardized investing portfolio.

Finally, the influence of COVID-19 confirmed and death cases shocks on international financial stock market indices has bidirectional spillover effects amongst American and European financial stock markets. The spread of the virus in the US negatively influence the dynamic conditional correlation between American and European financial stock market indices.

11.6. Policy Implications

Our results aid in the investigation of financial and economic effects of the pandemic by providing useful evidence that COVID-19 pandemic shocks have bidirectional spillover influences on the international financial stock markets. The present chapter is an indispensable focus for investors, policymakers, portfolio risk managers, and administrators. From a policy-making viewpoint, finding truthful and useful explanations of the volatility spillovers throughout the international financial stock markets is an important phase in creating beneficial monetary policy policies and healthy strategies. From the viewpoint of portfolio risk administrators and supervisors, our empirical findings are consistent with the suggestion of cross-market hedging. Our empirical results have practical implications. They are useful for policymakers who have to make assessments and choices on financial stability procedures. Moreover, the detection of unpredictable performance and bubbles is of immense significance considering the connections between international stock market indices. They are similarly important for various market contributors and members for the predictions of price changes, portfolio diversification, cross-hedging and cross-speculation, etc.

Acknowledgments

The authors are grateful to the guest editors of this book and the anonymous referees for their extremely helpful recommendations to enhance the quality of the chapter.

Declaration of Conflicting Interests

The author(s) declared no potential conflicts of interest with respect to the research, authorship and/or publication of this chapter.

Funding

The author(s) received no financial support for the research, authorship and/or publication of this chapter.

References

Ahmad, S., Abbasi, H.W., Shahid, S., Gul, S. and Abbasi, S.W. (2020). Molecular docking, simulation and MM-PBSA studies of Nigella sativa compounds: a computational quest to identify potential natural antiviral for COVID-19 treatment. *Journal of Biomolecular Structure and Dynamics*, **21**, 1–9. 1080/07391102.2020.1775129.

Ali, M., Alam, N. and Rizvi, S.A.R. (2020). Coronavirus (COVID-19). An epidemic or pandemic for financial markets. *Journal of Behavioral and Experimental Finance*, **27**(3), 1–6. https://doi.org/10.1016/j.jbef.2020.100341.

Arshad, A.S., Baloch, M., Ahmed, N., Arshad, A.A. and Iqbal, A. (2020). The outbreak of coronavirus disease 2019 (COVID-19) — An emerging global health threat. *Journal of Infection and Public Health*, **13**(4), 644–646. https://doi.org/10.1016/j.jiph.2020.02.033.

Ashraf, B.N. (2020). 'Stock markets' reaction to COVID–19: Cases or fatalities? *Research in International Business and Finance*, **54**(12), 1–7. https://doi.org/10.1016/j.ribaf.2020.101249.

Chebbi, T. and Derbali, A. (2015). The dynamic correlation between energy commodities and Islamic stock market: Analysis and forecasting. *International Journal of Trade and Global Markets*, **8**(2), 112–126. http://dx.doi.org/10.1504/IJTGM.2015.069425.

Chebbi, T. and Derbali, A. (2016a). A dynamic conditional correlation between commodities and the Islamic stock market. *Journal of Energy Markets*, **9**(1), 65–90. https://doi.org/10.21314.JEM.2016.137.

Chebbi, T. and Derbali, A. (2016b). On the role of structural breaks in identifying the dynamic conditional linkages between stock and commodity markets. *Journal of Energy Markets*, **9**(4), 71–81. https://doi.org/10.21314/JEM.2016.152.

Creti, A., Joëts, M. and Mignon, V. (2013). On the links between stock and commodity markets' volatility. *Energy Economics*, **37**, 16–28. https://doi.org/10.1016/j.eneco.2013.01.005.

Derbali, A. and Jouini, F. (2019). Analyzing the dynamic equicorrelation between Shanghai Composite (SSEC) and Austral African stock market indices. *Chinese Economy*, **52**(1), 83–106. https://doi.org/10.1080/10971475.2018.1523862.

Derbali, A. and Bouzgarrou, H. (2020). The dynamic dependence between the major US indices and the meat commodities indices. *PSU Research Review*, **4**(2), 149–168. https://doi.org/10.1108/PRR-09-2018-0027.

Derbali, A., Wu, S. and Jamel, L. (2020a). OPEC news and predictability of energy futures returns and volatility: Evidence from a conditional quantile regression. *Journal of Economics, Finance and Administrative Science* **25**(50), 239–259. https://doi.org/10.1108/JEFAS-05-2019-0063.

Derbali, A., Jamel, L., Ben Ltaifa, M., Elnagar, A.K. and Lamouchi, A. (2020b). Fed and ECB: Which is informative in determining the DCC between bitcoin and energy commodities? *Journal of Capital Markets Studies* **4**(1), 77–102. https://doi.org/10.1108/JCMS-07-2020-0022.

Dutta, A., Das, D., Jana, R.K. and Vo, X.V. (2020). COVID-19 and oil market crash: Revisiting the safe haven property of gold and Bitcoin. *Resources Policy*, **69**(1), 1–6. https://doi.org/10.1016/j.resourpol.2020.101816.

Engle, R. (2002). Dynamic conditional correlation: A simple class of multivariate generalized autoregressive conditional heteroskedasticity models. *Journal of Business and Economic Statistics*, **20**(3), 339–350. https://doi.org/10.1198/073500102288618487.

Gharib, C., Wali, S.M. and Ben Jabeur, S. (2020). The bubble contagion effect of COVID-19 outbreak: Evidence from crude oil and gold markets. *Finance Research Letters*, **38**(1), 101703. https://doi.org/10.1016/j.frl.2020.101703.

Harapan, H., Itoh, N., Yufika, A., Winardi, W., Keam, S., Te, H., Megawati, D., Hayati, Z., Wagner, A.L. and Mudatsir, M. (2020). Coronavirus disease 2019 (COVID-19): A literature review. *Journal of Infection and Public Health*, **13**, 667–673. https://doi.org/10.1016/j.jiph.2020.03.019.

He, Q., Liu, J., Wang, S. and Yu, J. (2020). The impact of COVID-19 on stock markets. *Journal of Economic and Political Studies*, **8**(3), 275–288. https://doi.org/10.1080/20954816.2020.1757570.

Kuttner, K.N. (2001). Monetary policy surprises and interest rates: Evidence from the fed funds futures market. *Journal of Monetary Economics*, **47**(3), 523–544. https://doi.org/10.1016/S0304-3932(01)00055-1.

Liu, H.Y., Manzoor, A., Wang, C.Y., Zhang, L. and Manzour, Z. (2020). The COVID-19 outbreak and affected countries stock markets response. *International Journal Environmental Research and Public Health*, **17**(8), 1–19. https://doi.org/10.3390/ijerph17082800.

Mensi, W., Sensoy, A., Vo, X.V. and Kang, S.H. (2020). Impact of COVID-19 outbreak on asymmetric multifractality of gold and oil prices. *Resources Policy*, **69**(1), 1–11. https://doi.org/10.1016/j.resourpol.2020.101829.

Nicola, M., Alsafi, Z., Sohrabi, C., Kerwan, A., Al-Jabir, A., Losifidis, C., Agha, M. and Agha, R. (2020). The socio-economic implications of the coronavirus pandemic (COVID-19): A review. *International Journal of Surgery,* **78**(6), 185–193. https://dx.doi.org/10.1016%2Fj.ijsu.2020.04.018.

Sansa, N.A. (2020). The impact of the COVID-19 on the financial markets: Evidence from China and USA. *Electronic Research Journal of Social Sciences and Humanities*, **2**(2), 29–39. https://ssrn.com/abstract=3562530.

Sharif, A., Aloui, C. and Yarovaya, L. (2020). COVID-19 pandemic, oil prices, stock market, geopolitical risk and policy uncertainty nexus in the US economy: Fresh evidence from the wavelet-based approach. *International Review of Financial Analysis*, **70**, 1–9. https://www.sciencedirect.com/science/journal/10575219.

Wagner, A.F. (2020). What the stock market tells us about the post-COVID-19 world. *Nature Human Behaviour*, **4**, 440. https://doi.org/10.1038/s41562-020-0869-y.

Zhang, D., Hu, M. and Ji, Q. (2020). Financial markets under the global pandemic of COVID-19. *Finance Research Letters*, **36**, 15–28. https://doi.org/10.1016/j.frl.2020.101528.

PART III

COVID-19: Effects on Financial Institutions, Money, and Instruments

https://doi.org/10.1142/9781800610781_0012

Chapter 12

Insuring Against Pandemics: A Private Sector Instrument for the Private Sector

Marco Rossi

MR Advisory,

Former Official at International Monetary Fund

mrossi@mradvisory.net

Abstract

The ongoing COVID-19 pandemic shows how quickly business resources can dry up against the backdrop of non-transient expenses. This has forced many businesses to proceed with large cuts in their workforce while facing the possibility of never getting back on their feet. Governments all over the world are trying to avoid such an outcome by providing guarantees on bank loans and upfront cash support, including grants. This chapter looks at the possibility of integrating such public response by developing an instrument — by the private sector and for the private sector — to help businesses of any size, including those with increasingly multinational operations, navigate the most perilous part of a pandemic. The instrument would release a contracted cash amount that could be calculated to provide a chosen grant element against an expected liquidity need, given a company's specific circumstances and preferences.

12.1. Introduction

The ongoing pandemic associated with the spread of COVID-19 across the globe is taking a heavy social toll in terms of human losses, anxiety, and disruption of daily routines. Governments are reacting, to various extents and speed, by implementing policies that are intended to limit the contagion and deal with the surge in the number of people needing medical assistance. Recognizing the financial impact of these measures on the economy, governments worldwide are also discussing ways to support the economy at the national and local level.

By grinding entire economies to a virtual halt, the impact of this pandemic goes far beyond that associated with the global financial crises we have dealt with over the years. Similar to the financial crises, the pandemic is global in its reach, but hits countries irrespective of their economic fundamentals. Moreover, by disrupting countries' productive systems at their core, it prevents the very generation of resources that are required to ensure a country's financial sustainability at the time when additional financial resources are needed. The analysis of the data after this pandemic will likely show us that, whereas its risk is symmetric, its longer-term impact may not be. Some countries have been hit by the pandemic before others or harder than others, some have faced it being more prepared than others, some have reacted to it in a more timely and deliberate fashion, while yet others had more political and financial space to intervene to offset its impact.

The number of casualties is likely to depend on the timeliness and effectiveness of governmental policies (and public adherence to them) to limit contagion, population structure (age and gender), and the ability of national health systems to rely on effective disease prevention protocols and to react efficiently and flexibly to new threats. Taking stock from this dramatic experience will require distilling best practices for national health systems — a task that would probably best be accomplished by the World Health Organization — in the way countries prepare for the future, including through possible reorientation or recalibration of policies and the strengthening of immediate and concerted global responses.

From an economic and financial standpoint, the issues are easier to grasp though their solution may prove equally challenging. Recent global financial crises have underscored the importance of having an adequate safety net to assist those countries, sometimes innocent bystanders, whose financial flows suddenly dry up. As mentioned, the financial risks associated with a pandemic are even greater because of the economic disruption it entails. Greater too are the financial resources that are required to cope because of the symmetric nature of the shock: all those affected will need to reach far into the public (and financial markets) purse at the same time, including, in some cases, when heavily constrained by their debt sustainability dynamics. In the face of a pandemic, the economic challenge of preventing a temporary shock from turning permanent by destroying a country's productive capacity becomes daunting.

Accordingly, most educated observers have called for the state to intervene with measures as draconian as those that have been put in place to mitigate the spread of the virus. Supporting the income of those who have lost their jobs, while necessary, is not enough. Governments should also absorb the private sector's increasing liabilities and greater financial sector's support directly onto their balance sheet, by issuing public debt and public sector guarantees. While the approach is correct, or rather inevitable *ex post*, it may not be feasible beyond a certain level for most countries as access to creditors becomes harder. To be sure, governments may agree to pool resources together to allay the borrowing costs for those countries whose individual access to financial markets is costlier — though, as shown these days in Europe, such agreement is neither certain nor immediate. Be that as it may, government intervention, even when political consensus can be expeditiously mustered, entails approval and administrative delays potentially undermining its efficacy in limiting the spreading of both household and corporate defaults.

International institutions, such the World Bank and the International Monetary Fund, and other regional cooperative agreements can already count on a substantial pool of resources to deal with cross-border financial crises and an array of instruments to deal with them, including some specifically tailored to helping the world's poorest countries cope with large-scale outbreaks and natural catastrophes. In line with their mandates, they negotiate their intervention with and rely on financing provided by the public sector. Political, rather than economic, considerations may, at times, deliver inferior solutions in terms of both program design and timeliness. Moreover, the inevitable need to safeguard their limited resources, while being able to support their entire membership, can also constrain the effectiveness of their actions.

Preparing for the next pandemic requires not only that the financial safety net be adequate, but also that the correct instrument be in place to make sure that access to the safety net is certain, effective, flexible, and timely. In fact, it is recommended to have in place as many instruments as possible to spread risks efficiently. The private sector should, therefore, be directly involved in building a buffer that could be accessed automatically without delays when needed through an instrument specifically designed to help the private sector help itself.

The goal here is to create a new instrument that (i) is predictable in terms of funds availability, (ii) would provide enough liquidity to minimize the risk of spreading liquidity shortages across the private sector, and (iii) would minimize adverse selection. Pricing is one key aspect in the design of any financing instrument consistently with the intended goals; this one would be no exception.

There are a number of variables to consider in assessing the cost/value of insurance, primarily among which the likelihood of a shock and the insuree's profile; the latter could boost or dampen the impact of any particular shock. For instance, the occurrence of a fire may be a *force majeure* type of event, but its destructiveness depends, to some extent, on how "diligent" the insuree has been in terms of taking care of the building and keeping first-aid props like fire extinguishers handy and in proper working order (moral hazard). In the case of a pandemic, the latter appears less relevant: while there are certainly practices that companies could explore to limit disruptions in their activities, including by migrating to artificial intelligence (AI) platforms, the scope to reduce the impact of a pandemic may remain limited until the bulk of economic activity still requires some sort of personal interaction across a mostly human workforce. One aspect, however, remains unchanged in the context of a pandemic: adverse selection, i.e. the likelihood that only those with high non-observable risks take up insurance.

Fixed fees or fees that are linearly increasing in the amount of liquidity (or its term) are usually intended to recoup administrative and opportunity costs, while building liquidity buffers in case of an adverse event. However, they are not completely satisfactory as they do not seem to rely on an appropriate *ex ante* market-based incentives structure, especially in situations of incomplete information. This calls for an instrument whose premium is calculated in a framework that explicitly incorporates the risk of a shock, the volatility of the insuree's cash flow, and the intrinsic value of the liquidity guarantee that the instrument provides. Since a balanced pool of good and bad risks helps maintain insurance actuarially sustainable and insurers in the market, such a framework should meet the favor of those mutually involved (insurers and insurees) and regulators alike. Premia could also be kept protected into an industry-wide fund to ensure that resources are available upon request, similar to the case of deposit insurance for the banking sector.

This chapter proposes a market-based liquidity instrument to assist corporates overcome the economic disruption associated with a pandemic. The proposed pricing framework is based on the isomorphic correspondence between the liquidity provided by the instrument and common stock put options; it modifies and expands Rossi (2008) to reflect the different setup as well as an explicit grant element. The simulations presented in this chapter are only illustrative, but show that the value of the liquidity guarantee provided by purchasing this type of instrument would depend on the risk of a pandemic pervasively affecting the economy, the volatility of the insuree's cash flow, and the amount of liquidity that would be potentially needed (contracted) to keep the insuree afloat during the pandemic.

The chapter is organized as follows. Section 12.2 describes the characteristics of the instrument and the context which its use is intended for. Section 12.3 presents the conceptual and operational pricing framework, while Section 12.4 reports some indicative simulations of the cost for corporates. Section 12.5 concludes.

12.2. The Instrument

The private sector comprises households and corporates, providing both goods and services. During a pandemic, the risk of default surges as it becomes increasingly unclear whether providers are able to fill their orders, whether clients are able to pay for those orders, and whether banks are prepared to extend credit to both or decide to call in outstanding credits: otherwise, solvent entities may risk default because of sudden illiquidity.

Under these circumstances, companies' revenues dry fast while fixed costs (employees, rents, utilities, etc.) remain. The ability of accessing liquidity but defraying the cost of such access, therefore, becomes key. To support economic activity, national and local governments are likely to act — as evidenced during the ongoing COVID-19 pandemic — and provide state guarantees on banks' loans and upfront financing to bridge companies's financing gap during the crisis. The grant element of such liquidity provision, however, is what matters the most to businesses since the extra financing is not required to support new productive initiatives but rather to compensate for an unexpected and exogenous drop in resources, and stay afloat. The proposed instrument is not intended to substitute any government-driven initiative but rather to help on the margin by adding yet another channel to support businesses of any size, including those with increasingly multinational operations, against the risks associated with a pandemic.

We usually associate risk with insurance. But what type of insurance? Against what type of risks? How do we trigger the insurance? How do we measure the risk? What is the payoff? How do we determine the premium? Who is underwriting the insurance? Who is buying it?

Type of insurance: The insurance provides coverage against a net loss of cash flow. It could also be thought as providing coverage of required service obligations under a contracted bank liquidity credit line. The insurance is provided by sector and/or an individual company basis. Once triggered, the insurance provides access to a specified amount of funds immediately upon request.

Type of risk: The risk is that which is associated with the drop in economic activity associated with a national epidemic or pandemic and the enactment of restrictive public health policies.

Triggering the insurance: To trigger the insurance, the following circumstances should materialize: (i) a national epidemic or pandemic is declared by the relevant national or international public authority, (ii) local (or international) authorities introduce restrictive social practices that affect the economy, and (iii) either the beneficiary is negatively affected by the implementation of these measures or national and local authorities approve measures to support the economy.

Measuring the risk: Not every disease outbreak turns into a pandemic or even an epidemic. In many cases, outbreaks are and remain local, limited in terms of people affected, and kept under control with normal health protocols. However, the risk that an outbreak morph into an epidemic/pandemic exists. Of interest here is to measure the probability of the insurance being triggered. Data on (i) previous outbreaks that have turned into national epidemic or pandemic, (ii) policy reactions to such outbreaks, and (iii) economic impact by industry should help derive a risk measure by country, by sector, as well as by disease.

Amount payable: The insured amount can be calculated to reach a desired share — full or partial coverage — of the net cash flow loss or the required service obligations under a bank liquidity credit line, which can be tailored specifically to each business (see discussion of the grant element in Section 12.3).

Premium: As for any insurance contract, the expected benefit for the insuree should be, at least, equal to the expected cost for the insurer. The premium on this instrument can be assessed as the value of a contingent claim.

Underwriting the insurance: The most obvious underwriter of this instrument is the insurance industry. Alternatively, or complementarily, banks could design specific credit lines that would offer subsidized terms under a pandemic, charging accordingly for such a commitment. This specific commitment fee could be set aside to fund the subsidies in case of a pandemic; in principle, very much like deposit insurance is funded. This fee could also take into account other financing charges that are customarily assessed on loans.

Purchasing the insurance: The insurance is valuable to all those affected by a pandemic. In practice, government programs are already in place to support households who lose their jobs through automatic stabilizers. Small businesses, whose financing requirements may be large from an individual business standpoint but are relatively manageable in aggregate for the public sector, could be effectively supported by local authorities too. Irrespective of size, firms find it of particular usefulness the ability to continue with their business as quickly and seemingly as possible. Whether government programs are sizable, flexible, and timely enough across countries is an open question at this point, with an assessment of the recent experience still pending.

12.3. The Operational Framework

A cash flow statement shows where a business gets its cash from and where it spends it over a specific period and is important for analyzing the liquidity and long-term solvency of a company. Table 12.1 illustrates a fictional simplified cash flow statement reporting a business' operating, investing, and financing activities under a baseline scenario and the alternative adverse scenario. The current pandemic shows that many businesses suffer through a drop in cash receipts. While each business can react differently to it — some by cutting employment and/or not paying suppliers, hence spreading its difficulties — the point is that most businesses may become illiquid and, depending on their financial structure, potentially insolvent. These businesses could manage through the crisis by accessing enough financial resources to offset the drop in net revenues, but without incurring in a higher debt burden.

At the time of requesting the insurance, the obligations over the following year — mainly labor and fixed costs — are projected in the budget and can be treated as known. These obligations or cash outflows, C_{outs}, can be met with expected cash inflows, C_{ins}, accumulated reserves, R, and market financing, F, which together define the company's liquidity position, L.

Hence, a company's liquidity position (L) can be defined as:

$$L = C_{\text{ins}} + R + F, \tag{12.1}$$

whose level and fluctuations depend on the behavior of C_{ins}, R, and F over time.

Specifically, C_{ins} are affected by the company's ability to market their products as well as by a change in its clients' preferences, which are both stochastic. A geometric Brownian motion can describe C_{ins}:

$$dC_{\text{ins}} = \mu C_{\text{ins}} dt + \sigma C_{\text{ins}} dz, \tag{12.2}$$

where dz is a Wiener process, implying a log-normal distribution for C_{ins}.

Table 12.1. Generic cash flow statement.

	Baseline scenario	**Pandemic scenario**
1. Operating Account		
A. Cash receipts from customers	\$10,000	\$3,000
B. Cash paid to suppliers and employees	\$4,000	\$4,000
C. Cash generated from operations (A–B)	\$6,000	\$(1,000)
D. Interest paid	\$1,000	\$1,000
E. Income taxes paid	\$1,000	\$1,000
F. Net proceeds from operations (C–D–E)	\$4,000	\$(3,000)
2. Investment Account		
A. Proceeds from the sale of equipment	\$1,000	\$1,000
B. Dividend received	\$1,000	\$1,000
C. Net proceeds from investments (A+B)	\$2,000	\$2,000
3. Financing Account		
A. Dividends paid	\$1,000	\$1,000
B. Net proceeds from financing (–A)	\$(1,000)	\$(1,000)
4. Net increase in cash and cash equivalents (1.F+2.C+3.B)	\$5,000	\$(2,000)
5. Cash and cash equivalents, beginning of year	\$1,000	\$1,000
6. Cash and cash equivalents, end of year (4+5)	\$6,000	\$(1,000)

Whereas R is known, access to financial markets, F, depends on a company's perceived ability to continue meeting its obligations. In normal times, solvent companies could resort to bank credit lines, for instance, to support temporary inflows/outflows mismatches; in a pandemic, even if available (for instance, as a result of the government issuing guarantees on bank loans), financing could be prohibitively expensive in the face of a drop in revenues. At any point in time, therefore, a company may or may not be able to rely on market financing to help service its obligations. Accordingly, F can be described by a stationary binomial stochastic process:

$$F = (> 0, \text{with probability}\, q; 0, \text{with probability} 1 - q), \quad (12.3)$$

where $1 - q$ is the probability of a pandemic.

The proposed instrument would allow a solvent business to obtain additional liquidity without burdening its balance sheet in case of a pandemic at any time over the lifespan of the instrument. In fact, purchasing the instrument would strengthen a company's solvency profile; very much like having an anti-burglary system is viewed as reducing the associated risk. The value to the company of being able to subsidize the cost of liquidity in a pandemic by purchasing this instrument can be expressed as:

$$V = [\max(C_{\text{outs}} - C_{\text{ins}}, 0)] \times \alpha \times (1 - q). \quad (12.4)$$

The first term in Equation (12.4) is akin to the payoff of a put option, where the level of operating resources, C_{ins}, is the stock price and the amount of known obligations, C_{outs}, is the strike price. By underwriting this instrument, the insurer would be writing a (notional) put option on the company's operating resources. By exercising the option, the company would obtain a cash payment when its operating resources fall short of its known obligations.

The term α is a scaling factor, which determines the actual payable amount in relation to the gap between operating resources and known obligations and according to the specific grant element the company wants to achieve on the additional financing.

From an operational viewpoint, calculating the premium on this instrument entails: (i) pricing the put option, (ii) specifying a certain grant element, and (iii) assessing the probability of a pandemic.

12.3.1. *Pricing the put option*

Calculating the option premium depends on the type of option being written. Payment under the instrument could be allowed (i) once to coincide with its expiration, (ii) a discrete number of times, or (iii) at any point in time. The option would, respectively, be European, Bermudan, or American, and its valuation present increasing complexity. To be sure, for Bermudan and American options no exact pricing formula, like Black–Scholes', exists; numerical procedures and analytic approximations are instead used. These include the binomial option pricing model and finite difference methods. Software is available to calculate option prices on the basis of these numerical and analytic methodologies. In practice, the instrument could be designed to mimic the property of a European option, while delivering payouts according to Bermudan or American schedules, by shortening its maturity and automatically rolling it over.

The value of a European put option is given by the Black and Scholes formula:

$$V(\tau) = \alpha \times (1 - q) \times [C_{\text{outs}} e^{-r\tau} N(d2) - C_{\text{ins}} N(d1)], \quad (12.5)$$

where $d_1 = \frac{1}{\sigma\sqrt{\tau}}[\ln \frac{C_{\text{outs}}}{C_{\text{ins}}} - (r + \frac{\sigma^2}{2})\tau]$, $d_2 = d_1 + \sigma\sqrt{\tau}$, σ^2 is the variance rate per unit of time for the logarithmic change in the value of C_{ins}, r is the discount factor, τ is the maturity of the option contract, and $N(di)$ is the cumulative normal density function.

12.3.2. *Specifying a certain grant element*

The insured amount can be calculated as a share of the net cash flow position or to reach a desired grant element under the liquidity credit line contracted with a bank, which can be tailored to each business. Specifically, a business would receive a lump sum from the insurance, which would be equivalent to the benefit from paying less in net present value terms for the given amount of liquidity that it has contracted to bridge the unfavorable circumstances. The difference between what the business would pay under the contracted credit line (in normal times) and the amount that it would pay under the alternative assumptions about interest rate and grace period that are considered sustainable under the circumstances of a pandemic is the amount payable by the instrument, whose size is determined by the desired grant element. Accordingly, α is a number between 0 and 1 that is chosen to define, *ex ante*, the size of the subsidy that the insuree receives in case of a pandemic. For $\alpha = 0$, the company receives nothing; this is tantamount to say that it is not interested in the instrument. For $\alpha = 1$, the company receives the entire gap between known obligations and actual operating resources. The cost of the pandemic would be zero, but the instrument would be expensive. In the spectrum $0 < \alpha < 1$, each company would choose the value that best fits its specific preferences.

12.3.3. *Assessing the probability of a pandemic*

To a large extent, this is uncharted territory for an economics-focused audience. It does not, however, need stay that way. In fact, epidemiology and data science can be of tremendous help. Specifically, the scientific community can already count on a rich and diverse database concerning origin, spread, and lethal impact associated with several diseases. At the same time, AI, neural networks, and big data analysis offer new ways of designing algorithms to analyze and extract information from complex systems and data sets.

Leveraging this knowledge, and cross-referencing it with evidence about the economic impact of past and current outbreaks — by sector of activity, by country, by public preparedness, etc. — could deliver specific measures about each disease that could pave the way for statistical inference and actionable insights. This is a line of research worth exploring.

12.4. Some Simulations

With the conceptual framework clarified, we can now move to simulate potential premia that could be charged on this instrument. For that we need values for the expected outflows and inflows and the following parameters: the volatility of the company's cash flow (σ^2), the share of the total potential liquidity shortfall that the company wants to insure against (as proxied by the grant element α), and the probability of a pandemic ($1 - q$). From Table 12.1, we have cash inflows (stock price) and cash outflows (strike price), showing that 60% of the company's inflows are required to service its fixed obligations; these values are used in the simulation.

Table 12.2 reports some illustrative simulations of the premium for this instrument, assuming a lower and higher scenario for each of these parameters. For the fictional company with an illustrative cash flow statement as shown in the baseline in Table 12.1, the premium could vary between less than a dollar to less than a couple of hundred dollars. It varies proportionally to each insuree's preference about its chosen grant element, the probability of being affected by a pandemic, the volatility of its own operating resources, the instrument expiration, and general monetary conditions proxied by the risk-free interest rate.

Table 12.2. Illustrative premia.

σ^2		α		$1-q$		
0.25	**0.5**	**0.2**	**0.8**	**0.3**	**0.7**	**Premium**
*		*		*		\$0.85
*		*			*	\$1.99
*			*	*		\$3.41
*			*		*	\$7.96
	*	*		*		\$18.05
	*	*			*	\$42.12
	*		*	*		\$72.20
	*		*		*	\$168.47

Note: The maturity of the instrument, τ, is 365 days. The risk-free interest rate, r, is the one-year US Treasury bill rate as of end April 2020 (0.2%).

12.5. Conclusions

In response to the COVID-19 pandemic, national governments and international institutions have strengthened assistance to the economy with a view to preventing a temporary crisis from morphing into a full-blown recession that could compromise the productive structure of the affected economies over the longer term. While some of the assistance is designed to not burden businesses' balance sheets, the reality is that, in many cases, these resources are provided as additional debt and/or their disbursement is marred with red-tape and hence are not as timely as they should be to ease the hardship. As for any crisis, prevention and effective management are key; with regard to the latter, a comprehensive set of tools is required. Given its potentially disruptive economic and social impact, a pandemic underscores the importance of complementing public efforts with private-sector involvement against the backdrop of sizable financing requirements.

This chapter proposes a new financial instrument to help businesses steer the course during a pandemic by accessing liquidity on sustainable terms. What are sustainable terms is clearly subjective; the proposed instrument would, in fact, be flexible enough to accommodate specific risk aversion and risk profiles, all within a market-based framework. The instrument would be issued by the private sector — clearly governmental agencies and multilateral institutions could also have a relevant role to play — for the private sector and could potentially provide that additional "grease" to prevent the economic engine from grinding to a halt at the least desirable moment.

The premium for this instrument is calculated based on the isomorphic correspondence between the contracted liquidity and common stock put options. It sets appropriate economic incentives for the prospective insuree while explicitly assessing the costs for the insurer. Illustrative simulations show that the premium could range between cents and hundreds of dollars depending on the chosen parameters, showing a wide scope for tailoring each instrument to businesses' specific preferences and risk profiles.

Further work should focus on quantitatively defining risk measures and triggers for pandemics. In this regard, this would require a multidisciplinary approach leveraging analytical research in economic literature, AI and neural networks, disease control and prevention, and data science. Crichton (1999), Kron (2002) and Pluchino *et al.* (2020), just to mention some, offer an interesting starting point.

References

Crichton, D. (1999). The risk triangle. In *Natural Disaster Management*, Ingleton, J. (ed.), (Tudor Rose, London), pp. 102–103.

Kron, W. (2002). Flood risk = hazard × exposure × vulnerability. In *Flood Defence*, Wu, M. *et al.* (eds.), (Science Press, New York), pp. 82–97.

Pluchino, A., Biondo, A. E., Giuffrida, N., Inturri, G., Latora, V., Le Moli, R., Rapisarda, A., Russo, G. and Zappala, C. (2020). A novel methodology for epidemic risk assessment: The case of COVID-19 outbreak in Italy. arXiv:2004.02739 (physics.soc-ph).

Rossi, M. (2008). Pricing IMF liquidity provision: The value of the IMF liquidity commitment. *Emerging Market Review*, **9**(1), March, 70–77.

https://doi.org/10.1142/9781800610781_0013

Chapter 13

From One Crisis to Another: Impact of COVID-19 Pandemic on Peer-to-Peer Lending Market

Asror Nigmonov* and Hussein Daradkeh†

University of Southern Queensland, Darling Heights, QLD 4350, Australia

**asrorrr@gmail.com*

†*hussein.daradkeh@usq.edu.au*

Abstract

This chapter empirically examines the liquidity risk experienced by peer-to-peer (P2P) lending market during the COVID-19 pandemic. This study utilizes time series and survival regression analyses to provide early evidence of the pandemic-induced exposure to liquidity risk in the P2P lending market. We use the daily number of listings and the probability of success in Bondora's secondary market as continuous dependent variables. The findings indicate that the secondary market listings substantially increased around the early days of the pandemic. Using the method of survival analysis, we also find that, despite increased volatility, the probability of successful listing increased during the pandemic period. Our findings improve the current risk management models and security mechanisms used by P2P lending platforms. However, the findings of this chapter should be used with caution because of the limitations imposed by third parties and rapid changes occurring in the industry.

13.1. Introduction

This chapter presents an empirical examination of the peer-to-peer (P2P) lending market during the COVID-19 pandemic. In this chapter, we explore the current trends in the P2P lending market and empirically investigate the main factors influencing the liquidity risk under the financial distress of the market. We compile the dataset consisting of secondary market listings at Bondora P2P lending platform based in Estonia. This platform is one of the early P2P lending platforms in Europe, which was launched in 2008. Bondora Secondary Market serves as a liquidity management feature offered to investors and creates a complementary marketplace for issued loans. This secondary marketplace offers an opportunity to exit the investment early and liquidate the loan portfolio. We examine the secondary market listings for the period from January 2016 to June 2020. We believe this platform is very suitable for our purpose, as it is one of the largest cross-border P2P lending platforms, working with investors in over 88 countries (including all countries of the EU).

Prior studies on P2P lending or crowdfunding did not examine the issues related to liquidity risk and behaviour of investors under the adverse economic conditions. For over a decade, P2P lending platforms benefited from favourable external conditions, and data was simply not available for observing the tendencies under financial distress. In fact, 2020 is expected to be the first year for the P2P lending market with a global economic downturn. However, we can evaluate the context of the issues raised in this chapter by relying on traditional financial and economics literature. An extensive amount of literature indicates that the pandemics have an enormous economic cost that can impact financial systems (Haacker, 2004; Santaeulalia-Llopis, 2008; Yach *et al.*, 2006). Specifically, pandemics are linked with the collapse of the banking sector, lower lending to the poor, and higher deposit withdrawals (Lagoarde-Segot and Leoni, 2013; Leoni, 2013; Skoufias, 2003). Agosto and Giudici (2020) highlight that the advancement in digital finance increased the exposure of financial markets to stressful events such as COVID-19. Hence, COVID-19 is expected to have a significant effect on financial technologies, in particular, crowdfunding and P2P lending.

This study offers several contributions to the existing literature in terms of its implications for risk management in P2P lending.

To this end, in this chapter, we provide early evidence of the pandemic induced exposure to liquidity risk in the P2P lending market. We examine the impact of the pandemic, as well as the related uncertainty on P2P lending investor sentiment. First, this study is the first research that evaluates the pandemic effect among technology-enabled financing (FinTech) practices. We present a regression model employing the daily number of listings and the probability of successful listing as continuous dependent variables. Second, we analyse the potential impact of the COVID-19 pandemic on the P2P lending industry using the method of survival analysis. For survival analysis, we use all listings in 2020 with the outcome of the listings as a binary dependent variable, which can be employed to understand the dynamics of external shocks in P2P lending markets. The proposed model allows for better prediction and monitoring the impact of external shocks like COVID-19 pandemic. Third, the data on secondary market listings is unique, since it combines multiple databases encompassing borrower- and country-specific characteristics of the listed loan stakes. Thus, our analysis provides a comprehensive view of the influence of COVID-19 risk on the liquidity risk.

We can summarize our empirical analysis as follows. Our data highlight that the number of listings and related volatility in Bondora Secondary Market substantially increased around the early days of the pandemic. Our regression estimations based on the daily number of listings indicate that, despite increased volatility, the probability of success[1] increased during the pandemic period. Furthermore, the findings from survival analysis indicate that, despite increased volatility, the probability of success increased during the pandemic period. However, we note that the findings of this study should be used with caution because of the limitations imposed by third parties and rapid changes occurring in the industry.

The remainder of the chapter proceeds as follows. Section 13.2 provides a discussion of the institutional background of the P2P lending market. Section 13.3 discusses the background literature and develops the hypothesis. Section 13.4 consists of a discussion of empirical analysis. Section 13.5 concludes with the discussion

[1]We define the probability of success as the probability of successfully selling the loan stake by the investor at the Bondora Secondary Market.

of the limitations of our study and promising avenues for further research.

13.2. Institutional background of P2P lending

The development of FinTech plays a vital role in securing funds for the development of small businesses, small consumer borrowers, and the overall economy. During the last decade, the market for FinTech experienced rapid expansion. As a critical response to the Global Financial Crisis of 2007–2008, digital P2P lending burst onto the world scene, together with cryptocurrencies and alternative financial instruments. Specifically, P2P lending[2] practices became innovative in terms of their ability to remove the intermediary from the lending process and raise debt-funding from investors via Internet-based platforms. The global P2P lending market was valued at US$120 billion in 2020 and expected to reach US$1.4 trillion by 2027 (ReportLinker, 2020). Tomlinson *et al.* (2016) reported a cumulative annual growth rate of 87.4% for the European market and 109.4% for the UK market between 2010 and 2015.

P2P lending is part of the growing industry of alternative lending practices. By its essence, it is considered to be a debt-based form of crowdfunding. The concept of crowdfunding is motivated from the notions of crowdsourcing and microfinance, and based on prior work of Morduch (1999), and Poetz Marion and Schreier (2012). It is generally perceived to be a distinct type of funding by fundraisers via numerous Internet sites devoted to the topic Poetz Marion and Schreier (2012). According to Schwienbacher and Larralde (2010), crowdfunding can be defined as an Internet-based call for funds to support initiatives for a specific purpose. The funds might come either in the form of a donation or in exchange for some form of reward. However, these various definitions of crowdfunding ignore certain types of investment that were also classified as "crowdfunding" in mainstream literature. Thus, crowdfunding may embrace such lending practices as Internet-based P2P lending (Lin *et al.*, 2013), or fundraising attempts that were launched by dedicated groups such as

[2]Also referred as "lending-based crowdfunding," "marketplace lending," "crowdlending," and "loan-based crowdfunding."

fans of music groups (Burkett, 2011). However, this study adopts the definition of "crowdfunding," which is described as initiatives for cultural, social, and for-profit reasons by collecting small contributions from numerous individuals, where the whole process does not involve any intermediaries and uses Internet platforms to make the connections between lenders and borrowers (Agrawal *et al.*, 2011).

Lending practices similar to P2P lending has been around as one of the non-bank financial intermediaries throughout history. One of the widely documented examples is the notarial credit entities in France that boomed in their prominence during the 18th century (Hoffman *et al.*, 2019). Working principles of these notaries, such as loan matching process and information networks, were similar to current P2P lending platforms. However, banks remained as the primary institutional lending party in the economy. With the emergence of digital technologies, such as the Internet, big data collection, blockchain cryptography, and smart contracts, the previous strengths of the centralised financial institutions have been diminished. These new technologies have made P2P lending extremely attractive and contributed to the early rapid growth of the P2P lending market. Through digital technologies and online social networking, P2P lending platforms simplified borrower experience and cut the traditional middleman (banks) from the funding flow equation (Welltrado, 2018). Instead, P2P lending platforms offer end-to-end loan solutions to borrowers and lenders with their active participation.

An overwhelming number of P2P lending platforms operate around the globe. Rau (2019) estimates that total P2P lending volume around the world was US$208.4 billion in 2016. In the European Union countries, 79 platforms successfully raised around €16.8 billion between 2010 and 2016 (Orcamoney, 2017). The report compiled by ReportLinker (2020) estimated a cumulative annual growth rate of 42.7% for the years 2020–2027. Despite its early rapid growth, P2P lending still represents a small fraction of total bank lending, whereas the growth rates considerable slowed during the last years. Even in the UK, where the P2P lending is most rapidly developing, it accounts for 0.53% of total unsecured consumer lending and 0.45% of total small and medium enterprise lending (Milne and Parboteeah, 2016). In the EU, the volume of lending raised through crowdfunding platforms increased on average by 60% yearly, between 2013 and

2016 (BIS, 2017). However, the pace of expansion has slowed after 2016.

The impressive early growth of this market rather indicates a favourable business environment than the strength of P2P lending markets. The industry has been sailing in safe waters since the Global Financial Crisis, with low interest rates and generally stable economies worldwide. In contrast, the expected global economic recession as the result of a global pandemic is the first one to be experienced by the P2P lending industry. The future of the industry is still uncertain, as it largely depends on complex and interrelated macroeconomic factors (Li *et al.*, 2016). Early indications of the survival of the platforms under the default wave came in China during 2018 and 2019. During this time, the US$190 billion Chinese P2P lending market considerably suffered when investors rushed to withdraw their money (Wildau and Jia, 2018). Regulatory changes and the wave of defaults created problems of "failing platforms" in China. As reported by Bloomberg (2018) and Liu (2019), the cumulative number of failed platforms in the Chinese P2P lending market reached staggering 4,334 platforms or 70% of active platforms. Tomlinson *et al.* (2016) admitted that the interest rate environment alone might lead to the expected divergence in penetration of P2P lending in the UK market from £0.5 billion (under normalized interest rate environment) to £35.5 billion (under current interest rate environment) by 2025. This forecast raises concerns about the future of an industry and cast doubt on underlying reasons hidden behind the emergence of these platforms. Accordingly, there is an urgent need for exploring loan loss and liquidity risk in the P2P lending industry under the conditions of financial distress. In view of this background, we concentrate on the exposure of P2P lending platforms to liquidity risk under the financial distress caused by a global pandemic.

13.3. Review of Existing Literature

13.3.1. *The extent of studies on crowdfunding and P2P lending*

In the 10 years between 2006 and 2016, crowdfunding and P2P lending practices have gained significant success. These models of lending practices have come forth as a viable process of raising funds and funding collaborative new ventures (Bessière *et al.*, 2020). However, there are limited studies published on the topic of P2P lending and crowdfunding in peer-reviewed journals. In addition to this, existing studies are thoroughly descriptive and narrow by nature. Schwienbacher and Larralde (2010) provided an early definition and comprehension of crowdfunding as a progressive technique of fundraising. The study was based on a case study involving a crowdfunding program for a French music start-up. They concisely examined and discussed the case study in the paper. Later on, numerous other studies intended to comprehend and signify the rationalities for attempting fundraising campaigns, such as crowdfunding, with the help of several theoretical frameworks (Belleflamme *et al.*, 2015).

The existing researches tend to comprehend crowdfunding and P2P lending platforms as a significant way of investment, which is also accompanied by additional benefits. As in this matter, the investigative studies conducted by Schwienbacher and Larralde (2010) and Mollick (2014) signified that the lending platforms of crowdfunding and P2P lending facilitate the testing of new products, marketing strategies, and campaigns. As advocated by Segal (2015), P2P lending can be a sustainable financing substitute for small-scale business organizations, particularly established after the recession in the credit marketplace.

Nevertheless, the research studies predominantly lack empirical investigation related to peculiar observational factors that largely influence the P2P lending. In addition to this, researches do not involve the existence of contradictory elements or the similarities among the conventional theories of financing mechanisms and P2P lending (Tan *et al.*, 2013). Consequently, as the practices and complementary policies related to P2P lending and crowdfunding develop, a crucial need emerges for empirical research related to this topic with proper evidence with an adequate understanding of extant theoretical aspects.

13.3.2. *Determinants of P2P lending*

A limited number of previous literature examined the determinants of the lender's strategies of bidding and the success rate of P2P loan funding. In this regard, the majority of existing articles examined factors that are extensively categorized as loan characteristics, user-related demographics, and soft information (Feng *et al.*, 2015). The studies of Freedman and Jin (2008), Puro *et al.* (2010) along with those of Lin *et al.* (2013), found a significant impact of interest rate, maturity of the loan, and lending amount on the probability of successful funding. Furthermore, several other papers on demographical data related to lending models demonstrated that females seem to better abide by the lesser rate of interest from both sides as a lender and borrower. Moreover, young recipients are mostly more successful than others. The studies also concluded that there is a racial disadvantage in the success rate of funding and the paid interest rate (Feng *et al.*, 2015).

Another set of studies focused on the determinant of default or non-payment among the lenders of the P2P platform. Serrano-Cinca *et al.* (2015) conducted a study in which they applied logistic regression with the loan book database from a LendingClub (USA). This study signified the value of rating assigned by the P2P lending platform for anticipating the loan defaults. Emekter *et al.* (2015) argued the role of credit score, debt to income ratio, FICO score, and revolving utilization rate in default of the loan. Various studies focused on the herding behaviour (Lee and Lee, 2012), the home bias (Lin and Viswanathan, 2016), and societal systems (Freedman and Jin, 2017) for explaining the likelihoods of default amongst P2P lending market.

13.3.3. *COVID-19 and financial sector*

The pandemic calamities are known to have a considerable economic cost attached to it that can significantly influence the financial systems ((Haacker, 2004); (Santaeulalia-Llopis, 2008); (Yach *et al.*, 2006)). The outbreak of COVID-19 at a global level has resulted in a worldwide pandemic, which in result instigated substantial constraints on various economies. According to Agosto and Giudici (2020), the digital form of financing based on online and social networking is anticipated to be primarily affected by the catastrophic outbreak of the highly contagious disease. The study performed contagion monitoring for establishing the impact of COVID-19 on digital financing. With the help of an application of statistical models, the short-term and long-term impact on economic changes were analyzed with changes of infection cases in the first country of the world affected by COVID-19, China. Agosto and Giudici (2020) highlight that in the first week of February 2020, as the cases of COVID-19 accelerated, contagion intensified and the Shanghai Stock Exchange composite index (SSE) plummeted. At a later stage of the epidemic, a negative correlation between SSE returns and reported COVID-19 cases, although weaker, is observed.

Bloom and Cadarette (2019) debated the numerous concerns regarding the impact of the pandemic on the healthcare system, loss of occupation, economic activities, holiday business, and foreign funding. The influence of a pandemic on the economy at the global level is undervalued, and as a result, financial prudence tends to underinvest in preparation for it ((Board, 2019), (Yach *et al.*, 2006)). This became more prominent when the spending behaviours changed globally after the outbreak of the COVID-19 pandemic. It resulted in a downtrend in the expenditure and home-based demands (Haacker, 2004). According to the study of Leoni (2013), the spread of the HIV pandemic was affirmatively associated with deposit withdrawals in developing countries. In addition to this, Lagoarde-Segot and Leoni (2013) forecast that a major pandemic could result in a downfall of the banking industry. Besides, advancing loans to the poor will be affected by the pandemic as investing groups and banks will be overstretched by the economic recession (Skoufias, 2003).

Goodell (2020) emphasized that there is a lack of studies related to the impact of the COVID-19 pandemic, but it can be paralleled to other incurred calamities, such as earthquakes, volcanic eruptions, air disasters, and terrorist attacks. In the earlier revealed adversities, the effect of such events is generally restricted, in contrast with COVID-19, which has an undesirable impact at the global level. Goodell (2020) also stated that, in the event of a non-survivable event, other outcomes are irrelevant, with almost no impact on market prices. However, with catastrophes like COVID-19 that is considered survivable, impact on financial markets is extremely relevant. COVID-19, as a survivable global pandemic, is projected to have a long-term imprint on financing and the cost of capital Goodell (2020).

Elnahas *et al.* (2018) debated that organizations located in a disaster-prone area tend to be less levered. For that reason, COVID-19 is estimated to bring together less levered principal structures. The COVID-19 pandemic is also instigating a direct global disparaging financial effect that is encountered by every organization in every part of the globe. Nevertheless, small businesses and low-income households can benefit from digital financing and online banking services (Ozili, 2018). There are several support programs for financing implemented by the governmental bodies to ease the financial problems of lending and fundraising for the small enterprises during this catastrophic incident of the outbreak of COVID-19. These online services will support in mitigating the downturn of the economy and fill the gaps to maintain and mitigate the economic challenges caused by the COVID-19 crisis (Civelek and Xiarewana, 2020).

Growth rates of the P2P lending market are impressive, and relatively low barriers to market entry, combined with low market interest rates, made this sector very dynamic. However, the future of the industry is still bleak, as it largely depends on complex and interrelated factors, while most of these factors are at a macro level (Li *et al.*, 2016). Potential risk factors resulting from variability of defaults, loan recovery, platform failure, fraud, or cybercrime pose threat to investors and platforms itself (Milne and Parboteeah, 2016). One of the early indications of vulnerability came in 2018 when a wave of defaults swept across the Chinese P2P lending market (Wildau and Jia, 2018). This precedent caused the withdrawal of funds by investors and the collapse of platforms unable to maintain liquidity. Most of the P2P lending platforms diversify across a large number of borrowers and maintain a certain level of "hardship funds." These measures allow them to protect themselves against borrower defaults and maintain the required level of liquidity (Cumming and Hornuf, 2018). What remains unprotected is loan loss and liquidity risk over the business cycle. Losses are expected to increase substantially over a major economic downturn, which could easily exhaust investor funds (Bolt *et al.*, 2012). At the same time, the current economic downturn as a result of the COVID-19 pandemic increased the likelihood of unsustainable losses by the industry. There is a need for better understanding of the dynamics of successful P2P lending under the conditions of financial distress. Thus, the central question of this chapter is: *How did COVID-19 affect the P2P lending market liquidity?*

Accordingly, it is expected that COVID-19 will have a significant effect on financial technology, such as crowdfunding and P2P lending. Specifically, we expect that the current pandemic negatively affects the liquidity of P2P lending platforms by creating a "bank-run" type scenario (Peckham, 2013). Following the typical behaviour in traditional financial markets, the pandemic might trigger "herding behavior" among P2P lending market investors who rush to turn their stakes into cash in masses. Accordingly, we hypothesise that the announcement of the COVID-19 pandemic by the World Health Organization (WHO) and subsequent increase in cases increased the number of listings in Bondora Secondary Market. We also predict that the developments related to the pandemic reduced the probability of successfully "cashing-out" investor holdings in Bondora P2P lending loans. To this end, the hypotheses to be tested in this chapter are the following:

COVID-19 pandemic and the secondary market listings.

H1a: Announcement of COVID-19 pandemic by WHO significantly increased the daily number of listings in Bondora Secondary Market.
H1b: Increase in daily COVID-19 case numbers significantly increased the daily number of listings in Bondora Secondary Market.
H1c: Increase in daily numbers COVID-19–related deaths significantly increased the daily number of listings in Bondora Secondary Market.

COVID-19 pandemic and the probability of a successful listing outcome.

H2a: Announcement of the COVID-19 pandemic by WHO significantly reduced the probability of success in Bondora Secondary Market.
H2b: Increase in daily COVID-19 case numbers significantly reduced the probability of success in Bondora Secondary Market.
H2c: Increase in daily numbers COVID-19–related deaths significantly reduced the probability of success in Bondora Secondary Market.

13.4. Empirical Analysis

13.4.1. *About Bondora*

The P2P lending market in continental Europe is experiencing remarkable continuous growth. Paired with its still developing regulations, the EU represents an excellent opportunity for analysing current tendencies in P2P lending. However, there is a lack of international or local authority that regulates P2P lending activities and that collects information on them. The scope of this research, therefore, is limited by the availability of the data. We limit the scope of this chapter as a case study of a single P2P lending platform. Within the framework of this chapter, we use the P2P lending platform data from Bondora Capital OÜ based in Estonia. Bondora is a marketplace for P2P consumer lending that covers most of the EU countries. Its marketplace allows users to invest in loans granted through the Bondora Group to borrowers in Estonia, Finland, and Spain. Bondora has historically financed the loans it originates by selling the associated receivables to a retail investor base drawn from 40 countries around the world, including all countries of EU. Bondora also makes most of its financials public, including the full loan-book and secondary market transactions. In this regard, the data available from Bondora is exceptionally suitable for analyzing investor sentiments across Europe.

Bondora has been in business since 2009 and is one of the leading non-bank digital consumer loan providers in Continental Europe. The consumer loans offered by Bondora are marketed in Finland, Spain, and Estonia through a fully digital process supported by advanced credit analytics and in-house servicing. All loans are unsecured consumer loans with principal amounts of €500 to €10,000 and repayment terms ranging from 3 to 60 months. It is possible to automate investments and trade loans secondary market. The secondary market offers an opportunity to exit the investment early and can be equivalent to cashing out a financial instrument in traditional financial markets.

Figure 13.1 depicts the loan portfolio of Bondora from January 2019 to June 2020 with the share of overdue loans. Following the financial market turmoil as a result of the COVID-19 pandemic, Bondora experienced certain disruptions in the loan portfolio

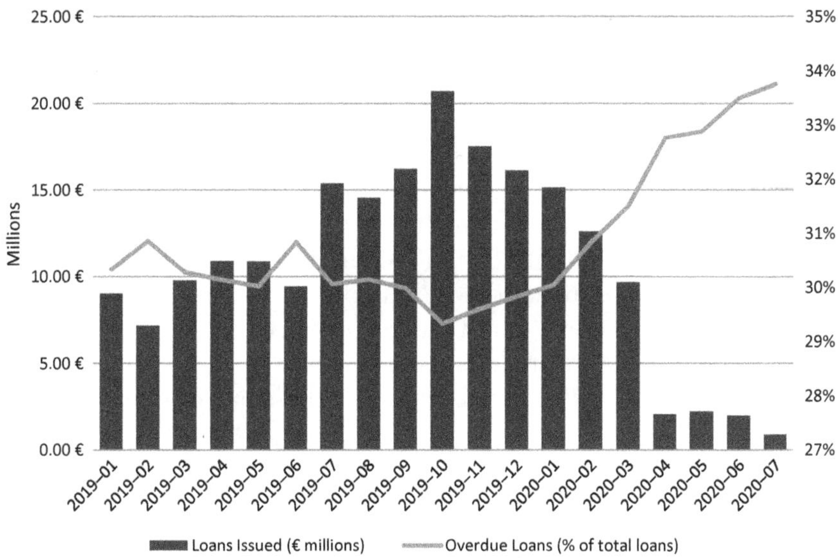

Figure 13.1. Loan portfolio and overdue loans issued by Bondora (Jan 2019–June 2020).

Source: Bondora (2020).

(Tomberg, 2020a). Certain actions were undertaken by the company to maintain steady returns for investors during these times. Loan originators based in Finland and Spain were suspended; partial pay-out feature of Go & Grow was automatically activated for most of the investor withdrawals; and new loan applications were stringently reduced (Bondora, 2020). As depicted in Figure 13.1, the volume of loans substantially dropped from April 2020. However, this was the result of reduced investor funding rather than the fall in loan applications (Tomberg, 2020b).

13.4.2. *Descriptive analysis*

Bondora provides its comprehensive secondary market and loan-book dataset with diverse features of each loan and loan holder. We combined secondary market transactions from 2016 to 2020 that amounted in over 5 million observations. We aggregated the number of failed and successful listings by listed date (daily observations) and country of loan origination. The dataset of the secondary market transactions was aggregated with country-specific variables obtained from other sources. For example, we added data on EU Economic sentiment indicator for each country of loan origination that was obtained from the statistical database of the Directorate-General for Economic and Financial Affairs of the European Commission. Our aggregated database consists of 1,629 valid observations, with some missing observations. Missing observations, because of non-availability of data, reduced the sampling size (N) and formed unbalanced panel data. This problem considerably reduces the degrees-of-freedom (df) in our regression analysis.

Observations in this modified database do not allow to fully grasp the gravity of the situation because of the small sample size that coincides with the pandemic period. This database also does not include important loan and borrower characteristics, which might create the problem of an omitted variable. Therefore, in the second stage of analysis, we use all the secondary market listing outcomes as a binary dependent variable. We combined each of the listings with the country-specific variables and corresponding loan details from the loan-book dataset. The updated database consists of over 20 explanatory variables, with over 5 million observations. It safeguards against the problem of omitted variables and substantially increases the df in our regression analysis. Each of the listings in the database also contains the observations for start and end time of the listing. This information allows us to examine the data using survival analysis, which facilitates estimating the timing of failure. The Appendix section provides Table 13.A.1 with the description of all variables used in this study.

Figure 13.2 provides a breakdown of the distribution of the daily number of listings in our sample database based on each month of 2020. We find that the daily listings considerably increased during March. This period was characterized by tumultuous behaviour of investors as the pandemic scare unfolded and WHO declared COVID-19 as a pandemic. Box plot in Figure 13.2 indicates a considerably higher average (median) daily listings in March compared to January and February of 2020. During March, the changes in the daily number of listings were also extremely high, as depicted by the standard deviation and quartiles in the box plot of Figure 13.2. Box plot also indicates that the numbers relatively stabilized by April and fell below pre-pandemic levels in May. However, the fall in secondary

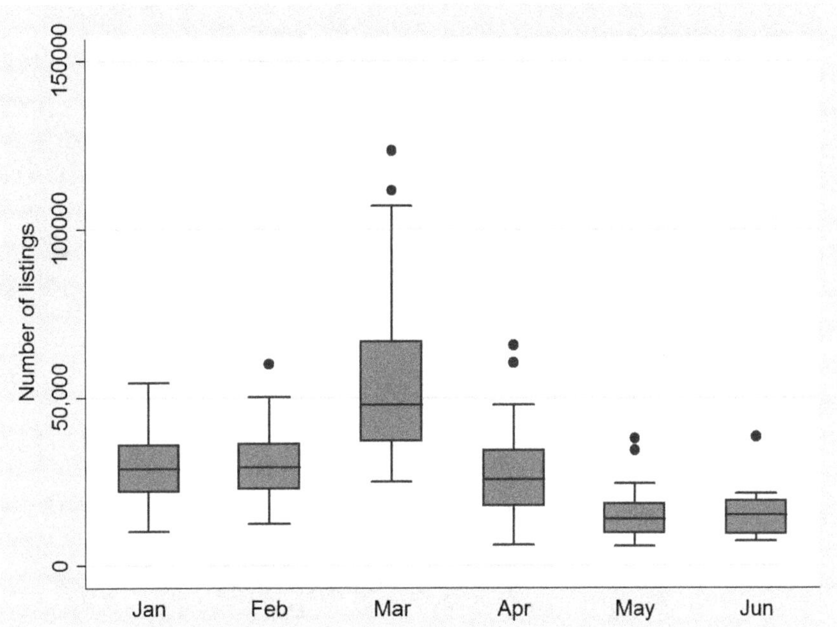

Figure 13.2. Monthly distribution of the daily number of listings in Bondora Secondary Market (Jan 2020–June 2020).

Source: Authors' calculations based on Bondora (2020).

market activity was the result of restrictions imposed by Bondora rather than the change in investor sentiment (Tomberg, 2020a).

Impact of disruptions related to the news cycles of the pandemic is particularly visible if the daily listings are presented in the form of a line chart. Figure 13.3 depicts the daily number of listings as a line chart, with the date of the pandemic declaration highlighted as a dashed line. The line chart visually indicates of contagion type conditions in Bondora Secondary Market around the dates of declaration of a pandemic. As the COVID-19–related negative news broke out, there were sharp and sudden spikes in secondary market listings. These types of spikes are incredibly detrimental for P2P lending market investors, as the market liquidity is much lower than the traditional financial markets. Crisis measures implemented by Bondora such as withdrawal limits safeguarded the liquidity of the platform to a certain degree. Nevertheless, restrictions are effective in the short term and might backfire in the long term, as the liquidity risk

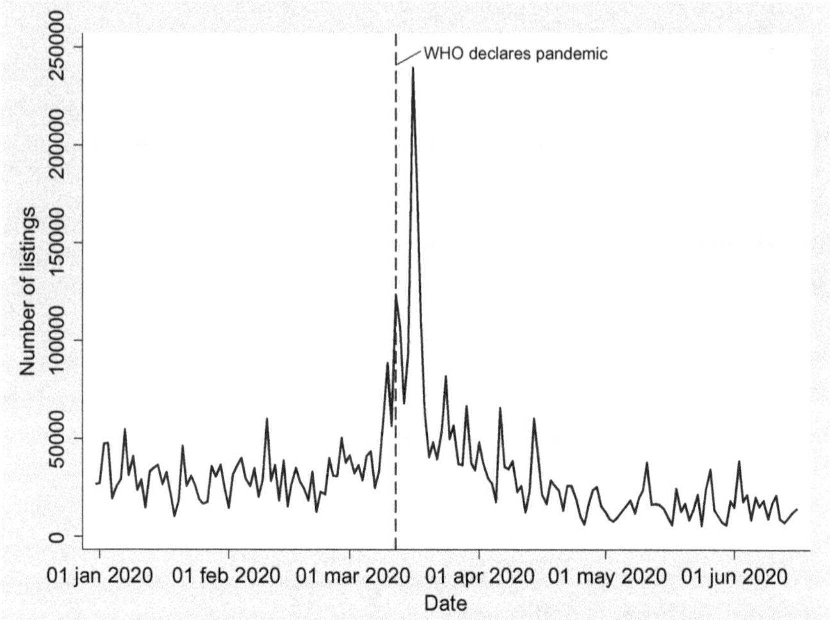

Figure 13.3. Daily number of listings in Bondora Secondary Market (Jan 1, 2020–June 30, 2020).

Source: Authors' calculations based on Bondora (2020).

transforms into insolvency. P2P lending platforms require specific long-term changes in their risk assessment and management, considering changed conditions in the business environment. The next section of this chapter empirically analyses the Bondora Secondary Market listings data that explains the changes in investor sentiment over the pandemic period. The findings also identify factors that further shape risk management in P2P lending market post-pandemic.

13.4.3. *Results of time series analysis with a continuous dependent variable*

In the first stage of regression analysis, we estimate the following equation using a continuous dependent variable:

$$\gamma_t = \alpha + \delta\gamma_{t-1} + \beta_d D + \beta_E X_t^E + \varepsilon_{it}, \tag{13.1}$$

where γ_t is the dependent variable represented by the number of listings and probability of success at Bondora Secondary Market at time t (daily observations, continuous variable). Probability success of the listing at time t is calculated as:

$$Probability\,of\,success_t = \frac{Number\ of\ successful\ listings_t}{Number\ of\ listings_t}, \quad (13.2)$$

where γ_{t-1} is the number of listings (probability of success) at time $t-1$ (lagged independent variable).

$\beta_d D$ is the variable representing the COVID-19 pandemic. Three proxies are used to represent the pandemic: (i) dummy variable equal to 1 for the dates later than March 11, 2020,[3] and 0 otherwise, (ii) change in the number of reported daily cases of COVID-19, and (iii) change in the number of reported daily COVID-19 related deaths.

$\beta_E X_t^E$ is the vector of economy-specific control variables (e.g. consumer confidence index).

The e_t is an error term that is unobserved factors. β is the independent variable coefficient that reveals the magnitudes of independent variables effects on γ_t. α is the intercept of the regression model.

The results of the regression are reported in Table 13.1. The table uses the number of listings as a continuous dependent variable. The results indicate high and significant values of Wald chi-squared for three of the regression models. This result indicates the fitness of the models and explains that there is a strong relationship between dependent variables and predictors. In terms of individual coefficients, the pandemic dummy variable has a significant positive coefficient (0.5934). This finding indicates that the daily number of listings increased by 0.59% after the declaration of COVID-19 as a pandemic by WHO. Based on the Models (1) and (2) of Table 13.1, the increase in the daily number of COVID-19 cases and deaths reduces the number of listings in the platform. However, the coefficients for these two variables are insignificant, preventing to draw a firm conclusion in this regard. Thus, we move into the analysis of time series data based on probability of success.

Table 13.2 reports the results of the regression model that employs the probability of success as the dependent variable. Pandemic

[3]The date WHO declared COVID-19 to be a pandemic.

Table 13.1. COVID-19 and the number of listings.

	(1)	(2)	(3)
	DV = LISTINGS	DV = LISTINGS	DV = LISTINGS
PANDEMIC_ DUMMY	0.5934***		
	(0.1149)		
CASES		−0.0115	
		(0.0575)	
DEATHS			−0.0208
			(0.0544)
INDEX	−1.7515***	−3.0934***	−3.0195***
	(0.2333)	(0.7493)	(0.5398)
ESI	0.0165***	0.0341***	0.0340***
	(0.0025)	(0.0045)	(0.0041)
AAR	−1.4522***	−2.2583	−2.0312
	(0.0419)	(5.1578)	(5.3835)
Wald chi square	2255.2733	198.0591	198.5992
Prob > chi square	0.0000	0.0000	0.0000
N	1629	1628	1628

Note: The table presents the results of time-series regression with a daily number of listings as the dependent variable. Refer to Appendix Table 13.A.1 for the variable description. All model specifications employ robust standard errors in parentheses ($^{*}p < 0.10$, $^{**}p < 0.05$, $^{***}p < 0.01$).

dummy significantly affects the daily probability of success of the listing in the Model (1) of Table 13.2. The probability of the successful listing of the loan stake by investors increased by 0.0548% during the pandemic period. Daily changes in the number of reported COVID-19 cases have a significant positive coefficient. So, a 1% increase in the number of cases leads to 0.0384% decrease in the probability of success of the listing. The coefficient is found to be significant at more than 99% confidence level.

On the contrary, the daily number of COVID-19–related deaths is found to be having a negative coefficient. The coefficient of this variable is −0.0322 with a confidence level of more than 99%. So, the number of COVID-19–related cases and deaths affect the probability of success in the opposite manner. We believe that this effect is the result of deaths being the lagging indicator (Langreth *et al.*, 2020). Cases usually indicate early changes in the pandemic turmoil

Table 13.2. COVID-19 and the probability of success.

	(1)	(2)	(3)
	DV = PROB_ SUCCESS	**DV = PROB_ SUCCESS**	**DV = PROB_ SUCCESS**
PANDEMIC_ DUMMY	0.0548^{*} (0.0323)		
CASES		0.0384^{***} (0.0111)	
DEATHS			-0.0322^{**} (0.0139)
INDEX	0.5291^{***} (0.0761)	0.0642 (0.1647)	-0.4398^{***} (0.1397)
ESI	-0.0117^{***} (0.0007)	0.0017 (0.0010)	-0.0015^{*} (0.0009)
AAR	−0.0128 (0.0126)	−1.0654 (0.9056)	−0.0436 (0.9721)
LR chi square	574.0610	53.4208	52.7498
Prob > chi square	0.0000	0.0000	0.0000
N	1629	1628	1628

Note: The table presents the results of time-series regression with the probability of success as the dependent variable. Refer to Appendix Table 13.A.1 for the variable description. All model specifications employ robust standard errors in parentheses ($^{*}p < 0.10$, $^{**}p < 0.05$, $^{***}p < 0.01$).

where investors are keen to cash-in, and the true impact of the pandemic-related disruptions did not hit the economy. This period is similar to the corporate bond market, where dealers absorb some of the "inventory" during the sell-off (Weill, 2007). However, as the pandemic progresses away from the early stage, withdrawals overweigh the liquidity provided by the market participants. During March 2020, a similar case was observed in the corporate bonds market, which faced withdrawals of almost US$100 billion (Scaggs, 2020). The number of COVID-19–related death numbers lagging a couple of weeks behind the number of cases represented this later period of pandemic-related market turmoil.

Other variables as it is reported in Tables 13.1 and 13.2 are modestly performing in terms of significance levels. However, the results are largely undermined by a small sample ($N = 1,629$) and the lack of borrower-specific variables. Therefore, in the next section, we explore the database of all the secondary market listing outcomes as a binary dependent variable. This database consists of over 5 million observations consisting of both country- and borrower-specific variables.

13.4.4. *Results of survival analysis*

The main empirical technique of this chapter is survival analysis, which facilitates estimating not only whether but also when the event occurs. We perform a survival regression analysis employing the listings posted in Bondora over the period from January 2020 to June 2020. The model based on survival analysis uses the same set of country-specific variables together with a wide range of borrower specific variables.

$$\gamma_t = \alpha + \delta\gamma_{t-1} + \beta_d D + \beta_E X_t^E + \beta_B X_t^B + \varepsilon_{it}, \tag{13.3}$$

where $\beta_E X_t^E$ is vector of borrower-specific control variables.

Other variables are defined as in Equation (13.1). Both techniques use the same data and the same explanatory variables, but the dependent variable differs. In Equation (13.1), the dependent variable is continuing variable, while in the survival analysis based on Equation (13.3) the dependent variable is the time until the occurrence of an event of interest. The event of interest is an unsuccessful listing where the investor cannot sell his/her stake in the loan. In the case of this research, the dependent variable is the risk of failure or how long the listing survived until the failure. We estimate the survival until the failure using Cox regression, which relates survival time and explanatory variables.

Table 13.3 shows the survival analysis results, using Cox regression, one for each explanatory variable. We report regression coefficients, standard errors, risk ratios and significance of p-values in the Table 13.3. The regression coefficient is interpreted as a k-fold increase in risk. Hence, a negative regression coefficient for an explanatory variable means that the risk is lower. Risk ratio can be interpreted as the predicted change in the risk for a unit increase in the explanatory variable. Table 13.3 reveals significant practical findings. All of the pandemic variables are consistent across the models. The goodness of fit for three models indicates the fit of the model around 0.03 and 0.0399, represented by pseudo R-squared values. Also evident from the Likelihood Ratio (LR) chi-square values is

Table 13.3. Cox regression analysis for survival time of secondary market listing.

	(1)		(2)		(3)	
	DV = SURVIVAL_TIME		**DV = SURVIVAL_TIME**		**DV = SURVIVAL_TIME**	
	Parameter estimate	**Hazard ratio**	**Parameter estimate**	**Hazard ratio**	**Parameter estimate**	**Hazard ratio**
PANDEMIC_DUMMY	-1.9793^{***}	0.1382^{***}				
	(0.0072)	(0.0010)				
CASES			-0.3778^{***}	0.6854^{***}		
			(0.0011)	(0.0008)		
DEATHS					-0.2873^{***}	0.7503^{***}
					(0.0019)	(0.0015)
INDEX	13.1924^{***}	536261.1679^{***}	9.1745^{***}	9647.6430^{***}	11.1360^{***}	68594.4742^{***}
	(0.0780)	(41812.2703)	(0.0748)	(721.9731)	(0.0641)	(4398.8638)
ESI	0.0093^{***}	1.0094^{***}	0.0080^{***}	1.0080^{***}	0.0549^{***}	1.0564^{***}
	(0.0004)	(0.0004)	(0.0003)	(0.0003)	(0.0003)	(0.0004)
POP	-0.1046^{***}	0.9007^{***}	0.2222^{***}	1.2489^{***}	-0.0964^{***}	0.9081^{***}
	(0.0029)	(0.0026)	(0.0030)	(0.0038)	(0.0032)	(0.0029)
RESTRUCTURED	0.1680^{***}	1.1830^{***}	0.1520^{***}	1.1642^{***}	0.1472^{***}	1.1586^{***}
	(0.0040)	(0.0048)	(0.0040)	(0.0047)	(0.0040)	(0.0047)

(Continued)

Table 13.3. *(Continued)*

	(1)		(2)		(3)	
	DV = SURVIVAL_TIME		DV = SURVIVAL_TIME		DV = SURVIVAL_TIME	
	Parameter estimate	**Hazard ratio**	**Parameter estimate**	**Hazard ratio**	**Parameter estimate**	**Hazard ratio**
AGE	0.0010***	1.0010***	0.0008***	1.0008***	0.0010***	1.0010***
	(0.0002)	(0.0002)	(0.0002)	(0.0002)	(0.0002)	(0.0002)
GENDER	0.0425***	1.0434***	0.0535***	1.0549***	0.0305***	1.0310***
	(0.0026)	(0.0027)	(0.0026)	(0.0028)	(0.0026)	(0.0027)
INTEREST	−0.0003***	0.9997***	−0.0008***	0.9992***	−0.0003***	0.9997***
	(0.0001)	(0.0001)	(0.0001)	(0.0001)	(0.0001)	(0.0001)
LOANDURATION	0.0015***	1.0015***	0.0030***	1.0030***	0.0006***	1.0006***
	(0.0001)	(0.0001)	(0.0001)	(0.0001)	(0.0001)	(0.0001)
INCOMETOTAL	−0.0001**	0.9999**	−0.0001***	0.9999***	−0.0002***	0.9998***
	(0.0000)	(0.0000)	(0.0000)	(0.0000)	(0.0000)	(0.0000)
DTI	0.0038***	1.0038***	0.0028***	1.0028***	0.0026***	1.0026***
	(0.0002)	(0.0002)	(0.0002)	(0.0002)	(0.0002)	(0.0002)
DISCOUNTRATE	0.0002***	1.0002***	0.0002***	1.0002***	0.0002***	1.0002***
	(0.0000)	(0.0000)	(0.0000)	(0.0000)	(0.0000)	(0.0000)
PRINCIPAL_DIFF	0.0160***	1.0162***	0.0154***	1.0155***	0.0146***	1.0147***
	(0.0001)	(0.0001)	(0.0001)	(0.0001)	(0.0001)	(0.0001)

Table 13.3 (*Continued*)

	(1)		(2)		(3)	
	DV = SURVIVAL_TIME		DV = SURVIVAL_TIME		DV = SURVIVAL_TIME	
	Parameter estimate	Hazard ratio	Parameter estimate	Hazard ratio	Parameter estimate	Hazard ratio
RATING						
A	0.1823***	1.2000***	0.1357***	1.1453***	0.0847**	1.0884**
	(0.0392)	(0.0470)	(0.0392)	(0.0449)	(0.0392)	(0.0426)
B	0.2693***	1.3090***	0.2292***	1.2576***	0.1819***	1.1995***
	(0.0305)	(0.0400)	(0.0305)	(0.0384)	(0.0305)	(0.0366)
C	0.4104***	1.5074***	0.3655***	1.4412***	0.2784***	1.3210***
	(0.0280)	(0.0422)	(0.0280)	(0.0404)	(0.0280)	(0.0370)
D	0.4973***	1.6443***	0.4575***	1.5801***	0.3807***	1.4633***
	(0.0276)	(0.0453)	(0.0275)	(0.0435)	(0.0275)	(0.0403)
E	0.5871***	1.7987***	0.4993***	1.6475***	0.3787***	1.4604***
	(0.0273)	(0.0491)	(0.0273)	(0.0450)	(0.0273)	(0.0399)
F	0.3470***	1.4148***	0.3014***	1.3518***	0.2406***	1.2721***
	(0.0275)	(0.0388)	(0.0274)	(0.0371)	(0.0274)	(0.0349)
HR	0.3486***	1.4171***	0.1884***	1.2073***	0.1832***	1.2010***
	(0.0283)	(0.0401)	(0.0283)	(0.0342)	(0.0283)	(0.0340)

(*Continued*)

Table 13.3. *(Continued)*

	(1)		(2)		(3)	
	DV = SURVIVAL_TIME		DV = SURVIVAL_TIME		DV = SURVIVAL_TIME	
	Parameter estimate	Hazard ratio	Parameter estimate	Hazard ratio	Parameter estimate	Hazard ratio
EMP_DUR						
Trial period	−0.0629*	0.9390*	−0.0281	0.9723	−0.0021	0.9979
	(0.0340)	(0.0320)	(0.0340)	(0.0331)	(0.0340)	(0.0340)
Up to 1 year	−0.0399***	0.9609***	−0.0241***	0.9762***	−0.0028	0.9972
	(0.0093)	(0.0090)	(0.0093)	(0.0091)	(0.0093)	(0.0093)
Up to 2 years	−0.0393***	0.9615***	−0.0429***	0.9580***	0.0119	1.0119
	(0.0134)	(0.0129)	(0.0134)	(0.0128)	(0.0134)	(0.0136)
Up to 3 years	−0.1693***	0.8443***	−0.1485***	0.8620***	−0.0966***	0.9079***
	(0.0148)	(0.0125)	(0.0148)	(0.0127)	(0.0148)	(0.0134)
Up to 4 years	0.0283*	1.0287*	0.0264*	1.0268*	0.0657***	1.0679***
	(0.0151)	(0.0155)	(0.0151)	(0.0155)	(0.0151)	(0.0161)
Up to 5 years	−0.0295***	0.9710***	−0.0216**	0.9786**	0.0014	1.0014
	(0.0089)	(0.0087)	(0.0089)	(0.0087)	(0.0089)	(0.0090)
More than 5 years	−0.0168**	0.9834**	−0.0147*	0.9854*	0.0193**	1.0194**
	(0.0084)	(0.0082)	(0.0084)	(0.0083)	(0.0084)	(0.0086)
Retiree	−0.0882***	0.9156***	−0.0736***	0.9291***	−0.0495***	0.9517***
	(0.0099)	(0.0091)	(0.0099)	(0.0092)	(0.0099)	(0.0095)

Table 13.3 (*Continued*)

	(1)		(2)		(3)	
	DV = SURVIVAL_TIME		DV = SURVIVAL_TIME		DV = SURVIVAL_TIME	
	Parameter estimate	Hazard ratio	Parameter estimate	Hazard ratio	Parameter estimate	Hazard ratio
EDUCATION						
Primary education	−0.1635	0.8492	−0.1410	0.8685	−0.3525	0.7029
	(0.2953)	(0.2508)	(0.2935)	(0.2549)	(0.2941)	(0.2067)
Basic education	−0.1835	0.8323	−0.1277	0.8801	−0.3323	0.7173
	(0.2955)	(0.2459)	(0.2936)	(0.2584)	(0.2942)	(0.2110)
Vocational education	−0.1516	0.8594	−0.1352	0.8735	−0.3422	0.7102
	(0.2953)	(0.2538)	(0.2935)	(0.2564)	(0.2941)	(0.2088)
Secondary education	−0.1302	0.8780	−0.0813	0.9219	−0.2964	0.7435
	(0.2953)	(0.2592)	(0.2934)	(0.2705)	(0.2940)	(0.2186)
Higher education	−0.1120	0.8941	−0.0910	0.9130	−0.2881	0.7497
	(0.2953)	(0.2640)	(0.2935)	(0.2679)	(0.2940)	(0.2204)
HOME OWNERSHIP						
Owner	0.2807	1.3241	0.2529	1.2878	0.2251	1.2525
	(0.2509)	(0.3322)	(0.2493)	(0.3211)	(0.2498)	(0.3129)

(*Continued*)

Table 13.3. (*Continued*)

	(1)		(2)		(3)	
	DV = SURVIVAL_TIME		DV = SURVIVAL_TIME		DV = SURVIVAL_TIME	
	Parameter estimate	**Hazard ratio**	**Parameter estimate**	**Hazard ratio**	**Parameter estimate**	**Hazard ratio**
Living with parents	0.2328	1.2621	0.2103	1.2340	0.1941	1.2142
	(0.2509)	(0.3167)	(0.2494)	(0.3077)	(0.2499)	(0.3034)
Tenant, pre-furnished	0.2105	1.2343	0.1878	1.2066	0.1624	1.1764
property	(0.2509)	(0.3097)	(0.2493)	(0.3008)	(0.2498)	(0.2939)
Tenant, unfurnished	0.2798	1.3228	0.2905	1.3370	0.2833	1.3275
property	(0.2510)	(0.3321)	(0.2494)	(0.3335)	(0.2499)	(0.3318)
Council house	0.1472	1.1585	0.1427	1.1534	0.1566	1.1695
	(0.2514)	(0.2912)	(0.2498)	(0.2882)	(0.2503)	(0.2928)
Joint tenant	0.2039	1.2262	0.2230	1.2498	0.2271	1.2550
	(0.2515)	(0.3084)	(0.2500)	(0.3124)	(0.2505)	(0.3143)

Table 13.3 (*Continued*)

	(1)		(2)		(3)	
	DV = SURVIVAL_TIME		DV = SURVIVAL_TIME		DV = SURVIVAL_TIME	
	Parameter estimate	**Hazard ratio**	**Parameter estimate**	**Hazard ratio**	**Parameter estimate**	**Hazard ratio**
Joint ownership	0.1481	1.1597	0.1405	1.1509	0.1287	1.1373
	(0.2515)	(0.2916)	(0.2499)	(0.2876)	(0.2504)	(0.2848)
Mortgage	0.2425	1.2744	0.2345	1.2643	0.2191	1.2450
	(0.2509)	(0.3198)	(0.2493)	(0.3152)	(0.2498)	(0.3110)
Owner with encumbrance	0.2329	1.2623	0.1756	1.1919	0.1983	1.2194
	(0.2528)	(0.3191)	(0.2513)	(0.2995)	(0.2518)	(0.3070)
MARITAL STATUS						
Married	−0.0891***	0.9148***	−0.1082***	0.8975***	0.0728***	1.0755***
	(0.0106)	(0.0097)	(0.0106)	(0.0095)	(0.0106)	(0.0114)
Cohabitant	−0.1085***	0.8971***	−0.0867***	0.9170***	0.0855***	1.0893***
	(0.0134)	(0.0120)	(0.0134)	(0.0123)	(0.0135)	(0.0147)
Single	−0.1163***	0.8902***	−0.1736***	0.8407***	0.0197*	1.0199*
	(0.0114)	(0.0102)	(0.0114)	(0.0096)	(0.0115)	(0.0117)

(*Continued*)

Table 13.3. (*Continued*)

	(1)		(2)		(3)	
	DV = SURVIVAL_TIME		DV = SURVIVAL_TIME		DV = SURVIVAL_TIME	
	Parameter estimate	Hazard ratio	Parameter estimate	Hazard ratio	Parameter estimate	Hazard ratio
Divorced	−0.1598***	0.8523***	−0.1683***	0.8451***	0.0085	1.0085
	(0.0147)	(0.0125)	(0.0147)	(0.0124)	(0.0147)	(0.0148)
Widow	−0.1758***	0.8388***	−0.1919***	0.8254***	−0.0216	0.9786
	(0.0389)	(0.0327)	(0.0389)	(0.0321)	(0.0390)	(0.0381)
LR chi square	248201.1066	248201.1066	271000.4306	271000.4306	164087.4244	164087.4244
Prob > chi square	0.0000	0.0000	0.0000	0.0000	0.0000	0.0000
Pseudo-R-squared	0.0300	0.0300	0.0328	0.0328	0.0399	0.0199
N	1541095	1541095	1541095	1541095	1541095	1541095

Note: The table presents the results of Cox regression analysis for survival time of listings. Refer to Appendix Table 13.A.1 for the variable description. Number of listings analyzed: 5,386,928. Failed: 1,158,162 (21.50%). Successful: 4,228,766 (78.50%). All model specifications employ robust standard errors in parentheses ($^{*}p < 0.10$, $^{**}p < 0.05$, $^{***}p < 0.01$).

that at least one of the predictors' regression coefficients is not equal to zero.

If coefficients are considered, the variable dummy of the pandemic has a significant negative coefficient. This negative coefficient for the variable largely counter-intuitive. It indicates a lower risk of failed listing for the period after the declaration of the pandemic. The Model (1) estimates that after the declaration of the pandemic expected log hazard ratio decreased by -1.9793, while holding all other predictors constant. We obtain similar results from the other variables representing the impact of the pandemic. Both COVID-19–related deaths and cases have negative coefficients. Each percentage increase in the number of reported daily COVD-19 cases reduces the risk of 0.6854 times, *ceteris paribus* (Model (2)). In contrast, the risk of an unsuccessful listing reduces 0.7503 times under each percentage increase in reported daily COVD-19–related deaths. The significance test for the coefficient tests the null hypothesis that it equals zero. In all three indicators of the pandemic, statistically significant differences have been found ($p < 0.001$). Results are coherent, to a certain degree, with the first stage of regression analysis of this chapter with continues dependent variable.

Another critical aspect of survival analysis is the survival curves indicating the probabilities of failure at a certain point of time (Figure 13.4). The chart in Figure 13.4 displays the survival curves for each period under consideration, before and after the pandemic. It can be appreciated that the probability of survival is higher during than before the pandemic.

13.5. Discussion and Concluding Remarks

This chapter discussed the implication of COVID-19 on the P2P lending market liquidity using the listings database of Bondora Secondary Market. To sum the finding of this chapter, loan defaults and the number of listing in Bondora Secondary Market significantly increased after the declaration of COVID-19 as a pandemic by WHO. This finding was confirmed in both graphical descriptive analysis and regression models. We can explain this impact by the surge in selling pressure and inventory accumulation by investors. This behaviour is typical during the pandemic when the market

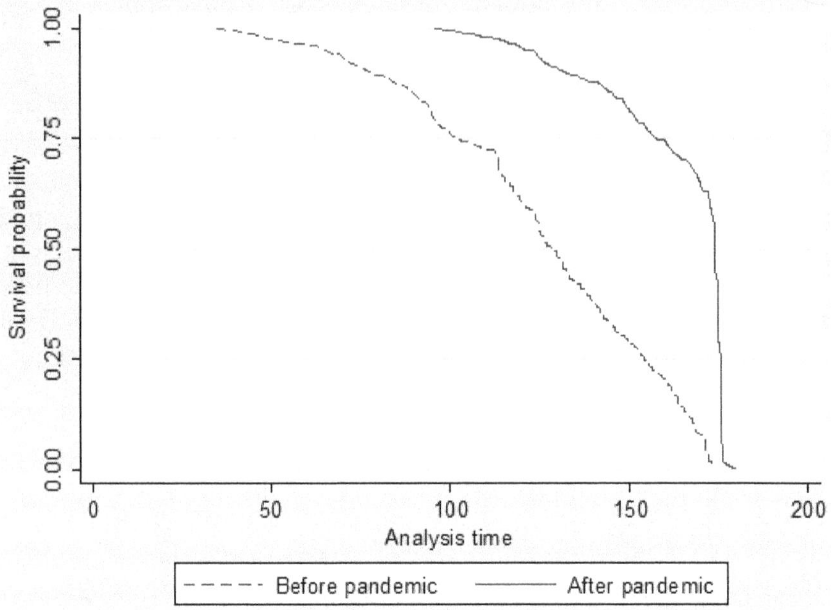

Figure 13.4. Survival function before and after the pandemic.

turmoil triggers so-called "dash for cash" when investors run for liquid assets (Gros, 2020). During this period, investors tend to sell risky assets (e.g. their stake in P2P lending loans) for cash and purchases of less risky assets (Wójcik and Ioannou, 2020). This finding falls in line with the early studies of Leoni (2013), Lagoarde-Segot and Leoni (2013), and Skoufias (2003). It also falls in line with the latest literature on the impact of the COVID-19 pandemic on liquidity provision in the financial markets (Haddad *et al.*, 2020; Kargar *et al.*, 2020; O'Hara and Zhou, 2020).

On the contrary, our findings indicated that the probability of successfully listing a loan stake increased during the pandemic period. Specifically, when we employed the survival analysis technique, the risk of unsuccessful listing reduced as the reported daily COVD-19–related deaths and cases increased. This result contradicts the latest studies of the impact of COVID-19 pandemic on the financial sector, such as Baig *et al.* (2020). Results of Baig *et al.* (2020) suggest that increases in COVD-19–related deaths and cases are associated with a significant increase in market illiquidity and volatility.

To sum, by concentrating around the liquidity risk, this study can improve current risk management models and security mechanisms used by P2P lending platforms. At the same time, the subsequent theoretical outcome of this study is the models of regional and cross-country diversification for P2P lending, just like in traditional finance. These models are also expected to contribute to the future best practices and sufficient growth of the market. However, the findings of this study should be perceived with caution and not conceived as a strong indication of certain tendencies in the market. Instead, this study just scratches the surface of the topic and opens broad room for further research. Thus, it is important to highlight several remarks related to the limitations of the current study and room for further research.

First, the impact of the pandemic on the financial sector, and the P2P lending market, has not been realized yet. For instance, the spike in withdrawals mainly occurred during March 2020 in Bondora P2P lending platform, while by April 2020, cash withdrawals mostly dropped to pre-crisis levels (Bondora, 2020). However, throughout March and June 2020, loan applications vastly surpassed available investments. Bondora also limited the loan originators and set the partial payout feature and most EU countries placed moratoriums on loan repayments. Thus, the findings of this study are largely distorted by various restrictions superimposed by third parties rather than defined by the market.

Second, as the current COVID-19–related crisis progresses into the later stage, liquidity problems experienced by households, businesses, and public sector organizations might also transform into a more severe stage. Issues related to liquidity might lead to a chain reaction of non-performing loans, insolvencies, and bankruptcies, sending the global economy into a vortex of financial and economic crises. P2P lending, as one of the risky sectors of financing, might experience a wave of defaults during 2021. This stream of defaults tends to seriously test the resilience of the industry and force platforms to reconsider their risk management models. Currently, most of the P2P platforms are revising their main tool of security against the financial hardship, i.e. "provision fund." P2P lending platforms now withhold up to 50% of investor interest income as a contribution to "provisional fund" (RateSetter, 2020). This type of extreme measures might be useful to solve short-term liquidity problems but drives away yield-hungry investors in the long term.

Third, the transformation of the financial sector that started after the Global Financial Crisis of 2007–2008 is expected to accelerate after the pandemic. The pandemic could help the transformation of "shadow banking" (banking by non-banks) with an extensive emphasis on alternative lending practices (Sindreu, 2020). The P2P lending market, as one of the prominent facets of alternative lending, might transform into the mainstream from its niche position currently held.

To sum, as the COVID-19 pandemic affected financial markets, there is a need for better understanding of the dynamics of successful P2P lending under the conditions of financial distress. By extending the modeling and findings of the current chapter, subsequent studies can concentrate on the dynamics of defaults in P2P lending under financial distress. Moreover, by concentrating on both liquidity and default risk, subsequent studies can improve current risk management models used by P2P lending platforms. P2P lending platforms, in turn, can improve their security mechanisms, such as contributions to provisional funds. In this regard, further studies might be enhanced with the models of diversification for P2P lending, just like in traditional finance, by paving the way for future best practices in the market.

Appendix

Table 13.A.1. Description of variables used in the chapter.

Variable	Description of variable	Source
Dependent variables		
LISTINGS	Number of daily listings at Bondora Secondary Market at time t (daily observations, continuous variable).	Bondora

Table 13.A.1. (*Continued*)

Variable	Description of variable	Source
PROB_SUCCESS	Probability of success at Bondora Secondary Market at time t (daily observations, continuous variable). Probability success of the listing at time t is calculated as in equation [2].	Bondora
Independent variables, pandemic indicator variables		
PANDEMIC_ DUMMY	Variable representing the COVID-19 pandemic. Dummy variable equal to 1 for the dates later than 11 March, 2020 (The date WHO declared COVID-19 as pandemic) and 0 otherwise.	World Health Organization (2020)
CASES	Variable representing the COVID-19 pandemic. Change in the number of reported daily cases of COVID-19 in country i at time t (daily observations, log values).	World Health Organization (2020), Johns Hopkins University & Medicine (2020)
DEATHS	Variable representing the COVID-19 pandemic. Change in the number of reported daily COVID-19 related deaths in country i at time t (daily observations, log values).	World Health Organization (2020), Johns Hopkins University & Medicine (2020)
Independent variables, borrower-specific variables		
INTEREST	Maximum interest rate accepted in the loan application.	Bondora
DTI	DTI score of borrower.	Bondora

(*Continued*)

Table 13.A.1. (*Continued*)

Variable	Description of variable	Source
INCOMETOTAL	Annual income of borrower. Log values.	Bondora
AMOUNT	Value of individual loan. Log values.	Bondora
LOANDURATION	Duration of loan.	Bondora
RATING	Rating of loan. Bondora Rating issued by the Rating model ranging between AA and HR (https://www.bondora.com/blog/introducing-bondora-rating/).	Bondora
AGE	Age of borrowers when signing the loan application.	Bondora
GENDER	Gender of borrower: 0-Male, 1- Woman, 2-Undefined.	Bondora
RESTRUCTURED	Dummy variable representing the restructuring of a loan. Equal to 1 if the original maturity date of the loan has been increased by more than 60 days, 0 otherwise.	Bondora
DISCOUNTRATE	The discount/mark-up set by the seller.	Bondora
PRINCIPAL_DIFF	The difference between the outstanding principal at StartDate and principal at EndDate of the listing.	Bondora
EMP_DUR	Employment time of borrower with the current employer: 0-Trial period, 1-Up to 1 year, 2-Up to 2 years, 3-Up to 3 years, 4-Up to 4 years, 5-Up to 5 years, 6-More than 5 years, 7-Retiree.	Bondora

Table 13.A.1. (*Continued*)

Variable	Description of variable	Source
EDUCATION	Education level of borrower: 1-Primary education, 2-Basic education, 3-Vocational education, 4-Secondary education, 5-Higher education.	Bondora
HOME OWNERSHIP	Home ownership type of the borrower: 1-Owner, 2-Living with parents, 3-Tenant, pre-furnished property, 4-Tenant, unfurnished property, 5-Council house, 6-Joint tenant, 7-Joint ownership, 8-Mortgage, 9-Owner with encumbrance, 10-Other.	Bondora
MARITALSTATUS	Marital status of borrower: 1-Married, 2-Cohabitant, 3-Single, 4-Divorced, 5-Widow.	Bondora
Independent variables, macroeconomic, and country-specific variables		
AAR	Annualized agreed rate by credit and other institutions in country i at time t (monthly, percentage points).	ECB Statistical Data Warehouse http://sdw.ecb.europa.eu/
ESI	The EU Economic sentiment indicator (composite measure, average = 100). Log values.	Full business and consumer survey results, European Commission https://ec.europa.eu/info/business-economy-euro/indicators-statistics/economic-databases/business-and-consumer-surveys_en

(*Continued*)

Table 13.A.1. (*Continued*)

Variable	Description of variable	Source
POP	Population of country i in year 2018. Log values	OECD (2020), Population (indicator). doi: 10.1787/d434f82b-en
INDEX	Average monthly stock market index values of country i at time t. Log values	Yahoo Finance, https://finance.yahoo.com/world-indices/

References

Agosto, A. and Giudici, P. (2020). COVID-19 contagion and digital finance. *Digital Finance*, Short Communication.

Agrawal, A.K., Catalini, C. and Goldfarb, A. (2011). The geography of crowdfunding. National Bureau of Economic Research Working Paper Series No. 16820.

Baig, A., Butt, H.A., Haroon, O. and Rizvi, S.A.R. (2020). Deaths, panic, lockdowns and US equity markets: The case of COVID-19 pandemic, SSRN 3584947.

Belleflamme, P., Omrani, N. and Peitz, M. (2015). The economics of crowdfunding platforms. *Information Economics and Policy*, **33**, 11–28.

Bessière, V., Stéphany, E. and Wirtz, P. (2020). Crowdfunding, business angels, and venture capital: An exploratory study of the concept of the funding trajectory. *Venture Capital*, **22**, 135–160.

BIS (2017). FinTech credit: Market structure, business models and financial stability implications. Bank for International Settlements and Financial Stability Board.

Bloom, D.E. and Cadarette, D. (2019). Infectious disease threats in the twenty-first century: Strengthening the global response. *Frontiers in Immunology*, **10**, 549.

Bloomberg (2018). How China's peer-to-peer lending crash is destroying lives. *Bloomberg Businessweek*. 3 October 2018.

Board, G.P.M. (2019). A world at risk: Annual report on global preparedness for health emergencies. World Health Organization, Geneva, Switzerland.

Bolt, W., De Haan, L., Hoeberichts, M., Van Oordt, M.R.C. and Swank, J. (2012). Bank profitability during recessions. *Journal of Banking & Finance*, **36**, 2552–2564.

Bondora (2020). June has most verified Estonian originations of 2020. *Bondora Blog* [Online]. Available from: https://www.bondora.com/blog/june-has-most-verified-estonian-originations-of-2020/ (Accessed July 10, 2020).

Burkett, E. (2011). A crowdfunding exemption? Online investment crowdfunding and U.S. securities regulation. *Transactions: The Tennessee Journal of Business Law*, **13**, 63–106.

Civelek, M.E. and Xiarewana, B. (2020). Effects of Covid-19 on China and the world economy: Birth pains of the post-digital ecosystem. *Journal of International Trade, Logistics and Law*, **6**, 147–157.

Cumming, D. and Hornuf, L. (2018). *The Economics of Crowdfunding. Startups, Portals and Investor Behavior* (Palgrave Macmillan, Cham).

Elnahas, A., Kim, D. and Kim, I. (2018). Natural disaster risk and corporate leverage. Available at SSRN 3123468.

Emekter, R., Tu, Y., Jirasakuldech, B. and Lu, M. (2015). Evaluating credit risk and loan performance in online Peer-to-Peer (P2P) lending. *Applied Economics*, **47**, 54–70.

Feng, Y., Fan, X. and Yoon, Y. (2015). Lenders and borrowers' strategies in online peer-to-peer lending market: An empirical analysis of ppdai.com. *Journal of Electronic Commerce Research*, **16**(3), 242.

Freedman, S. and Jin, G. (2008). Dynamic learning and selection: The early years of prosper. University of Maryland & NBER, 5–8.

Freedman, S. and Jin, G.Z. (2017). The information value of online social networks: Lessons from peer-to-peer lending. *International Journal of Industrial Organization*, **51**, 185–222.

Goodell, J.W. (2020). COVID-19 and finance: Agendas for future research. *Finance Research Letters*, **35**, July 2020, 101512.

Gros, D. (2020, 30 March, 2020). The West's COVID-19 Learning Curve. Project Syndicate. Retrieved from: https://www.nber.org/papers/w27168.

Haacker, M. (2004). The impact of HIV/AIDS on government finance and public services. In *The Macroeconomics of HIV/AIDS*, Haacker, M. (ed.), (International Monetary Fund, Washington, DC), pp. 167–181.

Haddad, V., Moreira, A. and Muir, T. (2020). When selling becomes viral: Disruptions in debt markets in the Covid-19 crisis and the Fed's response. National Bureau of Economic Research. May 2020, Working paper No. 27168, DOI 10.3386/w27168.

Hoffman, P.T., Postel-Vinay, G. and Rosenthal, J.-L. (2019). *Dark Matter Credit: The Development of Peer-to-Peer Lending and Banking in France* (Princeton University Press, Princeton, USA).

Kargar, M., Lester, B., Lindsay, D., Liu, S., Weill, P.-O. and Zúñiga, D. (2020). Corporate bond liquidity during the COVID-19 crisis. NBER Working Paper Series No. 27355.

Lagoarde-Segot, T. and Leoni, P.L. (2013). Pandemics of the poor and banking stability. *Journal of Banking & Finance*, **37**, 4574–4583.

Langreth, R., Court, E. and Cortez, M.F. (2020). Virus fatality picture is obscured by the ultimate lagging indicator. Bloomberg Prognosis. 27 June 2020.

Lee, E. and Lee, B. (2012). Herding behavior in online P2P lending: An empirical investigation. *Electronic Commerce Research and Applications*, **11**, 495–503.

Leoni, P.L. (2013). HIV/AIDS and banking stability in developing countries. *Bulletin of Economic Research*, **65**, 225–237.

Li, J., Hsu, S., Chen, Z. and Chen, Y. (2016). Risks of P2P lending platforms in China: Modeling failure using a Cox hazard model. *The Chinese Economy*, **49**, 161–172.

Lin, M., Prabhala, N.R. and Viswanathan, S. (2013). Judging borrowers by the company they keep: Friendship networks and information asymmetry in online peer-to-peer lending. *Management Science*, **59**, 17–35.

Lin, M. and Viswanathan, S. (2016). Home bias in online investments: An empirical study of an online crowdfunding market. *Management Science*, **62**, 1393–1414.

Liu, A. (2019). China P2P lending crackdown may see 70% of firms close. Bloomberg Technology. 2 January 2019.

Milne, A. and Parboteeah, P. (2016). The business models and economics of peer-to-peer lending. ECRI Research Report. European Credit Research Institute, Brussels, Belgium.

Mollick, E. (2014). The dynamics of crowdfunding: An exploratory study. *Journal of Business Venturing*, **29**, 1–16.

Morduch, J. (1999). The microfinance promise. *Journal of Economic Literature*, **37**, 1569–1614.

O'Hara, M. and Zhou, X.A. (2020). Anatomy of a liquidity crisis: Corporate bonds in the COVID-19 crisis. Available at SSRN 3615155.

Orcamoney (2017). *European P2P Lending Landscape* (ORCA Limited, Edinburg, UK).

Ozili, P.K. (2018). Impact of digital finance on financial inclusion and stability. *Borsa Istanbul Review*, **18**, 329–340.

Peckham, R. (2013). Economies of contagion: financial crisis and pandemic. *Economy and Society*, **42**(2), 226–248. Retrieved from: doi:10.1080/03085147.2012.718626

Poetz Marion, K. and Schreier, M. (2012). The value of crowdsourcing: Can users really compete with professionals in generating new product ideas? *Journal of Product Innovation Management*, **29**, 245–256.

Puro, L., Teich, J.E., Wallenius, H. and Wallenius, J. (2010). Borrower decision aid for people-to-people lending. *Decision Support Systems*, **49**, 52–60.

RateSetter (2020). RateSetter increases provision and temporarily reduces interest rates. Temporary Interest Reduction [Online]. Retrieved from https://www.ratesetter.com/blog/sp_announcement (Accessed May 4, 2020).

Rau, P.R. (2019). Law, trust, and the development of crowdfunding. *Trust, and the Development of Crowdfunding*, May 31.

ReportLinker (2020). Market impact survey - Covid-19 & looming recession. Global Peer-to-peer Lending Industry.

Santaeulalia-Llopis, R. (2008). Aggregate effects of AIDS on development. Washington University in St. Louis, Unpublished Manuscript.

Scaggs, A. (2020). Bond funds just had another week of record-setting investor withdrawals. *Barron's*. Dow Jones & Company.

Schwienbacher, A. and Larralde, B. (2010). Crowdfunding of small entrepreneurial ventures. In *The Oxford Handbook of Entrepreneurial Finance*. Edited by Douglas Cumming (Oxford University Press, Oxford, UK).

Segal, M. (2015). Peer-to-peer lending: A financing alternative for small businesses. *Issue Brief*. Office of Economic Research of the Office of Advocacy, Washington, DC.

Serrano-Cinca, C., Gutierrez-Nieto, B. and Lopez-Palacios, L. (2015). Determinants of default in P2P lending. *PLoS One*, **10**, e0139427.

Sindreu, J. (2020). Why Covid-19 Won't Stop the New Shadow Banks. *The Wall Street Journal*. 13 July 2020.

Skoufias, E. (2003). Economic crises and natural disasters: Coping strategies and policy implications. *World Development*, **31**, 1087–1102.

Tan, J., Shao, Y. and Li, W. (2013). To be different, or to be the same? An exploratory study of isomorphism in the cluster. *Journal of Business Venturing*, **28**, 83–97.

Tomberg, P. (2020a). Live Q&A with Pärtel Tomberg, CEO of Bondora. In Clannachan, M. (ed.). Bondora.

Tomberg, P. (2020, April 8, 2020). Live Q&A with Pärtel Tomberg, CEO of Bondora/Interviewer: M. Clannachan. Bondora. Interview link: https://www.youtube.com/watch?v=20bq8-bB_7g

Tomlinson, N., Foottit, I. and Doyle, M. (2016). A temporary phenomenon? Marketplace lending. An analysis of the UK market. Deloitte LLP, London.

Weill, P.-O. (2007). Leaning against the wind. *Review of Economic Studies*, **74**, 1329–1354.

Welltrado (2018). Don't let bitcoin whales eat your crypto. Welltrado White Paper.

Wildau, G. and Jia, Y. (2018). Collapse of Chinese P2P lenders sparks investor flight. *Financial Times*. July 13, 2020.

Wójcik, D. and Ioannou, S. (2020). COVID-19 and finance: Market developments so far and potential impacts on the financial sector and centres. *Tijdschrift voor economische en sociale geografie*, **111**, 387–400.

Yach, D., Stuckler, D. and Brownell, K.D. (2006). Epidemiologic and economic consequences of the global epidemics of obesity and diabetes. *Nature Medicine*, **12**, 62–66.

https://doi.org/10.1142/9781800610781_0014

Chapter 14

Equity Crowdfunding: Brave Market or Safe Haven for the Crowd During the COVID-19 Crisis?

Francesca Battaglia[*,‡], **Francesco Busato**[†,§], and **Maria Manganiello**[†,¶]

[*]*Department of Management Studies and Quantitative Methods, University of Naples Parthenope, Naples, Italy*

[†]*Department of Economic and Legal Studies, University of Naples Parthenope, Naples, Italy*

[‡]*francesca.battaglia@uniparthenope.it; francescabattaglia973@gmail.com*

[§]*francesco.busato@uniparthenope.it*

[¶]*maria.manganiello@uniparthenope.it*

Abstract

This chapter explores the impact of the COVID-19 pandemic on the Italian equity crowdfunding sector by analyzing a full dataset of 437 Italian equity crowdfunding campaigns over the period 2014–2020 and focusing on a sub-sample of 79 projects posted on the websites of platforms from January 2020 to June 2020. In detail, we investigate whether and to what extent the key drivers (i.e. *female founders*, *social capital*, and *equity offered*) that brought backers to finance a specific project before COVID-19 are the same nowadays, and which type of ventures backers are more prone to finance via equity crowdfunding in the aftermath of the crisis. We provide evidence that the strength of the effect of our key variables on the campaign's success has changed during the COVID-19

[‡]Corresponding author.

crisis. We also find that backers are more prone to finance companies with a high level of R&D expenditure and technological projects. Moreover, we point out that ventures not located in a red zone are more likely to be successfully financed by backers and that they are more willing to invest in projects launched in platforms implementing specific measures in response to COVID-19.

14.1. Introduction

New ventures face difficulties in attracting external sources to finance their initial stages of growth. Recently, as a consequence of the financial crisis, even traditional investors in start-ups, such as business angels and venture capitalists, have moved their investment activity upstream and focus more frequently on later-stage investments (Block and Sandner, 2009). In this context, equity crowdfunding is emerging as a new and alternative form of financing to the traditional funding markets, in which entrepreneurs make an open call to sell a specified amount of equity or bond like shares in a company, via an online platform, in order to attract a large group of investors (Ahlers *et al.*, 2015). As crowdfunding has the potential to foster innovation by offering new sources of capital and thereby to reduce the funding gap for innovative start-ups, it is growing at a rapid pace.

According to the 4th European Alternative Finance Benchmarking Report of the Cambridge Center for Alternative Finance (2019), in recent years, equity crowdfunding is experiencing an exponential growth in almost all European countries. Equity-based crowdfunding continued its regional growth, increasing 14.3% between 2016 and 2017. However, this growth camouflages a mixed and inconsistent dynamic on a country level among the regions. On one hand, Finland continued to experience a strong growth (76%). Its 2017 volume, €50.7 million, was a €21.9 million increase from 2016. On the other hand, while equity-based crowdfunding in Sweden raised €34.0 million in 2017, this was €12 million less than 2016, a decline of 26%. This may be explained by a combination of regulatory uncertainty and relatively high formal entry barriers for the existing regulations. Denmark's equity crowdfunding market has been limited by entry barriers like those in Sweden. Norway has only recently opened for equity-based crowdfunding, approving concessions for a few players. An equity market in Iceland has not developed yet, due to a combination of strict capital market regulations, limitations on cross-border transaction and foreign ownership, as well as a relatively small home market.

In Italy, the investment-based crowdfunding industry has been developing in a relatively rapid manner over the last few years. However, while it maintains relatively high annual growth rates, the absolute market values remain modest compared to countries like the US or the UK. To reduce this gap, the existing regulation was updated in 2017, with two main changes coming into force in 2018. The equity-based crowdfunding market has been opened to all types of small and medium-sized enterprises (SMEs), marking a critical turning point from the previous regulatory limitations. Previously, equity fundraising was only allowed for special cases of small start-ups ("innovative start-ups") and firms ("PMI innovative"), which represented a very small part of the overall Italian SME sector. These novelties have given a new impetus to the Italian industry, leading to the increase of amounts invested through crowdfunding and the development of new and innovative platforms.

Referring to the Italian context, Crowdfunding Buzz[1] shows that, in 2018, the equity crowdfunding platforms collected more than three times the amount gathered in 2017, with more than twice the number of successful campaigns. In 2019, the overall volumes were well above expectations. The Italian equity crowdfunding platforms collected €65.6 million, with an increase of 82%, compared to €36 million in 2018, for a total of 140 companies financed by 18,000 investors. Also the average amount of raised funds increased from €320,000 to €469,000. There is another extremely relevant signal related to the number of investments: in only the first half of the year 2019, there have been 9,000 investors against 9,300 in the whole of 2018. It is therefore clear that the use and trust of this new funding channel are being strengthened. As shown in Figure 14.1, if we

[1]Crowdfunding Buzz is an online magazine entirely devoted to gathering information about all forms of crowdfunding.

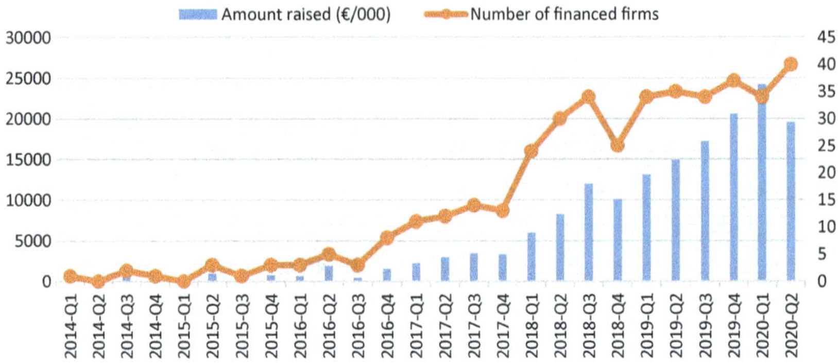

Figure 14.1. Quarterly trend of equity crowdfunding in Italy from 2014-Q1 to 2020-Q2.

Source: http://www.crowdfundingbuzz.it.

compare the first two quarters of 2020 (2020-Q1 and 2020-Q2) to the corresponding period in 2019 (2019-Q1 and 2019-Q2), the amount raised in 2020 is far greater than that of the same quarters of the previous year, highlighting a very good growth for the Italian equity crowdfunding market. Specifically, in the first quarter of 2020, the fundraising goal was 24,189 (€/000), an increase of around 84% compared to the same period in 2019 (13,078 €/000), while in the second quarter of 2020, the Italian equity crowdfunding platform collected 19,567 (€/000), with an increase of 31% compared to the second quarter of 2019. Moreover, the average amount invested by the crowd has increased significantly from €3,600 in 2019 to €5,000 in 2020.

Although the trend of the first quarter of 2020 is positive, a deeper analysis of the data referring to the month of March, the one most affected by the measures to contain the contagion from COVID-19, marked a setback. As Figure 14.1 and Table 14.1 show, while the overall collection in the first quarter of 2020 exceeded €16 million, and the number of successful campaigns is equivalent to the other two months, the amount raised in March is less than €3 million, but above all, the average funding is collapsed below €300,000 euros. In addition, the average number of investors per campaign decreased compared to the first two quarters of 2019, although the average investment increased. Obviously, the crisis has largely discouraged the "crowd" investors, but not

Table 14.1. Italian equity crowdfunding 2020-Q1 (€/000).

Month	N. firms	Amount raised	Average amount raised	Average number of investors
January	10	3.601 €	360 €	76
February	13	10.127 €	779 €	161
March	10	2.825 €	282 €	50
TOTAL Q1-2020	**33**	**16.553 €**	**502 €**	**101**

	Average investment	Max fundraising	Min fundraising
January	5,68 €	1.655 €	94 €
February	6,28 €	2.214 €	52 €
March	7,44 €	824 €	31 €
TOTAL Q1-2020	**6,45 €**	**2.214 €**	**31 €**

the ones who have the most financial resources and, therefore, they continue to invest and support the most promising young Italian companies.

Although the long-term economic effects of COVID-19 still remain to be seen, many studies are focusing on how previously identified relations have changed during the COVID-19 crisis (Conlon *et al.*, 2020; Conlon and McGee, 2020; Goodell and Goutte, 2020; Goodell and Huynh, 2020), by examining its short-term effect on financial markets (Akhtaruzzaman *et al.*, 2021; Aslam *et al.*, 2020; Zhang *et al.*, 2020; Baker *et al.*,2020a; 2020b; Ding *et al.*, 2020; Capelle-Blancard and Desroziers, 2020; Sansa, 2020), its impact across asset classes (Aloui *et al.*, 2020; Sharif *et al.*, 2020; Yarovaya *et al.*, 2020; Zhang *et al.*, 2020), and whether and to what extent the global pandemic has changed the retail investor behavior (Ortmann *et al.*, 2020 Baker *et al.*, 2020a; 2020b; Bu *et al.*, 2020; Bansal *et al.*, 2020; Papadamou *et al.*, 2020).

Another recent stream of literature explores how extreme uncertainty caused by the COVID-19 crisis events affects the levels and dynamics of entrepreneurial finance and the availability of entrepreneurial sources of finance for start-ups and SMEs (Baker *et al.*, 2020b; Brown and Rocha, 2020; Brown *et al.*, 2020; Wenzel *et al.*, 2020). This is a non-trivial issue, especially in light of the results obtained from previous studies assessing that during shocks and crisis events, the sudden increase of the uncertainty becomes highly debilitating for entrepreneurs and entrepreneurial actors, such as banks and investors (Block and Sandner, 2009; Conti *et al.*, 2019; McMullen and Shepherd, 2006; Packard *et al.*, 2017). Also policymakers have inevitably, and quite understandably, focused their attention on the immediate effects of the COVID-19 crisis on SMEs in terms of their ability to maintain staffing levels, avoid cash-flow problems, and prevent widespread bankruptcies in the wake of the lockdown (OECD, 2020a). Several studies suggest that access to bank finance becomes more problematic for innovative firms during crisis episodes such as the Global Financial Crisis (GFC) (Cowling *et al.*, 2012; Demirgüç-Kunt *et al.*, 2020; Lee *et al.*, 2015), few papers explore how these shock events influence the market for entrepreneurial sources of finance from venture capitalists and business angels and their impact on SMEs (Block and Sandner, 2009; Conti *et al.*, 2019; Hall and Lerner, 2020; Mason and Harrison, 2015), while to date there is no evidence on the role that crisis shocks play on the equity crowdfunding context.

That said, through a cross-platform analysis, spanning from January 2014 to June 2020, our chapter aims to analyze the impact of COVID-19 on the Italian equity crowdfunding context by investigating whether and to what extent the extreme uncertainty triggered by the COVID-19 crisis has changed the investor behavior toward this entrepreneurial funding channel. To the best of our knowledge, this is the first research to explore the effect of the COVID-19 pandemic on the equity crowdfunding in Italy. Our results show that, although the key drivers (i.e. *female founders*, *social capital*, and *equity offered*) that brought the crowd to finance a specific project before COVID-19 are the same, the strength of the relationship among them and the campaigns' success during the COVID-19 crisis has changed; moreover, we find that in the aftermath of the COVID-19 pandemic, investors are more prone to finance companies with a high level of

R&D expenditure and technological projects. We also provide evidence that firms not located in a red zone are more likely to be successfully financed by backers and that they are more willing to invest in projects launched in platforms implementing specific measures in response to COVID-19.

This chapter is structured as follows. Section 14.2 reviews the academic literature and specifies our research questions. Section 14.3 describes our sample and data sources, while Section 14.4 introduces the variables used in our models and presents the univariate analysis of the sample. Section 14.5 comments on our main results and Section 14.6 concludes.

14.2. Literature Review and Research Hypotheses

COVID-19 is the first global deadly pandemic after more than a century since the "Spanish Flu." The first known outbreak of COVID-19 was around the end of 2019 in China, and in less than three months, it spread across the globe, causing a huge number of infections and deaths over more than 200 countries. This outbreak has resulted in dramatic economic effects. This context of extreme uncertainty, characterized by market crashes (Akhtaruzzaman *et al.*, 2021; Aslam *et al.*, 2020; Zhang *et al.*, 2020 Baker *et al.*, 2020a; 2020b; Capelle-Blancard and Desroziers, 2020; Ding *et al.*, 2020; Sansa, 2020) also affects the availability of entrepreneurial sources of finance for start-ups and SMEs (Brown *et al.*, 2020; Brown and Rocha, 2020; Wenzel *et al.*, 2020; Baker *et al.*, 2020). Access to funding resources is crucial for entrepreneurs, especially for early-stage firms. External equity finance (i.e. venture capital and angel finance) is often not taken into consideration by entrepreneurs because of fear of losing their independence (Sapienza *et al.*, 2003). Recently, equity crowdfunding has emerged as a new opportunity of external equity finance, playing an important role in the financing of young entrepreneurial firms, and therefore policy and regulatory actions have been implemented or are being crafted to support further market growth (Ahlers *et al.*, 2015; Bruton *et al.*, 2015; Cumming *et al.*, 2019; Drover *et al.*, 2017; Vismara, 2016, 2018). As Italy was the first European country hardest hit by the COVID-19, in this setting, it would be interesting to investigate the early impact of COVID-19 on the investor's behavior toward this entrepreneurial funding channel.

Prior research focusing on the determinants of equity crowdfunding successful campaigns points out that female founders (Gorbatai and Nelson, 2015; Horvat and Papamarkou, 2017; Mohammadi and Shafi, 2017; Bapna and Ganco, 2019; Barbi and Mattioli, 2019; Battaglia *et al.*, 2021; Malaga *et al.*, 2018; McGuire, 2020), social capital (Battaglia *et al.*, 2021; Piva and Rossi-Lamastra, 2018; Polzin *et al.*, 2018; Angerer *et al.*, 2017; Lukkarinen *et al.*, 2016; Vismara, 2016; Ahlers *et al.*, 2015; Kromidha and Robson, 2016; Colombo *et al.*, 2015), and equity offered (Barbi and Mattioli, 2019; Battaglia *et al.*, 2021; Block *et al.*, 2018; Ralcheva and Roosenboom, 2020; Vismara, 2018; Hornuf and Neuenkirch 2016; Ahlers *et al.*, 2015; Busenitz *et al.*, 2005; Vismara, 2016) are the main uncontroversial key factors driving potential investors to finance equity crowdfunding projects. Our chapter is closely related to this stream of literature on the signaling theory in equity crowdfunding, by adding fresh evidence on the crowd behavior and its investment decisions during crisis periods. Several recent studies (Gorbatai and Nelson, 2015; Horvat and Papamarkou, 2017; Mohammadi and Shafi, 2017; Malaga *et al.*, 2018; Bapna and Gianco, 2019; Barbi and Mattioli, 2019; Battaglia *et al.*, 2021; McGuire, 2020) analyze the composition of the entrepreneurial team in terms of gender differences and emphasize indubitably the positive impact of women on the probability of the campaigns' success, by finding that *female founders* are more likely to lead to successful campaigns than their male counterparts.

In a similar vein, the literature on the signaling theory of equity crowdfunding highlights the paramount importance of the proponents' *social capital* of crowdfunding campaigns (Piva and Rossi-Lamastra, 2018; Polzin *et al.*, 2018; Angerer *et al.*, 2017; Lukkarinen *et al.*, 2016; Vismara, 2016; Ahlers *et al.*, 2015; Kromidha and Robson, 2016; Colombo *et al.*, 2015) as a key driver of successful fundraising, by pointing out that founders have a greater chance of reaching the funding goal in an equity crowdfunding campaign if they "possess" more social capital.[2] Moreover, the founders' social capital could reduce information asymmetries between entrepreneurs and investors, by helping proponents to find a way to signal the quality of their project in order to receive financing and to close a crowdfunding campaign successfully. Potential investors can evaluate the information on the entrepreneurs as well as their track record for previous projects posted on the platform. Under imperfect information about the quality of projects, social network may reassure investors and ingenerate information cascades (Battaglia *et al.*, 2021; Barbi and Mattioli, 2019; Block *et al.*, 2018; Piva and Rossi-Lamastra, 2018; Polzin *et al.*, 2018; Vismara, 2018; Angerer *et al.*, 2017; Lukkarinen *et al.*, 2016; Vismara, 2016; Ahlers *et al.*, 2015; Kromidha and Robson, 2016; Colombo *et al.*, 2015).

Finally, empirical evidence shows incontrovertibly that the percentage of *equity offered* by entrepreneurs is perceived by potential investors as a quality signal of the campaign. The rationale is that optimistic entrepreneurs, who are confident about the potential of their projects, retain as much equity as possible; conversely, those who are not confident in their firms are more prone to sell a higher amount of equity to investors (i.e. Barbi and Mattioli, 2019; Block *et al.*, 2018; Ralcheva and Roosenboom, 2020; Vismara, 2016; Ahlers *et al.*, 2015; Busenitz *et al.*, 2005). Backers may infer the quality of the project by observing the behavior of the founders, better and more informed about their own company than potential investors. Many authors (Barbi and Mattioli, 2019; Battaglia *et al.*, 2021; Block *et al.*, 2018; Ralcheva and Roosenboom, 2020; Vismara, 2016, 2018; Hornuf and Neuenkirch, 2016; Ahlers *et al.*, 2015; Busenitz *et al.*, 2005) show a negative relationship between the probability of a successful campaign and the percentage of equity offered.

[2]Social capital is defined by the OECD (2001) as "networks together with shared norms, values, and understandings that facilitate co-operation within or among groups." Social capital is a multidimensional concept, but we focus on its "structural" component, which is identified with social networks (Liang *et al.*, 2017; Bank of Italy, 2014; Sabatini, 2009). The existing crowdfunding literature on signaling theory (Colombo *et al.*, 2015; Mollick, 2014; Piva and Rossi-Lamastra, 2018) considers social network the most important dimension of social capital; accordingly, we use it as our proxy of social capital.

Since many studies focusing on the effect of COVID-19 in financial markets provide evidence that the global pandemic has changed the retail investors' behavior, moving them toward safer types of financial investments (i.e. Ortmann *et al.*, 2020; Baker *et al.*, 2020a,b; Bu *et al.*, 2020; Bansal *et al.*, 2020; Papadamou *et al.*, 2020), we first aim to investigate if the key drivers that brought the crowd to finance a specific project before COVID-19 are the same nowadays. Accordingly, our first research hypothesis is the following:

H1: Has the COVID-19 pandemic modified the key drivers of successful equity crowdfunding campaigns?

We believe that referring to the equity crowdfunding context, the effect of the crisis triggered by COVID-19 is not obvious, as it has caused a sudden and dramatic change in our way of living and of working (De Vos, 2020; Briscese *et al.*, 2020; Painter and Qiu, 2020 Lau, 2020; Brooks *et al.*, 2020; Coibion *et al.*, 2020). On one hand, the social distancing and lockdowns could have increased the usage of social media platforms and the time spent on surfing the Internet (OECD, 2020b[3]; World Bank, 2020[4]), and this aspect may have had a positive effect on the campaign success; on the other hand, the increasing uncertainty of the working, economic, and financial conditions (The World Bank, 2020; IMF, 2020; ECB, 2020) could have modified the investment strategies of the crowd, by increasing its risk aversion (ECB, 2020; OECD, 2020c; Baker *et al.*, 2020; Bansal *et al.*, 2019; Papadamou *et al.*, 2020). Overall, our opinion is that the redefinition of family priorities and the sudden and compulsory change in the way of living and working of people could have also modified their financial behavior. To address our first research question (H1), we analyze the signaling role of the presence of women in leadership positions, the share of equity retained by founders, and the size of their social network, on external investors by comparing the pre–COVID-19 period and the COVID-19 period (from January 2020 to June 2020).

[3]https://www.oecd.org/coronavirus/policy-responses/keeping-the-internet-up-and-running-in-times-of-crisis-4017c4c9/.

[4]https://www.worldbank.org/en/news/feature/2020/06/08/the-global-economic-outlook-during-the-covid-19-pandemic-a-changed-world.

Many authors (Hall *et al.*, 2016; Lome *et al.*, 2016) and supervisory reports (ECB, 2013) provide evidence that, during periods of international financial crises, R&D expenditures are more resilient to this economic negative downturn, and incentives for the firms to increase R&D investments have been a great and significant support to mitigate the aftermaths of the crises. Also during this period of great uncertainty, research and innovation are playing an essential role in the response to the COVID-19 outbreak (ECB, 2020). They are critical levers to ensure a sustainable and inclusive recovery, while boosting the resilience of our production sectors, the competitiveness of our economies, and the transformation of our socio-economic systems. Research and innovation actions are an essential part of the coordinated EU response to the public health and economic threat of COVID-19. Investments in innovative SMEs (including start-ups) are critical for recovery (ECB, 2020). R&D investment remains a critical driver of productivity, economic growth, and jobs and supports the EU's global competitiveness. Moreover, "The InvestEU Programme and the Recovery Package" provides support to the SMEs involved in research, innovation, and digitalization activities, by playing an important role in facilitating and accelerating access to debt and equity finance for high-growth, research- and innovation-driven SMEs and start-ups (ECB, 2020). In this setting, we are wondering if backers are more prone to invest in start-ups with a higher level of R&D expenditure and more willing to finance digital and high-tech projects. We thus propose our second hypothesis:

H2A: Are backers more prone to finance start-ups that invest more in R&D activities?

H2B: Are backers more willing to invest in digital and high-tech projects?

We specify that the two aforementioned hypotheses (H2A, H2B) deal with data referring to the pre–COVID-19 period and the COVID-19 period.

Our third and fourth research hypotheses (H3 and H4) relate only to the outbreak period, since we aim to analyze the tangible implications of the COVID-19 pandemic on the success of the equity crowdfunding campaigns. To that end we build up a sub-sample, by considering only projects launched in 2020. Since the COVID-19 pandemic has had a more severe impact on some geographical areas of Italy (i.e. Lombardy, Veneto, Piemonte, Emilia Romagna, and Marche), the so-called "red zones,"[5] where, due to the high number of deaths and infections, additional and more restrictive measures have been adopted by the Italian government (Buonanno *et al.*, 2020; Moderato *et al.*, 2020), we aim to investigate whether the probability of success of pitched projects (both in terms of total amount raised and number of investors) could be negatively related to the geographical location of ventures in the red zones. Accordingly, we formulate our third hypothesis:

H3: The geographical location of the company in a "red zone" reduces the probability of success of equity crowdfunding campaign.

In this scenario, some platforms are already implementing measures to support investors to continue to provide capital to new funding opportunities. In particular, they seek close and sometimes personal communication with their "investor base" in order to retain their confidence by providing more information on existing portfolios and on COVID-19 developments and measures. Some platforms proactively seek to reach out to new investors, others have implemented moratoria on capital repayments, where investors will only receive interest payments for the time being, while yet other platforms have waived their fees (ECN, 2020). For this reason, we aim to analyze whether the probability of the campaign's success is positively related to specific and non-conventional measures regarding COVID-19 implemented by the platforms, in addition to the standard due-diligence process (i.e. Cumming *et al.*, 2019; Rossi and Vismara, 2018) in order to reassure investors during this period of great uncertainty. Basing on this discussion, we propose our fourth hypothesis:

[5]First, at the inception of COVID-19 pandemic, the Italian Government defined a "red zone area" as a municipality where the first cases of COVID-19 were registered and with a high risk of spreading COVID-19. Later (March 1, 2020) this definition was introduced for five regions (i.e. Lombardy, Veneto, Piemonte, Emilia Romagna, and Marche) and then, (March 8, 2020) it was extended to the whole national territory. See https://www.gazzettaufficiale.it/eli/id/2020/03/08/20A01522/sg.

H4: The specific measures implemented by equity crowdfunding platforms regarding the COVID-19 crisis increase the probability of success of the campaigns.

14.3. Sample

We conduct a cross-platform analysis by investigating equity crowdfunding local platforms operating in Italy from January 2014 to June 2020. We build up a hand-collected dataset of 437 equity crowdfunding campaigns pitched on equity crowdfunding platforms active in Italy, at the date of data collection (the end of June 2020). The list of authorized Italian equity crowdfunding platforms is from the CONSOB registry. All the authorized equity crowdfunding platforms, according to the Italian regulation, are registered on this list. Our sample refers to the following 21 platforms with active campaigns: Action Crowd, Back To Work 24, Cofyp, CrowdFundMe, CrowdInvest, Ecomill, Extrafin, Forcrowd, Fundera, Idea Crowdfunding, Investi-re, Leonardo equity, Lita.co, Mamacrowd, Muum Lab, Next Equity, OpStart, Stars Up, TheBestEquity, 200Crowd, and We are starting.

All security crowdfunding platforms apply due diligence[6] on project selection. Due-diligence application is resource-demanding on platforms and cannot be fully overseen by regulators. Its application facilitates fundraising campaign success and also helps to increase the number of investors and the amount raised at the end of the campaign on a platform. Specifically, due-diligence application benefits the crowdfunding process by screening lower-quality or fraudulent projects and mitigating information asymmetries between project issuers and funders (Cumming *et al.*, 2019; Rossi and Vismara, 2018). Moreover, although all Italian equity crowdfunding platforms apply due diligence, not all of them have implemented special measures in response to COVID-19 (i.e. moratoria on capital repayments, disclosure of more information, reduction or cancellation of fees for the use

[6]Crowdfunding platform due diligence comprises background checks, site visits, credit checks, cross-checks, account monitoring, and third party proof on funding projects. It is related to legislation requirement, platform size, and type or complexity of crowdfunding campaigns (Cumming *et al.*, 2019).

Table 14.2. Italian equity crowdfunding platforms.

Platform	City	Foundation year	Registration date	Due diligence	Special measures regarding COVID-19
Action Crowd	Milan	2012	26/02/2014	YES	NO
BackToWork (ex Equinvest)	Milan	2014	14/01/2015	YES	YES
Cofyp	Macerata	2016	14/04/2016	YES	NO
CrowdFundMe	Milan	2013	30/07/2014	YES	YES
CrowdInvest Italia	Prato	2018	10/07/2018	YES	NO
Ecomill	Milan	2014	29/10/2014	YES	YES
Extrafin	Udine	2018	05/07/2018	YES	NO
Forcrowd	Milano	2019	12/06/2019	YES	NO
Fundera	Milan	2014	10/09/2014	YES	NO
Idea Crowd-funding	Rome	2017	29/11/2017	YES	NO
Investi-RE	Milan	2015	28/01/2015	YES	NO
Leonardo Equity	Florence	2018	17/04/2018	YES	NO
LITA.co Italy (ex 1001PACT. com)	Torino	2018	31/05/2018	YES	NO
Mamacrowd	Milan	2014	06/08/2014	YES	YES
Muum Lab	Lecce	2015	06/08/2014	YES	NO
Next Equity	Macerata	2014	16/07/2014	YES	YES
OpStart	Bergamo	2015	11/11/2015	YES	YES
StarsUp	Livorno	2013	18/10/2013	YES	YES
The Best Equity	Milan	2018	14/03/2018	YES	NO
Two-Hundred – 200 Crowd	Brescia	2014	18/06/2014	YES	NO
We Are Starting	Bergamo	2014	16/12/2014	YES	YES

of the platform, provision of information on government subsidies) to support and reassure potential investors. The list of the investigated platforms is reported in Table 14.2, which shows the city in which the platform is located, its foundation year, its registration date, and if it applies due diligence or has implemented specific measures to support investors during the COVID-19 period.

14.4. Variables

We gather information on equity crowdfunding campaigns from the platforms websites and from the original offering documents, where they are recorded and publicly available. We collected information on the offers (i.e. the fundraising goal, the amount raised, the equity offered, and the minimum investment allowed for each campaign) and on the founders, including their total number and their gender, as reported on the "Team" page of each campaign. Since we aim to investigate the impact of COVID-19 on the success of the projects, our dependent variable is a proxy for the campaign success. Following prior studies on the topic (Ahlers *et al.*, 2015; Colombo *et al.*, 2015; Vismara, 2016), we measure success in three different ways: (i) the (natural log of) number of investors (*number of investors*), (ii) the amount raised at the end of each campaign (*amount raised*), and (iii) success of campaign (*success*), a dichotomous variable, equal to one if the project reaches or exceeds its target capital and zero otherwise.

In order to answer our research hypotheses we build up the following variables:

(i) the dummy variable *covid* is a dummy variable, taking the value of 1 if the project was launched during the outbreak, and 0 otherwise;
(ii) the "red zones" variable (*red zones*) is a dichotomous variable equal to 1 if the project was launched by a company located in a "red zone,"[7] and 0 otherwise;
(iii) the dummy variable (*R&D*), equal to 1 if the start-up invests in R&D, and 0 otherwise;

[7]The Decree dated March 8 2020, Article 1 paragraph 1, identifies some areas in the Centre-North of Italy (in particular the whole of Lombardy and the provinces of Modena, Parma, Piacenza, Reggio-Emilia, Rimini, Pesaro and Urbino, Alessandria, Asti, Novara, Verbano-Cusio-Ossola, Vercelli, Padua, Treviso and Venice) as "red zone," by enforcing several strict limitations to their citizens.

For more information, see https://www.gazzettaufficiale.it/eli/id/2020/03/08/20A01522/sg.

(iv) the dummy variable (*tech*), which takes the value of 1 if the project belongs to the technology industry, and 0 otherwise; and

(v) the dichotomous variable (*special measures*) equal to 1 if the platforms have implemented special measures regarding COVID-19 to reassure the investors; and 0 otherwise.

We also include a set of additional control variables to account for other factors that, following previous studies, might be a relevant driver of success for equity-based crowdfunding campaigns. First, we consider the "size" of the campaign, proxied by its fundraising goal variable (*target capital*), measured as the natural logarithm of the amount that founders seek to raise using crowdfunding, in millions of euros (Block *et al.*, 2018; Mollick, 2014). Second, we include some variables to consider the perceived riskiness of the proposal. As outlined by Ahlers *et al.* (2015) and Vismara (2016), a relevant signal for investors is the amount of equity retained after an offering (*equity offered*), which is attentively set by entrepreneurs to signal the unobservable characteristics of their start-up. Entrepreneurs also have the opportunity to include in the offering document a more precise and detailed overview of the risks of the project, in order to reduce the problem of asymmetric information, so that investors will have a better basis to formulate their expectations (Epstein and Schneider, 2008). For this reason, we include a variable (*financial info*) equal to 1 if financial information about the company is available on the platform and 0 otherwise.

Another signal playing a relevant role in the setting of equity crowdfunding is the entrepreneurs' social capital. Some authors (Ahlers *et al.*, 2015; Lukkarinen *et al.*, 2016; Piva and Rossi-Lamastra, 2018; Vismara, 2016) find that a larger number of entrepreneurs' social network connections increase the probability of fundraising success. Accordingly, we record the number of connections of each founder on his (her) LinkedIn profile (*social capital*), to build up proxies of social capital. Since in equity crowdfunding, human capital plays a central role toward external investors in signaling the quality of the projects, we believe that internal corporate governance mechanisms, like the gender composition and the education level of the entrepreneurial team, are an important issue referring to that context. So, in order to take into account this feature, we first include a dummy variable related to the gender of the founders, *female founders*, equal to 1 if the founder is a woman and 0 otherwise. Moreover, we define a corporate governance dummy variable, related to the educational level of the founders, *team's education level,* equal to 1 if at least one founder has a high academic status, and 0 otherwise. Hsu (2017) shows that early-stage Internet companies whose team members hold a doctoral degree are more likely to get funded by venture capital investors. Also Backes-Gellner and Werner (2007) analyze the impact of a founder's educational signals on innovative start-ups. They find that entrepreneurs holding a university degree can more easily obtain credit. Ahlers *et al.* (2015) examine the role of education as an entrepreneurial signal for early-stage companies with a specific focus on equity crowdfunding. Many authors ((Kunz *et al.*, 2016) Vismara *et al.* 2017; Angerer *et al.*, 2017; Block *et al.*, 2018) also find that the number of comments increases the probability of the success of the campaign. Consequently, we include the variable number of comments (*number of comments*) in our regression models. Following Ralcheva and Roosenboom (2020) and Piva and Rossi-Lamastra (2018), we consider in our study the variable *patent,* a proxy of intellectual capital, equal to 1 if the start-up quotes a granted patent in an offering document; and 0 otherwise. Patents may serve as signals of the unobservable quality of equity crowdfunding campaigns. In this sense, Ralcheva and Roosenboom (2020) suggest that companies protecting their intellectual property significantly increase chances of success in equity crowdfunding. Also Piva and Rossi-Lamastra (2018) find a positive and highly significant impact of intellectual capital on crowdfunding campaigns, by confirming that patents positively affect investors' decision to fund entrepreneurs' projects. Table 14.3 reports a brief description of the variables used in our analysis.

14.4.1. *Univariate analysis*

Our sample consists of the full set of 437 campaigns conducted through the overall Italian platforms between January 2014 and June 2020. The average project in our sample raises about 135% (€241,384) of the target capital from 80 investors (Table 14.4). Some projects attracted more than 2,000 investors and raised more than three times their targets. About 77% of the Italian crowdfunding

Table 14.3. Variable definitions.

Variable name	Description
Dependent variables	
Success	Dummy variable equal to 1 for campaigns reaching or exceeding their capital, and 0 otherwise.
Amount raised (€)	The total amount raised at the end of the campaign.
Number of investors	The number of investors at the end of the campaign.
Explanatory variables	
Female founders	Dummy variable equal to 1 if the founder is a woman, and 0 otherwise.
Equity offered (%)	Percentage of equity offered by founders to external investors
Social capital	Number of proponent's LinkedIn connections.
R&D	Dummy variable equal to 1 if the firm spent resources in developing new innovative products and services.
Tech	Dummy variable equal to 1 if the company provides high technology products, and 0 otherwise.
Red zones[a]	Dummy variable equal to 1, if the project was launched by a company located in one of the following regions/ municipalities: the whole of Lombardy, Modena, Parma, Piacenza, Reggio Emilia, Rimini, Pesaro and Urbino, Alessandria, Asti, Novara, Verbano-Cusio-Ossola, Vercelli, Padua, Treviso, Venice, and 0 otherwise.
Covid	Dummy variable equal to 1 if the project has been launched during the outbreak, and 0 otherwise.
Special measures	Dummy variable equal to 1 if the platforms have implemented special measures to reassure investors during COVID-19, and 0 otherwise.
Control variables	
Financial info	Dummy variable equal to 1 if financial information on the company are available on the platform, and 0 otherwise.
Patent	Dummy variable indicating whether a start-up quotes a granted patent in an offering document. The variable equals 1 if so, and 0 otherwise.
Number of comments	Number of comments on the project page.

Table 14.3. (*Continued*)

Variable name	**Description**
Team's education level	Dummy which takes the value of 1 if there is at least one team member with an high academic status (i.e. university degree, Ph.D. or the title of Professor) within the company, and 0 otherwise.
Target capital (€)	Amount of target capital to be raised.

Note: This table shows the variables used in this study, distinguishing by dependent, explanatory, and control variables.

[a]A company is considered to be included in a red zone if the posted project starts in 2020, and if at least half of the campaign days has been extended after March 8, 2020.

Table 14.4. Descriptive statistics.

	# Observation	**Mean**	**Std. Dev.**	**Min**	**Max**
Dependent variables					
Success	437	0.771167	0.4205629	0	1
Amount raised	437	241384.5	254255.3	0	3435500
Number of investors	437	79.7	84.3231	0	2080
Explanatory variables					
Female founders	437	0.4184646	0.4502289	0	1
Equity offered	437	8.431851	7.066955	0.02	40
Social capital	437	424.9011	323.328	1	3389
R&D	437	0.7580247	0.4288091	0	1
Tech	437	0.4324943	0.4959898	0	1
Control variables					
Financial info	437	0.5860465	0.4931141	0	1
Patent	437	0.3496333	0.4774381	0	1
Number of comments	437	13.86702	18.00143	0	123
Team's education level	437	0.486513	0.382134	0	1
Target capital (€)	437	178788.2	153216.8	18000	2200000

Note: This table shows the descriptive statistics of our sample of crowdfunding campaigns launched on the Italian platforms from January 2014 to June 2020. *Amount raised* and *Target capital* are expressed in Euros. *Success, Female Founders, R&D, Tech, Red zones, Covid, Special measures, Financial info, Patent, Team's education level* are binary variables that take the value 1 if there is the presence of the qualitative attribute. *Number of investors* is expressed in absolute terms. *Social capital* is calculated as the number of the LinkedIn connections of all founders. *Number of comments* reports the number of comments on the project page expressed in absolute terms. *Equity offered* is the percentage of equity offered.

campaigns have been successful, while 23% of them have failed. The average entrepreneur in our sample has 424 LinkedIn connections, highlighting that the social connections seem to be very relevant in our sample. The average equity offered at listing is 8.43% and the average target capital is €178,788. About half of the team members (49%) have a high academic status (i.e. university degree, a Ph.D., the title of Professor), and 42% of founders are women. In our sample, less than half (35%) of firms have a patent, and about 76% of them spend resources in developing new innovative products and services. The number of the projects' comments range from 0 to 123, with an average of 13.8. Most companies (59%) provide a full disclosure of their financial information, and the 43% of them operate in the technology industry.

In order to test our third and fourth hypotheses (H3 and H4) relating to the outbreak period, we build up a sub-sample, by considering only projects launched from January 2020 to June 2020. Table 14.5 reports the descriptive statistics of our sub-sample. Looking at the summary statistics for our dependent variables, about 81% of the 79 pitches have been successful. On average, the projects of our sub-sample raise €283,624 (163%) of their target amount and attract 79 investors. About half (43%) of companies are located in a so-called "red zone," and 84% of Italian equity crowdfunding platforms have implemented special measures to reassure the investors during COVID-19. Table 14.5 shows more detailed information of our sub-sample, while Table 14.6 reports the correlation matrix of all our variables.

14.5. Empirical Analysis and Results

Consistent with prior studies (Ahlers *et al.*, 2015; Vismara, 2016), we run a negative binomial regression for the natural logarithm of the number of investors (*ln_invest*) that funded the project (Model 1). Then, following Piva and Rossi-Lamastra (2018), we run a Tobit regression for the amount of capital raised (*amount raised*) from a project at the end of the campaign (Model 2). Finally, we run a logistic regression by using a dichotomous measure of campaign success (Model 3), equal to 1 for campaigns reaching or exceeding their capital (Ahlers *et al.*, 2015; Colombo *et al.*, 2015; Vismara, 2016)

Table 14.5. Descriptive statistics of the sub-sample.

	Observation	Mean	Std. Dev.	Min	Max
Dependent variables					
Success	79	0.8101266	0.3947069	0	1
Amount raised	79	283624.5	255199.6	500	2179600
Number of investors	79	79.2	90.78323	1	505
Explanatory variables					
Female founders	79	0.3278481	0.4221243	0	1
Equity offered	79	9.755684	7.401884	0.95	32.26
Social capital	79	916	426.092	3	3826
R&D	79	0.7910488	0.4096308	0	1
Tech	79	0.4164557	0.4680649	0	1
Red zones	79	0.4303797	0.4982931	0	1
Covid	79	1	0	0	1
Special measures	79	0.835443	0.3731494	0	1
Control variables					
Financial info	79	0.7848101	0.4135799	0	1
Patent	79	0.3985075	0.4610569	0	1
Number of comments	79	9.672131	14.99858	0	64
Team's education level	79	0.4610569	0.3985075	0	1
Target capital (€)	79	173562.1	168359.4	14100	1000000

Note: This table shows the descriptive statistics of our sub-sample, referring to Italian crowdfunding campaigns from January 2020 to June 2020. *Amount raised and Target capital* are expressed in Euros. *Success, Female Founders, R&D, Tech, Red zones, Covid, Special measures, Financial info, Patent, Team's education level* are binary variables that take the value 1 if there is the presence of the qualitative attribute. *Number of investors* is expressed in absolute terms. *Social capital* is calculated as the number of the LinkedIn connections of all founders. *Number of comments* reports the number of comments on the project page expressed in absolute terms. *Equity offered* is the percentage of equity offered.

and zero otherwise. Since many our variables have large positive outliers, in all our model specifications we winsorized values at the 3rd and 97th percentiles (for a similar approach, see Ahlers *et al.*, 2015; Vismara, 2016; Vulkan *et al.*, 2016; (Piva and Rossi-Lamastra, 2018). Given that we might not have controlled for all relevant explanatory variables, in our empirical analysis, we include both year-fixed effects and platform-fixed effects, in order to remove any time-invariant heterogeneity from the focal campaign and to account for unobserved heterogeneity between the projects'

Table 14.6. Correlation matrix.

	#1	#2	#3	#4	#5	#6	#7	#8	#9	#10	#11	#12	#13	#14	#15	#16
#1 Success	1															
#2 Amount raised	0.261	1														
#3 Number of investors	0.168	0.430	1													
#4 Female founders	0.0305	0.0694	0.0186	1												
#5 Equity offered	−0.102	−0.0581	−0.0956	−0.0645	1											
#6 Social capital	0.101	0.246	0.304	0.0562	−0.0643	1										
#7 R&D	0.155	0.1477	0.249	−0.0644	−0.0280	0.0580	1									
#8 Tech	0.0837	0.146	0.0135	0.0929	−0.0392	0.0514	0.165	1								
#9 Red zones	−0.0668	−0.0730	−0.0313	0.0262	−0.0127	0.0271	0.0282	0.111	1							
#10 Covid	−0.0506	−0.0491	−0.0226	−0.0752	−0.172	0.0155	0.0384	0.117	−0.242	1						
#11 Special measures	−0.0205	−0.0176	0.0891	0.0682	−0.174	0.0200	0.129	0.0591	0.0405	0.0184	1					
#12 Financial info	0.0151	0.0350	0.0998	0.0553	−0.236	0.0667	0.157	−0.00198	0.156	0.210	0.369	1				
#13 Patent	0.0770	0.196	0.0918	0.0722	−0.0851	0.168	0.261	0.203	−0.0109	−0.0441	0.0228	0.0229	1			
#14 Number of comments	0.190	0.384	0.368	0.0562	−0.217	0.288	0.0564	0.127	−0.0581	−0.126*	0.238	0.172	0.00514	1		
#15 Team's education level	0.123	0.215	0.120	0.0499	−0.0212	0.140	0.166	0.130	0.0263	−0.113	−0.0135	−0.0564	0.183	0.0717	1	
#16 Target capital	0.244	0.120	0.201	0.121	−0.280	0.262	0.0326	0.137	0.114	0.161	−0.0408	0.0386	0.206	0.194	0.146	1

Note: The table shows the correlations between variables related to crowdfunding campaigns launched on the Italian platforms between January 2014 and June 2020.

attractiveness due to, e.g. varying degree of crowdfunding legitimacy over time or differing growth potentials between platforms. Robust standard errors are clustered at industry level. Table 14.7 shows the results of the first econometric analysis, with dependent variables measuring the crowdfunding campaign's success. Our first research question is to investigate if the key drivers that brought the crowd to finance a specific project before COVID-19 are the same nowadays.

Table 14.7. Determinants of the amount raised, number of investors, and success.

Variables	**(Model 1) Amount raised**	**(Model 2) Number of investors**	**(Model 3) Success**
Female founders	0.503^{***}	0.140^{***}	0.322^{***}
	(0.189)	(0.0211)	(0.282)
Female founders_covid	0.740^{***}	0.288^{***}	0.465^{***}
	(0.154)	(0.0382)	(0.167)
Social capital	0.000286^{***}	0.000383^{***}	0.0299^{***}
	(0.0000211)	(0.0000587)	(0.00483)
Social capital_covid	0.000722^{***}	0.000445^{***}	0.0506^{***}
	(0.0000629)	(0.0000260)	(0.00954)
Equity offered	-0.946^{***}	-0.356^{***}	-0.595^{**}
	(0.0229)	(0.0293)	(0.231)
Equity offered_covid	-0.426^{**}	-0.148^{*}	-0.423^{*}
	(0.0566)	(0.0348)	(0.210)
Financial info	0.235	0.146	0.669^{*}
	(0.738)	(0.158)	(0.210)
Patent	0.279^{***}	0.358^{**}	1.088^{**}
	(0.123)	(0.0343)	(0.341)
Team's education level	0.279^{***}	0.263^{**}	0.265^{*}
	(0.461)	(0.238)	(0.509)
Number of comments	0.0534^{***}	0.0654^{***}	0.156^{***}
	(0.00402)	(0.00749)	(0.0269)
Target capital	0.344	0.0478	1.309
	(0.150)	(0.0627)	(0.973)
Constant	5.795^{***}	2.941^{***}	16.61^{**}
	(3.383)	(0.688)	(11.01)
lnalpha		-2.011^{***}	
		(0.147)	
Observations	437	437	437

(*Continued*)

Table 14.7. (*Continued*)

Variables	(Model 1) Amount raised	(Model 2) Number of investors	(Model 3) Success
Year fixed effect	YES	YES	YES
Platform fixed effect	YES	YES	YES
Adj. R-squared	0.3615	0.1554	0.5506

Note: The table reports the coefficients of our empirical analysis with all variables winsorized at the 3rd and the 97th percentiles. Model 1 reports the coefficient of a Tobit regression of *Ln (Amount Raised)*, i.e. the natural logarithm of the amount raised by the company at the end of the campaign, on the chosen explanatory variables. Model 2 reports the coefficients of a negative binomial regression of *Number of Investors*, on the chosen explanatory variables. Model 3 reports the coefficient of a logit regression in which the dependent variable is *Success*, a binary variable that identifies the success of equity crowdfunding projects. In each analysis we include the key independent variables referring to the number of female company's founders (*female founders*), the equity offered (*equity offered*) and the social network information (*social capital*), by also analyzing the interaction between these three variables and COVID-19 (*female founders_covid, social capital_covid, equity offered_covid*) on the three dependent variables used as proxies of the campaign's success. We also include a set of control variables, such as, the financial information (*financial info*), the granted patents (*patent*), the team's academic status (*team's education level*), the number of comments on the project page (*number of comments*) and the information related to the target amount (*target capital*). The variables *equity offered, social capital, number of comments* and *target capital* are standardized. All the model specifications include year and platform fixed effects. Standard errors (in brackets) are clustered at industry level (sectors are defined by the NACE codes). ***, ** or * denote significance at the 1%, 5% and 10% levels, respectively. Robust standard errors in parentheses $^{***}p < 0.01$, $^{**}p < 0.05$, $^{*}p < 0.1$.

According to the signaling theory on equity crowdfunding focusing on the determinants of campaigns success, in our analysis we consider the main key drivers that impact on the success of an equity crowdfunding campaign, that is *female founders* (Bapna and Ganco, 2019; Barbi and Mattioli, 2019; Horvat and Papamarkou, 2017; Malaga *et al.*, 2018; McGuire, 2020), *social capital* (Ahlers *et al.*, 2015; Lukkarinen *et al.*, 2016; Piva and Rossi-Lamastra, 2018; Vismara, 2016), and the *equity offered* (Ahlers *et al.*, 2015; Vismara, 2016; Ralcheva and Roosenboom, 2020).

In order to test our first hypothesis, we build three interaction terms (*female founders_covid, social capital_covid*, and the *equity offered_covid*) between the dummy *covid* and each of our three key variables (*female founders, social capital* and the *equity offered*). We do not include the value of the *covid* variable standing alone, since its effect would be not distinguishable from other factors that are country-specific and time-variant. In Model 1, the campaign success is measured by using the amount raised; in Model 2, we use as proxy of campaign's success the (natural log of) total number of investors at the end of the campaign; while in Model 3, our dependent variable is the dummy variable *success*. Our results show that all our three key variables (*female founders, social capital*, and the *equity offered*), as well as all the coefficients of the interaction terms (*female founders_covid, social capital_covid*, and the *equity offered_covid*) are always significant at 10% confidence level or less. In detail, both *female founders* and *social capital* are strongly and positively associated with the campaign's success (always at the 1% confidence level), while the *equity offered* is negatively related to all our proxies of the success of the campaigns (at the confidence level ranging from 1% to 10%). Specifically, although all the variables are always highly significant, analyzing the regression coefficients and comparing the pre–COVID-19 period and the COVID-19 period, our results show that there has been an increase in the incidence of women and social networks on the campaign's success, but there has been a decrease in the impact of equity offered by founders. In this scenario characterized by a high level of the uncertainty over the economy, employment, finances, and relationships, *female founders* may be considered more trustworthy than men counterparty because of typical social roles, like domestic roles (e.g. mother) whose purpose is to put the goodwill of others first, that society associates to them, According to Gorbatai and Nelson (2015), women are more prone to use a highly communicative language that makes them capable of reaching a broad consensus among potential investors. Our findings are also in line with Horvat and Papamarkou (2017), Malaga *et al.* (2018), McGuire (2020), and Bapna and Gianco (2019), who show that female entrepreneurs benefit of higher success rates in fundraising.

Referring to *social capital*, our results show that it has a positive and significant effect on the campaign success (Ahlers *et al.*, 2015;

Lukkarinen *et al.*, 2016; Piva and Rossi-Lamastra, 2018; Vismara, 2016). By analyzing the coefficient of the interaction term between social capital and COVID-19 (*social capital_covid*), it can be observed that, during the lockdown, there has been an increase in the impact of social capital on the campaigns' success, in terms of the amount raised, the number of investors, and the campaign's success (at the 1% confidence level).

The most surprising result concerns the *equity offered* during the COVID-19 period. According to Ahlers *et al.* (2015), Vismara (2016), and Ralcheva and Roosenboom (2020), in all our model specifications, a larger percentage of equity offered is associated with a smaller amount of capital raised, a lower number of investors, and negatively with the campaign's success. Hence, overall, it can be argued that the amount of equity retained by founders is perceived as a quality signal of the crowdfunding campaign by external investors. By focusing on the coefficient of the interaction term *equity offered_covid*, we observe a decrease of its impact on the campaigns' success. Moreover, although the interaction term is still significant, its confidence level has greatly reduced.

To summarize, our results point out that the COVID-19 pandemic has modified the impact of key drivers of the successful equity crowdfunding campaigns.

Referring to our control variables, we find that the number of comments on the project page has a positive impact on the equity crowdfunding campaigns. In detail, in all our model specifications, the number of comments is always significant at 1%. This result is consistent with previous studies focusing on the relationship among the campaigns success probability and additional documents posted on the project page (i.e. videos, presentations, comments) useful for investors (Kunz *et al.*, 2016; Vismara *et al.* 2017; Angerer *et al.*, 2017; Block *et al.*, 2018; Piva and Rossi-Lamastra, 2018). Moreover, *patent* has a strongly positive impact both on the investor's decision to fund a project and on the amount raised, and it is also positively related to the likelihood of success (Barbi and Mattioli, 2019; Hoenig and Henkel, 2015; Piva and Rossi-Lamastra, 2018; Ralcheva and Roosenboom, 2020). Finally, consistent with the literature on the topic (Barbi and Mattioli, 2019; Piva and Rossi-Lamastra, 2018), the education level of the team members launching the campaign is positive and statistically significant at the 10% confidence level or less in all our empirical models, by playing an important role on the probability of the success of the projects.

In order to answer our second research hypotheses (H2A, H2B), we build two interaction terms, one between the dummy *covid* and the *R&D* (*R&D_covid*) and another between the variable *covid* and *tech* (*tech_covid*).

As reported in Table 14.8, findings show that *R&D* positively impacts the amount raised (Model 1, coefficient = 0.272, significant at 1%), as well as the number of investors and the campaign's success (Model 2, coefficient = 0.193; Model 3, coefficient = 1.486, both significant at 5%). Moreover, the technology firms (*tech*) also positively affect the amount raised, the number of investors (Model 1, coefficient = 0.288; Model 2, coefficient = 0.164, both significant at 5%), and the success (Model 3, coefficient = 0.386, significant at 10%). Taking a look at the coefficients of the interaction terms, it appears that by considering the COVID-19 outbreak, backers are more prone to invest in start-ups with a higher level of R&D expenditure and more willing to finance digital and high-tech projects. In detail, the coefficients of *R&D_covid* and *tech_covid* greatly increase their value (in some cases by doubling its impact on the campaign's success if compared to the pre-COVID period), and their level of significance (Model 1, coefficient = 0.964; Model 2, coefficient = 0.562, both significant at 1%; and Model 3, coefficient = 0.916, significant at 5%).

Our empirical evidence points out that the COVID-19 pandemic has modified the investors' behavior also in the equity crowdfunding context.

Italy has been the first country in Europe to put in place a nationwide lockdown to protect the population health, through the implementation of a stringent confinement approach. Since the COVID-19 epidemic has had a more severe impact on some geographical areas of Italy, the Decree dated March 8, 2020, identifies some areas in the Center-North of Italy (in particular Lombardy and the provinces of Modena, Parma, Piacenza, Reggio-Emilia, Rimini, Pesaro and Urbino, Alessandria, Asti, Novara, Verbano-Cusio-Ossola, Vercelli, Padua, Treviso, and Venice) as "red zones" by enforcing several strict limitations to their citizens. The lockdown imposed by the Italian government has put in place a number of economic policies, legal constraints, and social rules and measures to limit as much as

Table 14.8. Determinants of the amount raised, number of investors, and success.

Variables	(Model 1) Amount raised	(Model 2) Number of investors	(Model 3) Success
Female founders	0.523***	0.158***	0.584***
	(0.112)	(0.0252)	(0.296)
Female founders_covid	0.432***	0.279***	0.233**
	(0.122)	(0.0404)	(0.142)
Social capital	0.000269***	0.000630***	0.0358**
	(0.0000166)	(0.0000402)	(0.00120)
Social capital_covid	0.000969***	0.000361***	0.0773**
	(0.0000529)	(0.0000216)	(0.00249)
Equity offered	−0.326***	−0.147***	−0.773**
	(0.0211)	(0.0279)	(0.249)
Equity offered_covid	−0.159**	−0.197**	−0.893*
	(0.0541)	(0.0377)	(0.286)
R&D	0.272***	0.193**	1.486**
	(0.150)	(0.0379)	(0.545)
R&D_covid	0.301***	0.213***	1.613***
	(0.154)	(0.0324)	(0.423)
Tech	0.288**	0.164**	0.386*
	(0.0887)	(0.0133)	(0.265)
Tech_covid	0.964***	0.562***	0.916**
	(0.0855)	(0.0549)	(0.605)
Financial info	0.216*	0.1207	0.861*
	(0.700)	(0.163)	(0.243)
Patent	0.426***	0.477**	1.470**
	(0.141)	(0.0358)	(0.343)
Team's education level	0.350***	0.463*	0.416*
	(0.0734)	(0.220)	(0.337)
Number of comments	0.0539***	0.0648***	0.171***
	(0.00365)	(0.00783)	(0.0279)
Target capital	0.376	0.0460	1.482*
	(0.161)	(0.0253)	(0.836)
Constant	3.176***	2.900***	16.61**
	(1.161)	(0.654)	(12.25)
lnalpha		−1.680***	
		(0.232)	
Observations	437	437	437
Year-fixed effect	YES	YES	YES

Table 14.8. (*Continued*)

Variables	(Model 1) Amount raised	(Model 2) Number of investors	(Model 3) Success
Platform-fixed effect	YES	YES	YES
Adj. R-squared	0.3516	0.2545	0.4734

Note: The table reports the coefficients of our empirical analysis with all variables winsorized at the 3rd and the 97th percentiles. Model 1 reports the coefficient of a Tobit regression of *Ln (Amount Raised)*, i.e. the natural logarithm of the amount raised by the company at the end of the campaign, on the chosen explanatory variables. Model 2 reports the coefficients of a negative binomial regression of *Number of Investors*, on the chosen explanatory variables. Model 3 reports the coefficient of a logit regression in which the dependent variable is *Success*, a binary variable that identifies the success of equity crowdfunding projects. In each analysis we include the key independent variables referring to the number of female company's founders (*female founders*), the equity offered (*equity offered*), the social network information (*social capital*), the research and development (*R&D*), and the technology sector (*tech*), by also analyzing the interaction between these three variables and COVID-19 (*female founders_covid, social capital_covid, equity offered_covid, r&d_covid and tech_covid*) on the three dependent variables used as proxies of the campaign's success. We also include a set of control variables, such as, the financial information (*financial info*), the granted patents (*patent*), the team's academic status (*team's education level*), the number of comments on the project page (*number of comments*) and the information related to the target amount (*target capital*). The variables *equity offered*, *social capital*, *number of comments* and *target capital* are standardized. All the model specifications include year and platform fixed effects. Standard errors (in brackets) are clustered at industry level (sectors are defined by the NACE codes). ***, **, and * denote significance at the 1%, 5%, and 10% levels, respectively. Robust standard errors in parentheses $^{***}p < 0.01$, $^{**}p < 0.05$, $^{*}p < 0.1$.

possible the movement of Italian citizens and their physical contact, thus making the whole country a protected zone (Motta Zanin *et al.*, 2020).

In this scenario, our third research hypothesis aims to investigate whether the probability of success of pitched projects is related to the geographical location of the ventures (H3). To this purpose, we build the variable *red zones*, taking the value 1 if the project was launched by a company located in Lombardy or in one of the 14 nearby provinces specified on the Decree. Specifically, a company is considered to be included in a red zone if the posted project starts in 2020, and if at least half of the campaign days has been extended after March 8, 2020.

Table 14.9 reports the results of our regression models. Looking at our key independent variables, consistently with our conjectures, the geographical location of the company in a "red zone" reduces the probability of success of the campaign. It seems that the location of the firms in those municipalities severely affected by COVID-19 negatively impacts on the amount raised at the end of the campaign (Model 1, coefficient = −0.179, significant at 1%), on the number of investors (Model 2, coefficient = −0.397, significant at 1%) and on the campaign's success (Model 3, coefficient = −0.266, significant at 5%).

Table 14.9. Determinants of the amount raised, number of investors, and success.

Variables	(Model 1) Amount raised	(Model 2) Number of investors	(Model 3) Success
Female founders	0.500***	0.411***	0.610***
	(0.127)	(0.0160)	(0.287)
Social capital	0.000319***	0.000754***	0.0376**
	(0.0000777)	(0.0000317)	(0.00248)
Equity offered	−0.696***	−0.478**	−0.249**
	(0.0141)	(0.0225)	(0.217)
Red zones	−0.179***	−0.397***	−0.266**
	(0.0569)	(0.0463)	(0.277)
Financial info	0.245**	0.253	0.548*
	(0.0634)	(0.164)	(0.384)
Patent	0.683***	0.497*	0.792**
	(0.121)	(0.0340)	(0.262)
Team's education level	0.285***	0.432*	0.363**
	(0.0607)	(0.225)	(0.254)
Number of comments	0.0534***	0.0660***	0.159***
	(0.00344)	(0.00802)	(0.0289)
Target capital	0.334	0.0479	1.922*
	(0.136)	(0.0272)	(0.832)
Constant	5.767***	2.904***	14.96**
	(1.345)	(0.644)	(10.59)
lnalpha		−1.411***	
		(0.323)	
Observations	437	437	437

Table 14.9. (*Continued*)

Variables	(Model 1) Amount raised	(Model 2) Number of investors	(Model 3) Success
Year fixed effect	YES	YES	YES
Platform fixed effect	YES	YES	YES
Adj. R-squared	0.4651	0.2255	0.4123

Note: The table reports the coefficients of our empirical analysis with all variables winsorized at the 3rd and the 97th percentiles, by considering the subsample with only projects launched in 2020. Model 1 reports the coefficient of a Tobit regression of *Ln (Amount Raised)*, i.e. the natural logarithm of the amount raised by the company at the end of the campaign, on the chosen explanatory variables. Model 2 reports the coefficients of a negative binomial regression of *Number of Investors*, on the chosen explanatory variables. Model 3 reports the coefficient of a logit regression in which the dependent variable is *Success*, a binary variable that identifies the success of equity crowdfunding projects. In each analysis we include the key independent variables referring to the number of female company's founders (*female founders*), the equity offered (*equity offered*), the social network information (*social capital*) and the so-called "red zones," where, due to the high number of deaths and infections, additional and more restrictive measures have been adopted by the Italian Government (*red zones*). We also include a set of control variables, such as, the financial information (*financial info*), the granted patents (*patent*), the team's academic status (*team's education level*), the number of comments on the project page (*number of comments*), and the information related to the target amount (*target capital*). The variables *equity offered, social capital, number of comments*, and *target capital* are standardized. All the model specifications include year- and platform-fixed effects. Standard errors (in brackets) are clustered at industry level (sectors are defined by the NACE codes). ***, **, and * denote significance at the 1%, 5% and 10% levels, respectively. Robust standard errors in parentheses $^{***}p < 0.01$, $^{**}p < 0.05$, $^{*}p < 0.1$.

Moreover, many equity crowdfunding platforms have implemented specific measures referring to COVID-19 to support investors to provide capital to new funding opportunities. In detail, some platforms proactively seek to reach out to new investors, others have implemented moratoria on capital repayments, where investors will only receive interest payments for the time being, while yet other platforms have reduced or waived their fees. Moreover, many investigated platforms have also decided to implement measures that range from providing information on government support to stricter screening of projects in order to identify the businesses with the best survival chances in the current situation, while some financial services platforms have also introduced the possibility for donations.

To this purpose, we analyze whether the probability of the success of the campaign could be related to specific and non-conventional measures implemented by the platforms, in addition to the standard due diligence process (Cumming *et al.*, 2019; Rossi and Vismara, 2018). Table 14.10 shows the results of our regression analyses. The coefficient of *special measures* variable is always positive and strongly significant, thus providing support to our fourth hypothesis (H4). The adoption of specific measures by equity crowdfunding platforms for addressing the COVID-19 crisis seems to increase the probability of the campaign's success. In detail, the implementation of these

Table 14.10. Determinants of the amount raised, number of investors, and success.

Variables	(Model 1) Amount raised	(Model 2) Number of investors	(Model 3) Success
Female founders	0.790***	0.597**	0.310**
	(0.127)	(0.0160)	(0.287)
Social capital	0.000751***	0.000127***	0.0225**
	(0.0000183)	(0.0000829)	(0.00145)
Equity offered	−0.439**	−0.138**	−0.122*
	(0.0327)	(0.0126)	(0.172)
Special measures	0.214***	0.204***	0.176**
	(0.0891)	(0.0446)	(0.189)
Financial info	0.222*	0.197	0.258
	(0.0650)	(0.137)	(0.453)
Patent	0.521***	0.358*	0.591*
	(0.245)	(0.0432)	(0.151)
Team's education level	0.475***	0.418*	0.419**
	(0.135)	(0.220)	(0.130)
Number of comments	0.0414***	0.0643***	0.139**
	(0.00498)	(0.00819)	(0.0367)
Target capital	0.387	0.0333*	1.536
	(0.422)	(0.0163)	(0.874)
Constant	6.118***	2.223***	16.25*
	(1.753)	(0.398)	(11.89)
lnalpha		−1.661***	
		(0.433)	
Observations	437	437	437

Table 14.10. (*Continued*)

Variables	**(Model 1) Amount raised**	**(Model 2) Number of investors**	**(Model 3) Success**
Year fixed effect	YES	YES	YES
Platform fixed effect	YES	YES	YES
Adj. R-squared	0.5348	0.2183	0.3213

Note: The table reports the coefficients of our empirical analysis with all variables winsorized at the 3rd and the 97th percentiles, by considering the sub-sample with only projects launched in 2020. Model 1 reports the coefficient of a Tobit regression of *Ln (Amount Raised)*, i.e. the natural logarithm of the amount raised by the company at the end of the campaign, on the chosen explanatory variables. Model 2 reports the coefficients of a negative binomial regression of *Number of Investors*, on the chosen explanatory variables. Model 3 reports the coefficient of a logit regression in which the dependent variable is *Success*, a binary variable that identifies the success of equity crowdfunding projects. In each analysis we include the key independent variables referring to the number of female company's founders (*female founders*), the equity offered (*equity offered*), the social network information (*social capital*), and the special measures implemented by the platforms, in addition to the standard due diligence process, in order to reassure investors during COVID-19 (*special measures*). We also include a set of control variables, such as the financial information (*financial info*), the granted patents (*patent*), the team's academic status (*team's education level*), the number of comments on the project page (*number of comments*), and the information related to the target amount (*target capital*). The variables *equity offered*, *social capital*, *number of comments*, and *target capital* are standardized. All the model specifications include year- and platform-fixed effects. Standard errors (in brackets) are clustered at industry level (sectors are defined by the NACE codes). ***, **, and * denote significance at the 1%, 5%, and 10% levels, respectively. Robust standard errors in parentheses $^{***}p < 0.01$, $^{**}p < 0.05$, $^{*}p < 0.1$.

special measures is positively related to the amount raised at the end of the campaign, to the number of investors (Model 1, coefficient = 0.214; Model 2, coefficient = 0.204; both significant at 1%), and to the campaign's success (Model 3, coefficient = 0.176; significant at 5%).

14.6. Conclusions

A wide discussion nowadays concerns the Italian socio-economic "recovery" after the lockdown phase. Thus, assessing the impact of the COVID-19 pandemic on the investors' behavior in the equity crowdfunding context could provide crucial information on this new entrepreneurial funding channel to start-ups and SMEs, to the platforms' CEOs, and also to policymakers, giving important insights with regards to the potential opportunities to be seized in the future. In this regard, our chapter could be considered a pioneer study on how previously identified relations have changed during the COVID-19 crisis referring to the Italian equity crowdfunding sector.

By using a unique dataset of 437 successful and unsuccessful campaigns launched in Italy over the period 2014-2020, it aims to investigate whether and to what extent the key drivers (i.e. *female founders*, *social capital*, and *equity offered*) that brought backers to finance a specific project before COVID-19 are the same nowadays.

Although the long-term economic impact of crisis remains still to be seen, we provide suggestive evidence that the COVID-19 pandemic has modified the strength of the key drivers of successful campaigns (H1). By comparing the pre–COVID-19 period and the COVID-19 period, it is evident that there has been a stronger impact of *female founders* and of proponents' *social capital* on the campaign's success, and a lower impact of the *equity offered* (by founders toward external investors) on successful projects. In this period of great uncertainty triggered by the COVID-19, women in leadership positions may be considered more trustworthy than their male counterparts, and capable to obtain greater consensus among potential investors (Gorbatai and Nelson, 2015; Horvat and Papamarkou, 2017; Malaga *et al.*, 2018; McGuire, 2020 and Bapna and Gianco, 2019; Barbi and Mattioli, 2019). Regarding *social capital,* it can be observed that, during the lockdown, there has been an increase of its impact on the campaigns' success, in terms of amount raised, number of investors and successful projects.

The most surprising result concerns the *equity offered.* Although our results are consistent with prior studies on the topic (Ahlers *et al.*, 2015; Ralcheva and Roosenboom, 2020; Vismara, 2016), according to which a larger percentage of equity offered is negatively associated with the campaign's success, our findings show a strongly lower impact of the equity offered on the amount raised, on the number of investors and on the probability of campaigns' success during the COVID-19 pandemic.

Referring to our second research hypotheses (H2A and H2B), our results suggest that in the aftermath of the COVID-19 pandemic, backers are more prone to finance companies with a high level of *R&D* expenditure and technological projects (*tech*). In this regard, our opinion is that the redefinition of the family priorities imposed by the COVID-19 pandemic has probably lead to a change in the investors' behavior, both in financial markets in general and in the equity crowdfunding sector more specifically.

Moreover, we find that the COVID-19 outbreak has had a more severe impact on ventures located in the red zones (H3), where to limit the painful effect of the crisis, the Italian government has enforced several strict limitations to citizens. This result leads us to state that backers are more willing to finance ventures located in areas less affected by COVID-19, maybe for fear of losing their economic returns. As a consequence, the geographical location of the company in a "red zone" has a negative impact on the probability of successful campaigns.

The results of our fourth hypothesis (H4) confirm that, also in the equity crowdfunding sector, the COVID-19 pandemic has strongly increased the investors' risk-aversion (ECB, 2020; OECD, 2020b; Baker *et al.*, 2020a; 2020b; Papadamou *et al.*, 2020). We empirically demonstrate that backers are more prone to finance projects launched on platforms implementing special measures in response to the COVID-19 pandemic for a better protection of their investments.

Overall, our results show that equity crowdfunding could and should play a key role in supporting relevant attempts aimed at helping European businesses and the economy at large during and in the aftermath of COVID19.

The impact of COVID-19 on the Italian start-up ecosystem was truly devastating compared to what happened to "more traditional" Italian SMEs., as in their initial phase, start-ups could not gain profits. The Italian government has announced ad hoc measures to support them in adopting new work processes, speeding up digitalization, and finding new markets and innovative alternatives to traditional financial channels. Such policies aim to address urgent short-term challenges of SMEs and enable them to strengthen their post-crisis competitiveness.

With Decree-Law n. 34 dated May 19, 2020 (the "Decreto Rilancio"), the Italian government implemented several measures to support the Italian economy, hardly affected by COVID-19's emergency. At first, Italy has allocated resources to support high-tech start-ups: the endowment of the leading national subsidized finance program for innovative start-ups was increased by €100 million; €10 million was allocated to incentivize start-ups to use services by business incubators and accelerators. The thresholds for the national investor visa scheme for foreign citizens financing SMEs and start-ups were halved. Moreover, innovative start-ups are now assimilated into universities and research institutes to encourage research and development activities and cope with the COVID-19 emergency. This measure allows companies partnering with innovative start-ups to get a tax credit on the contract, according to Law n. 160 of December 27, 2019, for 150% of its amount.

In order to increase investment and economic recovery, the Italian government has provided, exclusively for individuals, a tax deduction of 50% of the amount invested in the share capital of one or more innovative start-ups or SMEs, either directly or through collective investments schemes (UCITS), which mainly invest in innovative start-ups or SMEs. The maximum deductible investment cannot exceed, in each tax period, the amount of €100,000, and each investment must be maintained for at least three years. This measure applies exclusively to innovative start-ups and SMEs registered in the Italian Business Register's respective special sections.

The Italian government has set up coordination mechanisms to monitor the outbreak and develop responses. The focus of such coordination mechanisms is on the health aspects, and the start-up aspects are explicitly considered in these coordinated efforts since regional and local governments play an essential role in the SME policy response.

References

Ahlers, G.K., Cumming, D., Günther, C. and Schweizer, D. (2015). Signaling in equity crowdfunding. *Entrepreneurship: Theory and Practice*, **39**(4), 955–980.

Akhtaruzzaman, M., Boubaker, S. and Sensoy, A. (2021). Financial contagion during COVID-19 crisis. *Finance Research Letters*, **38**, 101604. Available at SSRN: https://ssrn.com/abstract=3584898 or http://dx.doi.org/10.2139/ssrn.3584898.

Aloui, D., Goutte, S., Guesmi, K. and Hchaichi, R. (2020). COVID 19's impact on crude oil and natural gas S&P GS Indexes. Retrieved from https://papers.ssrn.com/sol3/papers.cfm?abstract_id=3587740, 29 April 2020.

Angerer, M., Brem, A., Kraus, S. and Peter, A. (2017). Start-up funding via equity crowdfunding in Germany – a qualitative analysis of success factors. *The Journal of Entrepreneurial Finance*, **19**(1), 1–34.

Aslam, F., Aziz, S., Nguyen, D.K., Mughal, K. and Khan, M. (2020). On the efficiency of foreign exchange markets in times of the COVID-19 pandemic. Available at SSRN 3632921.

Backes-Gellner, U. and Werner, A. (2007). Entrepreneurial signaling via education: A success factor in innovative start-ups. *Small Business Economics*, **29**(1–2), 173–190.

Baker, S.R., Bloom, N., Davis, S.J. and Terry, S.J. (2020). COVID-induced economic uncertainty. Nber Working Paper, No. 26983.

Baker, S.R., Farrokhnia, R.A., Meyer, S., Pagel, M. and Yannelis, C. (2020). How does household spending respond to an epidemic? Consumption during the 2020 Covid-19 pandemic. NBER Working Paper No. w26949.

Bank of Italy (2014). Social capital, economics and political economy, *Workshop and Conferences.*

Bansal, R., Croce, M.M., Liao, W. and Rosen, S. (2019). uncertainty-induced reallocations and growth. NBER Working Paper No. 26248.

Bapna, S. and Ganco, M. (2019). Gender gaps in equity crowdfunding: Evidence from a randomized field experiment. Retrieved from https://papers.ssrn.com/sol3/papers.cfm?abstract_id=3263533.

Barbi, M. and Mattioli, S. (2019). Human capital, investor trust, and equity crowdfunding. *Research in International Business and Finance*, **49**, 1–12.

Battaglia, F., Busato, F. and Manganiello, M. (2021). A cross-platform analysis of the equity crowdfunding Italian context: The role of intellectual capital. *Electronic Commerce Research*, 1–41.

Block, J., Hornuf, L. and Moritz, A. (2018). Which updates during an equity crowdfunding campaign increase crowd participation?. *Small Business Economics*, **50**(1), 3–27.

Block, J. and Sandner, P. (2009). Necessity and opportunity entrepreneurs and their duration in self-employment: Evidence from German micro data. *Journal of Industry, Competition and Trade*, **9**(2), 117–137.

Briscese, G., Lacetera, N., Macis, M. and Tonin, M. (2020). Compliance with Covid-19 social-distancing measures in Italy: The role of expectations and duration. NBER Working Paper No. w26916.

Brooks, S.K., Webster, R.K., Smith, L.E., Woodland, L., Wessely, S., Greenberg, N. and Rubin, G. J. (2020). The psychological impact of quarantine and how to reduce it: Rapid review of the evidence. *The Lancet*, **395**(10227), 912–920.

Brown, R. and Rocha, A. (2020). Entrepreneurial uncertainty during the Covid-19 crisis: Mapping the temporal dynamics of entrepreneurial finance. *Journal of Business Venturing Insights*, **14**, e00174.

Brown, R., Rocha, A. and Cowling, M. (2020). Financing entrepreneurship in times of crisis: Exploring the impact of COVID-19 on the market for entrepreneurial finance in the United Kingdom. *International Small Business Journal*, **38**(5), 380–390.

Bruton, G., Khavul, S., Siegel, D. and Wright, M. (2015). New financial alternatives in seeding entrepreneurship: Microfinance, crowdfunding, and peer–to–peer innovations. *Entrepreneurship Theory and Practice*, **39**(1), 9–26.

Bu, D., Hanspal, T., Liao, Y. and Liu, Y. (2020). Risk taking during a global crisis: Evidence from Wuhan. *Covid Economics*, **5**, 106–146.

Buonanno, P., Galletta, S. and Puca, M. (2020). Estimating the severity of COVID-19: Evidence From the Italian epicenter. Retrieved from: https://ssrn.com/abstract=3567093, 29 April 2020.

Busenitz, L.W., Fiet, J.O. and Moesel, D.D. (2005). Signaling in venture capitalist-new venture team funding decisions: Does it indicate long-term venture outcomes? *Entrepreneurship Theory and Practice*, **29**(1), 1–12.

Cambridge Center for Alternative Finance (2019). Shifting Paradigms – The 4th European Alternative Finance Benchmarking Report.

Capelle-Blancard, G. and Desroziers, A. (2020). The stock market is not the economy? Insights from the COVID-19 crisis. CEPR Covid Economics.

Coibion, O., Gorodnichenko, Y. and Weber, M. (2020). The cost of the Covid-19 crisis: Lockdowns, macroeconomic expectations, and consumer spending. NBER Working Paper No. w27141.

Colombo, M.G., Franzoni, C. and Rossi Lamastra, C. (2015). Internal social capital and the attraction of early contributions in crowdfunding. *Entrepreneurship Theory and Practice*, **39**(1), 75–100.

Conlon, T., Corbet, S. and McGee, R.J. (2020). Are cryptocurrencies a safe haven for equity markets? An international perspective from the COVID-19 pandemic. *Research in International Business and Finance*, **54**, 101248.

Conlon, T. and McGee, R. (2020). Safe haven or risky hazard? Bitcoin during the COVID-19 bear market. *Finance Research Letters*, **35**, 101607.

Conti, A., Dass, N., Di Lorenzo, F. and Graham, S.J. (2019). Venture capital investment strategies under financing constraints: Evidence from the 2008 financial crisis. *Research Policy*, **48**(3), 799–812.

Cowling, M., Liu, W. and Ledger, A. (2012). Small business financing in the UK before and during the current financial crisis. *International Small Business Journal*, **30**(7), 778–800.

Cumming, D.J., Johan, S.A. and Zhang, Y. (2019). The role of due diligence in crowdfunding platforms. *Journal of Banking & Finance*, **108**, 105661.

Demirgüç-Kunt, A., Peria, M.S.M. and Tressel, T. (2020). The global financial crisis and the capital structure of firms: Was the impact more severe among SMEs and non-listed firms? *Journal of Corporate Finance*, **60**, 101514.

De Vos, J. (2020). The effect of COVID-19 and subsequent social distancing on travel behavior. *Transportation Research Interdisciplinary Perspectives*, 100121.

Ding, W., Levine, R., Lin, C. and Xie, W. (2020). Social distancing and social capital: Why US counties respond differently to COVID-19. *Available at SSRN 3624495.*

Drover, W., Busenitz, L., Matusik, S., Townsend, D., Anglin, A. and Dushnitsky, G. (2017). A review and road map of entrepreneurial equity financing research: Venture capital, corporate venture capital, angel investment, crowdfunding, and accelerators. *Journal of Management*, **43**(6), 1820–1853.

ECB (2020). Economic and monetary developments. *Economic Bulletin.*

European Commission (2013). Effect of the economic crisis on R&D investment. Report 2013.

European Commission (2020). The role of research and innovation in support of Europe's Recovery from the COVID19 crisis. Report 2020.

ECN (2020). Early Impact of CoVid19 on the European Crowdfunding Sector. Report 2020.

Epstein, L.G. and Schneider M. (2008). Ambiguity, information quality and asset pricing. *The Journal of Finance*, **63**(1), 197–228.

Goodell, J.W. and Goutte, S., 2020, "Co-Movement of COVID-19 and Bitcoin: Evidence from Wavelet Coherence Analysis", https://papers.ssrn.com/sol3/papers.cfm?abstract_id=3597144

Goodell, J.W. and Huynh, T.L.D. (2020). Did Congress trade ahead? Considering the reaction of US industries to COVID-19. *Finance Research Letters*, Forthcoming.

Gorbatai, A.D. and Nelson, L. (2015). Gender and the language of crowdfunding. *Academy of Management Proceedings*, **1**, 15785.

Hall, B.H. and Lerner, J. (2010). The financing of R&D and innovation. In *Handbook of the Economics of Innovation from Elsevier*, Vol. 1, pp. 609–639. North-Holland.

Hall, B.H., Moncada-Paternò-Castello, P., Montresor, S. and Vezzani, A. (2016). Financing constraints, R&D investments and innovative performances: New empirical evidence at the firm level for Europe. *Economics of Innovation and New Technology*, **25**(3), 183–196.

Hoenig, D. and Henkel, J. (2015). Quality signals? The role of patents, alliances, and team experience in venture capital financing. *Research Policy*, **44**(5), 1049–1064.

Hornuf, L. and Neuenkirch, M. (2017). Pricing shares in equity crowdfunding. *Small Business Economics*, **48**(4), 795–811.

Horvat, E.A. and Papamarkou, T. (2017, September). Gender differences in equity crowdfunding. In *Proceedings of the AAAI Conference on Human Computation and Crowdsourcing*, Vol. 5, No. 1.

Hsu, D.H. (2007). Experienced entrepreneurial founders, organizational capital, and venture capital funding. *Research Policy*, **36**(5), 722–741.

International Monetary Fund (2020). World Economic Outlook report: A Crisis Like No Other, An Uncertain Recovery. June.

Kromidha, E. and Robson, P. (2016). Social identity and signalling success factors in online crowdfunding. *Entrepreneurship & Regional Development*, **28**(9–10), 605–629.

Kunz, M.M., Englisch, O., Beck, J. and Bretschneider, U. (2016). Sometimes you win, sometimes you learn—success factors in reward-based crowdfunding. *Multikonferenz Wirtschaftsinformatik* (MKWI), Ilmenau.

Lau, H., Khosrawipour, V., Kocbach, P., Mikolajczyk, A., Schubert, J., Bania, J. and Khosrawipour, T. (2020). The positive impact of lockdown in Wuhan on containing the COVID-19 outbreak in China. *Journal of Travel Medicine*, **27**(3).

Lee, N., Sameen, H. and Cowling, M. (2015). Access to finance for innovative SMEs since the financial crisis. *Research Policy*, **44**(2), 370–380.

Lome, O., Heggeseth, A.G. and Moen, Ø. (2016). The effect of R&D on performance: Do R&D-intensive firms handle a financial crisis better? *The Journal of High Technology Management Research*, **27**(1), 65–77.

Lukkarinen, A., Teich, J.E., Wallenius, H. and Wallenius, J. (2016). Success drivers of online equity crowdfunding campaigns. *Decision Support System*, **87**, 26–38.

Malaga, R., Mamonov, S. and Rosenblum, J. (2018). Gender difference in equity crowdfunding: an exploratory analysis. *International Journal of Gender and Entrepreneurship*, **10**(4), 332–343.

Mason, C.M. and Harrison, R.T. (2015). Business angel investment activity in the financial crisis: UK evidence and policy implications. *Environment and Planning C: Government and Policy*, **33**(1), 43–60.

McGuire, E. (2020). Can equity crowdfunding close the gender gap in startup finance? Available at https://papers.ssrn.com/sol3/papers.cfm?abstract_id=3233809, 29 April 2020.

McMullen, J.S. and Shepherd, D.A. (2006). Entrepreneurial action and the role of uncertainty in the theory of the entrepreneur. *Academy of Management review*, **31**(1), 132–152.

Moderato, L., Lazzeroni, D., Oppo, A., Dell'Orco, F., Moderato, P. and Presti, G. (2020). Acute stress response patterns and factors associated with impaired psychological status in health workers facing SARS-CoV-2: Saving Private Ryan. Available at SSRN: https://ssrn.com/abstract=3608122, 29 April 2020.

Mollick, E. (2014). The dynamics of crowdfunding: An exploratory study. *Journal of Business Venturing*, **29**(1), 1–16.

Mohammadi, A. and Shafi, K. (2018). Gender differences in the contribution patterns of equity-crowdfunding investors. *Small Business Economics*, **50**(2), 275–287.

Motta Zanin, G., Gentile, E., Parisi, A. and Spasiano, D. (2020). A preliminary evaluation of the public risk perception related to the COVID-19 health emergency in Italy. *International Journal of Environmental Research and Public Health*, **17**(9), 3024.

OECD (2001). *The Wellbeing of Nations: The Role of Human and Social Capital, Education and Skills*. OECD Centre for Educational Research and Innovation, Paris, France.

OECD (2020a). Coronavirus (COVID-19): SME policy responses. 15 July.

OECD (2020b). Policy responses to Coronavirus (COVID-19): Keeping the Internet up and running in times of crisis. 4 May.

OECD (2020c). Digital innovation and inclusiveness. 27 July.

Ortmann, R., Pelster, M. and Wengerek, S.T. (2020). COVID-19 and investor behavior. Available at SSRN 3589443, 29 April 2020.

Packard, M.D., Clark, B.B. and Klein, P.G. (2017). Uncertainty types and transitions in the entrepreneurial process. *Organization Science*, **28**(5), 840–856.

Painter, M. and Qiu, T. (2020). Political beliefs affect compliance with Covid-19 social distancing orders. Available at SSRN 3569098, 29 April 2020.

Papadamou, S., Fassas, A., Kenourgios, D. and Dimitriou, D. (2020). Direct and indirect effects of COVID-19 pandemic on implied stock market volatility: Evidence from panel data analysis. Munich Personal RePEc Archive.

Piva, E. and Rossi-Lamastra, C. (2018). Human capital signals and entrepreneurs' success in equity crowdfunding. *Small Business Economics*, **51**(3), 667–686.

Polzin, F., Toxopeus, H. and Stam, E. (2018). The wisdom of the crowd in funding: Information heterogeneity and social networks of crowdfunders. *Small Business Economics*, **50**(2), 251–273.

Ralcheva, A. and Roosenboom, P. (2020). Forecasting success in equity crowdfunding. *Small Business Economics*, **55**(1), 39–56.

Rossi, A. and Vismara, S. (2018). What do crowdfunding platforms do? A comparison between investment-based platforms in Europe. *Eurasian Business Review*, **8**(1), 93–118.

Sabatini, F. (2009). Social capital as social networks: A new framework for measurement and an empirical analysis of its determinants and consequences. *The Journal of Socio-Economics*, **38**(3), 429–442.

Sansa, N.A. (2020). The impact of the COVID-19 on the financial markets: Evidence from China and USA. *Electronic Research Journal of Social Sciences and Humanities*, **2**.

Sapienza, H.J., Korsgaard, M.A. and Forbes, D.P. (2003). The self-determination motive and entrepreneurs' choice of financing. Katz, J.A. and Shepherd, D.A. (ed.) *Cognitive Approaches to Entrepreneurship Research (Advances in Entrepreneurship, Firm Emergence and Growth, Vol. 6)*, Emerald Group Publishing Limited, Bingley, pp. 105–138.

Sharif, A., Aloui, C. and Yarovaya, L. (2020). COVID-19 pandemic, oil prices, stock market, geopolitical risk and policy uncertainty nexus in the US economy: Fresh evidence from the wavelet-based approach. *International Review of Financial Analysis*, **70**, 101496.

The World Bank (2020). The global economic outlook during the COVID-19 pandemic: A changed world. 8 June.

Vismara, S. (2016). Equity retention and social network theory in equity crowdfunding. *Small Business Economics*, **46**(4), 579–590.

Vismara, S. (2018). Information cascades among investors in equity crowdfunding. *Entrepreneurship Theory and Practice*, **42**(3), 467–497.

Vulkan, N., Astebro, T. and Sierra Fernandez, M. (2015). Equity crowdfunding: A new phenomena. *Journal of Business Venturing Insights*, **5**, 37–49.

Wenzel, M., Stanske, S. and Lieberman, M.B. (2020). Strategic responses to crisis. *Strategic Management Journal*, **41**(7/18).

Yarovaya, L., Matkovskyy, R. and Jalan, A. (2020). The effects of a 'Black Swan' event (COVID-19) on herding behavior in cryptocurrency markets: Evidence from cryptocurrency USD, EUR, JPY and KRW Markets. Available at https://papers.ssrn.com/sol3/papers.cfm?abstract_id=3586511.

Zhang, D., Hu, M. and Ji, Q. (2020). Financial markets under the global pandemic of COVID-19. *Finance Research Letters*, **36**, 101528.

https://doi.org/10.1142/9781800610781_0015

Chapter 15

The Nexus Between Oil and Gold Prices During the COVID-19 Pandemic

Saroja Selvanathan* **and Eliyathamby A. Selvanathan**†

Economics and Business Statistics Discipline,
Griffith Business School,
Griffith University, Nathan,
170 Kessels Road, Nathan, Queensland 6111, Australia

**s.selvanathan@griffith.edu.au*
†e.selvanathan@griffith.edu.au

Abstract

Oil prices play a major role in most countries' sustainable economic development. The fluctuation in oil prices significantly affects the economies of both developed and developing countries that depend heavily on oil imports. In uncertain times such as COVID-19, both governments and individual investors consider gold as a safe investment option. Using daily data, we empirically investigate the impact of COVID-19 on oil and gold prices. Our results reveal that the number of COVID-19 cases and deaths play a significant role in influencing the prices of oil and gold. In the long run, the impact on oil prices is "U" shaped while that on gold prices is "inverted U" shaped. In contrast to the pre–COVID-19 period, oil and gold prices both positively and significantly impacted each other during COVID-19, and the uncertainty during COVID-19 has a significant negative impact on both prices. During COVID-19, both economic uncertainty and world exchange rate increased the prices of oil

†Corresponding author.

and gold while the impact of volatility is the opposite. The above findings will also have practical implications for monetary policy with respect to inflation targeting. As the rise in oil price impacts heavily on the cost of production of goods and services for oil-importing economies, this would result in increased inflation. With no end to the COVID-19 pandemic at the time of writing, our findings will help government policymakers to devise appropriate policies to achieve sustainable development of their economies and investors to design their optimum portfolios.

15.1. Introduction

The coronavirus disease known as the COVID-19 pandemic was originally identified in the Wuhan Province in China in late December 2019. Since then, within 5 months as on May 8, 2020, this pandemic has spread at an alarming rate to more than 200 countries, infected more than 5.5 million people worldwide and resulted in more than 350,000 deaths and in the next 7 months, as on December 18, the virus has spread to more than 220 countries, infected well over 75 million people worldwide, and the death toll has reached more than 1.6 million Alarmingly, in the next 7 months, as of July 1, 2021, the number of infections have reached nearly 183 million people worldwide with the COVID-19 related death toll nearing 4 million.[1] The unimaginable shock inflicted by the COVID-19 pandemic has crippled the global economy and stagnated every stage of development globally (see Zimmermann *et al.*, 2020). It has created panic, fear, and uncertainty across the globe and has severely impacted people's health and livelihood, household operations, nations' economies, financial markets, and commodity markets (e.g. see Barro *et al.*, 2020; Bendavid and Bhattacharya, 2020; Chaney and Morath, 2020; Fauci *et al.*, 2020). While COVID-19 has not left many countries untouched, the number of cases and deaths differ vastly between countries based on the variations in response to the pandemic initiated by each country. The spread of the virus has not discriminated between developed or developing countries, or their geographical location. Some countries put their health interest ahead of their economies and have been able to manage to control the spread of the virus successfully for the time being (e.g. Australia and

[1] https://www.worldometers.info/coronavirus.

New Zealand). However, whether this success will continue when the economies reopen for normal business is not known. Some countries that relaxed their COVID-19–related restrictions (e.g. Singapore, South Korea, and Japan) have already reported that a second wave of COVID-19 cases are emerging. Also, the situation which arose in Victoria, Australia, in July 2020, when restrictions were relaxed and the Australian economy re-opened, is a good example to show how quickly things can go wrong and a second wave of the pandemic can commence. Even though developed countries, compared to developing or less developed countries, have the required resources and medical facilities to treat COVID-19 patients, it has not been easy to bring the situation under control (e.g. Italy, UK, and the US). On the other hand, many developing countries, such as Bangladesh, India, and Sri Lanka, are using lockdowns as the only means to control the spread of the virus. The lockdowns have severely impacted tourism, remittances, and export-related activities, which are the major source of income in most of the developing countries. Even though many of the developing countries were making good progress in improving the status of their economy and their living standards during the pre–COVID-19 period, currently the lockdown measures are crippling their economies. Coupled with their already existing poverty and lack of proper healthcare, the road to recovery for the developing countries seems to be a long stretch.

Crude oil plays a significant role in every economy and is one of the most commonly traded commodities in the world (Regnier, 2007). For the sustainable development of an economy, knowing the price movement of crude oil is crucial, especially in the COVID-19 environment. This is important to both developed and developing countries, which are heavily dependent on either imported crude oil for their development activities or crude oil exports for their economic development.

Among the precious metals, gold is considered to be a safer and less risky investment commodity by gold producers, investors, and gold traders in the financial markets. Based on the view that gold is considered to be a good buffer in any risky environment, investors try to increase their gold investment stocks when there is uncertainty in the world. Recognising the impact of gold prices on the price of crude oil, most central banks around the world also watch the movement of oil and gold prices. Investors in the financial markets always move their investments between oil and gold to diversify their portfolios (see Jain and Biswal, 2016; Sari *et al.*, 2010). The co-movement of the oil and gold prices have major implications on the global financial markets as well as local and global economies due to their huge tradability and high level of liquidity. Acknowledging the economic impact of price movements in these commodities, extensive research has been undertaken to analyse the movement of oil prices pre–COVID-19 (e.g. see Abhyankar *et al.*, 2013; Aloui *et al.*, 2016; Fattouh , 2010; Hailemariam *et al.*, 2019) and gold prices (e.g. see Baur and McDermott, 2010; Cai *et al.*, 2001) individually as well as the relationship between the oil price and gold price collectively (e.g. see Beckmann and Czudaj, 2013; Bildirici and Turkmen, 2015; Kumar, 2017; Le and Chang, 2012; Lee *et al.*, 2012; Malliaris and Malliaris, 2013; Reboredo and Ugolini, 2016; Tiwari and Sahadudheen, 2015; Yaya *et al.*, 2016). Other researchers have investigated the prices of oil and gold in relation to other variables such as stock markets (Miyazaki and Hamori, 2013; Baur and Lucey, 2010), US dollar (Azarl, 2015; Bonitsis and Rezvani, 2010; Zagaglia and Marzo, 2013) and global risk/uncertainty (Kang *et al.*, 2017; Sari *et al.*, 2011; Van Robays, 2016).

Le and Chang (2012) investigated the dynamic impact of oil price fluctuations on gold market returns using monthly data from May 1994 to April 2011 using a structural vector autoregressive approach. They reported that oil price shocks appear to have a significant positive impact on real gold returns contemporaneously. They concluded that observing oil price fluctuations can help predict movements in gold prices and such findings would help the monetary authorities and policymakers in monitoring the price movements of major commodities as well as help the investors and managers in optimizing their portfolios. Kumar (2017) considered the causal relationship between crude oil and gold prices and found strong evidence of bidirectional causal relationship between oil and gold prices. They also reported that positive shock in oil prices has a more pronounced effect than negative shock on gold prices. Another study by Bildirici and Turkmen (2015) analyzed the causality between the prices of oil and precious metals, including gold, and concluded bidirectional causality between oil and gold prices. Šimáková (2011) analyzed the relationship between oil and gold prices using various econometric techniques such as Granger causality and Johansen cointegration and found a long-term relationship between oil and gold prices.

Given the importance of oil and gold for a number of economies worldwide, understanding the relationship between oil and gold price movements is crucial for meaningful economic development. In addition, when there is turmoil in the economies of the world due to unexpected events like the Global Financial Crisis (GFC) or the COVID-19 pandemic, such analysis is crucial to understand and measure the overall impact of these events. A number of studies have appeared in the literature recently analysing the movement of oil and gold prices during the COVID-19 period. Using VARMA-GARGH approach together with data for the period January 2016 to August 2020 (including the COVID-19 period) Salisu *et al.* (2020a; 2020b) assessed the role of gold as a safe haven or hedge against crude oil price risks. They found that gold is a significant safe haven against oil price risks. Another study by Mensi *et al.* (2020) examined the impact of COVID-19 on the multifractality of the oil and gold prices based on upward and downward trends by applying the asymmetric multifractal detrended fluctuation analysis. They found that, before the COVID-19 pandemic, the gold (oil) market was more inefficient during downward (upward) trends. During the COVID-19 pandemic period, the gold (oil) market was more inefficient during upward (downward) trends. Oil and gold markets have been inefficient, particularly during the pandemic. On the safe haven property of gold, another study by Dutta *et al.* (2020) empirically investigated the time-varying correlations between oil and gold markets and examined and concluded that gold is a safe haven asset for the international crude oil markets during the COVID-19 period. Another more recent study by Adekoya *et al.* (2020) investigated how COVID-19 upturns the hedging potential of gold against oil and stock market risks using threshold regression and Markov-regime switching models. Contrary to most of the previous studies, Adekoya *et al.* found that market risks associated with global oil and stock markets can be effectively hedged by gold during the COVID-19 pandemic period. The paper by Gharib *et al.* (2020) investigated the causal relationship between crude oil prices and gold spot prices and assessed the impact of COVID-19 on the two prices. The study found a bilateral contagion effect of bubbles in oil and gold markets during the COVID-19 pandemic.

In the context of the economic disruption caused by the COVID-19 pandemic, the importance of further research into the price movements of these two commodities, which subsequently impact on the sustainable economic development of many countries, has intensified. Understanding the movements of oil and gold prices during the current COVID-19 pandemic would help financial market analysts and economic policymakers to design appropriate policies for the post–COVID-19 recovery phase. Since crude oil and gold markets are vulnerable to unexpected events such as the COVID-19 pandemic, a scientific analysis on the movement of oil and gold prices and the co-movement of their prices are of crucial importance to many parties who trade these commodities. This study aims to present an econometric analysis on the price movements of oil and gold in the current and pre–COVID-19 environment. This study differs from other recent oil–gold prices studies discussed earlier as we model the relationship between oil and gold prices by taking into account a number of other variables relevant to the current COVID-19 environment, such as the number of COVID-19 cases as well as deaths, economic policy uncertainty, volatility, and exchange rates.

Using daily data, in this study, we empirically investigate the impact of COVID-19 on oil and gold prices. Our results reveal that the number of COVID-19 cases and deaths play a significant role in influencing the prices of oil and gold. In the long run, the impact on oil prices is "U" shaped while that on gold prices is "inverted U" shaped. In contrast to the pre–COVID-19 period, oil and gold prices both positively and significantly impacted on each other during COVID-19, and the uncertainty during COVID-19 has a significant negative impact on both prices. During COVID-19, both economic uncertainty and world exchange rate increased the price of oil and gold while the impact of volatility is the opposite.

The organization of the chapter is as follows. In Section 15.2, we present the data sources and a preliminary analysis of the data. In Section 15.3, we present an econometric analysis on the price relationship between oil and gold for the pre–COVID-19 and COVID-19 impacted periods. In Section 15.4, we present concluding comments in the form of policy implications.

15.2. Data Source and Preliminary Data Analysis

Daily data for the variables crude oil prices (US$ per barrel) and gold prices (US$ per ounce), Global Economic Policy Uncertainty (GEPU) index, and Volatility index (VIX) for the period January 1,

1986, to May 8, 2020, and world total COVID-19–related cases and deaths for the period January 1, 2020, to May 8, 2020, are obtained from various sources. Crude oil price data are from FRED, Economic Research, Federal Reserve Bank of St Louis[2] and gold price data are from the World Gold Council.[3] Data for GEPU index are from the Policy Uncertainty website,[4] Baker *et al.* (2016), and Davis (2016), and the VIX data are from the CBOE VIX Index Historical Data website.[5] The value of the World Average Currencies Exchange Rate in US$ (WAEX) are downloaded from Economic Research, Federal Reserve Bank, St Louis website. Data for COVID-19–related deaths and confirmed cases are obtained from the website "Our World In Data."[6]

Figure 15.1 plots the daily oil prices and gold prices for the period January 1, 1986, to May 8, 2020. As can be seen, both the oil and gold prices move in a similar upward trend, with strong fluctuations and deviations during uncertain periods, such as the 2007–2009 GFC, the 2012–2014 Eurozone crisis, and the recent COVID-19 pandemic period (since December 2019). Around 2006, the oil prices started to increase at a higher rate compared to gold prices; however, with the onset of the GFC, the oil prices fell sharply to its lowest. Since then the price of oil has been very volatile but has been generally increasing. Gold price in general has had a steady increase until 2012, then a decreasing trend until 2016, but is steadily increasing after that. During the current COVID-19 pandemic period, the gold price has been generally increasing while that of oil is on the decline. The fall in oil prices commenced toward the end of 2019 due to the COVID-19 uncertainty, resulting in an oversupply of oil by some oil-producing countries, while more recent falls have been attributed to lack of demand due to COVID-19 lockdown of businesses and industries as well as the implementation of travel restrictions by many countries.

Figure 15.2 plots the oil price against gold price. As can be seen, a generally positive relationship exists between the two prices. Figure 15.3 presents the oil and gold prices for the period July 1,

[2]https://fred.stlouisfed.org/tags/series?t=oil.

[3]https://www.gold.org/goldhub/data/gold-prices.

[4]www.PolicyUncertainty.com.

[5]http://www.cboe.com/products/vix-index-volatility/vix-options-and-futures/vix-index/vix-historical-data.

[6]https://ourworldindata.org/coronavirus-source-data.

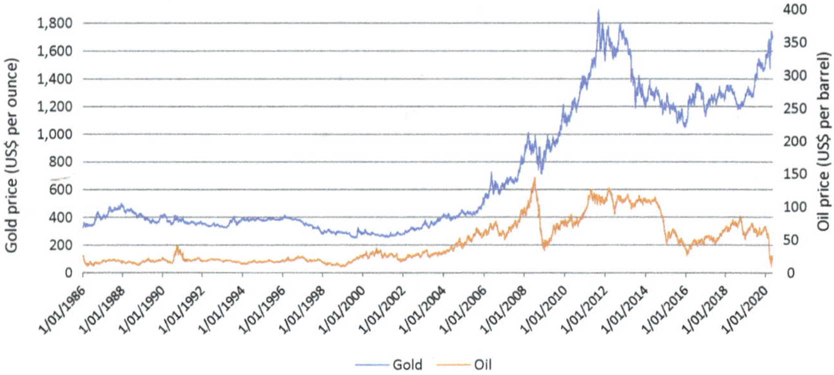

Figure 15.1. Daily gold price and oil price, Jan 1986–May 2020.

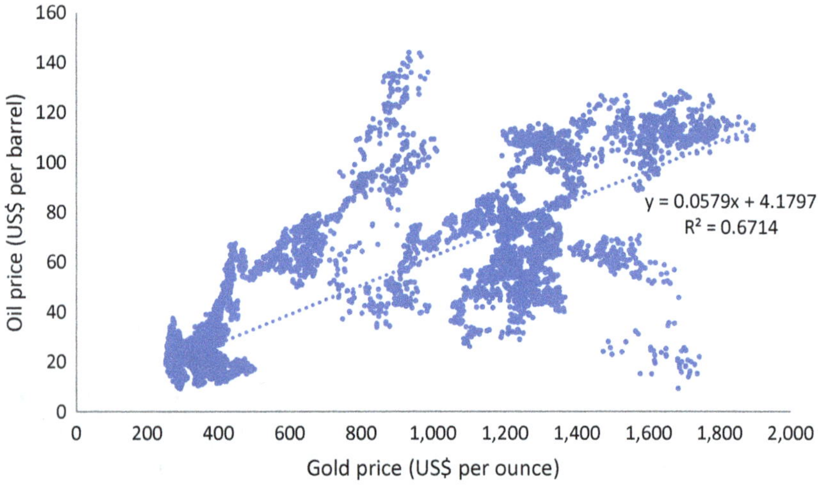

Figure 15.2. Daily oil price vs. daily gold price, Jan 1986–May 2020.

2019, to May 8, 2020, which includes a six-month time period of pre-COVID-19 conditions (July 1, 2019–December 31, 2019) and about five months of active COVID-19 conditions (January 1, 2020–May 8, 2020). Figure 15.3, clearly shows that during the pre-COVID-19 period, both prices moved reasonably in tandem. With the onset of COVID-19, the price of gold continued to increase but experienced two sudden drops: first during late Feb–early March when Italy reported a huge number of deaths following which the price

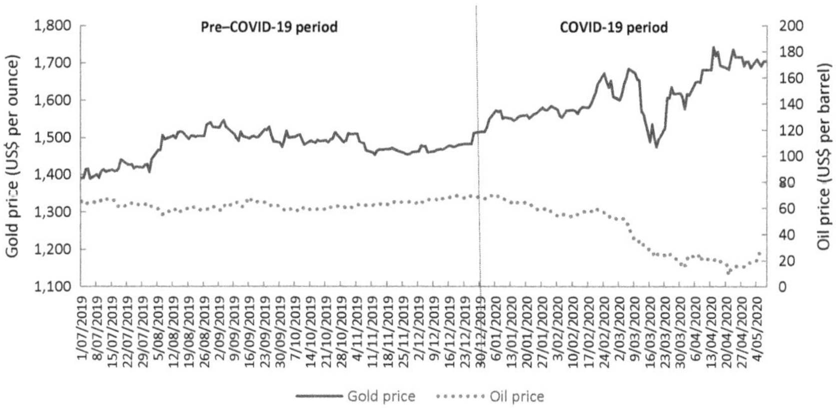

Figure 15.3. Daily gold and oil prices, pre- and during COVID-19, July 1, 2019–May 4, 2020.

recovered and continued to increase, and the second during mid-March 2020 at around the time that the UK and the US reported a sudden increase in the number of deaths. The price of gold is shown to have subsequently strengthened and continues on an increasing trend. In contrast, the oil price continued its declining path from the beginning of 2020 and from the beginning of May, as the easing of COVID-19–related restrictions commenced in some countries, the oil price is again on a slightly increasing path.

Next we consider the spread of the COVID-19 pandemic in terms of the number of cases and the number of deaths reported around the world. Figure 15.4 plots the total global COVID-19 confirmed cases and the number of deaths during the pandemic period January 1, 2020–May 8, 2020. Figure 15.5 plots the total COVID-19 cases and related deaths and the price of oil, and Figure 15.6 presents the same graph for gold price. As can be seen from Figure 15.5, the price of oil has been falling since the start of the pandemic in January 2020, while the number of COVID-19 cases and related deaths are on the increase. However, oil price resumed its upward trend in May even though the number of cases and deaths were still on the increase, probably due to expectation of increasing demand with the relaxation of lockdown restrictions in many countries. As can be seen from Figure 15.6, the price of gold, after a fall in March 2020 due to the pandemic shock, has been generally increasing during the

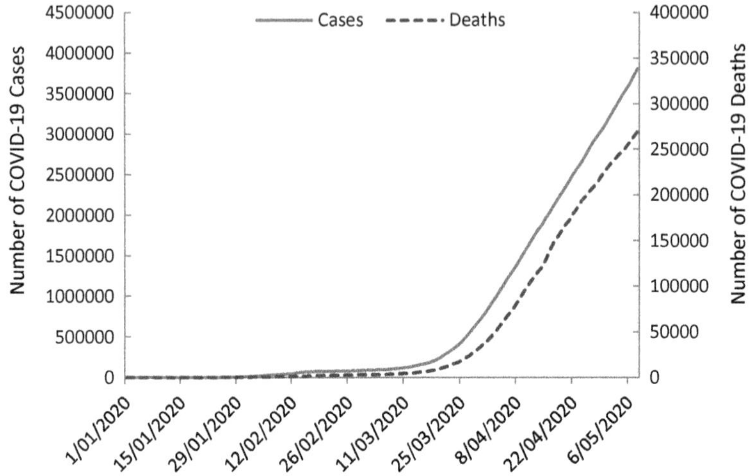

Figure 15.4. COVID-19 cases and deaths, January 1, 2020–May 8, 2020.

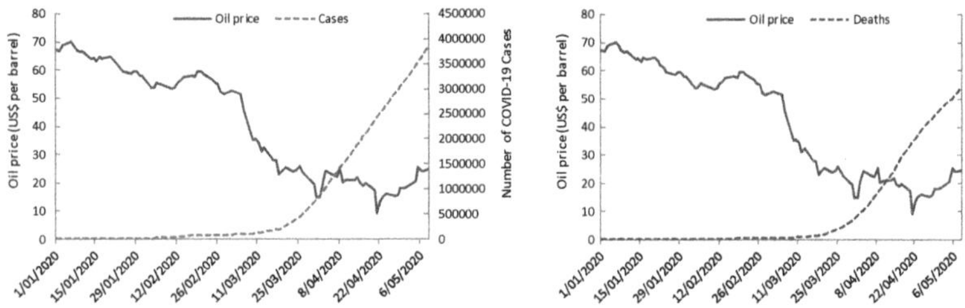

Figure 15.5. Oil price and COVID-19 cases and deaths, January 1, 2020–May 8, 2020.

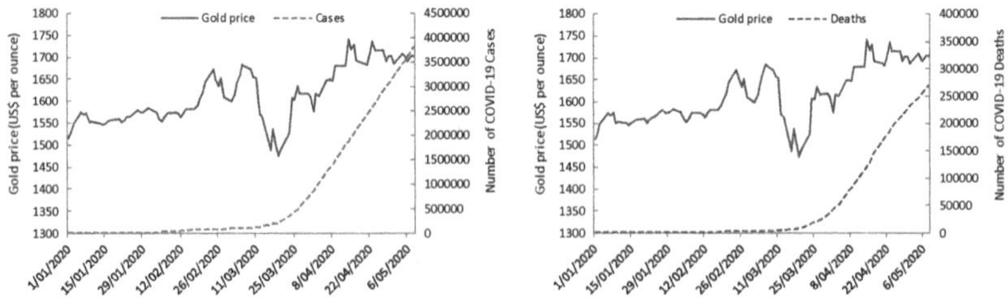

Figure 15.6. Gold price and COVID-19 cases and deaths, January 1, 2020–May 8, 2020.

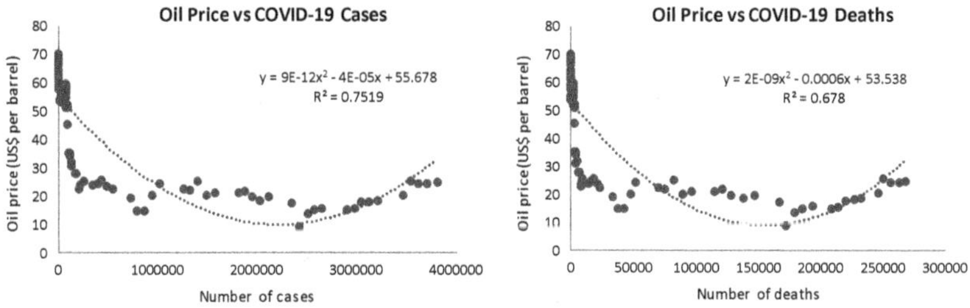

Figure 15.7. Oil price vs. COVID-19 cases and deaths, January 1, 2020–May 8, 2020.

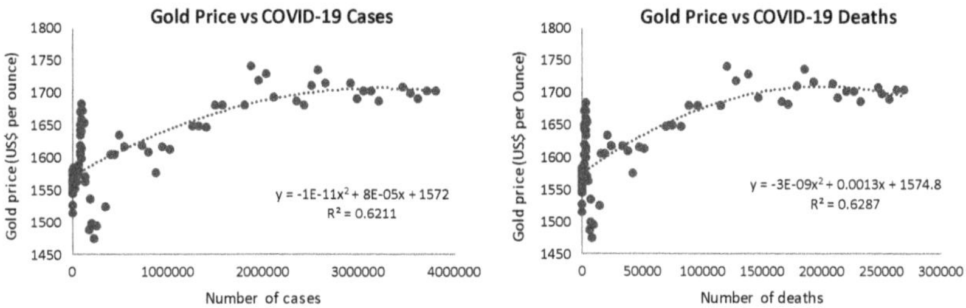

Figure 15.8. Gold price vs. COVID-19 cases and deaths, January 1, 2020–May 8, 2020.

COVID-19 period while increasing numbers of COVID-19 cases and related deaths were being reported daily.

Figures 15.7–15.8 present the oil price and gold price individually against the number of global COVID-19 cases and related deaths in the form of scatter plots. The scatter diagrams in Figure 15.7 indicate a second-order polynomial relationship between oil price and the number of COVID-19 cases or related deaths. As can be seen, when the number of COVID-19 cases or the number of related deaths increases, oil price declines up to a certain point and then starts to increase. On the other hand, gold price has increased with increasing number of COVID-19 cases or related deaths. The opposite behaviour of the oil and gold prices shows that, when there is uncertainty or shock in the world, oil prices are much more volatile compared to gold prices. The uncertainty created due to the pandemic encouraged oil suppliers to flood the market with the intent of making more revenue in the short term. However, demand for oil fell suddenly due to the global introduction of COVID-19 lockdowns, which resulted in reduced travel and production activity, and prices correspondingly fell sharply, reflecting the diminished demand. Since April 2020, a number of countries have started to relax their lockdown restrictions, leading to more demand for oil, and hence oil price is on the rise again. With gold (see Figure 15.8), since the short-term supply is limited, when the stock market started to fall due to the pandemic, there was a rush to buy more gold as it is considered a safe investment in uncertain situations and the price of gold continued to increase for a while and then stabilized.

Table 15.1 presents a number of summary statistics of the oil price, gold price, and other variables for the sample period July 1, 2019–May 8, 2020, which can be divided into two sub-periods, pre–COVID-19 period (July 1, 2019–December 31, 2019) and COVID-19 period (January 1, 2020–May 8, 2020). As can be seen, there is a significant difference in the oil price and gold price before and during the COVID-19 period. The average oil price (per barrel) has fallen from US$62.65 to US$41.21 (a fall of around 34.2%) while the average gold price (per ounce) has increased from US$1,477.24 to US$1,613.21 (an increase of 9.2%). There is also a noticeable increase in the variability of oil price, measured by the Standard Deviation (SD) and the Coefficient of Variation (CV) of the prices (from SD = US$3.28 to US$19.39 and CV = 5.2% to 47.1%) and gold price (from SD = US$37.18 to US$65.04 and CV = 2.5% to 4%). The VIX has more than doubled during the COVID-19 period (CV has increased from 18.0% to 57.8%) compared to the pre–COVID-19 period, and the GEPU index has also increased by 10% (CV has increased from 8% to 22.3%). The WAEX has remained more or less the same during pre–COVID-19 and the active COVID-19 periods. The oil prices were slightly positively skewed during the pre–COVID-19 period but has become approximately symmetric during COVID-19. On the other hand, gold prices were negatively skewed during the pre–COVID-19 period and has become positively skewed during COVID-19.

15.3. Methodology and Model Estimation Results

The main aim of this study is to analyse the interrelationship between oil price and gold price and other related variables. The chosen method for such analysis is the AutoRegressive Distributed

Table 15.1. Summary statistics for the variables, pre–COVID-19 and COVID-19 periods.

Variable	Mean	Median	Std dev	CV	Min	Max	Range	Excess Kurtosis	Skewness	JB test statistic	p-value	Obs
Oil price												
Pre-COVID-19	62.65	62.47	3.28	5.23	69.70	55.03	14.67	2.39	0.24	3.35	0.187	132
COVID-19	41.21	51.29	19.39	47.07	70.25	9.12	61.13	1.32	−0.05	10.96	0.004	93
Gold price												
Pre-COVID-19	1477.24	1485.20	37.18	2.52	1546.10	1388.65	157.45	2.71	−0.66	9.93	0.007	132
COVID-19	1613.21	1605.45	65.04	4.03	1741.90	1474.25	267.65	2.05	0.16	3.91	0.142	93
VIX												
Pre-COVID-19	14.95	14.01	2.69	17.98	24.59	11.54	13.05	3.48	1.07	26.58	0.000	132
COVID-19	33.20	33.42	19.18	57.78	82.69	12.10	70.59	2.46	0.64	7.43	0.024	93
EPUI												
Pre-COVID-19	261.66	251.94	21.05	8.05	306.83	244.55	62.28	3.69	1.52	53.42	0.000	132
COVID-19	288.96	348.39	64.53	22.33	348.56	217.26	131.30	1.03	−0.15	15.45	0.000	93
WAEX												
Pre-COVID-19	0.727	0.727	0.003	0.41	0.734	0.720	0.014	2.54	0.08	1.316	0.518	132
COVID-19	0.730	0.731	0.005	0.75	0.743	0.714	0.029	2.992	−0.140	0.305	0.858	93
Full sample (pre-COVID-19 and COVID-19) period (1/7/2019–8/5/2020)												
Oil price	53.79	60.42	16.52	30.71	70.25	9.12	61.13	3.34	−1.39	73.04	0.000	225
Gold price	1533.44	1509.20	83.96	5.48	1741.90	1388.65	353.25	2.68	0.65	16.83	0.000	225
VIX	22.49	15.18	15.38	68.36	82.69	11.54	71.15	5.86	1.89	211.00	0.000	225
EPUI	272.95	253.06	46.38	16.99	348.56	217.26	131.30	1.97	0.66	26.29	0.000	225
WAEX	0.728	0.728	0.004	0.59	0.743	0.714	0.029	3.780	0.311	9.318	0.009	225

Note: This table presents a comparison of the status of all the variables considered in the model in the form of summary statistics before and during the COVID-19 period. CV = Coefficient of variation, JB = Jargue, Min = Minimum, Max = Maximum.

Lags (ARDL) bounds test approach under the Vector Error Correction Model (VECM) framework. The ARDL bounds test approach is selected for the following reasons, namely (i) it does not require all the variables of the model to be integrated of the same order, i.e. all $I(0)$ or all $I(1)$, (ii) it can be used irrespective of the sample size (either small or large samples), and (iii) analysis based on long run and short run can be performed simultaneously.

We consider the following variables (all in natural log-form except the COVID-19 *CASES* and *DEATH* as they have some zero entries) in our system of equations: (1) oil price *OIL*; (2) gold price *GOLD*; (3) *GEPU* index; (4) *VIX*; (5) World Average Currency Exchange rate of US$ (WAEX), and; (6) Number of COVID cases (*CASES*) or Number of COVID deaths (*DEATH*). The scatter plot showing the relationship between oil price and gold price (Figure 15.2) as well as the high R^2 value observed for the error correction models indicate that a linear relationship can be used to model the relationship between oil and gold prices.[7] Therefore, we model *OIL* (oil price) as a linear function of *GOLD* (gold price) and vice-versa, *GEPU*, *VIX*, WAEX, and *COVID* (which is either *CASES* or *DEATHS*). Our focus is on the following two equations. In double-log form, we have

$$\begin{aligned} \ln OIL_t = \delta_0 + \delta_1 \ln GOLD_t + \delta_2 \ln GEPU_t + \delta_3 \ln VIX_t \\ + \delta_4 \ln \text{WAEX}_t + \delta_5 COVID_t + e_t. \end{aligned} \tag{15.1}$$

We also write *GOLD* as a linear function of *OIL*, *GEPU*, *VIX*, WAEX, and *COVID*. That is,

$$\begin{aligned} \ln GOLD_t = \delta_0 + \delta_1 \ln OIL_t + \delta_2 \ln GEPU_t + \delta_3 \ln VIX_t \\ + \delta_4 \ln \text{WAEX}_t + \delta_5 COVID_t + e_t. \end{aligned} \tag{15.2}$$

[7]There is very little evidence of a non-linear relationship between the two variables. Consequently, a non-linear autoregressive distributed lag (NARDL) model is not considered in this study.

The ARDL (p, q, r, s, v, k) formulations corresponding to long-run relationships given by Equations (15.1) and (15.2) can be written as

$$\begin{aligned}\Delta(\ln OIL_t) = {} & \beta_0 + \beta_1 \ln GOLD_t + \beta_2 \ln GEPU_t \\ & + \beta_3 \ln VIX_t + \beta_4 \ln \mathrm{WAEX}_t + \beta_5 COVID_t \\ & + \sum_{j=1}^{p} \gamma_{1j} \Delta(\ln OIL_{t-j}) \\ & + \sum_{j=0}^{r} \gamma_{3j} \Delta(\ln GEPUI_{t-j}) \\ & + \sum_{j=0}^{s} \gamma_{4j} \Delta(\ln VIX_{t-j}) \\ & + \sum_{j=0}^{v} \gamma_{5j} \Delta(\ln \mathrm{WAEX}_{t-j}) \\ & + \sum_{j=0}^{k} \gamma_{6j} \Delta(COVID_{t-j}) + u_t. \end{aligned} \tag{15.3}$$

$$\begin{aligned}\Delta(\ln GOLD_t) = {} & \beta_0 + \beta_1 \ln OIL_t + \beta_2 \ln GEPU_t + \beta_3 \ln VIX_t \\ & + \beta_4 \ln \mathrm{WAEX}_t + \beta_5 COVID_t \\ & + \sum_{j=1}^{p} \gamma_{1j} \Delta(\ln OIL_{t-j}) + \sum_{j=0}^{r} \gamma_{3j} \Delta(\ln GEPUI_{t-j}) \\ & + \sum_{j=0}^{s} \gamma_{4j} \Delta(\ln VIX_{t-j}) + \sum_{j=0}^{v} \gamma_{5j} \Delta(\ln \mathrm{WAEX}_{t-j}) \\ & + \sum_{j=0}^{k} \gamma_{6j} \Delta(COVID_{t-j}) + u_t. \end{aligned} \tag{15.4}$$

The ARDL bounds test can be used to test the long-run (or the cointegrating) relationship between the variables in the models based on a non-standard F-test by testing the null and the alternative hypotheses;

H_0: $\beta_1 = \beta_2 = \beta_3 = \beta_4 = \beta_5 = 0$ (no cointegration);

H_A: At least one of β_1 or β_2 or β_3 or β_4 or $\beta_5 \neq 0$ (existence of cointegration).

We use the critical values provided in Pesaran *et al.* (2001). There are two sets of critical values; one based on the assumptions that all variables are $I(0)$ and the other based on the assumptions that all variables are $I(1)$. If the calculated F-statistic is above the $I(1)$ critical value, then the null hypothesis should be rejected and conclude that there is support for cointegration. If the calculated F-statistic is below the $I(0)$ critical value, then the null hypothesis should not be rejected and conclude that there is no support for cointegration. If the calculated F-statistic is between the $I(0)$ critical value and the $I(1)$ critical value, then the test result is inconclusive. Even though the bounds test approach does not generally require the order of the integration of all the variables to be $I(0)$ or $I(1)$, it does require that none of the variables in the model equation are of order $I(2)$ or higher. In order to verify this, we perform the unit root tests. Table 15.2 presents the unit-root test results based on three tests for the variables for the two sub-sample periods. The first two unit-root tests, Augmented Dicky–Fuller test (ADF test) and Phillips–Perron test (PP test) have the null hypothesis that the series has a unit root (i.e. the series is non-stationary) and the third test Kwiatkowski–Phillips–Schmidt–Shin test (KPSS test) has the null hypothesis that the series is stationary. As can be seen, from the results reported in Table 15.2, we can conclude that all the variables in our models are $I(1)$.

Table 15.3 presents the bound test results for each model for the two sub-sample periods. As can be seen, all the values of the test statistics are higher than the $I(1)$ critical values, and we can conclude that there is support for co-integration between the variables in the models. This means that the model estimation results are not spurious and the least squares estimation results would still be valid.

Since co-integration exists between model variables, we can use an error-correction model to estimate the speed of adjustment of the disequilibrium caused by previous period shocks that re-converges to the long-run equilibrium. The error correction models, correspond to

Table 15.2. Unit root test results for the variables in level and first-difference forms.

Variable	Dicky-Fuller		Philip-Perron		KPSS		Conclusion
	Test statistic	Critical value	Test statistic	Critical value	Test statistic	Critical value	
Pre-COVID-19							
OIL	−2.843	0.185	−2.684	0.245	0.219	0.146	I(1)
D(OIL)	−9.846	0.000	−12.578	0.000	0.187	0.463	
GOLD	−2.372	0.392	−2.246	0.460	0.269	0.146	I(1)
D(GOLD)	−12.251	0.000	−12.530	0.000	0.143	0.146	
VIX	−2.972	0.144	−2.903	0.165	0.166	0.146	I(1)
D(VIX)	−12.811	0.000	−13.198	0.000	0.080	0.463	
GEPU	−2.115	0.532	−2.151	0.512	0.488	0.463	I(1)
D(GEPU)	−11.314	0.000	−11.314	0.000	0.105	0.463	
COVID-19							
OIL	−2.179	0.495	−2.179	0.495	0.147998	0.146	I(1)
D(OIL)	−10.194	0.000	−10.295	0.000	0.121724	0.463	
GOLD	−1.816	0.371	−1.977	0.297	0.812270	0.463	I(1)
D(GOLD)	−5.284	0.000	−10.074	0.000	0.035942	0.463	
VIX	−0.665	0.972	−0.773	0.964	0.209721	0.146	I(1)
D(VIX)	−11.061	0.000	−10.969	0.000	0.256760	0.463	
GEPU	−2.487	0.334	−2.561	0.299	1.068382	0.463	I(1)
D(GEPU)	−9.586	0.000	−9.586	0.000	0.123337	0.463	

Note: This table presents the stationarity test results of all the variables considered in the model based on three different tests, ADF, PP, and KPSS unit root tests for the pre–COVID-19 period and COVID-19 period.

Table 15.3. Bounds test for cointegration results for the oil and gold price variables.

		Critical values		
Variable	**Test statistics**	**I(0)**	**I(1)**	**Conclusion**
Pre-COVID-19				
Oil price	4.09	2.86	4.01	Cointegrated
Gold price	3.98	2.69	3.70	Cointegrated
During COVID-19 with number of CASES				
Oil price	5.17	2.43	3.52	Cointegrated
Gold price	6.28	2.43	3.52	Cointegrated
During COVID-19 with number of DEATHS				
Oil price	5.69	2.43	3.52	Cointegrated
Gold price	6.29	2.43	3.52	Cointegrated

Note: This table presents the test results on the long-run relationship between the model variables based on the bounds test for pre–COVID-19, current COVID-19 with number of cases, and current COVID-19 with number of deaths.

Equations (15.3) and (15.4) can be written as

$$\begin{aligned}\Delta(\ln OIL_t) = \gamma_0 &+ \sum_{j=1}^{p} \gamma_{1j}\Delta(\ln OIL_{t-j}) + \sum_{j=0}^{q} \gamma_{2j}\Delta(\ln GOLD_{t-j}) \\ &+ \sum_{j=0}^{r} \gamma_{3j}\Delta(\ln GEPU_{t-j}) + \sum_{j=0}^{s} \gamma_{4j}\Delta(\ln VIX_{t-j}) \\ &+ \sum_{j=0}^{\mathrm{v}} \gamma_{5j}\Delta(\ln \mathrm{WAEX}_{t-j}) + \sum_{j=0}^{k} \gamma_{6j}\Delta(COVID_{t-j}) \\ &+ \mu EC_{t-1} + u_t, \end{aligned} \tag{15.5}$$

$$\begin{aligned}\Delta(\ln GOLD_t) = \gamma_0 &+ \sum_{j=1}^{p} \gamma_{1j}\Delta(\ln GOLD_{t-j}) + \sum_{j=0}^{q} \gamma_{2j}\Delta(\ln OIL_{t-j}) \\ &+ \sum_{j=0}^{r} \gamma_{3j}\Delta(\ln GEPU_{t-j})\end{aligned}$$

$$+\sum_{j=0}^{s}\gamma_{4j}\Delta(\ln VIX_{t-j})$$

$$+\sum_{j=0}^{\text{v}}\gamma_{5j}\Delta(\ln \text{WAEX}_{t-j})$$

$$+\sum_{j=0}^{k}\gamma_{6j}\Delta(COVID_{t-j}) + \mu EC_{t-1} + u_t, \qquad (15.6)$$

where EC_{t-1} is the error correction term derived from the long-run relationships given by Equations (15.1) and (15.2) for Equations (15.5) and (15.6), respectively. The coefficients γ_{ij}'s measure the short-run dynamics associated with the long-run relationships and coefficient μ is the speed of adjustment that measures the long-run effect, which is expected to be a value in the range −1 and 0. Since the plots depicting the relationship between oil price or gold price and the *COVID* variable (either the number of COVID-19 cases or number of COVID-19–related deaths) in Figures 15.7 and 15.8 showed a quadratic relationship, we include a quadratic variable COVID^2 in Equations (15.5) and (15.6) in addition to the *COVID* variable.

Table 15.4 presents the short-run and long-run estimation results of Equations (15.5) and (15.6) for the pre–COVID-19 period. Table 15.5 presents the results during COVID-19 considering the *COVID* variable as the number of COVID-19 cases and Table 15.6 presents the results during COVID-19 considering the *COVID* variable as the number of COVID-19–related deaths. Each table presents the results for both the oil and gold price equations as well as the model diagnostics results. Considering the oil price equation, as can be seen from Table 15.4 based on pre–COVID-19 conditions in the long run, VIX and WAEX have a negative statistically significant (at the 10% level) influence on oil price, while gold price and GEPU have a positive influence on oil price but are not statistically significant. However, in the short run, oil price is significantly influenced by only its lagged-prices and gold price. During the pre–COVID-19 period, in the long run, a 10% increase in the VIX would have reduced oil prices by 2.7%. In the long run, a 10% increase in gold price would have reduced the price of oil by 7.13%.

Table 15.4. Results from model estimation — pre–COVID-19.

Oil Price: ARDL(3,1,0,0,0)			**Gold Price: ARDL(2,2,1,0,1)**		
Model estimation					
	Estimate	*p*-value		Estimate	*p*-value
Long-run			*Long-run*		
LGOLD	1.615	0.101	LOIL	−0.064	0.613
LGEPU	0.041	0.881	LGEPU	0.173	0.076
LVIX	−0.272	0.087	LVIX	0.100	0.124
LWAEX	−11.658	0.060	LWAEX	−1.790	0.441
			TREND	0.000	0.005
Short-run			*Short-run*		
C	−1.377	0.000	C	0.757	0.000
D(LOIL(-1))	−0.085	0.280	D(LGOLD(-1))	−0.181	0.025
D(LOIL(-2))	−0.172	0.028	D(LOIL)	−0.081	0.004
D(LGOLD)	−0.713	0.002	D(LOIL(-1))	−0.046	0.106
			D(LGEPU)	−0.022	0.398
			D(LWAEX)	−1.626	0.001
EC	−0.127	0.000	EC	−0.132	0.000
Model diagnostics tests					
	F-Statistic	*p*-value		F-Statistic	*p*-value
Serial correlation: LM test	0.030	0.863	Serial correlation: LM test	0.996	0.320
Heteroskedasticity test: ARCH	0.066	0.798	Heteroskedasticity test: ARCH	0.020	0.886
Ramsey RESET	0.403	0.527	Ramsey RESET	0.076	0.784

Note: This table presents the short-run and long-run estimation results for the oil price and gold price equations for pre–COVID-19. EC = Error Correction Term.

The estimation results of the oil price equation presented in Table 15.5 for the active COVID-19 period reveal that, in the long run, the effect of gold price (positive), VIX (negative), and the number of COVID-19 cases on oil price are statistically significant. That is, a "U shape" relationship exists between the number of COVID-19 cases and the oil price as the estimates of the CASE coefficient is negative and $CASE^2$ coefficient is positive. In the short run, the

Table 15.5. Results from model estimation — COVID-19 model with number of cases.

Oil Price: ARDL(1,0,0,0,0,2,0)			**Gold Price: ARDL(2,0,1,2,2,0,0)**		
		Model estimation			
	Estimate	***p*-value**		**Estimate**	***p*-value**
Long-run			*Long-run*		
LGOLD	2.510	0.029	LOIL	0.101	0.029
LGEPU	0.306	0.444	LGEPU	0.384	0.023
LVIX	−0.521	0.000	LVIX	−0.100	0.072
LWAEX	5.489	0.312	LWAEX	4.825	0.034
CASES	−0.751	0.000	CASES	0.091	0.025
$CASES^2$	1.540	0.000	$CASES^2$	−0.022	0.022
C	−12.843	0.121	C	6.690	0.000
Short-run			*Short-run*		
D(CASES)	−0.554	0.007	D(LGOLD(-1))	−0.202	0.029
D(CASES(-1))	−0.626	0.002	D(LWAEX)	0.025	0.352
			D(LVIX)	−0.001	0.896
			D(LVIX(-1))	0.038	0.002
			D(LWAEX)	−0.978	0.038
			D(LWAEX(-1))	−0.957	0.045
EC	−0.386	0.000	EC	−0.232	0.000
		Model diagnostics tests			
	F-Statistic	***p*-value**		**F-Statistic**	***p*-value**
Serial correlation: LM test	1.747	0.190	Serial correlation: LM test	2.008	0.161
Heteroskedasticity test: ARCH	0.270	0.604	Heteroskedasticity test: ARCH	1.325	0.253
Ramsey RESET	0.013	0.989	Ramsey RESET	1.963	0.053

Note: This table presents the short-run and long-run estimation results for the oil price and gold price equations for the current COVID-19 period with number of COVID-19 cases. ECT = Error Correction Term.

number of COVID-19 cases has a negative and statistically significant impact on oil prices. With regard to the gold price equation estimation presented in Table 15.5, in the long run, price of oil (positive), GEPU (positive), VIX (negative), WAEX (positive), and the number of COVID-19 cases, all have a statistically significant influence on gold prices. The impact of the number of COVID-19 cases

Table 15.6. Results from model estimation — COVID-19 model with number of deaths.

Oil Price: ARDL(1,0,0,0,0,2,0)			**Gold Price: ARDL(2,0,1,2,2,0,0)**		
		Model estimation			
	Estimate	***p*-value**		**Estimate**	***p*-value**
Long-run			*Long-run*		
LGOLD	2.584	0.048	LOIL	0.097	0.033
LGEPU	0.284	0.535	LGEPU	0.392	0.020
LVIX	−0.593	0.000	LVIX	−0.099	0.080
LWAEX	4.568	0.463	LWAEX	5.083	0.026
DEATH	−5.730	0.173	DEATH	1.190	0.028
$DEATH^2$	15.800	0.245	$DEATH^2$	−4.190	0.021
C	−13.383	0.156	C	6.748	0.000
Short-run			*Short-run*		
D(DEATH)	−0.720	0.016	D(LGOLD(-1))	−0.203	0.029
D(DEATH(-1))	−1.480	0.000	D(LWAEX)	0.024	0.357
			D(LVIX)	−0.002	0.849
			D(LVIX(-1))	0.037	0.003
			D(LWAEX)	−0.988	0.036
			D(LWAEX(-1))	−1.020	0.033
EC	−0.326	0.000	EC	−0.231	0.000
		Model diagnostics tests			
	F-Statistic	***p*-value**		**F-Statistic**	***p*-value**
Serial correlation: LM test	0.692	0.408	Serial correlation: LM test	2.218	0.140
Heteroskedasticity test: ARCH	0.586	0.446	Heteroskedasticity test: ARCH	1.254	0.266
Ramsey RESET	0.031	0.975	Ramsey RESET	2.305	0.024

Note: This table presents the short-run and long-run estimation results for the oil price and gold price equations for the current COVID-19 period with number of COVID-19 deaths.

has an "inverted U-shaped" effect on gold price as the CASE coefficient estimate is positive and the $CASE^2$ coefficient estimate is negative. The U-shaped relationship between the number of COVID-19 cases and oil price means that, when the number of COVID-19 cases increases, most of the governments implement lockdowns that lead to excess supply of oil in a situation of reduced demand and a subsequent fall in the price of oil. When the lockdown is slowly eased, the demand for oil increased and the price of oil also increased. The opposite would take place for gold as gold is mostly on a limited supply and with the news of increasing COVID-19 cases investors move away from oil investments and invest in gold as it is considered as a safe haven for investment during uncertainty. The short-run results reveal that the lagged VIX and the WAEX have a negative impact on gold price.

Results presented in Table 15.6 with the number of COVID-19–related deaths is generally similar to those presented in Table 15.5 with the number of COVID-19 cases. In the short run, the increase in the number of COVID-19–related deaths has had a negative effect on the price of oil but has no significant impact on the price of gold. However, in the long run, for the gold price equation, the statistically significant positive coefficient of the $DEATH$ variable and negative coefficient of the $DEATH^2$ variable indicate that the number of COVID-19–related deaths has an "inverted U shape" impact on the gold price. This means that, at the beginning when the number of COVID-19-related deaths increased, such uncertainty would increase the price of gold as investors prefer to invest in gold during uncertain times, and when the number of deaths peaked and started to stabilize, gold price would have reached a higher level and would stabilize at that level.

All the error correction terms in Tables 15.4–15.6 are statistically significant and are in the required range –1 to 0, indicating that there is a co-integrating relationship between oil price and gold price as well as a long-run bidirectional causality between them. The model diagnostics tests for serial correlation, AutoRegressive Conditional Heteroskedasticity (ARCH) effect and model validity (Ramsey's Regression Equation Specification Error Test — RESET) results presented in Tables 15.4–15.6 give confidence in our estimation results.

In summary, the significant positive long-run relationships found between oil and gold prices during COVID-19 (in both models with number of cases as well as number of deaths) reveal that an increase in the oil prices would lead to an increase in gold demand and therefore an increase in the price of gold. An increase in oil price negatively affects the economic growth and that leads to a reduction in asset prices. Therefore, investors prefer to move their investment from other assets to gold (Reboredo, 2003). Since our results show that the shocks in oil price have significant impact on gold price, such findings will have practical importance for monetary policy with respect to inflation targeting as a rise in oil price impact heavily on oil-importing economies' cost of production of goods and services, thereby increasing the inflation.

15.4. Concluding Comments

The COVID-19 pandemic has unleashed an unimaginable toll on the sustainability and development goals of the developed world as well as the developing world. The enormity of the effect via various channels can only be measured by considering these channels individually. In this study, we investigated one of these channels which affects virtually every developing as well as developed country in the world — the movement of oil price. In addition to this, we also considered the price movement of one of the safe investment channels of many countries, gold. We comparatively analyzed the movements of oil price and gold price before the COVID-19 pandemic and during the pandemic. In the literature, some studies have shown that there is some relationship between the price movements of oil and gold. Using the ARDL approach, we investigate the relationship between oil and gold prices in the short run and the long run. For this purpose, we use the daily price data of oil and gold, the number of reported COVID-19 cases and related deaths, and a few other related variables for the two periods, before COVID-19 and during COVID-19.

Our results reveal that pre–COVID-19, while both gold price and oil price significantly negatively impacted on each other in the short run, no significant influence is observed in the long run. In the long run, the gold price positively impacted on oil price and oil price impacted negatively on gold price, but both effects were not statistically significant. During the COVID-19 period, long-run results indicated that oil and gold prices both positively significantly impacted on each other's price when the number of COVID-19 cases or related deaths were included in the analysis. During COVID-19, in the short run, the number of COVID-19 cases and related deaths both negatively and significantly impacted on oil price but not on gold price. In the long run, the number of COVID-19 cases and related deaths impacted on oil price in a "U-shaped" form while they impacted on gold price in an "inverted U shaped" form.

As the COVID-19 situation is predicted to continue for the next 12–18 months, the above findings will help government policymakers to devise appropriate policies to achieve sustainable development of their economies and investors to design their optimum portfolios.

15.5. Conflict/Declaration of Interest Statement

The authors declare that they have no known competing financial interests or personal relationships that could have appeared to influence the work reported in this paper.

References

Abhyankar, A., Xu, B. and Wang, J. (2013). Oil price shocks and the stock market: evidence from Japan. *The Energy Journal*, **34**(2), 199–222.

Adekoya, O.B, Oliyide, J.A. and Oduyemi, G.O. (2020). How COVID-19 upturns the hedging potentials of gold against oil and stock markets risk: Nonlinear evidences through threshold regression and Markov-regime switching models. *Resources Policy*. https://doi.org/10.1016/j.resoupol.2020.101926.

Aloui, R., Gupta, R. and Miller, S.M. (2016). Uncertainty and crude oil returns. *Energy Economics*, **55**, 92–100.

Azar1, S.A. (2015). The relation of the US dollar with oil prices, gold prices, and the US stock market. *Research in World Economy*, **6**(1), 159–171.

Baker, S.R., Bloom, N. and Davis, S.J. (2016). Measuring economic policy uncertainty. *The Quarterly Journal of Economics*, **131**(4), 1593–1636.

Barro, R.J., Ursua, J.F. and Weng, J. (2020). The coronavirus and the great influenza pandemic – lessons from the 'Spanish Flu' for the coronavirus's potential effects on mortality and economic activity. NBER Working Paper 26866.

Baur, D.G. and Lucey, B.M. (2010). Is gold a hedge or a safe haven? Analysis of stocks, bonds and gold. *The Financial Review*, **45**, 217–229. http://dx.doi.org/10.1111/j.1540-6288.2010.00244.x.

Baur, D.G. and McDermott, T.K. (2010). Is gold a safe haven? International evidence. *Journal of Banking and Finance*, **34**, 1886–1898.

Beckmann, J. and Czudaj, R. (2013). Oil and gold price dynamics in a multivariate cointegration framework. *International Economics and Economic Policy*, **10**, 453–468. http://dx.doi.org/10.1007/s10368-013-0237-8.

Bendavid, E. and Bhattacharya, J. (2020). Is coronavirus as deadly as they say? *Wall Street Journal*, 24 March.

Bildirici, M.E. and Turkmen, C. (2015). Nonlinear causality between oil and precious metals. *Resources Policy*, **46**, 202–211. https://doi.org/10.1016/j.resourpol.2015.09.002.

Bonitsis, T.H. and Rezvani, F. (2010). Is there a U.S. dollar-petroleum price nexus? *Proceedings of the Northeast Business & Economic Association*, pp. 239–244.

Cai, J., Cheung, Y.L. and Wong, M.C.S. (2001). What moves the gold market? *Journal of Futures Markets*, **21**, 257–278.

Chaney, S. and Morath, E. (2020). Record 6.6 million Americans sought unemployment benefits last week. *Wall Street Journal*, 3 April.

Davis, S.J. (2016). An index of Global Economic Policy Uncertainty (GEPU). NBER Working Paper No. 22740.

Dutta, A, Das, D., Jana, R.K. and Vo, X.V. (2020). COVID-19 and oil market crash: Revisiting the safe haven property of gold and Bitcoin. *Resources Policy*, **69**. https://doi.org/10.1016/j.resoupol.2020.101816.

Fattouh, B. (2010). The dynamics of crude oil price differential. *Energy Economics*, **32**, 334–342.

Fauci, A.S., Lane, H.C. and Redfield, R.R. (2020). Covid-19 – Navigating the uncharted. *New England Journal of Medicine*, 26 March. doi: 0.1056/NEJMe2002387.

Gharib, C., Mefteh-Wali, S. and Jabeur, S.B. (2020). The bubble contagion effect of COVID-19 outbreak: Evidence from crude oil and gold markets. *Finance Research Letters*. https://doi.org/10.1016/j.frl.2020.101703.

Hailemariam, A., Smyth, R. and Zhang, X. (2019). Oil prices and economic policy uncertainty: Evidence from a nonparametric panel data model. *Energy Economics*, **83**, 40–51.

Jain, A. and Biswal, P.C. (2016). Dynamic linkages among oil price, gold price, exchange rate and stock market in India. *Resource Policy*, **49**, 179–185.

Kang, W., Ratti, R.A. and Vespignani, J.L. (2017). Oil price shocks and policy uncertainty: New evidence on the effects of US and non-US oil production. *Energy Economics*, **66**, 536–546.

Kumar, S. (2017). On the nonlinear relation between crude oil and gold. *Resources Policy*, **51**, 219–224. https://doi.org/10.1016/j.resoupol.2017.01.003.

Le, T. and Chang, Y. (2012). Oil price shocks and gold returns. *International Economics*, **131**, 71–104.

Lee, Y.H, Huang, Y.L. and Yang, H.-J. (2012). The asymmetric long-run relationship between crude oil and gold futures. *Global Journal of Business Research*, **6**(1), 9–15.

Malliaris, A.G and Malliaris, M. (2013). Are oil, gold and the euro inter-related? Time series and neural network analysis. *Review of Quantitative Finance and Accounting*, **40**, 1–14.

Mensi, W., Sensoy, A., Vo, X.V. and Kang, S.H. (2020). Impact of COVID-19 outbreak on asymmetric multifractality of gold and oil prices. *Resources Policy*, **69**. https://doi.org/10.1016/j.resoupol.2020.101829.

Miyazaki, T. and Hamori, S. (2013). Testing the causality between the gold return and stock market performance: Evidence for 'gold investment in case of emergency. *Applied Financial Economics*, **23**, 27–40.

Pesaran, M.H., Shin, Y. and Smith, R.J. (2001). Bounds testing approaches to the analysis of level relationships. *Applied Econometrics*, **16**, 289–326.

Regnier, E. (2007). Oil and energy price volatility. Energy Economics, **29**(3), 405–427.

Reboredo, J.C. (2013). Nonlinear effects of oil shocks on stock returns. *Resources Policy*, **38**(2), 335–346.

Salisu, A.A., Ebuh, H.U. and Usman, N. (2020a). Revisiting oil-stock nexus during COVID-19 pandemic: Some preliminary results. *International Review of Economics and Finance*, **69**, 280–294.

Salisu, A.A, Vo, X.V. and Lawal, A. (2020b). Hedging oil price risk with gold during COVID-19 pandemic. *Resources Policy*. https://doi.org/10.1016/j.resourpol.2020.101897.

Sari, R., Hammoudeh, H.M., Soytas, U. and Hacihasnoglu, E. (2010). Dynamics of oil price, precious metal prices, and exchange rate. *Energy Economics*, **32**(2), 351–362.

Sari, R., Soytas, U. and Hacihasnoglu, E. (2011). Do global risk perceptions influence world oil prices? *Energy Economics*, 33(3), 515–524.

Šimáková, J. (2011). Analysis of the relationship between oil and gold prices. *Journal of Finance*, **51**(1), 651–662.

Tiwari, A. K. and Sahadudheen, I. (2015). Understanding the nexus between oil and gold. *Resources Policy*, **46**, 85–91.

Van Robays, I. (2016). Macroeconomic uncertainty and oil price volatility. *Oxford Bulletin of Economics and Statistics*, **78**, 671–693.

Yaya, O., Tumala, M.M. and Udomboso, C.G. (2016). Volatility persistence and returns spill overs between oil and gold prices: Analysis before and after the global financial crises. *Resources Policy*, **49**, 273–281.

Zagaglia, P. and Marzo, M. (2013). Gold and the US dollar. *Quantitative Finance*, **13**(4), 571–582.

Zimmermann, K.F., Karabulutz, G., Bilgin, M.H. and Doker, A.C. (2020). Inter-country distancing, globalisation and the coronavirus pandemic. *The World Economy*, 1484–1498, DOI: 10.1111/twec.12969.

https://doi.org/10.1142/9781800610781_0016

Chapter 16

The Resilience of the Euro in the Era of COVID-19

Stelios Markoulis[*,†,‡] **and Neophytos Vasiliou**[†,§]

[*]*University of Cyprus, Cyprus*

[†]*Cyprus International Institute of Management, Cyprus*

[‡]*markoulis.stelios@ucy.ac.cy*

[§]*neofitos_basiliou@hotmail.com*

Abstract

In this chapter we examine the effect of the COVID-19 pandemic on foreign exchange markets and, in particular, on the price of the Euro versus other major currencies. We employ the event-study methodology to analyse a number of "key events" that occurred during the unfolding of the pandemic so far, and find that the Euro appears to show notable resilience, in most of the cases. It would appear that the policy responses of the European Commission and the European Central Bank were positively received by international markets. Our findings provide another building block in the academic literature related to the effects of exogenous shocks on international markets and could be of particular interest to market participants that engage in the foreign exchange market as well as policy markets.

16.1. Introduction

Since the end of 2019, the coronavirus disease 2019 (COVID-19) has been spreading globally at an unprecedented pace. The disease was initially detected in China, but soon the number of confirmed cases soared all over the world, causing the World Health Organization (WHO) to declare it a pandemic on March 11, 2020; according to the European Centre for Disease Prevention and Control, as of September 29, 2020, there have been 33.4 million cases of COVID-19 globally, and more than 1 million deaths. Although the epicentre of the pandemic has shifted since the beginning of the year from China to Europe and then the US, there is no doubt that this horrible disease — apart from grief and pain — will also leave its multifaceted mark on the world economy. Within this context, it is the aim of this chapter to focus on the effects of the pandemic on the foreign exchange market and, more specifically, on the price of the Euro versus other major global currencies.

Our findings seem to indicate that the performance of the Euro during the unfolding of the pandemic was quite resilient against other important global currencies, such as the US Dollar (USD), the Canadian Dollar (CAD), the British Pound (GBP), the Australian Dollar (AUD), and the New Zealand Dollar (NZD). Moreover, although during the earlier stages of the pandemic in Europe, the common currency tended to show depreciation against traditional "safe-haven" currencies, such as the Japanese Yen (YEN) and the Swiss Franc (CHF), later on it recovered against those currencies as well. It is possible that (i) the fact that Euro is a very liquid global currency (second only to the USD) and, probably more importantly, (ii) the common stance taken by European leaders toward tackling the crisis caused by the pandemic was well received by the markets. As such, it would appear that the unfolding of the pandemic provided an "opportunity" for the prominence of the Euro to rise; it seems that the opportunity was well utilized.

Events such as pandemics, natural disasters and terror attacks are often termed "black swan events" (Taleb, 2007) and tend to cause shock, fear, and panic among investors, which is often accompanied by a panic-selling response; e.g. Burch *et al.* (2016) documented that following the 9/11 attack on the US, retail investors sold vast amounts of stock, causing sharp price declines, even in assets where there was evidence of net institutional buying. Within this context, in recent time there has been a growing body of academic literature addressing the effects of such events on stock exchanges, and to a lesser extent on the foreign exchange market. For instance, Hood *et al.* (2013) examined the behaviour of investors after Japan's most powerful earthquake, which occurred in March 2011 and which resulted in a sharp downturn in the Nikkei index; the authors documented that domestic investors sold substantially more shares than they bought, while, interestingly, during the aftermath of the disaster, foreign investors "stabilized" the market by being net buyers. Along the same lines, Wang and Kutan (2013) investigated the effect of natural disasters on the stock markets of the US and Japan, as well as on the insurance sectors of these two markets. They found evidence of significant wealth effects in the insurance sectors of both countries but no evidence of such effects in the whole of both stock markets.

The literature on the effect of terror attacks on stock markets is much broader and has expanded substantially in recent time, especially after 9/11. For example, Chen and Siems (2004) focused on the impact of 14 major terrorist and military events on the capital markets of the US during the period 1915–2001 documenting that US capital markets have become more resilient over time. Baumert (2009) examined the effect of 9/11, the Madrid bombings in 2004, and the London bombings in 2005 on the major US, European, and Japanese stock markets, arguing that over time, the impact of such attacks has diminished, while Chesney *et al.* (2011) analyzed the effect of terror attacks that occurred in 25 countries over an 11-year period on the behavior of stock, bond, and commodity markets, pointing out that most of the events led to a significant negative impact. More recently, Markoulis and Katsikides (2018) examined 11 major terror attacks that occurred in the 21st century and their effect on international stock markets; the authors documented that earlier events resulted in higher negative abnormal returns for the affected markets in comparison to more recent ones. Papakyriakou *et al.* (2019) examined terror acts in G7 countries over the period 1998–2017, evaluating their impact on the stock market indices of several countries; they find that stock markets decline significantly on the day of the attack, as well as on the following trading day. Research related to the effects of terror attacks on the foreign exchange market is much scarcer; for example, Narayan *et al.* (2017) examined whether such events affect the exchange rates of 21 countries against the US dollar, documenting varying reactions between countries, in terms of magnitude and persistence. More recently, a comprehensive study by Park *et al.* (2018) analyse a large number of terror attacks across the stock and foreign exchange markets of 36 countries, during the period 1996–2015; the authors find almost no impact on stock markets and a rather small effect on foreign exchange markets.

Another layer of the literature, which is more closely related to our work, focuses on the effect of pandemics on stock markets. Nippani and Washer (2004) examined the effect of SARS on the stock market indices of Canada, China, Hong Kong, Indonesia, the Philippines, Singapore, Thailand, and Vietnam; the authors did not detect any evidence of negative returns, with the exception of the cases of China and Vietnam. Chen *et al.* (2007) also focused on the outbreak of SARS, examining its impact on hotel stocks in the markets of China and Taiwan and finding evidence of negative returns.

Despite the fact that the economic effects of COVID-19 are still unfolding, given the immense multidimensional global interest that the pandemic has "attracted," it is not surprising that its effects on international markets have already been the subject of several research papers. For instance, Ali *et al.* (2020) examined the reaction of global financial markets as the pandemic "moved" from China to Europe and then to the US, documenting that the initial epicentre China has managed to stabilize, while the rest of global markets have gone on a freefall, especially in the later phase of the spread. Along the same lines, Okorie *et al.* (2020) investigated the fractal contagion effect of the pandemic on 32 international stock markets, utilizing the Detrended Moving Cross-Correlation Analysis and Detrended Cross-Correlation Analysis techniques; the authors documented that there is indeed evidence of a contagion effect, which nonetheless "fizzles out" over time. Qing *et al.* (2020) focused on the stock markets of China, Italy, South Korea, France, Spain, Germany, Japan, and the US, documenting that the pandemic did have a negative impact, which nonetheless was of a short-term nature. He *et al.* (2020) utilized the event-study methodology to study the market response of various Chinese industrial sectors to COVID-19, documenting that industries such as transportation, mining, electricity and heating, and environment industries were adversely impacted, while others, such as manufacturing, information technology, education and healthcare industries showed resilience. Albulescu (2020) examined whether announcements of new cases of infection and fatalities of COVID-19 have had any impact on the volatility of US financial markets, documenting that the pandemic has indeed enhanced volatility. Under the same "prism," Seven and Yilmaz (2020) focused on the various rescue packages that were implemented by governments in an effort to mitigate the severe consequences of the pandemic and how these affected global equity market. The authors find that the recovery performance of markets varies significantly across countries; more specifically, it appears that fiscal stimulus support measures seem to be strongly and positively related to higher recovery, thus suggesting that such measures do in fact help to restore investors' confidence.

It becomes evident from the above paragraph that the effects of COVID-19 on global stock markets have been broadly analyzed in the literature; however, surprisingly, the same cannot be said about the foreign exchange market, where the only paper related to COVID-19 that we came across was Aslam *et al.* (2020), who employed multifractal detrended fluctuation analysis to examine the efficiency of forex markets during the initial period of the outbreak of COVID-19. The authors find evidence of a decline in market efficiency during the COVID-19 period, in comparison to the pre-pandemic level. They point out that this may be attributed to how investors perceive currencies and in the fundamentals that underline their value. This chapter aims to contribute further to the scarce literature related to the effect of COVID-19 on international foreign exchange markets, and more specifically provide a first assessment of the effect of the pandemic on the price of the Euro versus seven other important global currencies.

Within the context set out in the previous paragraph, our main research question is: have a number of important events which took place during the unfolding of COVID-19 affected the price of the Euro and to what extent? Moreover, within the framework of our main research question, we also address two further issues: the first one is whether the reaction of the Euro differs across different currencies, and the second one is whether the effect occurred only on the day of the specific event or it "spilled over" to the days that followed. To address these research questions, we employ the standard event-study methodology as proposed by MacKinlay (1997) and Kothari *et al.* (2007), in order to assess whether, as a result of each of the events examined, the Euro exhibited any abnormal appreciation or depreciation against each of the selected currencies.

The rest of this chapter unfolds as follows; Section 16.2 describes the data and the empirical method used; Section 16.3 presents and discusses our results; and Section 16.4 discusses policy implications and concludes.

16.2. Data and Methodology

A challenge when designing an event-study is how to compile the sample of events that will be examined. In this chapter, we are interested in events that might be considered to be "significant" in the unfolding of the pandemic in the Eurozone and as such potentially affect the foreign exchange market and more specifically the price of the Euro versus other important currencies. Within this context, we have selected the following five events (the fourth one consists of two sub-events), which we believe are adequate to address our research question, at least at this point in time; these events are summarized in Table 16.1.

The first event is the announcement of the WHO that COVID-19 may be transmitted from human to human; the second one refers to the first lockdown that occurred in the EU, which took place in parts of Italy (Lombardy and Veneto); the third event is another announcement by the WHO that COVID-19 can be characterized as a pandemic; the fourth event comprises of two sub-events, which refer to the start and the end of social distancing in the largest economy of the EU, Germany; and the fifth event is the announcement by the European Commission of its proposal for a recovery fund and an updated long-term budget, the aim of which is the support of the EU economy, given the negative repercussions of the pandemic.

As already noted in the introduction, the central hypothesis examined refers to the possible effect that the events mentioned above had on the price of the Euro. We analyse this relative to seven other currencies, and more specifically, the four traditional major ones (the USD, the YEN, the GBP, the CHF), plus three others, the CAD, the AUD, and the NZD. We choose these currencies given that they are the ones exhibiting the highest liquidity in global markets;

Table 16.1. Events and background information.

No.	Event	Date of event	Period of interest	Comment
1	Confirmation of human to human transmission	14/09/2020	14/01/2020–27/01/2020	Announcement of WHO that there may have been human-to-human transmission of COVID-19
2	Italy lockdown	23/02/2020	24/02/2020–06/03/2020	Announcement of the first lockdown in Italy (areas in Lombardy and Veneto)
3	COVID-19 characterized as pandemic (WHO)	11/03/2020	11/03/2020–24/03/2020	Announcement of WHO that COVID-19 can be characterized as a pandemic
4(a)	Start of social distancing in Germany	22/03/2020	24/03/2020–04/03/2020	Issuance of strict social distancing measures
4(b)	End of social distancing in Germany	29/06/2020	29/06/2020–10/07/2020	End of social distancing measures
5	Announcement of EU recovery plan	27/05/2020	27/05/2020–09/06/2020	European Commission issues proposal for an EU recovery fund and an updated EU long-term budget

Note: The above table depicts the five events that are analyzed in this chapter. It describes each event, presents the event-day (i.e. the announcement date) and the period of interest, which refers to the time-period utilized for the "event-windows," i.e. the period during which the effect of the event is assessed.
Source: Various sources; table compiled by authors.

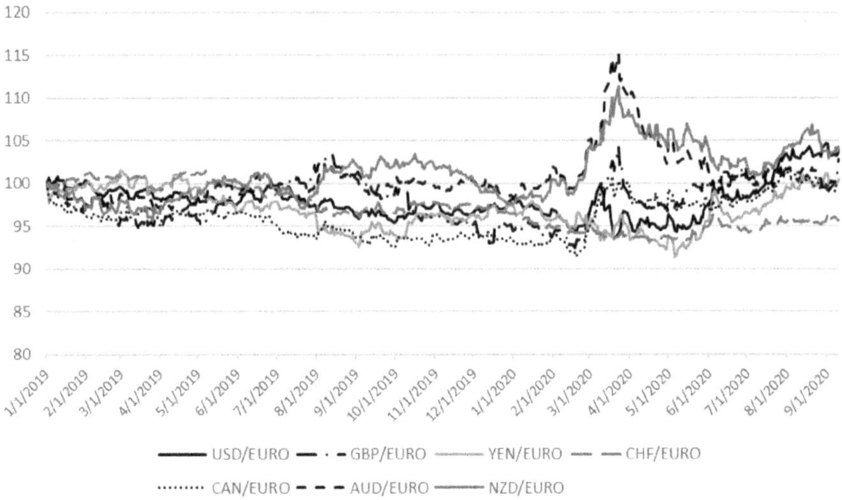

Figure 16.1. Euro versus other currencies.
Note: The above graph presents the price of the Euro in terms of seven other currencies; the USD, the GBP, the YEN, the CHF, the CAD, the AUD, and the NZD. All exchange rates have been indexed at 100, as on January 1, 2019.
Source: Exchange rates were collected from DataStream.

more specifically, according to the Triennial Central Bank Survey on Foreign exchange (2019), the USD appears in approximately 88% of the daily trades, the YEN in 17%, the GBP in 13%, the AUD in 7%, the CAD and the CHF in 5% each, and the NZD in 2%. For comparative purposes, we note that the Euro appears in 32% of the daily trades. Moreover, it is also worth pointing out that the choice of currencies adequately "covers" important geographical (and economic) areas.

Figure 16.1 depicts an initial "big picture" chart of the Euro versus the aforementioned currencies, for the period January 2019–September 2020.

Figure 16.1 clearly indicates that as from the beginning of 2020 — when it became clear that COVID-19 would be a major global issue — the price of the Euro versus the other currencies seems to behave differently when compared to the earlier time-period (i.e. during the whole of 2019). At first glance, it seems that the Euro appreciates versus the majority of the other currencies analyzed, with the exception of the YEN, the CHF, and to some extent the USD. It is the aim of the analysis that will follow to provide further insights to these initial observations.

Each currency pair was transformed into daily returns using the following equation:

$$R_{it} = \ln\left(\frac{P_{it}}{P_{it-1}}\right), \tag{16.1}$$

where R_{it} are the daily returns of currency pair I, and P_{it} and $P_{it}-1$ are the daily prices of currency pair i at time t and $t-1$. These refer to the value of one Euro in each foreign currency.

The methodology employed in this chapter is the "event-study" methodology. Typically, event studies examine the effects of an event on the value of assets, such as stocks and bonds, and, as in the case of our work, currencies. The methodology is based on the efficient market hypothesis put forward by Fama (1970), which asserts that as new information arrives at the market, it is immediately and accurately reflected in prices. This in turn implies that possible changes in prices may be attributed to specific events (e.g. the unfolding of the pandemic), which resulted in this new information being released. Given this property, it is not surprising that over the years "event studies" have been widely used in the finance literature; some of the more important papers that have employed it include Rendleman *et al.* (1982) and Ball and Brown (1968) to assess the impact of earnings announcements on stock prices; Brown and Warner (1980), Keown and Pinkerton (1981), and Bruner (1999), to assess the impact of M&A announcements on stock prices; Teoh *et al.* (1998a; 1998b) to examine the phenomenon of earnings management; Loughran and Ritter (1995) to examine initial public offerings; William (1981) to examine the effect of regulatory changes on stock prices; and Evans and Lyons (2008) to assess the effect of macroeconomic announcements on the foreign exchange market. Moreover, the methodology has also been used to assess the effects of "exogenous shocks" on markets; for example, Baumert (2009) and Baumert *et al.* (2013), Markoulis and Katsikides (2018), and Papakyriakou *et al.* (2019), among others, used it to assess the effect of terror attacks on stock markets, while Hassapis *et al.* (2018) used it to assess the effect of terror attacks on foreign exchange markets.

A framework of the analysis that needs to be followed to carry out an "event study" is provided in the work of MacKinlay (1997) and

Kothari and Warner (2007). More specifically, first, the date of the event needs to be determined; for the purposes of this work, this is the day on which specific important events related to the unfolding of COVID-19 in Europe have occurred; these have been described in Table 16.1. Next, as far as the time-series analysis is concerned, for each event, the "estimation period" and the "event period" need to be defined. The former is the period that will be used to determine the estimated or "expected" return predicted by the market around the "event date," while the latter is typically defined to be longer than the specific date of the event, in order to accommodate examination of periods surrounding the event.

For the purposes of this chapter, the "estimation period" is set at 60 trading days (September 10, 2019–December 3, 2019), which is the period ending 30 trading days prior to the first event that will be examined (January 14, 2020 — announcement of the WHO that there may have been limited human-to-human transmission of the coronavirus and that there might be a risk of a possible wider outbreak). There are two important points that need to be made here, the first is that the "estimation period" is not taken right before the occurrence of the first event so as to avoid "contaminating," it and the second is that we will use the same estimation period for all the events that will be analyzed, to make sure that COVID-19–related effects will not "spillover" from event to event. The "event period" is set at one, two, three, four, five, and ten days, i.e. we examine six "event-windows" (including the day of the event). The "event period" is extended beyond the day of the incident to assess how quickly the market absorbed (or did not absorb) the news; on the one hand, it is plausible that, on some occasions, initial worries might persist, while on the other hand, it is also possible that uncertainties might be eased somewhat through the release of new information.

To measure the reaction of the price of the Euro to each COVID-19–related event, an "expected" return for each currency pair employed must be estimated during the six "event-windows." This "expected" or "normalized" return must then be subtracted from the actual return ($R_{i,t}$), observed on the event-day and on subsequent days, so as to evaluate whether there is evidence of any abnormal return, which may have been caused by the specific COVID-19–related event.

This abnormal return is given by the following equation:

$$AR_{i,t} = R_{i,t} - E(R_{i,t}), \tag{16.2}$$

where $AR_{i,t}$ = the abnormal (or excess) return of currency pair i at time t, and $E(R_{i,t})$ = the expected return of currency pair i at time t.

An important element of Equation (16.2) is the estimation of $E(R_{i,t})$, where in this chapter we follow the methodology used in the work of Chen and Siems (2004) and Markoulis and Katsikides (2018), and compute $E(R_{i,t})$ as follows:

$$E(R_{i,t}) = \frac{1}{60} \sum_{t=-60}^{-1} R_{i,t}. \tag{16.3}$$

The date of the first event is $t = 0$ (January 14, 2020), hence the above equation estimates the expected return of currency pair i over 60 trading days, i.e. from $t = -90$ to $t = -30$ (as already noted, this will be the expected return that will be utilized in the analysis of all events).

To examine the immediate reaction of each currency pair to each event, the "event-day" abnormal returns need to be examined. Moreover, to assess the effect over the subsequent event-windows, the cumulative abnormal returns (CAR) for currency pair i must also be examined; these may be estimated using Equation (16.4):

$$CAR_{(t1,t2)} = \sum_{t=t_1}^{t_2} AR_{it}, \tag{16.4}$$

where: $t1$ and $t2$ are the start and end of the "event-window," respectively.

Given the above, the null and alternative hypotheses for each event-window can be defined as follows:

$$H0 : CAR_{(t1,t2)} = 0 \quad vs. \quad H1 : CAR_{(t1,t2)} \neq 0.$$

We will be examining each of the five events separately and as such, we will need to carry out standard t-tests for each event and for each "event-window," within the specific event.

The t-statistic that will be utilized is given by Equation (16.5):

$$t\text{-statistic} = \frac{CAR_{(t1,t2)}}{\sqrt{L\sigma^2(AR_t)}}, \tag{16.5}$$

where $\sigma^2(AR_t)$ is the variance of the one-period average abnormal return over the "estimation window"; L is the number of days corresponding to each "event-window," i.e. the CAR will have a higher variance the longer the L.

Effectively, the question we address through the above analysis, is whether, given each COVID-19–related event, the abnormal returns of the relevant currency pair (i.e. Euro versus each of the seven other currencies) are significantly different from zero on the day of the event and the cumulative abnormal returns are significant during the various subsequent "event-windows."

16.3. Event-Study Results

In this section, we present our results where, regarding each of the five events, we carry out t-tests for the abnormal returns of the relevant currency pairs (i.e. the price of the Euro in each of the seven other currencies), on the day of the event and for the CAR in the subsequent "event-windows," which consist of 2, 3, 4, 5, and 10 days; all our results are summarized in Table 16.2. Once this is done, we proceed with an analysis of these results.

The first event we analyse occurred on January 14, 2020, and refers to the announcement of the WHO that there may have been limited human-to-human transmission of the coronavirus and that there might be a risk of a possible wider outbreak. The announcement also noted that human-to-human transmission could be possible, given prior experience with SARS, MERS, and other respiratory pathogens. Results of our analysis regarding this event reveal no significant abnormal returns for the Euro against all currencies, except the YEN and the CHF, where we document negative cumulative abnormal returns in the 10-day event-window. More specifically, over the aforementioned event-window, the Euro depreciated by 2.36% versus the YEN and 1.28% versus the CHF; the former being significant at the 5% level, and the latter at the 10% level.

Table 16.2. Event-study results for the event day and 2-, 3-, 4-, 5-, and 10-day event-windows for all events.

	Event DAY (AR)	2-day CAR	3-day CAR	4-day CAR	5-day CAR	10-day CAR
Event 1. Confirmation of human to human transmission (January 14, 2020)						
USD/EURO	−0.0011	0.0015	0.0006	−0.0036	−0.0048	−0.0112
t-statistic	−0.4155	0.3905	0.1262	−0.6527	−0.7702	−1.2841
GBP/EURO	−0.0028	−0.0005	−0.0038	−0.0046	−0.0024	−0.0095
t-statistic	−0.4898	−0.0631	−0.3890	−0.4118	−0.1933	−0.5341
YEN/EURO	−0.0004	0.0015	0.0015	−0.0026	−0.0042	−0.0236**
t-statistic	−0.1328	0.3169	0.2595	−0.3826	−0.5528	−2.2109
CHF/EURO	−0.0039	−0.0046	−0.0065	−0.0069	−0.0063	−0.0128*
t-statistic	−1.5804	−1.3244	−1.5249	−1.4006	−1.1455	−1.6488
CAD/EURO	−0.0004	0.0008	−0.0007	−0.0039	−0.0053	−0.0033
t-statistic	−0.1224	0.1717	−0.1351	−0.6278	−0.7606	−0.3344
AUD/EURO	−0.0006	0.0014	0.0012	−0.0004	0.0002	0.0091
t-statistic	−0.1997	0.3290	0.2307	−0.0594	0.0233	0.9519
NZD/EURO	0.0022	0.0056	−0.0011	−0.0003	0.0008	0.0026
t-statistic	0.5507	0.9863	−0.1599	−0.0366	0.0881	0.2041
Event 2. Italy Lockdown (February 24, 2020)						
USD/EURO	0.0004	0.0011	0.0012	0.0122**	0.0120*	0.0411***
t-statistic	0.1418	0.2830	0.2454	2.2066	1.9478	4.7152
GBP/ EURO	0.0038	−0.0017	0.0067	0.0218*	0.0303**	0.0431**
t-statistic	0.6701	−0.2193	0.6906	1.9347	2.3999	2.4137
YEN/EURO	−0.0093***	−0.0137***	−0.0099*	−0.0045	−0.0245***	−0.0205***
t-statistic	−2.7459	−2.8615	−1.6939	−0.6667	−3.2435	−1.9201
CHF/EURO	−0.0003	−0.0008	0.0001	0.0033	0.0010	−0.0017
t-statistic	−0.1230	−0.2420	0.0315	0.6673	0.1898	−0.2185
CAD/EURO	0.0036	0.0054	0.0065	0.0214***	0.0261***	0.0546***
t-statistic	1.1542	1.2270	1.2143	3.4460	3.7575	5.5634
AUD/EURO	0.0024	0.0048	0.0126**	0.0199***	0.0394***	0.0400
t-statistic	0.7856	1.1310	2.4123	3.3085	5.8570	4.2017
NZD/EURO	0.0000	0.0042	0.0093	0.0175**	0.0356***	0.0418***
t-statistic	0.0046	0.7447	1.3401	2.1777	3.9541	3.2876
Event 3. COVID-19 characterized as pandemic (March 11, 2020)						
USD/EURO	−0.0059**	−0.0235***	−0.0247***	−0.0184***	−0.0335***	−0.0497***
t-statistic	−2.1549	−6.0222	−5.1581	−3.3372	−5.4294	−5.7003
GBP/EURO	−0.0010	0.0092	0.0201**	0.0371***	0.0447***	0.0516***
t-statistic	−0.1825	1.1539	2.0550	3.2882	3.5440	2.8910
YEN/EURO	0.0043	−0.0057	0.0068	−0.0014	−0.0006	0.0191*
t-statistic	1.2601	−1.1892	1.1604	−0.2119	−0.0761	1.7948
CHF/EURO	−0.0006	−0.0019	−0.0026	−0.0044	−0.0007	−0.0001
t-statistic	−0.2391	−0.5570	−0.6154	−0.8950	−0.1288	−0.0173
CAD/EURO	−0.0078**	−0.0166***	−0.0096*	−0.0046	−0.0047	−0.0014

(*Continued*)

Table 16.2. (*Continued*)

	Event DAY (AR)	2-day CAR	3-day CAR	4-day CAR	5-day CAR	10-day CAR
Event 3. COVID-19 characterized as pandemic (March 11, 2020)						
t-statistic	−2.5197	−3.7915	−1.7901	−0.7330	−0.6716	−0.1465
AUD/EURO	−0.0109***	0.0073*	0.0262***	0.0358***	0.0464***	0.0376***
t-statistic	−3.6299	1.7114	5.0294	5.9400	6.8983	3.9518
NZD/EURO	−0.0121***	0.0042	0.0108	0.0061	0.0210**	0.0298**
t-statistic	−3.0169	0.7453	1.5445	0.7557	2.3389	2.3410
Event 4(a). Commencement of social distancing in Germany (March 22, 2020)						
USD/EURO	0.0066**	0.0100**	0.0133***	0.0308***	0.0338***	0.0100
t-statistic	2.3737	2.5521	2.7753	5.5743	5.4811	1.1412
GBP/EURO	0.0291***	0.0083	0.0141	0.0010	−0.0130	−0.0254
t-statistic	5.1523	1.0364	1.4455	0.0869	−1.0329	−1.4226
YEN/EURO	0.0064*	0.0107**	0.0132**	0.0127	0.0036	−0.0188*
t-statistic	1.8925	2.2341	2.2614	1.8776	0.4794	−1.7665
CHF/EURO	0.0029	0.0048	0.0051	0.0084*	0.0026	0.0008
t-statistic	1.1739	1.3985	1.2156	1.7230	0.4772	0.1055
CAD/EURO	0.0192***	0.0183***	0.0114**	0.0084	0.0134*	−0.0096
t-statistic	6.1713	4.1781	2.1253	1.3553	1.9293	−0.9748
AUD/EURO	0.0218***	−0.0044	−0.0061	−0.0036	−0.0141**	−0.0197**
t-statistic	7.2270	−1.0240	−1.1789	−0.6019	−2.0940	−2.0729
NZD/EURO	0.0164***	0.0229***	0.0182***	0.0332***	0.0481***	0.0433***
t-statistic	4.0709	4.0249	2.6144	4.1234	5.3418	3.4007
Event 4(b). End of social distancing in Germany (June 29, 2020)						
USD/EURO	0.0039	0.0026	0.0052	0.0023	0.0035	0.0101
t-statistic	1.4121	0.6619	1.0844	0.4112	0.5659	1.1588
GBP/EURO	0.0087	0.0010	−0.0039	−0.0067	−0.0049	−0.0098
t-statistic	1.5387	0.1235	−0.3993	−0.5896	−0.3852	−0.5488
YEN/EURO	0.0071**	0.0071	0.0060	0.0038	0.0038	0.0073
t-statistic	2.1135	1.4866	1.0350	0.5576	0.5039	0.6845
CHFE/EURO	0.0044***	0.0005	0.0004	−0.0017	−0.0014	−0.0010
t-statistic	1.7952	0.1524	0.0869	−0.3419	−0.2489	−0.1331
CAD/EURO	0.0026	−0.0047	−0.0064	−0.0063	−0.0075	−0.0011
t-statistic	0.8335	−1.0679	−1.1844	−1.0170	−1.0811	−0.1156
AUD/EURO	0.0026	−0.0035	−0.0064	−0.0077	−0.0107	−0.0078
t-statistic	0.8565	−0.8114	−1.2359	−1.2717	−1.5924	−0.8158
NZD/EURO	0.0033	−0.0021	−0.0050	−0.0126	−0.0150*	−0.0148
t-statistic	0.8211	−0.3697	−0.7229	−1.5701	−1.6665	−1.1663

Table 16.2. (*Continued*)

	Event DAY (AR)	2-day CAR	3-day CAR	4-day CAR	5-day CAR	10-day CAR
Event 5. Announcement of EU recovery plan (May 27, 2020)						
USD/EURO	−0.0011	0.0064	0.0125***	0.0137**	0.0178***	0.0329***
t-statistic	−0.3880	1.6389	2.6162	2.4893	2.8834	3.7695
GBP/EURO	0.0115	0.0111	0.0145	0.0068	0.0057	0.0116
t-statistic	2.0454	1.3855	1.4804	0.6057	0.4537	0.6477
YEN/EURO	0.0009	0.0061	0.0129**	0.0122*	0.0254***	0.0310***
t-statistic	0.2537	1.2727	2.2079	1.8025	3.3730	2.9054
CHFE/EURO	0.0012	0.0041	0.0051	0.0060	0.0102*	0.0130*
t-statistic	0.4922	1.1970	1.1940	1.2310	1.8652	1.6852
CAD/EURO	−0.0001	0.0029	0.0133**	−0.0004	−0.0063	0.0032
t-statistic	−0.0351	0.6628	2.4665	−0.0648	−0.9118	0.3278
AUD/EURO	0.0099***	0.0050	0.0142***	−0.0067	−0.0183***	−0.0159*
t-statistic	3.2861	1.1696	2.7220	−1.1094	−2.7187	−1.6677
NZD/EURO	0.0082**	0.0055	0.0170**	0.0033	−0.0049	−0.0137
t-statistic	2.0299	0.9654	2.4423	0.4083	−0.5393	−1.0740

Note: The above table depicts abnormal returns, cumulative abnormal returns and t-tests for all the events that are analyzed in this chapter. Tests are presented for the "event-day" and "event-windows" of 2, 3, 4, 5, and 10 days. Abnormal returns are calculated using the equation:

$$AR_{i,t} = R_{i,t} - E\left(R_{i,t}\right),$$

where $AR_{i,t}$ is the abnormal return of currency pair i at time t and $E(R_{i,t})$ is the expected return of currency pair i at time t. $E(R_{i,t})$ is computed using the following equation:

$$E\left(R_{i,t}\right) = \frac{1}{60}\sum_{t=-60}^{-1} R_{i,t}.$$

The above equation estimates the expected return of currency pair i over 60 trading days, i.e. from $t = -90$ to $t = -30$ (starting date is January 14, 2020). Cumulative abnormal returns (CAR) for currency pair i are estimated using the equation:

$$CAR_{(t1,t2)} = \sum_{t=t_1}^{t_2} AR_{it},$$

where: $t1$ and $t2$ are the start and end of the "event-window," respectively. The null and alternative hypotheses for each event-window are defined as follows: $H0$: $CAR_{(t1,t2)} = 0$ vs $H1$: $CAR_{(t1,t2)} \neq 0$.

The t-statistic used to test the above hypothesis is:

$$t\text{-statistic} = \frac{CAR_{(t1,t2)}}{\sqrt{L\sigma^2\left(AR_t\right)}},$$

where $\sigma^2(AR_t)$ is the variance of the one-period average abnormal return over the "estimation window." L is the number of days corresponding to each "event-window," i.e. the CAR will have a higher variance the longer is L.

***denotes significance at the 1% level, **denotes significance at the 5% level, and *denotes significance at the 10% level.

The second event refers to the first introduction of a lockdown in Italy, specifically in Lombardy and Veneto regions, which occurred on February 23, 2020. Results regarding this event are quite rich and interesting in the sense that the Euro appears to exhibit significant reaction against all currencies examined, except the CHF. More specifically, it seems that the Euro appears to appreciate against the USD and the GBP, as well as the CAD, AUD, and NZD, and depreciates against the YEN. The appreciation of the Euro appears to "build up" and reaches its highest level at the 10-day event-window in all cases; for example, in the case of the USD, it is 4.11%, and in the case of the GBP, it is 4.3%. The highest appreciation is observed in the case of the CAD, where it is 5.46%. The depreciation against the YEN seems to start from the event day (–0.93%), reaches its higher level after 5 days (–2.45%) and shows persistence until the 10-day event-window (–2.05%). There does not appear to be any significant effect related to the price of the Euro relative to the CHF.

We next assess the impact of the third event, which is the declaration by the WHO that COVID-19 is indeed a pandemic (March 11, 2020), on the price of the Euro; again, results are quite rich and interesting. The Euro appears to depreciate modestly against the CAD (–0.96% up to the three-day event-window) and more profoundly against the USD; more specifically, the Euro depreciates against the USD in a rather monotonous manner, from –0.6% on the event-day to –4.97% in the 10-day event-window. On the other hand, the Euro seems to appreciate against the GBP (5.16% in the 10-day event-window) and interestingly against the YEN (1.91% in the 10-day event-window). Euro's behaviour against the AUD and NZD is remarkably similar; depreciation on the event day, followed by rising appreciation up to and including the 10-day event-window (+3.76% vs the AUD and +2.98% vs the NZD). As in the case of the previous event, there are no significant results regarding the CHF.

The fourth event comprises two sub-events, which are related to the start and the end of the social distancing in the EU's largest economy, Germany. As a result of the first sub-event, the Euro appreciates against the USD (5-day CAR of 3.4%), the CAD (5-day CAR of 1.3%), as well as the NZD (5-day CAR of 4.8%, which persists until the 10-day event-window). Moreover, the Euro also seems to appreciate against the GBP, but only on the event-day (abnormal return of 2.9%), while the change against the CHF is again quite negligible. Finally, the Euro seems to modestly appreciate against the YEN and the AUD in the earlier event-windows (e.g. positive CAR of 1.3% and 1.1%, respectively, in the 3-day event-window), with this being reversed later on (negative CAR of –1.9% and –2%, respectively, in the 10-day event-window). Interestingly, we note that despite the obvious negative nature of the event, the Euro exhibits noteworthy resilience. The second sub-event, which is related to the end of social distancing in Germany, does not provide such rich results; the Euro appears to exhibit very modest appreciation against the YEN and the CHF on the day of the event only (abnormal returns of 0.7% and 0.4%, respectively).

The fifth and final event that is analyzed in this study is the announcement of the European Commission's proposal for an EU recovery fund and an updated EU long-term budget, in a coordinated effort to combat the effects of the pandemic on the EU economy. Our results indicate that the Euro appreciates versus the USD, and the two "safe haven" currencies, the CHF and the YEN. More specifically, there is a 3.3% appreciation versus the USD in the 10-day window and a 3.1% appreciation versus the YEN in the same window; the appreciation versus the CHF is more modest, reaching 1.3%, again in the 10-day window. Moreover, the Euro seems to appreciate in the earlier event-windows versus the AUD, but this is reversed in the latter windows, reaching negative CAR of 1.6% in the 10-day event-window. There is also evidence of modest appreciation versus the GBP, the CAD, and the NZD, primarily in the earlier event-windows.

Table 16.3 summarizes the aforementioned findings and provides a platform for further discussion and analysis.

With the exception of the third event (characterization of COVID-19 as a pandemic by the WHO), the Euro either appreciates or exhibits no statistically significant change versus the USD. This is a particularly interesting result given the fact that the USD is the global reserve currency, which provides by far the most liquidity and the safest assets. A possible reason for this positive reaction of the Euro relative to the USD during the unfolding of the pandemic may be attributed to the common stance of EU leaders, which was epitomized by the pandemic rescue package presented by the European

Table 16.3. Summary of event-study results.

	Event 1	Event 2	Event 3	Event 4a	Event 4b	Event 5
Currency pair (Euro vs)						
USD	No effect	+ve	−ve	+ve	No effect	+ve
GBP	No effect	+ve	+ve	+ve	No effect	+ve
YEN	−ve	−ve	+ve	+ve/−ve	+ve	+ve
CHF	−ve	No effect	No effect	+ve	+ve	+ve
CAD	No effect	+ve	−ve	+ve	No effect	+ve
AUD	No effect	+ve	−ve/+ve	+ve/−ve	No effect	+ve/−ve
NZD	No effect	+ve	−ve/+ve	+ve	No effect	+ve

Note: The above table provides a summary of the significant results of our analysis; it shows the reaction of the Euro against each of the seven currencies following each of the five events. +ve means the Euro appreciated, −ve means the Euro depreciated, −ve/+ve means the Euro initially depreciated and then appreciated, +ve/−ve means the Euro initially appreciated and then depreciated, and no effect means there was no statistically significant reaction. Results are summarized across event-windows; e.g. +ve means that the Euro appreciated in at least one of the event-windows examined. Event 1 refers to the confirmation of human-to-human transmission (January 14, 2020); Event 2 to the Italy lockdown (February 23, 2020); Event 3 to COVID-19 being characterized as pandemic by the WHO (March 11, 2020); Event 4(a) to the start of social distancing in Germany (March 22, 2020) and event 4(b) to the end of social distancing in Germany (June 29, 2020); and Event 5 to the announcement of the EU recovery plan (May 27, 2020).

Commission on May 27, 2020, which comprised a € 750 billion economic stimulus plan along with a revised proposal for the EU 2021–2027 budget. This signalled that richer northern states were more willing to show solidarity toward their not-so-rich southern neighbours and thus lay the foundation for economic recovery and possibly further fiscal integration; there appears to be a notable difference in this response when compared to that during the Global Financial Crisis and the Euro sovereign debt crisis, which occurred a few years ago. At the same time, it is plausible that the management of the pandemic and the political debate surrounding it in the US was questioned by market participants, who were possibly also assuming that the central bank would need to lavish more and more stimulus on the economy, which in turn could put some downward pressure on the USD.

Regarding the GBP, it seems that the Euro either appreciates (4/6 cases) or there is no significant reaction (2/6 cases). This positive behaviour of the Euro versus the GBP can be attributed to reasons already noted when discussing the reaction of the Euro versus the USD but there are other factors that should also be noted; one of them is related to the fact that, like the USD, the Euro is a heavily traded currency and as such provides liquidity in times of crisis; a so-called funding currency. Moreover, the UK's persistent current account deficit implies a constant need for foreign investment, which is another reason for the GBP depreciating against the Euro, as is the general uncertainty surrounding the possibility of the UK achieving a trade deal with the EU; clearly, a so-called "cliff edge" Brexit will be bad for the GBP, especially during the unfolding of a pandemic.

As far as the YEN is concerned, results are not so clear-cut — there is significant reaction for all events, but the results are mixed; generally speaking, there appears to be depreciation of the Euro in the first two events, followed by appreciation in the ones that follow (with the exception of the fourth event, which provides mixed results). The pattern is not very different regarding the CHF; depreciation for the first event, no significant effect for the next two events, and appreciation later on. The earlier results can be attributed to the fact that investors may have turned to the so-called traditional "safe haven" currencies (CHF and YEN), thus their appreciation versus the Euro. This phenomenon has also been documented in studies examining the effects of terror attacks on currency markets; for instance, Hassapis *et al.* (2018) documented that after certain terror attacks (9/11, 2004 Madrid bombings, 2005 London bombings), the currency of the affected country/economic region depreciated versus the CHF and the YEN. The latter results, however, seem to provide further evidence regarding the resilience of the Euro during the unfolding of COVID-19.

Results regarding the CAD are quite similar to those observed in the case of the USD; again, we witness a rather positive reaction of the Euro in the majority of the events. In addition to the reasons cited above regarding the general strengthening of the Euro, it is also worth pointing out that in the case of the CAD there is another factor that must be considered; the CAD is a so-called commodity currency and as such, was disproportionately affected by the pandemic mainly due to the fact that the decreased oil demand from China pushed oil prices down and thus affected the CAD negatively. Finally, in the case of the AUD and the NZD, results are rather mixed; it would seem that the Euro appreciates against the NZD (except in the case of the third event, where it temporarily depreciates), while in the case of the AUD, results are clearly non-conclusive since we have three cases with mixed results and two that do not unveil any significant results.

16.4. Conclusion

The research question addressed in this chapter was how the common currency — the Euro — reacted against other major currencies during the unfolding of COVID-19 so far; as one might expect, our evidence, which is derived from event-study analysis is not clear-cut (as one might expect), as we obtain mixed results across events and currency pairs. However, if we were to "pass" a big-picture verdict on the reaction of the Euro, it would be a positive one; among other findings, the mere fact that in times of such a deep crisis, the Euro appears to strengthen versus the USD is quite important in itself.

So, what do we learn from this analysis, and what are the possible policy implications? The unfolding of COVID-19 and the subsequent economic crisis has conveyed an important message for Eurozone leaders: that the Euro deserves a greater international role. The key criteria that must be fulfilled for a currency to have such a role are a large and growing economy and developed financial markets, free movement of capital, the ability to supply safe assets, significant geopolitical power, and the willingness to be an important global "player"; within this context, it is not surprising that in recent times the Euro has been the world's "second currency" (in terms of trading). Clearly, to rise in global prominence, the Euro should be in a position to provide advantages that mimic those of the USD, which is something that we have not exactly seen in recent time. That is why the international use of the currency has been rather stalling and Eurozone countries have not been benefiting "equally" from the "privileges" stemming from the use of the common currency.

This is probably due to the fact that up to this point, the Eurozone has been characterized by market segmentation and a limited supply of "safe assets"; contrast this, for instance with US Treasury Bills and Bonds. To address this very important issue, there are two things that policymakers can do: (i) provide common instruments that would result in "safe assets" for all member states in times of crisis and (ii) use monetary policy to safeguard liquidity in the financial system.

The recently announced recovery fund of € 750 billion, which incidentally is the last event examined in this study, is a very good demonstration of the first one as it will provide a strong fiscal response to the COVID-19 crisis, which in turn is likely to help build confidence among investors that the common currency can be relied upon during times of major crisis. Moreover, at the same time, the bonds issued for the purposes of this fund will allow global investors to get more exposure to the Eurozone as a whole, rather than on individual member countries; this in turn could pave the way toward building a common capital market where high-quality assets will be traded. It should also be noted that joint issuance of "safe assets" should go hand-in-hand with central control of spending and a solid grip on revenues; the treaty-based EU framework is the closest to fulfilling such criteria with political accountability (through the European Parliament) and political control (through the Commission). Furthermore, it is also essential to make sure that a strong economic recovery is achieved in all Eurozone countries in order to make the Euro area an even more attractive destination for investment, which in turn could pave the way for a further increase in the supply of safe assets.

Regarding the second possible policy implication, it is clear that international investors trust the US Federal Reserve to "guarantee" the global role of the USD. Along these lines, we should note the ECB's pandemic emergency purchase program of up to € 1.35 trillion, which is expected to run until at least June 2021, as well as the fact that the ECB has activated a number of swap and repo lines to other central banks so as to provide liquidity in these times of need; this is another good example of what a central bank managing a truly global currency should do.

To conclude then, amidst the pain and the huge social and economic consequences of this horrible pandemic, it would appear that the common currency — the Euro — has showed noteworthy resilience against other major global currencies. It would appear that the actions taken by the European Commission and the ECB have been given a positive verdict by international markets and show the way forward in order to achieve the goal of bolstering the global standing of the Euro; clearly, the right combination of fiscal and monetary policy can help build a better functioning and more stable monetary union, which in turn could increase the global reach and influence of the Euro.

References

Albulescu, C.T. (2020). COVID-19 and the United States financial markets' volatility. *Finance Research Letters*. https://doi.org/10.1016/j.frl.2020.101699.

Ali, M., Alam, N. Rizvi, S.A.R. (2020). Coronavirus (COVID-19) - An epidemic or pandemic for financial markets. *Journal of Behavioral and Experimental Finance*, **27**. https://doi.org/10.1016/j.jbef.2020.100341.

Aslam, M., Aziz, S., Nguyen, K.D., Mughal, S.K. and Khan M. (2020). On the efficiency of foreign exchange markets in times of the Covid-19 pandemic. *Technological Forecasting and Social Science*, **161**. https://doi.org/10.1016/j.techfore.2020.120261.

Ball, R. and Brown, P. (1968). An empirical evaluation of accounting income numbers. *Journal of Accounting Research*, **6**, 159–177.

Baumert, T. (2009). Terrorism, news flows and stock markets. In: Richardson, H., Gordon, P. and Moore, J.E. (eds.). *Global Business and the Terrorist Threat* (Cheltenham, Northampton: Edward Elgar, 2009), pp. 119–135.

Baumert T., Buesa M. and Lynch, T. (2013). The impact of terrorism on stock markets: The Boston bombing experience in comparison with previous terrorist events. *Documento de Trabajo No. 88.*

Brown, S.J. and Warner, J.B. (1980). Measuring security price performance. *Journal of Financial Economics*, **8**, 205–258.

Bruner, R.F. (1999). An analysis of value destruction and recovery in the alliance and proposed merger of Volvo and Renault. *Journal of Financial Economics*, **51**, 125–166.

Burch, T.R., Douglas R.E. and Fuerst, M.R. (2016). Who moves markets in a sudden market wide crisis? Evidence from 9/11. *Journal of Financial and Quantitative Analysis*, **51**(2), 463–487.

Chen, A. and Siems, T. (2004). The effects of terrorism on global capital markets. *European Journal of Political Economy*, **20**, 349–366.

Chen, M.H., Jang, S.C.S. and Kim, W.G. (2007). The impact of the SARS outbreak on Taiwanese hotel stock performance: An event-study approach. *International Journal of Hospitality Management*, **26**(1), 200–212.

Chesney, M., Reshetar, G. and Karamana, M. (2011). The impact of terrorism on financial markets: An empirical study. *Journal of Banking & Finance*, **35**, 253–267.

Evans, M.D.D. and Lyons, R.K. (2008). How is macro news transmitted to exchange rates? *Journal of Financial Economics*, **88**(1), 26–50.

Fama, E. (1970). Efficient capital markets: A review of theory and empirical work. *The Journal of Finance*, **25**, 383–417.

Hassapis, C., Katsikides, S. and Markoulis S. (2018). Terror attacks, foreign exchange markets and class dynamics', classes — From national to global class formation. *IntechOpen*, 55–75.

He, P., Sun, Y., Zhang, Y. and Li, T. (2020). COVID–19's impact on stock prices across different sectors—an event study based on the Chinese stock market. *Emerging Markets Finance and Trade*, **56**(10), 2198–2212, doi: 10.1080/1540496X.2020.1785865.

Hood, M., Kamesaka, A., Nofsinger, J. and Tamura, T. (2013). Investor response to a natural disaster: Evidence from Japan's 2011 earthquake. *Pacific-Basin Finance Journal*, **25**, 240–252.

Keown, J.A. and Pinkerton, M.J. (1981). Merger announcements and insider trading activity: An empirical investigation. *Journal of Finance*, **36**(4), 855–869.

Kothari, S.P. and Warner, J.B. (2007). Econometrics of event studies. In: B. Espen Eckbo (eds), *Handbook of Corporate Finance: Empirical Corporate Finance* (North Holland/Elsevier, Amsterdam), pp. 3–36.

Loughran, T. and Ritter, J. (1995). The new issues puzzle. *Journal of Finance*, **50**, 23–51.

MacKinlay, A.C. (1997). Event studies in economics and finance. *Journal of Economic Literature*,(35), 13–39.

Markoulis, S. and Katsikides, S. (2018). The effect of terrorism on stock markets: Evidence from the 21st century, terrorism and political violence. doi: 10.1080/09546553.2018.1425207.

Narayan, P.K., Narayan, S., Khademalomoom, S. and Phan, D.H.B. (2017). Do terrorist attacks impact exchange rate behavior? New international evidence. *Economic Inquiry*, **56**(1), 547–561.

Nippani, S. and Washer, K.M. (2004). SARS: A non-event for affected countries' stock markets? *Applied Financial Economics*, **14**(15), 1105–1110. doi: 10.1080/0960310042000310579.

Okorie, D.I. and Lin, B. (2020). Stock markets and the COVID-19 fractal contagion effects. *Finance Research Letters*. https://doi.org/10.1016/j.frl.2020.101640.

Papakyriakou, P., Sakkas, A. and Taoushanis, Z. (2019). The impact of terrorist attacks in G7 countries on international stock markets and the role of investor sentiment. *Journal of International Financial Markets, Institutions and Money*, **61**, 143–160.

Park, J.S. and Khaleq, N.M. (2018). Do terrorist attacks harm financial markets? A meta-analysis of event studies and the determinants of adverse impact. *Global Finance Journal*, **37**(C), 227–247.

Qing, H., Liu, J., Wang, S. and Yu, J. (2020). The impact of COVID-19 on stock markets. *Economic and Political Studies*, **8**(3), 275–288. doi: 10.1080/20954816.2020.1757570.

Rendleman, R., Jones, P.C. and Latane, H.A. (1982). Empirical anomalies based on unexpected earnings and the importance of risk adjustments. *Journal of Financial Economics*, **10**(3), 269–287.

Seven, U. and Yilmaz, F. (2020). World equity markets and COVID-19: Immediate response and recovery prospects. *Research in International Business and Finance*. https://doi.org/10.1016/j.ribaf.2020.101349.

Taleb, N. (2007). *The Black Swan: The Impact of the Highly Improbable* (Random House and Penguin Books, New York).

Teoh, S.H., Welch, I. and Wong, T.J. (1998a). Earnings management and the long-run market performance of initial public offerings. *Journal of Finance*, **53**, 1935–1974.

Teoh, S.H., Welch, I. and Wong, T.J. (1998b). Earnings management and the underperformance of seasoned equity offerings. *Journal of Financial Economics*, **50**, 63–99.

Triennial Central Bank Survey Foreign exchange turnover (2019). Bank for International Settlements, April.

Wang, L. and Kutan, A. (2013). The impact of natural disasters on stock markets: Evidence from Japan and the US. *Comparative Economic Studies*, **55**, 672–686.

William S.G. (1981). Using financial data to measure effects of regulation. *Journal of Law and Economics*, **24**, 121–158.

World Health Organization (2020). Virtual press conference on Covid-19, 11 March. Retrieved from https://www.who.int/docs/default-source/coronaviruse/transcripts/who-audio-emergencies-coronavirus-press-conference-full-and-final-11mar2020.pdf?sfvrsn=cb432bb3_2. Accessed date 30/10/2020.

PART IV

COVID-19: Implications for Corporate Governance and Finance

https://doi.org/10.1142/9781800610781_0017

Chapter 17

Does a High ESG Score Pay Off During the Pandemic Outbreak?

Jędrzej Białkowski[*,‡] **and Anna Sławik**[†,§]

Department of Economics and Finance, UC Business School University of Canterbury, Christchurch, Private Bag 4800 Christchurch 8140, New Zealand

[†]*Institute of Economics, Finance and Management Jagiellonian University Prof. S. Łojasiewicza street, 30-348 Kraków, Poland*

[‡]*jedrzej.bialkowski@canterbury.ac.nz*

[§]*anna.slawik@uj.edu.pl*

Abstract

A key aspect of creating financially effective business strategies is the development of efficient management methods at the meeting point between the competing interests of an organization's diverse stakeholders, making it possible to generate added value for some of them. Stakeholder management, together with its underlying concepts such as corporate social responsibility (CSR), contributes to increasing the viability of an organization's system as well as the system of its environment, including the financial market. This is of crucial importance in times of crisis, when a system's viability is particularly put to the test. In this chapter, we tackle this actual problem under the unprecedented circumstances of the COVID-19 pandemic outbreak. In our research, we assume there is a positive relation between social responsibility, the stakeholder approach to corporate governance and a company's financial performance, and we take as a proxy for the latter the stock returns of publicly listed companies. We examine US and European companies with high and low environmental, social, and governance (ESG) scores in 18 countries and 11 industries in the period January–June 2020. Their ESG profile is determined using the SAM Corporate Sustainability Assessment (CSA) and Sustainalytics's ESG Risk Ratings. We find evidence that, under pandemic circumstances, delivering value to a broader spectrum of stakeholders (reflected by a high ESG score) does not necessarily immediately (in the short run) protect or enhance the value for shareholders (measured by annualized stock returns) but does not deteriorate the value either.

17.1. Introduction

Assuming the overriding goal of the sustainability of any system — be it of the economy, the market, or an enterprise — one of the basic problems of economics, finance, and management is to ensure balance by reconciling continuation with change, i.e. to continue operating in a time of change or to make changes in order to enable the continuation of a system's activity. The well-known stakeholder concept in social sciences can be, in our view, the catalyst for meeting this challenge of sustainability faced by all economic systems in the 21st century.

Stakeholder theory documents that addressing and balancing the conflicting claims of multiple stakeholders helps a company enhance performance and long-term viability and maximize shareholders' value (Bosse *et al.*, 2009; Paranque, 2017), and also increases the efficiency of its adaptation to external demands (Orlitzky *et al.*, 2003). This attitude can pay off during external crises thanks to more effective crisis management (Alpaslan *et al.*, 2009; Ndlela, 2019). Sustainable management, i.e. a management approach utilising the concepts of corporate social responsibility (CSR) and environmental, social and governance (ESG), which underline the stakeholder approach, can translate into higher and less volatile profitability in the long run and a better competitive position (Greenwald, 2010; Jo *et al.*, 2010), lower risk (Albuquerque *et al.*, 2018; Lee and Faff, 2009), better and cheaper access to finance (Boubaker *et al.*, 2020; El Ghoul *et al.*, 2011) or better resistance to crises, also in terms of higher stock returns and profitability during downturns (Lins *et al.*, 2017).

This chapter contributes to the literature of management and finance by shedding light on the well-known, though insufficiently explored/verified, problem of economic justification for CSR policies under the circumstances of the unprecedented pandemic crisis. It also makes the academic discourse more appealing/enquiring by proving that doing good does no harm (in monetary terms/to investors), even in this tough period faced by financial/capital markets.

The results of our study show that, by controlling for the sector and level of ESG scores, the impact of a company's ESG profile on its equity performance is positive during the period of the initial panic caused by the pandemic outbreak. It is rarely statistically significant, though. The sector-wise analysis provides weak evidence that ESG itself drives performance inside each sector. However, the leading companies in terms of their ESG score in each sector were able to generate a better return to investors than the rest, which was especially visible during the initial panic period of the COVID-19 downturn.

The remainder of the chapter is organized as follows. Section 17.2 links the concepts of social responsibility and sustainability with financial performance through stakeholder theory. Section 17.3 reviews empirical research on the impact of ESG on companies' value and performance. Section 17.4 provides evidence from both sides of the Atlantic on the returns of companies with high and low ESG scores during the COVID-19 outbreak. Section 17.5 provides the conclusion, including practical implications.

17.2. Linking Social Responsibility with Financial Performance

> *The first and foremost social responsibility of business is economic in nature.*
>
> A. Carroll (1979, p. 500)

17.2.1. *Under the stakeholder concept umbrella*

There seems to be no doubt that stakeholders[1] may play a significant role in resolving not only the social and environmental issues of

[1]We define a stakeholder as any identifiable "group or individual who can affect or is affected by the achievement of the organisation's objectives" (Freeman, 1984, p. 46).

a company but also, and foremost, the economic ones (e.g. Boubaker *et al.*, 2014). This is why the strategic management of stakeholders is seen as the means for increasing the likelihood of achieving the goals of a corporation, marketplace success, and financial performance (e.g. Donaldson and Preston, 1995; Choi and Wang, 2009; Jones, 1995; Sisodia *et al.*, 2007), and in general enhancing a firm's value (Freeman *et al.*, 2004) and long-term viability (Ackermann and Eden, 2011). To explain why it happens, Bosse *et al.* (2009) argue, based on an assumption of reciprocity, that the value created by a company is the aggregated value created in its stakeholder relationships. Importantly, the stakeholder approach — in the process of management — generates greater added value for shareholders (stockholders) than that which would be generated using the traditional shareholder value maximization model (see e.g. Paranque, 2017).

The stakeholder concept was first introduced in opposition to the shareholder value maximization model that was prevalent in management at that time. That model had its imperative in agency theory that used to be the dominant paradigm in the financial economics literature (Fama, 1980; Ross, 1973). We agree with Hill and Jones (1992) that agency theory, which is primarily concerned with the relationship between managers and shareholders, needed to be updated to a new paradigm — stakeholder-agency theory — which reflects the stakeholder approach to corporate governance (Freeman and Reed, 1983) and which is in line with current concepts of social responsibility and sustainability.

In our understanding, the stakeholder concept merges rather than contrasts the shareholder and stakeholder models. Interestingly, stakeholders are indeed the focal point of both models. The set of stakeholders being of a corporate interest under those models is just differently selected (due to different assumptions and motivations of their identification process). This is reflected in the instrumental versus normative approach of stakeholder theory.

The instrumental approach to the application of stakeholder theory is naturally closer to us, since it implies stakeholder management.[2] But more important, this is the one that advocates

[2]The instrumental stakeholder approach "establishes a framework for examining the connections, if any, between the practice of stakeholder management and the

discussion about the link between stakeholder management, CSR and companies' financial performance. The instrumental approach indicates that a stakeholder orientation, by creating stakeholder satisfaction, gives a company a source of competitive advantage (Hillman and Keim, 2001), which, in turn, can ensure the long-term survival and success of the firm (Freeman, 1984; Freeman and McVea, 2001), result in better financial performance (Berrone *et al.*, 2007) and even help to acquire and maintain industry leadership (Chakraborty *et al.*, 2004). Recognition of the importance of the stakeholder perspective in providing high financial returns has even been made by some finance scholars, such as Cornell and Shapiro (1987) and Zingales *et al.* (2020). A key assumption of the stakeholder approach is that firms' ultimate goal is market success and that satisfying stakeholder claims helps to achieve this goal (Donaldson and Preston, 1995; Freeman, 1984).

However, we support the opinion that normative and instrumental perspectives are not mutually exclusive or divergent, but that they are interrelated, and their integration — at least in the practice of management — is inevitable. To prove that, scholars have already attempted to integrate the two approaches (Gibson, 2000; Jones, 1995; Velamuri and Venkataraman, 2005). The underlying rationale of their studies is that ethical and socially responsible behaviours (a normative orientation) can result in a significant competitive advantage (an instrumental orientation) (Berrone *et al.*, 2007).

17.2.2. *Stakes in the context of crises*

By addressing and balancing the conflicting claims of multiple stakeholders (see, among others, Donaldson and Preston, 1995; Freeman and Phillips, 2002), managers can increase the efficiency of their firms' adaptation to external demands (Orlitzky *et al.*, 2003). It should be of critical interest to verify how this aptitude can pay off in the turbulent environment during external crises, such as natural distress, political unrest and pandemics.

On the one hand, crisis phenomena are an important context of management in the 21st century due to their being permanent. As a result of globalization, and the growing financial, economic, technical,

---

achievement of various corporate performance goals" (Donaldson and Preston, 1995, p. 66).

social and environmental interdependencies, crises are on the rise (e.g. Boin and Lagadec, 2000; Mitroff, 2005).

On the other hand, the importance and complexity of the influence of the environment is particularly strongly manifested during a downturn and events leading to crisis situations according to individual enterprises' assessment. An increase in the intensity and scope of the impact of modern crisis phenomena on businesses is closely related to the growing strength of the influence of stakeholders of different entities within the environment, which can be seen primarily in the industries and economies that are becoming gobalized. At the same time, as the interdependencies brought on by globalization increase, so does the impact of crises on various stakeholder groups (see e.g. Boin and Lagadec, 2000; Mitroff, 2005).

It is during crises that (e.g. Chandler, 1977, 2002) "visible hand of the market" manifests itself explicitly. Crisis phenomena and mechanisms that have been known throughout history prove that it is always the hand of specific stakeholders.[3] This is made crystal clear by the COVID-19 pandemic. Whether or not one denies the existence of the "visible hand," the stakeholder approach implies that managers can no longer rely on "the invisible hand" to resolve conflicts of interest among stakeholder groups, and they must instead deal directly themselves with ethics and social responsibility (Clarkson, 1995).

A common element of all crises is that they can harm organizational stakeholders (Mitroff *et al.*, 1996). Particularly important for both corporations' and financial markets' constituents is the fact that a crisis may drastically alter a stakeholder's salience and its potential influence on a firm's (shareholder) value in ways that the organization may not predict and which would not be covered by existing contracts (Agle *et al.*, 1999; Alpaslan *et al.*, 2009; Mitchell *et al.*, 1997). This should draw one's attention to a key feature of the Mitchell *et al.* (1997) stakeholder salience framework, namely, that no stakeholders' attributes are fixed in time (Magness, 2008).

A stakeholder theory of crisis management explains that the stakeholder model of corporate governance may be associated with

[3]This corresponds to J. Stiglitz's view that the invisible hand of the market does not exist, or rather reveals itself only under special conditions, since in many circumstances the market mechanism proves unreliable.

more successful crisis management outcomes due to higher frequencies of proactive and accommodating crisis management behaviour (Alpaslan *et al.*, 2009; Mitroff and Alpaslan, 2003). Alpaslan *et al.* (2009) argue that the stakeholder model of corporate governance may help firms prevent crises or recover from them more successfully. Similarly, Ndlela (2019) claims that by adopting a stakeholder approach, organizations can optimise their crisis management efforts.

In contrast, Sheaffer and Mano-Negrin (2003) find that firms that focused strictly on profit maximization were more prone to crisis. Their results suggest that the shareholder model is at least associated with higher frequencies of crises (Sheaffer and Mano-Negrin, 2003). The stakeholder model, which resonates with CSR, seems to lower the risk of potential and dangerous omission of some critical, though not obvious, influencers.

17.2.3. *Economically justified sustainability*

Concepts such as CSR, sustainability, or ESG go along with the idea that a company should deliver value not only to shareholders but also to different stakeholder groups by acknowledging their claims, rights, or needs. Since enterprises are "embedded in a society and draw all their resources from it, then they must act like responsible citizens" (Chakraborty *et al.*, 2004, p. 105). Taking such a perspective requires that corporate management empathise with and understand its stakeholders.

Stakeholder theory actually has deep roots in the notion of CSR, but at the same time, the stakeholder framework facilitates CSR application and evaluation (Carroll, 1979, 1991; Clarkson, 1995; Freeman, 1984; Parmar, 2010). The idea of CSR seems to have been announced earlier than the stakeholder concept itself. Barnard (1938) argued that the purpose of the corporation was to serve society, not noticing then that society is in fact the constellation of stakeholders of various entities. Today, it is undisputable that neither CSR nor the stakeholder concept can exist without each other.

We emphasize, however, that it is not our intention to present the two concepts as equivalent because they are not. Yet they are definitely intertwined with and reinforced and facilitated by each other. This was already noticed in the inclusive definition of

CSR by Carroll (1979), which underlines that the concept encompasses both the economic and social expectations toward organization, and that an economic emphasis is not separate and apart from a social emphasis. In the three-dimensional model of corporate social performance Carroll, 1979, and later in the pyramid of CSR Carroll, 1991, he distinguishes between economic, legal, ethical, and discretionary (or later philanthropic) components of social responsibility.

It is worth mentioning, however, that CSR is a concept that has been generated outside business (Clarkson, 1995). This is why its legitimization to corporate bodies has to be through management concepts.[4] The concept is also extremely unlikely to be incorporated as long as there is no visible/tangible link to a company's performance. As argued by Margolis *et al.* (2007), continuous efforts to identify the impact of CSR on companies' financial performance are also efforts to legitimise its social engagement and prove that business can do well by doing good. A stakeholder approach appears to be an appropriate framework to connect CSR to companies' performance, since this is the approach that has gone a long way from stakeholder influence on management toward stakeholder participation in it (as presaged by Dill (1975)).

One cannot agree more that success in satisfying multiple stakeholder interests constitutes the ultimate test of corporate performance (Donaldson and Preston, 1995). This success, however, is not possible without CSR and sustainability. Whenever stakeholders constitute a focal point of management, CSR policies must be in place. Findings of previous studies (Berman *et al.*, 1999; Berrone *et al.*, 2007; Hillman and Keim, 2001) clearly show that firms that satisfy stakeholder demands have higher economic benefits and achieve differentiation from their competitors.

An interesting avenue for exploring the relationship between ethics and performance is through the perspective of corporate identity (Berrone *et al.*, 2007). Since corporate identity is recognized as a source of competitive advantage (Balmer and Gray, 2020),

[4]Interesting evidence, on a similar note, can be found in Ackermann and Eden's (2007) robust empirical research, which showed that one of the most difficult aspects of considering stakeholders in strategy making was legitimising this activity.

Berrone *et al.* (2007) suggest that a firm's ethical stance or corporate ethical identity (i.e. its ethical values, behaviours, and communications on ethical commitments) can be seen as a component of the firm's corporate identity, which may enhance corporate performance. This relationship is also explained by Bosse *et al.* (2009), who claim that stakeholder perception of fairness is directly associated with the value created by a firm (since fair behavior is rewarded and unfair behavior is punished).

The concepts of CSR, sustainability, or ESG influence today not only business and management but also finance, with sustainable or green finance or socially responsible investing (SRI) becoming the capital markets' mainstream[5] (Global Sustainable Investment Review 2018, 2019; European SRI Study 2016, 2017). Potential explanations for this trend include a growing awareness that finance intertwines with matters of social responsibility and sustainability and the difficult aftermath of irresponsible finance that led to the Global Financial Crisis (GFC) (Boubaker *et al.*, 2020). Indeed, sustainable, green, or ethical finance has generated renewed attention due to notorious corporate scandals — like those of Enron, Worldcom, Arthur Andersen, Tyco International, Parmalat, Adelphia, Fannie Mae and Freddie Mac, and Lehman Brothers — and environmental accidents, such as Exxon, the Union Carbide, or BP, just to mention a few. Additionally, the growing importance of governmental regulations, including non-financial disclosure, the amplified scrutiny of the media, and increased pressure from various stakeholders have placed the ESG challenge on the strategic agenda of virtually all firms (e.g. Stevens *et al.*, 2005; Weaver *et al.*, 1999), and consequently of capital markets.

We want to round off this section with the following observation. Reflecting the high complexity and uncertainty of business and economic conditions, especially in the context of crises, and acknowledging the trend of boundaryless organizations and economic–social systems, we have moved from stakeholder management to

[5]Globally, sustainable investing assets amounted to US$30.7 trillion at the beginning of 2018, a 34% increase compared with 2016. The largest three regions — based on the value of their sustainable investing assets — were Europe, the US, and Japan (Global Sustainable Investment Review 2018, 2019).

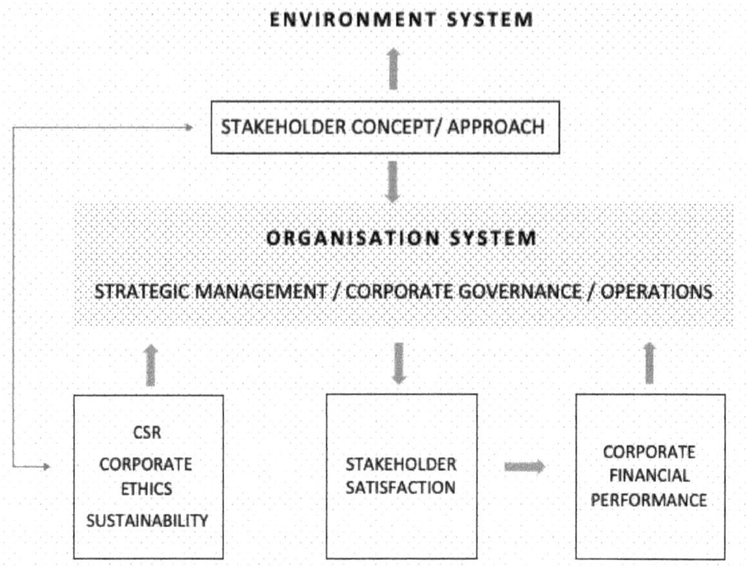

Figure 17.1. Linking CSR to a company's financial performance through stakeholder approach in the context of economic systems.

stakeholder accountability (Rasche and Esser, 2006) to let us operate in the turbulent, chaotic environment[6] of the Anthropocene.

Figure 17.1 presents the link between the concepts discussed in this section, showing that the interests of shareholders and stakeholders can merge through notions of social responsibility and sustainability, and that this can be shown in a company's financial performance.

17.3. Do Firms Practice What They Preach? Empirical Research Review

Academics have tried for decades to find and explain the relation between responsible and sustainable management (reflected in a firm's behavior) and a company's value and its financial performance. Although many questions are still open or answered by mixed results,

[6]Freeman views the turbulence of the business environment as the essential managerial justification for undertaking CSR activities for the benefit of stakeholders (e.g. Freeman, 1984; Parmar *et al.*, 2010).

numerous interesting implications have been observed based on academic research. In this section, we signal some of them, noticing they are in general related to three aspects of a company's success/performance: competitive advantage, financial results, and risk and volatility.

Companies that are managed in a responsible manner, or in other words are responsive to ESG factors, perform better (show higher and less volatile profitability in the long run) and enhance their competitive position (Greenwald, 2010; Jo *et al.*, 2010; Renneboog *et al.*, 2008). Engagement in CSR activities being the factor of financial performance improvement is, for example, reflected in the evidence from the global banking sector by Shen *et al.* (2016), who in particular reported that CSR banks overwhelmingly outperform non-CSR banks in terms of return on assets and return on equity. The positive impact of CSR on financial performance is also noticeable under economic downturn conditions. According to Lins *et al.* (2017), during the GFC, firms with high social capital, as measured by CSR intensity, had significantly higher stock returns than firms with low social capital. High-CSR firms also experienced higher profitability, growth, and sales per employee and raised more debt relative to low-CSR firms (Lins *et al.*, 2017).

CSR engagement can also translate into enhanced firm value, as examined by Jo and Harjoto (2011), whose findings show that firm value, measured by industry-adjusted Tobin's q, is positively related to the CSR choice. Moreover, their results indicate that CSR intensity plays an important role as well, since its impact on firm value is both statistically and economically significant (Jo and Harjoto, 2011).

The link between CSR and financial results can be explained by the fact that firms with a strong ethical identity achieve a greater degree of stakeholder satisfaction, which, in turn, positively influences financial performance (Berrone *et al.*, 2007). This satisfaction, also developed through close relationships with key stakeholders, creates intangible resources that are the basis for a sustainable competitive advantage (Berrone *et al.*, 2007). On a similar note, other scholars have found out that a positive impact of the (proactive) ethical initiatives on financial performance is possible because ethical behaviours generate intangible assets — good reputation (which we further refer to), trust, and commitment — which are vital to long-term business success (Fombrun *et al.*, 2000; Jones, 1995). Of interest are the findings of Berrone *et al.* (2007), which indicate that when distinguishing between corporate revealed ethics and corporate applied ethics, revealed ethics has informational worth and enhances shareholder value, whereas applied ethics has a positive impact through the improvement of stakeholder satisfaction. This might indicate that "practice what you preach" can magnify the effect of sustainable policies and ethical behaviours.

Whatever the explanation of the link between CSR and a company's financial performance, empirical evidence on how strong this relation is seems to be at least as crucial. A meta-analysis of 167 studies investigating effects between corporate social performance (CSP) and corporate financial performance since 1972, conducted by Margolis *et al.* (2007), indicates only a mildly positive relationship between CSP and financial results. Their prior meta-analysis in the same matter report that CSP, when treated as an independent variable, had a positive impact on financial performance in 53%, no impact in 24%, and a negative impact in 5% of 80 studies (Margolis and Walsh, 2001). This clearly calls for further research in this highly valid area.

There is strong evidence that, on the microeconomic level, firms can mitigate their risk exposure through effective CSR policies, whereas on the macroeconomic level, socially responsible behavior likely leads to a better corporate investment environment, better financial stability, and stronger and more crisis-resilient economies (Boubaker *et al.*, 2020). First of all, there is evidence that CSR decreases the systematic risk of a company, which may be critical in the context of crises. The model developed by Albuquerque *et al.* (2018) predicts that CSR decreases systematic risk and increases firm value, and that these effects are stronger for firms with high product differentiation.

There is also evidence that a high ESG score of a company is negatively related to its level of idiosyncratic risk (Luo and Bhattacharya, 2009; Mishra and Modi, 2013). For instance, socially responsible companies reduce the risk of very costly litigation (Koh *et al.*, 2014). This risk can materialise through stakeholders' activism (lawsuits, strikes, and protests). In this sense, companies with a low ESG score are generally exposed to higher operational risk.

In particular, numerous studies support the relationship between CSR performance and reporting and a company's reputation, showing that the reputation risk of socially responsible enterprises is lower than of those who are not (Bebbington *et al.*, 2008; Havemann and Webster, 1999; Perez, 2015). This is also because CSR activity creates a form of goodwill that acts as insurance-like protection for the company in case of negative events, and thus can represent added value for its shareholders (Godfrey *et al.*, 2009), especially if it manifests in a higher resistance to crises. A company's reputation, defined as an ability to deliver value to stakeholders, should be particularly noticeable to investors; hence, it constitutes a key asset of a company (Brady and Honey, 2007), which is not captured by its book value. According to Brady and Honey (2007, p. 6), "corporate reputation as a concept embodies the image and values of a company, and was therefore intimately linked with the concept of corporate responsibility." In turn, as stated by Havemann and Webster (1999), perceived ethical or unethical behaviour can have an impact on a company's reputation and share price.

The positive impact of company's responsiveness to ESG factors on its competitive advantage, and consequently on its competitive position, may be derived from cost advantages as well. For example, empirical research provides evidence that consideration of ESG factors in management systems can decrease operational costs in the long run, for example, by improving employees' motivation and thereby their productivity (Van Liedekerke, 2007). Waddock and Smith's (2000) corporate responsibility audits showed that adoption of proactive, stakeholder-inclusive, and morally responsible practices lowered costs, legal exposure, and risks to company reputation. Berrone *et al.* (2007) relate that ethical behaviours foster trusting and cooperative relationships with stakeholders, which, in turn, lead to a reduction in opportunism and contracting costs. In the end, there is an improvement in the firms' competitive advantage.

Empirical findings also associate the high ESG score of a company with lower cost of equity capital, lower cost of debt, and better access to finance. For example, El Ghoul *et al.* (2011) report that socially responsible companies have a lower cost of equity capital because of their lower perceived risk. Specifically, Sharfman and Fernando (2008) find that strategic improvements in environmental risk management reduce the cost of capital and improve the market's risk perception of a firm. Recently, Boubaker *et al.* (2020) provided evidence that firms with a better CSR performance exhibit lower financial distress and default risk due to better access to finance and creditworthiness, and that this relation is driven by the community, diversity, and employee dimensions of CSR (prevalent in firms operating in competitive markets and with strong governance).

Taking the above-mentioned arguments into account, companies positively screened against ESG factors and highly scored in sustainability ratings may offer greater utility (in terms of risk/return ratio) to investors. In such a case, they become appealing to a broader spectrum of investors, both those that are sensitive to CSR and those indifferent to ESG factors. In light of all prior arguments, we expect a positive relation between a company's ESG score and financial performance, measured by stock returns. In the following section, we examine whether the high-ESG stance of listed companies is positively interpreted by investors in the context of the recent crisis caused by the COVID-19 pandemic.

17.4. Does Sustainable Management Matter More in the Context of a Pandemic Crisis?

We seek an answer for the question of whether ESG values and activities embedded in corporate management practices are capitalized by the market during the unprecedented event of the COVID-19 pandemic. As a pandemic falls into the category of systemic risk, it has characteristics of a natural disaster. In contrast to the GFC, there is no sector to point to for blame, no structural problem. Also its impact on macroeconomic indicators seems to be different and of an unheard-of scale (e.g. the unemployment rate in the US was 10.6% in January 2010 vs 14.70% in April 2020).

Our aim is to examine if the performance of European and US companies during the February–June 2020 period depends on their ESG scores after controlling for sector. Such a natural experiment allows us to shed light on the issue of whether ESG makes a difference in times of natural disaster.

17.4.1. *Equity indices and ESG scores for Europe and the US*

We examined companies included in the main indices for Europe and the US, namely STOXX 600 and S&P 500, respectively. The

European index has a fixed number of 600 components representing large-, mid- and small-capitalization companies among 17 European countries, covering approximately 90% of the free-float market capitalization of the European stock market (not limited to the Eurozone). The countries that make up the index are the UK, France, Germany, Switzerland, Austria, Belgium, Denmark, Finland, Ireland, Italy, Luxemburg, the Netherlands, Norway, Poland, Portugal, Spain, and Sweden. The S&P 500 is one of the most commonly followed US equity indices; it measures the stock performance of 500 large companies listed on stock exchanges in the US.

As a proxy of companies' ESG profile, we use two leading global, comprehensive ESG ratings: the SAM Corporate Sustainability Assessment (CSA) (established in 1999 by RobecoSAM, and since January 2020 issued by S&P Global), and the ESG Risk Ratings prepared by Sustainalytics (established in 2009 as the result of a merger of a few ESG research providers). These ratings are based on information provided by the companies directly through questionnaires. This allows for analysis of sustainability at a much deeper level than frameworks based on public disclosure alone. We have chosen those ESG research providers also because they provide data for the S&P (SAM) and STOXX (Sustainalytics) indices.

ESG data providers are not regulated, unlike their counterparts that are focused purely on financial information. Therefore, the methodology, scope, and coverage of numerous available ESG ratings vary greatly. Berg *et al.* (2020), in their recent study, find that in a dataset of 6 ESG raters, correlations between scores of 823 companies were on average 0.61, correlations between all ratings were on average 0.54 and correlation between Sustainalytics and SAM ratings was 0.67. They also report that measurement of categories (attributes) is the main driver of ESG rating divergence, followed by scope of categories, whereas weight divergence is of minor importance (Berg *et al.*, 2020).

The divergence of ESG ratings is the reason a company's ESG score adopted for our research sample is compounded of both CSA and ESG Risk Ratings assessments and constitutes an average of those two scores. A broad portfolio of companies covered by both ratings as well as the identical scale used for reporting the final score allows us to merge the ratings results, providing a more adequate metric of CSR performance for our study.

The SAM CSA methodology pursues a best-in-class approach, which focuses on financially material, industry-specific sustainability issues (covering the economic, environmental, and social dimensions) that have a link to long-term financial performance. Factors that are considered to have the greatest impact on long-term financial assumptions are given the highest weighting in the CSA. Companies receive an S&P Global ESG Score between 0 and 100 and are ranked against other companies in their industry. A total of 61 industries derived from the GICS industry classification system are analyzed using industry-specific questionnaires. No industries are excluded from the assessment. The top 10% of companies within each industry are selected for inclusion in the DJSI World.

The Sustainalytics ESG Risk Ratings consider as relevant those ESG issues that have a potentially substantial impact on the economic value of a company and, hence, its financial risk-return profile from an investment perspective. A company is examined in two dimensions: ESG risks exposure, reflecting the extent to which a company is exposed to material ESG risks at the industry, sub-industry, and idiosyncratic level, and ESG risks management, reflecting how well a company is managing its exposure. The assessment focuses on preparedness — i.e. evaluation of management systems and policies in place to help manage ESG risks — and disclosure, i.e. whether company reporting meets international best-practice standards and is transparent in relation to ESG issues and actual performance.

In our research, we consider a sample of 1,034 companies: 484 from the S&P 500 and 550 from STOXX 600, as they are included both in CSA and ESG Risk Ratings.

17.4.2. *Design of a natural experiment*

The analysis is divided into three steps. In the first step, we examine performance in terms of the annualized return of sectors included in the S&P 500 and STOXX 600 indices. Our focus in on GICS sector breakdown, which includes following: Consumer Discretionary, Communication Services, Consumer Staples, Energy, Financials, Health Care, Industrials Information Technology, Materials, Real Estate, and Utilities. The analysis covers performance during two phases of the COVID-19 outbreak. The beginning of first period, which we call the panic period, is defined by the first reported cases in the US and Europe on the January 23 and 25, 2020, respectively[7]. The ending date for this phase is marked by the US Senate passing the historic US$2 trillion relief package on March 27, 2020. During the panic period of around 2.5 months, the main US indices experienced their worst days since the 1987 crash. We consider the period between the end of March and the end of June as a second phase of the COVID-19 outbreak, and we name it the bounce period, as this period was characterized by the rapid rebound of stock markets around the world.

The second step of our analysis focuses on sectors' ESG scores and whether those help explain performance during the panic and bounce periods. We select the sector as the main segment/entity of our analysis since it is the natural area of strategic management analysis, as it determines the competitive environment of an enterprise setting conditions for business operations and hence its profitability. The underlying drivers of profitability in the industry are shaped by the main forces, namely level of competition, bargaining power of customers and suppliers, threat of new entrants and substitute products (according to M.E. Porter's Five Forces model), as well as a company's relative position within the industry. Most importantly, in the context of our study, there are sector-specific risks and opportunities that focus on economic, environmental, and social challenges and trends that are relevant to companies within each industry or industries group.

We illustrate the relationship between a sector's average ESG score and annualized stock returns of its companies using a multivariable graph, such as a bubble chart. The third and final step of analysis focuses on the relationship between the performance of companies in each sector in relationship to their ESG score. By examining the Pearson correlation between annualized return and ESG score for companies from a given sector, we answer the question of whether there is a linear relationship between those two. In addition, we examine if the top 10% of a sector's constituents in terms of

[7]The first cases of COVID-19 infection were discovered in the US on January 23, 2020. Across the Atlantic, the first cases were discovered as follows: France on January 25, 2020; Germany on January 28, 2020; Finland on January 30, 2020; and Italy on January 31, 2020.

ESG score outperform the rest of the companies from a given sector during the panic and bounce periods. This analysis allows us to shed light on a potential non-linear relationship between ESG profiles and companies' performance within each of the 11 sectors.

17.4.3. *Results*

As the economy passes through different stages of the business cycle, the relative performance of different sectors might be expected to vary. The cyclical industries, those with above-average sensitivity to the state of the economy, tend to underperform during a recession and outperform during a recovery. For example, companies belonging to the Consumer Discretionary and Materials sectors are cyclical firms.

At the other end of the spectrum are companies from defensive industries, characterized by little sensitivity to the business cycle. Such firms produce goods and deliver services for which sales and profits are the least sensitive to the state of the economy. Defensive sectors include consumer staples, healthcare, and utilities. These industries will outperform others when the economy enters a recession.

Figure 17.2 shows the performance of the 11 sectors as part of the S&P 500 during the panic period (upper graph with grey bars) and bounce period (lower graph with hashed bars). The figures report annualized return calculated from average performance of daily log returns. The sectors suffering the biggest drop of share prices were energy, consumer discretionary, and financials. As the world was heading to lockdown, it became clear that there would be less demand for energy. A looming recession discourages discretionary spending, and uncertainty about liquidity contributes to bad performance of financials. The smallest losses were experienced by companies that are part of consumer staples and information technology. This is not surprising, as the former sector is a harbour for rainy days. The performance of the latter is more pandemic-specific. The graph showing the performance post the US$2 trillion rescue package reveals that the best-performing sectors were those experiencing the worst performance during the panic phase. The exception was IT companies, as their share prices not only did not drop much but also experienced a substantial increase during the bounce period. Taking into account the nature of the COVID-19 pandemic, special attention needs to be

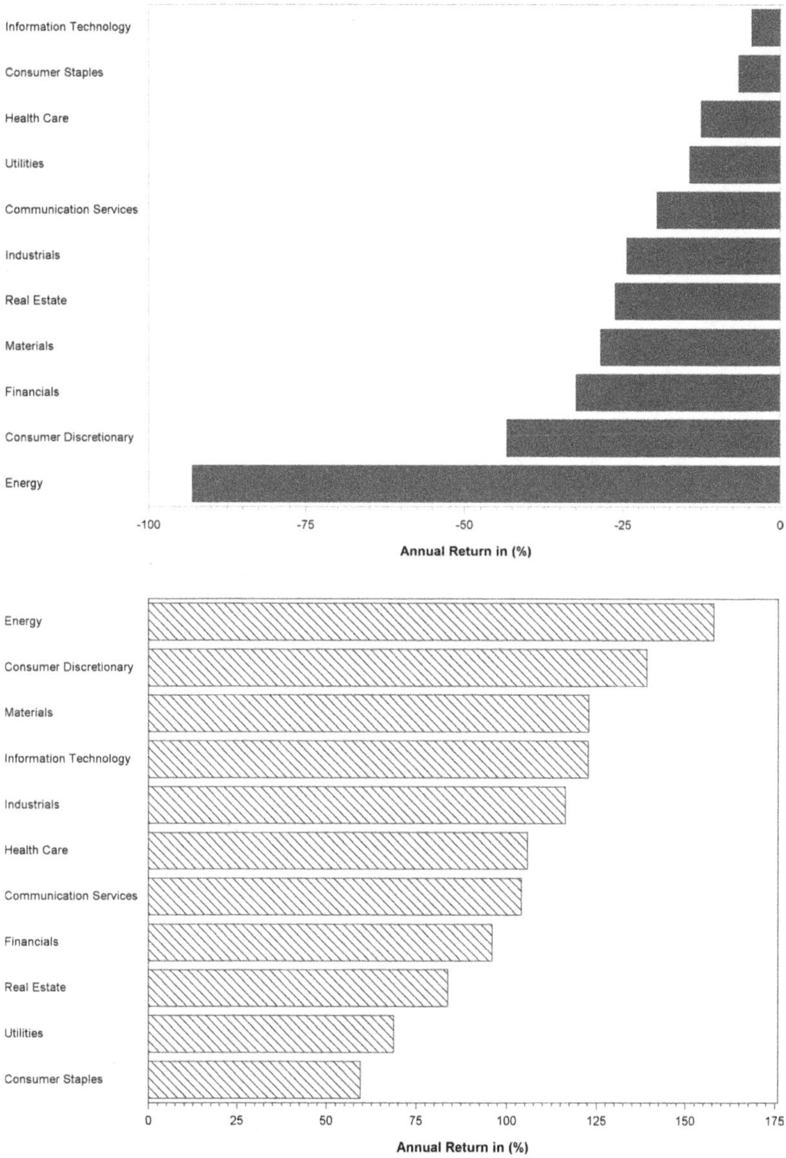

Figure 17.2. Performance of the US equity sectors part of S&P 500 index during the panic period of the COVID-19 pandemic (January 23–March 27, 2020) and the bounce period (April 1–June 30, 2020).

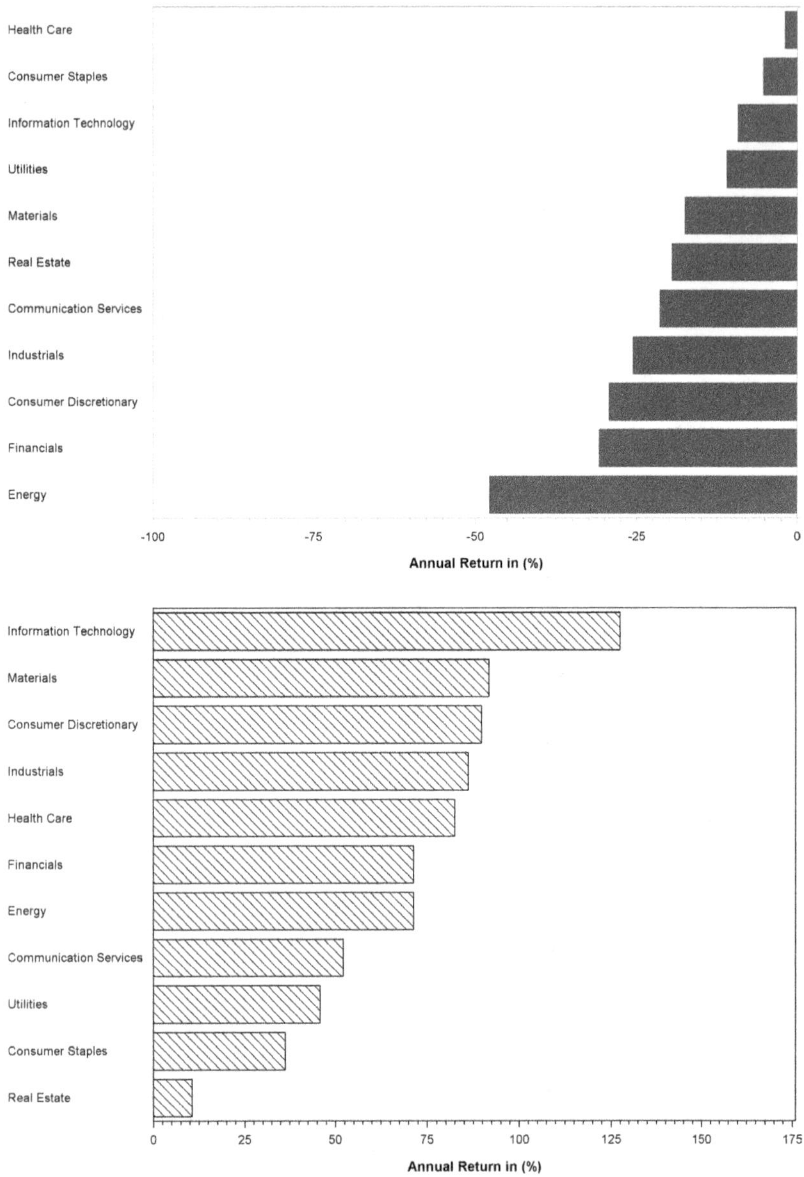

Figure 17.3. Performance of European equity sectors part of STOXX 600 index during the panic period of COVID-19 pandemic (January 23–March 27, 2020) and the bounce period (April 1–June 30, 2020).

paid to the health sector. In the case of the S&P 500, this sector was the third best performing during the panic period and its bounceback was average.

Next, we examine the performance of the 11 sectors on the European equity market (see Figure 17.3). The analysis of STOXX 600 reveals that the prices of European stocks on average were impacted less by the pandemic outbreak. The analysis of the upper graph with grey bars and the lower graph with hashed bars confirms it. As in the case of the S&P 500, the sectors most affected by the COVID-19 panic period were energy, consumer discretionary, and financials. The most immune to the panic were consumer staples, information technology, and healthcare industries. During the rebound between April and the end of June 2020, the best-performing sectors on the European equity market were consumer staples, information technology,

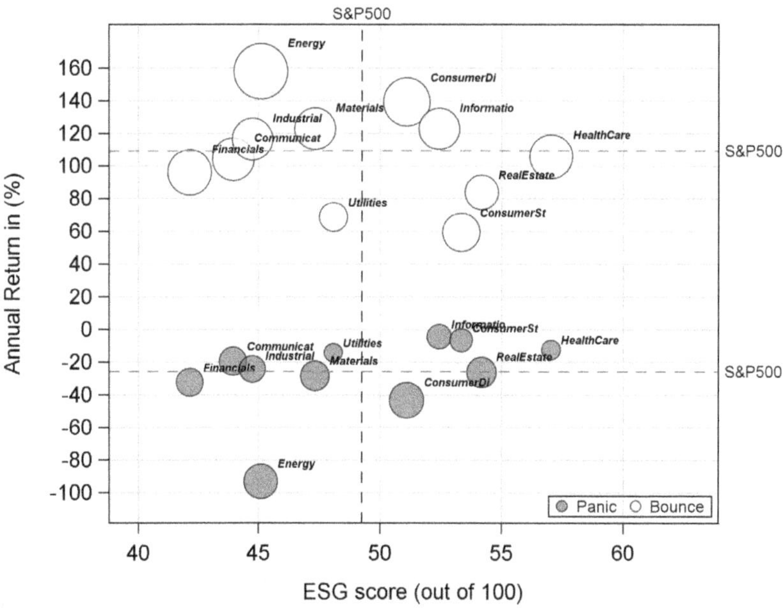

Figure 17.4. The impact of the COVID-19 outbreak on the annual return of 11 broad GICS sectors from the S&P 500 index during the panic period (grey bubbles) and bounce period (white bubbles). The two horizontal line corresponds to the average annual return of S&P 500 companies for the corresponding phase of the pandemic. The vertical line indicates an average ESG score for companies that are part of the S&P 500.

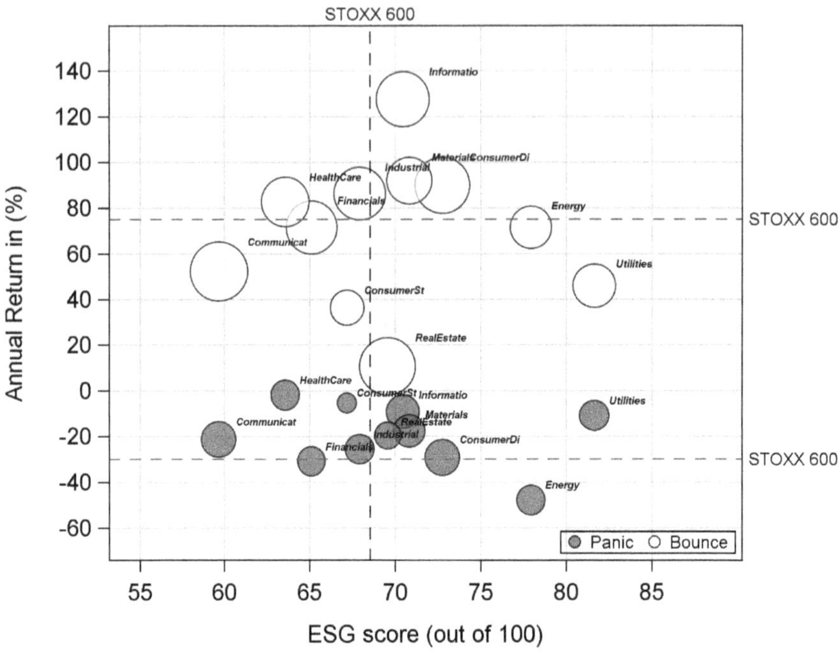

Figure 17.5. The impact of the COVID-19 outbreak on the annual return of 11 broad GICS sectors from the STOXX 600 index during the panic phase of the pandemic (grey bubbles) and the bounce period (white bubbles). The two horizontal lines correspond to the average annual return of STOXX 600 companies for the corresponding phase of the pandemic. The vertical line indicates an average ESG score for a STOXX 600 company.

and materials. In contrast to the US market, the companies included in the energy sector and part of the STOXX 600 index did not bounce back as much.

Figures 17.4 and 17.5 shed light on the relationship between industry performance and ESG scores. The size of the bubbles in the graphs corresponds to the variability of returns in each sector separately. The grey colour indicates the performance of a given sector during the panic period and white during the bounceback period. The position of bubbles is determined by annualized return (Y-axis) and ESG score. The two horizontal lines correspond to the average performance of companies that are part of the S&P 500 or STOXX 600, during the panic and rebound periods. The vertical line indicates the average ESG score for companies that are part of the index.

The analysis of both graphs reveals that, except for US market during the panic period, there is no clear indication that a higher ESG score (bubbles to the right) corresponds to better performance (bubbles are located higher). The white bubbles are bigger than the grey ones, suggesting that there was much more variability of returns during the bounce period.

The final step of our analysis is to examine if, among the companies belonging to a particular sector, there is relationship between ESG scores and the performance of stocks on equity market. Therefore, Tables 17.1 and 17.2 report the correlation between ESG score and annualized returns together with *p*-values. In addition, we show the difference in performance of the top 10% of companies in terms of ESG score versus the rest of a given sector. The *p*-values of a test for difference equal to zero are also reported.

The reported results provide weak evidence that ESG itself drives performance inside each sector. The correlation is mostly positive during the panic period of the pandemic, but low and, in most cases, insignificant. The results for the bounce period are mixed. It is worth highlighting that the best companies in terms of ESG score in each sector were able to generate better return to investors that the rest of the companies from a given sector. The observation applies mostly to the panic phase.

17.5. Conclusions

The reported results are tangible and have important implications for practitioners. Our analysis shows that, by controlling for sector and level of ESG score, the impact of a company's ESG profile on its equity performance is positive during the period of the initial panic caused by the pandemic outbreak. It is also rarely statistically significant. The financial implications of CSR performance/ESG profile in the context of the COVID-19 pandemic, therefore, should be understood as an interrelated set of the following findings.

First, the results are driven by the fact that a company's preparedness to a pandemic-type crisis only partly depends on its ESG profile. Equally important (or often more important!) are company cash holdings, lower debt ratios and overall profitability (see Ding *et al.*, 2020).

Table 17.1. The correlation between the performance of 11 GICS sectors from the S&P 500 index and their ESG scores, and the difference between the performance of the top 10% of companies in terms of ESG score in comparison with the rest from a given sector.

GICS sector	Pearson correlation	p-value	Top 10% vs. rest of sector (%)	p-value
Panel A: COVID-19 panic period				
Communication services	0.1906	0.3723	21.0	0.0029
Consumer discretionary	0.0013	0.9920	10.3	0.5448
Consumer staples	0.0149	0.9340	20.0	0.1037
Energy	−0.0198	0.9234	35.3	0.2216
Financials	0.0121	0.9242	12.8	0.2836
Healthcare	0.2238	0.0883	5.8	0.4346
Industrials	0.0359	0.7778	11.3	0.1608
Information technology	0.0495	0.6881	−8.6	0.4837
Materials	0.3119*	0.0990	28.0	0.4239
Real estate	−0.3981	0.0293	−12.8	0.2387
Utilities	0.0844	0.6691	−8.4	0.6082
Panel B: COVID-19 rebound period				
Communication services	−0.1169	0.5863	12.0	0.3172
Consumer discretionary	0.0264	0.8416	4.5	0.8991
Consumer staples	−0.1165	0.5254	−14.1	0.2948
Energy	0.2247	0.2297	−0.9	0.9615
Financials	0.3452	0.0052	31.3	0.0912
Healthcare	−0.3748	0.0034	−18.6	0.1554
Industrials	−0.3510	0.0048	−15.5	0.6115
Information technology	−0.2384	0.0520	−33.8	0.1386
Materials	0.0335	0.8756	−15.2	0.7181
Real estate	0.1010	0.5953	67.5	0.0972
Utilities	−0.1097	0.5785	−4.3	0.4720

Note: *Corresponds to statistical significance at the 10% level.

Table 17.2. The correlation between the performance of 11 GICS sectors from the STOXX 600 index and their ESG scores, and the difference between the performance of the top 10% of companies in terms of ESG score in comparison with the rest from a given sector.

GICS sector	Pearson correlation	p-value	Top 10% vs. rest of sector (%)	p-value
Panel A: COVID-19 panic period				
Communication services	−0.3544	0.0592	−3.1	0.8403
Consumer discretionary	−0.2346	0.1210	−6.9	0.5369
Consumer staples	0.1395	0.4242	3.5	0.7023
Energy	0.6682	0.0090	−0.4	0.9697
Financials	−0.0791	0.4694	3.5	0.7448
Healthcare	0.2032	0.2418	5.8	0.3718
Industrials	0.0502	0.6520	2.0	0.8288
Information technology	0.0219	0.9292	1.5	0.8782
Materials	−0.0921	0.5569	−4.9	0.7332
Real estate	−0.5384	0.0470	1.8	0.9275
Utilities	−0.0108	0.9573	13.3	0.8860
Panel B: COVID-19 rebound period				
Communication services	−0.3262	0.0842	−3.8	0.8556
Consumer discretionary	−0.2032	0.1806	−24.7	0.3498
Consumer staples	−0.0238	0.8923	15.5	0.6669
Energy	0.5754	0.0313	23.8	0.3075
Financials	0.0948	0.3853	12.8	0.5258
Healthcare	−0.1887	0.2776	−24.5	0.3322
Industrials	−0.0652	0.5584	−14.9	0.4923
Information technology	−0.3114	0.1944	8.0	0.8269
Materials	0.0783	0.6174	−7.6	0.7657
Real Estate	−0.2386	0.4112	−28.5	0.3886
Utilities	−0.1438	0.4744	−31.8	0.4610

Another key determinant of a company's stock price performance during the COVID-19 crisis is its industry/sector. The performance of sectors during the pandemic, to some extent, mirrors the relative performance thereof in different stages of the business cycle. The performance of cyclical industries, such as consumer discretionary or energy in our sample, with above-average sensitivity to the state of the economy, plummeted deeper during the panic period but outperformed others in the bounce period. On the other hand, defensive industries, such as consumer staples, utilities, and healthcare, with little sensitivity to the state of the economy, did better in the panic period but recovered slower in the bounce period. The picture of industries between the extremes, or those less representative for each category, might not be yet sharp enough since the crisis is not over, and there are probably more phases to come. The firms belonging to IT sectors are a particularly interesting case, as their stock price drop was minor and bounced back as the fourth-strongest for the US market and the strongest for the European market.

Moreover, the market/region variable matters a lot. There is a substantial difference between the level of ESG scores for the US and European sectors. The US healthcare industry, the industry with the highest ESG score (57.03), still scores lower than the worst-performing European sector, the communication sector with a score close to 60 (59.66). The difference may be at least partly explained by European regulations encouraging investing in companies with a high ESG profile.

Despite those market/region discrepancies, all companies in our sample have a relatively high ESG score, and this is particularly true for the European panel. It would be interesting to test them against enterprises that perform much worse in terms of ESG and/or to test them in a bigger, more varied (in terms of CSR performance) sample. Our results confirm that in the panel with the lower average ESG score (S&P 500), the correlation between ESG score and stock returns is positive and stronger than in the panel with a higher average ESG score (STOXX 600).

A crucial factor influencing the obtained results also seems to be the measure of a company's financial performance. Authors of prior studies acknowledged the importance of metrics adequateness in capturing intangible relationships (*e.g.* Berrone *et al.*, 2007; Hillman and Keim, 2001; Orlitzky *et al.*, 2003). Interestingly, as reported by

Orlitzky *et al.* (2003) and Margolis *et al.* (2007), CSR appears to be more highly correlated with accounting-based measures of corporate financial performance (e.g. ROA, ROE) than with market-based measures (e.g. stock returns, MVA stands for market value added).

Furthermore, the fact that our results are weaker can be explained by the fact that ESG ratings are heterogeneous (see Berg *et al.*, 2020). The general correlation of CSA and ESG Risk Ratings is at the level of 0.67, with the lowest correlation for the G dimension equal to 0.51, followed by $S = 0.55$ and $E = 0.66$. The divergence occurs not only at the aggregate level but is even more pronounced in specific subcategories of ESG performance. The biggest divergences of category scores (negatively correlated) are Community and Society (–0.19), Health and Safety (–0.16), and Customer Relationship (–0.13), and the average category scores correlation is only 0.32 (Berg *et al.*, 2020). Nevertheless, the fact that a large number of companies take part in the ESG evaluation and are positively screened by ESG raters proves that CSR practices are executed and the stakeholder approach is commonly adopted by public enterprises — 484 companies listed on the S&P 500 and 550 companies from STOXX 600 are present in both CSA and ESG Risk Ratings, with an average score of 49.26 for the first and 68.55 for the latter. The rankings criteria relate to numerous stakeholder groups and their diversified issues.

Overall, our results might suggest that delivering value to a broader spectrum of stakeholders (reflected by a high ESG score) does not necessarily immediately (in the short run) protect or enhance the value for shareholders (measured by annualized stock returns) under pandemic circumstances. This, however, does not clash with the various/abundant benefits (postulated by theorists and proved in empirical studies) of the stakeholder approach and the socially responsible and sustainable attitude of a company's management. Since these benefits can be observed mostly in the long term, they should be re-examined from the post-pandemic perspective.

Finally, there is one more straightforward lesson from our scrutiny, namely that ESG scores can be used as an additional tool for screening investments, but they are not suitable to replace a detailed fundamental analysis.

Despite numerous indisputable arguments in favour of socially responsible and sustainable corporations, as discussed in the theoretical section, CSR performance seems to be a relatively weak factor (as compared with other factors) for investors in their decision-making during the pandemic uncertainty. A high ESG stand-alone profile neither protects an enterprise from a negative impact of the pandemic crisis nor always helps it to be affected less or recover sooner. Even though the relationship between a company's ESG score and its equity performance is found to be weak, our contribution to the empirical knowledge in this area is two-fold: first, companies do not seem to be richly rewarded by the financial market for engaging in CSR, and second, companies are not penalised for their high ESG profile (and hence investments in CSR) either. These findings confirm the results of Margolis *et al.*'s 2007 meta-analysis, in which they reported that the overall effect of CSR on corporate financial performance is positive, with only 2% of the individual studies reporting a significant negative effect. They also concluded that "companies can do good and do well, even if companies do not always do well by doing good" Margolis *et al.* (2007, 22–23). Our findings similarly suggest that financial performance alone seems to be an unlikely rationale or justification for pursuing CSR policies/engagement. In our opinion, such engagement should be viewed rather as a long-term insurance than an instant protection, i.e. the "better safe than sorry" approach.

References

Ackermann, F. and Eden, C. (2011). Strategic management of stakeholders: Theory and practice. *Long Range Planning*, **44**(3), 179–196.

Agle, B.R., Mitchell, R.K. and Sonnenfeld, J.A. (1999). Who matters to CEOs? An investigation of stakeholder attributes and salience, corporate performance, and CEO values. *Academy of Management Journal*, **42**(5), 507–525.

Albuquerque, R., Koskinen, Y. and Zhang, C. (2018). Corporate social responsibility and firm risk: Theory and empirical evidence. *Management Science*, **65**(10), 4451–4469.

Alpaslan, C.M., Green, S.E. and Mitroff, I.I. (2009). Corporate governance in the context of crises: Towards a stakeholder theory of crisis management. *Journal of Contingencies and Crisis Management*, **17**(1), 38–49.

Balmer, J.M. and Gray, E.R. (2000). Corporate identity and corporate communications: Creating a competitive advantage. *Industrial and Commercial Training*, **32**(7), 256–262.

Barnard, C.I. (1938). *Functions of the Executive* (Harvard University Press, Cambridge, MA).

Bebbington, J., Larrinaga, C. and Moneva, J.M. (2008). Corporate social reporting and reputation risk management. *Accounting, Auditing & Accountability Journal*, **21**(3), 337–361.

Berg, F., Koelbel, J.F. and Rigobon, R. (2020). Aggregate confusion: The divergence of ESG ratings. Available at SSRN 3438533.

Berman, S.L., Wicks, A.C., Kotha, S. and Jones, T.M. (1999). Does stakeholder orientation matter? The relationship between stakeholder management models and firm financial performance. *Academy of Management Journal*, **42**(5), 488–506.

Berrone, P., Surroca, J. and Tribó, J.A. (2007). Corporate ethical identity as a determinant of firm performance: A test of the mediating role of stakeholder satisfaction. *Journal of Business Ethics*, **76**(1), 35–53.

Boin, A. and Lagadec, P. (2000). Preparing for the future: Critical challenges in crisis management. *Journal of Contingencies and Crisis Management*, **8**(4), 185–191.

Bosse, D.A., Phillips, R.A. and Harrison, J.S. (2009). Stakeholders, reciprocity, and firm performance. *Strategic Management Journal*, **30**(4), 447–456.

Boubaker, L., Djebabra, M. and Saadi, S. (2014). Contribution of stakeholder theory in the management of environmental quality of Algerian firms: Case study of the SONATRACH Group, Algeria. *Management of Environmental Quality: An International Journal*, **25**(3), 335–351.

Boubaker, S., Cellier, A., Manita, R. and Saeed, A. (2020). Does corporate social responsibility reduce financial distress risk? *Economic Modelling*, **91**, 835–851.

Boubaker, S., Cumming, D. and Nguyen, D.K. (eds.). *Research Handbook of Finance and Sustainability* (Edward Elgar Publishing, Cheltenham, UK, Northampton, MA, USA).

Brady, A.K.O. and Honey, G. (2007). Corporate reputation: Perspectives of measuring and managing a principal risk. Chartered Institute of Management Accountants. Available at https://issuu.com/cimaglobal/docs/corporatereputationperspectives/1?e=1740886/5033325.

Carroll, A.B. (1979). A three-dimensional conceptual model of corporate performance. *Academy of Management Review*, **4**(4), 497–505.

Carroll, A.B. (1991). The pyramid of corporate social responsibility: Toward the moral management of organizational stakeholders. *Business Horizons*, **34**(4), 39–48.

Chakraborty, S.K., Kurien, V., Singh, J., Athreya, M., Maira, A., Aga, A., ... and Khandwalla, P.N. (2004). Management paradigms beyond profit maximization. *Vikalpa*, **29**(3), 97–118.

Chandler, A.D. [1977] (2002), The visible hand: The managerial revolution in American business, Harvard University Press, Cambridge, MA.

Choi, J. and Wang, H. (2009). Stakeholder relations and the persistence of corporate financial performance. *Strategic Management Journal*, **30**(8), 895–907.

Clarkson, M.E. (1995). A stakeholder framework for analyzing and evaluating corporate social performance. *Academy of Management Review*, **20**(1), 92–117.

Cornell, B. and Shapiro, A.C. (1987). Corporate stakeholders and corporate finance. *Financial Management*, **16**(1), 5–14.

Ding, W., Levine, R., Lin, C. and Xie, W. (2020). Corporate immunity to the COVID-19 pandemic. National Bureau of Economic Research Working Paper No. w27055.

Donaldson, T. and Preston, L.E. (1995). The stakeholder theory of the corporation: Concepts, evidence, and implications. *Academy of Management Review*, **20**(1), 65–91.

El Ghoul, S., Guedhami, O., Kwok, C.C. and Mishra, D.R. (2011). Does corporate social responsibility affect the cost of capital? *Journal of Banking & Finance*, **35**(9), 2388–2406.

European SRI Study 2016 (2017). Retrieved from https://www.eurosif.org/wp-content/uploads/2016/11/SRI-study-2016-HR.pdf accessed date 9.07.2021.

Fama, E.F. (1980). Agency problems and the theory of the firm. *Journal of Political Economy*, **88**(2), 288–307.

Fombrun, C.J., Gardberg, N.A. and Barnett, M.L. (2000). Opportunity platforms and safety nets: Corporate citizenship and reputational risk. *Business and Society Review*, **105**(1), 85–106.

Freeman, R.E. (1984). *Strategic Management: A Stakeholder Approach* (Pitman Publishing Inc., Boston, MA).

Freeman, R.E. and McVea, J. (2001). A stakeholder approach to strategic management. In *The Blackwell Handbook of Strategic Management*, M. Hitt, E. Freeman, and J. Harrison (eds.). *Handbook of Strategic Management*, Oxford: Blackwell Publishing, pp. 189–207.

Freeman, R.E. and Phillips, R.A. (2002). Stakeholder theory: A libertarian defense. *Business Ethics Quarterly*, **12**(3), 331–349.

Freeman, R.E. and Reed, D.L. (1983). Stockholders and stakeholders: A new perspective on corporate governance. *California Management Review*, **25**(3), 88–106.

Freeman, R.E., Wicks, A.C. and Parmar, B. (2004). Stakeholder theory and "the corporate objective revisited." *Organization Science*, **15**(3), 364–369.

Gibson, K. (2000). The moral basis of stakeholder theory. *Journal of Business Ethics*, **26**(3), 245–257.

Global Sustainable Investment Review 2018 (2019). Retrieved from http://www.gsi-alliance.org/wp-content/uploads/2019/03/GSIR_Review2018.3.28.pdf. Accessed date 9.07.2021.

Godfrey, P.C., Merrill, C.B. and Hansen, J.M. (2009). The relationship between corporate social responsibility and shareholder value: An empirical test of the risk management hypothesis. *Strategic Management Journal*, **30**(4), 425–445.

Greenwald, C. (2010). ESG and earnings performance. Retrieved from https://www.thomsonreuters.com/content/dam/openweb/documents/pdf/tr-com-financial/case-study/esg-and-earnings-performance.pdf. Accessed date 9.07.2021.

Havemann, R. and Webster, P. (1999). Does ethical investment pay? EIRIS Report. Retrieved from http://www.eiris.org/files/research%20publications/doesethicalinvestmentpay99.pdf, accessed date 9.07.2021.

Hill, C.W. and Jones, T.M. (1992). Stakeholder-agency theory. *Journal of Management Studies*, **29**(2), 131–154.

Hillman, A.J. and Keim, G.D. (2001). Shareholder value, stakeholder management, and social issues: What's the bottom line? *Strategic Management Journal*, **22**(2), 125–139.

Jo, H. and Harjoto, M.A. (2011). Corporate governance and firm value: The impact of corporate social responsibility. *Journal of Business Ethics*, **103**(3), 351–383.

Jo, H., Saha, T., Sharma, R. and Wright, S. (2010). Socially responsible investing vs. vice investing. Paper presented at the *Academic and Business Research Institute Conference*, Las Vegas, NV, USA.

Jones, T.M. (1995). Instrumental stakeholder theory: A synthesis of ethics and economics. *Academy of Management Review*, **20**(2), 404–437.

Koh, P.S., Qian, C. and Wang, H. (2014). Firm litigation risk and the insurance value of corporate social performance. *Strategic Management Journal*, **35**(10), 1464–1482.

Lee, D.D. and Faff, R.W. (2009). Corporate sustainability performance and idiosyncratic risk: A global perspective. *Financial Review*, **44**(2), 213–237.

Lins, K.V., Servaes, H. and Tamayo, A. (2017). Social capital, trust, and firm performance: The value of corporate social responsibility during the financial crisis. *The Journal of Finance*, **72**(4), 1785–1824.

Luo, X. and Bhattacharya, C.B. (2009). The debate over doing good: Corporate social performance, strategic marketing levers, and firm-idiosyncratic risk. *Journal of Marketing*, **73**(6), 198–213.

Magness, V. (2008). Who are the stakeholders now? An empirical examination of the Mitchell, Agle, and Wood theory of stakeholder salience. *Journal of Business Ethics*, **83**(2), 177–192.

Margolis, J.D. and Walsh, J.P. (2001). *People and Profits? The Search for a Link Between a Company's Social and Financial Performance* (Lawrence Erlbaum, Mahwah, NJ, USA).

Margolis, J.D., Elfenbein, H.A. and Walsh, J.P. (2007). Does it pay to be good? A meta-analysis and redirection of research on the relationship between corporate social and financial performance. *Ann Arbor*, **1001**, 48109–1234. https://doi.org/10.2139/ssrn.1866371.

Mishra, S. and Modi, S. (2013). Positive and negative corporate social responsibility, financial leverage, and idiosyncratic risk. *Journal of Business Ethics*, **117**(2), 431–448.

Mitchell, R.K., Agle, B.R. and Wood, D.J. (1997). Toward a theory of stakeholder identification and salience: Defining the principle of who and what really counts. *Academy of Management Review*, **22**(4), 853–886.

Mitroff, I.I. (2005). *Why Some Companies Emerge Stronger and Better From A Crisis: Seven Essential Lessons for Surviving Disaster* (AMACOM/American Management Association, New York, NY, USA).

Mitroff, I.I. and Alpaslan, M.C. (2003). Preparing for evil. *Harvard Business Review*, **81**(4), 109–115.

Mitroff, I.I., Pearson, C.M. and Harrington, L.K. (1996). *The Essential Guide to Managing Corporate Crises* (Oxford University Press, New York).

Ndlela, M.N. (2019). A stakeholder approach to risk management. In *Crisis Communication*, Ndlela, M.N. (ed.), (Palgrave Macmillan, Cham), pp. 53–75.

Orlitzky, M., Schmidt, F.L. and Rynes, S.L. (2003). Corporate social and financial performance: A meta-analysis. *Organization Studies*, **24**(3), 403–441.

Paranque, B. (2017). The need for an alternative to shareholder value creation? The Ethomed student experience. *Research in International Business and Finance*, **39**, 686–695.

Parmar, B.L., Freeman, R.E., Harrison, J.S., Wicks, A.C., Purnell, L. and De Colle, S. (2010). Stakeholder theory: The state of the art. *Academy of Management Annals*, **4**(1), 403–445.

Pérez, A. (2015). Corporate reputation and CSR reporting to stakeholders: Gaps in the literature and future lines of research. *Corporate Communications: An International Journal*, **20**(1), 11–29.

Rasche, A. and Esser, D.E. (2006). From stakeholder management to stakeholder accountability. *Journal of Business Ethics*, **65**(3), 251–267.

Renneboog, L., Ter Horst, J. and Zhang, C. (2008). Socially responsible investments: Institutional aspects, performance, and investor behavior. *Journal of Banking & Finance*, **32**(9), 1723–1742.

Ross, S.A. (1973). The economic theory of agency: The principal's problem. *The American Economic Review*, **63**(2), 134–139.

Sharfman, M.P. and Fernando, C.S. (2008). Environmental risk management and the cost of capital. *Strategic Management Journal*, **29**(6), 569–592.

Sheaffer, Z. and Mano-Negrin, R. (2003). Executives' orientations as indicators of crisis management policies and practices. *Journal of Management Studies*, **40**(2), 573–606.

Shen, C.H., Wu, M.W., Chen, T.H. and Fang, H. (2016). To engage or not to engage in corporate social responsibility: Empirical evidence from global banking sector. *Economic Modelling*, **55**, 207–225.

Sisodia, R., Wolfe, D. and Sheth, J.N. (2003). *Firms of Endearment: How World-Class Companies Profit from Passion and Purpose* (Pearson Prentice Hall, New Jersey).

Stevens, J.M., Kevin Steensma, H., Harrison, D.A. and Cochran, P.L. (2005). Symbolic or substantive document? The influence of ethics codes on financial executives' decisions. *Strategic Management Journal*, **26**(2), 181–195.

Van Liedekerke, L., De Moor, L. and Vanwalleghem, D. (2007). Risk-return of Belgian SRI funds. Working Paper. Katholieke Universiteit Leuven, Faculty of Economics and Applied Economics, Department of Accountancy, Finance and Insurance.

Velamuri, S.R. and Venkataraman, S. (2005). Why stakeholder and stockholder theories are not necessarily contradictory: A Knightian insight. *Journal of Business Ethics*, **61**(3), 249–262.

Waddock, S. and Smith, N. (2000). Corporate responsibility audits: Doing well by doing good. *Sloan Management Review*, **41**(2), 75–83.

Weaver, G.R., Trevino, L.K. and Cochran, P.L. (1999). Integrated and decoupled corporate social performance: Management commitments, external pressures, and corporate ethics practices. *Academy of Management Journal*, **42**(5), 539–552.

Zingales, L. (2000). In search of new foundations. *The Journal of Finance*, **55**(4), 1623–1653.

https://doi.org/10.1142/9781800610781_0018

Chapter 18

Firm Liquidity During the COVID-19 Crisis

Valdonė Darškuvienė[*,‡], **Bernadeta Goštautaitė**[*,§], **Egidijus Kundelis**[*,¶], **Dalius Misiūnas**[*,**], and **Siuzana Ščerbina-Dalibagienė**[†,‡‡]

[*]*ISM University of Management and Economics, Arklių str. 18, Vilnius LT-01305, Lithuania, Europe*

[†]*Ministry of Finance, Lithuania, Europe*

[‡]*valdone.darskuviene@ism.lt*

[§]*bernadeta.gostautaite@ism.lt*

[¶]*egidijus.kundelis@ism.lt*

[**]*dalius.misiunas@ism.lt*

[‡‡]*siuzana.scerbina@gmail.com*

Abstract

The chapter examines how companies addressed the liquidity crisis which arose during the COVID-19 pandemic. It is based on CEO interviews and case studies of four companies with diverse corporate governance characteristics. This qualitative research of success and failure stories was designed to explain how the liquidity crisis evolved, what liquidity management tools and policies were used, and what links emerge between corporate governance, decision-making, and the impact on company performance. The study fills a gap in the research on company governance and financial performance under market uncertainty, with a focus on the effects of an unexpected large-scale crisis. While the research was

[‡]Corresponding author.

performed in Lithuania, it offers insights for understanding the business landscape and disruptions in general in the wake of a large-scale unexpected crisis.

18.1. Introduction

The vulnerability of companies to crisis has been much discussed in the academic literature, focusing, on the one hand, on specific features of crises and their links to company performance and failures, and on the other hand, on comparative crisis research. In this context, Ferraro *et al.* (2015) introduced the concept of "grand challenges," which they describe as typically being complex, with unknown solutions and intertwined technical and social elements.

The COVID-19 pandemic crisis emerged unexpectedly and has reached a scale such that it can be studied as one of the grand challenges facing economies globally. So far, little is known about this pandemic and its traits from the microeconomic perspective. The unprecedented scale of the crisis, with huge uncertainties locally as well as globally, has had diverse effects on society, healthcare systems, and economies in general. Amid the economic uncertainties, national governments have sought to balance lockdown measures, which have direct negative effects on business, particularly travel, hospitality, and entertainment, and measures to support employment and company liquidity. Research on companies' resilience to this crisis is just emerging. Thus, the chapter aims to examine how companies handled the liquidity crisis faced during the COVID-19 pandemic.

The literature tends to reflect two opposing views of liquidity management. One broad area of research focuses on the financial constraints of a company's operations and the key factors in managing liquidity, with an underlying emphasis on the continuity of the firm's operations. Prior studies provided different views on the underlying sources of liquidity in firm performance, examining the relationship between static versus dynamic liquidity and measures of company performance. Focusing on cash management, cash flows, working capital, earnings, and profitability has provided varied evidence of the effects on firm-level performance.

Another broad strand of research focuses on extreme factors leading to financial distress and on bankruptcy prediction. There is a common understanding that the inability to manage liquidity is one of the key factors leading companies to financial distress and insolvency. Crisis periods, usually characterized by economic downturn and market uncertainty, force re-examination of liquidity and solvency issues.

In this study, we point out the limitations of both strands of research when they ignore corporate governance characteristics and mechanisms. We build our argument on insights from studies which indicate that corporate governance influences the management behavior behind liquidity choices and, in extreme cases, financial distress and insolvency. Furthermore, we examine strong versus weak governance and its effects on company liquidity management and performance, in particular during the COVID-19 pandemic crisis.

To do so, we employ a qualitative study comprising CEO interviews and analysis of company cases. We take the success and failure stories of four companies with diverse corporate governance characteristics, seeking to explain how the liquidity crisis evolved, what liquidity management tools and policies were used, and what links existed between corporate governance, decision-making, and the effects on company performance.

The study provides several contributions to the research domain. First, it contributes to the understanding of the recent pandemic crisis as a liquidity crisis, identifying its features and providing supporting arguments. Second, it provides support for the argument that strong corporate governance enables better liquidity crisis management in companies.

The chapter provides an introductory overview of the impact of COVID-19 on businesses, with focus on liquidity and corporate governance, based on the most recent insights from the ongoing broader research. The study limited itself to examining companies' liquidity management and governance in Lithuania. However, since international as well as local companies were approached, the insights it offers are valid for understanding the broader business landscape and disruptions in general amid a large-scale unexpected crisis caused by a pandemic.

The rest of the chapter is organized as follows. Section 18.2 reviews the literature and discusses the strands of research on company liquidity management, insolvency, and governance. Section 18.3

describes the research methodology. Section 18.4 discusses the main insights obtained from the interviews and case studies. Section 18.5 concludes.

18.2. Literature Review

Generally speaking, there are two opposing views of liquidity management issues. The current study focuses on three strands in the literature. First, some prior studies have focused on examining the relationship between static versus dynamic liquidity and company performance measures such as cash flows, working capital, earnings, and profitability. There are different views on the underlying sources of liquidity in firm performance (Kim *et al.*, 1998; Lazaridis and Tryfonidis, 2006). Apart from traditional liquidity-related characteristics like cash holdings and working capital, empirical studies have examined such liquidity stress factors as increased drawdowns of credit and liquidity facilities by customers or counterparties, incapacity to roll-over short-term unsecured funding, redemption of funding at early stages, loss of credible counterparties, and reduced investment portfolio liquidity. Opler *et al.* (1999) addressed the contrast between the irrelevance of corporate cash holding in perfect markets and diverse evidence at the firm level. They support the static trade-off theory predictions of shareholder wealth maximization with empirical evidence that firms with strong growth opportunities and riskier cash flows tend to accumulate more cash holdings, hence improving their liquidity position. Lancaster and Stevens (1999) extended the research to test for industry effects when the relationships between liquidity and working capital and cash are industry-specific and cannot be generalized across all firms. However, there is a lack of consensus on the link between misalignments in corporate liquidity policies and long-term growth, dynamics along economic cycles, and specific types of economic crisis.

Another quite extensive strand of literature relates to company resilience and liquidity management with reference to the phenomenon of financial distress and insolvency. Financial instability induces market conditions that undermine or tend to undermine economic performance. A number of empirical studies have focused on the factors of external and internal environments that cause company financial distress and bankruptcies. While internal factors are related to management and corporate governance failures, external factors (economic, institutional, legal) are viewed as being beyond management's control. A broad and varied empirical literature focuses on financial distress and bankruptcy prediction.

Numerous studies have applied diverse explanatory variables (in many cases, though, based on liquidity performance) and a variety of empirical techniques. Since the seminal work by Beaver (1966), who introduced univariate discriminant analysis to contrast the performance of failing and successful companies, a number of different bankruptcy prediction models have been developed and tested by researchers. Altman (1968) introduced an extension to Beaver's model Beaver employing multiple discriminant analysis (MDA) to identify financial ratios, including liquidity-related ones, that allow for bankruptcy prediction. This approach was further tested under different settings (Agarwal and Taffler, 2007) and others), though with varying predictive accuracy. More recently, an empirical study of UK company data (Almamy *et al.*, 2016) reported a declining predictive accuracy of the original Z-score model when a longer time period is added into the analysis. This means there are limitations for using the models during periods of high market volatility and disruptions. Critiques of the model's restrictive assumptions about multivariate normality and the independence of explanatory variables led to further development of bankruptcy prediction models with improved financial distress predictability (Grice and Ingram, 2001; Jones *et al.*, 2015, 2017; Ohlson, 1980; Zavgren, 1985; Zmijewski, 1984).

In contrast to the criticized, inaccurate static bankruptcy prediction techniques, Shumway (2001) developed a dynamic discrete hazard model that included market-based variables. The predictive accuracy of the model, tested by Campbell *et al.* (2008) and others, was based on making it possible to assess the changing probability of bankruptcy over time as a function of a vector of explanatory variables that also vary with time. Further on, Agarwal and Taffler (2008), and others, acknowledged that market-based variables increase the overall predictability of distress prediction models, which led to the development of combined models, including both accounting performance ratios and market-based variables (Trujillo-Ponce *et al.*, 2014). In a review of the history of the development of bankruptcy prediction models, Balcaen and Ooghe (2006) summarized the problems, including the use of annual accounting information and the neglect of the multidimensional nature of failures.

In response to increased interest in developing effective corporate governance mechanisms to reduce risk-taking by company management and risks of financial distress and insolvency, a number of studies propose using an integrated set of variables — financial ratio-based predictors along with a set of corporate governance variables — in the distress prediction models (Liang *et al.*, 2020). Though the models are supported by theory, empirical studies do not provide conclusive evidence of their effectiveness.

To summarize, empirical studies give mixed results regarding the predictive ability of the traditional distress prediction models for different settings and groupings of companies. Many of the financial distress studies prefer simpler financial distress prediction models, often relying on liquidity and other accounting performance measures.

A third direction in the literature investigates the influence of corporate governance on the nature of management behavior leading to liquidity choices and financial distress. The earliest studies show that debt constrains managers by reducing free cash flow and potential cash diversion (Jensen, 1986). Based on this idea, Morellec *et al.* (2012) developed a dynamic trade-off model to examine manager–shareholder conflicts in capital structure choices relating to the firm's refinancing costs and to liquidation costs in bankruptcy.

A broad set of literature focuses directly on the relationship between liquidity and governance. The concepts of market liquidity and corporate governance and their relationship are widely examined, with better corporate governance generally implying higher liquidity for listed companies, subject however to the firm's performance characteristics Berglund (2020). Good corporate governance reduces agency problems in firms where the business is subject to a high degree of uncertainty. Yun (2009) suggested the choice of corporate liquidity as a channel for corporate governance and found large cash holdings may be a sign of confidence in good management. The studies confirmed the negative influence of low-quality governance. Research indicates that firms with weaker governance structures choose smaller cash holdings, which leads to liquidity risks (Harford *et al.*, 2008).

Recent studies have examined alternative approaches to corporate governance and liquidity management, with diverse outcomes. In examining corporate governance quality versus internal control, Chen *et al.* (2020) provide evidence that firms with higher-quality internal control are less likely to have abnormal cash holdings, either excesses or deficits of cash, and this effect is not driven by corporate governance quality. A study by Jebran *et al.* (2019) supports the impact of corporate governance attributes and the nature of the ultimate owner on the adjustment behavior of corporate cash holdings, and shows that the cash-holdings adjustment rate varies between normal and crisis periods. Dittmar and Mahrt-Smith (2007) documented that firms with poor corporate governance dissipate cash quickly in ways that significantly reduce operating performance.

Research on liquidity and corporate governance point to the existence of a relationship between agency cost, information asymmetry, and the quality of corporate governance. Yun (2009) showed that liquidity choices between cash and loan commitments are strongly influenced by the quality of corporate governance. Faleye *et al.* (2014) examined board composition and board members' reputation, busyness, and quality in relation to bankruptcy prediction. The various empirical studies offer insights on the complexity of the issues and their dependence on fundamental characteristic of the markets and the level of development of legal institutions in different settings and company groupings (large vs small companies, low vs high growth, financially constrained vs unconstrained firms; Zhang *et al.*, 2015). The majority of the studies use accounting-based company liquidity and performance measures, which, due to their lags in time and the application of accounting rules, have significant limitations for examining performance under crisis.

Overall, this literature review indicates a heterogeneity of approaches in theoretical and empirical studies on the relationship between liquidity, solvency, and corporate governance, as well as the inconclusiveness of insights. A few of the studies relate the COVID-19 crisis to these issues. In the most recent study, Ding *et al.* (2020) reported milder effects among firms with (i) stronger pre-2020 finances (more cash, less debt, and larger profits), (ii) less exposure to COVID-19 through global supply chains and customer locations, (iii) more CSR activities, and (iv) less entrenched executives. However, the resilience of firms to the pandemic is examined focusing on the differential, cross-firm stock price reactions to COVID-19 cases.

Against this background, we not only position our study at the intersection of liquidity management and corporate governance literature but also aim to investigate specifically how companies addressed the liquidity crisis faced during the COVID-19 pandemic. Furthermore, we focus on examining strong versus weak governance and its links to company liquidity management and performance in specific institutional/economic settings.

18.3. Methodology

This section describes our sample selection criteria and procedures, data collection, and analysis method.

18.3.1. *Sample and procedure*

To explore companies' experiences and responses to the challenges of the COVID-19 pandemic in Lithuania, we employed a qualitative, multiple-case-study research design, as that allows for rich and well-grounded explanations (Stake, 2005). Using criteria defined *a priori*, we purposefully selected four case companies based on previous research suggesting sector-based differences in company performance and vulnerability to failure (Ding *et al.*, 2020; Lancaster and Stevens, 1999; Zavgren, 1985), based on links between firm liquidity, cash holdings, and company failure (Zhang *et al.*, 2015), and based on corporate liquidity and governance traits (Ahmadjian and Okumura, 2006; Chen *et al.*, 2020; Faleye *et al.*, 2014; Morellec *et al.*, 2012; Yoshikawa *et al.*, 2007; Yun, 2009).

We used theoretically important selection criteria: (i) industry-specific company performance and liquidity traits and (ii) corporate governance influences on firms' choices to meet liquidity needs under external and internal constraints. Thus, the company cases represent diverse industries, including manufacturing (paper, furniture, refrigerators) and services (transportation), diverse size (large/medium-size and small companies), and strong versus weak corporate governance as reflected in ownership (local vs foreign, diversified vs individual/family, listed vs non-listed) and in two-tier versus one-tier board structures.

We chose four companies (see Table 18.1 for a more detailed description of each) which differ in regard to our selection criteria and provide contrasting illustrations of experiences, challenges, and measures taken to handle pandemic-induced liquidity problems. Company A is a publishing firm with a sales focus on local markets. It has the legal status of a limited liability company and is family-owned, with a one-tier corporate governance structure. Company B is a large to medium-size manufacturer of refrigeration equipment with a sales focus on international markets. The company is listed on a stock exchange, with concentrated foreign ownership. The company has a two-tier corporate governance structure. Company C is in the service industry, engaged in transportation and storage. It operates locally and abroad (Western Europe). It has the legal status of a limited liability company and a one-tier corporate governance structure. Company D is a medium-sized contract furniture producer (design, production, project management). It operates in local and foreign markets (Western Europe). It is a limited liability company with a one-tier corporate governance structure.

18.3.2. *Data collection and analysis*

We collected our data through interviews with senior executives in June–July 2020 using a semi-structured interview guide with at least two interviewers (Langley and Abdallah, 2011). We further triangulated our findings with archival data from publicly available databases (the Lithuanian Centre of Registers for company data) and media releases in order to better understand the social, political, and economic context (Stake, 2005). The interview guide included sections on firm characteristics, challenges experienced during the initial phase of the COVID-19 outbreak in the country, measures taken to manage the crisis, respondents' assessment of their current financial situation, changes in relationships with customers and providers of financing (owners, parent companies, commercial banks), respondents' evaluation of governmental financial support schemes, and their personal lessons learned. The interview guide thus contained both factual accounts (e.g. indicators, events) and respondents' subjective narratives. Given the pandemic-related restrictions, all interviews were conducted via a platform for video and audio conferencing. With the consent of our study participants,

Table 18.1. Descriptions of case companies.

Aspect	**Company A**	**Company B**	**Company C**	**Company D**
General characteristics				
Industry	Publishing, producer of commercial print media	Manufacturing of refrigerators and freezers	Transportation and storage	Manufacturing of furniture
Turnover, range	€1–10 million	€30–40 million	€20–30 million	€10–20 million
No. of employees	50–100	500–550	400–550	100–150
Financial results	Losses in 2019 and 2020	Losses in 2019 and 2020	Profits (€100,000–500,000 per year)	Profits (€100,000–500,000 per year)
Organization	Private (LLC), 24 years	Listed, established after privatization in late 1990s	Private (LLC), 11 years	Private (LLC), 20 years
Governance				
Board includes Independent members	N	Y	N	N
Supervisory board	N	Y	N	N
CEO duality	N	N	N	N
Ownership	Local ownership, one owner	Foreign ownership, not part of any corporate group	Local ownership, majority family	Local ownership, one owner

the interviews (60–75 minutes each) were audio-recorded and fully transcribed.

Although guided by the case study approach to analyzing qualitative data (Langley and Abdallah, 2011), we prioritized providing detailed narratives of each of the four case companies over the extraction of narrower supporting evidence for theory induction (Myers, 2013). We first conducted content coding of the interview transcripts to create a general framework to organize our findings. We then reconstructed the organizational narratives regarding the outbreak of the pandemic and its impact on each business. This resulted in rich empirical descriptions of our cases, illustrated with quotes of our informants, which we provide next.

18.4. Results

In this section we discuss the four cases chosen to examine how companies addressed the liquidity crisis which arose during the COVID-19 pandemic. The general characteristics, organization, and governance of the four case companies are described in Table 18.1.

We focused on these four chosen companies to reflect the diversity of experiences in specific industry settings. We began with semi-structured interview questions on topics such as what the company sees as the defining characteristics of the crisis and how it differs from previous economic crises, and the major challenges the company experienced during the first pandemic period and how it addressed them. Then we looked at the impact of COVID-19 on the company's performance, focusing on how their products, customers, suppliers, and distribution channels evolved over the same period of time. We also asked whether shareholders or creditors served as partners to the company in terms of providing funding or other types of aid. We inquired about the role of governance in the company's management of the crisis. Finally, we closed by encouraging interviewees to elaborate on anything that we might have missed and that had played a major role in their crisis management issues.

18.4.1. *Case A*

As a publishing company with a focus on sales in local markets, Company A did not experience direct government-imposed limitations on its activities during the pandemic. However, the crisis did impact the company significantly.

The CEO described this crisis as different from previous ones in nature and scale: "The scale and nature of crises are different. In 2008 there was a financial crisis and now there is a crisis due to the government restrictions. We expected the crisis to come and were preparing for it, but we were not ready to that extent."

The restrictions imposed on major clients of the company during the quarantine had a strong indirect negative effect on the company's operations. As clients' advertising, conferences, and exhibitions moved to virtual space, orders dropped by approximately 80%. The company experienced liquidity constraints as its cash flow turned negative. However, a previously accumulated financial reserve supported the company's solvency position. Revision of clients' credit limits and the introduction of a prepayment requirement followed. Suppliers adopted a similar strategy. Business resilience solutions became a top priority.

"We think it is not wise to stop ten years of business growth because of a three-month or one-year crisis," the CEO reflected.

The crisis was assumed to be short term, with the sole owner and CEO more focused on future industry trends as the company moves to online solutions.

18.4.2. *Case B*

For Company B, a manufacturer of refrigeration equipment, the crisis became "shock therapy." The CEO described the crisis as a liquidity crisis with a sudden, short-term, extremely negative impact on the company's operations caused by problems with customer payments as well as transportation and supply issues. Physical cash holdings did not decrease and the business did not interrupt its work; only market expectations and attitudes changed.

The major challenge for this company with a focus on international sales was cash-flow management, as customers suspended payments for goods and suppliers started changing contract terms and demanding prepayment. To manage its cash flows, the company itself began demanding prepayment and making use of government support measures, factoring, and bank financing.

According to the CEO, "attitudes to the crisis depend more on managers' level of stress tolerance than on their nationality or business background."

The CEO experienced strong control on the part of shareholders, conducted through the board. The company stresses transparency and information disclosure to the market, in keeping with investors' preferences.

18.4.3. *Case C*

For Company C, a fast-growing transportation company active in local and foreign markets, the pandemic had a moderate negative effect on business. The CEO characterized the crisis as a short-term liquidity crisis. Reflecting back on the 2008 crisis, he recalled the negative role of insurance companies, which at the time cancelled client credit limits immediately, resulting in substantial liquidity and solvency issues for many companies in the transportation sector. During the COVID-19 crisis, though, the CEO said, insurance companies were better prepared, more supportive, and showed a forward-looking attitude. Thus credit limits remained stable, which helped to stabilize liquidity. At the same time, providers of external finance (banks and leasing companies) introduced more flexible policies and long-term orientation. To maintain the company's resilience, strict cash-flow management, asset sales, and tax payment deferrals were needed, along with cost cuts and postponement of investment projects. The company saw a drop in transportation orders from clients strongly impacted by the pandemic. However, despite weakening performance, the company maintained its financial position.

The company's governance is characterized by the joint presence of owners and top management on the board. Strong governance was visible during the pandemic as the board reacted quickly to the deteriorating situation and made decisions to restructure the client base. The company terminated contracts with low-profit-margin clients, concentrating instead on services to higher-profit-margin clients and clients not impacted by COVID-19 restrictions. Thus, strong governance may be viewed as a key to fast and timely decisions to support the resilience of a company on a large scale.

18.4.4. *Case D*

For Company D, a mid-sized contract furniture producer (engaged in design, production, and project management) for local and foreign markets, the impact of the COVID-19 pandemic was significant. The company's CEO characterized the pandemic crisis as similar to the 2008 crisis in terms of an immediate drop in revenue and profitability, disruptions in the supply chain, and a larger long-term negative effect on operations. As the contract manufacturing industry in general shows strong inertia (due to a solid order backlog), the negative impact of the crisis on revenues is expected to be delayed by 6–12 months. The company experienced a high level of uncertainty about the future due to frozen capital investments in key export markets. It faced severe financial constraints, liquidity problems due to an increase in trade receivables, a lack of cash, and limited cash reserves. The company addressed its cash-flow management challenges during the pandemic by strengthening control over cash collection. Problems with working capital were magnified by a lack of flexible and cheap financing instruments. Banks limited commercial loans due to increased sector risk, declining to take more risk and provide additional financing. The company had to search for internal funding sources, such as accelerated cash collection. Its governance is characterized by strong involvement of the major shareholder in strategic and daily management of the company. Agency problems that arose were resolved by replacing non-performing top and middle managers.

These four cases permit a review of the range of issues faced in the crisis, which companies' management characterized as a liquidity crisis that was abrupt, sudden, and unexpected, with a strong impact either directly on company operations or indirectly through the supply chain. Table 18.2 provides a summary of the four cases based on the interviews with the companies' CEOs.

As the four cases show, both downsizing and growth in operations increase uncertainty for companies and cause financial constraints. A company's need for liquidity focuses the effect of financial constraints on corporate policies. This is reflected in companies' propensity to save and hold cash reserves, and in their ability to manage cash flows. An abrupt liquidity crisis forces management and shareholders to react, magnifying agency problems. The cases suggest that

Table 18.2. Liquidity crisis characteristics and challenges faced by companies during the COVID-19 pandemic.

Aspect	Company A	Company B	Company C	Company D
Characteristics of the COVID-19 crisis	Operational crisis	Liquidity crisis	Short-term negative effect on business, short-term liquidity crisis	Effect delayed by 6–9 months due to inertia. Expected long-term negative effect on business
The role of government in business failures/survival	Extremely negative due to lockdown of businesses that are major clients	Negative due to lack of support for large businesses	Negative. Limited positive effect of government support	Negative. Limited positive effect of government support
Major challenge during the first pandemic period	Loss of orders from clients	Cash-flow management	Cash-flow management, change of customer base, fast decision-making	Cash flow management, “opportunistic” behavior by some clients/debtors
Company performance during the initial pandemic period	Negative impact with slight recovery by the end of the period	Short-term (4–5 weeks) negative impact and rapid recovery	Negative impact and modest recovery. Decrease in revenues and profitability, postponement of investments, costs cuts	Negative impact and deteriorating liquidity position in longer term

(*Continued*)

Table 18.2. (*Continued*)

Aspect	Company A	Company B	Company C	Company D
Impact of COVID-19 on company's liquidity position	Negative impact (resolved by using the company's financial reserve)	Short-term unexpected negative impact	Short-term negative impact. Deteriorating liquidity reinstated	Increase in delayed trade receivables. Effect forecast to be medium to long-term negative
Impact of COVID-19 on company's relationships with customers and suppliers	Required prepayment by clients, and suppliers also required prepayment	Distinguishing of reliable "partners" (customers and suppliers)	Increased control of clients' creditworthiness. No cut of credit limits by insurance companies	Dramatic increase in delivery time by key foreign suppliers, disruption of own delivery
Role of corporate governance in managing the crisis	Hands-on management by owner	Strategy of continuous support by shareholders	Owners and top management are on the board. Active role of the board	Hands-on management by owner. Internal reorganization performed

success in resolving the crisis issues depends on whether governance mechanisms are strong or weak.

18.5. Conclusions

Whereas most previous studies focused on empirical research on company liquidity and performance based on secondary financial data applied to specific company samples, we analyzed the relationship between liquidity management and corporate governance in a specific organizational setting. We took the conceptual approach that good corporate governance reduces agency problems. In doing so, we looked for support for previous research which related stronger corporate governance to higher corporate liquidity. Moreover, we concentrated on characteristics of liquidity management in a crisis environment such as propensity to save cash, form reserve cash holdings, and control cash flows.

Our study offers insights for managers in designing and implementing liquidity management policies to improve a company's resilience to crisis. It suggests that in a sudden, unexpected crisis, the initial negative effect is caused by disruptions in supplier–company–customer relationships across the supply chain. Defensive actions for cash preservation and generation and breaches of financial agreements, may, on the one hand, support cash flow management, but on the other hand, they increase business risks.

Under such conditions, stakeholder relationship management and strengthening of corporate governance enable better liquidity crisis management in companies. This is a primary concern not only during a crisis but also might serve as the basis for forward-looking strategies to support company resilience over economic cycles.

While this research was conducted in Lithuania, the insights from the company case studies are valid generally for a better understanding of the business landscape and the disruptions of a large-scale unexpected crisis caused by a pandemic.

Our recommendations are based on qualitative case research, which may be further developed through quantitative studies investigating the relationships between corporate governance mechanisms and business liquidity management to support business resilience to a crisis.

Acknowledgments

This project received funding from the Research Council of Lithuania (LMTLT), agreement No. P-COV 20-77.

References

Agarwal, V. and Taffler, R. J. (2007). Twenty-five years of the Taffler z-score model: Does it really have predictive ability? *Accounting and Business Research*, **37**(4), 285–300.

Agarwal, V. and Taffler, R. (2008). Comparing the performance of market-based and accounting-based bankruptcy prediction models. *Journal of Banking & Finance*, **32**(8), 1541–1551.

Ahmadjian, C.L. and Okumura, A. (2011). Corporate governance in Japan. Chapter 8, In *Handbook on International Corporate Governance: Country Analyses*, C. A. Mallin (ed.), (Edward Elgar), pp. 130–147.

Almamy, J., Aston, J. and Ngwa, L.N. (2016). An evaluation of Altman's Z-score using cash flow ratio to predict corporate failure amid the recent financial crisis: Evidence from the UK. *Journal of Corporate Finance*, **36**, 278–285.

Altman, E. I. (1968). Financial ratios, discriminant analysis and the prediction of corporate bankruptcy. *The Journal of Finance*, **23**(4), 589–609.

Balcaen, S. and Ooghe, H. (2006). 35 years of studies on business failure: an overview of the classic statistical methodologies and their related problems. *The British Accounting Review*, **38**(1), 63–93.

Beaver, W. H. (1966). Financial ratios as predictors of failure. *Journal of Accounting Research*, **4**, 71–111.

Berglund, T. (2020). Liquidity and corporate governance. *Journal of Risk and Financial Management*, **13**(3), 54.

Campbell, J.Y., Hilscher, J. and Szilagyi, J. (2008). In search of distress risk. *The Journal of Finance*, **63**(6), 2899–2939.

Chen, H., Yang, D., Zhang, J.H. and Zhou, H. (2020). Internal controls, risk management, and cash holdings. *Journal of Corporate Finance*, **64**, 101695.

Ding, W., Levine, R., Lin, C. and Xie, W. (2020). Corporate immunity to the Covid-19 pandemic, NBER Working Papers 27055.

Dittmar, A. and Mahrt-Smith, J. (2007). Corporate governance and the value of cash holdings. *Journal of Financial Economics*, **83**(3), 599–634.

Faleye, O., Platt, H. and Platt, M. (2014). Board busyness and the risk of corporate bankruptcy. *Pratt's Journal of Bankruptcy Law*, **10**, 391–402.

Ferraro, F., Etzion, D. and Gehman, J. (2015). Tackling grand challenges pragmatically: Robust action revisited. *Organization Studies*, **36**(3), 363–390.

Grice, J.S. and Ingram, R.W. (2001). Tests of the generalizability of Altman's bankruptcy prediction model. *Journal of Business Research*, **54**(1), 53–61.

Harford, J., Mansi, S.A. and Maxwell, W.F. (2008). Corporate governance and firm cash holdings in the US. *Journal of Financial Economics*, **87**(3), 535–555.

Jebran, K., Chen, S., Tauni, M.Z. and Ahmad, H. (2019). Corporate governance, ultimate owner, and target cash holdings: Evidence from China. *SAGE Open*, **9**(4), 2158244019894293.

Jensen, M.C. (1986). Agency costs of free cash flow, corporate finance, and takeovers. *The American Economic Review*, **76**(2), 323–329.

Jones, S., Johnstone, D. and Wilson, R. (2015). An empirical evaluation of the performance of binary classifiers in the prediction of credit ratings changes. *Journal of Banking & Finance*, **56**, 72–85.

Jones, S., Johnstone, D. and Wilson, R. (2017). Predicting corporate bankruptcy: An evaluation of alternative statistical frameworks. *Journal of Business Finance & Accounting*, **44**(1–2), 3–34.

Kim, C.-S., Mauer, D.C. and Sherman, A.E. (1998). The determinants of corporate liquidity: Theory and evidence. *Journal of Financial and Quantitative Analysis*, **33**(3), 335–359.

Lancaster, C. and Stevens, J.L. (1999). Corporate liquidity and the significance of earnings versus cash flow: an examination of industry effects. *Journal of Applied Business Research (JABR)*, **15**(3), 37–46.

Langley, A. and Abdallah, C. (2011). Templates and Turns in qualitative studies of strategy and management. In *Building Methodological Bridges (Research Methodology in Strategy and Management, Vol. 6)*. Emerald Group Publishing Limited, Bingley, pp. 201–235.

Lazaridis I. and Tryfonidis, D. (2006). The relationship between working capital management and profitability of listed companies in the Athens Stock Exchange. *Journal of Financial Management and Analysis*, **19**(1), 26–35.

Liang, D., Tsai, C.-F., Lu, H.-Y.R. and Chang, L.-S. (2020). Combining corporate governance indicators with stacking ensembles for financial distress prediction. *Journal of Business Research*, **120**, 137–146.

Morellec, E., Nikolov, B. and Schürhoff, N. (2012). Corporate governance and capital structure dynamics. *The Journal of Finance*, **67**(3), 803–848.

Myers, M. (2013). *Qualitative Research in Business and Management*, 2nd edn (Sage, London).

Ohlson, J.A. (1980). Financial ratios and the probabilistic prediction of bankruptcy. *Journal of Accounting Research*, **18**(1), 109–131.

Opler, T., Pinkowitz, L., Stulz, R. and Williamson, R. (1999). The determinants and implications of corporate cash holdings. *Journal of Financial Economics*, **52**(1), 3–46.

Shumway, T. (2001). Forecasting bankruptcy more accurately: A simple hazard model. *The Journal of Business*, **74**(1), 101–124.

Stake, R.E. (2005). Qualitative case studies. In *Handbook of Qualitative Research*, 3rd edn Denzin, N.K. and Lincoln, Y.S. (eds.), (Sage, Thousand Oaks, CA), pp. 443–466.

Trujillo-Ponce, A., Samaniego-Medina, R. and Cardone-Riportella, C. (2014). Examining what best explains corporate credit risk: accounting-based versus market-based models. *Journal of Business Economics and Management*, **15**(2), 253–276.

Yoshikawa, T., Tsui-Auch, L.S. and McGuire, J. (2007). Corporate governance reform as institutional innovation: The case of Japan. *Organization Science*, **18**(6), 973–988.

Yun, H. (2009). The choice of corporate liquidity and corporate governance. *The Review of Financial Studies*, **22**(4), 1447–1475.

Zavgren, C.V. (1985). Assessing the vulnerability to failure of American industrial firms: A logistic analysis. *Journal of Business Finance & Accounting*, **12**(1), 19–45.

Zhang, W., von Eije, H. and Westerman, W. (2015). Does cash contribute to value? A comparison of constrained and unconstrained firms in China and Germany. *Eurasian Journal of Economics and Finance*, **3**(4), 22–38.

Zmijewski, M.E. (1984). Methodological issues related to the estimation of financial distress prediction models. *Journal of Accounting Research*, **22**, 59–82.

https://doi.org/10.1142/9781800610781_0019

Chapter 19

The Implications of the COVID-19 Pandemic on Corporate Governance: The Board of Directors' Response*

Grazia Dicuonzo* **and Francesca Donofrio**†

University of Bari Aldo Moro, Bari, Italy

*grazia.dicuonzo@uniba.it

†francescadonofrio@hotmail.it

Abstract

The COVID-19 pandemic poses a threat to the global economy, leading to the risk of a systemic crisis with devastating global economic impacts. These circumstances have put a strain on corporate governance systems, which have had to address major new problems and challenges. This chapter aims to investigate the board's reaction to the COVID-19, by providing an overview of the actions taken at the corporate governance level in the first phase of the pandemic. We first look at the actions taken by companies to support corporate governance; second, we examine the strategic actions implemented by companies; and finally, we investigate the actions taken by the board that had financial impacts on firms. In order to achieve our goal, we used the methodology of framing analysis. In particular, this study investigated the content of press releases of Italian FTSE MIB (Financial Times Stock Exchange – Milan Stock Exchange Index) companies. Our findings show that the corporate governance of the examined firms has implemented cost reduction actions, carrying out action plans aimed to mitigate the financial impacts related

*This chapter constitutes the results of a joint research project carried out by the authors. Sections 1, 3 and 4 have been contributed by G. Dicuonzo and Sections 2, 5 and 6 have been contributed by F. Donofrio.

to COVID-19. Regarding changes to top management remuneration policies, some companies have updated their short- and medium-term strategy or developed a new shareholder remuneration policy. In addition, most of the analyzed firms have put in place initiatives to actively support the country's efforts to overcome the current emergency by providing means and resources. The analysis of corporate press releases revealed that the COVID-19 pandemic challenged corporate survival. As such, our contribution has practical implications by providing an overview of the actions taken by corporate governance to respond to the COVID-19 pandemic. Moreover, our study can serve as a support tool for firms in the process of defining actions and strategies to respond to crisis events, especially if they affect the whole economic system.

19.1. Introduction

The COVID-19 pandemic began as a public health crisis and rapidly evolved into a financial and economic crisis of epic proportions. As the virus spread around the world, most national governors imposed a forced closure, which also affected the economic activity of many companies. Few or no companies were spared: some saw demand for their offerings plummet overnight, while others faced a noticeable increase in sales orders. Many companies have radically changed the way they work. Stock prices plummeted and then fell in an unprecedented pattern of volatility. Faced with uneven and, in some cases, ineffective responses from governments and with the economic recovery dependent on stopping the public health crisis, many companies have worked to close the gap. In the numerous meetings and updates during this period, the board members found themselves reviewing management's plans not only to guide the company through the crisis but also to support the company and help overcome the state of crisis.

In recent decades, there has been a need for greater and stronger business collaboration to combat systemic concerns such as rising income and wealth inequality, environmental degradation, climate change, racial and ethnic discrimination, declining public health and education, increasing corruption, the deterioration of public institutions, and the increased risk of pandemics. While some business leaders have heeded the call and found innovative ways to help address these problems, many others have looked the other way or referred to the problems as "social issues" or what economists call "public goods" problems and therefore, by definition, outside the scope of their legitimate interest as corporate executives and trustees for their shareholders.

COVID-19 has shown that these problems are not only legitimate areas of interest for businesses but also, and above all, sources of risk and opportunity. Like market forces, company forces can profoundly affect the business and competitive environment. In the wake of the COVID-19, boards of directors, institutional investors, governments, and the general public will renew their demands on companies to pay more attention to society's problems and play a more active role to help overcome them. For the same reason, boards of directors are increasingly expected to oversee the interface between business and society.

The new environment is characterized by an increasingly complex series of pressures and demands from various stakeholder groups, increased expectations of social commitment, and radical uncertainty about the future. These factors are complicating board decision-making and challenge the shareholder-centric governance model that has guided boards and business leaders over the past decades.

The shareholder-centric model, which is based on what academics' call "agency theory," appears to be giving way to a richer governance model that focuses on corporate health and resilience. COVID-19 pandemic has put a strain on the corporate governance that it has faced new problems and important challenges. In an ever-changing environment, the Board of Directors have to act quickly, prioritizing strategic initiatives and promoting action to preserve the company's financial structure and reputation (OECD, 2015). The governing body has strategic and supervisory functions, as well as a coordinated liaison with corporate stakeholders. The pandemic has radically changed the work of the Board of Directors. Indeed, COVID-19 has led to the definition of new tasks and greater responsibilities for the governing bodies, especially relating to employee health, organizational issues, and business continuity. In addition, in this crisis scenario, an assessment of the adequacy of governance structures to fully understand the business risks arising from the pandemic and the resulting economic downturn, a re-evaluation of business strategy with actions in the short and a proper balance between the need for immediate liquidity and the increase of indebtedness have been necessary.

In general, in case of extraordinary events, like natural disasters, wars, or terrorist attacks, the proper management of the emergency is crucial to reduce damages and recover rapidly the activities. In particular, corporate governance plays a key role in assuring business continuity. The Board of Directors of many companies has provided rapidly and constant information to reassure the investors. Indeed, during the first phase of spread of the COVID-19, financial markets have shown a high volatility of stocks due to the panic among the investors triggered by the alarming news on the pandemic (Haroon and Rizvi, 2020). In this context, it is important to remember that the Board has strategic and prospective supervision functions (European Central Bank, 2018). It guides and supports management in decisions related to the struggle for survival, ensuring that the company is able to emerge from the crisis stronger and more resilient.

In light of these considerations, the present study aims to investigate the Board's response to COVID-19. We want to understand the strategies implemented by Italian companies in response to the COVID-19 pandemic, specifically analyzing the actions taken by the Board of Directors to facilitate overcoming the crisis and ensure business continuity. We consider Italy an ideal context to investigate this issue because, during the pandemic, it was one of the first countries to impose the blockade and to count a high mortality rate from the coronavirus. For this reason, the perception of the risk of the severity of the spread of COVID-19 and of the negative economic and financial effects was immediately felt by Italian companies. This chapter offers an overview about the Board of Directors' responses in the first phase of the COVID-19 pandemic (March–October 2020), focusing on three key aspects.

First, we observe the actions taken by companies in order to support corporate management (Hopt, 2012; PWC, 2020). In order to deal with crisis situations, a crisis committee must first be set up to identify and know the reasons for the crisis itself (Deloitte, 2020a; FMO, 2020). Companies are called upon to define a plan of tangible interventions to remedy the situation (Schoenberg, 2005), as well as to prepare a communication plan to ensure that all stakeholders, both internal and external, are able to know all the efforts that the company has made and will do to overcome the crisis (Gupta, 2011; Lando, 2014). Some of these decisions have had financial impacts for companies, such as the revision of incentive plans and remuneration policies (Batish *et al.*, 2020; KPMG, 2020).

Second, we look at the strategic actions put in place by the companies. In times of crisis, such as the current one, the company should put in place strategies to define and plan remedial actions for overcoming the emergency and redefining the strategic guidelines that will guide the company in the medium term (Al Shobaki *et al.*, 2016). It would be interesting to study the impression management process, i.e. the process by which companies try to control the perception of stakeholders (Patelli and Pedrini, 2014).

Third, we identify the philanthropic actions disclosed to the stakeholders and decided by the management during the COVID-19 health emergency, which demonstrate the contribution of the companies for the community and the Board of Directors' interest to the social thematic.

To examine the above three key aspects we use framing analysis proposed by Pan and Kosicki (1993) and later developed by Choi (2012). Based on this research methodology, we investigate the content of press releases published in the period March 2020–October 2020 by a sample of Italian companies listed in the FTSE MIB.

The main results reveal a strong heterogeneity in the behavior of the companies, although the interest of all in facing the crisis at COVID-19 is evident. On the one hand, all the examined firms have implemented actions aimed primarily at ensuring business continuity, the health of their employees, and the interests of all stakeholders. On the other hand, companies have taken action to support the country in the process of managing and responding to the crisis.

This chapter is structured as follows: Section 19.2 presents the literature review; Section 19.3 illustrates research methodology; Section 19.4 describes the sample; Section 19.5 examines the results; and, finally, Section 19.6 refers to discussion and conclusions.

19.2. Literature Review

19.2.1. *Definition of crisis*

A crisis is often defined as a disturbance or sudden change in the life of an individual or a community, with more or less serious and lasting effects. In organizational terms, crises are described as disasters caused by people, organizational structures, economy, and/or technology that cause extensive damage to human life and the natural and social environment (Mitrof *et al.*, 1997).

Pearson and Clair (1998) define organizational crises as "a low-probability, high-impact event that threatens the viability of the organization and is characterized by ambiguity of cause, effect, and means of resolution, as well as by a belief that decisions must be made swiftly." From this definition, it is possible to identify the distinctive features of an organizational crisis. First, an organizational crisis refers to highly ambiguous situations in which causes and effects are unknown (Bachmann *et al.*, 2015; Sims, 2009). Second, crises are configured as situations with a low probability of occurrence, but which represent a serious threat to the survival of an organization (Bachmann *et al.*, 2015; Liu *et al.*, 2017) and for the organization's stakeholders (Alpaslan *et al.*, 2009; Liu *et al.*, 2017). Third, these are unexpected situations for the members of the organization and which require a very short response time (Williams *et al.*, 2017). Finally, organizational crises require necessary organizational changes, which can be either ameliorative or pejorative (Aguilera, 2019; Bao and Lewellyn, 2017; Renders and Gaeremynck, 2012). Therefore, these events are unplanned and produce unforeseen and significant consequences for the organization, such as temporary or permanent interruption of company activity, reduction of the company's performance, or threats to the corporate reputation (Williams *et al.*, 2017). Organizational crises are characterized by low probability of occurrence and high and negative consequences that threaten the objectives of an organization (Hällgren *et al.*, 2018). Many companies do not give the right emphasis to crisis planning due to the low probability of occurrence, and this behavior has negative repercussions both in terms of response to the crisis and in terms of countering it (Stern, 2003).

In general, crisis management theory should help to understand how to respond to an emergency, e.g. identify the priorities and actions to be taken to ensure business continuity and the satisfaction of the needs of all stakeholders (Comfort, 2007). Crisis management has two main phases. In the preparation phase, organizations aim to identify and interact with stakeholders in order to prevent crises from occurring and impacting stakeholders. In the response phase, organizations aim to minimize the negative effects of the crisis (Pearson and Clair, 1998).

19.2.2. *Corporate governance e-crisis management*

The effectiveness of corporate governance systems is affected various factors, such as national institutions (Renders and Gaeremynck, 2012; Van Essen *et al.*, 2013), national economic development (Chen *et al.*, 2011), ownership structure (Aguilera, 2019), and economic and financial condition of a company (Bundy *et al.*, 2017). The financial crisis that began in 2007 has highlighted important shortcomings in the systems of corporate governance (Erkens *et al.*, 2012). The origins of the crisis were initially attributed to governance failures in the financial sector and to the use of new and little-known financial instruments such as guaranteed debt obligations. On the one hand, the boards of directors were deemed inadequate in monitoring management and assessing the risks assumed by the company (de Haan and Vlahu, 2013; Muller-Kahle and Lewellyn, 2011). On the other hand, risk management, credit rating, and financial reporting standards have also proved ineffective in reporting underlying structural problems (John *et al.*, 2016).

The literature on managerial discretion (Williamson, 2008) emphasizes the value of decisive leadership in the context of uncertainty. In particular, it is argued that excessively restrictive controls have an impact on the effectiveness of response to the crisis (Erkens *et al.*, 2012). Particular ownership structures (Paniagua *et al.*, 2018), remuneration policies (Dell'Atti *et al.*, 2013), and government institutions at the national level (Akram *et al.*, 2019) can function differently and have different effects on company performance in stationary conditions and in crisis conditions.

The main functions of top management include communication with stakeholders, the identification of corporate stakeholders most affected by the crisis, and the involvement of these stakeholders in preparing and responding to the crisis (Freeman *et al.*, 2004). Assuming that top managers pursue the same objectives as the company (Laplume *et al.*, 2020), it is argued that the corporate governance perspective assessed and adopted by the company influences managers' perception of the relevance of stakeholders and therefore their behavior during crisis (Bundy *et al.*, 2017; de Gooyert *et al.*, 2017). In this sense, the literature has identified two models of corporate governance: the shareholder model, which focuses on maximizing shareholder value (Barry, 2018; Edmans *et al.*, 2017), and the stakeholder model, which focuses on legitimate rights and interests of any group or individual that can influence or be influenced by society (Freeman *et al.*, 2004).

According to the shareholder model, managers should make all decisions in order to increase the long-term value of the firm (Barry, 2018). The shareholder model is based on the idea that shareholders are motivated to ensure that the company manages its assets and resources efficiently and effectively (Clarke, 2004; Shao, 2019). Consequently, business managers must operate with a view to maximizing value, using the company's resources efficiently and effectively (Hart and Zingales, 2017). Ultimately, according to the shareholders' approach, a stakeholder should be considered in the preparation and response to crises if and only if the stakeholder has or is expected to have a significant influence on corporate value.

Conversely, according to the stakeholder model, all stakeholders have intrinsic value (Derakhshan *et al.*, 2019). Therefore, business managers should operate in the interest of all stakeholders and, consequently, companies should have multiple objectives (Freeman *et al.*, 2004).

The success of crisis preparedness or response efforts depends on at least two factors: the nature of an organization's relationship with its stakeholders, and the company's understanding of stakeholder attitudes in response to the crisis (Bundy *et al.*, 2017). In this second case, the creation of alliances, coordination, and sharing of information with corporate stakeholders will allow the company to better manage the crisis. Such circumstances will allow early detection of warning signs and minimize downtime. Consequently, there will be an effective containment of damages, and above all, the positive effects on the corporate reputation will be evident (Bundy *et al.*, 2017).

During a crisis, the stakeholder model facilitates the formation of alliances and the sharing of accurate information between stakeholders and company management. Stakeholders may have multiple interests (Gand *et al.*, 2005), experience the crisis subjectively, and request responses aimed at preserving their interests (Bundy *et al.*, 2017). The most efficient approach to crises requires the inclusion of as many stakeholders as possible in crisis preparedness and response, enabling all stakeholders to bring their perspective, identity, and knowledge to the analysis (Granville *et al.*, 2016). Thus, recognizing the intrinsic value of all stakeholders can coordinate the actions of different stakeholders in situations characterized by uncertainty about identities, interests, and relevant risks (Laplume *et al.*, 2020).

In summary, although a stakeholder-model–based approach to crisis management requires more time and resources to invest in crisis management and develop stakeholder relationships, managers following this model are more likely to be able to better manage crises and their consequences. While the board of directors can add value to a company by providing good advice and helping executives identify and access scarce resources, there is general agreement that the primary role of a board of directors is to act as a management supervisor (Clarke, 2004; Edmans *et al.*, 2017). The literature on managerial discretion suggests that overzealous monitoring and frequent interference in a company's affairs can discourage managerial initiatives (Lin *et al.*, 2020). Hence, CEOs tend to have a beneficial effect on business performance in uncertain environments where, hampered by fewer constraints, they can make quick decisions without the need to build consensus (Banzato and Sierra, 2016). Similarly, it is believed that non-executive directors are more vigilant monitors of corporate management, even if they have an information disadvantage compared to insiders and are typically slow to react in situations of adversity (Williamson, 2008). Consequently, although the characteristics of the board of directors associated with a precise supervisory activity may represent best practice under conditions of a stable state, these same characteristics can inhibit managerial discretion and limit their ability to respond to the contingencies of a crisis with deleterious effects to the financial performance of a company.

19.3. Research Methodology

To examine the implications of the COVID-19 pandemic on corporate governance, and in particular to understand the Board of Directors' response to COVID-19 pandemic, framing analysis was used (Pan and Kosicki, 1993). Starting from Choi's theoretical contribution, which examines how press releases were used to address the oil spill crisis, this study analyzed the content of the press releases of the companies belonging to the sample and identified and evaluated the frames used in these documents. We considered the information publicized following the rapid spread of COVID-19 and the subsequent lockdown imposed by national regulators.

On January 30, 2020, following China's reporting (December 31, 2019) of a cluster of pneumonia cases of unknown aetiology (later identified as a new SARS-CoV-2 coronavirus) in the city of Wuhan, the World Health Organization (WHO) declared the coronavirus epidemic in China to be a public health emergency of international concern. The following day the Italian government, after the first precautionary measures adopted starting from January 22, taking into account the particularly widespread nature of the epidemic, proclaimed a state of emergency and implemented the first measures to contain the contagion throughout the national territory. To identify the frames, we examined press releases (advertised directly by the companies through their websites) from March 1, 2020, to October 20, 2020. This information was initially coded for a specific frame used in each document. After identification through initial coding, three frames were identified. These patterns were identified by grouping similarly worded information, considering similar information, scope, structure, and message. The announcements were then coded again to refine the main frames. Initial and refinement coding eventually identified three frames that commonly occurred in news releases dealing with the COVID-19 pandemic. The three structures are as follows: social responsibility, impression management, and philanthropy.

Press releases classified under "social responsibility" convey information about corporate governance systems efforts to do the right things at the right time, taking into account relationships with stakeholders. Information on corporate governance systems commitment to work closely with state and local governments is included.

The "impression management" structure provides information on the actions taken by top management to communicate the desired image to all interested parties. According to the theory of impression management, a company has the possibility to define its image by pursuing different objectives: it may want to project an image that is as close as possible to the true corporate identity or, on the other hand, convey an impression of organization that is socially desirable, hiding all or part of the true corporate identity.

Press releases classified under "philanthropic" includes information relating to specific monetary donations that companies have made to support the country during the health emergency, regardless of whether the donation was to a person, organization, scientific foundation, etc. Any document discussing philanthropic donations in conjunction with COVID-19 has been classified here.

Each press release was individually coded, and then placed into only one of these three categories. In crisis communications, reassuring the public (or the reader of announcements) is one of the main objectives of companies. The identification of themes was developed by recording keyword patterns, citations, and other syntactic methods.

In addition to the three main frames, the information collected were analyzed by sub-themes. These sub-themes were decided by identifying themes or strategies used repeatedly throughout the information. In particular, in relation to the first frame, we have identified four sub-topics (going concern, remuneration/dividends, support to the nation, and task force/crisis management committee). With regard to the second frame, relating to impression management, there are two sub-themes: general information and employee protection. Finally, for the "philanthropic" frame, the sub-theme "monetary donations" is distinguished from the sub-theme "other donations."

By combining the analyses of the main frames with the main and secondary themes used in the press releases, this study produces a comprehensive account of the strategy put in place by companies during COVID-19.

19.4. Sample

Our analysis focuses on the companies of the FTSE MIB, the main benchmark index of the Italian equity markets. This index captures approximately 80% of the internal market capitalization and is made up of leading companies with high liquidity in the various ICB sectors in Italy. The FTSE MIB Index measures the performance of 40 Italian stocks and aims to reproduce the weightings of the broad sector of the Italian stock market.

The FTSE MIB is derived from the universe of trading stocks on the main stock market of Borsa Italiana (BIt). Each stock is analyzed by size and liquidity and the index provides a correct representation by sector overall. The index is weighted by market capitalization after adjusting the components by free float.

At the beginning of October 2020, there were 40 companies listed on the FTSE MIB. Banks and insurance companies were excluded

Table 19.1. Sample and number of press releases published by the companies.

No.	Company name	Super sector	Capitalization	No. of press releases
1	**A2A**	Utilities	3.993.827.647,00 €	30
2	**Amplifon**	Health care	6.417.551.405,00 €	14
3	**Atlantia**	Industrial goods and services	11.806.316.283,00 €	46
4	**Buzzi Unicem**	Construction & materials	3.467.156.701,00 €	38
5	**Campari**	Food and beverage	9.960.255.360,00 €	37
6	**CNH Industrial**	Industrial goods and services	8.901.483.319,00 €	50
7	**DiaSorin**	Health care	8.818.620.217,00 €	46
8	**Enel**	Utilities	80.100.221.291,00 €	104
9	**Eni**	Oil and gas	29.590.263.794,00 €	72
10	**Ferrari**	Automobiles and parts	31.798.702.710,00 €	25
11	**Fiat Chrysler Automobiles**	Automobiles and parts	14.927.440.171,00 €	42
12	**Hera**	Utilities	4.985.188.272,00 €	50
13	**Interpump Group**	Industrial goods and services	3.161.136.094,00 €	43
14	**INWIT**	Telecomunicazioni	8.205.389.100,00 €	29
15	**Italgas**	Utilities	4.569.188.180,00 €	39
16	**Leonardo**	Industrial goods and services	3.456.356.506,00 €	82
17	**Moncler**	Personal and household goods	8.542.377.842,00 €	5
18	**Nexi**	Industrial goods and services	9.315.154.988,00 €	18
19	**Pirelli & C**	Automobiles and parts	3.702.200.000,00 €	149

from these, obtaining a final sample of 27 companies. At the end of June 2020, they are worth €335 billion on the stock market and represent 76% of the total capitalization (excluding banks and insurance companies) (Mediobanca, 2020).

Table 19.1. (*Continued*)

No.	Company name	Super sector	Capitalization	No. of press releases
20	**Prysmian**	Industrial Goods and Services	6.046.625.933,00 €	41
21	**Recordati**	Health Care	9.445.388.621,00 €	17
22	**Saipem**	Oil and Gas	1.949.245.166,00 €	23
23	**Snam**	Oil and Gas	14.955.481.164,00 €	27
24	**STMicro-electronics**	Technology	22.686.712.047,00 €	88
25	**Telecom Italia**	Telecommunications	5.713.333.467,00 €	170
26	**Tenaris**	Basic Resources	6.085.549.305,00 €	21
27	**Terna**	Utilities	12.684.657.514,00 €	88
			335.285.823.097,00 €	**1.394**

Source: Borsa Italiana and companies' websites.

All companies included in the sample published at least one press release (see Table 19.1).

19.5. Results

We found a total of 1,394 press releases published by the companies from March 2020 to October 2020. Then, we analyzed the contents of the overall press releases and selected only those referring to the management of the COVID-19 crisis. In this way, we identified 126 press releases relating to the health emergency (Table 19.2). However, it should be noted that in some cases (28 out of 126 press releases) different types of information was provided in each press release, referring to different actions implemented by corporate governance. To this end, we have codified the messages provided in each document in order to obtain more precise and timely results. This further coding resulted in 157 pieces of information (sometimes including in the same document) made by the companies in the period between March and October 2020.

First, we analyzed the frequency of updates provided by companies regarding the actions taken to respond to the COVID-19 crisis.

Table 19.2. Number of the analyzed press releases.

Company name	No. of press releases
A2	4
Amplifon	7
Atlantia	2
Buzzi Unicem	1
Campari	5
CNH Industrial	11
DiaSorin	1
Enel	8
Eni	9
Ferrari	3
Fiat Chrysler Automobiles	8
Hera	1
Interpump Group	0[a]
INWIT	1
Italgas	2
Leonardo	9
Moncler	1
Nexi	0*
Pirelli & C	3
Prysmian	2
Recordati	1
Saipem	3
Snam	3
STMicroelectronics	1
Telecom Italia	39
Tenaris	1
Terna	0[a]
	126

Note: *,[a]These companies were excluded from the sample as they did not publish press releases useful for the purposes of this research. However, it should be noted that they have dedicated a page of their website to the health emergency or discussed the phenomenon in the Interim Financial Statements.
Source: Author's calculation.

Figure 19.1 shows the trend in the number of press releases releases published by the companies. The data show three main peaks, referring to March (outbreak of COVID-19 in Italy), April (first month of implementation of the precautionary measures put in place by the Government), and June (month of resumption of activities).

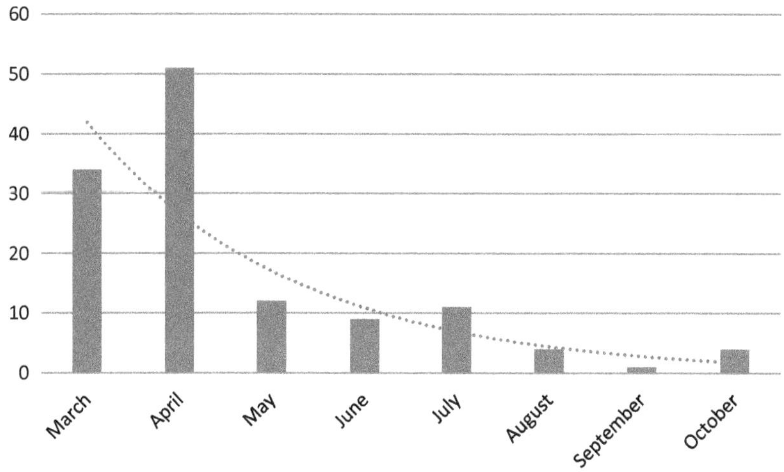

Figure 19.1. Timing of the publication of information.
Source: Author's illustration.

Table 19.3. Frames used in the press releases dealing with the COVID-19 crisis.

	Main announcements	
Frames	**Quantity**	**Percentage**
Social responsibility	74	47%
Impression management	58	37%
Philanthropic	25	16%
Total	**157**	

Source: Author's calculation.

Second, we classified the identified information in the three main frames (social responsibility, impression management, and philanthropic) (Table 19.3).

Subsequently, by aggregating the information found for each frame, we observed the temporal evolution of the publications of press releases. From Figure 19.2, it is noted that, at the origin of the pandemic (March 2020), most of the press releases (21 out of 44 in March) concerned the area of impression management. This result

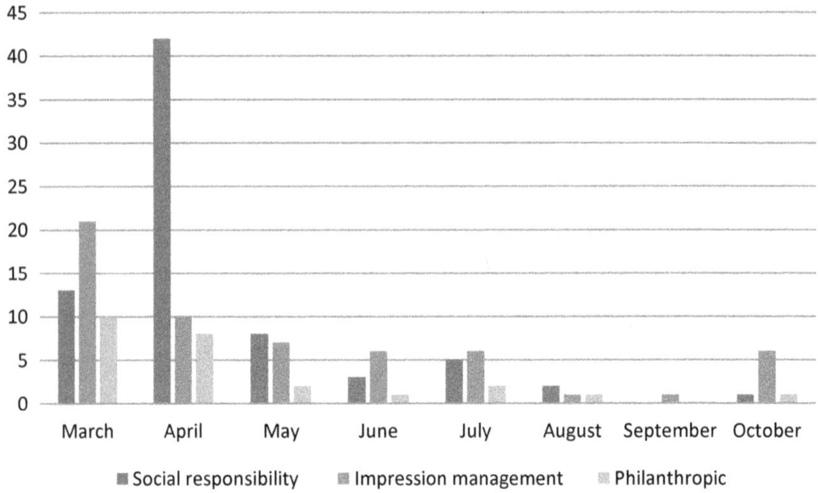

Figure 19.2. Timing of publication of information by frame.
Source: Author's illustration.

is in line with the evolution of the phenomenon under investigation, as when the pandemic broke out, the companies were primarily concerned with reassuring customers and protecting the interests of stakeholders and workers. The area of social responsibility also presents a modest number of press releases (13 out of 44 in March), although the latter frame reaches its maximum in April (42 out of 60 press releases). As for the philanthropic aspect, medium/high values are reported both in March and April 2020. Between May and July 2020, the number of press releases, relating to the three frames analyzed, remained almost stationary. Finally, from August to October, there was a sharp reduction in press releases.

According to the results of this study, the "social responsibility" and "impression management" frames were the most dominant frames used in the company's press releases. The information included in the social responsibility frame represents 47% of the total information releases examined. These information were very structured and coherent, and all included headlines such as "contributing to the fight against the pandemic" or "solidarity in support of institutions for the containment of the COVID-19 epidemic." It is clear that these documents use a very worded thematic approach, particularly through the unified use of these headlines, as well as through

Table 19.4. Main themes and sub-themes used in documents dealing with the COVID-19 crisis.

Frames	Main themes	Sub-themes	
Social responsibility	Meet local needs	Going concern (crisis management plan)	22
		Remuneration — dividends	7
		Support to the nation	42
		Task force — crisis management committee	3
Impression management	Information	General information	45
		Employee protection	13
Philanthropic	Donation	Monetary donation	22
		Other	3

Source: Author's calculation.

the ordering of information in each press release. These information releases were essentially a summary of the specific relief efforts of the companies examined, aimed at first of all guaranteeing the company's going concern, but also supporting the nation in this moment of crisis.

In addition to the three main frames, the press releases were analyzed by sub-themes. These sub-themes were decided by identifying themes or strategies used repeatedly throughout the press release. Table 19.4 shows the main and secondary themes found. The main themes were prevalent (more than the secondary themes) within each of the three frames of the information. Keywords were also used to identify each main theme and sub-theme.

In relation to the "social responsibility" frame, four sub-themes have been identified, referring to the corporate governance strategies implemented to ensure first and foremost business continuity. In detail, in four companies (15%), the CEO and the top management have committed to donate part of their remuneration to support solidarity initiatives to deal with the COVID-19 emergency; others have decided not to distribute an ordinary dividend in 2020 for the year 2019, in light of the impact of the current emergency due to COVID-19. Also, other companies (e.g. Eni, an energy company) have communicated, in addition to the actions to reduce investments and operating costs, to defer part of their long-term monetary incentive to next year, in order to reduce cash outflows for 2020. In addition, three of the companies examined decided to set up a crisis management committee or set up a task force both at group and individual levels, to coordinate and immediately activate all preventive measures aimed at protecting the health of their employees, customers, and other stakeholders, in line with the security measures indicated by the government authorities of the various countries. In 22 cases, companies announced the implementation by company managers of actions aimed at containing personnel costs, making use of social safety nets, rescheduling the expected hires, and using previous holidays. Some companies have adopted a plan to contain other operating costs, ensuring in any case adequate standards of safety and continuity of services. Finally, 42 announcements concerned the actions taken by companies to support the nation during the health crisis. In the difficult phase of health emergency that the country is going through, Italian companies have provided all their support in terms of resources, means, and people to support national institutions in the management and containment of the COVID-19 epidemic. In detail, a series of solidarity initiatives have been undertaken to support the effort of all those who are guaranteeing with their daily commitment the activities to contain the infection from COVID-19, as well as assistance to the sick and their families. Further measures concerned the production or acquisition of personal protective equipment, to support hospitals.

With regard to the second frame "impression management," two sub-themes have been identified. A total of 45 announcements were selected concerning general information disseminated by the company during the health emergency. By disclosing this information, the companies wanted to inform their stakeholders and shareholders day after day. Most of the time the information referred to the activities and procedures put in place by the company to protect internal and external human resources, to contain material and immaterial damage, and to guarantee the correct management of communication flows toward the outside and the continuity of the service offered. Through these messages, the companies have tried to reassure their stakeholders, safeguarding the reputation and corporate image. The second sub-topic refers to the protection of employees. In this case, 13 information announcements were selected. The latter report information about the health protocols implemented by companies to protect the health and safety of employees, which includes the possibility of carrying out swabs and serological tests. In this sense, three companies have taken out insurance coverage for an indemnity in the event of hospitalization caused by infection, a convalescence allowance, and a post-hospitalization care package to better manage the recovery of health and family management.

The last frame identified concerns philanthropic actions. In the difficult battle against COVID-19, the initiatives of companies to help show a very high human value. The philanthropic aspect of corporate initiatives was recognized in 25 press releases. In 88% of cases, the shares involved monetary donations made by companies in aid of the emergency. This results in the donation of thousands and sometimes millions of euros in favor of hospitals or voluntary associations. The remaining 22% instead deals with non-monetary philanthropic actions. In this case, the companies have decided to make all the means in their possession available to healthcare professionals or, more generally, the nation. In other cases, it was the company employees who made a contribution, donating hours of their salary for the strengthening of the National Health System and for the purchase of personal protective equipment.

19.6. Discussion and Conclusion

This study analyzed the Board of Directors' response to the COVID-19 health crisis. To this end we explore the types of frames used in the press releases of Italian companies listed on the FTSE MIB for the management of the COVID-19 pandemic. By analyzing these documents, we have identified three main frames to which all the announcements spread can be traced: social responsibility, impression management, and philanthropic. Among those identified, the "social responsibility" frame is associated with the total information releases concerning the COVID-19 pandemic. Of all 157 press releases, 47% are attributable to the "social responsibility" frame; 58 press releases (37%) refer instead to the second frame identified, relating to impression management. Finally, following the frame of "philanthropy," 16% of the information relate to philanthropic actions in terms of monetary donations or other types of donations.

This chapter offers an overview of the actions taken at the level of corporate governance in the first phase of the COVID-19 pandemic.

First, we looked at the decisions taken by companies in terms of social responsibility. The literature suggests that, in order to deal with crisis situations, it is necessary to establish a crisis committee to identify and know the reasons for the crisis itself (Deloitte, 2020a,b; FMO, 2020) companies are called upon to define a plan of concrete interventions to remedy the situation (Schoenberg, 2005), as well as to prepare a communication plan to ensure that all stakeholders, both internal and external, are able to know all the efforts that the company has made and will continue to do to overcome the crisis (Gupta, 2011; Lando, 2014). In line with the foregoing, we have identified the information referring to these aspects and have brought them back to the "social responsibility" frame. Social responsibility has been understood in a broad sense. In detail, the information relating to going concern, support to the nation, the creation of a crisis management committee, and the remuneration policy have been included in this frame. The results show that 14% of information refer to actions taken by the company to ensure business continuity. In response to COVID-19, corporate governance has put in place cost-containment actions and implemented action plans aimed at mitigating the financial impacts related to COVID-19. In addition, governance has extended the agile working method to remote personnel, ensuring the normal functioning of production assets, the continuity of the services offered, and the remote management of all activities relating to the market and the relationship with the customer.

With regard to the changes to the top management's remuneration policies, we set out to review the actions taken by the Board of Directors that have had financial impacts for companies, such as the review of incentive plans and remuneration policies (Batish *et al.*, 2020; KPMG, 2020). Only 5% of information relate to the remuneration of top management. In order to face the effects of the COVID-19 pandemic, seven companies belonging to the sample updated their short- and medium-term strategy or developed a new shareholder remuneration policy. In five cases, the CEO and/or top management decided to give up part of their fixed or variable remuneration to support the company, the sector to which they belong or, more generally, the country in the crisis management process.

The nation support sub-theme consists of 42 company announcements. Most of the companies examined have put in place active support activities to overcome the current emergency, making means and resources available to the nation. Some companies have taken part in national projects aimed at facilitating remote work and teaching by providing technical support. Others have made their own means available to transport personal protective equipment between the different regions. In other cases, company employees made themselves available for volunteer activities to support the elderly or sick in time of COVID-19.

The third sub-theme concerns whether the creation of a crisis management committee is necessary, which is crucial to identify and understand the reasons of the crisis itself. Only three of the companies surveyed formed a crisis management committee or participated in dedicated national task forces for this purpose.

Second, we analyzed the strategic actions implemented by the companies. In times of crisis, such as the current one, the company should implement strategies to define and plan corrective actions to overcome the emergency and redefine the strategic lines that will guide the company in the medium term (Al Shobaki *et al.*, 2016). In this sense we have identified the "impression management" frame made up of two sub-themes. The first refers to the general information disclosed by the companies regarding the strategies put in place to overcome the health crisis (45 press releases). The second refers to employee protection (13 information). From the examination of the information belonging to the second frame, it emerged that, since the outbreak of the pandemic, companies have put the health and protection of employees first, favoring smart working, reducing physical contact, and, in cases where it is impossible to do so, adopting protocols security for the same.

Finally, we considered the philanthropic actions, attributable to the support provided by companies to the nation. In 88% of cases, the shares involved monetary donations made by companies in aid of the emergency. The remaining 22% instead deals with non-monetary philanthropic actions.

The analysis of the company announcements revealed that the COVID-19 pandemic has put a strain on corporate survival. Since the crisis, companies have understood the importance of defining long-term strategies aimed at creating greater resilience and applying the lessons derived from this experience to design a roadmap of systems and talents capable of better preparing the company to face future discontinuities.

In this sense, our contribution has practical implications as it provides an overview of the actions taken by corporate governance to respond to the COVID-19 crisis. Our study could be a tool to support firms in the process of defining the actions and strategies to be implemented to respond to crisis events, especially if they affect the entire economic system.

Our chapter observed the press releases and therefore the intentions transmitted by the corporate governance to all stakeholders. Future research could have, as its objective, a parallelism between what was communicated during the first wave of the pandemic and what was actually achieved by the Italian firms. This will only be possible when the firm's official documents referring to 2020 are published. Furthermore, it would be interesting to observe the effects of the strategies implemented by firms to respond to the crisis on company performance.

Finally, this research is limited to the Italian context. Given the exponential diffusion of COVID-19, the study could be extended to the European context in order to understand the governance responses of firms belonging to different countries and compare them.

References

Aguilera, R.V. (2019). International corporate governance: a review and opportunities for future research. *Journal of International Business Studies*. https://doi.org/10.1080/03088837500000054.

Akram, F., Abrar-ul-Haq, M. and Raza, S. (2019). A role of corporate governance and firm's environmental performance: A moderating role of institutional regulations. *International Journal of Management Studies*, **25**(2), 19–37.

Al Shobaki, M.J., Abu Amuna, Y.M. and Abu Naser, S.S. (2016). The impact of top management support for strategic planning on crisis management?: Case study on UNRWA -Gazastrip. *International Journal of Academic Research and Development*, **1**(10), 20–25.

Alpaslan, C.M., Green, S.E. and Mitroff, I.I. (2009). Corporate governance in the context of crises: Towards a stakeholder theory of crisis management. *Journal of Contingencies and Crisis Management*, **17**(1), 38–49. https://doi.org/10.1111/j.1468-5973.2009.00555.x.

Bachmann, R., Gillespie, N. and Priem, R. (2015). Repairing trust in organizations and institutions: Toward a conceptual framework. *Organization Studies*, **36**(9), 1123–1142. https://doi.org/10.1177/0170840615599334.

Banzato, C.R. and Sierra, J. C. V. (2016). Implications of theory and research on strategic leadership: A critical review. *Revista Ibero-Americana de Estratégia*, **15**(03), 119–131. https://doi.org/10.5585/riae.v15i3.2331.

Bao, S.R. and Lewellyn, K.B. (2017). Ownership structure and earnings management in emerging markets - An institutionalized agency perspective. *International Business Review*, **26**(5), 828–838. https://doi.org/10.1016/j.ibusrev.2017.02.002.

Barry, B. (2018). Expression of concern regarding Jensen (2002). "Value maximization, stakeholder theory, and the corporate objective function." *Business Ethics Quarterly*, **28**(2), 237–239. https://doi.org/10.1017/beq.2018.9.

Batish, A., Gordon, A., Larcker, D.F., Tayan, B., Watts, E.M. and Yu, C. (2020). Sharing the pain. How Did Boards Adjust CEO Pay in Response to COVID-19? *Stanford Closer Look Series*, 1–22.

Bundy, J., Pfarrer, M.D., Short, C.E. and Coombs, W.T. (2017). Crises and crisis management: Integration, interpretation, and research development. *Journal of Management*, **43**(6). https://doi.org/10.1177/0149206316680030.

Chen, V.Z., Li, J. and Shapiro and D.M. (2011). Are OECD-prescribed "good corporate governance practices" really good in an emerging economy? *Asia Pacific Journal of Management*, **28**(1), 115–138. https://doi.org/10.1007/s10490-010-9206-8.

Choi, J. (2012). A content analysis of BP's press releases dealing with crisis. *Public Relations Review*, **38**(3), 422–429. https://doi.org/10.1016/j.pubrev.2012.03.003.

Clarke, T. (ed.) (2004). *Theories of Corporate Governance: The Philosophical Foundations of Corporate Governance* (Routledge, London), pp. 263–283.

Comfort, L.K. (2007). Crisis management in hindsight: Cognition, communication, coordination, and control. *Public Administration Review*, **67**(Suppl. 1), 189–197. https://doi.org/10.1111/j.1540-6210.2007.00827.x.

de Gooyert, V., Rouwette, E., van Kranenburg, H. and Freeman, E. (2017). Reviewing the role of stakeholders in Operational Research: A stakeholder theory perspective. *European Journal of Operational Research*, **262**(2), 402–410. https://doi.org/10.1016/j.ejor.2017.03.079.

de Haan, J. and Vlahu, R. (2013). Corporate Governance of Banks: A Survey. *SSRN Electronic Journal*, **386**. https://doi.org/10.2139/ssrn.2297770.

Dell'Atti, A., Intonti, M. and Iannuzzi, A.P. (2013). The effectiveness of remuneration committees in European banks: Regulation and best practices. *Journal of Financial Regulation and Compliance*, **21**(4), 373–396. https://doi.org/10.1108/JFRC-11-2012-0046.

Deloitte (2020a). Stepping in?: The board's role in the COVID-19 crisis (Issue March).

Deloitte (2020b). The heart of resilient leadership. Responding to COVID-19.

Derakhshan, R., Turner, R. and Mancini, M. (2019). Project governance and stakeholders: A literature review. *International Journal of Project Management*, **37**(1), 98–116. https://doi.org/10.1016/j.ijproman.2018.10.007.

Edmans, A., Gabaix, X. and Jenter, D. (2017). Executive compensation: A survey of theory and evidence. In *The Handbook of the Economics of Corporate Governance*, Edited by Benjamin E. Hermalin, Michael S. Weisbach, Volume 1, pp. 383–539. https://doi.org/10.2139/ssrn.2992287.

Erkens, D.H., Hung, M. and Matos, P. (2012). Corporate governance in the 2007-2008 financial crisis: Evidence from financial institutions worldwide. *Journal of Corporate Finance*, **18**(2), 389–411. https://doi.org/10.1016/j.jcorpfin.2012.01.005.

European Central Bank (2018). Good governance and the role of supervisory boards.

FMO (2020). Risk & crisis management. The role of good corporate governance.

Freeman, R.E., Wicks, A.C. and Parmar, B. (2004). Stakeholder theory and "The corporate objective revisited." *Organization Science*, **15**(3). https://doi.org/10.1287/orsc.1040.0066.

Gand, S., Acquier, A. and Szpirglas, M. (2005). Understanding organizational crisis management processes: An analytical framework drawn from a case study in a public company. *Euram*, 1–23. http://hal.archives-ouvertes.fr/hal-00748845/.

Granville, F., Mehta, A. and Pike, S. (2016). Destinations, disasters and public relations: Stakeholder engagement in multi-phase disaster management. *Journal of Hospitality and Tourism Management*, **28**, 73–79. https://doi.org/10.1016/j.jhtm.2016.02.001.

Gupta, R. (2011). Corporate communication: A strategic tool for crisis management. *Journal of Economic Development, Management, IT, Finance and Marketing*, **3**(September), 55–67.

Hällgren, M., Rouleau, L. and De Rond, M. (2018). A matter of life or death: How extreme context research matters for management and organization studies. *Academy of Management Annals*, **12**(1), 111–153. https://doi.org/10.5465/annals.2016.0017.

Haroon, O. and Rizvi, S.A.R. (2020). COVID-19: Media coverage and financial markets behavior—A sectoral inquiry. *Journal of Behavioral and Experimental Finance*, **27**, 100343. https://doi.org/10.1016/j.jbef.2020.100343.

Hart, O. and Zingales, L. (2017). Companies should maximize shareholder welfare not market value. *SSRN Electronic Journal*, August. https://doi.org/10.2139/ssrn.3004794.

Hopt, K.J. (2012). Corporate governance of banks after the financial crisis. *SSRN Electronic Journal*, 1–5. https://doi.org/10.2139/ssrn.1918851.

John, K., De Masi, S. and Paci, A. (2016). Corporate governance in banks. *Corporate Governance: An International Review*, **24**(3), 303–321. https://doi.org/10.1111/corg.12161.

KPMG (2020). Executive compensation during COVID-19.

Lando, A.L. (2014). The critical role of crisis communication plan in corporations' crises preparedness and management. *Global Media Journal, Canadian Edition*, **7**(1), 5–19.

Laplume, A., Walker, K., Zhang, Z. and Yu, X. (2020). Incumbent stakeholder management performance and new entry. *Journal of Business Ethics*. https://doi.org/10.1007/s10551-020-04629-8.

Lin, S., Chen, F. and Wang, L. (2020). Identity of multiple large shareholders and corporate governance: are state-owned entities efficient MLS? *Review of Quantitative Finance and Accounting*, **55**(4). https://doi.org/10.1007/s11156-020-00875-z.

Liu, Y., Shankar, V. and Yun, W. (2017). Crisis management strategies and the long-term effects of product recalls on firm value. *Marketing Science Institute*, **81**. https://doi.org/10.1509/jm.15.0535.

Mediobanca. (2020). Briefing note: impatto COVID-19 sul 1h 2020 (MNES mondiali e FTSE MIB).

Mitrof, I., Pearson, C. and Harrington, K.L. (1997). *The Essential Guide to Managing Corporate Crises: A Step-by-Step Handbook for Surviving Major Catastrophes* (Oxford University Press, Oxford, UK), p. 208.

Muller-Kahle, M.I. and Lewellyn, K.B. (2011). Did board configuration matter? The case of US subprime lenders. *Corporate Governance: An International Review*, **19**(5), 405–417. https://doi.org/10.1111/j.1467-8683.2011.00871.x.

OECD (2015). G20/OECD Principles of corporate governance. In *G20/OECD Principles of Corporate Governance*, OECD Publishing (ed.), (OECD). https://doi.org/10.1787/9789264257443-tr.

Pan, Z. and Kosicki, G.M. (1993). Framing analysis: An approach to news discourse. *Political Communication*, **10**(1), 55–75. https://doi.org/10.1080/10584609.1993.9962963.

Paniagua, J., Rivelles, R. and Sapena, J. (2018). Corporate governance and financial performance: The role of ownership and board structure. *Journal of Business Research*, **89**(January), 229–234. https://doi.org/10.1016/j.jbusres.2018.01.060.

Patelli, L. and Pedrini, M. (2014). Is the optimism in CEO's letters to shareholders sincere? Impression management versus communicative action during the economic crisis. *Journal of Business Ethics*, **124**(1), 19–34. https://doi.org/10.1007/s10551-013-1855-3.

Pearson, C.M. and Clair, J.A. (1998). Crisis management. *Academy of Management Review*, **23**(1), 59–76. https://doi.org/10.12816/0040783.

PWC (2020). Navigare in tempi di incertezza. Come rispondere alla sfida del COVID-19.

Renders, A. and Gaeremynck, A. (2012). Corporate governance, principal-principal agency conflicts, and firm value in European listed companies. *Corporate Governance: An International Review*, **20**(2), 125–143. https://doi.org/10.1111/j.1467-8683.2011.00900.x.

Schoenberg, A. (2005). Do crisis plans matter? A new perspective on leading during a crisis.

Shao, L. (2019). Dynamic study of corporate governance structure and firm performance in China: Evidence from 2001-2015. *Chinese Management Studies*, **13**(2), 299–317. https://doi.org/10.1108/CMS-08-2017-0217.

Sims, R. (2009). Toward a better understanding of organizational efforts to rebuild reputation following an ethical scandal. *Journal of Business Ethics*, **90**(4), 453–472. https://doi.org/10.1007/s10551-009-0058-4.

Stern, E.K. (2003). Crisis studies and foreign policy analysis: Insights, synergies, and challenges. *International Studies Review*, **5**(2), 155–202. https://doi.org/10.1111/1521-9488.5020016.

Van Essen, M., Engelen, P.J. and Carney, M. (2013). Does "good" corporate governance help in a crisis? The impact of country- and firm-level governance mechanisms in the European financial crisis. *Corporate Governance: An International Review*, **21**(3), 201–224. https://doi.org/10.1111/corg.12010.

Williams, T.A., Gruber, D.A., Sutcliffe, K.M., Shepherd, D.A. and Zhao, E.Y. (2017). Organizational response to adversity: Fusing crisis management and resilience research streams. *Academy of Management Annals*, **11**(2), 733–769. https://doi.org/10.5465/annals.2015.0134.

Williamson, O.E. (2008). Corporate boards of directors: In principle and in practice. *Journal of Law, Economics, and Organization*, **24**(2), 247–272. https://doi.org/10.1093/jleo/ewm059.

https://doi.org/10.1142/9781800610781_0020

Chapter 20

COVID-19 Pandemic: Impact of Lockdown on Firm-Level Returns in India

Nidhi Kaicker[*,¶], **Radhika Aggarwal**[†,**], **and Raghav Gaiha**[‡,§,††]

[*]*Ambedkar University Delhi, Delhi, India*

[†]*Faculty of Management Studies, University of Delhi, Delhi, India*

[‡]*Global Development Institute, University of Manchester, Manchester, UK*

[§]*Population Studies Centre, University of Pennsylvania, Philadelphia, USA*

[¶]*nidhi@aud.ac.in*

[**]*radhika.aggarwal25@gmail.com*

[††]*rgaiha@sas.upenn.edu*

Abstract

The present study is an important contribution to the sparse literature on the relationship between COVID-19 and stock market returns in India. It relies on a rigorous time-series analysis using firm-level data on a sample of 779 companies in India during the period March 13, 2020, till September 30, 2020. A panel data model is used to assess the impact of the COVID-19 pandemic on firm-level returns. The sectoral analysis provides empirical evidence on the sectors that have been worst and/or least affected as well as the degree of impact. The study also assesses the changing relationship between the pandemic and firm-level returns during the various lockdowns announced by the government of India. Some reflections are also offered on the post-pandemic scenario and policy measures that aid revival, drawing upon a few influential studies.

20.1. Introduction

The value of the BSE Sensitive Index on January 30, 2020, the date when India recorded its first COVID-19 positive case, was above the 40,000 mark. The value of this index dipped to below 30,000 levels in the last week of March 2020 when the first nation-wide lockdown was announced amidst the rising number of COVID-19 cases in the country. In the subsequent two months, the index rose but came nowhere close to its all-time high value. Such volatility has not been encountered previously, and undoubtedly this time is different. This study is an attempt to investigate the impact of COVID-19 on stock market outcomes. More specifically, using a panel data of Indian companies, the impact of this virus on the firm-level returns in the Indian stock market is examined.

The virus causing COVID-19 belongs to a large family of Coronaviruses that are known to cause the common cold and some major diseases such as the Severe Acute Respiratory Syndrome (SARS), which emerged in China in 2003, and the Middle East Respiratory Syndrome (MERS) in 2012 in Saudi Arabia. COVID-19 is known to have originated from bats in the seafood market of Wuhan, which is located in China's Hubei Province. According to the World Health Organization's (WHO) COVID-19 timeline, a cluster of cases of pneumonia were reported at Wuhan Municipal Health Commission on December 31, 2019. It was eventually determined as a novel coronavirus in January 2020. The first death in the world related to the deadly virus was reported on January 10, 2020, in Wuhan, China. Since then, there has been an exponential growth in the number of total affected cases and deaths due to this disease. By the end of February 2020, COVID-19 had spread to 86 countries and the epicentre of the outbreak moved from China to Europe in the month of March 2020, particularly Italy, which reported a rapid daily increase in the total number of cases and deaths related to this disease. On March 11, 2020, the rate at which the disease was spreading and its severity led WHO to declare COVID-19 as a pandemic. All countries across the world sealed their international borders in a bid to control the spread of the virus and initiated various measures such as lockdowns, quarantines, and social distancing to flatten the curve of the infection.

The first positive COVID-19 case was registered in India on January 30, 2020, in Kerala of a student who returned from China. While there were only three cases in India till the end of February 2020, the number started increasing rapidly in early March. India reported its first death due to COVID-19 on 13 March 2020, soon after which the Indian government sealed its international borders, suspended all visas to India, banned domestic travel by rail as well as air, and eventually announced a complete lockdown of the country to prevent community spread of the virus.

The nature of the COVID-19 virus and the measures taken to contain its spread such as sealing international borders and implementing lockdowns have greatly affected the global business environment. The International Monetary Fund (IMF) in its *World Economic Outlook* issue of October 2020 has projected that the global economy is expected to shrink by 4.4% in 2020. This would be the steepest economic slowdown since the Great Depression of the 1930s. Confining citizens inside their homes, travel restrictions, and shutting down factories have disrupted demand and supply chains across the world. Several industries such as tourism and hospitality, airlines, and thereby oil, have been the worst hit by the pandemic.

The stock markets across the world have also reflected the sentiments of the COVID-19 pandemic. A sense of fear and uncertainty about an impending recession looms over traders on stock markets who started exiting by panic selling. This led to large drops in major indices such as the S&P 500, Dow Jones, and NASDAQ, among others, triggering market-wide circuit breakers on four trading days in March 2020. The last time these market-wide circuit breakers were triggered since their creation was in the year 1997. The financial market in India also witnessed high volatility in line with the fall in global benchmark indices and lost 26% in dollar terms between February 1 and April 9, 2020. Trading had to be halted after Nifty 50 index crashed by 10.7% on March 13 and BSE Sensitive index plummeted by 10% on March 23 in less than an hour of market opening. It was the first time since the Global Financial Crisis of 2008–2009 that the circuit breakers were triggered in the Indian stock market. It is worth noting that the stock market fall of March 23 happened a day after the Janata curfew in India was imposed on March 22. With this background, we study the impact of nationwide lockdowns implemented to control the surge of COVID-19, on firm-level returns in India.

Our study contributes to the literature on the relationship between COVID-19 and stock markets, with particular reference to returns at the firm level. The sectoral analysis provides empirical evidence on the sectors that have been worst and/or least affected as well as the degree of impact on major sectors in the Indian context. Some reflections are also offered on the post-pandemic scenario and policy measures that are likely to aid revival, drawing upon a few influential studies.

We find that there is greater variation in the responsiveness (in terms of magnitude and the sign) of the firm-level returns to the confirmed number of cases/deaths in the various lockdown and subsequent unlock phases. On sectoral variation, we find that the average returns have been higher for sectors such as Chemicals and Fertilizers, Health & Pharma, and Telecom. The average returns, controlling for other factors, are lower for sectors such as Consumer Durables, Hotels and Restaurants, Financial Services, Real Estate & Construction, and Retail.

The scheme is as follows. Section 20.2 contains a review of selected studies. Section 20.3 examines the trends in COVID-19 cases and related deaths in India during the period of our study. Section 20.4 discusses the trends in stock price movements during the first six months of the COVID-19 pandemic in India. This is followed by results of an econometric analysis of the impact of the pandemic on firm-level returns in Section 20.5. Section 20.6 is devoted to a discussion of the significance of our findings from a policy perspective and some reflections on a likely post–COVID-19 scenario. Section 20.7 provides concluding observations.

20.2. Literature Review

The Capital Asset Pricing Model (CAPM) (Treynor, 1962; Sharpe, 1964; Lintner, 1965; Mossin, 1966) is a widely used model to price securities considering the going risk-free rate and market risk premium that the investor requires in compensation for the additional risk. The Fama–French three-factor model expands on the CAPM by identifying two additional factors associated with the returns on stocks — the size of the firm and the book-to-market equity of the firm (Fama and French, 1992, 1995). Few studies (Navy-Marx, 2013; Titman *et al.*, 2004) showed that the three-factor model is incomplete in explaining the expected returns as they are unable to explain much of the variation in average returns related to profitability and investment, respectively. This led Fama and French to include profitability and investment in their earlier model and develop a five-factor model (Fama and French, 2014), and this was found to perform better than the three-factor model.

Stock markets across the world are highly volatile and sensitive to major events such as economic and political events, sports, news, diseases, and epidemics. In March 2020, the global financial markets tumbled following an oil price war between Russia and Saudi Arabia. The US stock markets plunged sharply enough to trigger the market-wide circuit breaker in the early trading hours of March 9, a day after the price war began. On March 10, however, the market recovered more than half the losses incurred on the previous day. Bondt and Thaler (1985) analyzed whether the stock market overreacts and found that most people "overreact" to unexpected and dramatic news events. Such a reaction to events does not affect the profitability and investment factors of individual firms as instantly as it affects the three factors of market risk premium, size, and book-to-market ratio of the Fama–French asset pricing model and thus may not be adequately captured in the five-factor model.

Empirical literature on stock market returns has identified several major events that have affected these returns. A recent study (Kowalewski and Spiewanowski, 2020) examines stock market reaction to mining accidents — natural and man-made — in potash mines. A significantly strong negative response of the stock market to natural events is observed, along with a cumulative drop in the market value of affected mining firms in the first two days of the disaster.

Political events and news are also seen to affect stock market returns. A recent study (Bash and Alsaifi, 2019) measures the effect of the uncertain event of Jamal Khashoggi's disappearance using traditional event-study methodology. The findings indicate that this event led to a downward trend in cumulative abnormal returns across all companies listed on the Saudi Stock Exchange. The returns on the Tel Aviv Stock Exchange following political events are more extreme than the returns on days not followed by political events (Zach, 2003). Another study (Li, 2018) investigated the impact of breaking news, classified by different aspects such as sentiment, source, and origin of viewpoints, on stock market performance. Their results showed the existence of a positive correlation between news sentiment and stock market performance — positive news improving it, while negative news slowing it down. This study also confirmed larger effects on the stock market due to news from government sources, relative to news from other sources, while news with viewpoints from government has lesser effect compared with viewpoints from academia.

Similarly, stock market returns have been found to be affected by pandemics. In a study (Chen *et al.*, 2007), the cumulative abnormal returns of hotel stocks listed on the Taiwan Stock Exchange are measured, 10 days prior to the SARS outbreak and the results were compared with those after 10 and 20 days of the outbreak. Their findings showed that Taiwanese hotel stocks were sensitive to the SARS outbreak and would react negatively to the occurrence of similar diseases. The 2014–2016 Ebola outbreak events were followed by negative returns in the financial markets (Ichev and Marinc, 2018). Further, media-driven sentiments around the Ebola outbreak significantly influenced investors' decisions when investing in companies of different capitalization size and industry of operation.

A recent pioneering study (Al-Awadhi *et al.*, 2020), investigated the effect of COVID-19 on the Chinese stock market. Their findings indicate that both daily growth in total confirmed cases and in total deaths due to COVID-19 have significant negative effects on returns across all companies. They further investigated this virus' impact on a sectoral level and their results suggested that stock returns of the information technology and medicine manufacturing sectors performed significantly better than the rest of the market. On the other hand, stock returns of beverages sector, air, water, and highway transportation sectors performed significantly worse than rest of the market during the COVID-19 outbreak.

Another study (Ashraf, 2020) analyzed how the stock markets in 64 countries are responding to the COVID-19 pandemic, and found that stock markets responded negatively to the growth in confirmed COVID-19 cases. This response varies over time depending on the stage of the outbreak. The study also revealed that stock market's response to the growth in confirmed cases was more statistically significant, as compared to the growth in number of deaths. These findings are also supported by another recent study (Al-Awadhi *et al.*, 2020), which investigates the reaction of financial markets globally in terms of their decline and volatility as the epicentre of the COVID-19 pandemic moved from China to Europe and then to the US. Their findings suggest that, while the earlier epicentre, China has stabilized, the global markets have gone into a freefall — especially in the later stage of the outbreak.

The review of literature suggests that there is scant research on the impact of pandemics on individual firm-level returns, particularly for those listed on the Indian stock market. It is the first time that such a situation has touched global economies at such a rapid pace, which makes it imperative to study and quantify its impact.

This study evaluates the impact of the COVID-19 pandemic on firm-level returns in the Indian stock market and contributes to the literature on the relationship between infectious diseases and stock markets. It also provides empirical evidence on which sectors have been the worst and least affected in the Indian context. The results of the study are useful for fund managers and investors in rearranging their portfolios to maintain returns in case of a similar occurrence. The sectoral analysis in the study reflects the degree of impact on major sectors and likely aid policymakers to focus better on the revival measures and policy interventions accordingly. Some reflections are offered on the post-pandemic scenario, drawing upon a few influential studies.

20.3. Trends in COVID-19 Cases and Deaths in India

In early March 2020, India witnessed a sudden rise in the number of COVID-19–positive cases. This led state governments to ban public gatherings and instructed all schools and colleges to remain closed. The government of India suspended all visas and banned all international commercial passenger flights from landing in India as the country reported its first death due to COVID-19 on March 13, 2020. Three days later, the Indian government ordered all institutions, shopping malls, movie theatres, and gyms to remain closed until April 3. Since then, there has been first a gradual,

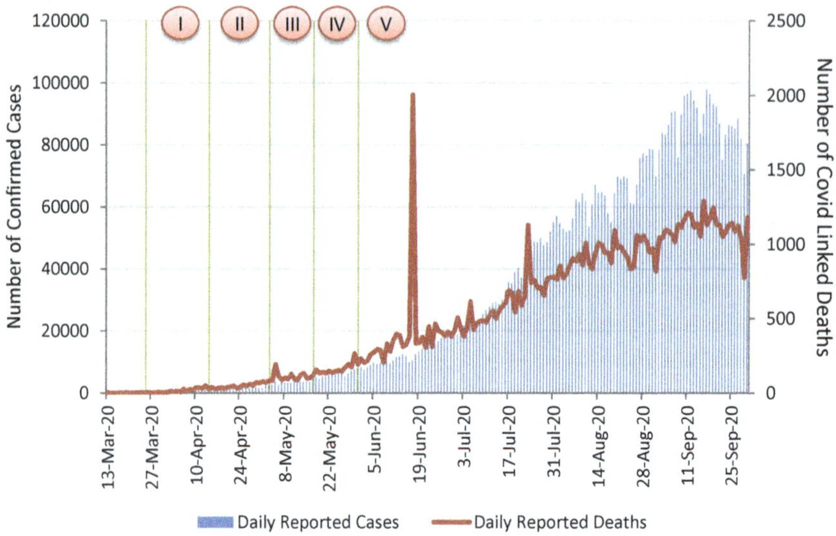

Figure 20.1. Daily reported COVID-19 cases and deaths in India (March 13–September 30, 2020).

Source: Official website of Ministry of Health and Family Welfare (MoHFW), Government of India. The Roman numbers indicate phases of the various lockdowns imposed by the government to curb the surge of the pandemic.

followed by a steep increase in both confirmed cases and deaths linked to the deadly virus.

Figure 20.1 shows the reported daily COVID-19 cases and related deaths in India for the period March 13, 2020, to September 30, 2020. Figure 20.2 shows the cumulative COVID-19 cases and related deaths for the same period. The data on recorded confirmed cases and deaths is taken from the official website of Ministry of Health and Family Welfare, Government of India.

The Roman numbers in each of the figures that follow indicate the phases of the various lockdowns imposed by the Indian government during this period. The first lockdown spanned a period of 21 days from March 25, 2020, to April 14, 2020, in which nearly all factories and services were suspended, barring "essential services." The second lockdown started on April 15, 2020, and continued till May 3, 2020, with conditional relaxations for regions where the COVID-19 spread had been contained. With additional relaxations, the phase three of the lockdown was from May 4, 2020, to May 17, 2020, and the

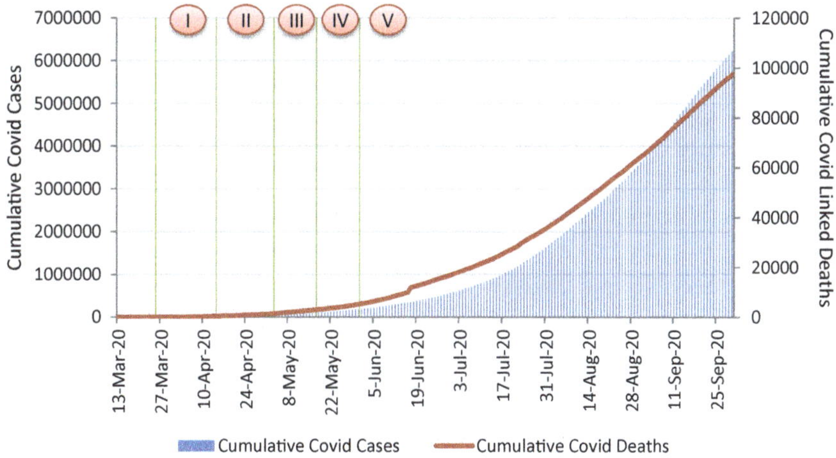

Figure 20.2. Cumulative COVID-19 cases and deaths in India (March 13–September 30, 2020).

Source: Official website of Ministry of Health and Family Welfare (MoHFW), Government of India. The figure represents COVID-19 cases September 30, 2020 from the start of the pandemic in India. The Roman numbers indicate phases of the various lockdowns imposed by the Government to curb the surge of the pandemic.

fourth phase was from May 18, 2020 to May 31, 2020. Phase five of the lockdown (June 1, 2020 to June 30, 2020), also known as Unlock 1.0, was the first phase of the reopening in stages, with an economic focus.

By the month of April 2020, most states appealed for the extension of lockdown to prevent further spread of the deadly virus. As a result, the lockdown was extended until May 3, 2020, across the entire nation. However, conditional relaxation was allowed in areas where the spread of the disease had been contained. Despite the efforts, COVID-19 continued to surge and India registered 29,310 new cases and 953 deaths related to the virus during the second phase of the lockdown.

A continuous increase in the number of confirmed cases and linked deaths forced the Government of India to further extend the nationwide lockdown by another two weeks until May 17. During this third phase of the lockdown, 733 districts of the country were classified into zones — red, orange, and green. The red zones or hotspot zones indicated the severely affected areas with the greatest number of active COVID-19 cases and had the most stringent regulations for movement of people and goods. Orange zones were those where there was one or more active case of COVID-19, but fewer than the red zones. The districts where there were no confirmed cases of the novel COVID-19 in the last 21 days were classified as the green zones. India had almost reached the mark of 100,000 confirmed cases and around 3,000 deaths by the end of this phase.

The phase four of the lockdown, which began on May 18, 2020, and continued till May 31, 2020, accounted for 47.2% of the total COVID-19 cases till that time. Hence, guidelines were issued to check the spread of COVID-19 along with resumption of economic activities in a staggered manner. Transport services such as buses, cabs, and auto-rickshaws were permitted. However, the restrictions on the interstate movement of buses were left to the mutual decision of the respective state governments. Other transport services such as air, metro, and rail continued to remain suspended. All shops were allowed to open except the ones in the containment zones (severely affected areas within the red zone classification) and malls. E-commerce platforms were allowed delivery of both essential and non-essential items. Mass political and religious gatherings remained prohibited. The country's infection tally surged to 177,652 and the death toll spiked to 5,165 by the end of this lockdown phase.

After spending almost 68 days in lockdown, the Government of India decided to lift the stringent restrictions in a phased manner with the stipulation of adherence to Standard Operating Procedures (SOPs). This phase is referred to as phase five of the lockdown or Unlock 1.0. The COVID-19 cases were increasing in the country but the fatality rate in India remained much lower than global fatality rate. Hence, the government introduced a three-phase unlock plan with an economic focus while keeping in check the spread of the novel coronavirus.

The Prime Minister of India also announced a COVID-19 relief package to the tune of Rs 20,000 billion, which was roughly around 10% of the country's GDP. The mega relief package was aimed at providing the Indian economy, the much-needed economic stimulus to recover from the contraction that was a direct result of the lockdowns.

20.4. Stock Market Returns in India During COVID-19 Pandemic

20.4.1. *Returns on BSE Sensex 30*

We start by examining the trends in the BSE Sensex 30. The Sensex (or the BSE-sensitive index) is like a barometer of the Indian stock market. It is calculated using the Market Capitalization-Weighted methodology of 30 component stocks representing large, well-established, and financially sound companies across key sectors. The base year of the Sensex is 1978–1979. Since September 2003, the Sensex is being calculated on a free-float market capitalization methodology. As the oldest index in the country, it provides time series data over a fairly long period.

As can be seen from Figure 20.3, the BSE Sensex experienced a huge fall coinciding with the announcement of Janata curfew on March 22, 2020, by the Prime Minister of India. It is interesting to note that the BSE Sensex rose by 1,862 points on March 25, when the first nationwide lockdown to control the surge of the COVID-19 pandemic in India began and economic activity in the country came

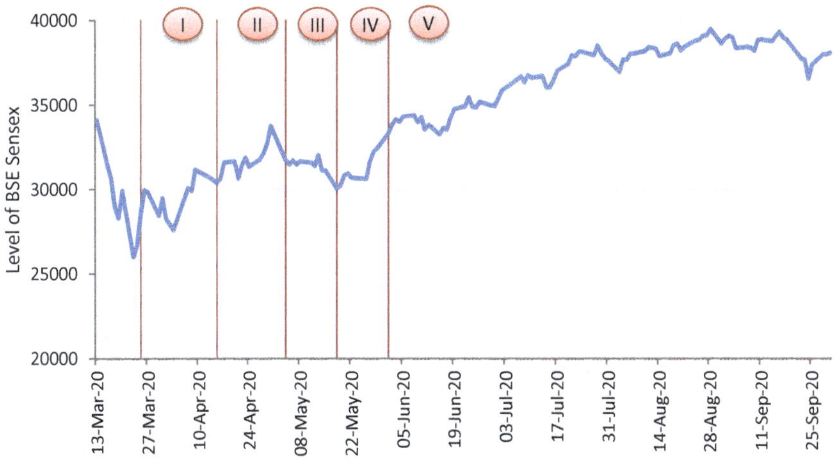

Figure 20.3. Movement in BSE Sensex during COVID-19 pandemic (March 13–September 30, 2020).

Source: Official website of BSE Historical Indices. The figure shows the level of the BSE sensitive index. The Roman numbers indicate phases of the various lockdowns imposed by the government to curb the surge of the pandemic.

to a standstill. This defying behaviour of the Indian stock market was a result of firm global cues. The market sentiment improved after the US President announced a massive economic stimulus in the wake of the pandemic's economic consequences, signalling a green day for Wall Street. Other global market indices were also trading with gains. On the same day, following reports of Facebook expected to buy a 10% stake in Reliance Jio, there was heavy buying of shares of its parent company — Reliance Industries — on the BSE Sensex, which also contributed to the upward rally in the Indian stock market.

However, the market situation changed soon enough. Even though the number of COVID-19 cases was low in March 2020 (an average of 56 new cases), during the first half of Phase I, the economic inactivity in the country created a bearish sentiment in the Indian stock market, resulting in the plunge in the BSE Sensex levels. While it was anticipated that the investor sentiment is likely to remain pessimistic during the lockdown period, to our surprise, during the latter half of the first COVID-19 lockdown, the Sensex started rising with the hope of the government announcing an economic relief package to revive the contracting Indian economy. This was also aided by the expectation of the lockdown being lifted bringing business activities back to their normal functioning. In fact, in the month of April 2020, the Indian share market outperformed its global peers.

While BSE Sensex climbed up for most of the second lockdown period, disappointment over an extended lockdown order by another two weeks dented the market outlook and led to sharp drops in the Indian benchmark equity index. The flaring up of tensions between the US and China further triggered the risk-off sentiment among the investors adding to the misery of the already fragile world economy.

Phase IV came with some easing of restrictions and was backed by stimulus measures as the government announced an economic relief package to combat the downside effects of the long stay-at-home order. It is worth noting that the BSE Sensex level has consistently increased thereafter. With the gradual opening up of the economy, investors expect slow return to normalcy.

It is also surprising to note that while COVID-19 cases and deaths have been rising at an exponential rate, and uncertainty exists over economic recovery, with India reporting a negative GDP growth rate to the extent of 23.9% in the first quarter (April–June) of the financial year 2020–2021, the stock market has rebounded and is following an upward trend. A possible reason for this dissonance could be that the markets are future-oriented, meaning that it is farsighted and in the long term is driven by economic fundamentals. Resumption of normal economic activities through several phases of unlock has led to the overall rising trend in the Sensex level. It took a period of 51 days (from March 14 to June 3, 2020) before the BSE Sensex was restored to its pre–COVID-19 level in India.

A higher-than-expected level of economic reopening has given the Indian stock markets a boost, and the BSE Sensex is less than 2% away from wiping out its losses for the year. Furthermore, monetary policy easing by the Reserve Bank of India to support the Indian economy, mild improvements in some economic indicators, and optimistic expectation over earning results from few major firms have helped improve investor sentiment, resulting in the rising trend of the BSE Sensex levels.

In Figure 20.4, it can be seen that the Indian stock market, and hence the daily returns on BSE Sensex, has fluctuated immensely.

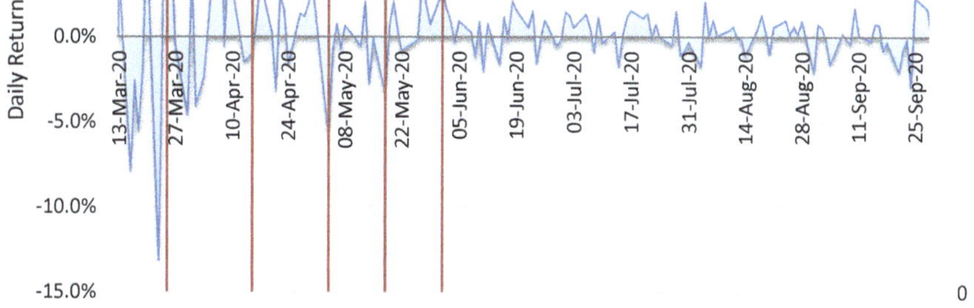

Figure 20.4. Movement in BSE Sensex daily returns (March 13–September 30, 2020).

Source: Authors' computations. The figure shows the percentage change in BSE Sensex value from the previous trading day's closing value. The Roman numbers indicate phases of the various lockdowns imposed by the government to curb the surge of the pandemic.

While there were significant highs and lows in daily returns during the initial period of nationwide lockdown, daily returns look less volatile as the unlock phases have progressed. Further, since the restrictions on economic activity were eased, there has been a significant surge in COVID-19 cases. The month of July, which coincided with Phase II, showed the highest variation in new cases and deaths associated with the deadly virus. Despite this, the Indian stock market including the BSE Sensex continued to rise.

The box plot graph in Figure 20.5 shows that the variation in BSE Sensex daily returns was at the maximum in the month of March and gradually decreased in the months that followed. As the whiskers of the box plot are longer toward the first quartile in the case of all months except July and September (where they are nearly equal in length), it can be seen that these returns are skewed to the lower side for most months of the study. A close look at the medians (which is represented by the line in the box) tells us that it has moved in the opposite directions in alternate months of the study. This reflects the great extent of fluctuations observed in the returns of

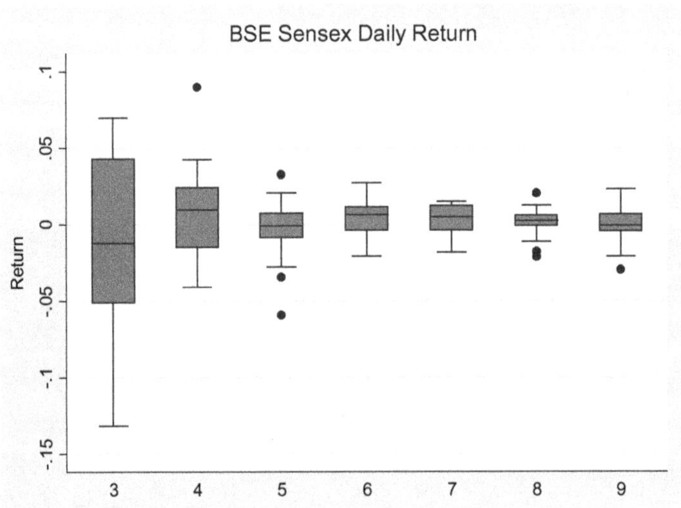

Figure 20.5. Monthly variation in BSE Sensex.
Source: Authors' computations. The figure shows the month-wise distribution of the BSE Sensex daily returns. The daily returns are calculated as a percentage change in BSE Sensex value from the previous trading day's closing value.

the Indian stock market equity index — i.e. the BSE Sensex. In Figure 20.5, the presence of outliers in the months of April, May, August, and September suggests that there have been abnormal gains and losses during these respective months of the study. As there are more outliers on the lower side of the graph below, we infer that even though the BSE Sensex levels have shown huge improvements, there have been more abnormal losses than gains.

20.4.2. *Sectoral variations in returns on BSE listed companies*

Next, we turn to the sectoral variations. Table 20.1 provides the average monthly return on the stocks belonging to a particular sector, during the pandemic period. It may be observed that all the sectors, including health and pharmaceutical, exhibited negative returns in the month of March, which, however, became positive in April. We use a panel of all companies belonging to the specified sectors included in the S&P BSE AllCap index, which comprises the BSE LargeCap, BSE MidCap, and BSE SmallCap companies.

The impact of the COVID-19 pandemic and subsequent lockdowns from March to May 2020 have varied across sectors. The performance of the retail sector has been abysmal and it gave an average negative return of 3.4% in March 2020. This sector has witnessed an immediate slump due to the closing down of shopping malls and other retail outlets to ward off the spread of the virus. The negative rate of return has been predominantly stark for those retailers dealing in non-essential items such as apparels, consumer durables, and footwear, among others. It is also worth noting that even as the lockdown has been lifted in a phased manner, the retail sector has still given a negative return in the alternate months that followed.

Other sectors such as hotels and restaurants and real estate have also performed poorly. The Indian hospitality sector has been grappling with the complete nationwide lockdown, including a ban on domestic and international travel. The demand for hospitality services has been significantly low even during the unlock phases, mainly catering to international travellers returning to India as ordained by the government. The real estate sector — both residential and commercial — has been hit hard due to the pandemic, subsequent lockdowns, and the resultant exodus of labour to their

Table 20.1. Monthly sectoral returns in 2020 (%).

Sector	March	April	May	June	July	August	September
Auto and Ancillaries	−2.11	1.30	0.03	0.66	0.08	0.65	0.06
Capital Goods	−2.16	1.12	−0.23	0.81	0.09	0.71	−0.13
Chemicals and Fertilizers	−1.45	1.43	0.03	0.54	0.32	0.49	0.13
Consumer Durables	−1.73	0.72	−0.10	0.60	−0.02	0.70	0.39
FMCG	−1.41	0.90	0.16	0.70	0.12	0.49	0.12
Financial Services	−2.41	0.74	−0.45	1.21	0.06	0.41	−0.30
Health & Pharma	−1.03	1.46	0.01	0.59	0.66	0.29	0.41
Hotels & Restaurants	−2.63	0.18	−0.42	0.79	0.05	0.86	−0.15
IT	−2.28	1.19	0.16	0.87	0.62	0.86	0.44
Logistics	−1.94	0.69	−0.16	0.54	0.39	0.56	0.13
Media & Entertain-ment	−1.87	0.87	−0.08	0.99	0.04	0.72	−0.23
Oil & NG	−1.71	1.38	−0.23	0.89	0.30	0.47	0.04
Power & Utilities	−1.13	0.93	−0.10	0.84	−0.19	0.40	−0.27
Real Estate	−2.44	1.12	−0.30	0.96	−0.15	0.73	−0.29
Retail	−3.41	0.52	−0.33	0.84	−0.41	0.87	−0.79
Telecom	−2.08	1.81	0.33	1.22	−0.12	0.58	0.00

Note: The table provides the average monthly return on the stocks of the various sectors.
Source: Author calculations based on data from Capitaline.com.

homes in rural areas. It bounced back in April to give a positive return of 1.12%, but has again slumped to a negative rate of return in the month of September, even as the country exited the nationwide lockdowns. The power sector's performance in the month of May has been the worst of all the months in our study. This is primarily because, during the lockdown period between March and May 2020, the industrial demand for electricity plummeted drastically. Of all sectors, telecommunications has attained highest positive returns for three consecutive months from April to June 2020. The nationwide

COVID-19 lockdown has resulted in a sharp increase in Internet usage, particularly in the wired broadband segment, which is usually underpenetrated. The higher dependency of businesses and education institutions on tools like video conferencing and other collaborative applications, mainly due to work-from-home and online classes, respectively, are driving up demand for telecom services. The IT sector displayed high average negative return of 2.28% in March 2020 but has been demonstrating positive average returns thereafter. IT services companies are expanding their cloud portfolio with greater investments as the demand for such services has risen, with clients increasingly opting for remote working solutions. This is expected to generate faster growth in digital revenues in the post-pandemic business environment. The returns of the media and entertainment sector have experienced maximum growth in the month of July. This coincides with the time when filming activities were partially resumed in the country although governed by strict and pre-defined health safety protocols. The auto sector experienced growth in the months of May and July due to an increase in the demand for private vehicles. This growth is also caused by the lack of public transport in the form of inoperative metro rail services in tier-1 cities and restrictions on seating capacity in public vehicles. The monthly returns of chemical sector have a correlation coefficient of 0.971 with the health & pharmaceutical sector, implying a strong positive linear relationship between the relative movements of the two sectors. These two sectors are among the few sectors along with IT and consumer durables, which have entered the green zone in September in terms of their monthly returns.

20.4.3. *Stock market volatility during COVID-19 pandemic*

The simplest measure of volatility is the standard deviation. For the period under study, a quick investigation of the ten-day trailing standard deviation shows spikes in the recent months, which have not been encountered previously.

As can be seen from Figure 20.6, the BSE Sensex witnessed sharp volatility due to the uncertainty and risk created by the COVID-19 pandemic as well as the lockdown policy adopted to curb the spread

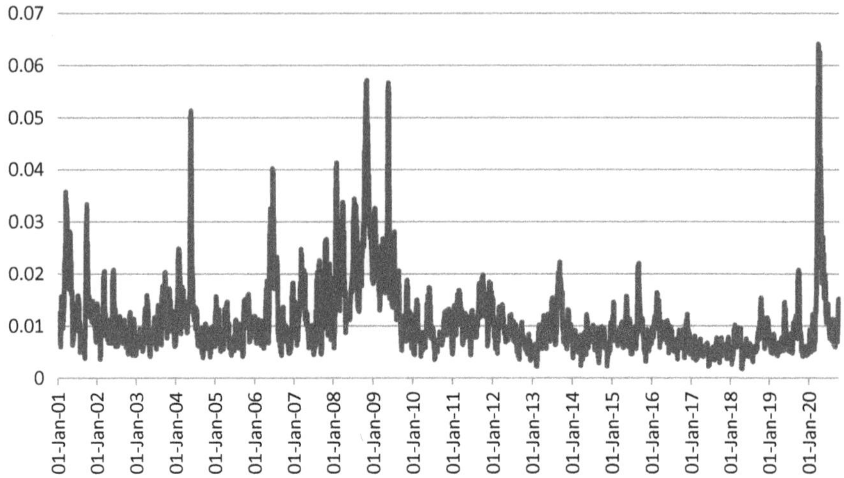

Figure 20.6. Ten-day trailing standard deviation on Sensex returns (January 1, 2001–September 30, 2020).

Source: Authors' computations. The figure shows the ten-day trailing standard deviation on BSE Sensex returns as a statistical measure of market volatility.

of the lethal virus. It is interesting to note that the fluctuations have been higher than those experienced during the Global Financial Crisis of 2008–2009. The intensity of the financial crisis of 2008–2009 is spread out over a longer time frame while that of the pandemic has been more immediate and severe. The volatility peaked in the month of March 2020, corresponding with the COVID-19 outbreak in India and the nationwide lockdowns that followed. The rift between Russia and Saudi Arabia over oil production also occurred around the same time, leading to low investor confidence in the markets across the world. As the lockdowns have been eased and economic activity is gradually returning to normal, the volatility has also subsided.

Figure 20.7 shows the ten-day trailing standard deviation on Sensex return in the last one year. It can be inferred from the graph that the volatility in the Indian stock market started increasing from the end of February 2020 when the first few cases of COVID-19 in the country came to light and continued as the nationwide lockdowns progressed. However, the fluctuations became smaller as the lockdown restrictions were eased through several phases of unlock and as resumption of economic activities boosted the market outlook as well as the path to economic recovery.

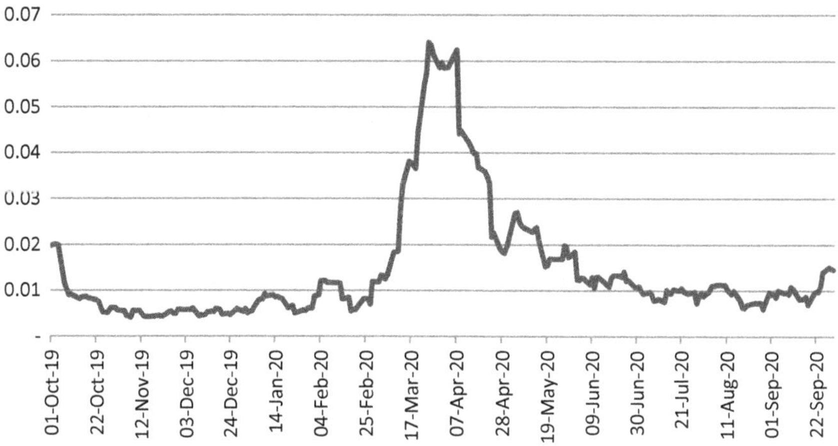

Figure 20.7. Ten-day trailing standard deviation on Sensex returns (October 1, 2019–September 30, 2020).

Source: Authors' computations. The figure shows the ten-day trailing standard deviation on BSE Sensex returns as a statistical measure of market volatility.

20.5. Econometric Analysis: Methodology and Results

20.5.1. *Methodology*

We use the period March 13, 2020, till September 30, 2020 (the cut-off date for this study) to examine the impact of the pandemic on stock returns. We use a panel of all companies included in the S&P BSE AllCap index, which comprises the BSE LargeCap, BSE MidCap, and BSE SmallCap companies. This index is a comprehensive rules-based index that measures the performance of the Indian stock market. Since its inception, it has been fully float adjusted and is designed to represent an index suite with a transparent and modular structure. In order to circumvent the effect of outliers, of the 856 companies that constitute this index, companies with negative price-to-book value (PBV) ratio on any day and PBV of more than 50 on any day were deleted. In addition to these, companies with market capitalization less than 100 on any day were removed. Our analysis is based on a sample of 779 companies.

A panel data regression model with the following specification is used:

$$R_{i,t} = \beta_0 + \beta_1 \mathit{Covid}\text{-}19_{i,t-1} + \boldsymbol{\rho F} + \boldsymbol{\vartheta S} + \boldsymbol{\tau L} + \epsilon_{it}, \qquad (20.1)$$

where $R_{i,t}$ is the return on stock i on day t, and is regressed on the lagged value of firm-specific characteristics (denoted by vector $\boldsymbol{F}$) and a measure of lagged pandemic (denoted by *Covid-19*). The measure of the pandemic used is: (i) number of deaths recorded on the previous day, and (ii) number of confirmed cases recorded on the previous day. Firm-specific characteristics include the lagged value of the firms' market capitalization (to capture the size effect), the price-to-book value ratio (to capture the value effect), and the Sensex Beta (to capture the risk premium). The database from where the firm data is captured, Capitaline, classifies companies into industries. The same classification is used, and sector-fixed effects are added to the above specification (captured by the vector $\boldsymbol{S}$).

We first examine the properties of our data by testing for stationarity. A stationary time series is one whose statistical properties such as mean, variance, and autocorrelation remain constant overtime. We examine the stationarity of the returns series using unit root test — Augmented Dicky Fuller (ADF) test (Wooldridge, 2006). Since the returns are a first difference of the stock prices, the series is found to be stationary.

In addition, time-fixed effects are used to capture the various lockdowns announced by the Indian government starting March 24, 2020, until the end of September 2020 (captured in the above specification by the vector $\boldsymbol{L}$). To see how the impact of pandemic indicators on firm-level returns has varied, the time dummies for the various months are interacted with the pandemic indicators. The data on stock prices, market capitalization, price-to-book value ratio for the period mentioned above (there are 138 trading days between March 13, 2020, to September 30, 2020) are taken from Capitaline database.

20.5.2. *Base specification*

Table 20.2 reports the results of the panel data regression. In specifications I and III, the firm-level stock price returns are regressed on the indicator of the pandemic (number of new cases registered on the previous day), the indicators of the firm size, value, and risk (based on the Fama–French three-factor model) and a set of time dummies for each month in our data. In Specification II and IV, the indicator of the pandemic is interacted with the time dummy to see if the relationship between the returns and the pandemic indicators varies as time progresses.

The firm-level stock returns are found to be negatively related to the confirmed number of new COVID-19 cases in the country but the relationship with the number of new COVID-19–related deaths is found to be statistically not significant (Specifications I and III). However, taking into account the coefficients of the interaction terms, we find that the relationship between the stock returns and the number of COVID-19 cases/deaths varied as the months progressed (Specifications II and IV). The coefficients of the interaction terms capture the varying coefficients for the different lockdown periods. The sum of the coefficient of the pandemic indicator in specifications (II) and (IV) in Table 20.2 and the coefficient of the interaction term denotes the overall coefficient for each month. The relationship between returns and cases/deaths is positive for the base month, i.e. March. However, a strong negative relationship between returns and cases is observed (an increase of 100 cases leads to a decline in the return by 0.1%) in the month of April, which coincides with the strict nationwide lockdown Phases I and II. With the lifting of restrictions during Phases III and IV of the lockdown, coinciding with the month of May, the relationship between returns and cases is almost negligible.

Similarly, a strong negative relationship between returns and deaths is observed (an increase of 100 deaths leads to a decline in the return by 1.3%) in the month of April. With the lifting of restrictions during Phases III and IV of the lockdown, coinciding with the month of May, the relationship between returns and deaths is positive (an increase of 100 deaths leads to an increase of 2.1% in the return). The positive trend continues in May with the magnitude reducing, and, finally, becoming negative again.

The coefficient with respect to the market capitalization (capturing the size effect) is negative, but with respect to price-to-book value ratio (capturing value effect) is positive, conforming to the Fama–French three-factor model. The coefficients of the time dummies suggest that the firm returns are found to be higher in April in comparison to March. The returns again drop in May and then increase in the subsequent months, reaching a peak in August and then dipping again in September. Thus, we find that there is greater variation in the responsiveness (in terms of magnitude and the sign)

Table 20.2. Regression results — Base specification.

DV: Daily stock return	Regular specification [I]	Using interaction with time dummies [II]	Regular specification [III]	Using interaction with time dummies [IV]
No. of observations	108281	108281	108281	108281
Lagged – reported confirmed cases	−0.000 (0.000)*	0.048 (0.000)*		
Lagged – reported confirmed deaths			0.000 (0.000)	1.259 (0.024)*
Log market capitalization	−0.022 (0.008)*	−0.016 (0.007)*	−0.023 (0.008)*	−0.020 (0.008)*
Price to book value ratio	0.011 (0.003)*	0.013 (0.003)*	0.011 (0.003)*	0.012 (0.003)*
Sensex Beta	0.070 (0.049)	0.071 (0.048)	0.070 (0.049)	0.070 (0.048)
Time factor variables:				
April	2.998 (0.049)*	6.439 (0.088)*	2.959 (0.049)*	5.122 (0.083)*
May	1.962 (0.049)*	1.298 (0.121)*	1.799 (0.049)*	0.861 (0.125)*
June	3.187 (0.052)*	7.097 (0.112)*	2.727 (0.054)*	4.223 (0.065)*
July	3.311 (0.076)*	4.977 (0.102)*	2.041 (0.062)*	4.467 (0.117)*
August	4.785 (0.123)*	11.694 (0.257)*	2.430 (0.079)*	9.440 (0.293)*
September	5.098 (0.163)*	4.992 (0.308)*	1.864 (0.088)*	4.240 (0.281)*
Reported cases/deaths interacted with:				
April		−0.049 (0.001)*		−1.273 (0.024)*
May		−0.048 (0.001)*		−1.239 (0.024)*
June		−0.048 (0.001)*		−1.259 (0.024)*
July		−0.048 (0.001)*		−1.261 (0.024)*
August		−0.048 (0.001)*		−1.265 (0.024)*
September		−0.048 (0.001)*		−1.260 (0.024)*
Constant	−1.828 (0.073)*	−4.231 (0.080)*	−1.824 (0.074)*	−3.556 (0.080)*

Note: *denote significance at 1%.
Source: Author's computations based on data from Capitaline.com.

of the firm-level returns to the confirmed number of cases/deaths in the various lockdown and subsequent unlock phases.

20.5.3. *Sectoral analysis*

In a variant of the base specification, we experiment to check the impact of pandemic indicators on stock returns for specific industry sectors by adding two additional sets of variables: the industry-fixed effects and interacting the industry-fixed effects with the pandemic indicator. The coefficient of the interaction term captures the variation in the elasticity of firm returns to the pandemic indicators across industries. For this analysis, we concentrate on specific industries, namely, Auto & Ancillaries; Chemicals & Fertilizers; Consumer Durables; E-commerce; Education; FMCG, Financial Services; Health & Pharma; Hotels & Restaurants; IT; Logistics; Media & Entertainment; Real Estate & Construction; Retail; and Telecom. Firms belonging to any sector apart from these are classified as *Others* (the reference category for our analysis).

The results are given in Tables 20.3(a) and 20.3(b). Table 20.3(a) reports the coefficients of the pandemic indicators (COVID-19 cases in Specification I and COVID-19–related deaths in Specification II), the coefficients of variables to capture the size effect, the value effect and the systemic risk, the coefficients of the time dummies, and interactions of the pandemic indicators with the time dummies. Table 20.3(b) reports the coefficients of the sector dummies and the interactions of the pandemic indicators with the sector dummies.

As in the base specifications, the firm-level stock returns are found to be positively related to both the confirmed number of COVID-19 cases in the country and the reported number of deaths linked to COVID-19, but this varies as time progresses. During the lockdown phases, this relationship is negative. The elasticity with respect to the market capitalization (capturing the size effects) is negative, and with respect to price-to-book value ratio (capturing value effect) is positive. The coefficient of Sensex Beta is also positive conforming to the Fama–French three-factor model. Similar to the base specification, the coefficients of the time dummies suggest that the firm returns are found to be higher in April in comparison to March. The returns again drop in May and then increase in the subsequent

Table 20.3. (a) Econometric results.

DV: Daily stock return	I	II
No. of observations	108281	108281
Lagged – reported confirmed cases	0.048 (0.000)***	
Lagged – reported confirmed deaths		1.259 (0.024)***
Log market capitalization	−0.014 (0.008)*	−0.017 (0.008)**
Price to book value ratio	0.010 (0.003)***	0.009 (0.003)***
Sensex beta	0.179 (0.050)***	0.180 (0.050)***
Time factor variables:		
April	6.438 (0.088)***	5.122 (0.083)***
May	1.298 (0.121)***	0.861 (0.125)***
June	7.097 (0.112)***	4.223 (0.065)***
July	4.978 (0.102)***	4.467 (0.117)***
August	11.694 (0.257)***	9.440 (0.293)***
September	4.993 (0.308)***	4.241 (0.281)***
Reported cases/deaths interacted with:		
April	−0.049 (0.001)***	−1.273 (0.024)***
May	−0.047 (0.001)***	−1.238 (0.024)***
June	−0.048 (0.001)***	−1.259 (0.024)***
July	−0.048 (0.001)***	−1.261 (0.024)***
August	−0.048 (0.001)***	−1.265 (0.024)***
September	−0.048 (0.001)***	−1.260 (0.024)***

Note: ***,**,*denote significance at 1%, 5%, and 10%, respectively.
Source: Author's computations based on data from Capitaline.com.

months, reaching a peak in August and then dipping again in September. Thus, we find that there is greater variation in the responsiveness (in terms of magnitude and the sign) of the firm-level returns to the confirmed number of cases/deaths in the various lockdown and subsequent unlock phases.

On sectoral variation, we find that the average returns have been higher for sectors such as Chemicals and Fertilizers, Health & Pharma, and Telecom. The average returns, controlling for other factors, are lower for sectors such as Consumer Durables, Hotels and Restaurants, Financial Services, Real Estate & Construction, and Retail.

20.6. Discussion

In an integrated global economy, domestic stock markets are heavily influenced through trade, exchange rate movements, and portfolio

Table 20.3. (b) Econometric results — sectoral analysis.

DV: Daily stock return	I	II
Sector dummies		
Auto & ancillaries	0.022 (0.065)	0.033 (0.072)
Chemicals & fertilizers	0.179 (0.062)***	0.257 (0.069)***
Consumer durables	−0.202 (0.117)*	−0.153 (0.130)
E-commerce	−0.064 (0.312)	0.158 (0.345)
Education	0.054 (0.221)	0.153 (0.245)
FMCG	0.074 (0.074)	0.118 (0.082)
Financial services	−0.129 (0.053)**	−0.162 (0.059)***
Health & pharma	0.292 (0.061)***	0.452 (0.067)***
Hotels & restaurants	−0.419 (0.168)**	−0.392 (0.186)***
IT	0.074 (0.071)	0.108 (0.078)
Logistics	−0.120 (0.113)	−0.128 (0.125)
Media & entertainment	0.105 (0.104)	0.134 (0.115)
RE & construction	−0.073 (0.066)	−0.142 (0.073)*
Retail	−0.527 (0.135)***	−0.596 (0.149)***
Telecom	0.354 (0.141)**	0.445 (0.156)***
Reported cases/deaths interacted with:		
Auto & ancillaries	0.000 (0.000)	−0.000 (0.000)
Chemicals & fertilizers	−0.000 (0.000)	−0.000 (0.000)**
Consumer durables	0.000 (0.000)**	0.000 (0.000)
E-commerce	0.000 (0.000)	−0.000 (0.000)
Education	−0.000 (0.000)	−0.000 (0.000)
FMCG	−0.000 (0.000)	−0.000 (0.000)
Financial services	−0.000 (0.000)	0.000 (0.000)
Health & pharma	−0.000 (0.000)	−0.000 (0.000)***
Hotels & restaurants	0.000 (0.000)**	0.000 (0.000)
IT	0.000 (0.000)***	0.000 (0.000)**
Logistics	0.000 (0.000)	0.000 (0.000)
Media & entertainment	−0.000 (0.000)	−0.000 (0.000)
RE & construction	0.000 (0.000)	0.000 (0.000)
Retail	0.000 (0.000)	0.000 (0.000)*
Telecom	−0.000 (0.000)	−0.000 (0.000)**
Constant	−4.346 (0.085)***	−3.690 (0.085)***

Note: ***,**,*denote significance at 1%, 5%, and 10%, respectively.
Source: Author's computations based on data from Capitaline.com.

flows. So, the evolution of the global economy has not just impacted India's stock market but will continue to shape its valuation and growth in the medium term. IMF's Global Financial Stability Report, October 2020, offers an optimistic and a pessimistic scenario, as the global economic prospects are contingent on policy choices to contain the second wave of the COVID-19 pandemic, availability of a vaccine, social distancing, and investor sentiment. While the sharp easing of financial conditions since late March has helped avert a financial crisis and contain the damage to the world economy by the COVID-19 pandemic, the deterioration of the economic outlook has moved the expected distribution of global growth in 2020 deeply into the negative zone. Global growth is projected at −4.4% in 2020. In 2021, a positive growth rate of 5.2% is projected by World Economic Outlook (WEO) (IMF, 2020b). Following the contraction in 2020 and recovery in 2021, the level of global GDP in 2021 is expected to be a modest 0.6% above that of 2019. Although the projected rebound and easy financial conditions imply that the odds of negative growth next year are low, the balance of risks is tilted to the downside. As observed by WEO, the uncertainty around the baseline projection is unusually large. The projection rests on public health and economic factors that are inherently difficult to predict. An important source of uncertainty relates to the path of the pandemic, the needed public health response, and the associated domestic activity disruptions, most notably for contact-intensive sectors. Another source is the extent of global spillovers from soft demand, weaker tourism, and lower remittances. A third source is financial market sentiment and its link to global capital flows. Lastly, and no less important, is uncertainty about the damage to supply potential — which will depend on the persistence of the pandemic shock, the size and effectiveness of the policy response, and the extent of sectoral resource mismatches. On the positive side, unprecedented policy actions have boosted investor sentiment and ensured the flow of credit to the economy; aggregate capital flows have recovered from their March lows, though half of emerging economies have witnessed capital outflows during recent months; global equity markets have rebounded strongly from pandemic lows, varying with the spread of the virus, the strength of policy support, and sectoral composition. Equity markets in China and the US have outperformed other markets, driven by technology stocks. In contrast, more contact-intensive sectors (hotels, restaurants, leisure) have suffered losses because of lockdowns and social distancing. Besides, underperformance of the energy sector reflects weak investors' assessment of growth prospects (IMF, 2020a). A worry is the "disconnect" between rising market valuations and the evolution of the economy. Market sentiment could easily turn negative if the momentum of policy support weakens and if it is not scaled up in response to deterioration in the economic outlook. Current risk asset valuation may be maintained for some time but not longer and a sharp adjustment could occur (IMF, 2020a). In brief, the growing market valuation could turn out to be illusory.

Some of the risks sketched above are more likely to prevail in India. The Reserve Bank of India/RBI (2020) offers a mixed blend of optimism and pessimism with a slightly heavier dose of the former. It reports that the Indian economy likely entered into a technical recession for the first time in history at the end of the first half of 2020–2021. It is not self-evident that even when output falls sharply in the second quarter and is followed by another fall in July–September quarter — sharp falls in output in two consecutive quarters characterise recession — the recession in India is referred to as a technical recession. In fact, RBI acknowledged a massive decline of 23.9% in GDP in April–June as estimated by the National Statistical Office on August 31, and another contraction of 8.6% in July–September. The fudge in fact goes deeper as the RBI is emphatic that data for October 2020 have brightened the near- term outlook for the Indian economy and stirred up consumer and business confidence.

Under the most likely scenario, the absolute value of real GDP may cross the GDP level of the Q4 of FY2020 almost after a year.[1] In other words, recovery will not get underway until the start of FY2022. The real GDP is likely to be at a substantially lower level than the pre–COVID-19 level. As the lockdown is being lifted partially and in stages and consumer sentiments are gradually improving, the surge in infections will influence consumer spending. Discretionary spending is likely to get delayed. With the continuing overhang of financial and economic uncertainties, demand will likely decline for most of 2021. Even before the COVID-19 pandemic, private investment had been declining for a while. Consequently, in FY2020, private investment shrank by −4.3% year-over-year. Post–COVID-19, the investment decline will be amplified due to uncertainty about demand, operational disruptions, and capacity and credit constraints. So, business spending is likely to contract in FY2021. In order to tackle the

[1]For different scenarios, see Deloitte (2020).

pandemic crisis and the economy's contraction, the Indian government announced a stimulus of 10.5% of GDP in May 2020, including direct transfers to the vulnerable sections, easing liquidity in the market, and addressing a mix of short-term and long-term challenges through policy reforms. If the entire amount is utilized, as assumed in the most likely scenario, the additional government spending with a fall in tax revenue due to low GDP is likely to aggravate the fiscal deficit in FY2021. WTO projects plummeting of world trade between 13% and 22% in 2020 due to the COVID-19 pandemic. Low exports are likely to be combined with lower imports due to poor domestic demand and rupee depreciation. Overall, the current account is likely to be positive in FY2021. However, if the economy bounces back in FY2022, imports will surge in response to higher domestic demand, and the current account is likely to turn negative.

The long and short of it is that India is expected to gradually rebound back in FY2022. However, if the pandemic prolongs, essential goods segment of retail, the pharmaceutical industry, and the technology and communication industry will scrape through. However, the hospitality and banking industry will struggle. On balance, the post–COVID-19 scenario for the stock market is likely to be grim but with a few bright spots.

20.7. Concluding Observations

The present study is an important contribution to the sparse literature on the impact of COVID-19 pandemic on the stock market in India. It assesses the impact on firm-level returns in the Indian stock market. A panel data model is used to assess the impact of the COVID-19 pandemic on firm-level returns.

The relationship between returns and cases/deaths is positive for the base month, i.e. March. However, a strong negative relationship between returns and cases is observed in the month of April, which coincides with the strict nationwide lockdown Phases I and II. With the lifting of restrictions during Phases III and IV of the lockdown, coinciding with the month of May, the relationship between returns and cases is almost negligible. Similarly, a strong negative relationship between returns and deaths is observed in the month of April.

With the lifting of restrictions during Phases III and IV of the lockdown, coinciding with the month of May, the relationship between returns and deaths is positive. The positive trend continues in May with the magnitude reducing, and, finally, becoming negative again. The coefficient with respect to the market capitalization (capturing the size effects) is negative, but with respect to price-to-book value ratio (capturing value effect) is positive. The firm returns are found to be higher in April in comparison to March. The returns again drop in May and then increase in the subsequent months, reaching a peak in August and then dipping again in September. On sectoral variation, we find that the average returns have been higher for sectors such as Chemicals and Fertilizers, Health & Pharma, and Telecom. The average returns, controlling for other factors, are lower for sectors such as Consumer Durables, Hotels and Restaurants, Financial Services, Real Estate & Construction, and Retail.

The results of the study are useful for fund managers and investors in rearranging their portfolios to maintain returns in case the pandemic is prolonged. Besides, our insights may help policymakers to focus better on the revival measures and policy interventions.

References

Al-Awadhi, A., Alsaifi, K., Al-Awadhi, A. and Alhammadi, S. (2020). Death and contagious infectious diseases: Impact of the COVID-19 virus on stock market returns. *Journal of Behavioral and Experimental Finance*, **27**, 100326.

Ali, M., Alam, N. and Rizvi, S. (2020). Coronavirus (COVID-19) - An epidemic or pandemic for financial markets. *Journal of Behavioral and Experimental Finance*, 100341.

Ashraf, B. (2020). Stock markets' reaction to COVID-19: Cases or fatalities? *Research in International Business and Finance*, **54**, 101249.

Baruah, A. (2020). IT firms ride on cloud to grow digital revenue. *LiveMint*, September 21.

Bash, A. and Alsaifi, K. (2019). Fear from uncertainty: An event study of Khashoggi and stock market returns. *Journal of Behavioral and Experimental Finance*, **23**, 54–58.

Bhargava, K. (2020). Indian share markets outperform global peers during lockdown; Sensex, Nifty jump 22% since March 23. *Financial Express*, April 30.

Chauhan, N. (2020). After Covid-19 lockdown, plan to unlock India in phases. *Hindustan Times*, May 31.

Chen, M., Jang, S. and Kim, W. (2007). The impact of the SARS outbreak on Taiwanese hotel stock performance: An event-study approach. *International Journal of Hospitality Management*, **26**(1), 200–212.

De Bondt, W.F.M. and Thaler, R. (1985). Does the stock market overreact. *Journal of Finance*, **40**, 793–805.

Deloitte (2020). Covid-19: Indian economic forecast amidst uncertainty, July.

Fama, E. and French, K. (1992). The cross-section of expected stock returns. *The Journal of Finance*, **47**(2), 427–465.

Fama, E. and French, K. (1993). Common risk factors in the returns on stocks and bonds. *Journal of Financial Economics*, **33**(1), 3–56.

Fama, E. and French, K. (1995). Size and book-to-market factors in earnings and returns. *The Journal of Finance*, 131–155, March.

Fama, E. and French, K. (2014). A five-factor asset pricing model. Fama-Miller Working Paper, September.

Ichev, R. and Marinc, M. (2018). Stock prices and geographic proximity of information: Evidence from the Ebola outbreak. *International Review of Financial Analysis*, **56**, 153–166.

IMF (2020a). Global Financial Stability Report. October, Washington, DC.

IMF (2020b). World Economic Outlook. October, Washington, DC.

Kowalewski, O. and Spiewanowski, P. (2020). Stock market response to potash mine disasters. *Journal of Commodity Markets*, **20**, 100–124.

Li, K. (2018). Reaction to news in the Chinese stock market: A study on Xiong'an New Area Strategy. *Journal of Behavioral and Experimental Finance*, **19**, 36–38.

Lintner, J. (1965). The valuation of risk assets and the selection of risky investments in stock portfolios and capital budgets. *Review of Economics and Statistics*, **47**, 13–37.

Mossin, J. (1966). Equilibrium in a capital asset market. *Econometrica*, **35**, 768–83.

Navy-Marx, R. (2013). The other side of value: The gross profitability premium. *Journal of Financial Economics*, **108**(1), 1–28.

Perapaddan, B.S. (2020). India's first coronavirus infection confirmed in Kerala. *The Hindu*, January 30.

Press Trust of India (2020). Fourth phase of lockdown accounts for nearly half of total Covid cases in India. *Hindustan Times*, May 31.

Raj, S. (2020). Bulls defy India lockdown: Sensex surges 1,862 points; what's behind the rally. *ET Markets*, March 26.

Reserve Bank of India (2020). Reserve Bank of India Bulletin, November.

Schnabel, J. (2020). Why is COVID-19 mild for some, deadly for others? *Cornell Chronicle*, April 20.

Sethuraman, S. (2020). Lockdown 3.0, global tension rattle markets; Sensex, Nifty crash nearly 6%. *Business Standard*, May 5.

Sharma, A. (2020). Coronavirus impact: India worst hit stock market; China least affected. *Business Today*, April 13.

Sharpe, W.F. (1964). Capital asset prices: A theory of market equilibrium under conditions of risk. *Journal of Finance*, **19**, 425–42.

The Economist (2020). The world economy: The peril and the promise, October 10.

The Hindu (2020). All about COVID-19. January 30.

The Hindu BusinessLine (2020). PM Modi calls for 'Janata curfew' on March 22 from 7 AM - 9 PM. March 19.

Titman, S., Wei, K. and Xie, F. (2004). Capital investments and stock returns. *Journal of Financial and Quantitative Analysis*, **39**(4), 677–700.

Treynor, J.L. (1962). Toward a theory of market value of risky assets. (Unpublished manuscript). In *Final version in Asset Pricing and Portfolio Performance, 1999*, Robert A. Korajczyk, (ed.), (London: Risk Books), pp. 15–22.

Vishnoi, A. (2020a). Indian stock markets are getting a boost from rising reopenings, falling Covid curve. *ThePrint*, October 12.

Vishnoi, A. (2020b). Indian stocks are set for their best run in 7 months as country exits lockdown. *ThePrint*, June 2.

Wooldridge, J.M. (2006). *Introductory Econometrics* (Thomson, South Western, Mason, OH).

World Health Organization (2020). Coronavirus diseases 2019 (COVID-19) Situation Report 40.

Zach, T. (2003). Political events and the stock market: Evidence from Israel. *International Journal of Business*, **8**(3), 243–266.

https://doi.org/10.1142/9781800610781_0021

Chapter 21

Business Group Affiliation and Resilience to COVID-19 Outbreak in India

Shreya Biswas* **and Nivedita Sinha**†

Department of Economics and Finance, Birla Institute of Technology and Science, Pilani, Hyderabad Campus, India

**shreya@hyderabad.bits-pilani.ac.in*

†nivedita.sinha@hyderabad.bits-pilani.ac.in

Abstract

The economic and market impact of COVID-19 in India has been quite disruptive, creating stress for Indian corporates. We observe the listed firms in India during the COVID-19 health crisis and the stringent lockdown period and investigate the performance of business group-firms as compared to a matched sample of standalone firms. We find that business group-firms outperformed the standalone firms during the nationwide lockdown as well as the extended lockdown period and attribute this short-term outperformance to the access to internal capital markets. Our results suggest that group-firms with better growth opportunities and affiliated to larger business groups had much higher returns, indicating an efficient transfer of resources amongst group-firms. Our results suggest that the presence of internal capital markets led to lower erosion of market value for shareholders.

21.1. Introduction

A business group is a collection of legally independent firms (publicly or privately held) doing business in different markets under common financial or administrative control. The affiliate group-firms have multiple ties through which they coordinate to achieve mutual objectives (Granovetter, 1995; Leff, 1978). Business groups are a prevalent organizational form in several world economies, such as Japan, China, South Korea, India, Latin American countries, Taiwan, Western Europe, etc. For example, 45, 40, and 20 out of the top 50 companies in India, South Korea, and China, respectively, belong to business groups (Ramachandran *et al.*, 2013). The group-firms in many emerging economies tend to be relatively large and economically more important than standalone firms. Khanna and Yafeh (2007) compared the size of affiliated and unaffiliated firms for 12 emerging markets and found that group-firms are relatively larger than standalone firms.

The institutional view of business groups suggests that group structure emerges in economies as a response to missing market institutions, high transaction costs, and ineffective mechanisms to enforce contracts. Extant literature (La Porta *et al.*, 1998, 1999) suggests that a consequence of weak contract enforcement mechanisms in emerging economies is a concentrated ownership structure of family-run business groups. As indicated by Leff (1978, p. 666), the "group pattern of industrial organization is readily understood as a microeconomic response to well-known conditions of market failure in the less developed countries." Business groups create value by spreading the costs of organizing such internal structures across several lines of business (Khanna and Palepu, 1997).

The business group structure has two defining characteristics. First, business groups have a family as an ultimate controller and have low to moderate cash-flow rights in several firms. This divergence in ownership and control leads to the principal–principal type of agency problem between the controller owner and the minority owners of the group-firms. In emerging economies with weak corporate governance laws and ineffective law enforcement mechanisms, agency problems exist between controlling and minority shareholders (Claessens and Fan, 2002). A business group is regarded as a device for the dominant shareholders to expropriate minority shareholders' wealth if their interests are not protected (Dharwadkar *et al.*, 2000). The controlling shareholders with higher cash flow rights in the higher-tier group-firms can often tunnel resources from lower-tier to higher-tier group-firms (Bertrand *et al.*, 2002). In addition to aligning the managers' interests with that of the shareholders, the boards of group-firms need to balance the interests of the minority and the controlling shareholders. There are additional complex corporate governance issues due to lack of transparency in internal functioning, equity ownership in other group affiliate firms, and possible rent-seeking by leveraging political associations (Khanna and Palepu, 2000).

The second feature of business group-firms is the presence of internal markets. The internal markets substitute for weak factor markets and missing institutions in emerging markets (Khanna and Palepu, 1997). Studies suggest three types of internal markets within business groups — internal labor market, internal capital market, and internal trade market. On the dark side, the internal capital markets facilitate the tunneling of resources (Bertrand *et al.*, 2002). Other studies have highlighted that internal capital markets ease group-firm's financing constraints through inter-company loans (Gopalan *et al.*, 2007). Diversified business groups also use their internal funds to invest in new lines of business and lend funds to other member firms to grow their business. Chang and Hong (2000) find that group-affiliated Korean *chaebol* firms benefit from group membership through sharing intangible and financial resources with other affiliate firms. Stein (1997) suggests that diversified firms can direct investment flows toward more productive divisions and allocate resources efficiently in an internal capital market. Recently, Tan *et al.* (2018) find that the presence of internal capital markets improves the investment efficiency and R&D investment of private business group-firms in China.

The role of the internal capital market can be essential to ease financing constraints, especially during crises. Santioni *et al.* (2020) show that affiliation to a business group reduced the probability of bankruptcy of the affiliates compared to standalone firms during the European crisis. The capital is transferred from cash-rich group-firms to the cash-poor group-firms, which helps the weaker firms weather the crisis by reducing reliance on bank capital. Using a dataset on loans between group companies in Chile, Bubchuk *et al.* (2020) find that intra-group loans increased during the Global Financial Crisis of 2008. The study also finds that the central firm in the group picks the "winners," i.e. the high-growth firms, and eases their financial constraints during the crisis period. During crisis events, external financing gets constrained, and internal capital markets play a crucial role by enabling the sharing of cash resources amongst group-firms.

Wang *et al.* (2005), studying Japanese *keiretsu* affiliate firms, and Almeida *et al.* (2015) studying Korean *chaebols*, during the Asian Economic Crisis, suggest that group-affiliated firms survive crisis events better than standalone firms due to access to internal capital markets. The group-firms can allocate resources efficiently by transferring funds to affiliates with better growth opportunities from low-growth firms, aiding them toward mitigation of adverse effects of the crisis (Almeida *et al.*, 2015). On the other hand, Zhang and Huang (2013) find that firms affiliated to business groups in China experience lower valuations than a matched sample of standalone firms during the financial crisis, suggesting expropriation of minority shareholders by controlling shareholders undertaking more related party transactions.

This chapter examines the importance of internal capital markets during the COVID-19 pandemic in India — an emerging market economy dominated by the business group-firms. The Indian setting is noteworthy for several reasons. First, the firms in the emerging economies are gaining importance in the global economy due to their international expansion (Khanna and Palepu, 2006). The companies in emerging economies like India have invested cumulatively more than US$344 billion in global expansion over the period 2003–2012 (Kapur *et al.*, 2014). Among the emerging economies, India has the highest number of overseas greenfield investments. India is the second-largest emerging economy, and actions taken by Indian firms have consequences for firms in the developed economies that aim to establish alliances or compete against Indian firms (Kim *et al.*, 2004).

Second, business groups play a crucial role in the Indian private sector. The study by Chakrabarti *et al.* (2008) provides a glance at India's 500 most valuable companies that together account for over 90% of the market capitalization of the Bombay Stock Exchange (BSE), revealing that about 60% (in terms of count) and 65% (in terms of market capitalization) of the Indian firms are business group-affiliates. The dominance of business group-firms in India did not reduce with the development of the Indian economy and deepening of capital markets, as suggested by the institutional view of business groups. Jadhav and Reddy (2017) find that top business group-firms are able to tap into growth opportunities, and this can explain the economic power enjoyed by the large business group houses in the Indian corporate sector. However, the small group-firms are losing relevance with economic development. Further, Ahmed and Srinivasan (2019) find that the recent corporate governance reforms in India have improved the corporate transparency of business group-firms and reduced the principal–principal agency problem associated with such a structure. Another recent study by Popli and Ladkani (2020), using data on 440 mergers and acquisitions between 2002 and 2013, also find evidence in favor of the value-enabling role of business groups in India.

Third, the Indian Prime Minister Narendra Modi announced a strict 21-day nationwide lockdown from March 24, 2020, to April 14, 2020, to contain the virus, shortly after COVID-19 was declared as a pandemic by the World Health Organization on March 11, 2020. According to the COVID-19 Government Response Stringency Index maintained by Oxford COVID-19 Government Response Tracker, India had a score of 100 (strictest) from March 25, 2020, to April 18, 2020. At the same time, the index was in the range of 72–75 for the US and 91–92 for Italy. Such a stringent government response in India was associated with short-term supply-chain disruptions, and demand suddenly fell to near-zero levels. During the 21-day lockdown, banking operations were curtailed, and many companies faced immediate cash-flow issues for paying salaries and other short-term creditors. The presence of internal capital markets can potentially ease the short-term financing needs of the group-firms in India due to sudden, stringent lockdowns. The prevalence of group structure and sudden, stringent lockdowns in India provides an ideal setting to test the short-run effects of internal capital markets on shareholder returns.

The analysis has two specific implications. First, it provides evidence in favor of the short-run benefits of internal capital markets for group-firms during a health crisis. Second, the higher returns of group-firms indicate that group affiliation can mitigate information asymmetry among the investor and the owner, especially during uncertain times. This chapter provides insights regarding the short-term benefits associated with internal capital markets. Given the ongoing nature of the COVID-19 pandemic, we can only assess the short-term outcome of the firm proxied by stock returns.

We consider the BSE-listed firms in India, excluding the state-owned firms, and match the set of group-firms with the standalone firms using observable firm characteristics like size, age, and industry. We find that in our matched sample, the returns of the group-firms were superior to the returns of the standalone firms during the lockdown period in India. Further, in line with the winner-picking hypothesis, we find that the returns on average were higher for the group-firms with higher growth opportunities given by high Q-ratio vis-à-vis group-firms with low Q-ratio. Further, we find that, during the lockdown period, the higher returns were mostly driven by the smaller firms in the group who are more likely to be financially constrained compared to larger firms in the group. Finally, the higher shareholder returns were mainly driven by the firms affiliated with large business groups, which is in line with the findings that large groups have intricate risk-sharing arrangements through its internal capital markets (Chu, 2004).

The remainder of the chapter is organized as follows. Section 21.2 discusses the data and the methodology employed in the study, Section 21.3 presents the results, and Section 21.4 summarizes the findings and highlights the implications of the study.

21.2. Data and Methodology

We consider the 5,075 BSE-listed firms in India for the analysis. We obtain the data for the firms from the Prowess database maintained by the Centre for Monitoring Indian Economy (CMIE). Prowess provides the classification of firms into group-, private-, and government-owned firms. We exclude 119 companies that are owned by the state or the central government from our analysis. Out of the remaining 4,956 companies, 1,345 companies belong to business groups (around 27%), and the rest were standalone firms. We also exclude the firms for which the year of incorporation, national industrial classification (NIC codes), or the information on total assets were unavailable for the financial year ending March 31, 2019.

The extant literature suggests that business group-firms are different from standalone firms in various observed and unobserved covariates. We match the business group and standalone firms in our sample based on age-groups, size-deciles, and two-digit NIC codes using a propensity score matching technique to produce robust inference in our regression analysis. The treatment variable is the *group* dummy, which takes the value one if the firm belongs to a business group and zero for standalone in the matching regression. The treatment variable is regressed on the *age-group*, *size-decile* based on total assets and industry dummies given by the *NIC-code* (two-digit NIC code) using a logit model. The nearest neighbor matching without replacement method with a caliper of 0.01 is used for matching the group-firms with the standalone firms in the sample. Post-matching, we obtain a sample of 1,772 firms consisting of 886 group-firms and 886 standalone firms for analyzing the effect of business group affiliation on weekly stock returns during the COVID-19 pandemic.

The outcome variable considered to assess the short-term effect of group affiliation is the daily stock returns (*return*) of the matched group and the standalone companies during January 1, 2020, to September 30, 2020, i.e. 187 trading days. The adjusted closing prices for the companies were obtained for the trading days for calculating the daily return. In our regression specification, we control for the market return given by the daily return of Sensex, which is a value-weighted index consisting of the top 30 companies in India. We define three *pandemic* dummies — *lockdown, extended lockdown,* and *COVID* to assess how the pandemic affected the returns of the companies. The timeline below gives the progression of the coronavirus pandemic in India since the beginning of 2020:

The Indian Prime Minister Narendra Modi addressed the nation on March 19, 2020, and appealed for a 12-hour voluntary "janata curfew" (people curfew). This was followed by a strict nationwide lockdown from March 24, 2020, to April 14, 2020, to curb the spread of the virus. During this 21-day period, economic activity and mobility, and all non-essential activities, had come to a virtual standstill. The *lockdown* dummy takes the value one from March 24, 2020, to April 14, 2020, corresponding to the 21-day nationwide lockdown period. The lockdown was further extended to May 2, 2020, with lesser restrictions in the country. Our *extended lockdown* dummy takes the value one from March 24, 2020, till May 2, 2020, and zero otherwise. The *COVID* dummy takes the value one from March 24, 2020, to September 30, 2020, i.e. till the end of the study period. There are 231,497 firm-day observations in our study.

The equation below gives the basic model specification:

$$\begin{aligned} return_{it} &= \beta_0 + \beta_1 Sensex_t + \beta_2 Group_i + \beta_3 Group_i * pandemic_t \\ &\quad + \beta_4 pandemic_t + \beta_5 Industry_i + \beta_6 Day_t + \varepsilon_{it}, \qquad (21.1) \end{aligned}$$

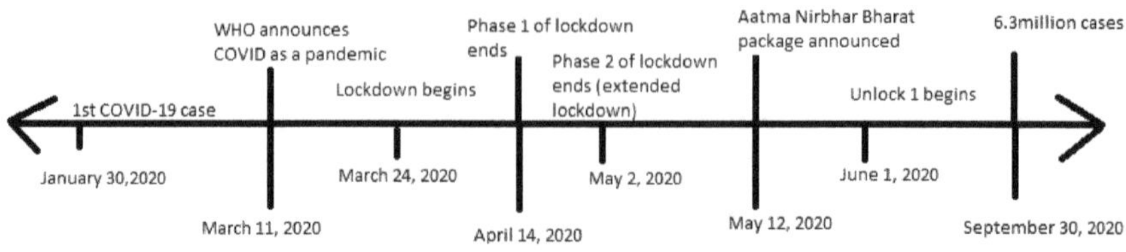

Figure 21.1. COVID-19 pandemic and various government interventions between January to September, 2020.

Sources: 1. https://indianexpress.com/article/india/coronavirus-covid-19-pandemic-india-timeline-6596832/.
2. https://www.who.int/news/item/27-04-2020-who-timeline---covid-19.

where $return_{it}$ is the return of company i on day t and $Sensex_t$ is the market return on the same day. The $Group_i$ is a dummy variable that takes the value one for group-firms and zero for matched standalone firms. The variable $Group_i * pandemic_t$ takes the value one for group-firms during the pandemic and zero otherwise. The variable $pandemic_t$ captures the three pandemic dummies *lockdown, extended lockdown,* and *COVID* and are used separately in the regression model. The coefficient β_3 gives the effect of group affiliation on returns during the COVID-19 crisis. A significant β_3 would suggest during the pandemic, returns for the shareholders of the group and standalone firms were different. Further, if $\beta_3 > 0$, it will suggest that shareholders benefited by investing group-firms during the crisis period, and a negative coefficient will suggest that the shareholder's return was lower for the group-firms during the pandemic vis-à-vis standalone firms. We control for industry effects using the two-digit NIC codes and also control for any news affecting the returns of the securities on a given day by introducing trading day fixed-effects.

21.3. Findings

Table 21.1 presents the mean returns for the group and standalone firms. We do not find any statistical difference in mean returns of a matched set of group and standalone firms for the entire period (column 1). Furthermore, the returns also do not differ between the group and standalone firms during the pre–COVID-19 period, suggesting that stock returns are unrelated to group affiliation in regular times. On the other hand, during the nationwide lockdown period

Table 21.1. Mean daily returns of the group and standalone firms during January–September, 2020.

All figures in %	**(1)**	**(2)**	**(3)**	**(4)**	**(5)**
	Overall Jan 1– Sep 30	**Pre–COVID-19 Jan 1– March 19**	**Lockdown period March 24– April 14**	**Extended lock-down March 24– May 2**	**COVID-19 March 24– Sep 30**
Standalone	0.063	−0.707	1.085	0.507	0.360
Group	0.082	−0.686	1.339***	0.634**	0.382
Observations	2,31,497	64,728	13,852	30,534	1,66,769

Note: $^{***}p < 0.01$, $^{**}p < 0.05$.

and the extended lockdown period, we find that group-firms' returns are superior to the matched set of standalone firms (columns 3 and 4). Interestingly the difference between the returns of the group and standalone firms reduced during the extended lockdown period. If we consider the entire COVID period, we do not find any difference in the returns of the group and standalone firms. This can be attributed to the fact that economic activity slowly picked up, and mobility restrictions were also eased in the country from May 2020. On May 12, 2020, the PM launched the "Aatma Nirbhar Bharat" scheme, a comprehensive economic package worth INR 200 billion (around 10% of GDP) to support the revival of economic and business activities in the nation during the pandemic (Press Bureau 2020 of India). The univariate results indicate the possibility that group-firms may perform better at the height of nationwide lockdown with severe mobility restrictions.

We explore this possibility further in a regression framework. Column 1 of Table 21.2 presents the results obtained from regressing daily returns[1] on Sensex returns and the *Group* dummy. We find that average returns of group-firms are not statistically different from that of standalone firms if we consider the entire 187-day period similar to the univariate results above. Column 2 gives the

[1]We checked for the stationarity of the return series using Augmented Dickey–Fuller test. The stock returns and Sensex returns were found to be stationary.

Table 21.2. Daily returns and effect of group affiliation.

	(1)	(2)	(3)	(4)	(5)	(6)
	Overall Jan 1– Sep 30	**Pre– COVID-19 Jan 1– March 19**	**Lockdown period March 24– April 14**	**Extended lockdown March 24– May 2**	**COVID-19 March 24– Sep 30**	**Non-extended lock-down period**
Group	***0.0002***	***0.0000***	***0.0031******	***0.0015******	***0.0003***	***0.0000***
	(0.0002)	***(0.0003)***	***(0.0009)***	***(0.0006)***	***(0.0002)***	***(0.0002)***
Sensex	0.4958***	0.6273***	0.2244***	0.3971***	0.4187***	0.5840***
	(0.0054)	(0.0113)	(0.0096)	(0.0083)	(0.0062)	(0.0073)
Constant	0.0059**	0.0019	0.0003	−0.0018	0.0080**	0.0074***
	(0.0026)	(0.0040)	(0.0126)	(0.0086)	(0.0032)	(0.0026)
Industry FE	Y	Y	Y	Y	Y	Y
Observations	231,497	64,728	13,852	30,534	166,769	200,963
R-squared	0.0801	0.1086	0.0588	0.1261	0.0596	0.0705

Note: The table presents the results obtained from regressing daily returns of the firms on group dummy and Sensex returns along with two-digit NIC codes for the matched group and standalone firms. Robust standard errors are reported in parenthesis. $^{***}p < 0.01$, $^{**}p < 0.05$.

pre–COVID-19 period's effect, i.e. the output obtained from regressing weekly returns between January 1 and March 20, 2020. The result of the pre–COVID-19 period is similar to that of the entire period. However, column 3 suggests that the returns for group-firms were, on average, 0.003% higher than the returns of similar standalone firms during the 21-day nationwide lockdown period. The group and standalone firms are comparable based on observable firm characteristics like age, size, and industry; hence, a plausible reason for the higher return for group-firms could be the access to internal capital markets or the reputation of the group-firms. Column 4 presents the result for the extended lockdown period, and we again find that the daily returns of group-firms were 0.001% greater than those of similar standalone firms. However, if we consider the entire COVID period since March 24, 2020 (column 5) or the period without the extended lockdown (column 6), we do not find any difference in returns on account of the firm's business group affiliation.

Next, we estimate Equation (21.1) specified in Section 21.2, and the results are presented in Table 21.3. If the higher returns for group-firms are due to internal capital markets, then the marginal benefit should be highest at the peak of a crisis. The 21-day lockdown period brought economic activities to a sudden halt and led to widespread supply-chain disruption. Even though the lockdown did not coincide with the pandemic's peak, it did represent the sudden sharp fall in economic activity. We find that, during the lockdown, the average returns of group-firms were 0.0025% greater than those of matched standalone firms (column 1), and this is significant at a 1% level of significance. The average daily returns were also significantly higher for group-firms during the extended lockdown period (column 2). The differences in returns of the group and standalone firms were higher during the 21-day nationwide lockdown period than during the extended lockdown period considered for this analysis, which is in line with our expectations. However, if we consider the COVID-19 pandemic period between March and September, we do not find any statistical difference in returns of the group and standalone firms (column 3). The preliminary results indicate that the internal capital market can be a potential reason that improves access to working capital, especially during the time period when the country's economic activity was negligible. With the reopening of the economy starting May 2020, the financial stress of the firms gradually reduced,

Table 21.3. Effect of group affiliation on returns during the COVID-19 pandemic.

	(1)	(2)	(3)	(4)	(5)	(6)
	Lockdown	**Extended lockdown**	**Pandemic**	**Lockdown**	**Extended lockdown**	**Pandemic**
*Group*Lockdown*	***0.0025******			***0.0024******		
	(0.0009)			*(0.0009)*		
*Group*Extended lockdown*		***0.0013*****			***0.0012*****	
		(0.0006)			*(0.0006)*	
*Group*COVID*			***0.0001***			***0.0002***
			(0.0004)			*(0.0004)*
Lockdown	0.0035***			0.0036***		
	(0.0007)			(0.0008)		
Extended lockdown		0.0007*			−0.0002	
		(0.0004)			(0.0006)	
COVID			0.0058***			0.0065***
			(0.0003)			(0.0006)
Group	0.0001	0.0001	0.0001	0.0001	0.0001	0.0002
	(0.0002)	(0.0002)	(0.0003)	(0.0002)	(0.0002)	(0.0003)
Sensex	0.4887***	0.4933***	0.4747***	0.3094***	0.3140***	0.3013***
	(0.0054)	(0.0054)	(0.0054)	(0.0078)	(0.0079)	(0.0075)
Constant	0.0057**	0.0058**	0.0017	0.0079***	0.0080***	0.0080***
	(0.0026)	(0.0026)	(0.0026)	(0.0026)	(0.0026)	(0.0026)
Industry FE	Y	Y	Y	Y	Y	Y
Day FE	N	N	N	Y	Y	Y
Observations	231,497	231,497	231,497	231,497	231,497	231,497
R-squared	0.0808	0.0802	0.0839	0.1299	0.1297	0.1305

Note: The table provides the results of regressing daily returns of firms on group and pandemic dummy interaction after controlling for group dummy, pandemic dummy, Sensex return, industry, and day effects. Robust standard errors are reported in parenthesis. $^{***}p < 0.01$, $^{**}p < 0.05$, $^{*}p < 0.1$.

and other sources of finance such as banking capital became available to the firms; hence, the difference in returns due to affiliation to a business group also vanished. As mentioned earlier, the Aatma Nirbhar Bharat package specifically tried to address the financial distress of firms in India by reducing the cost of debt capital along with debt moratorium provisions. Columns 4–6 reports the coefficients after controlling for trading day fixed-effects, and the results remain qualitatively similar. The results are in line with the findings of Santioni *et al.* (2020) and Wang *et al.* (2005) that group affiliation matters during a crisis. This chapter also supports other findings of studies that highlight the value-enabling role of business groups in India post-acquisition (Popli and Ladkani, 2020). However, our findings stand in contrast to the observations in China's context, wherein business group-affiliated firms had lower valuation than a matched sample of standalone firms during the financial crisis (Zhang and Huang, 2013).

21.3.1. *Heterogeneous effects*

We provide further evidence to support our hypothesis that the higher returns of group-firms can be primarily attributed to the existence of internal capital markets. The winner-picking hypothesis suggests that group companies having high growth opportunities benefit the most through the internal capital market. The Q-ratio is considered a proxy for the firm's growth opportunities in the corporate finance literature. Q-ratio greater than one suggests that the firm's market value is greater than its replacement cost; on the other hand, a value of Q-ratio below unity indicates that the firm is a low-growth firm and the replacement cost is more than the market value of the firm. We compute the Q-ratio of all the firms and analyze the results separately for the sub-sample of firms with a Q-ratio greater than one and those with a Q-ratio of one and below. We observe that group-firms with higher growth opportunities generated higher returns during the nationwide lockdown and the extended lockdown period (columns 1 and 2, Table 21.4). In contrast, low-growth group-firms did not generate higher returns during the extended lockdown period compared to standalone firms (column 5). The coefficient of interaction between the group and *COVID* dummy is insignificant for both high- and low-growth firms. This result is in line with the

Table 21.4. Effect of group affiliation on returns during the COVID-19 pandemic — high- and low-growth firms.

	(1)	(2)	(3)	(4)	(5)	(6)
	High-growth firms			Low-growth firms		
	Lockdown	Extended lockdown	Pandemic	Lockdown	Extended lockdown	Pandemic
*Group*Lockdown*	***0.0025****			***0.0022****		
	(0.0013)			***(0.0011)***		
*Group*Extended lockdown*		***0.0018*****			***0.0008***	
		(0.0009)			***(0.0008)***	
*Group*COVID*			***0.0005***			***−0.0004***
			(0.0005)			***(0.0006)***
Lockdown	0.0062***			0.0033***		
	(0.0017)			(0.0010)		
Extended lockdown		0.0001			0.0014**	
		(0.0006)			(0.0006)	
COVID			0.0042***			0.0076***
			(0.0003)			(0.0004)
Group	−0.0002	−0.0002	−0.0004	0.0005*	0.0005*	0.0009*
	(0.0002)	(0.0002)	(0.0004)	(0.0003)	(0.0003)	(0.0006)
Sensex	0.3647***	0.6139***	0.5986***	0.2734***	0.4115***	0.3896***
	(0.0235)	(0.0086)	(0.0085)	(0.0074)	(0.0068)	(0.0069)
Constant	0.0081**	0.0087**	0.0041	0.0075**	0.0037	−0.0003
	(0.0041)	(0.0041)	(0.0041)	(0.0034)	(0.0033)	(0.0033)
Industry FE	Y	Y	Y	Y	Y	Y
Day FE	Y	Y	Y	Y	Y	Y
Observations	111,765	111,765	111,765	119,732	119,732	119,732
R-squared	0.1660	0.1156	0.1180	0.1100	0.0592	0.0642

Note: The table provides the results of regressing daily returns of firms on group and pandemic dummy interaction after controlling for group dummy, pandemic dummy, Sensex return, industry, and day effects separately for the sub-sample of firms with Q-ratio greater than one (High growth) and Q-ratio less than equal to one (Low growth). Robust standard errors are reported in parenthesis. $^{***}p < 0.01$, $^{**}p < 0.05$, $^{*}p < 0.1$.

findings of Almeida *et al.* (2015), wherein they find that internal transfers helped high-growth Korean group-firms during the Asian Financial Crisis.

Further, the literature suggests that internal capital markets are crucial for financially constrained group-firms. The larger firms are, in general, less financially constrained than smaller firms (Han *et al.*, 2015). To provide additional evidence in favor of the importance of internal capital markets, we separately consider the sub-samples of matched small group and standalone firms and matched large group and standalone firms. In our analysis, a firm is considered *small* if its total assets at the end of the financial year 2019 were below the mean and *large* otherwise. Results in Table 21.5 indicate that the average returns for smaller group-firms were higher than smaller standalone firms during the lockdown and extended lockdown periods (columns 1 and 2). However, for the *large* group-firms, returns were not different from the matched standalone counterpart during the lockdown period or the extended lockdown (columns 4 and 5). This suggests that smaller group-firms that are likely to be financially constrained are likely to outperform their standalone counterpart during the crisis period; however, such return differential owing to group affiliation does not exist for large firms. Again similar to our main results, we do not find any return premium for group affiliation during the entire pandemic period for either *small* or *large* firms sub-samples (columns 3 and 6).

Almeida *et al.* (2011) found that, in Korean *chaebols,* the family owner of the group would have higher direct ownership in high net present value (NPV) firms, and low-NPV firms would be placed at the lower level of the pyramid structure. The efficiency argument of internal capital markets suggests that the funds during a severe crisis should be diverted toward the group affiliates with the potential to use the capital optimally, i.e. toward high-NPV firms. If the higher return for the group-firms during the lockdown is due to the presence of internal capital markets, then one can argue that the effect should be driven by the set of group-firms with a high promoter's ownership (high-NPV firms). Next, we analyze whether there is a heterogeneous effect based on the promoter's ownership. We separately analyze the relation for the sub-samples of firms with a high promoter's ownership and those with less than average promoter's ownership. Table 21.6 present the results of this sub-sample

Table 21.5. Effect of group affiliation on returns during the COVID-19 pandemic — small and large firms.

	(1)	(2)	(4)	(5)	(6)	(8)
	Small firms			Large firms		
	Lockdown	Extended lockdown	Pandemic	Lockdown	Extended lockdown	Pandemic
*Group*Lockdown*	***0.0030*****			***0.0010***		
	(0.0009)			***(0.0028)***		
*Group*Extended lockdown*		***0.0016*****			***−0.0004***	
		(0.0004)			***(0.0027)***	
*Group*COVID*			***0.0002***			***0.0003***
			(0.0004)			***(0.0014)***
Lockdown	0.0038***			−0.0041*		
	(0.0010)			(0.0022)		
Extended lockdown		−0.0010			−0.0039	
		(0.0006)			(0.0025)	
COVID			0.0079***			0.0019*
			(0.0008)			(0.0012)
Group	−0.0000	−0.0002	0.0001	−0.0004	−0.0002	−0.0005
	(0.0002)	(0.0002)	(0.0003)	(0.0007)	(0.0006)	(0.0011)
Sensex	0.3557***	0.3630***	0.3477***	0.0915***	0.0910***	0.0866***
	(0.0087)	(0.0087)	(0.0088)	(0.0109)	(0.0109)	(0.0107)
Constant	0.0092***	0.0094***	0.0093***	0.0001	0.0001	−0.0002
	(0.0026)	(0.0026)	(0.0026)	(0.0026)	(0.0026)	(0.0026)
Industry FE	Y	Y	Y	Y	Y	Y
Day FE	Y	Y	Y	Y	Y	Y
Observations	209,790	209,790	209,790	21,707	21,707	21,707
R-squared	0.1549	0.1547	0.1553	0.0216	0.0224	0.0215

Note: The table provides the results of regressing daily returns of firms on group and pandemic dummy interaction after controlling for group dummy, pandemic dummy, Sensex return, industry, and day effects separately for the sub-sample of small and large firms. Robust standard errors are reported in parenthesis. $^{***}p < 0.01$, $^{*}p < 0.1$.

Table 21.6. Effect of group affiliation on returns during the COVID-19 pandemic — high and low promoter's ownership.

	(1)	(3)	(4)	(5)	(7)	(8)
	High promoter's ownership			**Low promoter's ownership**		
	Lockdown	**Extended lockdown**	**Pandemic**	**Lockdown**	**Extended lockdown**	**Pandemic**
*Group*Lockdown*	***0.0023****			***0.0029*****		
	(0.0012)			***(0.0013)***		
*Group*Extended lockdown*		***0.0013*****			***0.0013****	
		(0.0005)			***(0.0007)***	
*Group*COVID*			***0.0006***			***0.0000***
			(0.0005)			***(0.0006)***
Lockdown	0.0047***			0.0022*		
	(0.0011)			(0.0012)		
Extended lockdown		−0.0013**			−0.0001	
		(0.0006)			(0.0005)	
COVID			0.0054***			0.0067***
			(0.0007)			(0.0004)
Group	0.0002	−0.0000	−0.0001	−0.0001	−0.0002	0.0001
	(0.0002)	(0.0002)	(0.0004)	(0.0003)	(0.0003)	(0.0006)
Sensex	0.3060***	0.3128***	0.3011***	0.3087***	0.4895***	0.4664***
	(0.0089)	(0.0089)	(0.0089)	(0.0145)	(0.0081)	(0.0082)
Constant	0.0040***	0.0041***	0.0040***	0.0080***	0.0061**	0.0013
	(0.0013)	(0.0013)	(0.0013)	(0.0027)	(0.0026)	(0.0026)
Industry FE	Y	Y	Y	Y	Y	Y
Day FE	Y	Y	Y	Y	Y	Y
Observations	126,334	126,334	126,334	100,215	100,215	100,215
R-squared	0.1406	0.1402	0.1408	0.1202	0.0726	0.0770

Note: The table provides the results of regressing daily returns of firms on group and pandemic dummy interaction after controlling for group dummy, pandemic dummy, Sensex return, industry, and day effects separately for the sub-sample of firms with high and low promoter's ownership. Robust standard errors are reported in parenthesis. $^{***}p < 0.01$, $^{**}p < 0.05$, $^{*}p < 0.1$.

analysis. We do not find evidence that the higher returns in group-firms during the lockdown and extended lockdown period were driven by the group-firms with higher promoter's ownership. The returns for group-firms were greater than standalone firms during the lockdown and extended lockdown for both the sub-samples, indicating a return premium associated with group affiliation during a severe crisis period, irrespective of the promoter's direct ownership in the group-firm.

Studies have also highlighted that group affiliation benefits accrue only when the firms are affiliated to large business groups (Chu, 2004). If a firm is affiliated with small or mid-sized business groups, the cost of affiliation could be higher than the associated benefits. On the other hand, affiliation to a large business group in emerging markets may help the firm to circumvent factor market inefficiencies. We consider the total assets at the group level as the proxy for group size in our analysis. We separately compare firms belonging to large business groups to large standalone firms and those belonging to small business groups to small standalone firms, and the results are presented in Table 21.7. We find that the higher return during the lockdown and extended lockdown period is mostly driven by firms affiliated with large business groups (columns 1 and 2). On the other hand, the returns of firms affiliated to smaller business groups were lower than their standalone counterparts. This finding highlights that mere group affiliation may not be beneficial for the shareholders; however, affiliation to a large business group could be value-enhancing during a severe crisis scenario.

Our findings suggest that business group-firms in India appear to be more resilient in the short run during the height of the economic crisis posed by the ongoing COVID-19 pandemic. The shareholders of the group-firms enjoyed higher returns during the 21-day nationwide lockdown period and during the extended lockdown period vis-à-vis similar standalone firms. This chapter provides evidence in favor of the advantages of group affiliation in the context of an emerging market economy like India, especially during crisis scenarios. Our study also suggests that such benefits may not be apparent once the economic conditions become more conducive for businesses. Further, external policy interventions (Aatma Nirbhar Bharat) can create a level playing field between the group and standalone firms by easing the firm's capital constraints.

Table 21.7. Effect of group affiliation on returns during the COVID-19 pandemic — Business group size.

	(1)	(2)	(3)	(4)	(5)	(6)
	Large business group and standalone firms			**Small business group and standalone firms**		
	Lockdown	**Extended lockdown**	**Pandemic**	**Lockdown**	**Extended lockdown**	**Pandemic**
*Group*Lockdown*	***0.0111*** ***			***−0.0049*** *		
	(0.0039)			***(0.0026)***		
*Group*Extended lockdown*		***0.0057*** **			***−0.0055*** ***	
		(0.0024)			***(0.0016)***	
*Group*COVID*			***0.0037*** **			***−0.0017*** *
			(0.0016)			***(0.0010)***
Lockdown	−0.0048			0.0043^{***}		
	(0.0040)			(0.0009)		
Extended lockdown		−0.0040			0.0013^{***}	
		(0.0025)			(0.0004)	
COVID			0.0045^{**}			0.0060^{***}
			(0.0018)			(0.0007)
Group	0.0012^{*}	0.0011	−0.0012	0.0015^{***}	0.0012^{**}	0.0017^{**}
	(0.0007)	(0.0007)	(0.0015)	(0.0005)	(0.0005)	(0.0008)
Sensex	0.3348^{***}	0.3396^{***}	0.3268^{***}	0.2889^{***}	0.4450^{***}	0.2810^{***}
	(0.0113)	(0.0115)	(0.0113)	(0.0102)	(0.0074)	(0.0096)
Constant	0.0091^{***}	0.0093^{***}	0.0115^{***}	0.0017	0.0014^{***}	0.0015
	(0.0029)	(0.0029)	(0.0031)	(0.0012)	(0.0005)	(0.0012)
Industry FE	Y	Y	Y	Y	Y	Y
Day FE	Y	Y	Y	Y	Y	Y
Observations	110,868	110,868	110,868	120,629	120,629	120,629
R-squared	0.1464	0.1461	0.1469	0.1172	0.0695	0.1178

Note: The table provides the results of regressing daily returns of firms on group and pandemic dummy interaction after controlling for group dummy, pandemic dummy, Sensex return, industry, and day effects separately for the sub-sample of large group and standalone firms and smaller group and standalone firms. Robust standard errors are reported in parenthesis. $^{***}p < 0.01$, $^{**}p < 0.05$, $^{*}p < 0.1$.

21.4. Discussion and Conclusion

The presence of business groups is ubiquitous in emerging market economies like India. The business groups have survived many crises in the last few decades, including the more recent Global Financial Crisis. The business group structure helps the affiliates to function in an environment characterized by less than fully developed capital markets, weak legal enforcement, and inefficient factor markets due to the presence of internal markets. In this chapter, we examine whether group-firms have outperformed the standalone firms in India during the ongoing COVID-19 pandemic. Using a set of matched listed standalone and group-firms, we find that the average weekly returns of group-firms were higher during the 21-day nationwide lockdown and the extended lockdown period than their standalone counterparts. On the other hand, the returns do not differ during the pre-pandemic period and the overall pandemic period considered in this study.

The main results suggest that returns to group affiliation increase during a severe crisis due to risk-sharing arrangements. We attribute the higher short-run performance to the presence of internal capital markets. Among the group-firms, the returns are higher for the high-growth firms in line with the winner-picking hypothesis. We also find that smaller business group-firms generated higher returns than the smaller standalone firms in the group, highlighting the possibility that the presence of internal capital markets eases the financing constraints of small group-firms in India. Finally, the returns during the lockdown period were higher for firms affiliated with large business groups, suggesting that mere group affiliation may not be value-enhancing for the shareholders. This reiterates that the returns to group affiliation vary with the size of the business group.

The study has two specific limitations. First, in the absence of transaction-level data, we are unable to directly test whether the higher returns of group-firms can be attributed to the presence of internal capital markets. However, our results suggest that the higher returns for the group-firms are likely due to the existence of internal capital markets. Further, research can explore the direct relation using group-level transaction data. Second, the present analysis is indicative of the resilience of group-firms in India during the height of the economic crisis during the ongoing COVID-19 pandemic. Given that the pandemic in India is still far from over drawing definite conclusions remains difficult. Future studies can shed further light on whether group-firms' performance was superior relative to the standalone firms using accounting data.

The findings provide insights regarding the advantages of group affiliation in an emerging market economy, especially during uncertain times. The study highlights that, even though group-firms face several corporate governance challenges, the group structure has several benefits, and the returns to group affiliation are higher in the very short run. The access to internal capital markets can reduce the reliance of group-firms on external bank capital during periods with limited institutional functioning, such as a nationwide lockdown. Our results suggest that the investors do not discount shares of the group-firms due to their lack of transparency. Instead, we find that the group-firms generated higher returns during a severe crisis than the standalone firms in India. There is a need to integrate institutional and agency views to understand the role of business groups in emerging markets. Finally, this chapter also suggests that active policy intervention in the form of access to cheap capital can act as a substitute for internal capital markets and create a level playing field for the group and standalone firms in financial markets.

References

Ahmed, M. and Srinivasan, M.K. (2019). Governance reforms and corporate transparency in business groups: Evidence from India, *Academy of Management Proceedings*, 1. https://journals.aom.org/doi/abs/10.5465/AMBPP.2019.16418abstract.

Almeida, H., Park, S.Y., Subrahmanyam, M.G. and Wolfenzon, D. (2011). The structure and formation of business groups: Evidence from Korean Chaebols. *Journal of Financial Economics*, **99**, 447–475.

Almeida, H., Kim, C.S. and Kim, H.B. (2015). Internal capital markets in business groups: Evidence from the Asian financial crisis. *The Journal of Finance*, **70**, 2539–2586.

Bertrand, M., Mehta, P. and Mullainathan, S. (2002). Ferreting out tunneling: An application to Indian business groups. *The Quarterly Journal of Economics*, **117**, 121–148.

Bubchuk, D., Larrain, B., Prem, M. and Infante, F.U. (2020). How do internal capital markets work? Evidence from the great recession. *Review of Finance*, **24**, 847–889.

Chakrabarti, R., Megginson, W. and Yadav, P. (2008). Corporate governance in India. *Journal of Applied Corporate Finance*, **20**, 59–72.

Chang, S. and Hong, J. (2000). Economic performance of group-affiliated companies in Korea: Intragroup resource sharing and internal business transactions. *The Academy of Management Journal*, **43**, 429–448.

Claessens, S. and Fan, J.P. (2002). Corporate governance in Asia: A survey. *International Review of Finance*, **3**, 71–103.

Chu, W. (2004). Are group-affiliated firms really more profitable than non-affiliated? *Small Business Economics*, **22**, 391–405.

Dharwadkar, B., George, G. and Brandes, P. (2000). Privatisation in emerging economics: An agency theory perspective. *Academy of Management Review*, **25**, 650–669.

Gopalan, R., Nanda, V. and Seru, A. (2007). Affiliated firms and financial support: Evidence from Indian business groups. *Journal of Financial Economics*, **86**, 759–795.

Granovetter, M. (1995). Coase revisited: Business groups in the modern economy. *Industrial and Corporate Change*, **4**, 93–130.

Han, L., Zhang, S. and Greene, F.J. (2015). Bank market concentration, relationship banking, and small business liquidity. *International Small Business Journal*, **35**, 365–384.

Jadhav, A.M. and Reddy, V.N. (2017). Indian business groups and their dominance in the Indian economy. *Economic and Political Weekly*, **52**, 85–92.

Kapur, M., Allen, A. and Gupta, A. (2014). Indian paths to global growth: Developing successful business strategies for international expansion. *Go Global India Report.* Accenture. Retrieved from https://www.accenture.com/_acnmedia/accenture/conversion-assets/dotcom/documents/global/pdf/dualpub_23/accenture-indian-paths-to-global-growth.pdf (Accessed August 29, 2020).

Khanna, T. and Palepu, K. (1997). Why focused strategies may be wrong for emerging markets. *Harvard Business Review*, **75**, 41–51.

Khanna, T. and Palepu, K. (2000). Emerging market business groups, foreign investors, and corporate governance. In *Concentrated Corporate Ownership*, Morck, R. (ed.) National Bureau of Economic Research Conference Report (University of Chicago Press, 1427 E. 60th Street Chicago, IL 60637 USA), pp. 265–294.

Khanna, T. and Palepu, K. (2006). Emerging giants: Building world-class companies in developing countries. *Harvard Business Review*, **84**, 60–69.

Khanna, T. and Yafeh, Y. (2007). Business groups in emerging markets: Paragons or parasites? *Journal of Economic Literature*, **45**, 331–372.

Kim, D., Kandemir, D. and Cavusgil, T. (2004). The role of family conglomerates in emerging markets: What Western companies should know? *Thunderbird International Business Review*, **46**, 13–38.

La Porta, R., Silanes, F. Lopez-de, and Shleifer, A. (1998). Law and finance. *Journal of Political Economy*, **106**, 1113–1155.

La Porta, R., Silanes, F. Lopez-de, and Shleifer, A. (1999). Corporate ownership around the world. *Journal of Finance*, **54**, 471–517.

Leff, N. (1978). Industrial organization and entrepreneurship in the developing countries: The economic groups. *Economic Development and Cultural Change*, **26**, 661–675.

Oxford COVID-19 Government Response Tracker. Retrieved from https://www.bsg.ox.ac.uk/research/research-projects/coronavirus-government-response-tracker (Accessed August 29, 2020).

Popli, M. and Ladkani, R.M. (2020). Value constraining or value enabling? The impact of business group affiliation on post-acquisition performance by emerging market firms. *Management and Organization Review*, **16**, 261–291.

Press Bureau of India. Retrieved from https://pib.gov.in/PressReleasePage.aspx?PRID=1638112 (Accessed August 29, 2020).

Ramachandran, J., Manikandan, K.S. and Pant. A. (2013). Why conglomerates thrive (outside the US). *Harvard Business Review*, December Issue.

Santioni, R., Schiantarelli, F. and Strahan, P.E. (2020). Internal capital markets in times of crisis: The benefit of group affiliation. *Review of Finance*, **24**, 773–811.

Stein, J. (1997). Internal capital markets and the competition for corporate resources. *Journal of Finance*, **52**, 111–134.

Tan, W., Yu, S. and Ma, Z. (2018). The impact of business groups on investment efficiency: Does capital allocation matter? *Emerging Markets Finance and Trade*, **54**, 3539–3551.

Wang, H-M., Huang, H. and Bansal, P. (2005). What determined success during the Asian economic crisis? —The Importance of experiential knowledge and group affiliation. *Asia Pacific Journal of Management*, **22**, 89–106.

World Health Organization (2020). Retrieved from https://www.who.int/news-room/detail/27-04-2020-who-timeline---covid-19 (Accessed August 29, 2020).

Zhang, T. and Huang, J. (2013). The value of group affiliation: Evidence from the 2008 financial crisis. *International Journal of Managerial Finance*, **9**, 332–350.

PART V

Perspective Transformations in the Era of COVID-19

https://doi.org/10.1142/9781800610781_0022

Chapter 22

Two Questions on the Banking Sector After the Pandemic Hit

Magdalena Grothe[*,‡] **and Antonio Sánchez Serrano**[†,§]

[*]*European Central Bank, Sonnenmannstrasse 22, 60314 Frankfurt am Main, Germany*

[†]*European Systemic Risk Board, Sonnenmannstrasse 22, 60314 Frankfurt am Main, Germany*

[‡]*magdalena.grothe@ecb.europa.eu*

[§]*antonio.sanchez@ecb.europa.eu*

Abstract

The pre-pandemic state of the EU banking system was determined by several intertwined elements related to structural, economic, and policy factors. In view of these characteristics, this chapter discusses the potential impact of the pandemic shock on the EU banking system, focusing on the risks arising from the weakening performance of non-financial corporations and the related decline in bank asset quality. It reviews two key concerns related to the banking sector that the COVID-19 health crisis has brought to the forefront: the outlook for non-performing loans and bank profitability. Considering the financial soundness of the different sub-sectors within non-financial corporations along with the size of the COVID-19–related shock, we find that retail and wholesale trade sectors could face most challenges to absorb the shock. These challenges could further translate into an increase in non-performing loans on banks' balance sheets, higher impairments, and drag on bank profitability.

22.1. Introduction

There is never a suitable time for a crisis, but the COVID-19 pandemic arrived in a particular unfortunate moment for the European banking system, as it was still healing the wounds caused by the Global Financial Crisis and the sovereign debt crisis. The pre-pandemic state of the EU banking system was determined by several intertwined elements, related to structural, economic, and policy factors. In recent years, the European banking system has shown growing capitalization and increasing loan intermediation, underpinned by favourable funding conditions. At the same time, the profitability performance of many EU banks has been relatively weak, which has also been reflected in the equity pricing of the sector. The key drivers behind the underperformance of the EU banking system were, to different degrees across banks, the burden of non-performing loans still in their balance sheets, low margins related to the macroeconomic environment of low growth and low-interest rates, and cost inefficiencies. And then, COVID-19 arrived. The immediate impact on the banking sector of financial market tensions and the decline in the economic activity caused by the pandemic was alleviated by a strong, coordinated, and unprecedented policy support from fiscal, monetary, and prudential authorities. When the shock of the spreading pandemic spurred market volatility, the banking sector was among the most affected. The market effects of the pandemic shock were heterogeneous across banks, mainly reflecting their pre-pandemic characteristics (see, e.g. Aldasoro *et al.*, 2020). Policymakers answered with a strong response to alleviate economic and funding shocks as well as provide additional space for bank intermediation (see, e.g. Drehmann *et al.*, 2020; European Central Bank, 2020a; Hutchinson and Mee, 2020; International Monetary Fund, 2020a). Policy measures eased the adverse impact on banks, but the pockets of weakness and vulnerabilities are still present (see Demirgüç-Kunt *et al.*, 2020; European Central Bank, 2020c; International Monetary Fund, 2020b).

This chapter reviews the potential impact of the pandemic shock on the European banking system, focusing on the risks arising from increasing private and public sector indebtedness and interlinkages with banks' balance sheets. Significant academic and regulatory resources have been devoted to understanding the nature of the shock generated by the COVID-19 pandemic and its impact on the real economy and the financial system. Carletti *et al.* (2020) discuss the impact of the COVID-19 on the banking system, with a particular focus on the challenges to the main business model of banks and the increasing digitalization of our society. In a related approach, this chapter aims to contribute to the existing literature on the impact of the COVID-19 pandemic in the banking system by discussing key issues affecting the banking sector that are directly triggered by the COVID-19 health crisis, such as determining the outlook for non-performing loans and bank profitability and considering the legacy of the global financial and the sovereign debt crises.

We find that the impact of the COVID-19 pandemic on the financial position of non-financial corporations is expected to be larger for the sectors of retail and wholesale trade, with other sectors also suffering important drops in revenues. Considering the financial soundness of the different sub-sectors within non-financial corporations in terms of existing equity, we find that a non-immaterial number of non-financial corporations may be left with negative equity, possibly leading to insolvency. As bank loans are the main source of funding for European corporations, we see an important transmission channel of this stress to the balance sheets of European banks, first through an increase in impairments. The subsequent deterioration of European banks' profits, already starting from very low profitability levels in the recent pre–COVID-19 years, could bring their overall solvency position into question. The response of banks to these challenges is going to determine how banking would function in the post–COVID-19 environment as the provider of credit to the real economy.

The chapter is structured as follows. Section 22.2 includes a brief discussion of the state of the EU banking system, in particular focusing on the legacies of the global financial and the sovereign debt crises. Section 22.3 addresses the important questions about the outlook for profitability and non-performing loans of the EU banking sector following the COVID-19 pandemic. Section 22.4 concludes.

22.2. The Legacy of the Global Financial and the Sovereign Debt Crises

Large and persistent stocks of non-performing loans — a legacy of the Global Financial Crisis — are one of the key issues characterising the

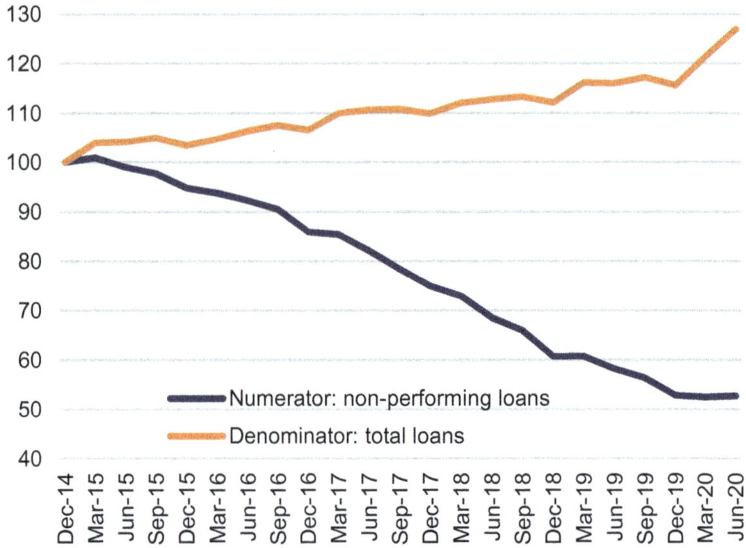

Figure 22.1. Ratio of non-performing loans and advances: Numerator and denominator trends (*index: Dec–14=100*).

Note: The chart shows the evolution of the numerator (non-performing loans) and of the denominator (total loans) of the ratio of non-performing loans as reported to the EBA Risk Dashboard, for a sample of around 190 banks.

Source: European Banking Authority (2020), panel 7.

EU banking sector, notwithstanding the improvement in asset quality observed over the recent years, at the aggregate EU level and for most EU countries (see European Banking Authority, 2016, 2019). The overall EU ratio of non-performing loans declined from 6.5% in December 2014 to 2.7% in December 2019 for significant banks. This decline is due to both the declining stock of non-performing loans and increasing overall loans (Figure 22.1, see also European Banking Authority (2019) for a more detailed discussion). The progress has been achieved in all EU countries (Figure 22.2, see also e.g. European Systemic Risk Board, 2019b). Still, the rate of non-performing loans is much higher in the EU than in other advanced economies. For example, the ratio of non-performing loans to total loans for all US banks was 0.85% in 2019.[1] At the country level, the stock of non-performing loans has been associated with a negative impact on

[1]Based on Federal Reserve Bank of St. Louis database FRED.

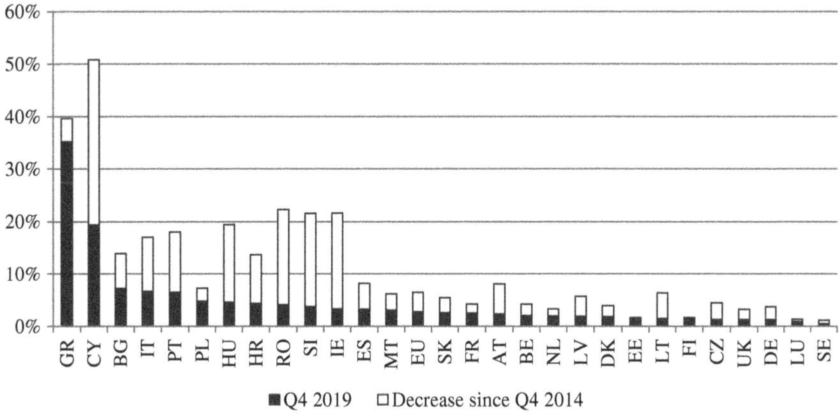

Figure 22.2. Ratio of non-performing loans and advances *(% of total gross loans and advances).*

Note: The chart shows the weighted average ratio of non-performing loans and advances to total gross loans and advances for banks in EU countries as at the fourth quarter of 2019 (blue bars). It also shows the decrease (blue rectangles) since the fourth quarter of 2014. Data for Slovenia and Malta refers to the fourth quarter of 2015 and for Estonia to the third quarter of 2016, due to data availability. The data are based on a sample of 134 banks for the fourth quarter of 2014 and 182 banks for the fourth quarter of 2019.

Source: European Banking Authority and authors' calculations.

GDP growth, productivity, and employment (Balgova *et al.*, 2018; Espinoza and Prasad, 2010; Klein, 2013; Nkusu, 2011).

While the quality of the loan portfolios has been improving across individual banks, some of them still have exceptionally high ratios of non-performing loans and a relatively slow pace of reduction of non-performing loans (Figure 22.3). Indeed, many banks in Europe have been operating with ratios of non-performing loans above 10% for several years. An overview of the publicly available bank-level information in Figure 22.3 shows that almost all European banks managed to reduce the ratios of non-performing loans between 2014 and 2018, although, at the same time, the challenges related to legacy assets still remain significant in some banks (mainly, because the reduction is too slow).

High levels of non-performing loans are a drag on the cost side of banks' profit and loss accounts. They prevent new lending opportunities (Fell *et al.*, 2018; Segura and Suarez, 2019), thus continually weakening bank profitability. The persistence of non-performing

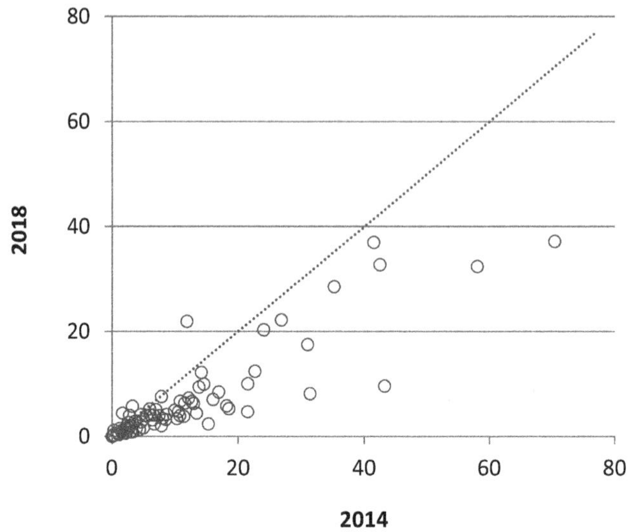

Figure 22.3. Progress of individual banks with the reduction of non-performing loans between 2014 and 2018 *(percentages).*

Note: The chart shows the ratios of non-performing loans of significant EU banks at the end of 2014 (x-axis) and at the end of 2018 (y-axis). The 45 degrees lines is represented to indicate which banks have reduced their ratios of non-performing loans between 2014 and 2018 (those below the line) and which ones have increased their ratios (those above the line).

Source: European Banking Authority transparency exercises and SNL.

loans in the balance sheet of European banks can be explained by several factors (Suarez and Sánchez Serrano, 2018), some of which may be unintended. Consequently, fostering the resolution of legacy assets at the level of individual banks, as advocated in recent years by European authorities (Council of the EU, 2017; European Systemic Risk Board, 2017; European Systemic Risk Board, 2019b), is important to have a sound banking sector that can provide financial services to the real economy. That can also improve confidence in banking systems. Following coordinated policy efforts (European Central Bank Banking Supervision, 2018a,b, 2019), progress in the reduction of non-performing loans has been visible in recent years (see Enria, 2019; European Banking Authority, 2019). More recently, since mid-2018, the distribution of the ratios of non-performing loans across significant institutions has been less skewed, with the reduction in the tail of very high ratios of non-performing loans (Figure 22.4).

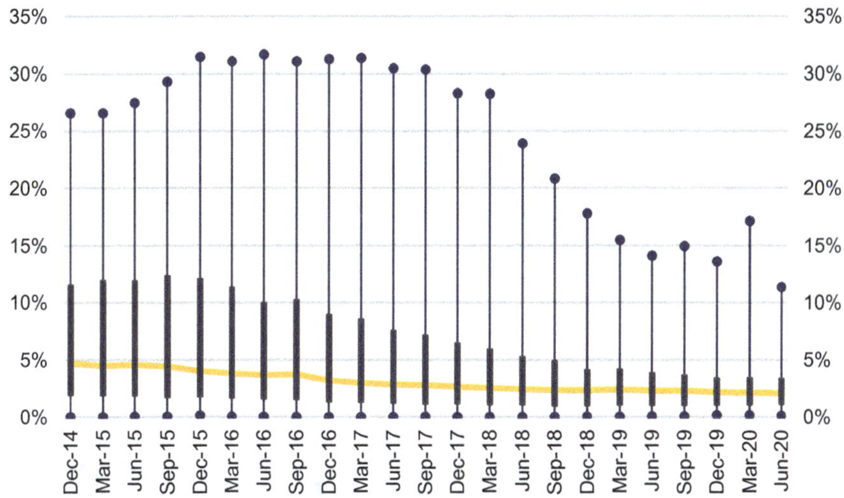

Figure 22.4. Ratio of non-performing loans and advances — dispersion *(% of total gross loans and advances).*

Note: The chart shows the 5th and 95th percentiles, interquartile ranges, and medians for the ratio of non-performing loans and advances, as published by to the EBA Risk Dashboard. From Q1 2020 onward, EU aggregates no longer include figures for UK banks and they include data for subsidiaries of UK banks in EU countries.

Source: European Banking Authority (2020), panel 7.

Turning to profitability, financial market pricing of EU banks has been already relatively weak in the aftermath of the Global Financial Crisis and before the COVID-19 crisis. EU banks' equity prices have been relatively weak, as compared to other sectors or banks in other jurisdictions. For example, compared to 20 years ago, EU banks trade at around one-third of the past value, while the overall EuroStoxx50 index trades around 2.5 times higher (European Systemic Risk Board, 2020, Chart 5.1). The price-to-book ratios for the EU banking sector have been below one for several years (Figure 22.5; see also Basten and Serrano, 2019). Equity market pricing of the EU banking sector implies relatively little market confidence in its medium-term profitability prospects, which is likely related to vulnerabilities of some EU banks. Profitability in the EU banking sector has been close to or below zero for a significant tail of bank distribution over recent years (Figure 22.6). This relatively weak performance

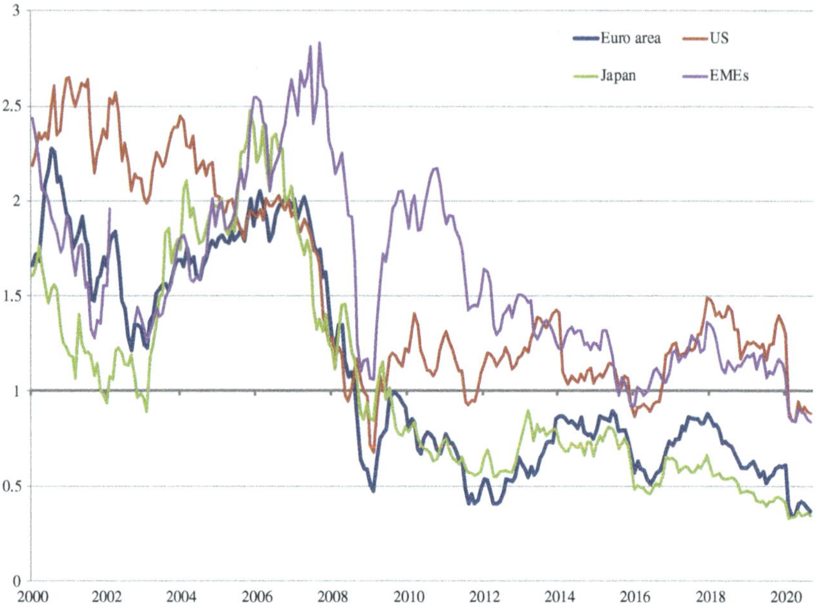

Figure 22.5. Bank price-to-book ratios across regions *(ratio)*.
Note: The chart shows the price-to-book ratios of banks, with monthly frequency, in the Euro area (based on Euro Stoxx Banks index), US (based on S&P 500 Banks index), Japan (based on Topix Banks index), and emerging markets economies (based on MSCI EM Banks index) since year 2000. Last observation: October 1, 2020.
Source: Bloomberg.

for some banks may be related to the large size of the EU banking system and the resulting inefficiencies, as flagged by previous research (see, e.g. European Central Bank, 2017; Pagano *et al.*, 2014).

A detailed analysis of bank profitability drivers has been conducted by European Central Bank Banking Supervision (2018c). The findings suggest that profitability and business models were under pressure with declining net interest income in many banks and pressures from non-performing loans and/or heavy cost structures in some banks. The environment of low growth and low-interest rates was putting and is likely to put further pressure on bank profits, in particular via suppressed net interest margins (see European Systemic Risk Board, 2016a,b). Beyond these more longer-term developments, cyclical factors have been one of the important drivers

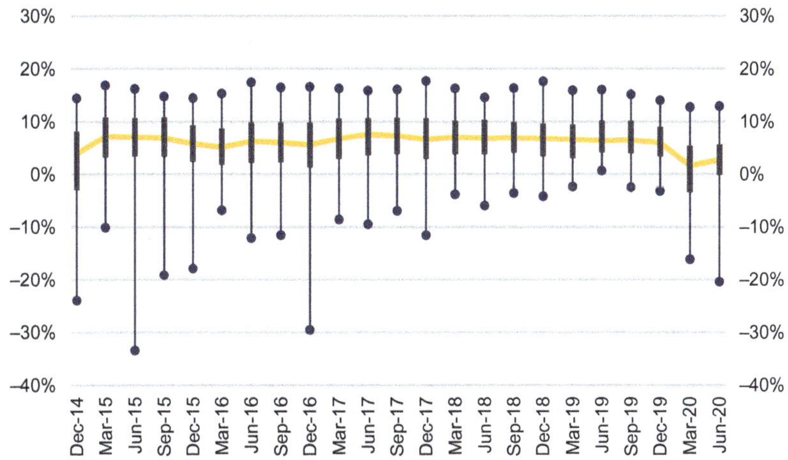

(a) Return on equity

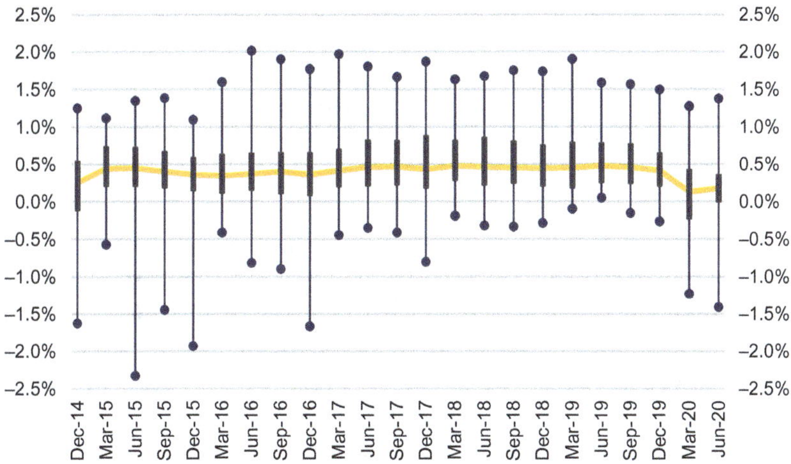

(b) Return on assets

Figure 22.6. Profitability measures for EU significant banks *(%)*.

Note: The charts show the 5th and 95th percentiles, interquartile ranges, and medians for the two main ratios of profitability of banks: return on assets and return on equity. From Q1 2020 onward, EU aggregates no longer include figures for UK banks and they include data for subsidiaries of UK banks in EU countries.

Source: European Banking Authority (2020), panels 11 and 12.

of bank profitability in Europe (see, e.g. Athanasoglou *et al.*, 2008; Kok *et al.*, 2015; Menicucci and Paolucci, 2015; Andersson *et al.*, 2018).

22.3. How Can the COVID-19 Pandemic Impact the Outlook for Non-Performing Loans and Profitability?

The financial turmoil caused by the outbreak of the COVID-19 pandemic in March 2020 resulted in increased volatility and tighter funding conditions for all market participants (including banks), which called for an unprecedented policy response. In the particular case of bank equities, the decline in share prices further reflected worsening future profits. In the first half of 2020, income of European banks plunged, resulting in weaker profitability (see also Figure 22.6). It was also in this context of reduction of the stock of non-performing loans in the balance sheet of some European banks that the COVID-19 pandemic appeared. Looking ahead, the outlook for non-performing loans, as well as bank profitability, is relatively gloomy.

The academic literature has found a strong link between macroeconomic conditions and non-performing loans (see Beck *et al.*, 2015; Ghosh, 2015; Louzis *et al.*, 2012, among others). Already before the onset of the COVID-19 crisis, the European economy was characterized by a prolonged period of relatively low growth (European Systemic Risk Board, 2016a,d, 2020). As a result of the pandemic, the growth outlook for Europe, as for the majority of world economies, is muted. The year 2020 is expected to witness a decline in GDP not seen since war times, and a weak recovery is expected in 2021 and 2022 (see, e.g. International Monetary Fund, 2020c). One important vulnerability expected to materialise in the balance sheets of banks relates to the declining asset quality and increasing non-performing loans. During the COVID-19 crisis, a significant wave of downgrades has been observed, and further downgrades could be expected to follow, at least judging by the prevailing balance of negative versus positive ratings outlook (see, e.g. Aramonte and Avalos, 2020; European Systemic Risk Board, 2020c).

The outlook for non-performing loans remains relatively uncertain, as uncertainty prevails over the short-term evolution of the

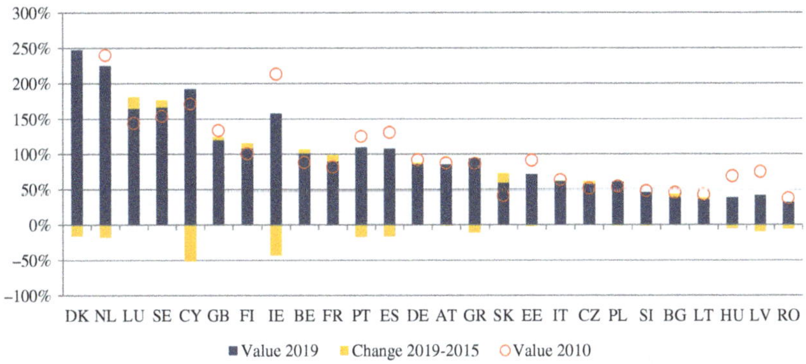

Figure 22.7. Household debt to gross disposable income ratio *(%)*.
Note: The blue bars represent the value of the ratio household debt to income for EU countries and the yellow bars the change since 2015. Red dots represent the value of the ratio in 2010. No data available for Croatia and Malta.
Source: Eurostat and authors' calculations.

pandemic across Europe and over its economic consequences. Some studies predict as much as one-fourth increase in bankruptcies across countries over a one-year horizon (see Banerjee *et al.*, 2020) while others find that national factors are going to determine the impact of the COVID-19 pandemic on the corporate sector (Gourinchas *et al.*, 2020).

In this regard, some important distinguishing aspects of the COVID-19–related recession need to be considered in relation to the outlook for the banking sector.

First, already at the end of 2019, indebtedness of households and, particularly, that of non-financial corporations, was very high in historical terms (see Figures 22.7 and 22.8). Entering a recession with high indebtedness makes economic agents more fragile and vulnerable. In the last years, concerns have arisen about developments in various funding segments, which appeared to some extent disconnected from the credit risks and the rising indebtedness in the real economy (European Systemic Risk Board, 2016a,b; International Monetary Fund, 2020b). For example, corporate bond issuances were high, with relatively low spreads even for higher-risk corporates; leveraged loans markets grew substantially; and lending to real estate markets seemed to boom in some countries (European Systemic Risk

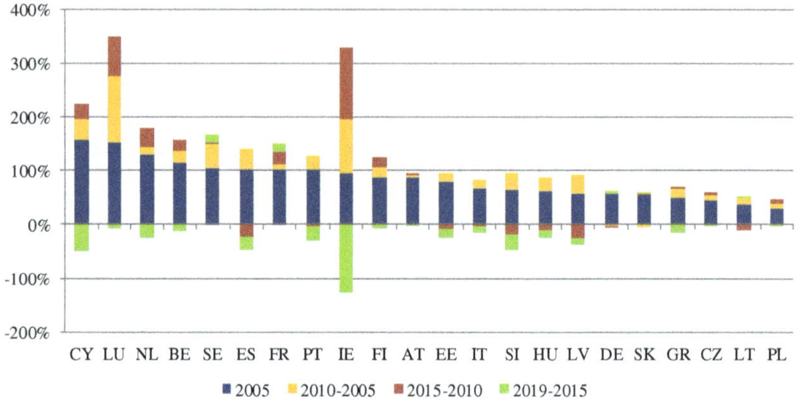

Figure 22.8. NFC debt to GDP ratio *(%)*.

Note: The blue bar represents the value of the debt (debt securities and loans) of non-financial corporations to GDP in 2005. Yellow, red, and green bars represent the change between 2005 and 2010, 2010 and 2015, and 2015 and 2019, respectively. No data is available for Bulgaria, Croatia, Denmark, Romania, and United Kingdom.

Source: ECB and authors' calculations.

Board, 2019d; Financial Stability Board, 2019; International Monetary Fund, 2018).

Second, unlike the Global Financial Crisis or the sovereign debt crisis, the COVID-19 recession is not limited to economic sectors or some countries. The Global Financial Crisis affected sectors such as real estate and was, to a large extent, a crisis originating in the financial sector, which fed through to the economic downturn. The COVID-19 recession, on the contrary, is directly affecting wide economic activity, albeit some sectors (travel, tourism or hospitality), and some countries are likely to be hit stronger than others. Battistini and Stoevsky (2020) compute losses of up to 60% of gross value added in the sector of retail trade, transport, accommodation, and food services activities, with other sectors (industry, manufacturing, and construction) facing losses of up to 40% of their gross value added. Similarly, Gourinchas *et al.* (2020) identify accommodation and food services; arts, entertainment, and recreation; education; and other services as the most affected sectors by the pandemic.[2]

[2]This would be in line with the findings in the Spanish Flu pandemic (see Garrett, 2008).

Overall, the significant reduction in real activity affects the main sources of income for households (wages) and non-financial corporations (sales). Consequently, we can observe a significant drop in consumption, driven by these supply- and demand-related factors, which largely feeds to the negative growth rates of the gross domestic product seen in the first half of 2020 (see European Central Bank, 2020a, Chart 10).

Third, policy measures have focused on ensuring that the net worth of economic agents does not deteriorate excessively as a result of the reduced economic activity. They have been swift and strong, providing relief to more troubled borrowers in the form of loan guarantees, payment moratoria, or suspensions of bankruptcy filings.[3] While these policy interventions have avoided that the COVID-19 outbreak turns into a systemic crisis and have maintained the stock of non-performing loans relatively stable, they cannot be maintained forever. Most of them are currently expected to terminate at the end of 2020, a time when it seems that the pandemic will still be severely affecting economic activities. As a result of the deep recession caused by the COVID-19 pandemic, the substantial indebtedness of economic agents, even already before the pandemic outbreak, and the termination of most policy support measures at the end of 2020 (or in the first months of 2021), it can be expected that non-performing loans start to rise during 2021, with estimations under a severe scenario of non-performing exposures around € 1.4 trillion in the euro area (see, e.g. Enria, 2020).

To gauge the possible outlook for corporate loans quality, we approximate the amount of corporate distress that could be associated with the reduction in economic activity in spring 2020 during the COVID-19 outbreak. Our approach is based on the losses for the second quarter of 2020 in gross value added by sector, as assessed by Battistini and Stoevsky (2020). We compare these losses with the corporate revenues and equity, comprising capital, reserves, and retained earnings, as observed before the onset of the COVID-19 crisis. For our calculations, we use the data from the ERICA database

[3]For an overview of the measures implemented in the EU, see https://www.esrb.europa.eu/home/search/coronavirus/shared/data/esrb.covidpm.xlsx.

of the European Central Balance Sheet Data Offices (ECCBSO),[4] which contains the main accounting variables and ratios for a sample of around 1,000 European non-financial corporations.

We make several assumptions. First, the ERICA database does not contain information on gross value added, so we approximate this as revenue, which captures sales of non-financial corporations in accounting terms. Second, the data are aggregated in the ERICA database with further information on quartiles. We assume that the first, second, and third quartiles can be interpreted as representative of weak, average, and sound non-financial corporations in a given sector of activity. Third, we map sectors of activity between our two reference datasets, as shown in Table 22.1. Fourth, due to data availability in the ERICA database, we use data as of end-2018. We use structural variables, which, in principle, should not vary significantly from year to year, so we can consider that they are representative of the values observed before the COVID-19 pandemic at the end of 2019.

Non-financial corporations typically retain, in aggregated terms, a significant proportion of their balance sheet as equity (30% or even more), providing them with a substantial cushion to withstand losses. Figures 22.9 and 22.10 show the interquartile range of the ratios of total equity to total assets and turnover to total liabilities for the non-financial corporations in the ERICA database, as of the end 2018.

Based on the above, we assume that corporate distress arises if the following inequality is met:

$$\alpha_{h,i,t}\left(\frac{Revenue}{Total\ Assets}\right)_{h,i,t} > \left(\frac{Equity}{Total\ Assets}\right)_{h,i,t}, \qquad (22.1)$$

where α is the reduction in revenue (gross value added) taken from Battistini and Stoevsky (2020) as a consequence of the COVID-19 pandemic, and h, i, and t represent the quartile (including the minimum), the sector of activity, and the time period, respectively.

The first term of the inequality would represent the loss in revenues caused by the reduction in economic activity following the

[4]See https://www.bach.banque-france.fr/index.php?page=telechargementFile&file=Erica_Brochure.pdf.

Table 22.1. Equivalence of sectorial breakdown of non-financial corporations.

ERICA database	**Battistini and Stoevsky (2020)**
	Agriculture
Chemistry	
Machinery and equipment	Industry excluding manufacturing and construction
Metal products, components and optical product/equipment	
Vehicle manufacturing	Manufacturing
Other manufacturing	
Energy	
Construction	Construction
Retail trade	Retail trade, transport, accommodation, food service activities
Whole sale	
Transportation and storage	
Food products	
Information and communication	Information, communication
	Financial and insurance activities
Real estate	Real estate activities
Other services	Professional, scientific, administrative and technical activities
	Public administration
	Arts, entertainment, recreation and other activities

Note: The table shows different sectors upon which the aggregate of non-financial corporations is broken down in the two data sources for the simulation. Battistini and Stoevsky (2020) are used to determine the loss in gross value added while the ERICA database is used to determine whether accumulated resilience of non-financial corporations can be used to absorb these losses.
Source: ECCBSO, Battistini and Stoevsky (2020), and authors' mapping.

COVID-19 pandemic, while the second term of the inequality represents the equity cushion in the balance sheet of non-financial corporations to withstand these losses.

Since the ratio of revenue to total assets is not included in ERICA, we need to transform the above equation to use the ratios of revenues to total liabilities and the total liabilities to total assets:

$$\alpha_{h,i,t}\beta_{h,i,t}\left(\frac{Revenue}{Total\ Liabilities}\right)_{h,i,t} > \left(\frac{Equity}{Total\ Assets}\right)_{h,i,t}, \quad (22.2)$$

where β is the ratio between total liabilities and total assets.

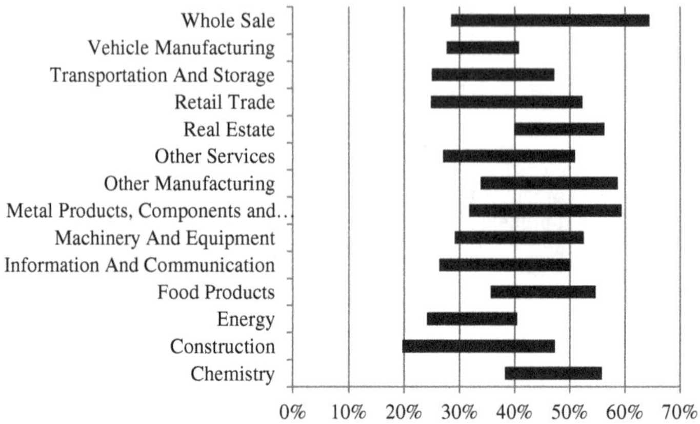

Figure 22.9. Ratio of total equity to total assets of non-financial corporations in the ERICA database, interquartile range (%).

Note: The blue bars represent the interquartile range (first and third quartiles) of the ratio total equity/total assets at the end of 2018 for the non-financial corporations included in the ERICA database.

Source: ERICA database of the European Committee of Central Balance Sheet Data Offices and authors' calculations.

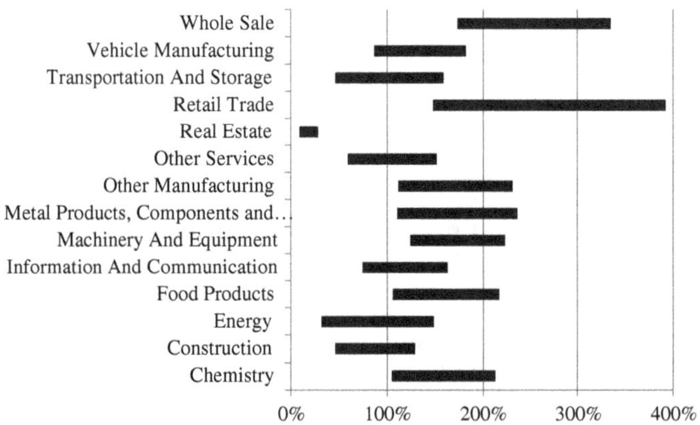

Figure 22.10. Ratio of total revenues to total liabilities of non-financial corporations in the ERICA database, interquartile range (%).

Note: The blue bars represent the interquartile range (first and third quartiles) of the ratio revenue/total liabilities at the end of 2018 for the non-financial corporations included in the ERICA database.

Source: ERICA database of the European Committee of Central Balance Sheet Data Offices and authors' calculations.

Figure 22.11 presents an overview of the approximated initial pandemic-induced loss in the lowest-quartile of the ratio of corporate revenues to total corporate assets, as compared to corporate equity in percentage of total assets. The comparison shows that the equity in the balance sheet of non-financial corporations in the first quartile would be enough to absorb the losses related to the COVID-19 outbreak, for all sectors except two: retail trade and manufacturing. Retail trade would be affected until the third quartile, while manufacturing would only be affected in the first quartile. Translating the corporate losses to the corresponding impact on banks would further require accounting for the size and distributions of the loan books, the reliance on market-based debt financing, as well as the impact of ambitious loan guarantees government schemes over time.

Likely increasing non-performing loans will make a negative impact on profitability, already under pressure from the macroeconomic environment of low growth and low-interest rates (Albertazzi and Gambacorta, 2009; European Systemic Risk Board, 2016a,b). Weak profitability patterns seem to have been relatively persistent in Europe over the recent years. While many institutions improved profitability between 2014 and 2018, the returns on assets remained low or even negative for some banks, without any clear sign of improvement (Figure 22.12).

In a stylised way, the profit and loss account of a bank can be represented as follows:

$$PR_t = II_t - IE_t + F_t + T_t + FV_t - AE_t - I_t + O_t, \qquad (22.3)$$

where PR_t denotes the profit of the year, II_t the interest income, IE_t the interest expense, F_t the net fee and commission income, T_t trading income, FV_t fair value gains or losses, AE_t administrative expenses, I_t impairment charges, and O_t other income and expenses.

We can elaborate further on the determinants of interest income, interest expense, and impairments. By doing so, we obtain the following equation:

$$\begin{aligned} PR_t = {} & (r_t + \delta_t)L_t(1 - npl_t) - r_t D_t + F_t + T_t + FV_t \\ & - AE_t - \tau npl_t + O_t, \end{aligned} \qquad (22.4)$$

where r_t denotes the risk-free rate, δ_t the credit spread, npl_t the rate of non-performing loans, L_t the outstanding stock of loans,

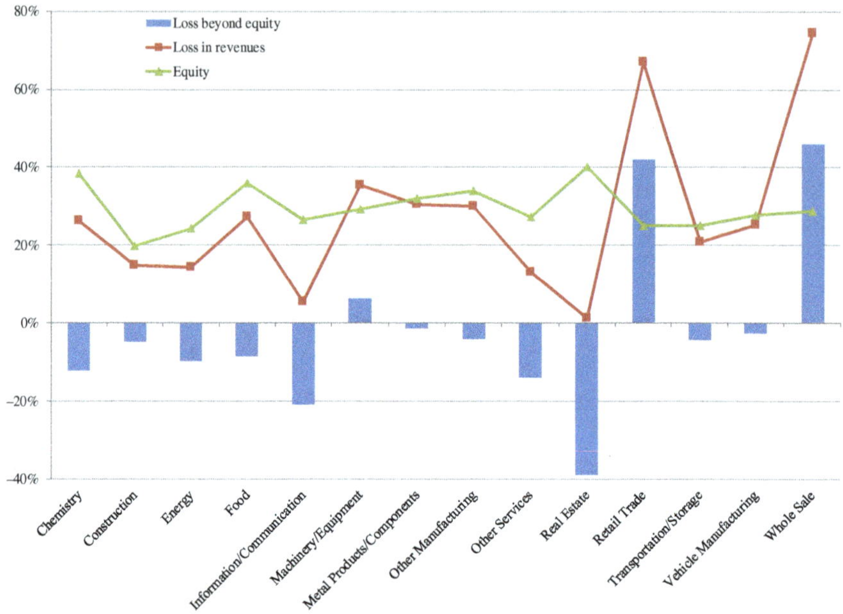

Figure 22.11. Approximated initial pandemic-induced losses in the lowest revenue quartile of non-financial corporations %.

Note: The figure shows the approximated initial loss in revenues from the pandemic, as based on Battistini and Stoevsky (2020), to total (red line). The green line represents the ratio of total equity to total assets and the blue bars to the difference between the two. Negative values would indicate that total equity to total assets is larger than the loss in revenue, and positive differences that total equity to total assets is smaller than the loss in revenue. The data refers to the first quartile of corporates in the ERICA database, according to their revenue/liability ratio.

Source: ECCBSO, Battistini and Stoevsky (2020), and authors' calculations.

D_t deposits, and τ the annual impairment charges related to non-performing loans.

It is important to note that non-performing loans are entering into the profit equation above through two channels: first, they determine the amount of impairment charges in the period, and, second, indirectly, they reduce interest income, as International Financial Reporting Standard (IFRS) 9 currently does not allow for full accrual of interest of non-performing loans.

The profit and loss account of a bank is particularly sensitive to the evolution of the economy in general, and of GDP growth,

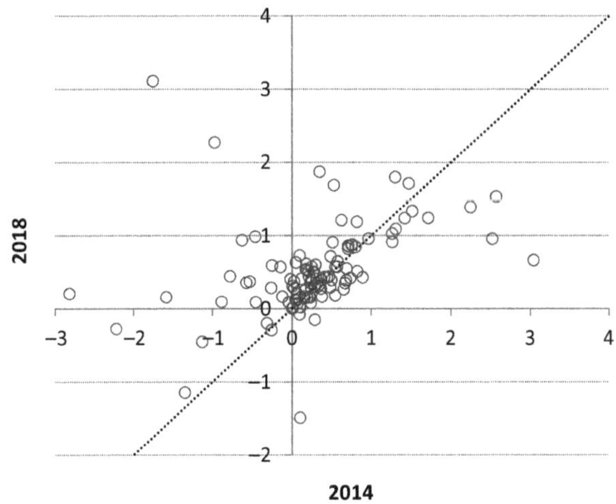

Figure 22.12. Profitability developments of individual banks between 2014 and 2018 *(percentages)*.

Note: The chart shows the returns on assets of significant EU banks at the end of 2014 (x-axis) and at the end of 2018 (y-axis).

Source: European Banking Authority transparency exercises and SNL.

in particular. The total volume of loans, which is going to determine interest income, the main source of profit for the bank, depends heavily on growth (Calza *et al.*, 2001; Pool *et al.*, 2015). We have mentioned above that the amount of non-performing loans also depends on the evolution of the real economy. However, also trading income and fair value gains can be affected, as in periods of financial turmoil or with weak macroeconomic fundamentals, financial markets may be volatile, leading to the recognition of substantial trading losses and large losses in the fair value of financial instruments, particularly those held for trading of a more complex nature (Boot and Ratnovsky, 2016; European Systemic Risk Board, 2020c).

To understand how the COVID-19 pandemic can affect the profitability of banks in Europe, it is useful to consider how their profit and loss account looked like at the end of 2019, following Equation (22.3). Figure 22.13 shows how interest expenses and administrative costs almost entirely absorb the interest income generated by European banks. The profit or loss of the year becomes greatly determined by other income and expenses, since the other items in the

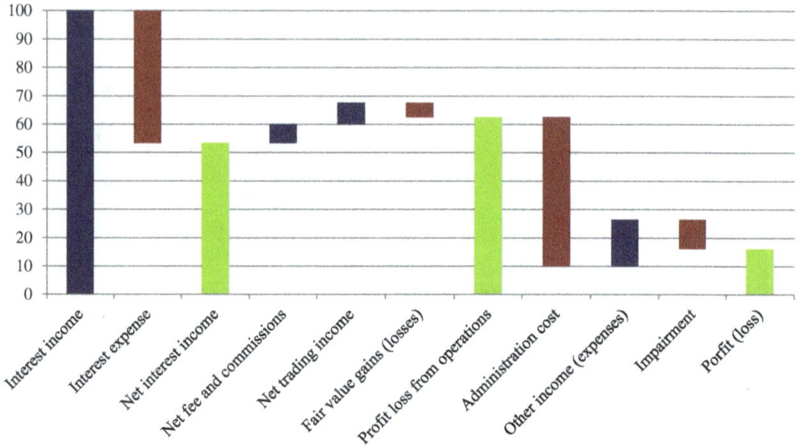

Figure 22.13. Profit and loss account of European banks (index: interest income = 100).

Note: Data as reported to the Consolidated Banking Data of the ECB, referring to all domestic and stand-alone banks, as of end 2019. The chart shows the main items in the profit or loss account of banks, scaled to the size of interest income (interest income = 100). The blue bars represent income and the red bars expenses in the profit and loss account. Green bars are balancing items.

Source: ECB and authors' calculations.

profit or loss account (fee income, trading income, fair value gains, and impairment charges are practically netting each other).

Figure 22.13 represents the situation of a banking system with a very limited amount of non-performing loans, resulting in small impairment charges. It is expected that the non-performing loans to arise from the COVID-19 recession would indeed force European banks to post significant losses, something that could already be observed in the results for the first half of 2020 (see also Figure 22.6). In this regard, the latest European Banking Authority (EBA) stress test exercise, which was conducted before the outbreak of the COVID-19 pandemic, foresees an increase in impairment charges of 586%, 303%, and 237% in the three years of the adverse scenario, for the median bank, in comparison with the latest real data (European Banking Authority, 2018; European Systemic Risk Board, 2019c). Increases in impairment losses of a similar scale would imply that impairments would represent almost 50% of total interest income for banks in the short-term, while they were around 10% in 2019

(Figure 22.13). Losses will then erode the equity of banks, with the possibility of putting into question their solvency position.

However, for the medium-term sustainability of banks, once the hit from deteriorating asset quality is dealt with, it would be crucial that the macroeconomic environment recovers and returns to positive and robust growth. A scenario with subdued growth over a long period would slowly but decisively hamper the profitability of banks (see European Systemic Risk Board, 2016a,b). Besides, banks themselves should also go through an important effort to understand the optimal size of their business and the most efficient way to provide services to customers. That could translate in the adoption of new technologies to reduce administrative expenses, and possibly also in a decrease of the size of the balance sheet to accommodate it to the capacity of the bank to generate profits (addressing thus the issue of overbanking as identified by Pagano *et al.* (2014)) or in mergers and acquisitions to benefit from synergies with other banks.

22.4. Conclusions

Before the onset of the COVID-19 pandemic, the profitability performance of many EU banks had already been relatively weak, which was also reflected in the sector's equity pricing. The burden of non-performing loans, while on a continuing declining trend, was still significant for some banks. The COVID-19 shock arrived in a particular unfortunate moment, putting further pressure on shorter- and medium-term performance outlook.

Looking ahead, the COVID-19 outbreak is likely to increase the amount of non-performing loans in the balance sheet of European banks. While policy support provides a critical help to non-financial corporations and the economy as a whole, revenue losses are likely to translate to non-performing loans if they are prolonged and some of policy support measures expire. Recent literature tries to estimate the impact of the pandemic on sectoral revenues (Battistini and Stoevsky, 2020) and the prospects for corporate defaults (e.g. Banerjee *et al.*, 2020). Our analysis adds to these results, suggesting that corporate distress could become a significant burden for European banks in the coming years.

The COVID-19 crisis is also likely to affect the profitability of EU banks. This could happen through two channels. First, the probable increase in non-performing loans is going to lead to higher impairments in the profit and loss account of banks. Second, the further prolongation of the low-growth and low-interest-rate environment is likely to affect bank loan revenues through compressed interest margins. On the positive side, the COVID-19 pandemic may be seen as an opportunity for EU banks to remove overcapacity, at the entity and country levels, by adopting new technologies, removing inefficiencies, and fostering consolidation in the banking sector.

Disclaimer

The views expressed in this paper are those of the authors and do not necessarily represent the views of the European Central Bank, the European Systemic Risk Board or any of its Member Institutions. The analysis of this chapter has been completed and accepted for publication in Autumn 2020.

References

Albertazzi, U. and Gambacorta, L. (2009). Bank profitability and the business cycle. *Journal of Financial Stability*, **5**(4), 393–409.

Aldasoro, I., Fender, I., Hardy, B. and Tarashev, N. (2020), Effects of Covid-19 on the banking sector: The market's assessment. *BIS Bulletin*, No. 12, May.

Andersson, M., Kok, C., Mirza, H. , Móré, C. and Mosthaf, J. (2018). How can euro area banks reach sustainable profitability in the future? *ECB Financial Stability Review*, November.

Aramonte, S. and Avalos, F. (2020). Corporate credit markets after the initial pandemic shock. *BIS Bulletin No. 26*, July.

Athanasoglou, P.P., Brissimis, S.N. and Delis, M.D. (2008). Bank-specific, industry-specific and macroeconomic determinants of bank profitability. *Journal of International Financial Markets, Institutions and Money*, **18**(2), 121–136.

Balgova, M., Nies. M. and Plekhanov, A. (2018). Reducing non-performing loans: Stylized facts and economic impact. Paper presented at the 2018 Annual Meeting of the American Economic Association 5 January 2018, Philadelphia.

Banerjee, R., Cornelli, G. and Zakrajšek, E. (2020). The outlook for business bankruptcies. *BIS Bulletin No. 30*, October.

Basten, M. and Sánchez Serrano, A. (2019). European banks after the global financial crisis: A new landscape. *Journal of Banking Regulation*, **20**, 51–73.

Battistini, N. and Stoevsky, G. (2020). Alternative scenarios for the impact of the COVID-19 pandemic on economic activity in the euro area. European Central Bank Economic Bulletin May 2020, Box 1.

Beck, R., Jakubik, P. and Piloiu, A. (2015). Key determinants of non-performing loans: new evidence from a global sample. *Open Economics Review*, **26**, 525–550.

Boot, A. and Ratnovsky, L. (2016). Banking and trading. *Review of Finance*, **20**(6), 2219–2246.

Calza, A., Gartner, C. and Sousa, J. (2001). Modelling the demand for loans to the private sector in the euro area. ECB Working Paper No. 55.

Carletti, E., Claessens, S. Fatas, A. and Vives, X. (2020). The bank business model in the post-Covid-19 world. CEPR Reports on the Future of Banking, No. 2.

Council of the EU (2017). Report of the FSC Subgroup on Non-Performing Loans.

Demirgüç-Kunt, A., Pedraza, A. and Ruiz, C. (2020). A banking sector pandemic. World Bank Blog, 21 August.

Drehmann, M., Farag, M., Tarashev, N. and Tsatsaronis, K. (2020). Buffering Covid-19 losses — the role of prudential policy. *BIS Bulletin*, No. 9, April.

Enria, A. (2019). Non-performing loans in the euro area — where do we stand? Speech at the Conference *EDIS, NPLs, Sovereign Debt and Safe Assets*, organised by the Institute for Law and Finance, Frankfurt, 14 June.

Enria, A. (2020). Supervisory challenges of the pandemic and beyond. Keynote speech at the *Handelsblatt European Banking Regulation Conference*, Frankfurt, 3 November.

Espinoza, R. and Prasad, A. (2010). Non-performing loans in the GCC banking system and their macroeconomic effects. IMF Working Paper No. 10/224.

European Banking Authority (2016). EBA report on the dynamics and drivers of non-performing exposures in the EU banking sector. July.

European Banking Authority (2018). 2018 EU-wide stress test results. November.

European Banking Authority (2019). EBA report on NPLs — progress made and challenges ahead. November.

European Banking Authority (2020). Risk dashboard. Q2 2020.

European Central Bank (2017). Report on financial structures. October.

European Central Bank (2020a). Economic Bulletin. 24 September.

European Central Bank (2020b). Banks in the coronavirus crisis. ECB Podcast, 10 June.

European Central Bank (2020c). Financial Stability Review. May.

European Central Bank Banking Supervision (2018a). ECB announces further steps in supervisory approach to stock of NPLs. 11 July.

European Central Bank Banking Supervision (2018b). ECB sets out its supervisory expectations for new NPLs. 15 March.

European Central Bank Banking Supervision (2018c). SSM thematic review on profitability and business models. September.

European Central Bank Banking Supervision (2019). CB revises supervisory expectations for prudential provisioning for new non-performing loans to account for new EU regulation. 22 August.

European Systemic Risk Board (2016a). Macroprudential policy issues arising from low interest rates and structural changes in the EU financial system, November.

European Systemic Risk Board (2016b). The impact of low interest rates and ongoing structural changes on the banking system: Assessment of vulnerabilities, systemic risks and implications for financial stability, November.

European Systemic Risk Board (2016c). The low interest rate environment and structural changes in the real economy, November.

European Systemic Risk Board (2016d). The ESRB issues eight warnings on medium-term residential real estate vulnerabilities. 28 November.

European Systemic Risk Board (2017). Resolving non-performing loans in Europe. July.

European Systemic Risk Board (2019a). Annual Report. July.

European Systemic Risk Board (2019b). Macroprudential approaches to non-performing loans. January.

European Systemic Risk Board (2019c). The cyclical behaviour of the ECL model in IFRS 9. March.

European Systemic Risk Board (2019d). Vulnerabilities in the residential real estate sectors of the EEA countries. September.

European Systemic Risk Board (2020a). Risk dashboard. September.

European Systemic Risk Board (2020b). Issues note on liquidity in the corporate bond and commercial paper markets, the procyclical impact of downgrades and implications for asset managers and insurers. May.

European Systemic Risk Board (2020c). Macroprudential implications of financial instruments in Levels 2 and 3 for accounting purposes, February.

Fell, J., Grodzicki, M., Metzler, J. and O'Brien, E. (2018). Non-performing loans and euro area bank lending behaviour after the crisis. Financial Stability Review of Banco de España No. 35.

Financial Stability Board (2019). Vulnerabilities associated with leveraged loans and collateralised loan obligations. December.

Garrett, T. (2008). Economic effects of the 1918 influenza pandemic: Implications for a modern-day pandemic. *Federal Reserve Bank of St. Louis Review*, **90**(2), 75–93.

Ghosh, A. (2015). Banking-industry specific and regional economic determinants of nonperforming loans: Evidence from US states. *Journal of Financial Stability*, **20**, 93–104.

Gourinchas, P-O., Kalemli-Ozcan, S., Penciakova, V. and Sander, N. (2020). COVID-19 and SME failures. IMF Working Paper No. 20/207.

Hutchinson, J. and Mee, S. (2020). The impact of the ECB's monetary policy measures taken in response to the COVID-19 crisis. *ECB Economic Bulletin*, (5), Box 3.

International Monetary Fund (2018). Global Financial Stability Report, October.

International Monetary Fund (2020a). Policy responses to COVID-19. IMF **Policy Tracker**.

International Monetary Fund (2020b). Global Financial Stability Report, October.

International Monetary Fund (2020c). World Economic Outlook, October.

Klein, N. (2013). Non-performing loans in CESEE: Determinants and macroeconomic performance. IMF Working Paper No. 13/72.

Kok, C., Móré, C. and Pancaro, C. (2015). Bank profitability challenges in euro area banks: The role of cyclical and structural factors. *ECB Financial Stability Review*, May.

Louzis, D., Vouldis, A. and Metaxas, V. (2012). Macroeconomic and bank-specific determinants of non-performing loans in Greece: A comparative study of mortgage, business and consumer loan portfolios. *Journal of Banking and Finance*, **36**(4), 1012–1027.

Menicucci, E. and Paolucci, G. (2016). The determinants of bank profitability: Empirical evidence from European banking sector. *Journal of Financial Reporting and Accounting*, **14**(1), 86–115.

Nkusu, M. (2011). Non-performing loans and macrofinancial vulnerabilities in advanced economies. IMF Working Paper No. 11/161.

Pagano, M., Acharya, V., Boot, A., Brunnermeier, M., Buch, C., Hellwig, M., Langfield, S., Sapir, A. and van den Burg, I. (2014). Is Europe overbanked? Reports of the Advisory Scientific Committee, No 4, ESRB, June.

Pool, S., de Haan, L. and Jacobs, J. (2015). Loan loss provisioning, bank credit and the real economy. *Journal of Macroeconomics*, **45**, 124–136.

Segura, A. and Suarez, J. (2019). Optimally solving banks' legacy problems. CEMFI Working Paper No. 1910.

Suarez, J. and Sánchez Serrano, A. (2018). Approaching non-performing loans from a macroprudential angle. Reports of the Advisory Scientific Committee of the European Systemic Risk Board No. 7.

https://doi.org/10.1142/9781800610781_0023

Chapter 23

How Will the 2020 Crisis Accelerate the Evolution of the Banking System?

Frederic de Mariz
Columbia University, New York, USA
fm2136@columbia.edu

Abstract

An exogenous shock triggered a simultaneous collapse in supply and demand, which coincided with an oil price shock and led to a financial crisis. We compare and contrast the COVID-19–related Financial Crisis (CFC) with previous shocks. Policy responses included the traditional toolkit of lower policy rates, more flexible rules on loan loss provisioning and capital rules, injection of liquidity through direct lending and asset repurchase, and expanding public balance sheets, among others. Banks implemented their own response to the crisis by tapping into funding lines to increase their liquidity cushions, offering loan forbearance, and serving as distribution agents for government subsidies. Capital markets played their role via record-high levels of debt issuance and convertibles. The CFC will accelerate trends that were visible in the financial industry. From branch closures to a rise in contactless payments and the growth of super apps, the health crisis is leading to new practices by financial institutions, being a catalyst for digital banking. Moreover, it is impacting the demand for financial products, with a rise in demand for insurance protection and increased interest in sustainable investment strategies. Accelerated digitization and sustainability represent the dual impact for the financial sector, while at the same time paving the way for opportunities.

23.1. Introduction

What started as a health crisis rapidly spread to become an economic, financial, and, in some countries, political crisis. The 2020 COVID-19–related Financial Crisis (CFC) is not without precedents and led to policy responses that were largely inspired by the 2008 Global Financial Crisis (GFC). However, while policy responses were not new, their speed and size were. The 2020 event differs in its essence from 2008, being characterized by an exogenous shock, and in its vast consequences. The 2020 crisis will change many consumption, work, and economic habits. Beyond the COVID-19 health crisis, how is the 2020 CFC going to impact the financial sector? How will it change the way we bank?

From branch closures to a rise in contactless payments and the rise of super apps, the health crisis is leading to new practices by financial institutions, being a catalyst for digital banking. Moreover, it is impacting the demand for financial products, with a rise in demand for insurance protection and increased interest in sustainable investment strategies. Accelerated digitization and sustainability represent the dual impact for the financial sector, while at the same time paving the way for opportunities.

This chapter contributes to the current literature with the support of market data, detailed case studies, and interviews of market participants. A brief review of the academic literature on shocks shows the similarities and differences of the 2020 event and how the financial sector has been impacted during previous crises. We argue that the 2020 crisis will accelerate a trend of convergence between large banking incumbents and digital natives. Within the category of digital natives, we observe a bifurcation between robust digital models, which are set to benefit from the crisis and will continue to diversify their product offering, and weaker ones, which have either less access to capital to withstand the shock or uncertain monetization models. CFC also strengthens the position of large financial institutions that presented strong balance sheets and operating models when the shock hit. The crisis will accelerate the trends that the financial industry has been experiencing in the past decade, including digitization, search for sustainable profitability, and client-centered business models.

We first detail the impact of the current crisis on the financial sector, comparing and contrasting it with previous shocks. We then delve into the trends that COVID-19 is accelerating, including digitization of processes, branch closures, the rise of super apps and platforms, and changes in operating models. We also detail how innovation can support development goals. Finally, we describe the challenges exacerbated by the crisis for financial institutions, customers, and regulators, including the digital divide, misplaced regulations, and cyber risks.

23.2. Using the 2008 GFC Playbook, But the 2020 CFC Is Different

23.2.1. *The impact of crises on financial systems*

The CFC is unique in the sense that an exogenous shock triggered a simultaneous collapse in supply and demand, which coincided with an oil price shock. We compare and contrast the CFC with previous shocks.

There is a rich literature on the impact of crises on asset valuations and economic growth. Kaminsky *et al.* (1998) looked at warning signals or symptoms of an imminent currency crisis. The authors found that declining exports, deviations of the foreign exchange from trend, ratio of broad money to gross international reserves, output, and equity prices were relevant signals that a currency crisis may take place in the coming 24 months.

Research from 2009 explained the differences in the crisis impact in the form of growth forecast revisions, using cross-country regressions. IMF (2009) found that "a small set of variables explain a large share of the variation in growth revisions" — in particular, "countries with more leveraged domestic financial systems and more rapid credit growth tended to suffer larger downward revisions to their growth outlooks." For emerging markets, the financial channel was more relevant than a collapse in trade to explain revisions in growth forecasts. The authors also find (a weaker) evidence that countries with a stronger fiscal position before the crisis fared better, while exchange-rate flexibility buffered some of the impact of the shock.

Reinhart and Rogoff (2009) note that "banking crises are associated with profound declines in output and employment." Unemployment rises an average of seven percentage points over the down phase of the cycle, which lasts on average over four years, while output falls an average of over 9%. The authors also note that "government debt tends to explode, rising an average of 86 percent in the major post–World War II episodes." Importantly, the authors note that the main cause of debt explosion is not the widely cited bailing out and recapitalizing of the banking system, but rather a "collapse in tax revenues."

In an influential paper, Reinhart and Rogoff (2014) analyzed the pace of recovery from financial crisis using evidence from 100 episodes. In particular, the authors examined the evolution of real per capita GDP around 100 systemic banking crises. They found that "it takes about eight years to reach the pre-crisis level of income," with a median at six and a half years. Considering the GFC of 2008, "only Germany and the US (out of 12 systemic cases) [had] reached their 2007-2008 peaks in real income" by 2014. They also found that 45% of episodes recorded double dips. While they acknowledge that every crisis has its specificities, they note that post-war business cycles are not the relevant comparator for the recent crises in advanced economies. Their approach recognizes that policymaking and crisis management follows a pendulum, and that the "current phase of the official policy approach is predicated on the assumption that growth, financial stability and debt sustainability can be achieved through a mix of austerity and forbearance (and some reform)." Harsher policies, including debt restructurings, higher inflation, capital controls, and other forms of financial repression are typically observed in emerging markets alone.

Looking in more details at the financial sector, Adrian and Shin (2010) look at select features of the 2008 crisis, especially leverage, which is procyclical and increases during boom periods. They explain that bank lending and capital markets are intertwined, leading to a complementarity of micro- and macro-policies. In the same vein, Tirole (2010) notes that the 2008 crisis was "characterized by massive illiquidity." He reviews "what we know and don't know about illiquidity and all its friends: market freezes, fire sales, contagion, and ultimately insolvencies and bailouts," and other types of market breakdowns. Tirole explains why liquidity cannot easily be apprehended through a single statistic. He emphasizes the need for macroprudential policies, where liquidity should be regulated in conjunction with capital adequacy requirement.

Evidence suggest that "banks in countries with stricter capital requirement regulations and with more independent supervisors performed better," and that differences in corporate governance did not have a statistically meaningful correlation with bank performance (Beltratti and Stulz, 2009). Anginer and Demirguc-Kunt (2014) analyze the importance of capital rules to reduce systemic risk. They find that "capital is effective to reduce systemic risk, and the type of capital matters." They also find that there is "some suggestive evidence that the increased regulatory focus on macroprudential regulation after the [2008] crisis has strengthened the capital," providing a strong basis for the stricter capital rules that were implemented following 2008.

Evidence from select countries also suggest that regulations can reduce the duration of a crisis. This is the conclusion of Tchana (2014), who assessed empirically this hypothesis in the case of Indonesian banks, using a monthly index of banking fragility under a Markov-switching model. He noted that "at the end of the 1997–2002 episode, the Bank of Indonesia had closed 70 banks and nationalized 13, out of a total of 237." The non-performing loans for the banking system were "estimated at 65–75% of total loans at the peak of the crisis and fell to about 12% in February 2002." He stressed the relevance of regulations such as capital adequacy, deposit insurance, and reserve requirements to reduce the duration of the crisis.

Moreover, a stream of the literature looks at the contagion effect of the crisis from one segment of the economy to another. Bekaert *et al.* (2014) find evidence of only a small contagion from the US and the global financial sector to domestic portfolios and valuations in the GFC. By contrast, "there has been substantial contagion from domestic markets to individual domestic portfolios, with its severity inversely related to the quality of countries' economic fundamentals." This confirms that, in the case of the 2008 crisis, markets focused more on country-specific characteristics. Contrary to the GFC, the CFC is exogenous in nature — it was not caused by a credit crunch, a banking, or an exchange crisis (Baldwin, 2020). Banking crises are always characterized by a cumulative stress on solvency and liquidity. However, the combination of causes is unique to each. The 2020 crisis did not present warning signals.

Baldwin and Weder di Mauro (2020) note that the "damage in every systemic crisis in history is caused by endogenous risk amplification, even if the trigger can be an exogenous shock as it was in the 1914 systemic crisis." While the COVID-19 trigger is exogenous, the authors ask whether the financial system absorbs this shock, as it usually does for exogenous shocks, or "whether the shock interacts adversely with the latent feedback loops in the financial system and exposes existing vulnerabilities that culminate in a systemic financial crisis." Banks are better prepared in 2020 than in 2008, with higher capital and liquidity levels. That said, a long period of historically low interest rates had led companies and households to increase debt levels, representing a risk for lenders, putting debt and loan repayments under stress (Bank of International Settlements, 2019). The authors advocate that "the appropriate policy response cannot be limited to reducing interest rates or purchases of corporate or sovereign bonds on the open market but should also encompass forbearance and targeted help and similar policies."

While the uncertainty remains on the pace of economic recovery, most economic forecasts point to a full recovery by 2022 (IMF, 2020), i.e. more than two years after the beginning of the crisis, if we use the start date of March 11, 2020 when the WHO made the assessment that COVID-19 could be characterized as a pandemic (World Health Organization, 2020). The market response to the rising threat of COVID-19 anticipated the WHO announcement starting in February, as evidenced by measure of asset valuation and risk such as S&P and VIX data. IMF Chief Economist Gita Gopinath noted that the Great Lockdown represented the worst recession since the Great Depression, with a "cumulative loss to global GDP over 2020 and 2021 from the pandemic crisis [...] around 9 trillion dollars, greater than the economies of Japan and Germany combined" (IMF, 2020).

By contrast, asset valuations and market expectations experienced a rapid recovery already by May 2020, just two months after the beginning of the crisis, supported by unprecedented policy measures (Figure 23.1). Observers noted that the "speed of recovery surprised the markets," with "a bull market in the middle of the outbreak" (Franco, 2020). In fact, the S&P index reached a trough on March 23, 2020, and at the end of the first half of 2020, it was just

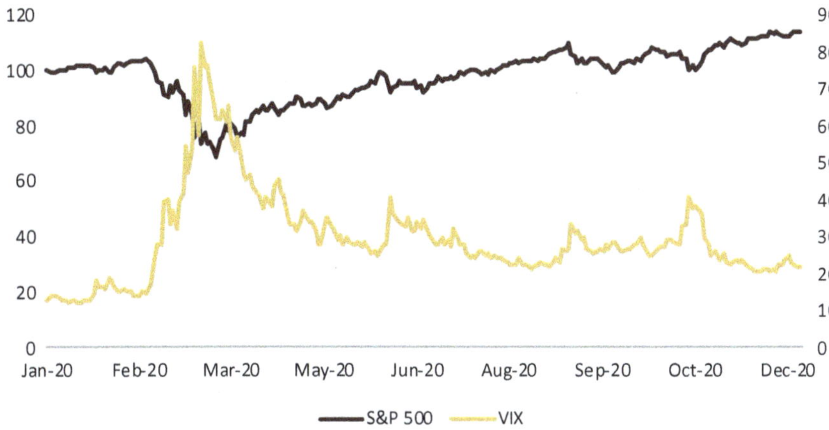

Figure 23.1. Rapid recovery in asset prices despite volatility (S&P, VIX).
Source: Factset.

4% below its January 1 level. Similarly, VIX, a measure of market volatility, reached a peak of 82.7 on March 16, 2020, and declined somewhat after that date, while not returning to its 2019 levels.

23.2.2. *2020 policy responses impacting financial systems*

The 2020 policy responses were swift and aggressive, mostly using 2008 as a playbook. If the first order impact was not unusual, the CFC stands out because of several unique characteristics. What is the role of the Financial Sector and FinTech in the context of the crisis?

Contrary to the 2008 GFC, this crisis did not start in the financial sector. In 2008, banks were, to a large extent, at the origin of the crisis, with rising defaults in select consumer segments, opaque accounting in off-balance sheet vehicles, loss of confidence, and stress in interbank liquidity. The GFC led to banking bankruptcies and consolidation, favoring larger, domestic deposit-taking institutions (Claessens, 2006). Unsurprisingly, the response to the 2008 crisis involved an increased focus on banking supervision and a crackdown on lax regulations with the definition of Basel III rules.

In 2020, financial institutions presented more robust balance sheets, with limited foreign exchange mismatch, stronger liquidity, and capital ratios. There is limited evidence of a "flight to quality" or "flight to size" in deposit-taking institutions or a preference for domestic institutions versus foreign-controlled banks, contrary to 2008. In 2008, financial institutions faced a perfect storm with a dual impact on their liquidity and capital positions. In 2020, the short-term impact on the financial sector included a shock to asset quality, leading to higher levels of loan loss provisions. Funding availability and cost were impacted, while interest rates decreased as a result of accommodating public policies, leading to margin compression. Banks acted as "shock absorber for the system, liquidity providers of second to last resort," as drawdowns on credit lines increased meaningfully (Oliver Wyman, 2020), reaching a peak in May 2020, 29% before pre–COVID-19 level, and subsequently normalizing (Figure 23.2). From the perspective of capital markets, the shock to asset valuations and rating downgrades resulted in a decrease in the value of collaterals and provisions, in particular for asset managers and insurance companies.

Outside of credit and insurance, payments experienced an acceleration in adoption of contactless solutions, with COVID-19

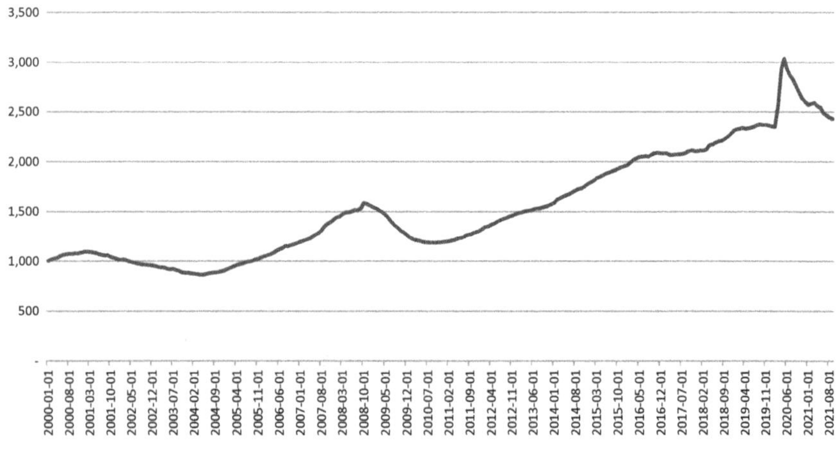

Figure 23.2. Strong increase in drawdowns on banks' credit lines (US$ billions).

Source: Federal Reserve Economic Data, Federal Reserve Bank of St Louis. Commercial and Industrial Loans, All Commercial Banks, Billions of US Dollars, Monthly, Seasonally Adjusted.

helping to "speed up the shift toward digital payments" (Bank of International Settlements, 2020b), with consumers massively mentioning hygiene as an important factor to prefer electronic means of payments over cash for the first time. Lagarde (2020) highlights a European survey showing that "40% of respondents [...] say they have reduced their use of cash." Brazilian FinTech company Ebanx (2020) noted that "contactless payments grew fivefold in Brazil comparing with March 2019," citing data from the Brazilian Card Association ABECS, mostly driven by the near-field communication technology embarked on plastic cards. Moreover, electronic payments are the financial backbone of e-commerce companies, which benefited from lockdowns and restrictions put in place during the pandemic.

In 2020, banks and payment companies can be part of the solution of the crisis, offering innovative solutions to customers via digital channels, widening their service offering to support the resilience they are looking for, becoming agents of public policies in government social programs, and renegotiating credit terms with their borrowers.

The first policy responses to the crisis have focused on safeguarding the liquidity and capital base of banks, while allowing for flexibility in credit risk management. The BIS offered a quick response to the crisis, and defined in April 2020 that "relief measures include a range of different payment moratoriums and government guarantees" (Bank of International Settlements, 2020a). With a character of exception, regulators have authorized that capital treatment and the definition of non-performing assets be more flexible. While "the Basel Framework applies higher capital requirements to loans that are categorised as past due or defaulted [...] the Committee has agreed that when jurisdictions apply this criterion, payment moratorium periods (public or granted by banks on a voluntary basis) relating to the COVID-19 outbreak can be excluded by banks from the counting of days past due." Accounting of loan loss provisions, based on IFRS 9 rule and expected loss considerations, was also made more flexible, acknowledging the high level of uncertainty surrounding future projections.

In Europe, the crisis reshaped policy priorities and the reaction to it was "sizeable and prompt" (IIF, 2020). State aid frameworks were made flexible; the European Central Bank offered fresh quantitative easing (Q.E.), while strict clauses under the Stability and Growth Pact were suspended. Measures included a collaboration between the

European Central Bank, the Commission, the European Banking Authority EBA and national governments. IIF (2020) noted that "although the shock, by its very nature, is a symmetric one – hitting all countries in similar fashion – the ability of different nations has been hampered by differences in policy, with Italy and Spain doing relatively modest fiscal stimulus compared to Germany." The 2020 crisis therefore revived the debates over risk-sharing among countries and proposals to issue "Coronabonds, a special, one-time version of Eurobonds" (IIF, 2020). In October 2020, the European Commission (2020) announced the issuance of EU SURE bonds of up to €100 billion as social bonds, being a "clear demonstration of the E.U.'s long-term commitment to sustainable financing." The first tranche issued on October 20 generated strong market demand and was close to 14 times oversubscribed. The funds "will be transferred to the beneficiary Member States in the form of loans to help them cover the costs directly related to the financing of national short-time work schemes and similar measures as a response to the pandemic."

As expected, policy responses included the traditional toolkit of lower policy rates, more flexible rules on loan loss provisioning and capital rules, injection of liquidity through direct lending and asset repurchase, and expanding public balance sheets, among others. Banks implemented their own response to the crisis by tapping into funding lines to increase their liquidity cushions, offering loan forbearance, renegotiating loans, and serving as distribution agents for government subsidies. Capital markets, in turn, played their role, via record-high levels of debt issuance and convertibles.

In the context of COVID-19, policymakers globally have revived a series of measures and discussions, both old and new. Among the stricter rules, policymakers have recommended caps on rates, increasing taxes on banks, cutting dividends, or tampering with credit data reported to credit bureaus (De Mariz, 2020a).

23.2.3. *Financial innovation that accelerates development*

Before the CFC, regulators faced the difficult task of fostering enough innovation while avoiding jumps that could jeopardize the health of the financial system and harm customers (De Mariz, 2020b). Innovation and financial digitization bear the promise of a greater financial inclusion. Financial inclusion has become a key policy objective in most emerging economies, but is also topical in developed markets.

Regulators globally have embraced the challenge of FinTech, favoring new business models in the financial sector, which can increase contestability and improve both the access to and the quality of financial services. Overall, innovation in financial services is accelerating. FinTech is an industry composed of companies that use technology to make financial systems and the delivery of financial services more efficient. FinTech is an essential tool to boost financial inclusion.

The example of Europe sheds light on the key principles that are guiding regulators and influencing policymakers globally. Recent directives have moved the focal point on the customer, under the principle that banking data should belong to citizens. Directives from the European Commission on transparency, portability, and interoperability are putting more emphasis on customers' rights and protection. By contrast, the previous consensus implied that data belonged to financial intermediaries in exchange for the classic functions they performed, such as deposit taking. Regulators globally are encouraging innovation, including open banking.

The banking sector is an essential contributor to output creation due to its intermediary role between deposit taking and loan concessions. The financial sector has also traditionally performed other financial functions, including investments and insurance. Levine (2005) notes that banks perform five functions that can impact economic growth: (i) they produce information, (ii) invest, (iii) diversify risk, (iv) capture savings, and (v) enable the interchange of goods and services.

There is a large literature offering support for a link between financial inclusion and development, while excessive or inappropriate inclusion can also bring risks. The World Bank (2016) estimates that more than 1.6 billion people and more than 200 million businesses lack financial services worldwide. Additionally, hundreds of millions are underserved and are not able to reach their full productive potential for lack of financials access. Access to and usage of financial services have traditionally improved, thanks to deeper branch networks and innovations, such as banking correspondents in Brazil and the creation of group lending in Bangladesh, both in the 1970s. Over the past two decades, technology and regulations are forces that have boosted inclusion. While access has improved, it is far from ubiquitous.

Cermeño and Roa (2013) review the channels between financial development and economic growth. While most research shows a positive relationship, the crisis calls to revise and refine those links. Evidence suggests that countries with a sounder financial system experience better growth. Financial institutions strive due to information and transaction costs. The authors note that "traditional economic model derived from Arrow-Debreu do not incorporate asymmetries of information and therefore do not include financial institutions in the drivers of growth": they consider capital accumulation and technological change as drivers of growth. An underdeveloped financial system is most likely to lead to credit rationing. Other research (La Porta *et al.*, 2000) shows a positive correlation between financial development and economic growth. More academic research recognizes the need to refine the proxy used for financial development, and not focus just on financial depth (quantity of credit) but incorporate the dimensions of wide access and quality.

There are several definitions of financial inclusion. For the World Bank, "financial inclusion means that individuals and businesses have access to useful and affordable financial products and services that meet their needs – transactions, payments, savings, credit and insurance – delivered in a responsible and sustainable way." The Center for Financial Inclusion (CFI) states that financial inclusion allows everyone to have "access to a full suite of quality financial services at affordable prices, with convenience, dignity, and consumer protection, delivered by a range of providers in a stable, competitive market to financially capable clients" (Kelly and Rhyne, 2015). The definitions illustrate that being financially included is different from — and much more complex than — being banked: having a bank account at a formal bank institution, including banks, cooperatives and credit unions. Mas (2009) notes that financial inclusion consists in having access to a wide range of financial services, not just credit. Financial inclusion considers all economic agents, either individuals or corporates, with a special attention for the more vulnerable and excluded segments, such as the poorer segments of the population in emerging markets and small- and medium-sized businesses.

Importantly, the reverse concept of financial exclusion is a growing concern in developed economies, such as the US (Burhouse and

Osaki, 2014), and is likely to accelerate under the CFC. The World Bank (2013) notes that 20% of the US adult population is underbanked, which the authors define as having a bank account but using financial services from another alternative, i.e. a non-FDIC (Federal Deposit Insurance Corporation) insured financial provider. Financial inclusion is based on three dimensions of access, usage, and quality (Roa, 2015). Claessens (2006) explains: "access refers to supply, whereas use is the intersection of the supply and demand schedules." Quality is the catalyst that converts the potential access to actual usage (De Mariz, 2020b).

Electronic payments are an entry door for inclusion, including payments with credit, debit, prepaid cards, and other electronic means such as online and mobile payments. The growing use of electronic payments can open the door to a wider range of financial services, including credit, especially via the constitution of payment history. The rise in electronic payments brings various development-related benefits to a country, while cash usage is associated with informality. Reaching a higher level of electronic payments is a positive achievement but is not sufficient to guarantee inclusion.

Research shows that asymmetries of information can be detrimental to the market as a whole. The credit market is imperfect in a sense that there may not be a price that clears the supply and demand for credit, if banks simply refuse to lend for lack of information (Akerlof, 1970; Stiglitz and Weiss, 1981, 1992), and credit market conditions amplify and propagate the effects of real monetary shocks, under a phenomenon described as the financial accelerator (Bernanke *et al.*, 1994). Bernanke *et al.* (1991) explain that borrowers who face relatively high agency costs in credit markets will bear the brunt of economic downturns. Agency costs stem from the situation where a principal (the lender) cannot, without cost, acquire information on the agent (the borrower). Credit is different from other goods, due to the central role of information, and sunk costs from information gathering act as barriers to entry for borrowers (Greenwald and Stiglitz, 2003).

Stiglitz (1989) stressed the importance of asymmetries of information in the credit market, explaining that screening and monitoring of clients are two essential functions of financial institutions. Loans are different from other goods and markets, since they are not contemporaneous: money is repaid in the future, loans are heterogeneous, and they bear information problems. Stiglitz and Weiss (1992) developed a theory of credit rationing. According to the model, charging a higher interest rate can reduce profits for a lender, as the interest rate (price of money) does not play its normal clearing function. The authors advance two reasons for the negative correlation: an adverse selection and an incentive effect. Pinheiro and Moura (2003) argue that asymmetries of information lead some borrowers to be "informationally captured," and credit bureaus can reduce those asymmetries.

As a result, there is a growing attention on financial market infrastructure companies, such as information repositories. In Brazil, companies like Experian, Equifax, and SPC dominate the Brazilian market of credit bureaus and should experience enhanced quality of the credit scores they produce on the back of a 2019 regulation that incorporates positive credit information into scores (De Mariz, 2020a).

In the case of Brazil, there were 742 active FinTech firms as of 2020, according to Brazilian venture capital fund Distrito, and half of them (49.6%) had been created between 2016 and 2019 (Distrito, 2020). The two largest categories are payments (16.4%), and lending (15.8%). About 30% offer solutions that are Business-to-Consumer (B2C), 54% are Business-to-Business (B2B), and the rest are mixed models. Meanwhile, incumbents are also investing heavily to enhance their platforms and service offering, either via internal projects or via inorganic growth. Latin America's largest private bank, Itaú, has been an important seed investor in FinTech via its incubator and co-work venture called Cubo and has launched its own 100% digital bank called Iti. Digitization bears the promise of more inclusion, more efficient macroeconomic policies, and a better allocation of capital to unlock opportunities.

23.3. The 2020 Crisis Will Accelerate Existing Trends in the Financial Sector

23.3.1. *The crisis is a catalyst for FinTech*

Faster digitization can offer benefits, e.g. leading to a "less resource-intensive economy, allowing carbon emissions to be decoupled from economic growth more quickly," boosting productivity, and "democratizing access to essential services, such as health and education" (Lagarde, 2020). The CFC will accelerate trends that were visible in the financial industry, rather than alter the course of events. The crisis increases the digitization of the industry, branch closures, and potentially transforms banks as channels for policymakers.

In general terms, commentators point to a number of changes that will impact societies and economies, defining COVID-19 as a turning point. Changes in the economy at large may include a preference for shorter supply chains, higher reliance on remote working, consumer patterns relying more on e-commerce, a different form of globalization, and more focus on sustainable practices and investment strategies, including green bonds (Deschryver and De Mariz, 2020). UBS (2020) notes that such changes could involve large changes in retail, a return of select industries such as pharmaceuticals in developed countries, a lower reliance on international air travel, or a migration to smaller cities with lower populational densities. Research also suggests a possible industry consolidation into the hands of a small group of international companies, driven by an intensification of mergers and acquisitions, supported by historically low cost of financing, the search for synergies, and a desire to maintain supply chains. In the retail sector, a McKinsey survey of Brazilian consumers showed that 40% started making online purchases during the pandemic and plan to continue shopping online post–COVID-19, and 35% indicated that they would visit less brick-and-mortar stores in a post–COVID-19 world (McKinsey, 2020).

In banking, the most relevant and irreversible trend that has been visible for the past 20 years is digitization, while some underline that "digitization is the key to resilience in the banking segment" (BCG, 2020). Health and hygiene considerations are a boost to low-touch or no-touch service offerings across industries, ranging from telemedicine, e-commerce, and notaries to online education. In the financial sector, 2020 will be a turning point for digital banking and contactless payments. Oliver Wyman (2020) noted in May 2020 an increase of 30% YOY in card-not-present transactions in the US, while fraud attempts increase 700% YOY, suggesting a need to strengthen risk management.

Digitization will lead to an acceleration in branch closures and redesign, a trend that started post GFC. In Latin America, the peak in branch numbers was reached in 2017, with an expected acceleration in closures (Figure 23.3), leading to a smaller number of transaction-focused locations, causing meaningful impact on employment or commercial real estate. In some segments, the CFC will create new opportunities, with renewed demand for insurance protection.

The perception of FinTechs may also evolve as they navigate through the crisis and prove the resilience and sustainability of their business models. The 2008 crisis made apparent a trend of flight to quality or flight to size, especially in deposits (Federal Reserve Bank of Saint Louis, 2010). FinTechs still represent a very small percentage of deposit-taking, particularly because most of them are not formally regulated as banks. FinTechs' business models are based mostly on credit concession and ancillary services, such as payments, brokerage, or foreign exchange transfers.

The evolution of the financial system is inherently based on innovation, but recent years have shown an acceleration in this trend, and technology bears the promise of a radical transformation in the sector. New business models and companies are challenging incumbents. FinTech is growing rapidly, driven by three factors: high margins in select financial products attracting new players, lower costs of technology and the ubiquity of cell phones, and a stronger support for innovation by regulators. FinTech has thereby created high expectations.

For banks, financial innovation and digitalization provide opportunities for cost savings and revenue gains, as well as transforming the customer experience. Traditional banks are innovating in order to boost efficiency gains, which are meant to offset some of the margin pressure stemming from competition. Physical branch reduction and rationalization bring meaningful cost savings for banks, while many processes are migrated to digital platforms (Figure 23.4). Digital channels (mobile and Internet) are now the main transaction channels for the largest Brazilian banks, according to the Brazilian Central Bank. Banks have experienced a meaningful decrease in profitability over the past decade, and digitization represents an opportunity to reduce costs.

On top of cost savings, the mobile distribution channel generates revenue opportunities. Brazilian banks originate an increasing percentage of personal loans via mobile, including payroll-deducted consumer loans. Banks have also been exploring cross-selling

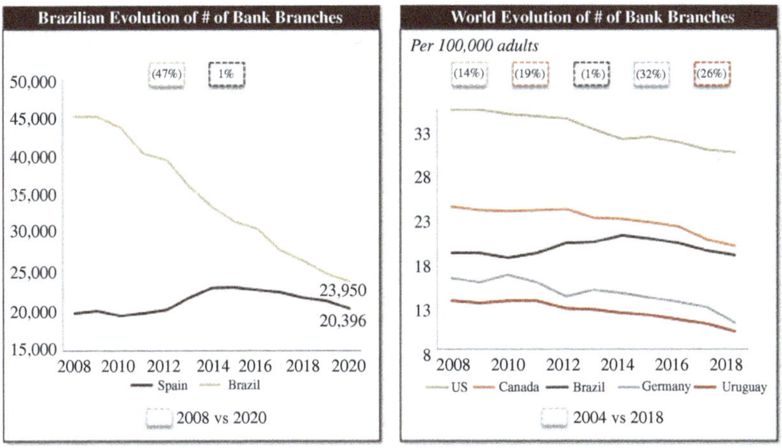

Figure 23.3. Branch closures have accelerated.
Source: WorldBank.

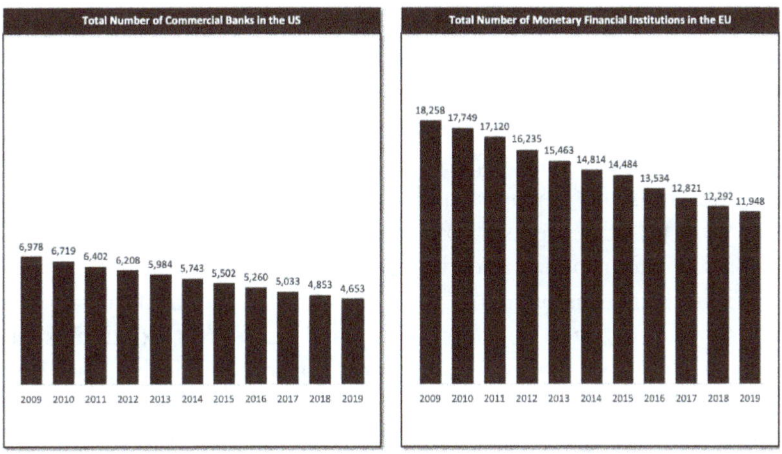

Figure 23.4. The reduction in the number of banks may also accelerate.
Source: BCG (2020).

opportunities — e.g. proposing foreign exchange or travel insurance when clients activate the international feature on their credit cards. Brazilian banks also offer loan renegotiation options on their mobile apps. Going forward, banks note that there is additional revenue potential with the upcoming inclusion of fee-generating services such as insurance products. Moreover, mobile banking is becoming more important for building customer relationships and as a channel that can potentially engage with users 24/7 and enhance the customer experience as well as customer loyalty.

With the use of financial services from non-traditional providers set to rise sharply, banks have responded to threats from FinTech competitors via partnerships. In many cases, FinTech ventures are not disrupting existing players but searching for opportunities to collaborate, as incumbents bring the benefits of deeper pockets and proximity with the regulators. FinTech firms benefit from low client acquisition cost and target the low- to middle-income clients, offering niche solutions and often a smarter customer online experience. In many cases, FinTech firms are not necessarily implementing a disruptive technology but rather building on existing tracks laid by incumbents.

23.3.2. *Is there a convergence between traditional banks and FinTechs?*

FinTechs are no doubt a large beneficiary of the digitization, but not all will benefit. Meanwhile, traditional banks have also invested large amounts to modernize their infrastructure and better serve their customers. The crisis may represent an opportunity for incumbents, as they benefit from deeper liquidity and capital reserves than rising FinTechs. Which category stands to benefit the most from the CFC, comparing incumbents and digital native business models?

While FinTechs are likely to accelerate the number of clients they serve, they will be under increased pressure to deliver sustainable profitability. We expect a concentration in the FinTech sector, with some clear FinTech winners emerging. FinTechs are likely to experience a "winner-takes-all" phase in business-to-consumer models, as platform and scale effects favors size. Meanwhile a convergence of product offerings and perception between select traditional players and FinTechs will emerge. Cyber risks and frauds will be a growing consideration. Moreover, customer perception on FinTechs may become stronger if they manage to withstand the crisis and prove their reliability and safety — two traditional customer concerns.

Within FinTech, electronic payments are evolving. Payments present the triple advantage of having high operating margins for newcomers, requiring less capital investment (compared to credit, for example) and gathering valuable data on customers (which can generate other types of revenues). Payments are a logical entry product for FinTechs. In fact, before resorting to credit, customers need to have a transaction account, build a transaction history, and need to evidence their ability to manage their resources over time.

Electronic payments include online transfers; card-based instruments, such as debit, credit, or prepaid cards; and e-money (World Bank, 2016). Electronic payments, also referred to as digital payments, are often opposed to cash usage and payments by checks. An essential goal of electronic payments is to reduce transaction friction, with better convenience and cost for users. "The practical applicability of the neoclassical modeling approach is now challenged by at least two alternative theoretical paradigms" (Merton and Bodie, 2004). First, "New Institutional Economics, focuses explicitly on transaction costs, taxes, computational limitations, and other frictions." The other paradigm is that: "Behavioral Economics, introduces non-rational and systematically uninformed behavior by agents" (Merton and Bodie, 2004). Humphrey *et al.* (1996) analyze 12 European countries and estimate a reduction in operating costs of €32 billion, or 0.38% of GDP, between 1987 and 1999, driven by the 36% increase in electronic payments and 32% increase in ATM in the total segment of payments. According to Banco Central do Brasil (2007), fully migrating to electronic payments would generate a cost saving of 0.7% of Brazilian GDP, using 2005 data, or approximately BRL R$15 billion.

Payments have been the focus of policymakers, considering all kinds of connections between the different potential parties (GBP or Government, Business, People). For example, Government to People (G2P) payments have largely benefited from a move to electronic channels, as this slashes the costs associated with the disbursement of benefits and wages. The World Bank calls for leveraging on "government payment programs to promote financial inclusion," as "the large volume of payments issued by governments, as well as the nature of some specific programs like social spending programs, represents an opportunity to promote or facilitate financial inclusion on a large scale" (World Bank, 2016).

Brazil has a tradition in innovation in financial technology, especially in payments and transfers, due to a high level of frauds and very high inflation, which demanded both sophisticated and fast payment mechanisms. The Brazilian Central Bank announced the implementation of a peer-to-peer (P2P) system, launched in November 2020, called PIX. This is different from other countries, such as China, where the platform was developed by private entities as a closed system. In Brazil, more than 900 market participants initially declared their intention to connect to PIX. PIX provides P2P payments, with a financial settlement in a few seconds, 24/7 availability, zero cost for person-to-person transactions, and a small cost for payments to merchants. This system is likely to reduce the use of cash, contributing to a key public policy. The system is also expected to compete against other electronic payment methods and may lead to a migration from debit cards to PIX, especially for smaller tickets.

In Mexico, the success of a G2P program had two simultaneous dimensions: a move toward electronic payments and toward centralized payments. In 2012, "97% of pension payments were made by electronic transfers" (Babatz, 2013, p. 23). The unification and digitalization of payments to government employees, retirees, and social transfers was a wide success. By digitizing and centralizing its payments, the Mexican government has "saved USD $1.27 billion per year," equivalent to "3.3% of all its total expenditure on wages, pensions and social transfers" (Babatz, 2013, p. 37). Savings came in the form of float revenues, with no more anticipation in payment, lower transaction fees, and less leakage and operational errors.

Many new acquiring companies emulate the existing ecosystem but propose a faster technology, better antifraud intelligence, and lower prices to their retail clients. Plastic cards are often dematerialized, to be supported by smartphones, removing the need for plastic. The acceptance of Near-Field Communication (NFC) and Quick Response (QR) codes is picking up in Latin America, with heavy investments being made by Big Tech companies such as e-commerce giant Mercado Libre throughout Latin America or digital banks such as Agibank in Brazil. P2P payments are picking up, following the outstanding success of Chinese platforms WeChat and Alipay and Indian platform Paytm. Brazil is scheduled to implement P2P payments in September 2020, thanks to a new switch developed and controlled by the Brazilian Central Bank. For P2P, the main barrier to overcome is often interoperability across systems and software.

23.4. The Crisis Raises Challenges for Companies, Customers, and Regulators

23.4.1. *Access is not enough, the service offering needs to evolve*

Access to digital financial services is on the rise, but quality is an essential dimension of financial inclusion to lead to optimal economic development. The CDC is a unique opportunity for the financial sector to dust off its client service and product offering.

Business models will evolve, not just providing access to a larger number of customers, but effectively creating loyalty with a large service offering. Financial institutions of all types will focus more on the life-time value (LTV) of their clients. In that sense, customer satisfaction, a low level of customer complaints, and sustainable service offerings are likely to become paramount and will reduce the investor excessive focus on customer acquisition cost (CAC). Business focusing on fees will become more attractive for investors in the short term, as credit origination becomes complicated by COVID-19 and uncertain asset quality patterns.

For customers, the digital divide will become even more apparent, with a renewed need for financial education. The current crisis raises unprecedented challenges for customers, who may find that the digital provision of services creates unforeseen barriers, as the accelerated "shift toward digital payments [...] could open a divide in access to payments instruments, which could negatively impact unbanked and older consumers" (Bank of International Settlements, 2020b). Access to a well-functioning Internet as well as readily available hardware are an issue for millions of users. The digitization of banking services may simply reproduce the digital divide observed since the advent of the Internet. This time, the divide may become more critical as many services move to digital means, including banking services, but also education, consumption via e-commerce, telemedicine, or select public services, to name some of the most mentioned during the

COVID-19 crisis. Along with a digital divide, cyber risks are rising as more citizens rely on digital services.

Access is a first necessary step but may not be sufficient. The well-known examples of government subsidies distributed to citizens may provide access to a bank account and sometimes a debit card but does not automatically translate into recurrent usage and the development of financial capabilities.

In Brazil, the Bolsa Familia, the largest conditional redistribution program in the developing world, is a case study in G2P transfers, as the program delivers financial assistance to nearly a third of the total population, and 99% of the recipients receive digital payments into a card or bank account, representing a public policy success (World Bank, 2012). The program "seeks to reduce poverty and inequality" and "break the intergenerational transmission of poverty by conditioning these transfers on beneficiary compliance with human capital requirements," such as "school attendance, vaccines, pre-natal visits" (Lindert *et al.*, 2007, p. 2). There are over 32,000 retail locations where benefits can be withdrawn, and 65% of benefits are received at lottery locations. G2P payments reduce the administrative cost of the program for the government and offer an entry point into the financial system for recipients. According to the World Bank, moving to electronic payment and consolidating four programs into one "improved efficiency by reducing administrative costs" from 14.7% to 2.6% of the value of the grants disbursed (Lindert *et al.*, 2007, pp. 112–113). However, while electronic G2P payments bring efficiency to the system, they are not always associated to an effective inclusion of people: 88% withdraw all the money right away in Brazil, and the use of bank accounts for cash management purposes is still limited. The poorer the household, the more likely they are to withdraw their full transfer at once.

While the existing literature has focused on the dimensions of access and usage, quality of payments is the third dimension that bridges the gap between access and effective usage. What are the characteristics of good quality payment systems? What best practices can be shared when establishing new payment systems and regulations? If citizens have access to the payment capability, why would they not use them? What constrains their usage?

The three main reasons for being unbanked include the costs associated with bank accounts, distances traveled to reach a bank or financial agent, and the various requirements involved in opening a financial account (Allen *et al.*, 2012). World Bank (2013) shows that 34% of firms in developing economies have a bank loan, versus 51% in developed markets. The World Bank (2016, p. 4) estimates that "200 million enterprises in developing economies are still constrained in terms of financing, even though small and medium enterprises generate the greatest number of new jobs, employ the largest number of people in aggregate." Being financially excluded is also linked to income level: the richest 20% of adults in developing countries are more than twice as likely to have a formal account as the poorest 20%. Regulations relating to banking correspondents, simplified financial services, mandatory free basic financial offering, investments into branch opening, and mobile banking have helped meaningfully increase the convenience for citizens to be banked. Those who have access but choose not to use services pose less of a problem for policymakers. Among survey participants without an account in the 2014 Findex survey, only 4% said they do not need one (Demirgüç-Kunt *et al.*, 2015).

The financial capability of the customer has become an increasingly central aspect of the thinking about financial inclusion. Authors define financial capabilities for customers who "have knowledge, skills, and behaviors that enable them to make sound financial decisions" (Kelly and Rhyne, 2015). Financial education is multifaceted: it does not necessarily precede an uptake of financial services but rather goes hand in hand with experimenting new financial solutions and improving one's financial capability.

23.4.2. *Is the crisis leading to new government–bank relationships?*

On the one hand, governments may prefer to use banks as a part of the solution, supporting funding and emergency programs for enterprises and people (G2B, G2P). On the other hand, government may be tempted to use the credit channel with unorthodox policies.

In the case of *Caixa Tem* in Brazil, the program launched by government-owned bank Caixa added 40 million new customers to its client base during the CFC. On the other end, legislative proposals in Brazil in April and May 2020 included proposed caps on credit card lending rates, a removal of negative data from credit bureaus, or an increase in corporate taxes for banks. At the same time, several banking supervisory bodies allowed for flexible provisioning policies, justifying investors' questions about the true solidity of banks. In the context of a full legislative agenda, policymakers are also accelerating measures in favor of digital adaptation of banks, with the case study of P2P payments and open banking in Brazil.

While COVID-19 is certainly not the direct cause of some policies that were years in the making, it has proven to be a formidable catalyst for digitization of the delivery of public services. For example, Brazil Decree No. 10,332, dated April 28, 2020, complemented a policy agenda focused on microreforms whereby the "Brazilian federal government launched a two-year strategic initiative, which establishes the objectives and goals for the digitalization of public services" (Hogan Lovells, 2020). The goal of this strategy is "to improve service quality, by promoting transparency in interactions between the Brazilian public and the Brazilian federal government," using technology to "reduce bureaucracy and corruption, prevent fraudulent activity, protect information and regain the confidence of Brazilians and companies involved in government processes, in addition to reducing overall costs to Brazilians and to the Brazilian government." The government also plans to cut on the number of websites (with 1,500 government websites currently) to one single portal "gov.br" by the end of 2020, and to integrate all of the Brazilian state governments onto the portal by the end of 2022. Only one login will be necessary for Brazilian citizens to access all federal and state public services and as well as broad access to government information. Business creation and closure and work permits will also be facilitated. As a result of the digital government strategy, the Brazilian federal government predicts a saving of BRL 37.9 billion in the next five years (approximately US$800 million). Furthermore, Brazilian citizens will save 147 million hours collectively through the digitalization of governmental services, which is equivalent to one full workday per capita.

The crisis may lead to a new government–bank relationship, or at least a closer partnership. In fact, governments have been quick to identify banks and FinTech as potential channels for public policies, be it via the credit channel, or more simply as a distribution agent for subsidies. Caixa became the exclusive distribution agent of a specific emergency subsidy, nicknamed "coronavoucher," which close to 40 million citizens received throughout Brazil. Strikingly, the program allowed the government in collaboration with Caixa to identify 40 million citizens who were excluded from the banking system and whose needs may be better identified in future social policies. Another focus of policymakers and supervisors has been to ensure that liquidity is not frozen at some large banking institutions, preventing "money to flow to the edges of the system" (Franco, 2020), but that the credit channel is well functioning and performs its mission to reach consumers and corporates, both large and small.

23.5. Conclusion

The CFC is having a profound impact on financial institutions. While some policy measures were not unusual and reminded of previous crises, the evolution of banks, insurance, payments companies, and other financial institutions is unique in many ways. The 2008 GFC no doubt offered an important playbook, but the response to the 2020 CFC was unique, swift, and sizeable. The crisis accelerated existing trends in the industry, including digitization, branch closures, customer-centric models, and the need for sustainable profitability.

The CFC also accelerated a convergence between traditional players that embraced change and select FinTech players who had reached critical mass. In that sense, the CFC confirms the emergence and consolidation of FinTech models, while some traditional financial providers were able to take advantage of the crisis, benefiting from their comfortable balance sheets grouped with a large existing client base.

On the flip side, the crisis exacerbated some challenges for financial institutions, customers, and regulators, including the digital divide, misplaced regulations, and cyber risks. Financial innovation can once again be a formidable tool to include more citizens and support development goals.

References

Adrian, T. and Shin, H.S. (2010). The changing nature of financial intermediation and the financial crisis of 2007-09, Federal Reserve Bank of New York Staff Reports, Staff Report no. 439, March 2010.

Akerlof, G.A. (1970). The market for lemons: Quality uncertainty and the market mechanism. *The quarterly journal of economics*, 488–500.

Allen, F., Demirgüç-Kunt, A., Klapper, L., *et al.* (2012). The foundations of financial inclusion: Understanding ownership and use of formal accounts. World Bank, *Policy Research Paper 6290.*

Anginer, D. and Demirguc-Kunt, A. (2010). Bank capital and systemic stability, *Policy Research Working Paper 6948*, World Bank June 2014.

Babatz, G. (2013). Sustained effort, saving billions: Lessons from the Mexican government's shift to electronic payments. *Better Than Cash Alliance Case Study.* Retrieved from http://betterthancash.org.

Baldwin, R. (2020). Keeping the lights on: Economic medicine for a medical shock, VoxEU CEPR. Retrieved from https://voxeu.org/article/how-should-we-think-about-containing-covid-19-economic-crisis. Accessed March 13, 2020.

Baldwin, R. and Weder di Mauro, B. (2020), Mitigating the COVID economic crisis: Act fast and do whatever it takes, VoxEU CEPR. Retrieved from https://voxeu.org/content/mitigating-covid-economic-crisis-act-fast-and-do-whatever-it-takes. Accessed March 18, 2020.

Banco Central do Brasil (2007). Custo e Eficiencia na Utilizacao de Instrumentos de Pagamento de Varejo. Reforma do sistema de pagamentos de varejo. BCB, Brasilia.

Bank of International Settlements (2019). Annual Report.

Bank of International Settlements (2020a). Measures to reflect the impact of Covid-19, Basel Committee on Banking Supervision.

Bank of International Settlements (2020b). Covid-19, cash, and the future of payments, Raphael Auer, Giulio Cornelli and Jon Frost, BIS Bulletin 03.

BCG (2020). Global Risk 2020, It's Time for Banks to Self-Disrupt, April.

Bekaert, G., Ehrmann, M., Fratzscher, M. and Mehl A. (2014). The global crisis and equity market contagion. DIW, Discussion papers 1352.

Beltratti, A. and Stulz, R.M. (2009). Why did some banks perform better during the credit crisis? A cross-country study of the impact of governance and regulation, European Corporate Governance Institute, Finance Working Paper No 254/2009.

Bernanke, B.S., Lown, C.S. and Friedman, B.M. (1991). The credit crunch. *Brookings Papers on Economic Activity*, **1991**(2), 205–247.

Bernanke, B., Gertler, M. and Gilchrist, S. (1994). The financial accelerator and the flight to quality. NBER Working Paper No. w4789.

Burhouse, S. and Osaki, Y. (2014). FDIC National survey of unbanked and underbanked households. Federal Deposit Insurance Corporation.

Cermeño, R. and Roa M.J. (2013). Desarrollo financiero, crecimiento y volatidad: Revisión de la literatura reciente. Centro de Estudios Monetarios Latinoamericanos, CEMLA, *WP No. 9*.

Claessens, S. (2006). Access to financial services: A review of the issues and public policy objectives. *The World Bank Research Observer*, **21**(2), 207–240.

De Mariz, F. (2020a). Using data for financial inclusion: The case of credit bureaus in Brazil. *Columbia University Journal of International Affairs*. Retrieved from https://jia.sipa.columbia.edu/online-articles/using-data-financial-inclusion-case-credit-bureaus-brazil. Accessed July 6, 2021.

De Mariz, F. (2020b). Fintech for impact: how can financial innovation advance inclusion? Wiley Press. In *Global Handbook of Impact Investing: Solving Global Problems Via Smarter Capital Markets Towards A More Sustainable Society*, De Morais Sarmento, E. and Paul Herman, R. (eds.), (Wiley), pp. 1159–1192.

Demirgüç-Kunt, A., Klapper, L.F., Singer, D. *et al.* (2015). The Global Findex Database 2014: Measuring financial inclusion around the world.

Deschryver, P. and De Mariz, F. (2020). What future for the green bond market? How can policymakers, companies and investors unlock the potential of the green bond market? *Journal of Risk and Financial Management*, **13**(3), 61. Retrieved from https://doi.org/10.3390/jrfm13030061

Distrito (2020). Fintech Report Brasil.

Ebanx (2020). Contactless payments grew 5 times in Brazil over one year. 8 May. Retrieved from https://labs.ebanx.com/en/news/payments/contactless-payments-grew-5-times-in-brazil-over-one-year. Accessed July 11, 2020.

European Commission (2020). European Commission to issue EU SURE bonds of up to €100 billion as social bonds. 7 October. Retrieved from https://ec.europa.eu/commission/presscorner/detail/en/ip_20_1808. Accessed December 19, 2020.

Federal Reserve Bank of Saint Louis (2010). Flight to safety and U.S. Treasury securities. St Louis: The Regional Economist, July 1, 2010.

Franco, G. (2020). Interview with Gustavo Franco. *UBS Conference*, 23 June 2020, Sao Paulo.

Greenwald, B. and Stiglitz, J.E. (2003). *Towards a New Paradigm in Monetary Economics* (Cambridge University Press) Cambridge, Mass.

Hogan Lovells (2020). Brazil's digital government strategy takes effect. Retrieved from https://ehoganlovells.com/rv/ff00623553824c7b5420f64e3c42adf0f4ac174e. Accessed July 11, 2020.

Humphrey, D.B., Pulley, L.B. and Vesala, J.M. (1996). Cash, paper, and electronic payments: A cross-country analysis. *Journal of Money, Credit and Banking*, **28**(4), 914–939.

IIF (2020). European Conference: The E.U., Covid-19 and the Future of Financial Services, May 26, 27.

IMF (2009). The global financial crisis: Explaining cross-country differences in the output impact. IMF Working Papers WP/09/280.

IMF (2020). The great lockdown: Worst economic downturn since the great depression, April 14. Retrieved from https://blogs.imf.org/2020/04/14/the-great-lockdown-worst-economic-downturn-since-the-great-depression (Accessed July 5, 2020).

Kaminsky, L. and Reinhart, C. (1998). Leading Indicators of Currency Crises, IMF Staff Papers.

Kelly, S. and Rhyne, E. (2015). By the numbers: Benchmarking progress toward financial inclusion. Center for Financial Inclusion, Accion.

Lagarde, C. (2020). Fostering sustainable growth in Europe. 20 November. Keynote speech by Christine Lagarde, President of the ECB, at the European Banking Congress.

La Porta, R., Lopez-de-Silanes, F., Shleifer, A., *et al.* (2000). Investor protection and corporate governance. *Journal of Financial Economics*, **58**(1), 3–27.

Levine (2005). Finance and growth: Theory and evidence. In *Handbook of Economic Growth*, Volume 1, pp. 865–934.

Lindert, K., Linder, A., Hobbs, J., *et al.* (2007). The nuts and bolts of Brazil's Bolsa Família Program: implementing conditional cash transfers in a decentralized context. Social Protection Discussion Paper 39853.

Mas, I. (2009). The economics of branchless banking. *Innovations*, **4**(2), 57–75. doi: 10.1162/itgg.2009.4.2.57.

McKinsey (2020). O novo consumidor pós-Covid - Pesquisa Mesa Redonda McKinsey. Retrieved from https://www.acileme.com.br/noticias:o-novo-consumidor-pos-covid----pesquisa-mesa-redonda-mckinsey. Accessed July 5, 2020.

Merton, R.C. and Bodie, Z. (2004). A conceptual framework for analyzing the financial system. In *The Global Financial System: A Functional Perspective*, pp. 3–31.

Pinheiro, A.C. and Moura, A. (2003). Segmentation and the use of information in brazilian credit markets. *Credit Reporting Systems and the International Economy*.

Oliver Wyman (2020). Webinar: Covid-19 and the Impact on the U.S. Financial System – Payments, June 3.

Reinhart, C. and Rogoff, K. (2009). The aftermath of financial crises, NBER Working Paper No. 14656.

Reinhart, C. and Rogoff, K. (2014). Recovery from financial crises: Evidence from 100 Episodes, NBER, January.

Roa, M.J. (2015). *Financial Inclusion in Latin America and the Caribbean: Access, Usage and Quality* (CEMLA, Mexico City).

Stiglitz, J.E. (1989). Financial markets and development. *Oxford Review of Economic Policy*, **5**(4), 55–68.

Stiglitz, J.E. and Weiss, A. (1981). Credit rationing in markets with imperfect information. *The American Economic Review*, **71**(3), 393–410.

Stiglitz, J.E. and Weiss, A. (1992). Asymmetric information in credit markets and its implications for macro-economics. *Oxford Economic Papers*, **44**(4), 694–724.

Tchana, F. (2014). Banking regulation effective to prevent crisis. *Emerging Markets Review*. Retrieved from https://jia.sipa.columbia.edu/online-articles/using-data-financial-inclusion-case-credit-bureaus-brazil. Accessed July 6, 2021.

Tirole, J. (2010). Illiquidity and all its friends, BIS Working Paper 303.

UBS (2020). Future reimagined: Propelled to the thinking economy. UBS Research, 18 June.

World Health Organization (2020). WHO Timeline — COVID-19. Retrieved from https://www.who.int/news-room/detail/27-04-2020-who-timeline—covid-19. Accessed July 5, 2020.

World Bank Group (2012). *General Guidelines for the Development of Government Payment Systems, Financial Infrastructure Series* (World Bank Publications), Cambridge, Mass.

World Bank Group (2013). Global Financial Development Report 2014: Financial Inclusion, **2**, (World Bank Publications), Cambridge, Mass.

World Bank Group (2016). *Innovation in Electronic Payment Adoption: The Case of Small Retailers* (World Bank Publications), Cambridge, Mass.

https://doi.org/10.1142/9781800610781_0024

Chapter 24

Future Research Avenues for Finance in Transformation*

Wissem Ajili-Ben Youssef[†,§] and Yves Rakotondratsimba[‡,¶]

[†]*ESLSCA — Paris Business School, Paris, France*

[‡]*ECE Paris, INSEEC U, France*

[§]*wbenyoussef@eslsca.fr*

[¶]*yves.rakotondratsimba@ece.fr*

Abstract

The world has been changing long before the onset of the economic and financial crisis related to COVID-19. However, the pandemic precipitated the setting in motion of several events: economic and financial crises, social and political tensions, and ecological transition. The digital transformation in companies is reshaping the finance landscape. Not only businesses and organizations but also the academic world and researchers are affected by the changes. Disruption in the finance generates both challenges and opportunities. The authors put forward recommendations and research lines, inspired by both literature and existing practices, to highlight finance transformation.

24.1. Introduction

Even though the COVID-19 health crisis seems to have a somewhat disconnected origin from the finance sphere, it is bound to

---

*In memory of Professor Yves Rakotondratsimba for his research, generosity, and humbleness.

leave unprecedented traces because of the magnitude of the ensuing economic crisis. However, before the pandemic outbreak, the world of finance has already been disrupted by digital transformation (DT) and environmental and energetic transitions (EET). DT and EET were described and analyzed by many academic and professional authors, including Andersson *et al.* (2018), Financial Stability Board (2017), Fenwick and Vermeulen (2018), UNEP-FI (2018), UN-Environment Inquiry (2019), and Chenet (2019).

Gomber *et al.* (2017) and Kavuri and Milne (2019) studied research gaps in FinTech and digital finance. Their research suggestions focus on organizational behavior, interactions between the involved parties, and technological innovations. Moreover, it is not only companies that are impacted by significant changes but also the world of education. In particular, teacher-researchers must self-reinvent in line with changing times (Accenture, 2018; Arnett, 2014; Iberdrola, 2020; Singh, 2017).

By analyzing academic work and professional reports from consulting firms, various think tanks, and supranational organizations, this chapter aims to provide forecasts and research lines to highlight finance transformation. In this work, the authors develop 10 research avenues for integration by researchers, educators, and the other concerning parties in the professional environment (i.e. companies, decision-makers, and regulators).

The 10 proposals are: (i) Dealing with emerging factors, (ii) interacting with platforms, (iii) use of smart financial products, (iv) adjustments to market frictions, (v) development of personalized solutions, (vi) investigations in explainable machine learning (xML), (vii) reworking on models, (viii) multi-time steps prediction, (ix) development of research on research, and (x) coupling education and research.

The first eight research propositions are about the frameworks of approaches and concepts at the heart of the DT and EET. They are essentially linked to quantitative techniques but are described qualitatively in this chapter. The two remaining leads are on research and the coupling of research with education. The idea is that part of it requires training for human resources for trade and business transformation.

The remainder of the chapter is organized as follows: Section 24.2 discusses transformations in the finance industry. It analyses some elements relating to DTs and EETs, drawing on the research of many scholars (Andersson *et al.*, 2018; Chenet, 2019; Jagtiani *et al.*, 2018; UNEP-FI, 2019; Zetzsche *et al.*, 2018). Section 24.3 identifies 10 future research avenues to highlight digital finance transformation. Section 24.4 concludes the chapter.

24.2. Transformations in Finance Sphere

24.2.1. *Digital transformation*

Scholarly articles related to DTs and EETs in the finance sphere are available freely in the Internet. They are abundant and comprise academic literature or professional reports from consulting societies, various think tanks, and supranational bodies.

Many digital changes and transformations in the finance sphere are visible over the past five years. For example, there has been significant restructuring in the financial industries through. The disapperance of trades in various global banks (BNP, SG, HSBC, among others). There is also a substantial increase in retail bank customers (increased bank rates) and changes in their relationships and behaviors toward banks, mainly through digital means. It is crucial to point out that these changes are linked to increasing financial cost reductions and tailor-made offerings. These profound changes have been driven by new entrants such as FinTech. The latter took over and transformed financial services exclusively held by traditional banking institutions. FinTech has demonstrated abilities that have ended up upsetting the lack of inertia specific to traditional financial institutions.

The DT period has also led to the emergence of new assets, such as digital assets and cryptocurrencies. Initially, conventional institutions and some customers have downplayed the impact of virtual currencies since their volume was initially marginal compared to traditional assets. However, as the underlying technologies are still in substantial evolution, higher authorities, such as central banks, have taken the phenomenon of cryptocurrencies seriously. It will likely shake up both the role of traditional assets and the entire financial system (Bank of England, 2019; Financial Stability Board, 2017; Jung *et al.*, 2019).

Existing regulations, primarily for financial institutions, reach their limits (Jagtiani *et al.*, 2018). Regulatory constraints (always increasingly restrictive since the crises beginning in 2007) will lead to traditional institutions losing their competitiveness in the face of new players such as FinTech and TechFin Zetzsche *et al.* (2018). The new players have taken over parts of the banks' activities while not being subject to the same rules. The prudential measures were developed to preserve the entire financial system. However, these measures assume that financial institutions are the leading players. Nowadays, there are severe systemic risks in the world of DTs, where traditional financial institutions become heavily dependent on very few third-party technology players. Financial regulations, such as Basel II and III, were carefully developed by the financial sector and the Basel Committee after extensive deliberations. The rapid progress of technologies and the emergence of new players means that the regulatory development efforts, spread over time, are no longer sustainable. Finance is facing DT, which is destroying conventional organizations and constructing new rules for organizations and players. Knowledge of the structures and operations of traditional trades no longer address DT. The irony is that financial regulators and supervisors, with their eyes on the control of adverse effects of technologies, will also have to integrate and use these technologies as tools.

On the other side, within the DT framework, it is necessary to go back to the decryption aspect to identify the factors and mechanisms that underlie these transformations. Both in practice and literature, it is now known that behind the visible changes, as mentioned in points (ii)–(iv) earlier, are technologies and data. Significantly, the latter is still increasing exponentially since storage and calculation capabilities are available. Machine Learning Algorithm (MLA) concepts also play a role in extracting knowledge from data. The creation of new values, more interesting (for several stakeholders at once) than those obtained with conventional approaches, arises from the exploration of the combined effects of the use of MLAs, data, and above all the agility to link these technical devices with the business side, whose choice is crucial. The financial institution's front-end business model, which is primarily geared toward shareholder interest, gives way to the business model, which focuses mainly on the customer experience. This change was noticeable, as the banks' direct competitors highlighted customer satisfaction and demonstrated agility, which a rigid traditional structure had difficulty implementing. FinTech's agility, cost reduction, and custom-made product and service offerings were only possible through data and technology exploration.

For example, banks such as JP Morgan have moved toward the massive use of new technologies and have even declared their statutes' evolution from a financial institution to a technology company. Whether in finance or other fields, it is more important to seize technologies and data for survival in activities. The ability to define and have a strategy, considering both the holistic aspect of the business ecosystem considered and the mastery of the specific and local part of the business, will ensure prosperity and differentiation among competitors. Also, for the players of traditional financial institutions, there is the concern not to be overwhelmed to ensure and participate in experiments based on new technologies, which have not yet sufficiently reached a certain degree of maturity.

As mentioned in the previous overview of the DT's directly visible aspects, the changes have brought new finance opportunities and created new problems. These include emerging risks from technology use, mainly cyber risks, systemic risk due to dependence on a few technology companies, risks related to data usage, and algorithm risks (Mishra, 2019a,b).

24.2.2. *EET*

The finance sector is also currently facing EET (Sachs *et al.*, 2019; UN-Environment Inquiry, 2019). The process followed by finance in sustainable development has had a long history. Many scholars described the prominent historical landmarks of this process, mainly the Paris Agreement (2015) and the publication of the EU Action Plan on Financial Sustainability Growth (2018) (Chenet, 2019). The finance sector has long participated in the fight against global warming through the creation of carbon markets. There is also the contribution to accelerate and encourage investors in the investment field to exclude activities that contribute to environmental degradation and instead focus on investing in sustainable activities (e.g. renewable energy).

Although the necessary organizational foundations are now established for sustainability, and it seems to be an opportunity, also probably an obligation, there are several economic and technical issues, making it challenging to align finance with environmental objectives. Nowadays, finance knows the emergence of physical and transition risks. These risks are entirely different from traditional risks (Chenet,

2019; Ducruet and Roux, 2019; Ganguly *et al.*, 2017; Le Guenedal, 2019), and actors are not yet armed for their measures and management. As a result, green products' development supports products (BNP Paribas, 2019; UNEP-FI, 2018; UNEP-FI, 2019).

Although the COVID-19 health crisis has accelerated DT in finance and even other areas, the case of EETs seems to be more scrambled. During the containment period beginning in March 2020, observers and supporters believed that the commitment to climate would have gathered favorable elements for the acceleration of its implementations. While the COVID-19 health crisis continues with the degradation of the economic conditions (massive destruction of employment) and the increase of political and social tensions, the trajectory for implementing environmental conservation initiatives is compromised.

Membership in the finance DT appears to be easier to impose than with EETs. Indeed, at the firm level (or the traditional financial institution), indifference to the DT can be immediately sanctioned by losing competitiveness or foreclosing on the market. For the EET, a reluctance to move does not necessarily lead to a company's rapid disappearance. Even if deterrents (through penalties or taxes or purchases of emission rights) exist, they may be less effective in the face of fine-tuning that the company implements. In addition, in the context of the alignment of finance with environmental objectives, economic efficiencies through incentive mechanisms are not yet entirely convincing.

Although a global awareness of the environment appears to be present, the divergent economic interests between involved parties make it challenging to implement initiatives. These initiatives developed from above by various bodies (experts, supporters, regulators, legislators, citizens) based on global analyses (mainly statistical, macroeconomic models) cannot accurately consider adequate considerations at the local level of companies to environmental initiatives (Robert, 2017). We can also not forget the impact of Greenwashing, which arises from the overzealousness of the proponents of environmental and climate protection.

The lack of credibility and adherence to climate and environmental initiatives can give credence to developing alternative approaches. Indeed, official initiatives cannot sufficiently consider local objectives and technical reserves (Le Guenedal, 2019). Global initiatives and related laws are organizational tools introduced by the governing bodies for the concerned parties' move (by incentive or obligation) toward a sustainable environment. Artificial Intelligence (AI) techniques can also relate to local situations (Nassiry, 2018; Oxford Sustainable Finance Programme, 2018; Rolnick *et al.*, 2019). However, the massive use of AI-based technological approaches, although of interest, may run counter to preserving the environment.

24.3. Research Avenues for Finance Transformation

Section 24.2 has provided some decryption or deciphering of the changing world, particularly that of finance under the combined effect of DT and EETs. In this section, the authors develop ideas to move forward. To achieve this, the authors sketch ideas from general or global organizations. Going in this direction may be structured and inspiring, but the result may be subject to controversies due to the somewhat contradictory interests of various concerned parties. The proposal is likely to be followed by little impact or concrete actions and become a dead letter, as shown through several research works. To have more impact, the authors focus on the academic world, mainly researchers and educators whose interests are quite convergent.

The themes developed do not exhaustively cover possible research avenues in the context of finance in transformation. However, these themes reflect the field of action that the authors are acting in. The authors have distinguished ten tracks for convenience. However, some are dependent and probably may be classified otherwise. The authors have gathered here ideas that can help concerned parties (academics, among others) better bounce back in the current disruptions of all kinds.

Until the financial crisis of 2008, academic research focused on problems according to the point of view and the interests of the institutions (financial and insurance). The situation has completely changed, with the entry of new players that are not necessarily financial but mainly technology companies, and the business model has moved toward the customer experience. Consequently, the approaches in finance research and their content is expected to be entirely disrupted.

The characterization of disruption is not exaggerated insofar as the research knowledge acquired up to 2008, in the financial industry and institutions, does not include the operational aspects of digital assets, risks, and transactions. The current transition period (where both old and emerging practices coexist, intermediated- disintermediated products, etc.) does not yet have a conceptual and structural framework identified as was the case before — a framework is supposed to guide and enlighten practices, trades, and especially education.

24.3.1. *Dealing with new risk factors*

Even for standard financial risks, knowledge (already quite advanced) must evolve since the fundamental problems have not been entirely solved. Nevertheless, solutions can be defined as technologies evolve. Since the needs have been designed, solutions have been found and based mainly on reductive models. Such a restriction is motivated by the need to understand the phenomena and consider their implementation's technical feasibility.

As data becomes more abundant and technologies are captured and addressed, the same market problem (e.g. valuation and coverage of financial products) will be discussed through data-driven approaches. Approaches based on econometric or stochastic models (although sparingly chosen by the modeler) are insufficient and outdated. Researchers and educators must build the training materials and documents corresponding to these evolutions toward data approaches (similar to those available before with conventional models).

In the meantime, with DTs and EETs, emerging risks (not necessarily financial) with significant physical, economic, and financial impacts need to be incorporated into the standard and well-established framework of risk management. The increasing use of digital assets (such as cryptocurrencies) creates new risks (Ganguly *et al.*, 2017). The coexistence between traditional assets, digital assets, and digital technologies changes the risk landscape and, consequently, actions and approaches to risk management (Mishra, 2019a,b; UNEP-FI, 2019).

Emerging non-financial risks (physical and environmental, technology-related, or transition risks) can result in financial losses, either local (individual or corporate) or global or systemic.

Nowadays, finance can identify the global change in the risk landscape and qualitatively describe the possible interactions between different types of risks and various transactions/operations. However, quantification (allowing good management and hedging) is still the fundamental challenge that finance research must undertake.

For example, quantitative measures and analyses of the risks associated with environmental transitions are essentially infancy (Ducruet and Roux, 2019; Dunz *et al.*, 2019; Le Guenedal, 2019; Oxford Sustainable Finance Programme, 2018). Cyber risks are an essential investigation field because of the difficulties associated with their complex nature (involving both technology and the human nature). Coverage of such types of risks is a challenge for two reasons: conventional quantitative approaches cannot be directly implemented, and technological alternatives (using ML techniques via blockchains) must be improved (Carter and Mainelli, 2018).

The problems of assessing, managing, and hedging risks (or those associated with product valuation, market regulation, etc.), can be addressed using several approaches, both conventional (as with stochastic models) and technological (based on data and associated concepts). The solution must be in the multidisciplinary approaches focusing on the global aspect and the complexities inherent in the socio-economic phenomena.

Technical knowledge development can turn risks into (monetary) opportunities. The monetization of the risk associated with a phenomenon (adverse) is possible, e.g. through the offer of an insurance product or compensation of losses in the event of a contractually defined event. However, the hedging product may generate additional risk for the seller and that it is necessary to manage. The point is that all types of risks (financial or not) are increasing and becoming interdependent and complex to manage. Management should be based on both qualitative and quantitative approaches. The two approaches are complementary and feed on each other.

Studies of non-financial emerging risk factors and their links to financial risks are challenges and opportunities that still need to be explored. For example, as in the cyber risk case, it is hard to quantify the non-financial risk factor. The challenge is whether to assess the economic/monetizable impact directly or to persevere on a proper technique of filtration of the risk factor or to proceed otherwise using a proxy-based on a carefully chosen algorithmic approach.

24.3.2. *Platforms*

In the context of DT that impacts human activities, platforms are ubiquitous, either to serve as an intermediatory between various stakeholders or as a medium for the exchange of material or intangible goods and services. Increasingly growing and important value creations are taking place across platforms by exploring and exploiting data.

Thus, even if it is not yet an essential focus of the academic world (both for research and education), the study of platforms may stimulate an exciting investigation field. Several issues (organizations, structures, business models, technologies, techniques, scientific, ethical, social, political, legal, etc.) are increasingly embedded across platforms.

On one hand, there is the analysis and decryption of organizations' behaviors and exchanges around platforms. For example, it will enable the evolution of traditional business models and value creations in this changing world. In addition to the structural aspect, there is also the utility of better understanding the interdependencies in the digital ecosystem to better address and appreciate the dimensions of societal issues such as workaround platforms.

On the other hand, the platforms' quantitative aspects deserve special attention and actions that should be carried out and not neglected. It is crucial to understand how exactly valuations are performed across platforms. This valuation provides a better appreciation of both implicit structures and decisions that directly affect certain parties involved.

Having precise and formalized structures on the platforms makes it possible to assess the parties' decisions. Are some workers using the platforms exploited to benefit others who capture a significant part of their values? Or is it the business model itself with limits so that it does not live up to what one should expect and thus generates disillusionment or inequalities that are difficult to accept socially?

Intense research, both qualitative and quantitative, on the specific characteristics of platforms is thus to be carried out. In principle, a multidisciplinary approach should be put in place to achieve relevant, actionable results. Qualitative descriptions currently exist on how platforms work across some businesses (Cennamo, 2019; Choudary, 2018; Dhar and Stein, 2016; Pollari, 2018). There are also dispersed studies on technical and scientific considerations (e.g. dynamic pricing) (Liu *et al.*, 2019; Ye *et al.*, 2018). However, materials, books, or references are not yet available that combine the conceptual and generic aspects that allow students, researchers, and other stakeholders to explore and exploit the platforms' depth and richness.

24.3.3. *Smart financial products*

There is now a constant need to imagine new or innovative practical use cases offered by blockchain technology. This technology allows the automatization and disintermediation of some operations. It provides information and assets stocking with a strong guarantee of protection against falsification.

The blockchain's use requires, on the one hand, some technical notions about the practical use of aspects related to the technology itself. On the other hand, the primary objective of one whats to do on the business side (transfer of value, execution of a contract, an offer of intangible content, etc.). Even if a classic product is offered (e.g. an option on a given underlying asset), the technical support switch should slightly or even substantively amend the contract's offer and execution. Blockchain technology expands contract offerings on both the "tailor-made" nature and the efficiency of performance.

Blockchain technologies generate broad opportunities for strategic and technical research. For example, one can imagine and want to create innovative products that meet efficient supply and demand. To fix ideas, we can compare with the case of conventional financial contracts that are options on a given underlying asset. The smart contract version reduces costs and allows flexibility in executions and just as well in the contract's very structure and just as well in the conventional contracts, varying structure to meet the needs of customers. As a second example, one may start by noticing the difficulty one has with some support of risks or investments (challenging to observe and not having very little statistical data for the associated side in noticeable impact). This difficulty can be overcome or bypassed with the use of the technique related to blockchain. Indeed, for the cyber risk case, one can even help construct a new index or observable support, not contestable, promoting the emergence of useful products that a conventional market cannot offer (Carter and Mainelli, 2018).

Given the substantial change in delivery support and even the agreements' nature compared to conventional contracts, it is crucial to develop theoretical and conceptual approaches (ISDA, 2018). The derivative valuation assumes that the market is essentially directed at institutional actors. In contrast, the logic for a "tailor-made product" aimed at a few, not necessarily institutional, players is very different (Fries and Kohl-Landgraf, 2018). The researcher thus sees himself offering new research opportunities, either by improving existing knowledge or by inventing new ones.

The smart contract use goes through its theoretical construction base (which should be more or less comparable to the conventional construction), its implementation through codes, and other aspects, commercial and legal. (Fries *et al.*, 2019). The smart contract encompasses several disciplines, such as traditional classical finance with qualitative and quantitative aspects, technologies of blockchains, development of codes, and legal aspects.

24.3.4. *Adjustment to market frictions*

Standard financial theories taught at least until the financial crisis of 2008, and on which industrial practices are based, have been quite often developed in simplified frameworks, such as that with the assumption of the absence of transaction costs. Among the fundamental reasons for the appearance of FinTech is the cost reduction for parties (buyer and seller). Thus, adjusting theories within the transaction costs framework becomes a crucial concern in finance research (Buhler *et al.*, 2018).

For a product or object taken in isolation, neglecting friction can be acceptable and even desirable in the benefit of a better understanding of the issue. However, if at the same time several phenomena or objects (interdependent) are considered, then the frictions can become integral so they should be regarded as even modifying or amending the basic theory of an item taken in isolation. Research in finance would have to go back in no small part, if not completely, to the theories where friction is rejected. So, it is a huge undertaking that awaits the interested researcher.

It is important to note that the incorporation of transaction costs through a conventional approach was essentially considered a margin adjustment. For example, in the portfolio theory literature, transaction costs have been additional constraints associated with the scrubbed friction decision equation. However, transaction costs must be incorporated into the expectation of the portfolio's random loss and profit. We simplified to avoid calculation problems. When more resources are available (including various algorithmic approaches), and care is taken to reduce costs, it is high timc that the researcher came to the full consideration of the phenomenon. Transaction costs were neglected since the reasoning is from a financial institution's point of view, which has had the opportunity to reduce its costs by, e.g. influencing the volume of its transactions. In the era of "bespoke" for the customer, it is different, and this is where we can find the agility we recognize that defines FinTech.

24.3.5. *Developing custom solutions*

One of the strengths of the new technologies is that they address specific local situations where global recommendations cannot work well. With Big Data, insurance companies can offer individualized contracts and pricing and consequently detach themselves from the strong constraints linked to mutualization. Also, the strength and essential differentiation of a FinTech comes from its agility to offer increasingly individualized services at a lower cost, which a traditional institution like the bank cannot provide because of the rigidity related to its very structure.

Quite often, services or products provided by traditional financial institutions arise from a set of academic thoughts or practical requirements established in past contexts that may be very different from the present. The portfolio theory (dating from the 1950s) is still taught in schools although it ignores transaction costs, digital assets, and data availability. Furthermore, the portfolio theory is based on the presence of a fictitious market serving as a reference.

Traditional learning should be reconsidered and reworked to adapt to the current new context. The achievements, coming from various academic researchers' joint efforts, have been developed from the specific point of view of a financial institution intended for clients but whose business model is primarily geared to the investors' interests. For example, the traditional portfolio theory was developed from the perspective of an institution. It completely ignores the profile of an individual investor client whose wealth is low and to whom the impact of transaction costs could be severe.

In the current context, where the business model is focused on the customer experience, it becomes crucial to develop models that make it possible to create "tailor-made" products and services. Therefore, it is a new avenue for the researcher, who should be concerned not only with traditional financial institutions' problems but also with those of alternative entities such as FinTech and TechFins and individual clients.

The logic of tailored product development can be very different from that used for conventional standardized products. Traditional tools, or even the foundations of some approaches, cannot be used. Determining a price based on a probabilistic risk-neutral approach, assuming the existence of a market without arbitrage, makes no sense if one considers just the case of an isolated customer. It is essential to know that digital financial assets do not behave like traditional financial assets, so the latter's asset class theories will not be suitable for the former class. Also, the mixtures between classical and digital active ingredients give rise to fundamental problems. In any case, the "tailor-made" framework opens a new research avenue for finance.

24.3.6. *xML survey*

The use cases that provide startling results, thereby jostling the finance field, come from exploring knowledge from data and through the MLA techniques (Bank of England, 2019; BNP Paribas, 2019; Financial Stability Board, 2017; Jagtiani *et al.*, 2018). It also now appears that ML is becoming paramount in various areas other than finance (Carter and Mainelli, 2018; Fenwick and Vermeulen, 2018; Oxford Sustainable Finance Programme, 2018; Rolnick *et al.*, 2019; UN-Environment Inquiry, 2019).

The ML studies have focused mainly on the descriptions of use cases or applications in everyday life and the algorithms used to perform the tasks related to these cases. Studies have focused on the importance of ML and scope for both practical applications and classical theoretical approaches. Nowadays, the challenge is to consider the three following notions: transparency, interpretability, and explainability. These concepts are now a concern for some academic researchers and involved parties (Moody, 2019; Roscher *et al.*, 2020;

Xie *et al.*, 2020). Throughout the rest of this chapter, xML will designate the research and analysis field whose concerns revolve around these three questions.

Although xML appears to be more philosophical or abstract, it also has important implications for many stakeholders (legislators, regulators, decision-makers, even ML users) (Bracke *et al.*, 2019; Faggell, 2020). For example, xML makes it possible to decide better on aspects of discrimination that the algorithm may generate and, just as well, build trust for users in the black box that some MLAs represent but whose results can mobilize considerable financial amounts. With xML, it is possible to better integrate machine returns to detect some unsuspected effects thanks to the algorithm's functionalities.

xML research then becomes a matter that researchers should allocate more time to. The results of this research deserve to be taught and popularized to benefit all non-academic stakeholders. Finally, one should be aware that xML research can mobilize technical knowledge (by entering the algorithms) and exceptional attention to the structures and organizations within the application scope.

24.3.7. *Reworking on models*

Both the world before and the world of today, that is undergoing a complete transformation and transition, have the need to introduce and make use of models, which can have several purposes: to explain phenomena, to predict facts, to manage positions, and to support operational decision-making.

Interdependent economic and environmental phenomena lead to the usefulness of stacking (sub) models. Since the classical models (econometric, stochastic) taken in isolation have evolved and are now clubbed with approaches based on data or algorithms, it is possible to review the integrated models (Dunz *et al.*, 2019; Le Guenedal, 2019).

The model's stacking raises overall credibility, given that component models do not have the same degree of maturity and credibility (Robert, 2017). Macroeconomic models (Grandjean and Giraud, 2017) are constructed according to a question posed and differ structurally. In contrast, climate/weather models all seek to represent the same types of physico-chemical processes. The model construction's logic varies depending on whether one's field is in economics or basic sciences.

With the phenomena studied becoming increasingly complicated, there are issues of a practical nature that cannot just be decided by logical arguments or partisan convictions. The models are there to reduce arbitrariness, but they cannot do this completely. It is up to the researcher to thwart the traps while also making efforts to popularize the content of complex models crucial for significant decisions that involve many individuals or a nation. Revealing or disassembling the mechanism of a model cannot be enough. It is essential to transmit the reflex to the learner to formulate an event or fact in education. This reflex is not necessarily the modeling itself. Apart from explaining the origin of the model and its very logic, it is crucial to focus on its concrete implementation and step back from the digital rendering.

A model is based on assumptions (even the thoughts or convictions of a particular group of individuals) used in its construction. Consequently, the modeler should be vigilant about what the model brings to enlighten a theory or perspective. He must be aware that the model is only a relativization (so nothing absolute). Alternative approaches, based on other qualitative or qualitative explanations, should simultaneously be used. Generally, in practice, a position or decision's credibility is based on a convergence of conclusions from various models. The result of a model is favored only by the analyst. It is, therefore, clear that researchers need to develop multiple models.

A scientific model is very different from an economic model. The underlying model interacts with human evolutionary actions. Thus, with an adaptive system, a standard model (based on stochastic processes) should have had difficulty representing. Integrated models (of the energy/environment/economic type to consider the global challenges that characterize the world in transformation and transition) make a natural mix between natural phenomena and models representing human actions. Therefore, a multidisciplinary approach is needed, where various researchers from different backgrounds should bring and share the best of their expertise (qualitative, quantitative, and technical approaches).

It is always important to keep in mind that, being imperfect approximations of reality, all models are inherently false. Only the modeler needs it to operate, so he should be modest and vigilant about what a model can produce. To reduce bias within the model and accept that there is always a subjectivity dose, the researcher must amend the model or propose an alternative approach. In the current state, where facts engage society for decades, it is essential to look at the models used to make long-term decisions. Most of the models commonly used to represent financial asset changes are instead adapted to describe phenomena for a few years (no more than five years). While considering the type of model to be used, the alignment of finance with climate and environmental objectives requires models that allow to integrate data accumulated for decades. Researchers should think about and develop projection models that address this need.

Decision-makers are called upon to make decisions that commit society for several decades, on the one hand relying on (questionable) convictions and orientations, and on models whose foundations are fragile and probably doubtful. The researcher must inspect or evaluate the models to identify their tolerance levels and make them transparent to concerned parties.

24.3.8. *Multi-time step prediction*

One of the current essential points to align finance with climate and environmental objectives is considering long-term facts. However, the dominant attitude among market players, at least in the first decade since the year 2000, favors short-term profits, which is not good for global development and wreaks havoc on humanity.

Stochastic models used at the heart of the financial market, such as with financial assets, are not adapted to adequately describe developments for long maturities of several years (e.g. beyond five years). Beyond finance, which naturally calls for predictions and forecasts, the idea of predictive analysis is ubiquitous in many areas. It is at the heart of the MLAs used to explore and exploit knowledge from data. This knowledge is the basis for developing use cases and various financial activities (detecting fraud in transactions, asset allocation, etc.).

Predictive analysis is a topic that has been widely studied (Dataman, 2019) by many authors and is still the case today, especially with algorithmic approaches (Ben Taieb, 2014; Liu *et al.*, 2019; Mohajerin and Waslander, 2019). However, most of the studies have focused on prediction for a relatively short time horizon. For example, in the context of trading, practitioners work as time progresses. Good predictive analysis for each period is adequate and should be better than a study that suddenly anticipates what will happen on several future dates. However, in other cases, such as in counterparty risk management, it is necessary to have an analytical vision of what will happen for several future moments at a time.

Adopting a long-term strategic vision, as with financing or investment decision-making while considering environmental or climate risks, requires an appropriate approach to predictive analysis in a single development at several future moments. This requirement is still part of the current challenges for researchers and practitioners and paves the way for a research field. A very minimal contribution on our part is found in Jun *et al.* (2020), and currently, we are still working on this issue by exploring the data-based approach instead of stochastic approaches. However, if one considers an analysis of a very-long-term horizon, comprising several decades, for example, the data can no longer be used correctly. Nevertheless, we will soon generate coherent scenarios for very long maturities, such as that needed in the financing or investment framework that aligns with the climate goals.

24.3.9. *Developing research on research*

At present, it is evident that (i) the volume of knowledge available (thanks to new technologies) continues to grow exponentially, (ii) research is becoming increasingly sophisticated and in all directions, and (iii) problems, at least those that directly affect society, are increasingly numerous, interdependent, and complex.

This situation should not dissuade the researchers. Some acquired knowledge will give way to others. Naturally, there is the question of deciding what knowledge to preserve or develop. Researchers can ask themselves what types of knowledge can be produced now, that will not be forgotten too quickly and serve to address at least some of society's pressing needs. Thus, underlying it is the very logic of academic publications and research topics that are questioned and reviewed.

Excessive specializations are detrimental to research, especially its dissemination and the very creation of new knowledge. Indeed, the researchers justify the seriousness and level of their work through peer judgments. However, some of the knowledge produced serve only a few people's interests and remain useless for society's welfare. If the detailed knowledge produced is likely to advance the common interest, it would be a matter of concern to popularize it, at least in the direction of specialists in other fields. The synergy between knowledge advances a large section of the society.

The DT and EET show problems requiring both global approaches and specific local approaches, which may be technically advanced. The interdependence between energy, the (natural) environment, and the economy makes it necessary to have a holistic view, which concerned parties can share and exploit. Global initiatives and directives, developed at the top and likely approved by citizens, are likely to fail. These directives may be economically unsustainable or even counterproductive since the resultant technical effects and details cannot be sufficiently integrated through macroeconomic models.

Faced with the complexities of the issues that impact them, concerned parties such as researchers, educators, and even companies/industries are interested in having a synthetic and explicit view of the interdependencies between the various, increasingly specialized, research fields. Indeed, each involved party, being too engaged by their challenges, does not necessarily have time or required knowledge to see what is happening in other fields.

This above-mentioned situation requires the need for a new branch of research called Research on Research (R/R). R/R can be conducted by researchers or educators who can mobilize their efforts to analyze, decipher, synthesize, and especially popularize research across various fields that are somehow connected, at least with issues related to global initiatives.

The current complexities around the issues require coordination and multidisciplinarity. The latter's concrete implementation is not always easy because it mobilizes many material and human resources. Moreover, the differences in sensitivities and cultures between researchers may pose obstacles. R/R inputs at least allow concerned parties to operate more efficiently than just undertaking actions taken in isolation and that risk being disconnected from the overall challenge. Currently, research should face a need for multidisciplinary collaborations. One way to achieve this is through R/R.

Although some are not always aware, the disruption affects the academic world and especially R/R. The latter will now have to reinvent itself to continue to exist effectively but not just continue as before — e.g. in the restricted logic of academic publications between peers and remaining in a mono-disciplinary framework. The researcher should be aware that he can play an essential role through the enlightening and support of concerned parties, including companies. Nowadays, anyone with goodwill can become an expert and make himself more useful for the society's advancement with the available information and knowledge. Indeed, some consulting companies and informed individuals have understood this fact and directed their actions. Thus, the traditional activity of the researcher is threatened. The very financing to produce knowledge quite disconnected from reality (therefore very little use for society as a whole) no longer seems justified in this world in transformation and increasingly scarce precious resources.

The teacher-researcher's missions are now expanded. Apart from persevering in the field where he has been academically productive, the teacher-researcher should also be concerned with popularizing his themes and defending them to non-specialist audiences or non-academic stakeholders. The teacher-researcher should commit himself to a type of research coupled with his educational mission, of which we will expand in detail below.

Nowadays, research is multidisciplinary to align with the needs and recognition of society or involved parties. Pure academic recognition (by peers) is no longer sufficient and even tends to be unnecessary. From the entrepreneurial point of view, for example, what counts is the ability to transform knowledge to real solutions or ideas actionable in the face of the problem. Having publications is an academic rite for the quest for legitimacy among peers. The publications' monetary value is increasingly questioned in an academic world in transformation, and where resources become increasingly scarce, teacher-researchers fail to reinvent themselves and function differently. Multidisciplinary research with a real purpose (which non-academic involved parties can appreciate and benefit from) should be easily monetizable. By participating in this research type, the researcher would have the society's legitimacy and subsequently strengthen his activities.

24.3.10. *Education and research coupling*

Traditionally research is present to build new knowledge, either (i) to feed previous knowledge (deny, improve, prolong), (ii) to accompany practices (decipher the issues, develop models or methodological approaches, develop experiments or prototypes), and above all (iii) to serve the needs of education (reconcile fundamental knowledge with uses in professional practices).

Although some are not aware of it, the world of education and research is being disrupted due to the reinvention of digital and data technologies (Accenture, 2018; Arnett, 2014; Iberdrola, 2020; Singh, 2017). The traditional roles of the schools (standardized and uniform mass training with an increasing and exorbitant financial cost) and of the educator (supposed to master and possess the knowledge that the learner would need) are disrupted.

On the one hand, we are now witnessing training that is increasingly personalized and best meets learners' specific needs in their job quest. These training courses are either delivered physically by institutions outside conventional standards (42 and Microsoft, among others) or disseminated through the digital medium by trainers who have specialized in aligning the education on offer with the trades' realities. On the other hand, the traditional educator (with his primary knowledge offerings established and supported by research for decades) seems increasingly out of step with the immediate needs of a changing world. Although they do not have the characteristics of academic support as in the past, tutorials seem to meet the learners needs better. These tutorials go directly to the essentials and do not dwell on non-practical aspects, such as references that do not add value to the practical point of view.

Moreover, it is a fact that at least in the last two decades, successes in economic activities have been achieved by people outside the academic world (i.e. without having degrees). These people have been able to grasp the meaning of the evolution of the world and to make the most of their common sense and willingness to succeed, relying mainly on the opportunities offered by the new technologies associated with digital and data. Traditional schools with their standardized training, their diplomas referred to by bodies (such as the state), and academicians behind (teacher-researchers) trained in the same mold have evident difficulties in adequately coping with the challenges and opportunities of the changing world with DTs and EETs.

The functioning of the education and research world should be reviewed or reinvented. The task is enormous, and the authors do not claim to be able to do it here. Nevertheless, they are trying to make a few points here, at least to feed the reflection. Moreover, for convenience, the analysis focuses only on the academic research-teacher's situation, who so far has played an important role both in the transfer and the construction of knowledge. When it comes to education, there is the transmission of knowledge on the one hand and the development of knowledge content on the other. Here the chapter focuses instead on the latter aspect.

The development of the content of "tailor-made knowledge" for education is not simple. First, the purpose should be clear. Do we want to build knowledge that enables the leader to cope with traditional professions in full transformation, or new works that have recently appeared or new businesses that are not yet visible in the current state? The development of training content for the learner requires a variety of considerations. For example, the spirit and scope of continuing training for a learner already at work should be different from that of a learner in initial training who can favor a global culture and try to cast a wider net in the choice of occupations.

Changes in occupations such as finance, concepts, and techniques related to new technologies were not necessarily part of the educator or teacher-researcher's training context. As a result, they may not be able to develop the learner's knowledge and may not teach the learner what is needed. Also, the available and structured learning support, such as those coming from research, may not exist, or that the educator or teacher-researcher cannot integrate them. He may need to train himself or seek training elsewhere before transmitting to himself that he has learned in the right conditions.

Decryption through various research works (on technological and scientific advances, on the behavior of organizations and society, on trades, on education) may be used to formulate ideas for reshaping adequate education provision. Conversely, current needs and deficiencies in education may, in turn, feed into new themes for research. The academic researcher can thus capture at the same time decryptions of what is happening and elaborations of new training that align with the needs of society (i.e. detect when decrypting). If the researcher fails to assume this coupling between research and education, the responsibility then falls directly on consulting companies or trainers wo have forged appropriate expertise and are in charge. Thus, it makes sense to postulate the need for interest in the coupling between research and education. It presents a vital activity that the classical research-teacher could undertake to sustain its existence.

There is indeed a problem of existence (or even legitimacy) for the researcher. On the one hand, the classical courses that he is accustomed to providing may be available at a lower cost online and may no longer be relevant to the learner's needs. The contents of some classical courses do not correspond to the immediate realities and conditions of the world. The facts encountered are not yet really part of the knowledge elements established in the available literature. Research on research (R/R) can help address this deficiency. On the other hand, the classical (non-committed) research themes that the researcher leads can remain uninterested in the global demand of the socio-economic world, ready to subsidize anyone who brings relevant and actionable solutions.

In ERC (Education and Research Coupling) work, the researcher can no longer work in isolation or remain with colleagues in the same discipline. As the world's environment becomes increasingly complex and global, the researcher should be open to collaborate with other stakeholders (companies and professionals) that are not necessarily academic. Education and training must accompany the changing world, and therefore the development of the related educational content should always be on the move. This elaboration creates challenges and opportunities that the teacher-researcher can assume. Suppose he does not have sufficient technical knowledge or is not comfortable with techniques (such as coding), he could outperform in the decoding of organizational structures and behaviors, which are very useful to the learner. The more technological or technical part could be entrusted to a stakeholder (non-academic) who knows the trades better.

The ERC is a path of diversification for the researcher, which was confined to research topics that were essential of interest only to peers. This coupling can also constitute an indispensable bulwark for surviving in the face of threats from non-academic actors, who find education to have an enormous potential to face the failures of the traditional actors of the education world.

24.4. Concluding Comments

The chapter started by recalling that both DT and EET have substantially changed finance. The COVID-19 health crisis, resulting in a global economic crisis of unprecedented magnitude, has accelerated DT and disrupted the scheduled launch of EETs.

In this work, the authors have proposed ten avenues of research likely to be of particular interest to researchers, educators, and other stakeholders in the professional environment (companies, decision-makers, regulators, etc.). These tracks are based partly on the authors' experience and analyses of academic work and professional relations (consulting companies, various think tanks, and supranational organizations).

In contrast to research suggestions developed in the related literature (Gomber *et al.*, 2017; Kavuri and Milne, 2019, among others), the first eight proposed research lines focus on the frameworks of approaches and concepts that are at the heart of DTs and EETs. They are based on quantitative techniques but described qualitatively.

It is not only finance that has been disturbed by DT and EET but also other fields, especially the academic world (education and research). Consequently, the chapter had devoted the two remaining tracks to the themes of research on research and the coupling of research with education. On the one hand, it is necessary to develop appropriate training to provide human resources for the professions that are being transformed, emerging, or appear due to DT and EET. On the other hand, this development can only be carried out correctly based on appropriate research.

The objective of this study is to generate actionable ideas, especially for the research-teacher, to properly integrate and face the disruptions related to DT and EET. Instead of focusing on the usual academic approaches (such as empirical approaches, interviews, analyses of work in the literature) in line with the ruptures analyzed and considered, the authors followed an idea that is now common in the field of start-ups. Indeed, with the volume of knowledge currently available and just at the cost of attention and time, the claim of authorship of ideas counts little. The important point now is to have the agility to transform the knowledge compiled, bring an idea actionably, and advance the goal in sight.

Table 24.1. Research gaps in finance transformations.

Number	Research gaps
1	Dealing with emerging factors
2	Platforms
3	Smart financial products
4	Adjustments to market frictions
5	Development of personalized solutions
6	Investigations in xML
7	Reworking on models
8	Multi-time steps prediction
9	Research's development of research
10	Coupling education and research

This chapter can be considered the result of the R/R presented through the ninth research avenue. Some ideas proposed are actionable since they have already been implemented in the authors' activities. Other proposals can be integrated to enrich those in this study. Moreover, the tracks proposed could have been more detailed and in-depth. Instead of staying with qualitative descriptions, more technical formulations could be brought. In the context of multidisciplinary collaborations, it is useful to have two versions of the same paper. One emphasizes the qualitative aspects to provide a global vision of all issues. And another version, more developed on the quantitative side, orients to readers who are sensitive to the technical sides. Writing this latest version could be one of the authors' upcoming projects.

The chapter's main findings demonstrate that there are numerous gaps in the finance-transformation–related literature. Although there are many potential areas of interest regarding DT and EET in the finance industry, the authors identify ten crucial gaps in both the literature and practices (see Table 24.1), which other researchers can hopefully use to further knowledge in this field.

References

Accenture (2018). Digital disruption in education. Retrieved from http://fr.slideshare.net/accenture/digital-disruption-in-education. Accessed October 18, 2020.

Andersson, P., Mavin, S., Mähring, M., Teigland, R. and Wennberg, K. (2018). Managing digital transformation, Stockholm School of Economics Institute for Research (SIR). Retrieved from http://www.hhs.se/contentassets/a3083bb76c384052b3f3f4c82236e38f/managing-digital-transformation-med-omslag.pdf. Accessed October 18, 2020.

Arnett, T. (2014) Why disruption innovation is important for education. Retrieved from https://www.christenseninstitute.org/blog/why-disruptive-innovation-matters-to-education/. Accessed October 18, 2020.

Bank of England (2019). Machine learning in UK financial services, October. Retrieved from https://www.bankofengland.co.uk/report/2019/machine-learning-in-uk-financial-services. Accessed October 18, 2020.

Ben Taieb, S. (2014). Machine Learning Strategies for multi-step-ahead time series forecasting, September. Retrieved from https://souhaib-bentaieb.com/pdf/2014_phd.pdf. Accessed October 18, 2020.

BNP Paribas (2019). FinTechs and the ESG data challenge. Six case studies of emerging technologies, November. Retrieved from https://securities.bnpparibas.com/insights/fintechs-esg-data-case-studies.html. Accessed October 18, 2020.

Bracke, P., Datta, A., Jung, C. and Sen, S. (2019). Machine learning explainability in finance: An application to default risk analysis, Bank of England Staff Working Paper No. 816. Retrieved from https://www.bankofengland.co.uk/working-paper/2019/machine-learning-explainability-in-finance-an-application-to-default-risk-analysis. Accessed October 18, 2020.

Buhler H., Gonon, L., Teichmann, J. and Wood, B. (2018). Deep hedging. *ArXiv*, February. Retrieved from https://arxiv.org/pdf/1802.03042.pdf. Accessed October 18, 2020.

Carter, S. and Mainelli, M. (2018). Cyber-catastrophe insurance-linked securities on smart ledgers, long finance — distributed futures. Cardano Foundation Working Paper, November. Retrieved from https://www.longfinance.net/media/documents/Insurance-Linked_Securities_and_Cyber_Catastrophe_v3.4_for_online_use.pdf. Accessed October 18, 2020.

Cennamo, C. (2019). Competing in digital markets: A platform-based perspective. *Academy of Management Perspectives*, July. Retrieved from https://doi.org/10.5465/amp.2016.0048 (Accessed October 18, 2020).

Chenet, H. (2019). Climate change and financial risk. Energy and Prosperity Chair Working Paper, April. Retrieved from http://www.chair-energy-prosperity.org/publications/climaTE-change-and-financial-risk/. Accessed October 18, 2020.

Choudary, S.P. (2018). The architecture of digital work platforms: Policy recommendations on the design of platforms for workers' well-being. ILO Future of Work Research Paper Series. Retrieved from https://www.ilo.org/wcmsp5/groups/public/---dgreports/---cabinet/documents/publication/wcms_630603.pdf. Accessed October 18, 2020.

Dataman (2019). Machine learning or econometrics? To explain or predict? October. Retrieved from https://medium.com/analytics-vidhya/machine-learning-or-econometrics-5127c1c2dc53. Accessed October 18, 2020.

Dhar, V. and Stein R. (2016). Fintech platforms and strategy. MIT Sloan Research Paper No. 5183-16, December. Retrieved from https://ssrn.com/abstract=2892098 or http://dx.doi.org/10.2139/ssrn.2892098. Accessed October 18, 2020.

Ducruet, P. and Roux, A. (2019). Climate risk in Finance: concepts, methods, and assessment tools. Finance for Tomorrow Working Paper, Paris Europlace. Retrieved from https://financefortomorrow.com/en/actualites/publication-launch-climate-risk-in-finance/. Accessed October 18, 2020.

Dunz, N., Naqvi, A. and Monasterolo, I. (2019). Climate transition risk, climate sentiments, and financial stability in a Stock-Flow Consistent approach, Ecological Economic Paper 23, WU Vienna University of Economics and Business. Retrieved from https://econpapers.repec.org/paper/wiwwus045/6911.htm. Accessed October 18, 2020.

Faggell, D. (2020) AI transparency in finance - Understanding the black box, January. Retrieved from https://emerj.com/partner-content/ai-transparency-in-finance/. Accessed October 18, 2020.

Fenwick, M. and Vermeulen, E. (2018) Technology and corporate governance: Blockchain, crypto and artificial intelligence. European Corporate Governance Institute Law Working Paper No. 424/2018, November. Retrieved from https://ecgi.global/sites/default/files/working_papers/documents/finalfenwickvermeulen1.pdf. Accessed October 18, 2020.

Financial Stability Board (2017). Artificial in the context of machine learning in financial services, market developments, and the implications of financial stability, November. Retrieved from https://www.fsb.org/wp-content/uploads/P011117.pdf. Accessed October 18, 2020.

Fries, C.P. and Kohl-Landgraf, P. (2018). Intelligent derivative contracts (detaching transactions from counterparty credit risk: Specification, parameterization, valuation). April. Retrieved from https://ssrn.com/abstract=3163074 or http://dx.doi.org/10.2139/ssrn.3163074. Accessed October 18, 2020.

Fries, C.P., Kohl-Landgraf, P., Paffen, B., Weddigen, S., Del Re, L., Schütte, W., Bacher, D., Declara, R., Eichsteller, D., Weichand, F. and Streubel, M. (2019). Implementing a financial derivative as smart contract. February. Retrieved from https://ssrn.com/abstract=3342785 or http://dx.doi.org/10.2139/ssrn.3342785. Accessed October 18, 2020.

Ganguly, S.H., Margolis, B. and Rowshankish, K. (2017). Digital risk: Transforming risk management for the 2020s, McKinsey & Company, February. Retrieved from https://www.mckinsey.com/business-functions/risk/our-insights/digital-risk-transforming-risk-management-for-the-2020s. Accessed October 18, 2020.

Gomber, P., Koch, J. and Siering, M. (2017). Digital finance and FinTech: Current research and future directions. *Journal of Business Economics*, **87**, 537–580. Retrieved from https://doi.org/10.1007/s11573-017-0852-x. Accessed October 18, 2020.

Grandjean, A. and Giraud, G. (2017). Comparaison des modèles météorologiques, climatiques et économiques: quelles capacités, quelles limites, quels usages? (Comparison of weather, climate, and economic models: What capacities, what limits, what uses?), Chaire Energie et prosperité Working Paper, May. Retrieved from http://www.chair-energy-prosperity.org/wp-content/uploads/2017/03/publication-2017-comparaison-modeles-grandjean-giraud-1.pdf. Accessed October 18, 2020.

Iberdrola (2020). Disruptive education to meet the challenges of the future. Retrieved from https://www.iberdrola.com/talent/disruptive-education. Accessed October 18, 2020.

ISDA (2018). Contracts for smart derivatives, from concept to construction. ISDA White Paper, October. Retrieved from https://www.isda.org/a/cHvEE/Smart-Derivatives-Contracts-From-Concept-to-Construction-Oct-2018.pdf. Accessed October 18, 2020.

Jagtiani, J., Vermilyea, T. and Wall, L. (2018). The roles of big data and machine learning in banking supervision. The Clearing House, Bank Policy Institute. Retrieved from https://www.theclearinghouse.org/banking-perspectives/2018/2018-q1-banking-perspectives/articles/big-data-ml-bank-supervision. Accessed October 18, 2020.

Jun, J.Y., Lebreton, V. and Rakotondratsimba, Y. (2020). Forecasting negative yield-curve distributions. *Journal of Forecasting*, August. Retrieved from https://doi.org/10.1002/for.2727. Accessed October 18, 2020.

Jung, C., Mueller, H., Pedermon, T.E., S., Boards, S. and Thew, O. (2019). Machine learning in UK financial services. BoE and FCA, **16**(10).

Retrieved from https://www.bankofengland.co.uk/report/2019/machine-learning-in-uk-financial-services. Accessed October 18, 2020.

Kavuri, A.S. and Milne, A. (2019). Fintech and the future of financial services: What are the research gaps? CAMA Working Paper 18/2019, February. Retrieved from https://cama.crawford.anu.edu.au/siTEs/default/files/publication/cama_crawford_anu_edu_au/2019-02/18_2019_kavuri_milne.pdf. Accessed October 18, 2020.

Le Guenedal, T. (2019). Economic modelling of climate risks. Amundi Asset Management Working Paper, Quantitative Research. Retrieved from https://research-cenTEr.amundi.com/page/Publications/Working-Paper/2019/Economic-Modeling-of-ClimaTE-Risks?search=true. Accessed October 18, 2020.

Liu, J., Zhang, Y., Xiaoqing, W., Yuming, D. and Xingyu, W. (2019) Dynamic pricing on e-commerce platform with deep reinforcement learning. Retrieved from https://arxiv.org/abs/1912.02572. Accessed October 18, 2020.

Liu, X., Gherbi, A., Li, W. and Cheriet, M. (2019). Multi features and multi-time steps LSTM based methodology for bike sharing availability prediction. *Procedia Computer Science*, **155**, 394–401. Retrieved from https://www.sciencedirect.com/science/article/pii/S187705091930969X https://doi.org/10.1016/j.procs.2019.08.055. Accessed October 18, 2020.

Mishra, R.N. (2019a). Changing the contours of risk management in a digital financial space: The future started yesterday, January. Retrieved from https://ssrn.com/abstract=3407153 or https://dx.doi.org/10.2139/ssrn.3407153. Accessed October 18, 2020.

Mishra R.N. (2019b). New risks – New concerns. Reserve Bank of India, June. Retrieved from https://ssrn.com/abstract=3407179 or https://dx.doi.org/10.2139/ssrn.3407179. Accessed October 18, 2020.

Mohajerin, N. and Waslander, S.L. (2019). Multi-step prediction of dynamic systems with recurrent neural networks. *IEEE Transactions on Neural Networks and Learning Systems*, **99**, 1–14. doi: 10.1109/TNNLS.2019.2891257 or https://arxiv.org/abs/1806.00526. Accessed October 18, 2020.

Moody's (2019). Analysis of Moody's analytic. A BoE paper examines the explicability of machine learning in the finances. August. Retrieved from https://www.moodysanalytics.com/regulatory-news/aug-09-19-boe-paper-examines-explainability-of-machine-learning-in-finance. Accessed October 18, 2020.

Nassiry, D. (2018). The role of Fintech in unlocking green finance: Policy insights for developing countries, Asian Development Bank Institute, ADB Working Paper Series 917, November. Retrieved from https://www.adb.org/publications/role-finTEch-unlocking-green-finance. Accessed October 18, 2020.

Oxford Sustainable Finance Programme (2018). Climate risk analysis from space; remote sensing, machine learning, and the future of measuring climate-related risk. July. Retrieved from https://www.smithschool.ox.ac.uk/research/sustainable-finance/publications/Remote-sensing-data-and-machine-learning-in-climate-risk-analysis.pdf. Accessed October 18, 2020.

Pollari, I. (2018). The rise of the digital platform's in financial services, KPMG, January. Retrieved from https://home.kpmg/xx/en/home/insights/2018/02/rise-of-digital-platforms-fs.html. Accessed October 18, 2020.

Robert, S.P. (2017). The use and misuse of models for climate policy. *Review of Environmental Economics and Policy*, **11**(1), Winter, 100–114. Retrieved from https://doi.org/10.1093/reep/rew012. Accessed October 18, 2020.

Rolnick, D., Donti, P.L., Kaack, L.N., Kochanski, K, Lacoste, A., Sankaran K., Ross, A.S., Milojevic-Dupont, N., Jaques, N., Waldman-Brown, A., Luccioni, A., Maharaj, T., Sherwin, E.D., Mukkavilli, S.K., Kording, K.P., Gomes, C., Ng, A.Y., Hassabis, D., Platt, J.C., Creutzig, F. and Chayes, J. (2019). Tackling climate change with machine learning. *arXiv*, **1906**, 05433v2. Retrieved from https://arxiv.org/abs/1906.05433. Accessed October 18, 2020.

Roscher, R., Bohn, B., Duarte, M. and Garck, J. (2020). Automatic learning explicable for scientific ideas and discovery. *arXiv*, January. Retrieved from https://arxiv.org/pdf/1905.08883.pdf. Accessed October 18, 2020.

Sachs, J., Woo, W., Yoshino, N. and Taghizadeh –Hesary, F. (2019). Why green finance is important. ADBI Working Paper No. 917, January. Retrieved from https://www.adb.org/publications/why-green-finance-important. Accessed October 18, 2020.

Singh, D. (2017). Digital disruption in the education sector. Retrieved from http://bwdisrupt.businessworld.in/article/Digital-Disruption-in-the-Education-Sector/24-10-2017-129263/. Accessed October 18, 2020.

UN-Environment Inquiry (2019). Digital finance and citizen action: In financing the future of climate-smart infrastructure. Funding for Climate Futures, Rethinking infrastructure, February. Retrieved from https://www.oecd.org/environment/cc/climaTE-futures/case-study-digital-finance-and-citizen-action.pdf. Accessed October 18, 2020.

UNEP-FI (2018a). Explore natural capital opportunities, risks, and exposure. A practical guide to financial institutions. Alliance Natural Capital Financing Working Paper, December. Retrieved from https://www.unepfi.org/publications/ecosysTEms-publications/exploring-natural-capital-opportunities-risks-and-exposure-a-practical-guide-for-financial-institutions/. Accessed October 18, 2020.

UNEP-FI (2018b). Rethinking impact to finance SDGs: A position paper and call to action prepared by The Positive Impact Initiative, November. Retrieved from https://www.unepfi.org/wordpress/wp-conTEnt/uploads/2018/11/Rethinking-Impact-to-Finance-the-SDG.pdf. Accessed October 18, 2020.

UNEP-FI (2019). Integrating natural capital in risk assessments. A step-by-step guide for banks. Working Paper, Natural Capital Finance Alliance and PricewaterhouseCoopers (Geneva, Oxford, and London). Retrieved from https://naturalcapital.finance/wp-content/uploads/2019/01/NCFA-Phase-2-Report.pdf. Accessed October 18, 2020.

Xie, N., Ras, G., Van Gerven, M. and Doran, D. (2020). Explainable deep learning: A field guide for the uninitiated. *arXiv*, April. Retrieved from https://arxiv.org/abs/2004.14545. Accessed October 18, 2020.

Ye, P., Qian, J., Chen, J., Wu, C.H., Zhou, Y., De Mars, S., Yang, F. and Zhang, L. (2018). Customized regression model for Airbnb dynamic pricing. Retrieved from https://www.kdd.org/kdd2018/accepted-papers/view/customized-regression-model-for-airbnb-dynamic-pricing. Accessed October 18, 2020.

Zetzsche, D.A., Buckley, R.P., Arner, D.W. and Barberis, I.N. (2018). From FinTech to TechFin: The regulatory challenges of data-driven finance. *New York University Journal of Law and Business*, **14**(2), 393–447. Retrieved from https://5e1dd987-5f71-42ac-ab22-142046bfae62.filesusr.com/ugd/716e9c_2d238eae54ac4d35abb655dddb91f256.pdf. Accessed October 18, 2020.

https://doi.org/10.1142/9781800610781_0025

Chapter 25

Impacts of COVID-19 on Digital Financial Transformation: Insights from Consumer Behaviors in Vietnam

Jasmine T. Ha[*,§], **Jason Q. Nguyen**[†,¶], **and Quan V. Le**[‡,||]

[*]*Department of Sociology, Western University, London, Ontario, Canada & Center for Studies in Demography and Ecology, University of Washington, Seattle, Washington, USA*

[†]*Ivey Business School, Western University, London, Ontario, Canada & The Institute for Circular Economy Development, Vietnam National University, Ho Chi Minh City, Vietnam*

[‡]*University of Management and Technology, Ho Chi Minh City, Vietnam & The Institute for Circular Economy Development, Vietnam National University, Ho Chi Minh City, Vietnam*

[§]*jasmine.tpd.ha@gmail.com*

[¶]*jnguyen@ivey.ca*

[||]*quan.le@umt.edu.vn*

Abstract

The usage of e-commerce platforms and digital financial services in Vietnam surged dramatically during COVID-19. An important question for the financial service industry is whether and how the surge will translate into long-term industry reconfigurations. Current literature on digital financial services, which has typically focused on changes driven by corporate stakeholders and investors, provides little room to consider the role of customers. Our proposed chapter fills this gap by integrating conceptual and empirical ideas from service quality research, focusing on customer perceptions and behaviors. Using empirical survey data, we examine whether and how customer behavioral changes during COVID-19 impact digital financial transformation in Vietnam. We further combine survey findings with three case studies of digital transformation to evaluate whether customer behavioral changes are in sync with relevant corporate transformation strategies. By connecting two sources of changes, our work will help investors, managers, and policymakers envision long-term industry reconfigurations in the post–COVID-19 era.

25.1. Introduction and Related Literature

The COVID-19 pandemic and related social isolation periods, while devastating to the overall Vietnamese economy, initiated a spurt in customer demand for online/cashless transactions and e-commerce, thereby generating unprecedented growth in both revenue and transactions for various FinTech businesses in Vietnam in the first six months of 2020. Statistics from a leading e-commerce site report massive numbers of online orders, peaking at 5,000 orders per minute in the first quarter of 2020.[1] Concurrently, the usage of digital financial services, including Internet banking, e-wallet, and mobile money, have also risen significantly.[2] Corporates across different industries have responded with various strategies, including expanding the workforce, widening their range of services, and speeding up digital transformation projects.

Vietnam's e-commerce and FinTech industry have enjoyed impressive growth in recent years, reaching US$4.4 billion in 2017 and estimated to accelerate to US$7.8 billion in 2020. Within the industry, digital payment dominates over other segments, as it accounts for close to 90% of the total market share.[3] Accordingly, there have been significant investments in FinTech payments, major deals involving large international and national stakeholders, and a steady rise in the number of new Vietnamese FinTech payment companies. Vietnam's FinTech industry also receives support from the government with various regulations and proposed policies that set the legal foundation and pave the way for digital financial services. Decree 999,

---

[1]https://tinyurl.com/yyh8v2to (Accessed November 26, 2020).
[2]https://tinyurl.com/y6dzvweu (Accessed November 26, 2020).
[3]https://tinyurl.com/y6nfvbmc (Accessed November 26, 2020).

passed in 2019, introduced various measures to accelerate online payments. The national and most prominent utility company, Vietnam Electricity, was asked to facilitate payments of power bills through electronic and mobile payments. Ho Chi Minh City, the largest city in Vietnam, further requested all schools, hospitals, and other city agencies to accept and encourage online payments. Online shopping and ride-sharing platforms have also been quick in catching on this trend by continuously dishing out promotions through their in-house e-wallets.

Despite the encouraging development and government support, Vietnamese consumers' high resistance to both financial and digital services remains an important roadblock impeding the further growth of the FinTech industry. Compared to other nation-states in Southeast Asia and around the world, the proportion of financial service users in Vietnam is low, reflected in the sub-par ratio of bank account users amongst the population aged 15 years and older. This ratio is only 30.8% in Vietnam, much lower than the 48.9% and 81.6% in the neighboring countries of Indonesia and Thailand, respectively. According to a 2019 report by Standard Chartered,[4] among users of e-commerce and other digital services, cash remains the dominant mode of payment such that over 90% of Internet purchases in Vietnam are paid with cash on delivery. As such, the increased usage of online shopping and digital financial services during the COVID-19 social isolation period is a welcome boost for Vietnam's FinTech industry, bringing new opportunities as well as potential challenges. On the one hand, this may ignite a consumer-led revolution in terms of receptiveness and usage of e-commerce and digital financial services. On the other hand, consumers' interests might well disappear when normalcy resumes after the pandemic. It is thus important to understand the drivers of increases in usage of e-commerce and digital financial services during the social isolation period. This would enable FinTech firms, as well as in other industries, and the government, to adopt appropriate practices, policies, and regulations that leverage the momentum to overcome consumers' resistance and achieve the growth that sustains beyond the pandemic. Unfortunately, such an understanding has not been established in the current literature on

[4]https://tinyurl.com/yy9hybv3 (Accessed November 26, 2020).

e-commerce and digital financial services, which has typically focused on changes driven by corporate stakeholders, investors, and government regulations (Basol and Patel, 2018). In this chapter, we look to fill this gap by focusing on the impact of consumer-related factors on the growth of e-commerce and digital financial services sector. In particular, we seek to answer two research questions:

(i) What factors are associated with e-commerce/online shopping activities and usage of digital financial services *during* and *after* the COVID-19 social isolation period in Vietnam?
(ii) How can e-commerce, FinTech companies, and the government leverage this demand surge to expand their customer bases beyond the pandemic?

To that end, we collect primary data from a survey examining whether and how customer online shopping behaviors and usage of e-finance services have changed during and after the COVID-19 social isolation period in Vietnam. Our survey considers both months of March and April 2020 to be the effective period of interest, as online shopping and e-commerce activities started picking up in early March when the Vietnamese Government Decree 15 on social distancing was issued to limit face-to-face contact. The Vietnamese government later announced Government Decree 16 on March 29, officially mandating a social isolation period starting from April 1 and lasting until April 28, 2020. The social isolation order requested individuals to stay home, except for crucial activities (e.g. buying necessities, medical supplies). Most non-essential brick-and-mortar businesses, such as coffee shops, restaurants, or cinemas, were to stop their on-premises services during the period. In our study, the social isolation period provided a quasi-experiment setting to examine consumers' usage of e-commerce and digital financial services *before, during*, and *after* this period. The survey was launched between July 15–25, 2020, yielding a total sample of 556 completed responses.

Our empirical results show that technology savviness and connectedness are, unsurprisingly, the main drivers that increase online shopping activities and FinTech usage. Furthermore, consumers in the older age groups, who are typically less technology savvy and more resistant to digital and financial services, are also more likely to increase their online activities during the social isolation period. A possible explanation for this result is that elderly consumers may have greater health and safety concerns that override their resistance to digital and financial services. Our results also indicate the increases in usage of e-commerce and digital financial services are likely to remain even after the social isolation period. We further combine findings from the survey with case studies of digital transformation during COVID-19 in three businesses (one e-commerce platform, one FinTech company, and one traditional non-digital service provider in the F&B industry) to evaluate whether customer behavioral changes are in sync with relevant corporate transformation strategies.

With these results, this chapter provides several important implications, both academically and practically. Theoretically, this chapter complements the literature on the drivers of e-commerce and digital financial services, which typically highlights the importance of corporate stakeholders, investors, government regulations, and technology innovations as the key drivers (see e.g. Basol and Patel, 2018; Mattila *et al.*, 2018; Breidbach *et al.*, 2019; Abad-Segura *et al.*, 2020). There have been a few scattered calls in the literature to consider consumers perceptions on digital financial services and e-commerce. For instance, Malady and Buckley (2014) suggested financial regulators should address local context and customer value, which may vary significantly across different countries. Other studies emphasize the salience of indirect costs, such as travel distance to service provider, forgone activities (Bachas *et al.*, 2018), and negative feelings from previous experience (Finau *et al.*, 2016), on customers' level of service usage. In a case study of FinTech development in China, Chen (2016) coined the term "Finlife" to highlight the crucial role of customer satisfaction in determining the success of a new FinTech service. Specifically, a FinTech service must make an impactful improvement in customers' life to gain customer acceptance and subsequent viral promotion through a customer's personal network. Our work enriches this stream by focusing on the unique aspect of consumers' health and safety concerns, which have been made particularly important by the COVID-19 pandemic.

Practically, this chapter provides insights into the best practices for business and service reconfiguration that leverages consumers' behavioral changes to move forward to the post-pandemic recovery and potential growth. The encouraging sign is that businesses in Vietnam have transformed in a way that better support equal access to healthcare, enhanced safety measures, and strong collaborations across industries. As consumers' favorable receptiveness toward digital and financial services could likely remain beyond the pandemic and the customer base would expand toward people with various forms of vulnerability, e.g. age and other health risks for COVID-19, our study also calls for governmental regulations that can quickly catch up to the trends and provide more transparency to the legal processes relating to e-commerce and digital financial services.

The rest of the chapter proceeds as follows. Section 25.2 discusses the related theory, followed by a discussion of the survey results in Section 25.3 as well as the three case studies in Section 25.4. Section 25.5 provides the concluding remarks.

25.2. Theoretical Background

Since we are interested in consumers' receptiveness and perceptions toward e-commerce and digital financial services, we build upon the literature on customer satisfaction in services, particularly on the SERQUAL model. The SERQUAL model, first developed by Parasuraman *et al.* (1988), which has been widely tested and used to measure customer perceptions of service quality, contains five dimensions: tangibles (physical facilities and the appearance of personnel), reliability (ability to perform the promised service dependably and accurately), responsiveness (willingness to help customers and provide prompt service), assurance (employee knowledge base), and empathy (caring and individualized attention provided to customers). In an online environment, customers interact mainly with technology rather than with service personnel, hence the model needs to be adjusted for e-services (Lee and Lin, 2005).

Research on customer satisfaction in e-services emphasizes the importance of trust to replace the dimension of assurance from the SERQUAL model in the context of adoption and usage of online shopping and e-commerce services (see, e.g. Grabner-Kraeuter, 2002; Gefen *et al.*, 2003; Pavlou and Gefen, 2004; Pavlou and Fygenson, 2006; Shin *et al.*, 2013). Ratnasingam *et al.* (2002) distinguish trust in the offline versus online environment and state that, "whereas the traditional notion of trust primarily focuses on trust in a trading partner, trust in e-business also incorporates the notion of trust in the infrastructure and the underlying control mechanism (technology trust) which deals with transaction integrity, authentication, confidentiality, and non-repudiation." It is also established that trust in e-commerce and digital financial services, as well as online stores, induces digital safety, i.e. the assurance that personal and financial information is safe throughout the online interactions (Ha and Stoel, 2008; Chang *et al.*, 2016; Vu, 2017). Trust is a crucial factor leading to online purchase decisions. After the initial purchase, the customer perceptions of trust and other service quality dimensions affect their loyalty (as returned customers) and viral promotion of a given e-service. In our context, the lack of trust is often cited as the main reason for consumers' resistance to digital financial services and e-commerce in Vietnam (Vu, 2017).

The COVID-19 pandemic, with its spread through close physical contacts, has brought forth an important aspect of safety that was previously unlinked to consumers' adoption and usage of e-commerce and digital financial services, which is health and safety concerns. The World Health Organization (WHO) has recommended that people should avoid large crowds and restrict making cash payments to avoid infection since the coronavirus can survive several days on the surface of exchanged notes. In Vietnam, the government, banks, and FinTech firms encouraged people to switch to e-commerce and online shopping to limit physical contact and exposure to the coronavirus. Given the impressive growth in e-commerce and cashless transactions during the social isolation period, one may speculate that health concerns have overridden the lack of consumers' trust in digital services, driving non-users to switch to digital financial and shopping services. A counter perspective, however, is that the growth was driven mainly by "connected" users, i.e. those already savvy in digital services (Keely, 2017), who intensify their online activities during the social isolation period. It is thus crucial to use empirical data to delineate the individual impact as well as the interplay between these two forces in the uptake of e-commerce and digital financial services in Vietnam.

With respect to the development of FinTech and online shopping platforms, the takeaway is to consider the multiple dimensions of customer demand. Specific to the growth during the COVID-19 pandemic, increased usage of digital services may be considered in various measures: the number of transactions, the amount of money spent digitally, the variety of payment methods, and the variety of items purchased. By tracking the changes in each of these measures and charting them to the key dimensions of trust and necessity (health concerns), we can then make informed suggestions on how the COVID-19–spurred growth may translate into long-term transformation in digital financial services.

25.3. Empirical Strategy

25.3.1. *Survey data collection procedure*

We collected original data through a self-administered survey questionnaire about customer online shopping behaviors during and after the social isolation period. In Vietnam, the second wave of COVID-19 cases started on March 7, 2020, when Patient 17 tested positive to the virus after returning from Europe. The government quickly applied quarantine protocols to the locations near the newly infected cases and issued advice for the public to limit face-to-face contact and large group gatherings. A formal nationwide social distancing order was announced on March 29, to be effective between April 1 and April 28, 2020. The social distancing order requires individuals to stay home, except for crucial activities such as buying necessities and medical supplies and other emergency travels. Most non-essential brick-and-mortar businesses, such as coffee shops, restaurants, or cinemas, were required to close during the social distancing period. In our survey, we consider both months of March and April 2020 to be the effective social distancing period, as online shopping and cashless payments began to pick up in early March when the government's advice to limit face-to-face contact was issued.

To obtain accurate responses and reduce ambiguity, a preliminary questionnaire was distributed to a pilot group of five people, selected based on convenient sampling. The pilot group not only answered the questions but also suggested some changes in the language and ordering of questions. Their suggestions were incorporated to refine the questionnaire. The final survey was launched through the Qualtrics platform, with respondents recruited through Qualtrics'

Panel Service. The targeted population for this research is individuals who have some experiences with online shopping (in other words, people who have never shopped online are excluded from the survey). Respondents aged 18–64 years were drawn from 5 big cities in Vietnam, namely Ha Noi, Ho Chi Minh City, Hai Phong, Can Tho, and Da Nang. The survey was launched between July 15 and 25, yielding a total sample of 556 completed responses.

Table 25.1 provides a glimpse at some descriptive attributes of the sample. Most respondents reside in two largest cities, with roughly 33% in Ha Noi and 31% in Ho Chi Minh City. Our respondents are also quite evenly distributed across the three prime working-age groups of 20–29, 30–39, and 40–49 years, with the percentage being 36.5%, 29.14%, and 23.92%, respectively. The youngest category has fewer respondents because the age range is much smaller, i.e. only 18- and 19-year-olds. It was most challenging to locate respondents in the oldest age group of 50–59 years, thus only about 4% of our sample belongs to this category. In terms of gender, the sample is balanced between male and female respondents. Over 60% of all respondents indicate that they are the main shopper in the household. Beyond demographic characteristics, we also ask questions about their usage of digital and financial services, including time spent on the Internet, number of bank accounts, number of e-wallets, and their satisfaction with online shopping services during COVID-19.

25.3.2. *Data analysis*

It is important both theoretically and practically to understand whether the growth in customer activities in online shopping and FinTech usage are stable and sustainable after the COVID-19 pandemic. In Table 25.2, we provide a summary of the online shopping behaviors of customers during and after the COVID-19 social isolation period with four measures: the number of orders placed, the amount of money spent, the variety of items bought online, and the variety of payment methods.

The first set of columns in Table 25.2 displays measures of behavioral change during the social isolation period (t_1), compared to before social isolation (t_0). We denote these changes as $\Delta_{t_1-t_0}$. Each measure of behavior change is recorded through a 5-point Likert scale

Table 25.1. Descriptive statistics of survey respondents.

		Mean or percentage	**Std. Dev.**	**Min**	**Max**
City	Ho Chi Minh City	32.73			
	Ha Noi	31.12			
	Da Nang	12.23			
	Can Tho	17.45			
	Hai Phong	0.47			
Age	Under 20	6.47			
	20–29	36.51			
	30–39	29.14			
	40–49	23.92			
	50 or older	3.96			
Gender	Male	49.46			
	Female	49.64			
	Prefer not to say	0.90			
Main household shopper	No	36.87			
	Yes	63.13			
Household income	Under 2 million VND	1.26			
	2–3 million VND	0.54			
	3–5 million VND	2.70			
	5–10 million VND	13.49			
	10–20 million VND	43.17			
	Over 20 million VND	38.85			
Change in household income during COVID-19	Decreased a lot	17.81			
	Decreased a little	53.60			
	No change	14.75			
	Increase a little	13.13			
	Increase a lot	0.72			
Education level	Less than high school	2.88			
	High school graduate	11.15			
	Some college	21.58			
	College graduate	42.27			
	Master's or Ph.D.	22.12			
Time spent on the Internet daily	Less than 3 hours	6.29			
	3–5 hours	32.37			

question, with 1 being “A lot less,” 2 being “A little less,” 3 being “No change,” 4 being “A little more,” and 5 being “A lot more.”

Table 25.1. (*Continued*)

	Mean or percentage	Std. Dev.	Min.	Max.
5–7 hours	26.26			
7–9 hours	23.20			
More than 9 hours	11.87			
Number of bank accounts	2.04	1.17	0	8
Number of e-wallets	2.05	1.33	0	11
Overall satisfaction with online shopping during social isolation (1 = Strongly disagree, 5 = Strongly agree)	4.04	0.78	1	5
Number of observations	556			

Accordingly, a mean score larger than 3 suggest an increase in each measure at the aggregate level. Further t-test statistics show that the means are significantly larger than 3. A similar pattern is observed in the second set of columns in Table 25.2, where we display measures of customer behavioral change after the social isolation period (t_2) compared to during social isolation (t_1), or $\Delta_{t_2-t_1}$. All mean values are significantly larger than 3 as well, yet the values are smaller compared to the those in the previous set. We verified this observation with the t-test displayed on the right-most column of Table 25.2. The test statistics indicate that the change in the second set is indeed smaller than the change in the first set. The results indicate that there has been an increase in the usage of online shopping and digital payments during the social isolation period to prevent the spread of COVID-19. Further, the increases are sustained after the social isolation period, albeit in smaller increments. Taken together, these initial results are promising signs for the FinTech market, as they support the idea that new digital habits formed during COVID-19 likely continued beyond the pandemic.

We next examined whether the increased usage of digital financial services was driven by already-savvy users or new and less connected users. It is important to answer this question because increased usage in the second group, if confirmed, signals a real expansion of the

Table 25.2. Changes in customer e-commerce behaviors during and after the COVID-19 social isolation period.

	Change during the social isolation period, compared to before ($\Delta_{t_1-t_0}$)			**Change after the social isolation period, compared to during ($\Delta_{t_2-t_1}$)**			**Difference ($\Delta_{t_2-t_1} - \Delta_{t_1-t_0}$)**		
	Mean	**Std. Dev.**	**T-test ($\Delta_{t_1-t_0} > 3$)**	**Mean**	**Std. Dev.**	**T-test ($\Delta_{t_2-t_1} > 3$)**	**Mean**	**Std. Dev.**	**T-test (Diff < 0)**
Number of orders	3.39	1.20	7.65***	3.22	1.11	4.74***	−0.17	1.19	−3.32***
Money spent	3.42	1.16	8.46***	3.30	1.11	6.47***	−0.12	1.15	−2.44**
Variety of items	3.65	1.07	14.38***	3.45	1.09	9.75***	−0.20	1.02	−4.68***
Variety of payment methods	3.54	0.96	13.15***	3.42	0.92	10.77***	−0.12	0.91	−3.04**

Note: $^{**}p < 0.01$; $^{***}p < 0.001$.

customer base for e-commerce and FinTech business — a welcome significant change given the Vietnam context where lack of trust has kept many people away from digital financial services. According to a report by Keely (2017), the "connected" users tend to be young, between with the age of 21 and 34 years and so we will use the higher age group as a proxy of the less-connected users. During the pandemic isolation, these elderly people (and less "connected" users) are deemed to be at higher risk of death and complications when they contract the virus. With the possibility of the virus surviving up to several days on surfaces, cash can be the source of coronavirus transmission, especially since money can exchange hands frequently in daily transactions. The WHO has recommended that people should restrict making cash payments to avoid infection. In Vietnam, the government encourages people to switch to e-commerce using FinTech to limit exposure to the coronavirus. Consequently, we conjecture that health concerns might drive elder consumers toward digital services to limit infection risks due to close physical contact. A quick cross-tabulation of the data provides an initial confirmation to the conjecture. In Figure 25.1, we display the change in online shopping and digital payment by age group. Panel A reflects the change during the social isolation period, compared to before. The age groups are shown in bars of darkening blue, where the darker shade indicates older ages. It is clear that those in their forties and fifties increases their online shopping orders, expenditure, variety of purchased items, and variety of payment methods in larger increments compared to the younger age groups. In particular, the mean change for the variety of payment methods is larger for the oldest age group (50 years and older), compared to the rest. In Panel B, a similar pattern is observed across different age groups, suggesting that the changed behaviors are sustained in the months of May and June, after the social isolation order was removed.

To further understand behavioral changes across different age groups of users, we ran two sets of exploratory multivariate regressions, and display the results in Table 25.3 and Table 25.4. In the first set, we seek to understand which characteristics are correlated with an increased usage of online shopping and digital payment during the social isolation period. Our results confirmed the intuition that technology savviness and connectedness, as indicated

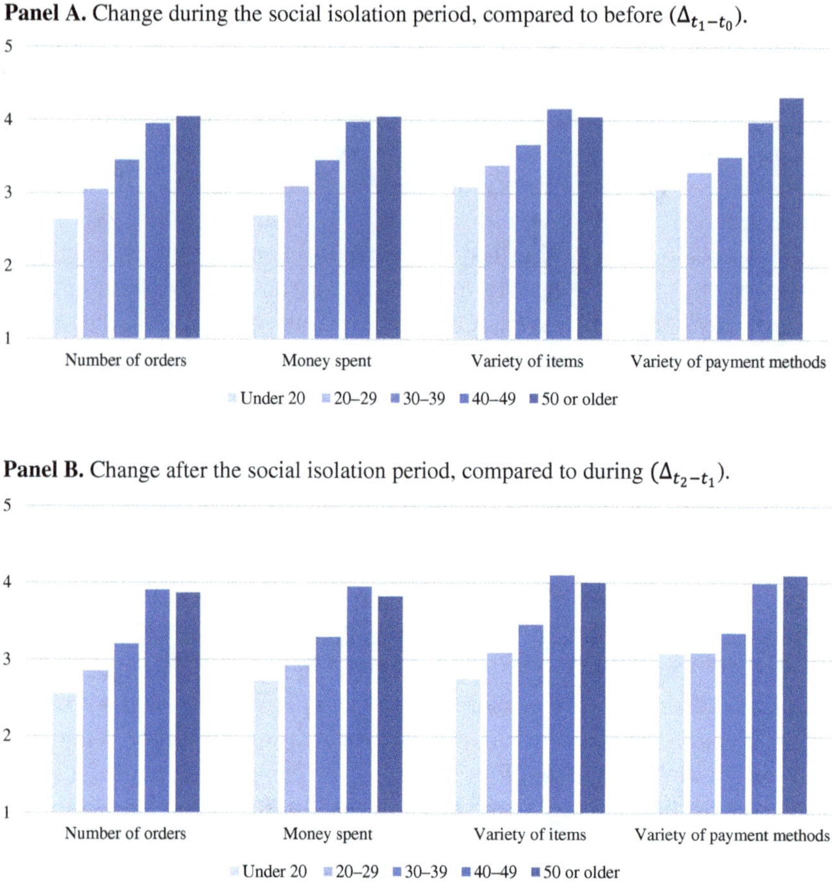

Figure 25.1. Changes in e-commerce behaviors by customer's age.

by *time spent on the Internet*, *the number of e-wallets*, and to some extent, *education level*, unsurprisingly contribute positively to more digital service usage. In addition, we verified our previous observation that those in *the oldest age group* are indeed more likely to have a positive change in their online shopping and digital payment behaviors, even after controlling for all other factors. All aspects of behavioral changes were significantly stronger for *main shoppers* of the household versus non-main shoppers. *Household income*, expectedly, is only positively related to increased orders and expenditure, but not to the variety of purchased items

Table 25.3. Multivariate regression models of customer behavioral change during the social isolation period, compared to before ($\Delta_{t_1-t_0}$).

	Number of orders (1)	Money spent (2)	Variety of items (3)	Variety of payment methods (4)
City (Ref = Ha Noi)				
Da Nang	0.31^{+}	0.13	0.08	0.54^{**}
	(0.17)	(0.17)	(0.16)	(0.14)
Can Tho	0.09	0.21	0.58^{**}	0.57^{**}
	(0.17)	(0.17)	(0.16)	(0.14)
Hai Phong	0.03	0.30	0.39^{*}	0.45^{*}
	(0.20)	(0.19)	(0.18)	(0.16)
Ho Chi Minh City	−0.07	−0.02	0.05	0.05
	(0.11)	(0.11)	(0.11)	(0.09)
Age (Ref = Under 20)				
20-29	−0.21	−0.22	−0.14	−0.10
	(0.21)	(0.21)	(0.20)	(0.17)
30-39	0.00	−0.03	0.04	−0.01
	(0.23)	(0.22)	(0.21)	(0.18)
40-49	0.43^{+}	0.35	0.17	0.15
	(0.24)	(0.24)	(0.23)	(0.20)
50 and older	0.85^{*}	0.75^{*}	0.55^{+}	0.81^{*}
	(0.30)	(0.30)	(0.28)	(0.25)
Gender (Ref = Male)				
Female	0.24^{*}	0.16^{+}	0.11	0.02
	(0.10)	(0.09)	(0.09)	(0.08)
Prefer not to say	−0.43	−0.40	−0.53	0.24
	(0.50)	(0.50)	(0.47)	(0.41)
Main shopper	0.26^{*}	0.34^{**}	0.23^{*}	0.26^{*}
	(0.10)	(0.10)	(0.09)	(0.08)
Household income	0.12^{*}	0.13^{*}	0.05	0.07
	(0.06)	(0.06)	(0.05)	(0.05)
Change in household income during COVID-19	0.11^{+}	0.13^{*}	0.10^{+}	0.02
	(0.06)	(0.06)	(0.05)	(0.05)

(Continued)

Table 25.3. (*Continued*)

	Number of orders (1)	Money spent (2)	Variety of items (3)	Variety of payment methods (4)
Highest education qualification	0.16*	0.15*	0.12*	0.14*
	(0.06)	(0.06)	(0.05)	(0.05)
Time on the Internet daily	0.09*	0.08*	0.12*	0.07*
	(0.04)	(0.04)	(0.04)	(0.03)
Number of bank accounts	0.03	0.02	−0.05	−0.08*
	(0.05)	(0.05)	(0.04)	(0.04)
Number of e-wallets	0.16**	0.08*	0.11*	0.12**
	(0.04)	(0.04)	(0.04)	(0.03)
Constant	0.21	0.69*	1.64**	1.76**
	(0.35)	(0.35)	(0.32)	(0.29)
Observations	556	556	556	556
Adjusted R-squared	0.244	0.212	0.187	0.220

Note: Standard errors in parentheses; $^{+}p < 0.10$; $^{*}p < 0.05$; $^{**}p < 0.01$.

and the variety of payment methods. Finally, *the degree to which one's household income is impacted* during COVID-19 are significantly correlated to online shopping behaviors but not to payment choice.

We further examine the behaviors after the social isolation period. In Table 25.4, the regression models are similar to the previous set, with two additional variables. First, we controlled for consumers' *earlier behavior changes* that occurred during the social isolation period, and second, we considered *the satisfaction* with the online shopping experience during that time. The results show that those who increase their online shopping and digital payment activities during social isolation are more likely to continue their behaviors even further after social isolation. This reiterates the point that new digital habits formed during COVID-19 will help expand the

Table 25.4. Multivariate regression models of customer behavioral change after the social isolation period, compared to during ($\Delta_{t_2-t_1}$).

	Number of orders (5)	Money spent (6)	Variety of items (7)	Variety of payment methods (8)
Change during COVID-19 ($\Delta_{t_1-t_0}$)	0.29**	0.31**	0.42**	0.37**
	(0.04)	(0.04)	(0.04)	(0.04)
Overall satisfaction during COVID-19	0.08	0.08	0.13*	0.07
	(0.05)	(0.05)	(0.05)	(0.04)
City (Ref = Ha Noi)				
Da Nang	0.30*	0.29*	0.47**	0.14
	(0.15)	(0.14)	(0.14)	(0.12)
Can Tho	0.21	0.43*	0.21	0.17
	(0.15)	(0.14)	(0.14)	(0.12)
Hai Phong	0.28	0.48*	0.29+	0.08
	(0.17)	(0.17)	(0.16)	(0.14)
Ho Chi Minh City	0.01	−0.01	−0.14	−0.06
	(0.10)	(0.10)	(0.09)	(0.08)
Age (Ref = Under 20)				
20-29	0.10	−0.02	0.16	−0.18
	(0.19)	(0.18)	(0.17)	(0.15)
30-39	0.26	0.15	0.37*	−0.03
	(0.20)	(0.19)	(0.18)	(0.16)
40-49	0.57*	0.31	0.55*	0.21
	(0.21)	(0.21)	(0.20)	(0.17)
50 and older	0.55*	0.33	0.49+	0.32
	(0.27)	(0.26)	(0.25)	(0.22)
Gender (Ref = Male)				
Female	−0.09	−0.11	−0.05	0.09
	(0.08)	(0.08)	(0.08)	(0.07)
Prefer not to say	−0.77+	−0.33	−0.34	−0.62+
	(0.44)	(0.43)	(0.41)	(0.35)

(*Continued*)

Table 25.4. (*Continued*)

	Number of orders (5)	Money spent (6)	Variety of items (7)	Variety of payment methods (8)
Main shopper	0.11	0.15^{+}	0.05	−0.04
	(0.09)	(0.09)	(0.08)	(0.07)
Household income	−0.05	−0.03	−0.00	0.01
	(0.05)	(0.05)	(0.05)	(0.04)
Change in income during COVID-19	0.19^{**}	0.14^{*}	0.05	0.07^{+}
	(0.05)	(0.05)	(0.05)	(0.04)
Highest education qualification	0.00	0.04	0.04	0.06
	(0.05)	(0.05)	(0.05)	(0.04)
Time on the Internet daily	0.01	0.00	0.04	0.02
	(0.04)	(0.03)	(0.03)	(0.03)
Number of bank accounts	−0.06	−0.03	−0.05	-0.10^{*}
	(0.04)	(0.04)	(0.04)	(0.03)
Number of e-wallets	0.06^{+}	0.04	0.05	0.07^{*}
	(0.03)	(0.03)	(0.03)	(0.03)
Constant	1.27^{**}	1.20^{**}	0.66^{*}	1.53^{**}
	(0.36)	(0.35)	(0.33)	(0.29)
Observations	556	556	556	556
Adjusted R-squared	0.327	0.324	0.394	0.370

Note: Standard errors in parentheses; $^{+}p < 0.10$; $^{*}p < 0.05$; $^{**}p < 0.01$.

customer base for the FinTech industry. *Satisfaction* with the service during social isolation only has a significant impact on the increased variety of items purchased online. This means for people to continue venturing out of their comfort zones, they first need to be satisfied with the actual experiences of online shopping and digital payment. Finally, it is noticeable here that the indicators for connected users became less significant. *Time on the Internet* daily does not have a significant relationship with any behavior measure. *The number of e-wallets* only impact the variety of payment methods and to a less significant extent, the number of online orders. These results are unsurprising, given that their impact is probably nested in the earlier behavioral changes, which are controlled for.

25.4. Service Reconfiguration by Businesses

Beyond survey data, we also consider case studies of how three businesses — one FinTech company, one e-commerce platform, and one traditional (non-digital) service provider — are transformed during COVID-19. We rely on these cases to evaluate whether corporate transformation strategies are in sync with customer behavioral changes.

25.4.1. *MoMo wallet*

The FinTech industry in Vietnam has about 27 e-wallet platforms, including the top five companies — MoMo, ViettelPay, Moca, AirPay, and ZaloPay. MoMo, owned by Di Dong Truc Tuyen Service Joint Stock Company, is the largest e-wallet and the fastest growing payment service provider in Vietnam, with the growth rate and transaction value at around 15% per month. Established in 2007, MoMo is the first mobile money platform in Vietnam. In 2009, the State Bank of Vietnam granted a trial license to MoMo in partnership with Vietcombank to provide mobile payment services. MoMo has received investment from Warburg Pincus, Goldman Sachs, and Standard Chartered Private Equity.

As of November 2019, MoMo has nearly 13 million iOS and Android app users. Currently, MoMo has more than 20,000 payment partners and 100,000 locations nationwide that accept its e-wallet and linkage to 23 major banks and 43 domestic and international cards. In 2018, MoMo was ranked among the top 50 emerging companies; and in 2019, the company was in the top established companies, ranked 36 out of 50 in Southeast Asia. This recognition is based on criteria such as innovative activities of products and services, ability to mobilize capital, scale, and coverage.

With the percentage of bank account users in Vietnam remaining low at 20% and the number of people with credit cards at only 3%, MoMo has the capacity to provide digital financial services in all provinces across Vietnam, allowing consumers in remote areas, where banking and mobile phone services are not yet reachable, to be financially inclusive. As a mobile payment platform, MoMo promotes a cashless economy and provides consumers with a one-touch payment experience, including money transfers, bill payments, airline and train ticket purchases, movie tickets, and other financial service extensions. MoMo currently has about 2 million transactions per day with a daily average of VND520,000 per user.

Reflecting on the company performance during the social isolation period, the CEO of MoMo said that the company has seen significant shifts in its customer segments (MoMo, 2020).[5] For instance, digital payment through prominent cinemas used to generate millions of transactions per month dropped to virtually zero in April 2020 when the cinemas closed. However, the company was surprised to find that online donation campaigns for various causes, including health, safety, and economy recovery post-isolation performed exceptionally well on its base of 5 million MoMo e-wallet users. In June 2020, the company collaborated with Saigon Co.op, a prominent supermarket chain, to initiate new programs to support agriculture recovery through a promotion program on the FinTech platform. Based on the programs' successes, the CEO of MoMo stated that they will expand in the direction of collaborations and aiming at supporting social causes in the post-COVID recovery period. This strategic change of MoMo, which focuses more on grocery items, also provides support for our results that main shoppers of the household could be an important driving force to promote online shopping and the use of FinTech services.

25.4.2. *Tiki*

Vietnam's Big Four in B2C e-commerce platforms are Lazada, Sendo, Shopee, and Tiki. Established in 2010, Tiki is currently ranked the top two e-commerce platform in Vietnam and the top six in

[5]https://tinyurl.com/es9ase84 (Accessed November 26, 2020).

Southeast Asia. Tiki aspires to become the Amazon of Vietnam. Similar to Amazon, Tiki was initially established as a start-up selling books online, but since then the company has grown to a full e-commerce business offering over 4 million products stored in 33 fulfilment centers and warehouses in 13 major cities. Recently, Tiki is also venturing into the service sector, including travel and entertainment bookings and insurance. Today, Tiki employs about 3,500 workers. Tiki was voted the number 1 workplace in Vietnam in the Internet/e-commerce industry by Anphabe in 2018, and the company was recognized by HR Asia as the Top 50 Best Places to Work in Asia in 2019. The company's strategic investors are VNG and China-based JD.com. In 2019, Tiki successfully raised US$75 million in a round led by Northstar Group, a leading Singapore-based private equity fund manager.

In 2017, the company introduced TikiNOW, a two-hour delivery service to major metropolitan areas, including Ha Noi, Ho Chi Minh City, and Da Nang. The average shopping frequency of customers with TikiNOW membership is five times higher than the regular customers. This has demonstrated the benefits that the membership package brings to the customers, thus raising consumer satisfaction and loyalty. In addition, Tiki has invested heavily in FinTech to provide online payment security and protect private information of the customers to build trust and credibility.

In the first quarter of 2020, Tiki ranked second in terms of web traffic with 24 million visitors, only after Shopee with 43 million visitors. During the social isolation period between April 1 and April 22, 2020, the Tiki platform experienced a surge of 15% revenue growth compared to the peak holiday period of November–December 2019 due to the two-hour delivery service and delivery safety. The most purchased items during the social isolation period were masks, hand sanitizers, and air purifiers. Books also experienced high growth rates, particularly on general medical and family knowledge topics, reflecting our observed impact of education level and health concerns on online shopping behavioral changes.

25.4.3. *The Coffee House*

The Coffee House (TCH) is a latecomer in the rapidly growing, but highly competitive, coffee chains in Vietnam. It was established in 2014 with its first coffee shop in Ho Chi Minh City. The strategic investor of TCH is Seedcom, established in 2014 as a venture capital company to invest in retail and retail-servicing companies. The main objective of Seedcom is investment in technology to support retail chain store development.

Today, TCH has 160 coffee shops in major cities across the country. The company's slogan is "Everyone has one TCH in the neighborhood." The goal of TCH is to capture the market segment between Highlands Coffee, which typically attracts office workers, and Starbucks, which mainly targets the local affluent class and foreign tourists. The targeted market and consumer base of TCH is the middle-class group, who is capable of using technology. Based on the concept "from farm to cup," TCH has invested in a 50-hectare coffee farm in Cau Dat region of Lam Dong province in 2018, hoping to bring the highest quality beans to the consumers. The company also invested in a roaster in District 7 in Ho Chi Minh City with a capacity of 20 tons/month.

The COVID-19 pandemic has revolutionized the mindset of brick-and-mortar in the F&B industry. In 2020, TCH planned to open 100 new shops. However, the plan has been delayed due to the pandemic. Instead, TCH shifted its focus on investing in technology to provide rapid online order, delivery, and pick-up service and QR codes for faster payment process. TCH technology platform integrates many different departments within the organization, including service management, operations, and TCH app (for online service and customer care) to provide the highest quality service and satisfaction.

For example, the introduction of pick-up service in June 2020 differentiated TCH from other F&Bs in Vietnam. With pick-up service, customers make an order in advance using the app, then stop by the store for pick up, and the order will be ready in 1 minute. This service has been launched in stores nationwide, mainly in Hanoi, Ho Chi Minh City, and Da Nang, reaching one million TCH app users. This is faster compared to the take-away service, were customers have to wait in line to make an order, pay, and wait for the order to arrive, which may take between 7–10 minutes. Previously, TCH often introduced new services necessary for the current needs of the market, now they are taking a step forward by introducing the services for future demand. TCH believes that, in the post-pandemic era, businesses who want to become a pioneer in the F&B industry need to build a strong network between technology and the consumers, reflecting the importance of savvy and connected customers observed through our surveys.

25.4.4. *Discussions*

The three case studies have shown that businesses are rather agile to adjust their strategies quickly and tap into the right group of customers (i.e. savvy and connected users and main shoppers) who can drive the major behavioral changes both during and after the COVID-19 social isolation period. For digital businesses like MoMo and Tiki, the pandemic has highlighted the role of online activities to address real-life needs. The two companies have taken on a transformative path that further aligns their corporate interests with social causes, such as addressing inequality in access to proper healthcare and health safety, boosting economic recovery post–COVID-19, and collaborating with a broad range of industry partners to provide a better and wider range of e-commerce experiences to their customers. For a brick-and-mortar business like TCH, the pandemic has effected a change in their growth strategy, from extending physical chain outlets to an online expansion through the TCH app. All of these represent significant reinvention of the business, which are expected to make them even more resilient in the condition of uncertainty post–COVID-19. In addition, our survey results suggest that companies could also explore strategies to leverage the health-concern momentum and expand further toward the elderly people, which could be an important new customer base.

25.5. Concluding Remarks

In this chapter, we have examined empirical evidences from both customer behaviors and business case studies to understand how the e-commerce and digital markets have changed during the COVID-19 pandemic, and to further consider how the changes would be sustained after the pandemic. Evidences from our survey of 556 online shoppers confirmed that there has been indeed an increased in the usage of e-commerce and online payments during the social isolation period in March and April 2020. Further, such behavior changes continued even after the isolation period, which is a promising sign to conclude that the new digital habits would be sustained in the future post–COVID-19 era. From the business case studies, we observed that the three different types of business, including a FinTech company, an e-commerce platform, and a non-digital service provider, have actively reinvented themselves to better suite their customers' concern for cashless payments and quick-and-easy purchases that minimize direct contact.

Further, as we examine the factors associated with e-commerce and digital service demands during and after the social isolation period, we find that although technology savviness and connectedness remain important to drive the increase in online shopping activities and FinTech usage, customer in the older age groups, and particularly those in their fifties and beyond, are also more likely to increase their online activities. This is an encouraging sign to explore new segments to expand the customer base. Our results also indicate that increases in online activity during the social isolation period is significantly correlated with further increases in online activity after social isolation, net of various controlled factors. This might point toward a hidden construct for a customer segment that is well conscious of health risks during COVID-19.

Our results also shed an important light for firms in terms of post-pandemic recovery and potential expansion of the customer base. As mentioned earlier, our study asserts the key roles of connected spenders, suggesting that firms' recovery efforts should pay close attention to this emerging segment of customers, which has been carried out successfully by Vietnamese firms. Our results also suggest that consumers in the older age groups, and particularly those in their forties and beyond, are more likely to increase their online shopping and e-commerce activities during and beyond the pandemic due to their concerns for health and safety. This is a significant change given that the traditional population of "connected" and technology-savvy users tend to be aged below 30 years. It also creates new opportunities in the post-pandemic expansion of the customer base by strengthening and increasing the loyalty of this new elder customer segment. Educational campaigns, targeted promotional and loyalty programs, and targeted product and service offerings will make e-commerce and digital financial services easier and more convenient for these consumers.

Both customers' changes in receptiveness and perceptions, as well as business strategies, surprisingly, suggest a positively disruptive growth of Vietnam's e-commerce and digital financial service because of the COVID-19 pandemic. The encouraging sign is that the businesses in Vietnam have transformed in a way that better support equal access to healthcare, enhanced safety measures, and strong collaborations across industry. This also poses some important challenges from a policy perspective. First, it is crucial to increase users' connectedness to further spur Vietnam's e-commerce and boost the digital economy market. This could be done through providing public information and education and implementing policies to expedite digital transformation and improvements in digital infrastructure. The recent issuance of licenses for commercial testing of 5G mobile network to telecom giants, Viettel and Mobifone, suggest that Vietnam's digital infrastructure will be ready for the anticipated boom of e-commerce and digital financial services. Second, since the customer base for the industry likely expand toward people with various forms of vulnerability, e.g. age and other health risks for COVID-19, it is essential that governmental regulations can quickly catch up to the trends to provide a legal framework that ensures transparency, security, and safety of all involved stakeholders, especially vulnerable consumers. The Vietnam government has recently greenlighted the legalization process of mobile money, with plans for pilot commercial uses in 2021. Mobile money is a form of electronic money, allowing users to pay for goods or services directly with mobile phone accounts, without the need to link with bank accounts. Since mobile phone usage is widespread in Vietnam, with subscriptions substantially over 100% population ratio, mobile money is expected to deepen the market penetration of e-commerce and digital financial services, especially in rural and mountainous areas, where consumers typically do not have access to, or are highly resistant to, traditional financial services. In summary, there have been promising signals that Vietnam is on course to develop a resilient digital economy, supported by well-developed infrastructure, supporting regulations and decent market penetration. Such a digital economy is the best preparation for both businesses and consumers in case of a similar global disruption like the COVID-19 pandemic.

References

Abad-Segura, E., González-Zamar, M.D., López-Meneses, E. and Vázquez-Cano, E. (2020). Financial technology: Review of trends, approaches and management. *Mathematics*, **8**(6), 951.

Bachas, P., Paul, G., Sean, H. and Enrique, S. (2018). digital financial services go a long way: Transaction costs and financial inclusion. *AEA Papers and Proceedings*, **108**, 444–448.

Basol, R.C. and Shiv, S.P. (2018). Transformation through unbundling: Visualizing the global fintech ecosystem. *Service Science*, **10**(4), 379–396.

Breidbach, C.F., Keating, B.W. and Lim, C. (2019). Fintech: Research directions to explore the digital transformation of financial service systems. *Journal of Service Theory and Practice*, **30**(1), 79–102.

Chang, S.E., Shen, W.C. and Liu, A.Y. (2016). Why mobile users trust smartphone social networking services? A PLS-SEM approach. *Journal of Business Research*, **69**(11), 4890–4895.

Chen, L. (2016). From Fintech to Finlife: The case of Fintech development in China. *China Economic Journal*, **9**(3), 225–239.

Finau, G., Rika, N., Samuwai, J. and McGoon, J. (2016). Perceptions of digital financial services in rural Fiji. *Information Technologies & International Development* [Special Issue], **12**(4), 11–21.

Gefen, D., Karahanna, E. and Straub, D.W. (2003). Trust and TAM in online shopping: An integrated model. *MIS Quarterly*, **27**(1), 51–90.

Grabner-Kraeuter, S. (2002). The role of consumers' trust in online-shopping. *Journal of Business Ethics*, **39**(1–2), 43–50.

Ha, S. and Stoel, L. (2009). Consumer e-shopping acceptance: Antecedents in a technology acceptance model. *Journal of Business Research*, **62**(5), 565–571

Keely, L. (2017). Your business is going to depend on connected spenders, so 0you'd better understand who they are. *Harvard Business Review*, 8 February.

Lee, G.G. and Lin, H.F. (2005). Customer perceptions of e-service quality in online shopping. *International Journal of Retail & Distribution Management*, **33**(2), 161–176.

Malady, L. and Buckley, R. (2014). Building consumer demand for digital financial services: the new regulatory frontier. Center for International

Finance and Regulation (CIFR) Research Working Paper Series, Paper No. 035/2014.

Mattila, J., Seppala, T. and Lahteenmaki, I. (2018). Who holds the reins? – Banks in the crossfire of global platforms. The Research Institute of the Finnish Economy. Working Paper.

Parasuraman, A., Zeithaml, V.A. and Berry, L.L. (1988). SERVQUAL: a multiple item scale for measuring customer perceptions of service quality. *Journal of Retailing*, **64**(1), 12–40.

Pavlou, P.A. and Fygenson, M. (2006). Understanding and predicting electronic commerce adoption: An extension of the theory of planned behavior. *MIS Quarterly*, **30**(1), 115–143.

Pavlou, P.A. and Gefen, D. (2004). Building effective online marketplaces with institution-based trust. *Information Systems Research*, **15**(1), 35–62.

Ratnasingam, P., Pavlou, P.A. and Tan, Y. (2002). The importance of technology trust for B2B electronic commerce. In *Proceeding of the 15th BLED Electronic Commerce Conference 2002*, Bled, Slovenia, June 17–19, pp. 384–398.

Shin, J.I., Chung, K.H., Oh, J.S. and Lee, C.W. (2013). The effect of site quality on repurchase intention in Internet shopping through mediating variables: The case of university students in South Korea. *International Journal of Information Management*, **33**, 453–463.

Van Noort, G., Kerkhof, P. and Fennis, B.M. (2008). The persuasiveness of online safety cues: The impact of prevention focus compatibility of Web content on consumers' risk perceptions, attitudes, and intentions. *Journal of Interactive Marketing*, **22**(4), 58–72.

Vu, Diep V. (2017). The current status of digital payments in Vietnam and some recommendations (in Vietnamese). *Industry and Trade Magazine*. Retrieved from https://tinyurl.com/y5jxqem2.

https://doi.org/10.1142/9781800610781_0026

Chapter 26

Transformation of Derivatives Securities in Emerging Markets: Policy Implications in Light of the 2007–2009 Global Financial Crisis and COVID-19 Pandemic

Mazin A. M. Al Janabi

(Retired) Tecnologico de Monterrey, EGADE Business School, Santa Fe Campus, Mexico City, Mexico

mazinaljanabi@gmail.com

Abstract

During the last three decades, trading of derivatives products in emerging markets has undergone a number of adaptations and modernizations to different scales, depending on each market's early stages of infrastructure. This chapter discusses some of the central barriers to the launch of rewarding derivatives products in emerging economies and proposes some possible responses, pragmatic solutions, policy measures, and implications, in light of the outcomes of the 2007–2009 Global Financial Crisis and the COVID-19 pandemic. The objective is to set unambiguous operational platforms, sound regulations and effective oversights to deter misconducts, frauds, manipulations, abusive practices, and rogue trading within financial markets and institutions.

26.1. Introduction

Since the mid-1980s, the total number of derivatives exchanges operating in both emerging market and developed economies has multiplied several-fold. Nevertheless, despite the remarkable growth in the global derivatives markets, there is significant heterogeneity in their degree of advancement across countries (Fernandez, 2006).

Currently, derivatives contracts are created and traded on organized futures and options exchanges and over-the-counter (OTC) through authorized dealers. For many assets, the trade in derivatives products is now far larger in total monetary terms than in cash securities. Furthermore, highly standardized derivatives securities, mainly futures and options contracts, are traded on organized exchanges with well-run clearinghouses. Thus, derivatives exchanges have greatly expanded in number and range of traded products they offer in recent years. However, OTC derivatives still account for a substantial portion of the notional value outstanding.

Emerging markets have commenced playing a fundamental role in the trading of derivatives products since the last decade of the 20th century. Even though these markets are seen, by and large, as politically insecure, segmented, illiquid, lacking of sound and consistent regulations, and deficient in reliable financial datasets, they do provide certain benefits to the diverse market participants (i.e. both speculators and hedgers alike). Accordingly, in an emerging-market setting, the challenges for regulatory bodies and the burdens and duties of portfolio managers, risk managers and financial treasurers will undeniably be increased several-fold (Al Janabi, 2012a).

As a result, emerging markets can obtain significant advantages from launching of derivatives trading activities, which include, but are not limited to, the capability to transfer risks, lower transactions costs, and the accessibility of public information. Nevertheless, the success of a reliable derivatives market rests on the completeness of the fundamentals on which it was designed, the embraced structure and trading platforms, and the varieties of traded securities (Tsetsekos and Varangis, 1997, 2000; Al Janabi, 2006, 2012a).

The surge in the use of derivatives securities in the recent years, along with large and widely reported losses by well-known corporations and financial institutions, have given rise to many concerns, debates, and confusions on the appropriate use of derivatives products (see for instance, Boyle and Boyle, 2001; Steinherr, 2000). Indeed, this seems like a paradox — instruments that should reduce financial risks are themselves accused of introducing new risks. However, are these losses caused by derivatives, or just by the improper use of derivatives products?

Derivatives products and structured securities can successfully control and hedge financial and commodity risks, but their unrestrained use can be extremely risky. The leverage effects in derivatives products that makes them price-effective, when hedging standing market risk exposures or merely for speculation motives, can also make them the cheaper way to take part in new trading contracts. Though derivatives products can be customized to eliminate most risks, their complexity and potential for large profits lead some market participants to disregard the embedded multifaceted residual risks and inspire others to take advantage of these facts and misuse them in practice (Al Janabi, 2012a).

Lately, the development of state-of-the-art technology for the administration and control of integral risk is on the rise, and particularly for the assessment of derivatives securities and other complex structured products. As a result, financial institutions in emerging markets have formally started in designing and implementing risk management procedures, rigorous valuation models, and systems mainly due to the following reasons:

(i) The mistreatment and abuse in derivatives securities was evident during the 2007–2009 subprime Global Financial Crisis, and particularly within credit derivatives products. In other words, the issue was not with the derivatives securities per se, but more exactly how they were manipulated and exploited in practice by certain market players in the course of the 2007–2009 global financial meltdown (Acharya *et al.*, 2009a).

(ii) Major competitions between financial institutions, derived from policies of deregulation and openness, have reduced earnings and shrunk margins. This has forced financial entities to think twice with respect to the value of the limited capital available to support the various global transactions.

(iii) The presence of new structured products, such as derivatives products and hybrid instruments, and the level of complexity required for the valuations of positions and estimation of risk profiles.

(iv) Major transparency and globalization of financial markets have obliged local authorities and regulators to enhance risk management practices and setting up clear "rules of the game," based on international standards as issued by the Bank of International Settlements (BIS), Basel Committee on Banking Supervision, and the Financial Stability Board (FSB).

(v) The impacts of previous and recent global crises (including the impact of the latest COVID-19 pandemic) on financial markets and the consequential effects that have led to the bankruptcy of countries and the insolvency of several key institutions (both financial and corporate entities).

(vi) While the 2007–2009 Global Financial Crisis and the COVID-19 pandemic have different origins and characteristics, as the first is a financial meltdown in nature whereas the other is a health crisis, there are certain similar traits as related to their effects on derivatives markets, particularly its impacts on the operations and clearance of OTC derivative securities.

(vii) The effects of the COVID-19 health crisis on the global financial markets (including derivatives markets) is unprecedented. With the ongoing spread of the COVID-19 health crisis on globe scale, and the economic slump as a result of its aftershocks, its total consequences continue to be undetermined. For OTC derivatives market participants, COVID-19 provoked various concerns that financial and non-financial entities should take into consideration as they exploit different risk management strategies and policies, and adjust to the continuing events.

In this backdrop, the aim of this chapter is to provide practical and operational guiding principles for the launch of effective derivatives products in emerging markets and within sound and consistent frameworks of contemporary regulations, transparency, policy measures, and oversights. This chapter addresses a number of operational and regulatory issues for derivative market participants to consider in light of the 2007–2009 Global Financial Crisis and the ongoing COVID-19 pandemic. The goal of this chapter is to fill a gap in financial market regulations and contemporary risk management literature, particularly in the emerging markets viewpoint, by presenting a practitioner's opinions on how to structure reliable and operational derivatives products and markets in emerging economies. The attempt here is to propose several robust strategies and guidelines that can aid emerging markets in the launch of reliable derivatives markets and trading platforms within a well-structured framework of regulations and operational policies, predominantly in the wake of the COVID-19 health crisis and the aftermath of 2007–2009 credit crunch and its end-results in the collapse and insolvency of a number of well-known financial service institutes and entities worldwide. This chapter can be of interest to those involved in the design of consistent, coherent, and reliable operational platforms for the trading of derivatives products in emerging markets, predominantly in light of the aftermaths of the 2007–2009 subprime global financial crunch and the COVID-19 health crisis.

The remainder of this chapter is organized as follow. In Section 26.2, regulatory challenges in emerging markets and contemporary risk management issues are examined and certain obstacles (including, but not limited to, markets and regulatory concerns) are then acknowledged. In Section 26.3, proposals of regulatory challenges for the reliable operations of derivatives products in emerging markets are discussed. In Section 26.4, financial market misconducts and some possible responses and proposals are examined. Section 26.5, discusses the regulatory challenges for effective operations of derivatives products, including the assessments of embedded risks and the role of datasets and statistical tools. Section 26.6 highlights key responses to efficient regulatory challenges, including relevant Basel Accords and Financial Stability Board (FSB) rules on the COVID-19 health crisis. Section 26.7 concludes the chapter.

26.2. Regulatory Challenges in Emerging Markets and Contemporary Risk Management Issues

In many emerging markets, proprietary trading has turned out to be a fundamental activity of financial markets and institutions; therefore, besides the risks usually expected in the day-to-day business of financial intermediation, financial entities are taking operational views about the movements and tendencies of these markets. These developments and changes have reinforced the necessity for better risk management systems and internal regulatory compliances and controls (Al Janabi, 2008a).

The need for risk management products and processes by emerging countries is now substantial and will persist all the way through the 21st century. This definitely will put more burden and strain on banking regulators and supervisors to assure the safety and soundness of their corresponding financial systems by means of pertinent regulations and prudential policies. To that end, the regulatory and supervisory challenges are even more complex and important to tackle in emerging markets for many reasons. Emerging markets have a series of traits that necessitate different regulatory oversights and risk management tactics and methods than those of developed countries. Some of these characteristics can affect regulations, risk methodologies, assessment, and modeling techniques of potential exposures, while the others influence and modify the execution process, detailed as follows (Al Janabi 2006; 2008a; 2008b):

(i) The traded financial securities are, in many cases, insufficient and/or deficient for launching acceptable benchmarks and settings for the valuation of certain transactions, such as long-term interest rate, currency swaps, exotic derivatives, and hybrid and structured derivatives products. Likewise, low trading volume (i.e. illiquid financial markets with wide bid-ask spreads and long span for unwinding of holding assets) and the unavailability of historical datasets for various financial securities form suspicions concerning the validity of quoted prices.

(ii) Generally used risk assessment methods and practices were devised in developed countries for securities traded in their markets. These securities usually function under steady, well-established, liquid, and deregulated financial systems. When applied in emerging market settings, however, these approaches and modeling techniques may produce useless outcomes as a result of the existing gaps of information and technology in such environments.

(iii) The risk characteristics of emerging markets differ from those of more mature markets in fundamental ways. Standard statistical measures, such as correlation and volatility, must be suitably interpreted before being applied in risk assessment. Besides, the relationships between these risk measures can undergo abrupt and dramatic changes — for instance, correlation factors can switch signs under stressed market situations.

(iv) These emerging markets are well characterized by frequent government interferences in financial markets to alleviate the short-term influence of an existing event or crises. Therefore, the assessment of risk on the short-end will reveal a fairly risk-steady market and it might pass along the erroneous message, given that the effect of present disturbances and crises is watered down with government interventions. Nevertheless, once risk is determined on a long-time horizon, one should not be astonished to discover immense swings in the level of potential risks. In these conditions, risk techniques, such as downside-risk measures, stress testing, and event-risk, are more suitable in this case than recognized market risk methods — such as the Value-at-Risk (VaR) risk measure that assumes normal distributions of financial asset's returns.[1]

(v) Event risk (or markets under severe crisis conditions) is a widespread spectacle in emerging markets and is correlated to the risk of considerable losses owing to extreme changes in risk factors because of unforeseen political, economic, or other events, which can affect the value of financial contracts. In fact, event risk can be manifested in those state of affairs where prices are greatly reliant on certain structural factors — e.g. a political restructuring and reforms in case of emerging-markets debt trading or the aftermath of an insolvency filing in case of corporate distressed debt trading — or where price performance is influenced (for instance, foreign exchange rate pegging systems).

(vi) Emerging countries are distinguished by lower investment in information technology (IT) systems that can manage and control front office (trading units), middle office (risk management and legal and regulatory compliance), and back office

[1]For other relevant literature on Value-at-Risk, internal risk models, and portfolio selection, one can refer as well to Asadi and Al Janabi (2020); Al Janabi (2020a); Al Janabi (2020b); Arreola-Hernandez and Al Janabi (2020); Grillini *et al.* (2019); Al Janabi *et al.* (2017); Al Janabi *et al.* (2019); Arreola-Hernandez *et al.* (2017); Arreola-Hernandez *et al.* (2015), among others.

(accounting and settlement). In addition, they are in shortage of staffs with technical qualifications in economics and finance, such as traders, arbitrageurs, quantitative analysts, financial engineers, and risk managers.

(vii) The market structure of financial services and banking activities is concentrated in just a small number of key financial institutions, on which the stability of the entire macroeconomy depends. In essence, local financial markets are commonly distinguished as thin and illiquid, requiring appropriate IT infrastructures, and rigorously volatile, making them even more challenging for local financial and non-financial institutions to assess and manage their risks efficiently. In certain emerging markets, banks and other financial service intermediary's functions are conducted and interlinked with other corporate entity shareholders, producing serious moral hazard problems and shortcomings.

(viii) Illiquid securities such as bonds, equities, and foreign exchange rates are very familiar in emerging markets. Typically, these instruments are traded infrequently (with very low volumes as well as widespread bid-ask spreads).[2] This of course implies a real problem to anyone who tries to assess the market risk of these instruments with techniques that are built on correlation matrices and historical volatilities. Therefore, the selection of the time horizon (or the required number of days to unwind a position) is a crucial aspect and has critical influence on Value-at-Risk (VaR) statistics (Al Janabi, 2012a).

(ix) The political structure and government strategies of preserving stability of the financial system are fragile, inconsistent, unpredictable, and less developed. These markets are commonly distinguished with regular government involvements to soothe and absorb the short-term effects of existing events, crises, and disorders. As such, banks and other financial institutions may have a high degree of political impact in their countries, but only

[2]For further discussion on liquidity risk and Liquidity-Adjusted Value-at-Risk (LVaR) literature using the Al Janabi model, we can refer the readers to Madoroba and Kruger (2014) and Al Janabi (2011, 2012b, 2013, 2014) research papers. In their paper, Madoroba and Kruger (2014) review and compare 10 liquidity risk VaR models, including the Al Janabi model.

a partial understanding and acceptance of the necessities for autonomous regulations and supervisions.

(x) Financial superiority for the valuations of complex, multidimensional financial instruments and reporting of potential exposures are inadequate, opaque, and less rigorous than in front-line economies. Furthermore, accounting and auditing criteria and standards differ broadly from market to market. Likewise, financial entity management and regulatory supervisors are less skilled in innovative methods and modeling techniques for the identification, measurement, management, and control of the different kinds of financial risks.

(xi) The lack (or, in many instances, the non-existence) of sufficient historical and current datasets for most of these markets macroeconomic variables can complicate and render difficult the logistics of an effective and integral risk management system. Certainly, slight tangible progress can be made without decent datasets, and it will definitely take substantial efforts to gather them.

26.3. Proposals of Regulatory Challenges for Reliable Operations of Derivatives Products in Emerging Markets

In the following paragraphs, my aim is to highlight some of the key issues related to the assessment, management and control of different risks allied with the trading and operations of derivatives products and with particular emphasis on emerging markets.

As a practitioner in derivatives products trading floors and risk management marketplace — first, as a trader of derivatives products and later on as a trading risk manager and global director of market risk — and based on my prior operational experience, studies and observations in emerging markets, I strongly recommend that any emerging market in the phase of organizing and/or preparing its own facilities and infrastructure to enter into the derivatives business should, at a minimum, examine refining the following operational, regulatory, and supervisory factors, described along these lines:

(i) Launching of liquid cash markets for the trading of common stocks, foreign exchange transactions, and debt instruments (i.e. bonds and short-term interest rate products). In fact, the lack of continuous liquidity in the trading of stocks, foreign exchange, and debt instruments can undeniably lead to complications in the hedging of pertinent risks arising from reporting derivatives products on corporation's balance sheet. Indeed, the later played a large role in the course of the 2007–2009 subprime global financial crunch.

(ii) It is advised to commence first with OTC markets for the trading of derivatives products of important local market underlying assets, such as interest rates (debt instruments), foreign exchange contracts, and stock market indices. This preliminary stage can help in constructing the basic building blocks for standard derivatives exchanges thereafter. As such, during the course of this provisional phase, regulatory and supervisory authorities can enhance on the next operational, regulatory, and oversights requirements, detailed as follows:

(a) Conducting an assessment process of likely OTC market participants, such as market-makers (traders and dealers), speculators, arbitrageurs, and hedgers, who can contribute as requested invitees in outgoing brainstorming groups, with legislators and policymakers, with the objective of setting up the necessary steps of adequate microstructures for effective and fruitful standardized derivatives exchanges.

(b) Development and improvement on existing key regulatory requirements for setting up accounting procedures and settlements, operations, and risk management. This act can aid in encouraging market participants and policymakers to set the basis of acceptable market microstructures of formal derivatives exchanges. These market microstructures should include, at the minimum: (1) regulatory oversight; (2) clearing and settlement methods and procedures; (3) trading and risk management infrastructure and systems; (4) varieties of derivatives products to be traded; (5) memberships of the derivatives exchange; and (6) ownership of the clearing corporation (clearinghouse).

(c) The selection of the different types of derivatives products to be traded afterward in standard derivatives securities exchanges. This can aid in measuring the benefits and advantages of the chosen securities and to decide whether local market participants are enthusiastic enough about developing local derivatives securities exchanges. The obtained outcomes should be judged against the risks and benefits of using already recognized derivatives exchanges — largely in developed foreign nations that are trading derivatives products on key local market variables and indicators — that are more liquid and emphasize prudential regulations and oversights. In fact, derivatives exchanges challenge and compete with one another to list futures and options contracts that have the likelihood of turning into actively traded product, hence the first-mover effect (i.e. which exchange lists first a potential contract), in my judgment, plays a fundamental role in the likely outcome of any derivatives products' listing tactic. In addition, the first-mover effect can have more impact than trading-platform selections — electronic trading versus open-outcry trading (for further details on this topic, one can refer to Holder *et al.*, 1999). Furthermore, I have recognized that emerging economies' participants are keener to trade derivatives products that are associated with equities and equity market indices (i.e. index-based derivatives). Indeed, the idea of introducing index-based derivatives falls also in line with the results of other researchers (see, for instance, Tsetsekos and Varangis, 2000).

(d) Assembling of adequate current and historical databases and time-series of assets prices and other macroeconomic variables is at the core of any pricing and risk management process. In fact, this quality data collection process should be considered by financial corporations, markets, and regulatory bodies as vital assets to be actively managed and as a strategic resource necessitating its own specialist custodians (Glasser, 2013). To that end, at this stage, datasets and time-series of assets prices and other essential macroeconomic variables should be collected, classified, filtered, matched, analyzed, and verified, as decision-making will be based on such crucial information, otherwise "garbage-in can most likely lead to garbage-out."

(e) Setting up the basis for the implementation of management information systems (MIS) according to the need and level of sophistication of each emerging country and institution. Trading, booking, and settlement systems that can handle front, middle, and back offices should be devised and outfitted. It is recommended that local IT providers get involved in the design process of these systems rather than importing off-the-shelves foreign MIS systems. This is because imported commercial systems might not satisfy the needs of each country and it might also include very rigorous and tedious tools, which are not required at this stage.

(f) In addition, the design of an OTC market can help in speeding up an investor's learning process on advance finance topics, especially for treasury department's managers and financial markets analysts who most likely are the first market players interested in participation and acquiring solid knowledge in advanced financial engineering aspects. Furthermore, retailers can possibly find such a market an opportunity for hedging purposes and for choosing a carefully analyzed bet-side on local-market macroeconomic variables.

26.4. Financial Market Misconduct and Some Possible Responses and Proposals

In the next paragraphs, my objective is to underline some of the main concerns associated with the possibility of fraudulent actions, manipulations, abusive practices, rogue trading, and misconduct within financial markets and institutions and provide some insights on how to deter these kinds of imprudent behaviors, detailed as follows:

(i) Financial institutions and markets must first make every effort to employ and retain responsible, liable, and mature traders who comprehend and question what they are doing and trading. Next is recognizing that many traders (if left alone without clear trading policies and procedures, regulations, and sufficient supervision) have the encouragement and tendency to break the rules.

Therefore, at this stage, the management must assure capable monitoring tools and accurate implementation of trading rules and policies. As a minimum, this requires independent reporting of a trader's action, as well as a readiness to question the roots of abnormal profitable activity and why a particular trader is speculating with high-risk instruments or whether he is operating beyond the risk-budgeting or risk-appetite trading limits of the institution (Al Janabi, 2012a).

(ii) Given the leverage of derivatives securities, a single trader can easily bankrupt a large financial institution — the Barings case may be an exceptional one, but it is far from being a confined case. Indeed, the leverage inherent in derivatives makes them a price-effective way to manage risk, but at the same time, it magnifies possible losses. Most derivatives investments require only a small initial outlay, so their value fluctuates much more than an equivalent sum placed in the underlying cash instruments.

(iii) Likewise, specific attention should be devoted to the newly structured derivatives on natural disasters, weather conditions and forecasts, etc. For instance, nowadays, derivatives products can be used for both speculation and hedging on natural disasters such as earthquakes, extreme weather conditions, etc. Some of the recent innovations are the trading of forward agreements and future contracts on electricity and other kinds of structured products on different energy and greenhouse effects underlying variables. In the case of electricity agreements, these contracts call for the delivery of and payment for electric power in a future period and are used much like oil derivatives contracts to fix or hedge energy costs. However, in fact, electricity derivatives contracts are quite different and complex than other commodities contracts.

26.5. Regulatory Challenges for Effective Operations of Derivatives Products – Assessments of Embedded Risks and the Role of Datasets and Statistical Tools

In the consecutive paragraphs, my goal is to discuss and emphasize the importance of some other embedded risks, such as liquidity risk, counterparty risk, and event risk, and their role in the 2007–2009 global financial meltdown and the COVID-19 health crisis. Moreover, I debate on some of the main issues that were raised in the trading of derivatives, and particularly credit derivatives, in OTC operations during the course of the 2007–2009 global financial crunch. As a final point, I discuss the issue of availability of datasets and statistical tools and their role and influence in the Global Financial Crisis and the COVID-19 pandemic, and provide some insights that were revealed during these crises and markets disorders on the following issues: (i) The financial crunch disclosed that regulatory authorities did not have satisfactory and sufficient data in usable format for assessing and analyzing rising risks in the global financial system and (ii) The failure to foresee the 2007–2009 Global Financial Crisis and the reaction to the COVID-19 health crisis was not the result of flawed statistics, detailed as follows:

(a) Liquidity risk management is of critical significance to entities in the financial service sectors, and exceptional attention should be dedicated to assessment, management, and control of this class of trading risk. In fact, many collapses and failures of financial entities have surfaced in large part due to scarce liquidity resulting from undesirable crisis and events. In view of that, the necessity for better measurement, management and control tools of liquidity risk is rising in the global financial markets, and particularly in emerging economies. This is with the main aim of setting a broad set of liquidity and funding rules that are intended to preserve significant flexibility to address market liquidity events and to allow core trading activities to continue to generate revenues even under adverse market conditions (Al Janabi, 2008c, 2012a).
(b) In less-developed financial markets, there is a great level of involvement and intervention by local authorities as they look for preserving economic permanence. As such, the exposure of businesses operating in this situation is ruled by risk factors that cannot be regarded as "genuine" market variables, which are governed by supply and demand forces. In such a case, it becomes critical to incorporate crisis risk (or event risk under adverse market situations) in any wise risk calculations and management. In the emerging markets context and under the notion of government-controlled risk factors, event risk can surface, for example, under abrupt and considerable currency depreciation or severe devaluation (Al Janabi, 2012a).

(c) Correlation assumptions in emerging markets must be taken seriously as correlation can break down or even change signs. Correlation assumptions can either be explicit or implicit. In some ways, the implicit assumptions are more dangerous in that they are more easily overlooked. A typical implicit assumption is a correlation of either zero or one. For example, some emerging markets currencies are pegged to the US dollar, and one can assume that the correlation is very close to one. This is not really a statistical fact, but rather reflects a policy decision that could change abruptly. A concrete example of an implicit assumption of zero is the correlation between the local exchange rate and credit risk spreads for an emerging market country. While this may be correct for mature markets, in emerging market it is not the case.

(d) The 2007–2009 global financial crunch and the COVID-19 health crisis have underlined a number of drawbacks of OTC trading of some derivatives securities (such as credit derivatives), particularly counterparty and operational risk concerns and the effects of the lack of transparency among market players. The key issue is that collaterals and margin requirements and obligations are established bilaterally in OTC trading platforms and do not take into consideration the externality that can be inflicted on the rest of the financial system for each trading position and its interrelated counterparty risk. This can permit systemically significant exposures to expand without enough capital-cushion to support the overall OTC market transactions (Acharya *et al.*, 2009b). To that end, regulators should endorse the use of well-functional, centralized clearinghouses and demanding better transparency on the counterparty exposures of systemically key financial institutions — whose possible failure would put other institutions at severe risk. In effect, these institutions should be demanded to assess, in real time, their enterprise-wide counterparty risk exposure and to disclose the obtained information with regulatory bodies. Lastly, systematically important financial institutions should be required to run stress-testing techniques to verify the changes in the values of their assets and liabilities and to demonstrate that they could withstand the collapse of their main trading counterparties (Stulz, 2009).

(e) Counterparty risk related to OTC trading of derivatives products, and particularly credit derivatives, played a major role during the course of the 2007–2009 financial crisis and the COVID-19 pandemic. Indeed, OTC disposition of trading in credit derivatives, and the consequential obscurity, added considerably to counterparty risk anxieties surrounding the collapse or near failure of major players such as Lehman Brothers, Bear Stearns, and AIG. Yet again, the main problem can be attributed to the nature of trading in these kinds of derivatives products rather than to the products per se. Hence, it is recommended that, instead of regulating these special kinds of derivatives products straightforwardly, the emphasis should be focused on the root cause of counterparty risk concerns — which is the lack of centralized counterparty clearing, or in other words a single counterparty for all trades (Acharya and Richardson, 2009; Acharya *et al.*, 2009a,b). In fact, there has been several discussions about making the use of centralized clearinghouses compulsory for all derivatives products, or even demanding that all derivatives products to be traded on organized exchanges. A typical clearinghouse would almost remove counterparty risk on the assumption that it is well capitalized and run properly (Stulz, 2009). While such a tactic would work appropriately for some derivatives contracts, it could be very costly to employ for some classes of complex derivatives securities (Stulz, 2009). As such, demanding the use of a centralized clearinghouse mechanism for all derivatives securities can probably reduce the diversity of derivatives products obtainable in international markets. On the other hand, Das (2010) questions the ability of a centralized clearinghouse to manage risk effectively, at least for all derivatives products, owing to the lack of availability of prices, constraints on market liquidity, and the inherent derivatives products features that may be problematic to model.

(f) The 2007–2009 Global Financial Crisis revealed that regulatory authorities did not have satisfactory and sufficient data in compatible and usable formats that were needed on a timely basis for assessing threats to financial stability and to analyze rising risks in the global financial system. In addition, the 2007–2009 global financial meltdown disclosed that the generated data was incomplete, inadequate, or not straightforward to assemble and leverage because of an absence of standards and classifications for their description and application (Glasser, 2013). Furthermore, it demonstrated that the data was not well structured, comprehended, or analyzed, neither in anticipation of the 2007–2009 subprime crisis nor for the duration of its worst days. As a result, regulators were not capable of evaluating the different kinds of risks generated by firms or to analyze risks on an aggregate level merely because each regulatory entity maintained its own opinion on the collected data (Glasser, 2013).

(g) The failure to foresee the 2007–2009 global financial crunch and prior crises was not the result of flawed statistics, rather it is a consequence of the defective lens through which those statistics were examined, analyzed, and interpreted. Ultimately, the lens through which we should examine, analyze, and interpret the data is more crucial than the data itself (Borio, 2013). This boils down to the point that we like to see what we really want to see — a well-known phenomenon that was described by psychologists as cognitive dissonance. As such, what some market players regard as a favorable redistribution of risk in the global financial system, other market participants perceive it as a dangerous and excessive risk-taking practice. Likewise, policies with respect to regulating derivatives securities that some regulatory entities consider as wise, others regard as reckless and imprudent — or to put it in other words "one man's meat is another man's poison."

26.6. Responses to Efficient Regulatory Challenges — Principles and Proposals Including Relevant Basel Accords and Financial Stability Board Rules on COVID-19 Health Crisis

It is a common phenomenon that the pressure on regulators to regulate further raises noticeably during and instantaneously after financial crises; and the sub-prime credit crunch has been no different on this front (Acharya and Richardson, 2009). Lamentably, quite often different market participants, commentators, policymakers, as well as some academics misjudge symptoms for causes and back regulations that pretend to repair symptoms instead of getting at the root causes of the issue (Acharya and Richardson, 2009).

Nevertheless, I do believe that the 2007–2009 global financial crunch and the COVID-19 health crisis have underlined some inadequacies in the trading platforms and infrastructure of derivatives products — especially the relatively newer ones, such as credit derivatives. These shortcomings call for timely regulatory attentiveness and intervention. As discussed earlier in the chapter, regulations for the trading of derivatives products are indispensable elements, and the shortcoming of reinforcement of these components had led to widespread scandalous misconducts, insolvencies, collapses and crises. These regulations have to include several items such as accounting standards and settlement processes, legal business environment, risk management systems, transparency, oversights, operational platforms, pricing and valuation of diverse derivatives, and structured products.

In essence, regulations and supervisions in developed and developing countries are at the heart of any risk measurement, management, and control process. To that end, I discuss below some of the contemporary and essential issues in existing regulatory reforms, and provide insights on other imperative aspects related to internal models and operational risk, and the impact of counterparty risk and credit derivatives on the 2007–2009 Global Financial Crisis and the COVID-19 pandemic, detailed along these lines:

(i) The Basel Committee on Banking Supervision and the Bank of International Settlements (BIS) have set and applied certain capital adequacy and regulations requirements on banks in major industrialized countries. In 1993, the BIS implemented risk-based capital ratios for all commercial banks, which are member-countries of the BIS, under what has become recognized as the Basel I Agreement. The 1993 Basel Agreement explicitly integrated the diverse credit risks of assets (both on and off-balance-sheet) into capital adequacy methods and processes. This was followed with a revision in 1998, in which market risk measures were incorporated into risk-based capital ratios. In 2001, the BIS issued a consultative document, currently is called Basel II, which recommended the incorporation of operational risk into capital requirements and updated the credit risk assessments in the 1993 agreement. In the reformed Basel II Accord, the assessment of market risk (the so-called "standard model") did not change from that implemented in 1998. In fact, Basel II's overall intention is to endorse adequate capitalization of banks and encourage improvements in risk measurement, management, and control, thereby strengthening the stability of the entire financial system. Basel II Accord does so by implementing three complementary pillars: one concerning capital adequacy methodology and calculation, another on supervisory review, and a third setting disclosure terms to enable market discipline. Nevertheless, Basel II did not explicitly address the regulation of liquidity risk management. As a result, the Basel Committee has proposed a third regulatory accord (thus, termed Basel III) on bank capital adequacy. This proposed agreement is intended to improve supervisory practices and strengthen market liquidity risk management and stress-testing techniques. In fact, the Basel III Accord was developed in response to the shortcomings in financial market regulations uncovered by the 2007–2009 global financial crunch. The Basel III Accord is expected to reinforce bank capital requirements by boosting liquidity and reducing bank leverage.

(ii) The Financial Stability Board (FSB), which coordinates financial rules for the Group of 20 leading economies (G20), has set regulatory mandates and policy & procedures after the 2007–2009 Global Financial Crisis to make trading in derivative products more efficient and transparent. This global regulator has issued several regulatory mandates, peer review reports, and frequent implementation progress reports among the G20 counties for the clearing of transactions in the trillions of dollars worth OTC derivatives markets. These regulatory measures became mandatory after the 2007–2009 global financial meltdown to make trading in OTC derivative securities more transparent, and with tighter scrutiny for clearinghouses to withstand extreme stress as well as to hold enough funds to deal with big losses.

(iii) The COVID-19 health crisis is presenting the global financial markets (including derivatives markets in emerging economies) with unparalleled complications and hurdles. Governments and financial markets and institutions are striving to assess and adjust to the social and economic effects of COVID-19 on the disruptions to global financial markets, including emerging derivatives markets.

(iv) While COVID-19 pandemic is not a sub-prime credit-driven incident in comparison to what happened during the 2007–2009 Global Financial Crisis, the ongoing health crisis has caused remarkable disruptions to financial and derivatives markets across the globe. It is not easy to estimate the consequences this extraordinary event will have on global economy and financial markets, at large. Nevertheless, we have already seen that the COVID-19 health crisis is presenting global derivative markets participants with hitherto unfamiliar paradigms and dramatic changes in operations and settlements.

(v) There are many ways in which the COVID-19 pandemic could interrupt the operations and settlement of global financial markets as well as derivatives markets. To that end, entities should identify transactions in their multiple-asset portfolios that are vulnerable to interruption due to the shutting down of financial markets, trading delays and suspensions, early closing of markets, and the absence of market rates as well as other pricing and valuation data for marking-to-market and settlements of transactions across different financial products.

(vi) Market volatility has been one of the main concerns of the COVID-19 health crisis thus far. The volatility caused by the COVID-19 pandemic was due to unprecedented events that caused large variations in performance margin requirements (i.e. collateral liabilities) and margin calls. These extreme markets volatilities demanded unexpected volumes of intraday margin calls. Thus, the failure to meet the margin calls mandate can cause the closeout of all outstanding derivatives transactions.

(vii) One more important issue to bear in mind is whether COVID-19 could cause massive invocation of force majeure covenants in frequently used trading contracts under the International Swaps and Derivatives Association (ISDA) Master Agreement and related ISDA collateral agreements. Force majeure provisions usually provide protections for unanticipated events that preclude a counterparty from carrying out its commitments under a specific agreement. Nonetheless, it stays an open uncertainty whether counterparts would essentially be capable to depend on force majeure provisions, predominantly with regard to transactions where performance may basically hinge on the aptitude to get an access to settlement systems, which can be retrieved distantly.

(viii) The FSB published two recent documents in the year 2020 regarding the financial stability implications and policy measures taken during the period of enhanced economic uncertainty arising from the COVID-19 pandemic. In the first report of the Financial Stability Board (2020b), the FSB published a report on international cooperation to address the financial stability implications of COVID-19. This FSB report was delivered to the G20 economies and includes an overview of the types of measures taken by FSB member jurisdictions as well as policy measures for international cooperation and coordination to address the financial stability implications from COVID-19. Below are some excerpts and highlights from the first report:

(a) "The COVID-19 pandemic represents the biggest test of the post-crisis financial system to date. The global financial system faces the dual challenge to sustain the flow of credit amidst declining growth and manage heightened risks. Nevertheless, the global financial system is more resilient and better placed to sustain financing to the real economy as a result of the G20 regulatory reforms in the aftermath of the 2008 global financial crisis" (Financial Stability Board, 2020b).

(b) "The FSB is closely monitoring the resilience of key nodes in the financial system that are critical for financial stability. These include: the ability of financial institutions and markets to channel funds to the real economy; the ability of market participants around the world to obtain US dollar funding, particularly in emerging markets; the ability of financial intermediaries, such as investment funds, to effectively manage liquidity risk; and the ability of market participants and financial market infrastructures (including central counterparties) to manage evolving counterparty risks" (Financial Stability Board, 2020b).

(c) "The report sets out five principles that underpin the official community's rapid and coordinated response to support the real economy, maintain financial stability and minimize the risk of market fragmentation. Using these principles, authorities will: monitor and share information on a timely basis to assess and address financial stability risks from COVID-19; recognize and use the flexibility built into existing financial standards to support our response; seek opportunities to temporarily reduce operational burdens on firms and authorities; act consistently with international standards, and not roll back reforms or compromise the underlying objectives of existing international standards; and coordinate on the future timely unwinding of the temporary measures taken" (Financial Stability Board, 2020b).

(d) "On the basis of these principles, the FSB is supporting international cooperation and coordination on the COVID-19 response in three ways. First, the FSB is regularly sharing information among financial authorities on evolving financial stability threats, on the policy measures that financial authorities are taking or are considering, and on the effects of those policies. Second, the FSB is assessing potential vulnerabilities in order to better understand the impacts of COVID-19 on financial markets in individual jurisdictions and across the globe and inform discussions of policy issues. Third, FSB members are coordinating on their responses to policy issues, including measures that standard-setting bodies and national authorities take to provide flexibility within international standards or reduce operational burdens" (Financial Stability Board, 2020b).

The second FSB publication (Financial Stability Board, 2020a) was a public consultation report that assists central counterparty (CCP) resolution authorities on issues related to the operations of OTC derivatives markets. Below are some excerpts and highlights from the second report:

(a) "Central clearing of standardized over-the-counter (OTC) derivatives is a key pillar of the G20 Leaders' commitment to reform OTC derivatives markets in response to the 2008 financial crisis. Increased central clearing has simplified the previously complex and opaque web of derivatives exposures. In addition, more collateral is in place to reduce counterparty credit risks. At the same time, CCPs' criticality to the overall safety and soundness of the financial system means that authorities must take steps to ensure that CCPs do not themselves become a source of systemic risk and that they can be successfully resolved without exposing taxpayers to loss" (Financial Stability Board, 2020a).

(b) "Part I of the guidance proposes five steps to guide the authorities in assessing the adequacy of a CCP's financial resources and the potential financial stability implications of their use. The authorities should:

Step 1: Identify hypothetical default and non-default loss scenarios (and a combination of them) that may lead to a resolution of a CCP.
Step 2: Conduct a qualitative and quantitative evaluation of existing resources and tools available in the resolution of the CCP.
Step 3: Assess potential resolution costs.
Step 4: Compare existing resources and tools to resolution costs and identify any gaps.
Step 5: Evaluate the availability, costs and benefits of potential means of addressing any identified gaps" (Financial Stability Board, 2020a).

(c) "Part II of the guidance addresses the treatment of CCP equity in resolution. It provides a framework for resolution authorities to evaluate the exposure of CCP equity to losses in recovery, liquidation and resolution and how (where it is possible) the treatment of CCP equity in resolution could be adjusted" (Financial Stability Board, 2020a).

(ix) Local regulators and financial entities should give exceptional importance to regulating operational risk. The complexity and rapid speed of advances in the derivatives market put certain pressure on the control role to endure. If it does not keep up, the financial entity will be vulnerable to unintentional errors and internal fraud, delinquencies and misconducts. Undoubtedly, there is no placement for the human element and its judgment in any risk management process.

(x) One of the areas of operational risk that requires specific attention is "model risk." In fact, model risk refers to the subtle danger that the model used to value trading positions and its related risks is flawed. Indeed, model construction is as much art as science, and people too often think that complex mathematical models can solve any problem. It is important to recognize (and to admit) that once you have built your own statistical/mathematical models, there is a big temptation to fall in love with them. In essence, models and mathematics are only the medium through which to express a set of assumptions and views about market behavior; and model implementation, in fact, is context-specific.

(xi) Counterparty risk played a central role during recent financial meltdown. There are several calls (see for instance, Acharya and Richardson, 2009; Acharya *et al.*, 2009a,b) for the establishment of a centralized clearinghouse to act as a single counterparty for all trading in the OTC derivatives products, and particularly the newer ones — namely credit derivatives. The justification for regulatory interference in making credit derivatives instruments to trade across a centralized clearinghouse is twofold. First, when one counterparty trades with another, the two counterparties do not restrain the counterparty risk externality they inflict on other market participants (Acharya and Richardson, 2009). Indeed, all OTC contracts contain some collateral or margin requirements, in which counterparties set a deposit guarantees whose purpose is to minimize counterparty risk among entities. This deposit margin is marked-to-market on a daily basis, based on variations in the value of the underlying assets as specified by bilateral contract and the creditworthiness of the concerned counterparties. The complexity, however, is that such collateral provisions are negotiated and set on a mutual agreement. As such, counterparties in each negotiated contract do not take complete account of the fact that the counterparty risk exposure they are willing to accept in a bilateral contract also concerns other market players. Without a doubt, they quite often cannot take into consideration this counterparty risk externality in an OTC background, as a result of the insufficient transparency about the counterparty's other trading positions and its interconnection with the rest of the OTC market (Acharya and Richardson, 2009; Acharya *et al.*, 2009b).

(xii) Excessive, unnecessary, and incompetent regulations are generally perceived as generating new risks of its own and in the long-run causing greater costs of regulatory compliance for financial markets and institutions (Al Janabi, 2012a). Undeniably, derivatives products played both positive and negative roles in the way the 2007–2009 Global Financial Crisis unfolded; and by the same token, it suggests that some sort of regulations of derivatives products make common sense in light of this crunch as well as the COVID-19 health crisis. Nevertheless, regulations that obstruct innovation for the sake of saving investors from the real and fictional threats of risk-taking would unquestionably face a high price. As a result, the failure to picture the impact of derivatives products in proper viewpoint could lead to regulations that do more damage than good (Stulz, 2009).

(xiii) Without a doubt, one of the key raising concerns in emerging markets is that the evolution in contemporary regulations and oversights was not being matched by the trait and quality of the regulators themselves; therefore, a gap is opening up. Financial engineering processes and valuation models have opened the doors for cutting-edge and sophisticated instruments and different valuation methods and techniques that are years ahead for regulators and supervisors in emerging markets to catch up. In fact, financial innovations have led to the creation and structuring of very complex risk exposures not fully understood and evaluated by both targeted investors and the financial entity's own risk management systems. Furthermore, derivatives trading systems and trade processing and confirmation architecture are generally insufficient, with infrastructure lagging well behind innovation in financial markets (Das, 2010). Accordingly, cultivating the competence, independence, and strength of the regulatory and oversight authorities to guarantee that they can appropriately regulate derivatives trading is a critical issue of supreme significance for a prosperous trading of these complex instruments in emerging economies. This indeed requires full knowledge of the true operation of the derivatives products industry and the necessary matters that need to be addressed (Das, 2010).

26.7. Concluding Remarks

The growth and development of derivatives products will carry on in spite of the surge of losses, bankruptcies, and misconducts reported in their use. These losses and fraudulent actions unveil that derivatives securities are not risk-free, even though they can diminish risks when used correctly. In addition, these massive losses and shocking misconducts can serve as a reminder that complexity does not guarantee safety, and those leveraged bets on interest rate, foreign exchange rate, and stock market indices are still bet unless they are based on serious and applicable analysis and information. However, these losses and misuses do not modify the fact that many prospective users of these adaptable and inexpensive financial instruments have not yet acknowledged their full usefulness and value.

Nevertheless, certain emerging markets have rushed the process of opening of their derivatives exchanges, to compete and "keep up with the Joneses" among neighboring markets, and without having in place the full markets' microstructures and foundations. This is unfortunate indeed; however, it was natural due to the lack of knowledge and responsibility of policymakers. After about two decades of operations, however, some of these makers are still small for the size of their economies, and the traded contracts are not so significant in volume.

In a nutshell, based on prior real-world involvement and observations in emerging markets (as a practitioner of derivatives products and witness of brutal financial crises, bankruptcies and collapses), I have observed that emerging countries which have ignored or ill-treated most of the "rule of thumb" that I have debated on in the earlier sections of this chapter, have indeed fallen into the trap of launching of inefficient and illiquid derivatives products and markets — with many loopholes for rogue participants, fraudulent actions, manipulations, abusive practices, and other outrageous misconducts.

Finally, while the COVID-19 pandemic is not a sub-prime credit event in comparison to what have happened during the 2007–2009 Global Financial Crisis, the ongoing COVID-19 health crisis has created new challenges for global financial markets as well as derivative markets and caused remarkable disruptions to financial and derivatives markets across the globe.

In terms of clearing and settlement for the operations of derivative products, the past decade since the 2007–2009 Global Financial Crisis has been characterized by regulatory amendments as defined by the Financial Stability Board (FSB) in response to the G20 mandates to deal with the operational shortcomings uncovered in 2007–2009 financial meltdown.

While the financial and social impact of the COVID-19 health crisis has yet to be fully unearthed, derivatives market participants could implement evaluations of its effects on their trading agreements and counterparties. The COVID-19 outbreak has already influenced the derivatives market in many aspects and will continue to trigger interruptions in the near future. To that end, OTC derivatives' market participants must perform exhaustive revisions of the terms of their trading master agreements with key counterparties, with special emphasis on the operational and force majeure provisions under the ISDA Master Agreement and related ISDA collateral agreements to identify potential complications and to evade inadvertent systematic defaults.

Conflict of Interest

The author declares no conflict of interest in this chapter.

Funding

This research study did not receive any funding from any entity or organization.

References

Acharya, V.V. and Richardson, M. (2009). *Restoring Financial Stability: How to Repair a Failed System* (John Wiley & Sons, Inc., NJ, USA), pp. 57–376.

Acharya, V.V., Brenner, M., Engle, R.F., Lynch, A.W. and Richardson, M. (2009a). Derivatives: The Ultimate financial innovation. In *Restoring Financial Stability: How to Repair a Failed System*, Acharya, V.V. and Richardson, M. (eds.), (John Wiley & Sons, Inc., NJ, USA), pp. 233–249.

Acharya, V.V., Engle, R.F., Figlewski, S., Lynch, A.W. and Subrahmanyam, M.G. (2009b). Centralized clearing for credit derivatives. In *Restoring Financial Stability: How to Repair a Failed System*, Acharya, V.V. and Richardson, M. (eds.), (John Wiley & Sons, Inc., NJ, USA), pp. 251–268.

Al Janabi, M.A.M. (2006). On the inception of sound derivative products in emerging markets: Real-world observations and viable solutions. *Journal of Financial Regulation and Compliance*, **14**(2), 151–164.

Al Janabi, M.A.M. (2008a). Internal regulations and procedures for financial trading units, *Journal of Banking Regulation*, **9**(2), 116–130.

Al Janabi, M.A.M. (2008b). On the appropriate function of trading risk management units: Principal objectives and adequate use of internal models. *Journal of Banking Regulation*, **10**(1), 68–87.

Al Janabi, M.A.M. (2008c). Integrating liquidity risk factor into a parametric value at risk method. *Journal of Trading*, summer issue, 76–87.

Al Janabi, M.A.M. (2011). A generalized theoretical modeling approach for the assessment of economic capital under asset market liquidity risk constraints. *The Service Industries Journal*, **31**(13 & 14), 2193–2221.

Al Janabi, M.A.M. (2012a). Derivatives securities in emerging mena markets: structuring lessons from other financial markets. *Journal of Banking Regulation*, **13**(1), 73–85.

Al Janabi, M.A.M. (2012b). Optimal commodity asset allocation with a coherent market risk modeling. *Review of Financial Economics*, **21**(3), 131–140.

Al Janabi, M.A.M. (2013). Optimal and coherent economic-capital structures: evidence from long and short-sales trading positions under illiquid market perspectives. *Annals of Operations Research*, **205**(1), 109–139.

Al Janabi, M.A.M. (2014). Optimal and investable portfolios: An empirical analysis with scenario optimization algorithms under crisis market prospects. *Economic Modelling*, **40**, 369–381.

Al Janabi, M.A.M. (2020a). Is optimum always optimal? A revisit of the mean-variance method under nonlinear measures of dependence and non-normal liquidity constraints. *Journal of Forecasting*. Early View Articles: https://doi.org/10.1002/for.2714.

Al Janabi, M.A.M. (2020b). Multivariate portfolio optimization under illiquid market prospects: A review of theoretical algorithms and practical techniques for liquidity risk management. *Journal of Modelling in Management.* EarlyCite Articles: https://doi.org/10.1108/JM2-07-2019-0178.

Al Janabi, M.A.M., Arreola-Hernandez, J.A., Berger, T. and Nguyen, D.K. (2017). Multivariate dependence and portfolio optimization algorithms under illiquid market scenarios. *European Journal of Operational Research*, **259**(3), 1121–1131.

Al Janabi, M.A.M., Ferrer, R. and Shahzad, S.J.H. (2019). Liquidity-adjusted value-at-risk optimization of a multi-asset portfolio using a vine copula approach. *Physica A: Statistical Mechanics and Its Applications*, **536**, 122579.

Arreola-Hernandez, J. and Al Janabi, M.A.M. (2020). Forecasting of dependence, market and investment risks of a global index portfolio. *Journal of Forecasting*, **39**(3), 512–532.

Arreola-Hernandez, J., Al Janabi, M.A.M., Hammoudeh, S. and Nguyen, D.K. (2015). Time lag dependence, cross-correlation and risk analysis of U.S. energy and non-energy stock portfolios. *Journal of Asset Management*, **16**(7), pp. 467–483.

Arreola-Hernandez, J., Hammoudeh, S., Khuong, N.D., Al Janabi, M.A.M. and Reboredo, J.C. (2017). Global financial crisis and dependence risk analysis of sector portfolios: A vine copula approach. *Applied Economics*, **49**(25), 2409–2427.

Asadi, S. and Al Janabi, M.A.M. (2020). Measuring market and credit risk under Solvency II: Evaluation of the standard technique versus internal models for stock and bond markets. *European Actuarial Journal*, **10**(2), 425–456.

Borio, C. (2013). The Great Financial Crisis: Setting Priorities for New Statistics. *Journal of Banking Regulation*, **14**(3 and 4), 306–317.

Boyle, P. and Boyle F. (2001). *Derivatives: The Tools that Changed Finance*, Risk Books.

Das, S. (2010). Regulation and the derivatives markets, *Financial Times*. Retrieved from www.ft.com/markets, Published on June 7, 2010, UK.

Fernandez, V. (2006). Emerging derivatives markets: The case of Chile. *Emerging Markets Finance and Trade*, **42**(2), 63–92.

Financial Stability Board (2020a). Guidance on financial resources to support CCP resolution and on the treatment of CCP equity in resolution: Consultative document FSB website, www.fsb.org. Available at: https://www.fsb.org/wp-content/uploads/P020520.pdf. Published on May 4, 2020, Basel, Switzerland.

Financial Stability Board (2020b). COVID-19 pandemic: Financial stability implications and policy measures taken FSB website, www.fsb.org. Available at: https://www.fsb.org/wp-content/uploads/P150420.pdf. Published on April 15, 2020, Basel, Switzerland.

Glasser, T. D. (2013). Leveraging data for financial stability monitoring. *Journal of Banking Regulation*, **14**(3 and 4), 195–208.

Grillini, S., Sharma, A., Ozkan, A. and Al Janabi, M.A.M. (2019). Pricing of time-varying illiquidity within the Eurozone: Evidence using a Markov switching liquidity-adjusted capital asset pricing model, *International Review of Financial Analysis*, **64**, 145–158.

Holder, M. E., Thomas III, M. J. and Webb, R. I. (1999). Winners and Losers: Recent Competition Among Futures Exchanges for Equivalent Financial Contract Markets. *Derivatives Quarterly*, Winter Issue.

Madoroba, S. B. W. and Kruger, J. W. (2014). Liquidity effects on value-at-risk limits: Construction of a new VaR model. *Journal of Risk Model Validation*, **8**, 19–46.

Steinherr, A. (2000). Derivatives the Wild Beast of Finance: A Path to Effective Globalisation? (John Wiley & Sons, Inc., NY, USA).

Stulz, R. M. (2009). Financial derivatives: Lessons from the subprime crisis. *The Milken Institute Review*, First Quarter.

Tsetsekos, G. and Varangis P. (1997). The structure of derivatives exchanges: Lessons from developed and emerging markets, Policy Research Working Paper No. 1887. (World Bank, Development Economics Department, Washington, D.C).

Tsetsekos, G. and Varangis P. (2000). Lessons in structuring derivatives exchanges. *The World Bank Research Observer*, **15**(1), 85–98, February.

https://doi.org/10.1142/9781800610781_0027

Chapter 27

Impact on Financial Markets and Institutions

Qiyu Wang

China Academy of Financial Research,
Zhejiang University of Finance and Economics,
Hangzhou, China
Department of Applied Mathematics,
The Hong Kong Polytechnic University, Hong Kong
qiyu.wang@connect.polyu.hk; qiyu.wang@9q.com

Abstract

In this chapter, we investigate the impact of the COVID-19 health crisis on multi-dimensional financial markets and institutions in a quantitative manner. For the stock market, we use statistical methodologies to quantify the abnormalities, investigate the hedging strategies, and compare the asset classes to find safe havens in a flash crashes. For the bond market, we investigate the Treasury yields and corporate bonds. For the alternative market, we track the mutual fund market globally, and document the hedge fund performances. Based on these respective research studies across the market, we then synthesize the financial market by testing the cross-border co-integration, correlations to measure contagion, sentiments by text analysis, and the role of the financial institutions.

27.1. Introduction

The first serious alarm bells regarding the widespread nature of COVID-19 began ringing in December 2019. Early in the summer of 2018, the signs of the pandemic began to show. For example, it was reported that a flu was discovered in the US in the summer of 2018. The virus, which finally erupted on a large scale globally, has been named as severe acute respiratory syndrome coronavirus 2 (SARS-CoV-2). Unexpectedly, its impact has been deep and worldwide. In fact, a recent paper published in the journal *Science* predicts that the transmission dynamics could continue to be sustained as late as 2024 (Kissler *et al.*, 2020).

COVID-19 began to sweep across the world from December 2019, the month that has been considered to be the official start of the pandemic by the official sources. At first, it seemed to spread rapidly in China, but became to be out of control in the US and Europe. Some research results showed COVID-19 may potentially turn into another black death pandemic (Kissler *et al.*, 2020). In this chapter, we aim to fill the research gap through a quantitative analysis of the financial markets that is lacking at present. We use worldwide stock indices to measure the stock market performance. We investigate US representative Treasury and corporate bonds yields. The Exchange Traded Funds (ETFs) across the asset classes and hedge funds of different styles are also discussed. The mechanism behind them is considered by analyzing the actions of broker-dealer and institutional investors. Last but not the least, we briefly introduce the text information such as daily reports of COVID-19.

The quantitative analysis, especially the statistical tests such as abrupt points, stationarity tests, correlation, and cointegration tests, confirm the negative impact of COVID-19 on the financial markets. The behavior and performance of broker-dealers and institutional investors partially explain the relationship with policy management. The resulting economic implications of COVID-19 have been serious.

The structure of this chapter is as follows. In Section 27.2, we introduce a series of models. The financial markets we quantitatively investigate include the stock market, bond market, and fund market. In Section 27.3, we provide the conclusion.

27.2. Model

27.2.1. *Stock market impact*

27.2.1.1. *Analysis of the stock market indices*

The stock market, as the most accessible financial market, reflects the economic impact on the stock prices. After COVID-19 erupted, the stock markets fell. For example, the S&P 500 index, the most widely used stock market performance indicator, has slumped dramatically since the COVID-19 crisis became serious in March 2020 (see Figure 27.1(a)). Similar stock price dynamics are shown in the Dow Jones price index in Figure 27.1(b). The stock price dynamics of the Nasdaq slightly differed from the other two major indices, although it also suffered a downturn in March 2020 (see Figure 27.1(c)). The Russell 2000 index is plotted in Figure 27.1(d). It also suffered from the COVID-19 crisis and rebounded afterward. The bottoming of the stock prices occurred a little later than the other indices for the Nikkei 225 index, as shown in Figure 27.1(e).

We introduce the data source briefly. The worldwide stock market prices, including the S&P 500, Dow Jones 30, Nasdaq, Financial Times Stock Exchange (FTSE 100), Nikkei 225, and Russell 2000, are collected from Yahoo Finance. The S&P 500, Dow Jones 30, and Nasdaq are the three major US stock indices. FTSE is an index covering British stocks. The Nikkei index measures the Japanese stock market. Russell 2000 indicates the Russian market. The time span of data series is from October 2019 to October 2020. The S&P 500, Dow Jones 30, Nasdaq, and Russell 2000 have 252 data points. The Nikkei 225 has 242 data points. At the time of writing the COVID-19 crisis is sweeping the global population, imposing huge challenges on public health management, notwithstanding the ensuring economic costs.

The summary statistics of the data time series is provided in Table 27.1. We illustrate the mean, the maximum, the minimum, standard deviation, skewness, and value-at-risk (VaR) of the stock

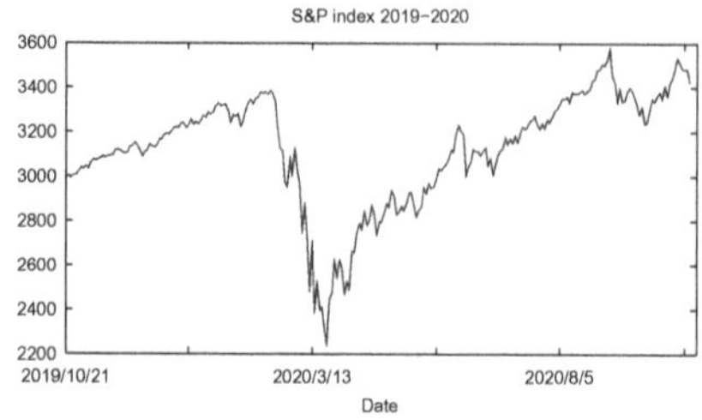

(a) S&P 500 time series

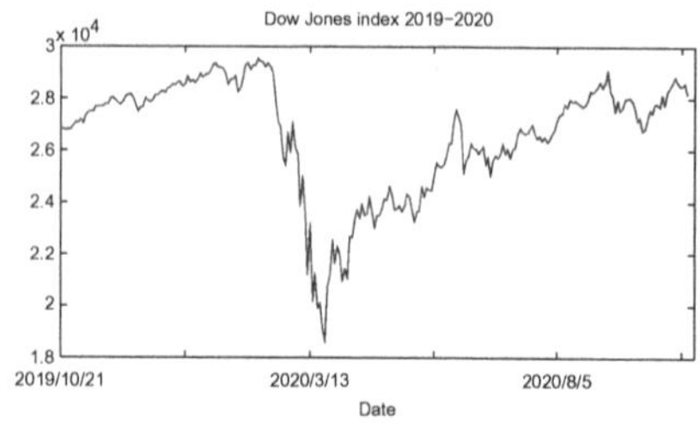

(b) Dow Jones time series

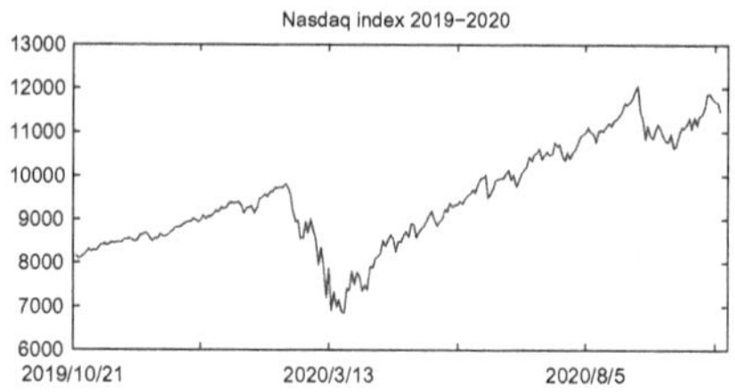

(c) Nasdaq time series

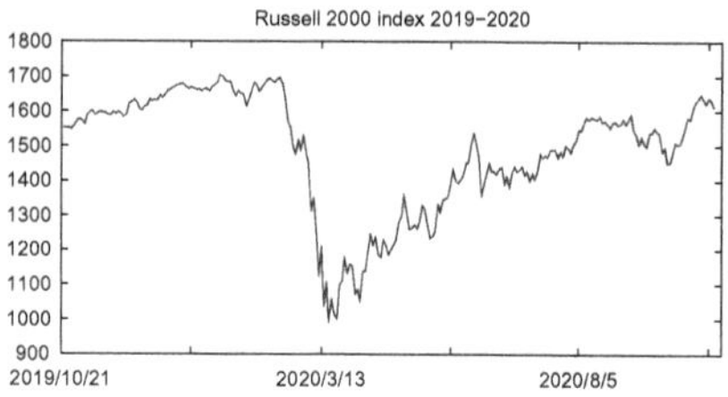

(d) Russell 2000 time series

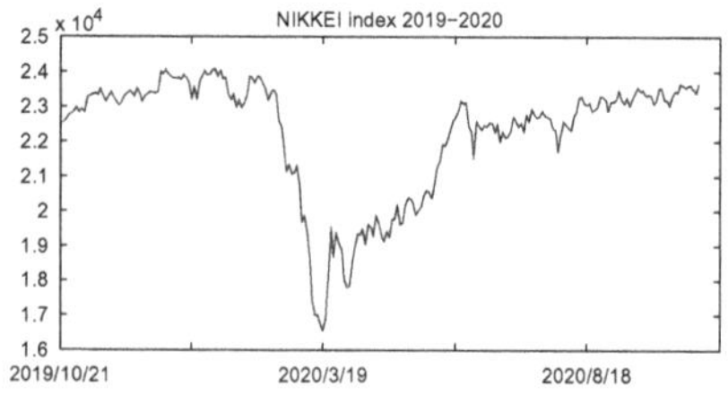

(e) NIKKEI 225 time series

Figure 27.1. The financial time series of stock indices during the COVID-19 crisis.
Note: We plot the stock indices time series in this figure. These figures cover stock indices globally. We could observe that all of these markets slumped during the COVID-19 crisis.

indices returns. From the statistics, we can find that the Nasdaq component stocks have been relatively steady among the three major US stock market indices during the crisis. The Nikkei seems the least affected stock market, concluding from the relatively higher returns, low standard deviation, and positive skewness. The Russell 2000 index shows the most volatile standard deviation, with a strong skewness.

We conduct tests for anomaly detection. Using methodology in stationarity statistics, we quantitatively detect the stock market

Table 27.1. Summary statistics of the stock indices.

	Mean	**Max.**	**Min.**
DJI	1.9800E−04	1.0764E−01	−1.3842E−01
GSPC	5.2116E−04	8.9683E−02	−1.2765E−01
IXIC	1.3582E−03	8.9347E−02	−1.3149E−01
RUT	1.5409E−04	8.9763E−02	−1.5399E−01
NIKKEI	2.0154E−04	7.7314E−02	−6.2736E−02
	Std	**Skew**	**VaR**
DJI	2.3010E−02	−8.5771E−01	−3.6231E−02
GSPC	2.1550E−02	−8.8905E−01	−3.4268E−02
IXIC	2.2095E−02	−1.0492E+00	−3.8588E−02
RUT	2.6582E−02	−1.3236E+00	−3.7513E−02
NIKKEI	1.6024E−02	2.4000E−01	−2.7539E−02

Note: This table illustrates the statistics of the stock indices. We compared the global markets and determined which market is more against the pandemic risk. DJI (Dow Jones Index); GSPC (Standard&Poor); IXIC (Nasdaq); RUT (Russel); NIKKEI (NIKKEI 225).

anomalies during and beyond the COVID-19 health crisis. We conduct break point and stationarity (Tsay, 2005) tests[1] using Matlab code.

We introduce the methodology of the tests. First, the detection of an abrupt change point means that the probability characteristics change around that point. Several methods could detect the change point, such as CUSUM, probability density estimation, direct compute, probability method, and clustering method. The breakpoint statistic we use in this chapter is a non-parametric method called Pettitt.

Second, the stationarity test is a preparatory step in the time series studies. Because the ARIMA model usually requires that the time series is stationary, the stationarity test is of vital importance. The source of non-stationarity comes from the trend in the mean, explosive volatility, and autocorrelation. Several methods are used to test stationarity, such rolling statistics, and the Dickey–Fuller Test. A mainstream stationarity test we use in this chapter is the

[1]http://finzi.psych.upenn.edu/R/library/bfast/html/bfast.html.

Table 27.2. Abnormality of the stock indices.

	Abrupt	Min.	Stationary
DJI	105	106	1
GSPC	105	106	1
IXIC	112	106	1
RUT	105	103	1
NIKKEI	109	100	1

Note: This table illustrate the statistics of the abrupt test, minimum values, and stationarity states.

Table 27.3. Correlation of the stock indices.

Corr	GSPC	IXIC	RUT
DJI	9.8598E−01	9.2805E−01	9.2980E−01
GSPC	1	9.6739E−01	9.1833E−01
IXIC		1	8.6624E−01
RUT			1

Note: This table illustrates the correlations between the stock indices.

Dickey–Fuller test. In this chapter, we will not fit the ARIMA model, therefore we do not report the ACF and PACF orders.

We show the results in Table 27.2. The first column documents the abrupt points of the time series. The second column records the minimum point of the time series. The third column is the hypothesis test results of the stationarity test. The results are in accordance with the price numbers and the summary statistics of the returns. The Nasdaq had a delayed touchdown response to the crisis. The Nikkei is relatively independent of the Western stock markets. The stationarity tests show that the time series are stationary.

In a co-movement investigation, we calculate the correlations and co-integrations of the indices. We construct the correlations for the stock indices. The statistics test for the co-integration is the Johansen test in Matlab. There are two major co-integration tests: the Engle–Granger co-integration test and the Johansen test.

The results are presented in Tables 27.3 and 27.4. The interpretation of the results is that DJI, GSPC, IXIC, RUT and NIKKEI stock indices are highly correlated. They simultaneously respond

Table 27.4. Co-integration of the stock indices.

CoI	**GSPC**	**IXIC**	**RUT**
DJI	1	1	1
GSPC	1	1	1
IXIC		1	1
RUT			1

Note: This table shows the co-integration between the stock indices pair.

Table 27.5. The statistical summary and the hedge ratio of stock indices futures.

Spot/Fut	**Mean**	**Std**	**Hedge**
DJI	1.8916E−04	2.2500E−02	9.7987E−01
GSPC	5.1660E−04	2.1184E−02	9.6669E−01
IXIC	1.5234E−03	2.1711E−02	9.7146E−01
RUT	1.5067E−04	2.6147E−02	9.7911E−01

Note: This table illustrate the statistics and hedge ratios of the stock indices futures.

to the COVID-19 crisis, which we learn from the co-integration tests.

27.2.1.2. *Hedge by the futures*

To hedge the risk from the underlying stocks, we could use futures. The trading time period of futures is longer than that of stocks. We conduct calendar match by adopting the common trading days.

The hedging ratio is computed by

$$h^* = \rho\sigma_S/\sigma_B,$$

where ρ is the correlation between the stock indices and stock indices futures; σ_S is the standard deviation of the stock indices; σ_F is the standard deviation of the stock indices and futures (Table 27.5).

27.2.2. *Bond market impact*

To investigate the impact of COVID-19 on the bonds market, we look at the Treasuries (He *et al.*, 2020) and the corporate bonds market.

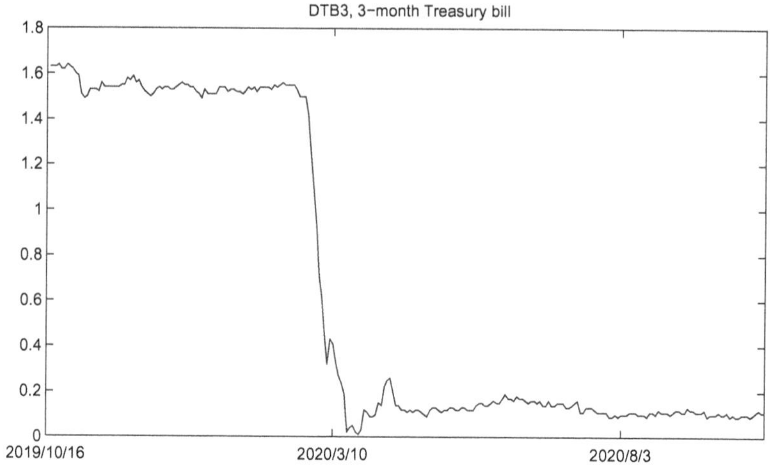

(a) DTB3 time series

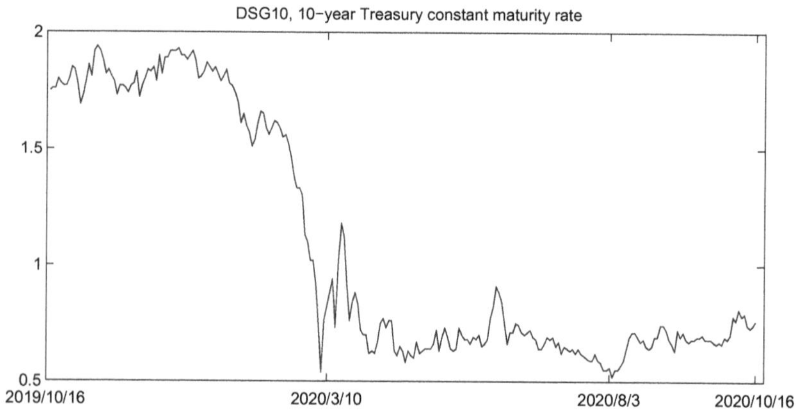

(b) DGS10 time series

Figure 27.2. The financial time series of treasuries during the COVID-19 crisis. *Note*: This figure illustrate the time series of the 3-month and 10-year Treasuries.

27.2.2.1. *Treasuries*

The data we collected was from the Federal Reserve Bank of St Louis, including the 3-month Treasury bill and 10-year Treasury constant maturity rate. We plot the time series of DTB3 (3-month debenture) in Figure 27.2(a) and DGS10 (10-year debenture) in Figure 27.2(b).

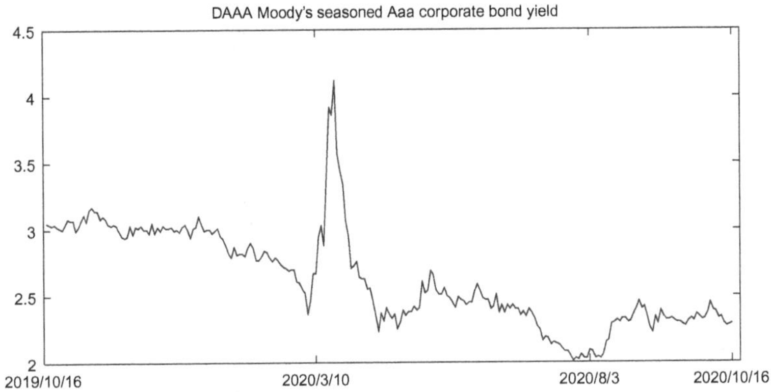

(a) DAAA time series

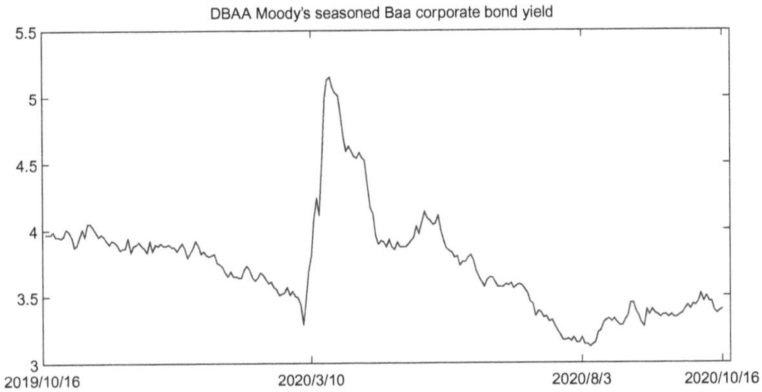

(b) DBAA time series

Figure 27.3. The financial time series of corporate bonds during the COVID-19 crisis.
Note: This figure illustrates the time series of the DAAA and DBAA corporate bonds.

We could observe from the figures that the yield curve was already at a high level before the crisis peak in March 2020.

27.2.2.2. *Corporate bonds*

The data was collected from the Federal Reserve Bank of St Louis. We use two representative corporate bond time series of the Moody's seasoned Aaa corporate bond yield.

We plot the yields in Figures 27.3(a) and 27.3(b). From the figures, we observe the yield peaks in March 2020. It clearly shows that

Table 27.6. The statistical summary and statistical tests of bonds.

Bonds	Mean	Std	Abrupt	Min.	Stationarity
DTB3	1.0824	0.5182	111	201	0
DGS10	0.6616	0.6800	104	109	1
DAAA	2.6268	0.3718	120	194	0
DBAA	3.7382	0.3888	160	203	0

Note: This table illustrates the illustrative statistics and test statistics.

the COVID-19 crisis influenced the bond markets. Shortly afterward, the yield curves became flat.

Kargar *et al.* (2020) analyze the corporate bond liquidity during the COVID-19 crisis. They have examined the actions the US government has taken to address the crisis. Their explanation is that the liquidity conditions deteriorated substantially, causing the yield curve variation.

27.2.2.3. *In-depth analysis*

We illustrate the summary statistics and statistical results in Table 27.6. The returns of the corporate bonds are on an average higher than that of the Treasury yields. However, the volatility of the Treasuries is higher than that of the corporate bonds. The abrupt points of the Treasuries are earlier than that of the corporate bonds. The abrupt points are not the minimum points, but appear earlier than the bottom of the yield curve. In contrast to the stock markets, we could observe that the bond market time series are not stationary, except for the long-term Treasury yields. When modeling with the time series, we should transform the non-stationary time series into stationary time series (Table 27.6).

27.2.3. *Fund market impact*

27.2.3.1. *ETF market*

To investigate the fund market impact, we investigate the ETFs worldwide, the same fund asset classes studied in Wang and Chong (2019). The names of the funds are provided in Table 27.7. The

Table 27.7. Classes of postmodern asset allocation.

Asset type	Class	Benchmark	Tick
Stock	Large Cap	Russell 1000	iShares Russell 1000 Value ETF (IWD)
	Small Cap	Russell 2000	iShares Russell 2000 ETF (IWM)
	Emerging	MSCI EM	iShares MSCI Emerging Markets ETF (EEM)
	Derivatives	MSCI EAFE	iShares MSCI EAFE ETF (EFA)
Fixed income	Government Bond	Barclay Gov.	SPDR Blmbg Barclays 1-3 Mth T-Bill ETF (BIL)
	Convertible Securities	Barclay Conv.	SPDR Blmbg Barclays Convertible Securities ETF(CWB)
	High-yield Bond	Barclay High-Yield	SPDR Blmbg Barclays High Yield Bd ETF (JNK)
Alternative	PE	S&P PE index	Invesco Listed Private Equity ETF (PSP)
Assets	Real Estate	FTSE nareit	Invesco Active US Real Estate ETF (PSR)
	Spot	SP GSCI	iShares S&P GSCI Commodity-Indexed Trust (GSG)

Note: This table illustrates the ETFs that we study in this chapter.

private equity and real estate indices are from Invesco asset management. SPDR covers a wide range of ETF and mutual fund products, including BIL,[2] CWB and JNK.

Table 27.8 shows the interpretation of the results. The returns of these ETFs during the COVID-19 crisis are prevalently low. The volatility of the alternative investment is comparatively high. The returns of fixed income without rights are low.

27.2.3.2. *Hedge fund market*

We have downloaded the hedge fund data from Hedge Fund Research.[3] The data is documented in Bloomberg. Their Bloomberg codes are EHI166, EHI90, EHI80, and EHI473, respectively and these are the monthly price data.

The interpretation of the results is as follows. The performance of the hedge funds during the crisis is worse than their performance in the long run (Table 27.9). The returns of Asian hedge fund markets are relatively unrelated to the other markets and are higher but are also accompanied by a higher volatility and VaR.

Boyson *et al.* (2008) investigate the relationship between the contagion and the liquidity of hedge funds. Following their analysis, the explanation of the hedge fund performance during the COVID-19 crisis.

27.2.4. *Comparison of the asset classes*

We have quantitatively analyzed the performance of the asset classes. The stocks, bonds, ETFs, and hedge funds are influenced by the COVID-19 to different degrees. We could see there is no absolutely safe haven for investment. The Asian market is weakly influenced by the COVID-19. Alternative investments show the strongest performance. However, they are accompanied by a higher risk.

[2] https://www.ssga.com/us/en/individual/etfs/funds/spdr-bloomberg-barclays-1-3-month-t-bill-etf-bil.

[3] https://www.eurekahedge.com/Research.

Table 27.8. The performance of ETFs.

ETF	Return	Sigma	VaR	Sharpe	Ret_VaR
IWD	−1.2245E−04	2.2590E−02	−3.2636E−02	−5.4207E−03	3.7521E−03
IWM	2.2001E−04	2.5236E−02	−3.6576E−02	8.7179E−03	−6.0151E−03
EEM	3.8601E−04	2.1430E−02	−2.8043E−02	1.8012E−02	−1.3765E−02
EFA	−2.8700E−05	1.9397E−02	−2.6912E−02	−1.4772E−03	1.0647E−03
BIL	2.7100E−05	1.2096E−04	−2.1828E−04	2.2388E−01	−1.2407E−01
CWB	1.3305E−03	1.6693E−02	−2.5074E−02	7.9701E−02	−5.3062E−02
JNK	8.2700E−05	1.0926E−02	−1.8394E−02	7.5679E−03	−4.4951E−03
PSP	−1.2631E−03	2.0515E−02	−2.9484E−02	−6.1572E−02	4.2841E−02
PSR	4.0071E−04	7.3501E−01	−6.9315E−01	5.4518E−04	−5.7811E−04
GSG	4.0071E−04	7.3501E−01	−6.9315E−01	5.4518E−04	−5.7811E−04

Note: This table illustrates the performance of the ETFs.

Table 27.9. The performance of hedge funds.

Hedge fund	Return	Sigma	VaR	Sharpe	Ret_VaR
NA	7.2088E−01	1.6223E+00	−2.1300E+00	4.4435E−01	−3.3844E−01
NA COVID	6.2727E−01	3.3774E+00	−7.2600E+00	1.8572E−01	−8.6401E−02
Euro	5.2606E−01	1.7179E+00	−2.2300E+00	3.0622E−01	−2.3590E−01
Euro COVID	1.1091E−01	3.1518E+00	−8.1600E+00	3.5189E−02	−1.3592E−02
Asian	6.2831E−01	2.1362E+00	−3.4800E+00	2.9413E−01	−1.8055E−01
Asian COVID	9.1000E−01	3.5932E+00	−7.9700E+00	2.5326E−01	−1.1418E−01
Main	6.6361E−01	1.4409E+00	−1.6600E+00	4.6056E−01	−3.9977E−01
Main COVID	5.3091E−01	2.8091E+00	−6.4000E+00	1.8900E−01	−8.2955E−02

Note: This table illustrates the performance of the hedge funds.

27.2.5. *Financial markets, broker-dealer, and market-makers*

We briefly summarize the behavior of dealers in the treasury markets. On the dealer balance sheet, the holdings of treasuries and reverse repo of dealers are subject to regulations, (see He *et al.*, 2020).

The dealer behavior for corporate bonds has also been seriously influenced by COVID-19. The dealers appeared unwilling to absorb corporate debt onto their balance sheets, see (Kargar *et al.*, 2020). The Federal Reserve's corporate credit facilities impose eligibility requirements for bond purchase.

Ramelli and Wagner (2020) analyze the impact of COVID-19 on the stock market. Actively managed mutual funds underperform compared to the passive managed funds (see Alfaro *et al.*, 2020). Pastor and Vorsatz (2020) find that losses in market value at the firm level rise with capital intensity and leverage and are greater in industries that are more conducive to disease transmission.

27.2.6. *Text information and sentiment*

The media reports on COVID-19 are becoming highly frequent. The mainstream media in the US, such as CNN, has special daily columns on the pandemic.[4] As of the end of October 2020, COVID-19 cases in the US has surpassed 9 million. The media texts contain the sentiments of investors who face COVID-19. In the future, it is highly meaningful to set up a COVID-19 dictionary for text analysis.

The John Hopkins Coronavirus Resource Center[5] maintains a daily count of the global cases and cases by country.

27.3. Conclusion

In this chapter, we review the conditions of several financial markets during the COVID-19 crisis, including stock markets, bond markets, and the fund markets. In the stock market analysis, we investigate major stock indices. In the bond markets, we investigate Treasuries and corporate bonds. In the fund markets, we investigate ETFs and hedge funds. The abrupt tests show the breakpoints in the financial markets. The stationarity test show that the stock markets are mainly stationary, while most of the bond markets are not.

On the other hand, we also review the mechanisms behind the financial market performance, mainly the dealers in the Treasury and corporate bonds market and the institutional investors' performance. The bond-market dealers respond to the policy shock and transform the market trends. The institutional investors have been found to perform corresponding to the COVID-19 impact.

[4]https://us.cnn.com/2020/10/31/health/us-coronavirus-saturday/index.html.
[5]https://coronavirus.jhu.edu/us-map.

References

Alfaro, L., Chari, A., Greenland, A.N. and Schott, P.K. (2020). Aggregate and firm-level stock returns during pandemics, in real time. NBER Working Papers.

Boyson, N.M., Stahel, C.W. and Stulz, R. (2008). Hedge fund contagion and liquidity. Working Paper Series.

He, Z., Nagel, S. and Song, Z. (2020). Treasury inconvenience yields during the COVID-19 crisis. Working Paper 27416. National Bureau of Economic Research. Retrieved from http://www.nber.org/papers/w27416, doi: 10.3386/w27416 (September 30th, 2020).

Kargar, M., Lester, B., Lindsay, D., Liu, S., Weill, P.O. and Ziga, D. (2020). Corporate bond liquidity during the COVID-19 crisis. NBER Working Papers.

Kissler, S.M., Tedijanto, C., Goldstain, E., Yonatan H. and Grad, M.L. (2020). Projecting the transmission dynamics of SARS-COV-2 through the postpandemic period. *Science*, **368**, 860–171.

Pastor, L. and Vorsatz, B. (2020). Mutual fund performance and flows during the COVID-19 crisis. Social Science Electronic Publishing.

Ramelli, S. and Wagner, A. (2020). COVID-19 and the stock market. In A New World Post COVID-19 Lessons for Business, the Finance Industry and Policy Makers edited by Monica Billio and Simone Varotto, 111–123. https://edizionicafoscari.unive.it/libri/978-88-6969-443-1/covid-19-and-the-stock-market/.

Tsay, R.S. (2005). *Analysis of Financial Time Series.* Wiley Series in Probability and Statistics. 2nd edn. (Wiley, US).

Wang, Q. and Chong, T.L. (2019). How effective is the tail mean-variance model in the fund of fund selection: An empirical study by using various risk measures. *Financial Research Letters*, **29**, 239–244.

https://doi.org/10.1142/9781800610781_bmatter

Index

N

Q

R

www.ingramcontent.com/pod-product-compliance
Lightning Source LLC
LaVergne TN
LVHW012052011026
849162LV00018B/162
9781800610774